Oxford Paperback Reference

Oxford Dictionary of **Rhymes**

The most authoritative and up-to-date reference
books for both students and the general reader.

Oxford Paperback Reference

ABC of Music
Accounting
Allusions
Animal Behaviour
Archaeology
Architecture and Landscape
   Architecture
Art and Artists
Art Terms
Arthurian Legend and
   Literature*
Astronomy
Battles*
Better Wordpower
Bible
Biology
British History
British Place-Names
Buddhism
Business and Management
Card Games
Catchphrases
Celtic Mythology
Chemistry
Christian Art
Christian Church
Chronology of English
   Literature
Century of New Words
Classical Literature
Classical Myth and Religion
Classical World*
Computing
Contemporary World History
Countries of the World
Dance
Dynasties of the World
Earth Sciences
Ecology
Economics
Encyclopedia
Engineering*
English Etymology
English Folklore
English Grammar
English Language
English Literature
English Surnames
Euphemisms
Everyday Grammar
Finance and Banking
First Names
Food and Drink
Food and Nutrition
Foreign Words and Phrases
Geography
Humorous Quotations
Idioms
Internet

Islam
Kings and Queens of Britain
Language Toolkit
Law
Law Enforcement*
Linguistics
Literary Terms
Local and Family History
London Place-Names
Mathematics
Medical
Medicinal Drugs
Modern Design
Modern Quotations
Modern Slang
Music
Musical Terms
Musical Works
Nicknames
Nursing
Ologies and Isms
Philosophy
Phrase and Fable
Physics
Plant Sciences
Plays*
Pocket Fowler's Modern English
   Usage
Political Quotations
Politics
Popes
Proverbs
Psychology
Quotations
Quotations by Subject
Reverse Dictionary
Rhymes*
Rhyming Slang
Saints
Science
Scientific Quotations
Shakespeare
Ships and the Sea
Slang
Sociology
Space Exploration
Statistics
Superstitions
Synonyms and Antonyms
Weather
Weights, Measures, and Units
Word Histories
World History
World Mythology
World Place-Names
World Religions
Zoology

*forthcoming

Oxford
Dictionary of
Rhymes

OXFORD
UNIVERSITY PRESS

OXFORD

UNIVERSITY PRESS

Great Clarendon Street, Oxford OX2 6DP

Oxford University Press is a department of the University of Oxford.
It furthers the University's objective of excellence in research, scholarship,
and education by publishing worldwide in

Oxford New York

Auckland Cape Town Dar es Salaam Hong Kong Karachi
Kuala Lumpur Madrid Melbourne Mexico City Nairobi
New Delhi Shanghai Taipei Toronto

With offices in

Argentina Austria Brazil Chile Czech Republic France Greece
Guatemala Hungary Italy Japan Poland Portugal Singapore
South Korea Switzerland Thailand Turkey Ukraine Vietnam

Oxford is a registered trade mark of Oxford University Press
in the UK and in certain other countries

Published in the United States
by Oxford University Press Inc., New York

© Oxford University Press 2006, 2007

British Library Cataloguing in Publication Data
Data available

Library of Congress Cataloging in Publication Data
Data available

Designed by Jane Stevenson
Typeset in Frutiger and Parable
by Laserwords Private Limited, Chennai, India
Printed in Great Britain by
Clays Ltd., Bungay, Suffolk

ISBN 978-0-19-280688-8

Contents

Preface

The *Oxford Dictionary of Rhymes* is a completely new work of reference, combining not only a vast range of rhyming words but also practical usage notes and examples in order to meet as far as possible the needs of today's rhyme-makers.

The rhymes of this dictionary are based directly on the pronunciations held in the wider Oxford Dictionaries databases, and are organized primarily on aural rather than orthographic principles. This emphasis on sound is important for at least three reasons. First, organization by sound—and not by the order of the letters of the alphabet—ensures that sounds that are closest together are grouped together. Secondly, the way the rhymes are organized does not depend on spelling: in English, spelling is notoriously irregular in the way letters represent sounds. Finally, the entries in the *Oxford Dictionary of Rhymes* relate to the standard pronunciation of British English and, where two possible pronunciations are correct, the word in question is listed in two different places.

The editorial contributions of Sheila Ferguson to the compilation of this dictionary, and the technical expertise of James McCracken in its inception, are gratefully acknowledged.

Introduction

Rhyme is heard everywhere—because it **works**. In advertising jingles, football chants, birthday-card greetings, tabloid headlines, political slogans, and catchphrases, rhyme makes the sentiments more powerful and more memorable. If you can't beat them, join them; Arrive Alive—Don't Drink and Drive; Dennis the Menace; No More War; hang 'em and flog 'em: in all, words are slammed together, echoed and re-echoed, as one rhyme-word prompts another or confirms the word that prompted it. Listen to any crowd chant or sing, and the punched emphasis on any rhyme shows clearly how important it is to each singer, and to all in keeping time; listen to almost any song on the radio, and its use of rhyme, for better or worse, is a primary factor in what you hear.

This widespread commercial, political, and social use of rhyme is a testimony to its commanding power over our attention and memory; so too, of course, is the artistic use of rhyme by poets and singers, which may in addition to power seek range and subtlety. And as anyone who reads contemporary poetry or listens to contemporary music knows, the idea that rhyme is somehow 'old-fashioned' or has fallen by the wayside is simply nonsense. Many of the best living poets are confirmed rhymers, middle-of-the-road easy-listening ballads and rock anthems rely as much as ever on strong rhymes, and the great innovators of rhyme in recent years have been rappers, from Grandmaster Flash to the Beastie Boys and Eminem: you may like or loathe the songs, but the cleverness and frequent sting of the tumbling rhymes cannot be denied. And unwelcome as the connection might be to some, Eminem, as a heavy and complex rhymer with social purpose, is a descendant of songwriters like Cole Porter, Ira Gershwin, and W. S. Gilbert (of Gilbert & Sullivan), whose comic-operatic songs like "I am the very model of a modern Major-General" were a nineteenth-century equivalent of rap.

Whatever your own concerns with it, rhyme is thus worth attending to for many reasons, and to understand it helpfully some history and analysis are necessary. This introduction is therefore divided into three sections: 'I. Rhyme in history and by type' gives some historical context and explains how rhyme has traditionally been analysed in English; 'II. Rhyme in use and by demonstration' applies those lessons, first tracking one particular type of rhyming-stanza from 1591 to the twentieth century, then ranging over a wide variety of modern poets and singers; and 'III. How to use this book' explains how to find the various kinds of rhyme that exist so you can use them for your own purposes. The technical vocabulary defined in Section I is used without further explanation in Section II, so if you are unfamiliar with such terms as *stressed* and *unstressed rhyme*, or *arch* and *chain rhyme*, it is advisable to read the sections in order. A table listing all the varieties of rhyme appears on pages xvi–xvii and there are inset panels throughout the book which give additional examples and tips.

Rhyme in history and by type

I'm a poet
And I know it.

Rhyme is a basic possibility of language, and must have occurred (if only by chance) in the earliest human speech. It was formalized early in Chinese and Arabic poetry, but in the West the idea of rhyme as a formal characteristic of poetry is relatively recent. No classical Hebrew, Greek, or Latin poets normally used rhyme, depending instead on parallel grammar or metres based on vowel-length, while Anglo-Saxon poets used the repetition of vowels or consonants known as *assonance* and *alliteration*. When rhyme was formally organized in the West as a poetic tool, principally in the twelfth to fourteenth centuries, it was in part its new and striking audibility that enabled it so rapidly to spread across Europe, first as a poetic vogue, and then as an established norm for lyric verse and song.

Rhyme was able to displace alliteration and assonance because both earlier modes depend on the repetition of individual letters that may occur anywhere in a word, and so do not necessarily connect the meanings of the words in which they occur. Charles Churchill's famous tag in *The Prophecy of Famine* (1763) about "apt Alliteration's artful aid" is remembered precisely because it is self-referentially witty, as most alliterative volleys are not. Rhyme, conversely, is based not simply on whole syllables, but on a word's last stressed vowel and all sounds that follow it, so that larger, grammatically significant elements of a word are likely to be involved.

As a formal principle of poetry rhyme thus represented a paradigm shift, one of many during the transition from 'Late Medieval' to 'Renaissance' and 'Early Modern'. Metrically, for example, the new importance of stress signals a shift from classical metres using duration to new metres using accent, and amid such shifts, 'rhyme' and 'rhythm' (both from Greek *rhythmos* and ultimately *rhein*, 'to flow') became distinct. Where alliteration or assonance, however rhythmic, link words only lightly within a line, relying on single sounds without individual meaning, rhyme, by linking multiple syllables (usually) in distinct lines, binds much larger parcels of sense. It is also an intrinsically complex phenomenon, interacting with spelling, poetry's distinctive use of lines, and regional accents, and richly invites variation, while alliteration or assonance can only shift from letter to letter. Rhyme thus helped poets and singers to organize, learn, and present their material, and helped readers or audiences to understand and remember it: a powerful and distinct resource, as Oscar Wilde insisted in calling rhyme "the one chord we have added to the Greek lyre".

His "we" is more dubious. The immediate sources of Western rhyme were Arabic poetry, in which various kinds of rhyme had been used since at least the 8th century CE, and perhaps some Celtic poetry; the primary European distribution system was the Troubadours, Provençal poet-musicians of the twelfth and thirteenth centuries who travelled and corresponded across Europe, the Middle East, North Africa, and Asia Minor. Traces of Late Mediaeval rhyme are as widespread as their contacts, but once rhyme had been adopted (via the 'Sicilian school' at the court of Frederic II Hohenstaufen in Palermo) by the great Italian poets Dante (Dante Alighieri, 1265–1321) and above all Petrarch (Francisco Petrarca, 1304–74), a massive and decisive secondary distribution began, initially in manuscript, then in print also, through the pan-European cultural and educational movement known as Humanism. Though exact dating is contested and uncertain, the 'Gawain-Poet' in the mid-late fourteenth century probably represents the first English sign of Petrarch's influence: *Sir Gawain and the Grene Knyght* itself has a rhyming 'wheel' ending its alliterative stanzas, and the notorious formal complexity of *Pearl* (preserved in the same manuscript) arises precisely from combining rhyme with alliteration. Geoffrey Chaucer (*c*.1344–1400), writing at the same time, was rarely so elaborate, but his *Canterbury Tales* established rhyming couplets as a narrative mode, while *Troylus and Criseyde* did as much for complex stanzas; shorter lyric verse, like the songs to which it is close, was already there. The older traditions of *blank* or unrhymed verse still prospered towards their dramatic flowering in Shakespeare and his fellows, but new traditions of rhymed verse rapidly joined them as normative within both folk and elite poetic cultures.

Notwithstanding some bad-tempered outbursts, like Milton's famous jibe in the 1667 Preface to *Paradise Lost* about "the troublesome and modern bondage of rhyming", rhymed and blank verse co-existed happily until the early twentieth century. Poetic tastes swung this way and that, but no one seriously thought less of Pope or Tennyson for rhyming, nor of Wordsworth or Browning for using blank verse. In the first quarter of the twentieth century, however, some Modernists began to proclaim the supposed death of rhyme and other formal devices. Patently, with Modernism and the birth of *free verse*, a new energy infused and transformed the blank tradition; equally patently, neither rhyme nor other formal devices were wholly absent even from High Modernism (think of T. S. Eliot or e. e. cummings), and both within and around Modernism rhyme flowed unabated, in W. B. Yeats, Robert Frost,

W. H. Auden, Philip Larkin, Robert Lowell, Elizabeth Bishop, Sylvia Plath and a hundred more. The 'New Formalism' announced by critics in the 1980s was certainly a reaction against the formlessness of some (late) Modernist work, but even so, it was not in any serious sense new, and in practice the augmented blank and rhyming traditions continue, now as then, to co-exist to their mutual benefit.

Despite its long prosperity, however, categorizations of rhyme vary in differing national traditions. In French poetry, for example, there are particular concerns with euphony (sweetness of sound) and punning, while in German, alliteration and assonance are designated as types of rhyme. English has a rich vocabulary for rhyme, but names are unstable: in what follows, therefore, alternative names are sometimes provided in parenthesis. Fortunately, however, there is more variation in labelling than understanding, for the basic definition of rhyme as involving two elements (the last stressed vowel + all following letters) creates an obvious structure of **degree**. In *full* (or *perfect*) *rhyme* both elements are correctly matched (as in 'hand/band'), and this can be intensified into *rime riche* (which as a French term always keeps its italics) by extending the rhyming sequences backwards from the last stressed vowels ('right hánd/fright ánd'). The obvious next step is *half-* (or *imperfect, near, slant*) *rhyme*, with only one element correctly matching, which divides into *vowel rhyme*, with the same last stressed vowel but different following letters ('hand/hang'), and *pararhyme*, with the same letters following different vowels ('hand/bind'). For the mathematically-minded, these four primary variants might be represented as $\{(+1,1), (1,1), (1,0), (0,1)\}$.

A second common analysis is by **type**. If the last stressed vowels are in last syllables ('hánd/bánd', 'cáre/bewáre', 'disgúst/entrúst'), the rhyme is *stressed* (the older term, abandoned as sexist, was *masculine rhyme*). If the last stressed vowels are followed by one or more metrically unstressed syllables ('hánding/stánding', 'Atlántic/gigántic'), the rhyme is *unstressed* (or *feminine*). The use of multiple words to form a rhyme ('poet/know it'), or of rhyming phrases ('on the run/in the sun'), creates *mosaic rhyme*, which if deliberately silly or outrageous ('hypotenuse/lot o' news') is known as *Hudibrastic rhyme*, from Samuel Butler's practice in

Hudibras. There are also three oddities: the logical *auto-* (or *null* or *identical*) *rhyme*, of a word with itself; the illogical *eye-* (or *printers'*) *rhyme*, when words that look as if they rhyme are not so pronounced ('-ough' is notorious: cough, bough, rough, dough); and the playful variety of *spelling rhymes*, using humorous distortion or abbreviations (compare '& Co./although' with '& Co./dump any'). To these can be added *wrenched rhyme*, when 'normal' pronunciation is overridden to create a rhyme by distorting one last vowel into conformity with the other ('hand/brigánd'); and two further types of distorted rhyme, *embedded rhyme*, of one word with a medial part of another ('band/handfast'), especially popular in song when the rhyme can be sounded in delivery, and which can be displayed on the page as *broken rhyme*, when the word containing the medial rhyming syllable is split between lines. In his last collection, *A Scattering of Salts* (1995), the underrated American poet James Merrill (1926–95) combined both in 'Snow Jobs', a wicked take on twentieth-century political integrity: "Like blizzards on a screen the scan-/dals thickened at a fearful rate / Followed by laughter from a can / and hot air from the candidate."

Expanding slightly, a third common analysis is by the **position** of rhyming words within lines. *Terminal rhyme*, between words ending lines, is predominant, but *medial rhyme* (at least one non-terminal word) remains common in song lyrics, libretti, and comic poetry—think of Gilbert & Sullivan, Tom Lehrer, or Eliot's *Old Possum's Book of Practical Cats*. There is one strict form of *medial rhyme*, *leonine rhyme*, when the word in the middle of the line (technically, preceding the caesura) rhymes with the end-word of the same line (as in "And louder rose the ragged crows" or "And blessed with bread the waters red", both from Charles Causley's 'Christ at the Cheesewring'). *Initial rhyme*, with at least one word beginning a line, is rarer, but as *autorhyme* can be created by repeated lines and formulae (as in the Psalms) or refrains that vary only slightly (as in many ballads).

Expanding again, the final common analysis is of **relation**, the pattern in which rhymes are combined (or *rhyme scheme*). Using the quatrain as an example, and the standard notation of rhyme schemes (in which successive letters, *a b c* ..., represent rhyming lines), if all lines rhyme, it is *monorhyme* (*aaaa*); if two lines rhyme and two are blank, it is *single rhyme* (*aabc, abac, abca, abbc, abcb, abcc*); if successive pairs of lines rhyme, it is *couplet rhyme* (*aabb*); if alternating lines rhyme, it is *cross-rhyme* (*abab*); and if the rhymes have mirror symmetry, it is *arch-* (or *chiasmic*) *rhyme* (*abba*). Once a pattern is sufficiently established to generate expectations of rhyme, rhymes may be *accelerated* by shortening the line (as in lines 3–4 of limericks) or by bringing a line forward (as *ababcdd*, where the second *d* is earlier than expected); or equally be *delayed*, by lengthening the line (as at the end of Spenserian stanzas) or by putting a line back (as *ababcdced*, where the second *d* is later than expected). And if a rhyme-sound is carried over from one stanza to another—as in the *terza rima* made famous by Dante, rhyming *aba bcb cdc* and so on—it is *chain rhyme*.

Finally, critics also talk of *semantic rhyme*, between words with related meanings (as 'glass/vitreous' or 'cake/bake'), and *thematic rhyme*, between words that are linked in a given work ('free/ slavery' or 'redeem/dream', for example, in a poem about Emancipation). There is also, therefore, *counter-semantic rhyme*, between words with opposed meanings, as 'make/break', 'raise/ raze', or, famously, 'death/breath'. In theory these are all desirable qualities in a rhyme, but in practice are intimately dependent on diction, the verbal range and register of a poem: if a semantic or thematic rhyme fits, all well and good, but if diction is forced, to admit for the sake of a rhyme a word that stands out as one the speaker of the poem would not use, even a perfectly semantic rhyme will not turn any profit.

These four kinds of analysis, by degree, type, position, and relation, enable accurate discussion, and offer writers a way forward in composition and revision. They are not complete— the effects and uses of rhyme exceed all handy analysis, especially where accents and non-standard spelling are involved, and it can *always* surprise—but there are nevertheless connections between particular poetic effects and particular combinations of rhyme, awareness of which can guide writers to control, as much as readers to understand, what is going on.

The varieties of rhyme

Degree

rime riche	full rhyme + preceding elements	right hand / fright and
full rhyme	last stressed vowel + following elements	hand / band
vowel rhyme (half-rhyme)	last stressed vowel only	hand / hang
pararhyme (half-rhyme)	following elements only	hand / bind

Type

stressed rhyme (masculine)	last stressed vowel in last syllable	hand / band
unstressed rhyme (feminine)	last stressed vowel not in last syllable	handing / standing
mosaic rhyme	involving multiple words	tanned hands / bandstand
Hudibrastic rhyme	deliberately silly mosaic rhyme	handstand / grand, planned
autorhyme (identical or null rhyme)	repetition	hypotenuse / lot o'news
eye rhyme	in spelling only, not pronunciation	cough / bough
spelling rhyme	with distorted orthography	Charles II / beckoned
wrenched rhyme	last vowel mis-stressed	hand / brigánd
embedded rhyme	with a medial syllable in a word	handout / band
broken rhyme	displays embedded rhyme	band / hand-/out...

Position

terminal rhyme (end rhyme)	between words ending lines
medial rhyme (internal rhyme)	at least one rhyme-word is not terminal
leonine rhyme	between the mid- and end-words of the same line
initial rhyme	between words beginning lines

Relation

monorhyme	*aaaa*	hand / band / sand / land
single rhyme	*aabc*	hand / band / foot / arm
	abac	hand / foot / band / arm
	abca	hand / foot / arm / band
	abbc	hand / foot / put / arm
	abcb	hand / foot / arm / put
	abcc	hand / foot / arm / harm
couplet rhyme	*aabb*	hand / band / foot / put
cross-rhyme	*abab*	hand / foot / band / put
arch-rhyme	*abba*	hand / foot / put / band
delayed, accelerated	relative to any established pattern	
chain rhyme	chaining successive stanzas together with a shared rhyme	
semantic	between words with related meanings	alive / survive
counter-semantic	between words with opposed meanings	save / grave
thematic	between meanings thematic to a given work	

Rhyme in use and by demonstration

I'm a poet
And I know it:
Thus I show it
And sometimes blow it.

The broadest rules of thumb are that:

(1) the consonance of full rhyme tends to confirm sense, while the dissonance of half-rhyme tends to question or ironize sense;

(2) stressed rhyme tends to affirmation, and unstressed rhyme to comedy;

(3) medial rhymes tend to call for accelerated delivery;

(4) cross-rhyme marches while arch-rhyme curvets, monorhyme hammers, couplets epigrammatize, and so on.

As with all such rough rules there are infinite exceptions, and one can always work against the grain—but to try, for example, to write a grave or joyous anthem using unstressed pararhymes ('handing/ binding', 'finger/clanger') is a needlessly uphill task: real anthems prefer stressed full rhyme, in couplets (such as 'high/die/sneer/ here' in 'The Red Flag') or even triplets ('glare/air/there', 'victorious/glorious/over us'). This last, from the British national anthem, 'God Save the Queen', is a warning as well as an example: the unstressed 'victorious/glorious' and mosaic pararhyme '/over us' are in practice neither as comedic nor as dissonant as one might in theory expect; deliberately overstated lyrics and a clever melody (falling on 'victorious' and 'glorious' but rising with 'over us') enable the anthem to carry its risky rhymes, usually without difficulty. More private poems are unlikely to command such resources, and risk will be correspondingly higher.

An interesting lesson in the powers of rhyme is offered by *ottava rima*, an eight-line Italian stanza rhyming *abababcc*. Now strongly associated in English with the wicked comedy of Lord Byron's *Beppo* and *Don Juan*, *ottava rima* started in Italian as a straightforward narrative stanza, and its earliest major appearances in English are translations, beginning in 1591 with Sir John Harington's of *Orlando Furioso* by Ludovico Ariosto (1474–1533). Harington was Elizabeth I's godson, and having translated one canto about an orgy to circulate among the ladies of the Queen's Bedchamber, he was set to translating the other 45 as a punishment; one that he took in good part:

> Of Dames, of Knights, of armes, of loves delight,
>   Of curtesies, of high attempts I speake,
> Then when the Moores transported all their might
>   On Affrick seas the force of France to breake,
> Incited by the youthfull heate and spite
>   Of *Agramant* their king that vowd to wreake
> The death of king *Trayano* (lately slayne)
> Upon the Romane Emperour *Charlemaine*.

I will no less *Orlandos* acts declare
    (A tale in prose ne verse yet song or sayd)
Who fell bestraught with love, a hap most rare
    To one that erst was counted wise and stayd.
If my sweet Saint that causeth my like care
    My slender muse afford some gracious ayd,
I make no doubt but I shall have the skill
As much as I have promist to fulfil.

Vouchsafe (O Prince of most renowmed race,
    The ornament and hope of this our time)
T'accept this gift presented to your grace
    By me your servant, rudely here in rime,
And though I paper pay and inke in place
    Of deeper debt, yet take it for no cryme:
It may suffise a poore and humble debter
To say and if he could it should be better.

                            (Book I, stanzas 1–3)

Ottava rima breaks down into a cross-rhymed sestet + terminal couplet (6+2, *ababab-cc*), and works well as a beast of narrative burden because the tick-tock sestet can carry action while the couplet offers space for a summary comment or moral reflection. In English, however, the need for two triple rhymes tests skill, and Harington's first *b*-rhyme, 'speake/breake/wreake', signals that pararhyme will be allowed. It also begins with witty self-deprecation, "I speake"—Virgil's famous formula opening his *Aeneid* was "*Arma virumque cano*", meaning 'Arms and the man *I sing*'—and the rhyming reminders of "speake" underscore that humility. Similarly, allowing his second *c*-rhyme, 'skill/fulfil', as mildly wrenched, Harington sticks to stressed rhyme (even in 'lately slayne/*Charlemaine*') until the third *c*-rhyme, 'debter/better'—a fine example of the link between unstressed rhyme and (ironic) comedy. The third stanza aptly served Harington's private needs (his book is fulsomely dedicated to Elizabeth), and the rhyming sequences in the sestet, 'race/place/grace' and 'time/rime/cryme', skilfully insinuate a personal apology to his godmother into the fabric of his penance.

Little is known about Edward Fayrfax other than that in 1600 he published a translation of Torquato Tasso's *Il Goffredo* (later retitled *Gerusalemme Liberata*) as *Godfrey of Bulloigne or The Recoverie of Ierusalem*. Tasso (1544–95), fearful of the Inquisition, produced a sombre Christian epic about the Crusaders' conquest

of Jerusalem in 1099, lacking Ariosto's lively fantasy but also in
ottava rima; Fayrfax followed suit:

> The sacred armies and the godly knight
>   That the great sepulchre of Christ did free
> I sing; much wrought his valour and foresight,
>   And in that glorious war much suffer'd he:
> In vain 'gainst him did hell oppose her might,
>   In vain the Turks and Morians armed be;
> His soldiers wild, to brawls and mutines prest,
> Reduced he to peace; so heaven him blest.
>
> O heavenly muse, that not with fading bays
>   Deckest thy brow by th' Heliconian spring,
> But sittest, crown'd with stars' immortal rays,
>   In heaven, where legions of bright angels sing,
> Inspire life in my wit, my thoughts upraise,
>   My verse ennoble, and forgive the thing,
> If fictions light I mix with truth divine,
> And fill these lines with others' praise than thine.
>
> Thither thou know'st the world is best inclined
>   Where luring Parnass most his sweet imparts,
> And truth convey'd in verse of gentle kind,
>   To read perhaps will move the dullest hearts;
> So we, if children young diseas'd we find,
>   Anoint with sweets the vessel's foremost parts,
> To make them taste the potions sharp we give;
> They drink deceived; and so deceiv'd they live.
>
> (Book I, stanzas 1–3)

As that last line attests, Fayrfax was capable of power and delicacy,
and he was a more faithful translator than Harington, but it isn't
only Tasso's epic subject and often gloomy tone that weigh him
down. Metrically Fayrfax is too often flat-footed ("Reduced he to
peace; so heaven him blest"); syntactically he tends as unhappily
to echo Spenser ("Anoint with sweets the vessel's foremost parts")
as to anticipate Milton ("Where luring Parnass most his sweet
imparts"); but his rhymes do not help. In the first *a*-rhyme the
wrenching of 'foresíght' to match 'knight/.../might' is earlier and
more awkward than Harington's 'skill/fulfil', and the first *c*-rhyme,
'prest/blest', is, if then allowable, unfortunate. But most tellingly,
there is no unstressed or half-rhyme in these stanzas, and readers
must wait until stanza 17 for the first variation from stressed full
rhyme ('asunder/wonder') and stanza 30 for the second
('given/uneven'). Such constant and heavy chiming may work well

in an anthem or in shorter stanzas demanding only double rhymes, but in an epic with triple rhymes it soon begins to thump and annoy.

Listened to one-by-one, Fayrfax wasn't doing anything particularly wrong in his lines or his rhymes. A verse-translator's lot is never easy, and there are anxieties and a grimness in Tasso's work that Fayrfax perhaps catches in what may seem like stumbles and relentlessness. The slalom of each sestet and halt of each couplet are constantly demanding, and freedom of movement always burdened by fidelity of translation. Yet with the best will in the world, Fayrfax (some shining moments excepted) is duller to read than Harington, and failure in variety, especially of rhyme, is a primary reason. Though complex, this phenomenon is familiar to everyone who has written in rhyme: each line seems fine in itself, each achieved rhyme acceptable; but as lines accumulate the whole seems more and more a botch-job, a series of local solutions without larger purpose.

Primo Levi pinned part of the problem in 'Rhyming on the Counterattack', when he observed that the rhyming poet:

is committed to ending a verse not with the word dictated by discursive logic but with another, strange word, which must be drawn from the few that end 'in the right way'. And so he is compelled to deviate, to leave the path that is easier because it is predictable; now, reading what is predictable bores us and so does not inform us. The restriction of rhyme obliges the poet to resort to the unpredictable: compels him to invent, to 'find'; and to enrich his lexicon with unusual terms; to bend his syntax; in short, innovate.

        (*The Mirror Maker: Stories and Essays* (trans. Raymond Rosenthal, 1989; London: Minerva, 1990), p.113)

Just so: but such innovation cannot, especially in a long poem, be allowed to accumulate higgledy-piggledy, and the "restriction of rhyme" is not a restriction to stressed full rhyme. One need not go as far as Vladimir Nabokov, who in creating chess-problems liked "form to bulge and burst like a sponge bag containing a small furious devil", to recognize that variation of rhyme is necessary in any extended use of a stanza-form; and to discipline such variant rhymes over thousands of lines demands a coherent attitude—an overarching capacity to govern expedience and guide virtuosity.

Enter Byron. He knew Harington's and Fayrfax's translations as

well as their originals, and having taken the form for a brisk spin in
the 99 stanzas of *Beppo* (1818), promptly embarked on the 2,000+
stanzas of *Don Juan* (1818–24), left unfinished at his premature
death:

> I want a hero: an uncommon want,
> When every year and month sends forth a new one,
> Till, after cloying the gazettes with cant,
> The age discovers he is not the true one;
> Of such as these I should not care to vaunt,
> I'll therefore take our ancient friend Don Juan,
> We all have seen him in the pantomime
> Sent to the devil, somewhat ere his time.
>
> Vernon, the butcher Cumberland, Wolfe, Hawke,
> Prince Ferdinand, Granby, Burgoyne, Keppel, Howe,
> Evil and good, have had their tithe of talk,
> And fill'd their sign-posts then, like Wellesley now;
> Each in their turn like Banquo's monarchs stalk,
> Followers of fame, 'nine farrow' of that sow:
> France, too, had Buonaparté and Dumourier
> Recorded in the Moniteur and Courier.
>
> Barnave, Brissot, Condorcet, Mirabeau,
> Petion, Clootz, Danton, Marat, La Fayette,
> Were French, and famous people, as we know;
> And there were others, scarce forgotten yet,
> Joubert, Hoche, Marceau, Lannes, Dessaix, Moreau,
> With many of the military set,
> Exceedingly remarkable at times,
> But not at all adapted to my rhymes.
>
> (Canto I, stanzas 1–3)

It is Byron's personality that is so compelling, but from the outset
rhyme is foregrounded as a principal pleasure. The first *a*-rhyme,
'want/cant/vaunt', sharply establishes semantic pararhyme, while
an outrageous unstressed mosaic *b*-rhyme, 'new one/true one',
comically imposes English pronunciation on '/Juan'. In the second
stanza 'Howe/now/sow' is disrespectfully close to 'How now,
brown cow?', while the notably unstressed 'Dumóur-i-er/
Cóur-i-er', if better pronounced than 'Juan', undermines the
dignity of being mentioned in Parisian dispatches. The third
stanza opens (like the second, but this time using French names)
with a clever catalogue, improbably establishing the *a*-rhyme as
'Mirabeau' and *b*-rhyme as 'La Fayette', awakening readers'
anticipation. Both are stressed, and after the experience of

'Dumourier/Courier' apparently demand French rhymes—but Byron promptly supplies English ones, 'as we know' and 'forgotten yet', making such interlingual rhyming sound easy, which it isn't. By way of comparison, William Aytoun's 'To Britain' (in *The Oxford Book of Sonnets*) wobbles perilously when its rhyme for 'Waterloo' is *'sauve qui peut'*, and James Lasdun's 'Powder Compact' has to labour to earn its last rhyme of *'memento mori'* and 'reliquary'.

Critically, and like Harington ("this gift presented to your grace / By me your servant, rudely here in rime") but unlike Fayrfax, who was more worried about irreverence, Byron then addresses the issue of rhyming directly. Without Harington's need for personal apology, he has no call to be self-deprecating, and his downbeat return in the third couplet to plain speech and stressed monosyllabic rhyme (times/rhymes) declares a personal presence that will be mediated largely through manipulations of rhyme. Every stanza thereafter has some new rhyming delight to offer, but always contained within the tonal mesh Byron generates by patterning voices, and supported by his narrative presence and wit. It is a mode many have attempted, but in which few have succeeded in Byron's measure; Auden perhaps came closest, in his long *Letter to Lord Byron* (1936), but abandoned *ottava rima* for the more English rhyme royal (a heptet rhyming *ababbcc*). Yet if *ottava rima* has not since Byron found an English-language poet able to handle it at its traditional narrative length, it has not, thanks to William Butler Yeats (1865–1939), fallen into disuse.

Much of what Yeats achieved with form is remarkable, but nothing more so than his late adoption of *ottava rima* as a lyric stanza, most famously in 'Sailing to Byzantium', most devastatingly in 'The Circus Animals' Desertion'. Part of his skill lies in his handling of *end-stopping*, the reinforcement of line-breaks with punctuation—marks, and *enjambent*, the wrapping of syntax from one line to the next, helping to blur and digest the necessary triple rhymes; but even in the earlier and easier 'Sailing to Byzantium' there is also a discord generated by pararhyme:

> THAT is no country for old men. The young
> In one another's arms, birds in the trees
> —Those dying generations—at their song,
> The salmon-falls, the mackerel-crowded seas,

> Fish, flesh, or fowl, commend all summer long
> Whatever is begotten, born, and dies.
> Caught in that sensual music all neglect
> Monuments of unageing intellect.

The awkward additional near-pararhyme of 'men' and 'young' across a disruptive full stop anticipates the *a*-pararhyme, 'young/song', and any comfort in the fullness of the first *b*-rhyme, 'trees/seas', and second *a*-rhyme, 'song/long', is lost in the second *b*-rhyme, '/dies' (again medially augmented, with 'is'), and the wrenching of 'intelléct' into conformity with 'neglect'.

In 'Among School Children' the discord grows worse:

> I WALK through the long schoolroom questioning;
> A kind old nun in a white hood replies;
> The children learn to cipher and to sing,
> To study reading-books and histories,
> To cut and sew, be neat in everything
> In the best modern way—the children's eyes
> In momentary wonder stare upon
> A sixty-year-old smiling public man.

There is a problem with stressing '-ing' endings as rhymes (as Shakespeare showed in sonnet 87, 'Farewell thou art too deare for my possessing'), and the extra stress on 'quéstioníng' is not helped by its rhyme: in any poetic opening 'sing' summons Virgil and the epic tradition, but here its subject is 'The children', not the Yeatsian 'I' who 'walks' and is briefly stared at, and smiles in practised habit or with nerves. Wrenching recurs with 'everything', while pararhyme sounds immediately in 'replies/ histories', and again, despairingly, in 'upon/man'.

Such discord could be traced in other late poems in *ottava rima*; its terminus is 'The Circus Animals' Desertion':

> I sought a theme and sought for it in vain,
> I sought it daily for six weeks or so.
> Maybe at last, being but a broken man,
> I must be satisfied with my heart, although
> Winter and summer till old age began
> My circus animals were all on show,
> Those stilted boys, that burnished chariot,
> Lion and woman and the Lord knows what.

The wrenched or pararhyming couplet has a Byronic gravity-in-levity, so that mock-seriousness and serious mockery are hard to tell apart, but it sounds rather hollow after the initial autorhyme of 'I sought' (picked up in 'at last'), the discordant *a*-pararhymes 'vain/man/began' (interacting with 'daily', 'broken', and 'animals'), and the qualifying or negative *b*-rhymes 'or so/although/on show'. So potent are these systematic dissonances that they become, in Eliot's phrase, the 'objective correlative' or physical embodiment of Yeats's dissatisfaction with himself: fuller rhymes and greater harmony would not correct a fault, but undo the whole.

Few of us can hope to redesign the coachwork of a major stanza in this way, but the general lesson holds good for all rhymers. Rhyme in any concentration demands sharp attention from the writer (and subsequently all readers); which does not mean slavish adherence to one sort of rhyme, but rather a plan within which variations can be marshalled. Harington, Byron, and Yeats share a professional poetic understanding of rhyme as in counterpoint to itself and to other prescribed elements of a form, an understanding that Fayrfax did not really have: and in 'free verse' (which means only a lack of prescription, not any proscription) the stakes will usually be higher, for rhyme will be operating in relative isolation. Hence (in part) Auden's wry observation that in free verse an 'infallible ear' is always required: a single bad rhyme, awkwardly wrenched or introducing a false note in diction or syntax, can bring ruin, yet a great poet can all but bend our ears to his or her will.

T. S. Eliot (1888–1965) went as far as anyone in the 'Dante' section of *The Dry Salvages*, the third of his *Four Quartets* (1942), abandoning rhyme itself but substituting a pattern of alternating stressed and unstressed endings ('re-enáctment/sháme/awáreness', 'hárm/vírtue/stáins' etc.) that manage with the faintest vowel rhymes and some help from layout to be heard as equivalent to full rhyme in Dantean *terza rima*—a lesson well learned by the Canadian poet-performer Leonard Cohen (b.1934), whose persistently 'mournful' sound owes much to unstressed endings (some rhyming, some blank). Almost as radical as Eliot though in a different manner, a recent sonnet called 'In Iowa' by the Irish Nobel Laureate Seamus Heaney (b.1937), has the quatrain rhyme-sequences 'Mennonites/afternoon/windscreen/

flits', 'gap/snow/seat/brow', and 'gears/wilderness/darkness/
tatters', plus the couplet 'hiss/waters'. This 4-4-4-2 structure
suggests a Shakespearean sonnet (rather than the Petrarchan 4-4-
3-3), which should properly have the rhyme scheme *abab cdcd
efef gg*, comprising three cross-rhymed quatrains and a couplet; in
Heaney's version, the third quatrain is arch-rhymed (*effe*) rather
than cross-rhymed, but otherwise, allowing for the persistent
pararhyme, the pairings of '-noon/-screen', '-ites/flits', 'snow/
brow', and 'hiss/waters' seem to be in the right places. The
supposed *c*-rhyme, 'gap/seat', however, is not a rhyme at all—
neither vowels nor following sounds match—and yet the pairing
seems in this company to strain towards being one. There is in the
poem no syntactical connection between "the open gap/of a field"
and the "iron seat" of a "mowing machine", but as expectation of
(para)rhyme tries to bind the words together I find myself
imagining the kinds of gaps iron seats often have, how
uncomfortable they are, and the elevated view the seats of farm-
machines offer over rolling farmland; even, ranging more widely
with the ideas of 'gap' and 'seat', that for Heaney, as intensely Irish
as he is cosmopolitan, to be 'In Iowa' is to be strikingly out of place.
In almost anyone else's work, 'gap/seat' would simply be a duff
moment, a failure of form or at best a shrug of defeat; in Heaney's
it is the free stroke of a master.

As in Yeats, and persistently in the First World War poems of
Wilfred Owen, half-rhyming serves Heaney by generating but also
containing anxieties and questionings; it is equally possible to go
the other way, and build intensities of full rhyme. Perhaps the
most notorious of all post-1945 lyrics, the terrifying 'Daddy' by
Sylvia Plath (1932–63), returns again and again, always unevenly,
to the same crooning rhyme-sound, 'do/shoe/blue/you/achoo/
gobbledygoo', while only occasionally and with tremendous power
delivering the rhyme that demands that sound, 'Jew'. Many other
aspects of 'Daddy' are irregular—the rhythm can sound jaunty,
which for some adds insult to injury, and the diction is sometimes
wilfully childish—but it is the hammering rhymes that most
people remember.

Such an extreme strategy is necessarily a one-off, but insistence of
rhyme can be very profitably harnessed. The lyrics of The
Waterboys' great lament 'Old England', from *This is the Sea* (1985),

for example, written by Mike Scott (b.1958) builds through triple and quadruple rhymes to a climactic description of a place "where criminals are televised politicians fraternize/journalists are dignified and everyone is civilised/and children stare with Heroin eyes". The complex beat and wrenched delivery more acceptable in song allows each of the medial and terminal rhymes, 'televised-fraternize/dignified-civilised', to sound clearly, building through their variations (-ised, -ize, -ied) an arch that apparently ends with 'civilised' as the full rhyme for 'televised'; only to be trumped, after the blow of the blank 'stare' where another medial rhyme might be expected, by the delayed, now hideously unexpected "Heroin eyes" and its horrible closeness to "fraternize". As the phrase is repeated it begins to sound like 'heroinise', and so to suggest (in a corporate-style word) a strategy of heroin-induced anaesthesia as a means of dulling exclusion and poverty, yet remains "Heroin eyes", a glassy pin-pointedness that is vile to see in anyone, and in massed children a peculiarly terrible thing. Rap lyrics and slam poetry also tend to try this route, often with real success, but can easily fall into the trap parodied by Blondie in 'Rapture', where a "man from Mars" who knows about "stars" hungrily eats up "cars", "bars", and "guitars" only because they rhyme.

Relatedly, one might think of Bob Dylan (Robert Zimmerman, b.1941), often accused of 'just trying to make it rhyme', but to many, a rhymer of astonishing skill. Helped in performance by the ambiguity between long lines with regular medial rhymes and enjambed short rhyming lines, one of his tricks is the use of prepositions as rhyme-words, as in 'Like a Rolling Stone': "Ain't it hard when you discover that / He really wasn't where it's at". The preceding "diplomat / Who carried on his shoulder a Siamese cat" is embarrassing for Dylan's defenders, but the rhymes on 'that' and 'at' carry in performance (if not on the page) a vengeful and insistent sneer made all the more powerful by the simple, functional words. Like most live performers Dylan also knows the value of stretching his vowels, and in the same song his recurrent rhymes for 'feel', as each stanza ends with an elongated 'meal' or 'steal', offset the far curter rhymes on the prepositions.

If a rhyming rock-and-roll villain is sought, the better candidate is Jim Morrison (James Douglas Morrison, 1943–71) of The Doors, who immortally declared both in the song 'Riders on the Storm' and the poem 'The Hitchhiker' that 'There's a killer on the road', but ruined things by adding—very much with rhyme but wholly without reason—that 'His brain is squirming like a toad'. It isn't that one cannot accept a squirming toad, nor that toads aren't killers, nor even that some connection between the look of a killer's brain and a toad squirming is beyond imagination, but that the rhyme is lazy, an obvious and weak choice when several far more interesting possibilities were readily available ('goad', 'mode', 'load'), never mind a raft of pararhymes beginning with 'mad' and 'bad', and vowel rhymes beginning with 'roam' and 'lone'. In a looping and self-consciously eerie (or portentous) song like 'Riders on the Storm', the clang of 'road/toad' cannot be easily borne without clear and apparent justification, and the results are notorious even among Morrison's most ardent defenders as a poet.

Rhyme of course has humbler and more homely uses than poetry and song, in proverbs, slogans, jingles, and birthday cards, but even when literary quality is in no way necessary, the rules of thumb remain useful. The notorious tweeness of printed birthday-card rhymes has much to do with tin-eared metre, but their stale sentimentality is equally to do with tired and rehashed rhymes, devoid of any effort to refurbish their meaning. Compare 'love/dove', 'love/above', 'dear/near' and the rest of their ilk with 'love/prove', 'love/give', and 'dear/far': yes, the dissonances could spiral out of control to undo a loving or celebratory tone, but they could equally introduce sufficient spine to lift the verse from limp servility to convention. The celebrated awfulness as a poet of William McGonagall (1830–1902) also has as much to do with his clumsy strivings after full rhyme as his obsession with commemorating transport disasters at interminable length. And I suspect that the condescension often shown to the plaintive or jolly (and once hugely popular) poems of Pam Ayres (b.1947), collected in such volumes as *Thoughts of a Late-Night Knitter* and *Some of Me Poetry* (both 1978), similarly has as much to do with her forced rhymes as her everyday subjects and calculated self-presentation as an amateur.

Finally, the issues that regional or national accents pose for rhyme are also best treated as resources, not problems. Occasional use of regional accent to create a rhyme in a poem that is otherwise accentless on the page is unwise; even intended comedy readily slides into snideness or jeering, and neither readers nor audiences tend to be forgiving. Systematic use of one's own regional accent, however, once derided by the establishment, is back with a vengeance, and may be indicated by spelling, as in 'giver/nivver' (for 'never'), or left to a reader's discretion. Tony Harrison, born to working-class parents in Leeds in 1937, famously pointed out in 'Them and [Uz]' (freely available is a wonderful reading by Harrison at the British Council website) that to Wordsworth, born in Cumberland, 'matter/water' was a full rhyme—but poetry "you see / 's been dubbed by [ʌs] into RP". '[Uz]' and '[ʌs]' represent the northern- and southern-English pronunciations of the pronoun 'us'—'[Uz]' rhymes with southern 'buzz' or 'booze', and '[ʌs]' with 'bus'—while 'RP' is Received Pronunciation, the supposedly accentless but in fact specifically southern sound that is 'normal' or 'proper', the 'Queen's' or 'BBC' English, in terms of which northerners (among others) are deemed to speak with an 'inferior' accent. Harrison's trenchant claim is that much great poetry has been rendered 'southern' on the page when its creators would in life have spoken with a northern (or whatever) accent, and even so small a thing as the short northern 'a' (making 'past' like 'pasta', not 'parsed') can have tremendous effects. His English teacher at Leeds Grammar School, to which he won a scholarship, once stopped him from reading Keats's 'Ode to a Nightingale' aloud because his accent 'barbarised' our "glorious heritage". Instead Harrison "played the drunken porter in *Macbeth*", and he has described his career as a "long, slow-burning revenge" on that teacher, poetically bringing home to the English the bigoted class and regional snobberies that divide them as a nation. Beyond domestic politics, in 'A Cold Coming', published in the news pages of *The Independent* during the First Gulf War in 1991, Harrison persistently rhymed 'Iraq' with a short 'a'— 'Iraq/back', or '/sack', or '/black', but never '/park' or '/dark'—and the snap of the short vowels is integral to a poem of bitter questions.

Similar issues recur fiercely in post-colonial poetry. The St Lucian Nobel Laureate Derek Walcott (b.1930), for example, late in 'Nearing Forty' (from *The Gulf*, 1969) rhymes 'clerk' with 'work', forcing readers to choose between the received southern-English pronunciation, 'clark', a pararhyme ('clark/work'), and a common but non-standard and *déclassé* pronunciation, 'clurk', a full rhyme ('clurk/work') that semantic harmony (clerks working) and the peaceful resolution of Walcott's poem seem to want. Or again, the Jamaican poet Edward Baugh (b.1937), responding in 'Nigger Sweat' (from *A Tale from the Rainforest*, 1988) to a notice in the Visa Section of the U. S. Embassy in Kingston requiring applicants to 'Kindly keep [documents] dry', pointedly rhymes the affirmatory patois pronoun 'weself' with 'life', fighting with semantic pararhyme against the humiliation of a place seemingly designed to "bruk-spirit" in those who must wait there.

The most general lessons, then, are variety and control. Those committed to verse may wish to experiment systematically with given stanzas using full and half-, or monosyllabic and mosaic, or stressed and unstressed rhyme; much may be learned in doing so. Those desiring rhymes only for light or occasional verse may equally profit by considering carefully the kind of rhyme they want, as well as their desired content. And for the comically or satirically minded, rhyme is a calculation that should never be ignored.

How to use this book

I'm a poet
And I know it:
As proud as William of Orange
I rhyme my way ... ~~cringe range binge~~ zorange

The Oxford Dictionary of Rhymes offers a toolkit to writers of all kinds. It will allow you to look up rhymes for specific words; browse sets of rhymes for inspiration; use the tips in the notes to create extra sets of rhymes; and learn from the poetry panels how other writers past and present have used rhyme.

The first half of the book is set out in 35 sections, each representing the sound of a word ending. The sounds (or phonic elements) are indicated using the most common spelling in English, starting with the vowel sounds, such as '-ay', '-ee', '-ow', '-oo', and moving on to consonant sounds, such as '-b', '-g', '-k', '-sh', and '-z'. There are 13 sections of words ending in vowel sounds, and 22 sections of words ending in consonant sounds. The sections are divided in approximately alphabetical order by sound, so that in the '-b' section you will find the following subsections: '-ab', '-arb', '-eb', '-airb', '-abe', '-eeb', '-ib', '-ibe', '-ob', etc. The consistent sequencing of subsections in this manner will enable you to source vowel rhymes across sections. Once you are familiar with the book, all this will allow you to browse the text, as well as to use the index to guide you. Browsing is a good way to make exciting and unexpected rhyming connections.

To find rhymes for a specific word, simply go to the index (which has 45,000 words to choose from, including proper names); there you will find a number which directs you to a corresponding section in the main text (e.g. 1.1 or 12.55). At that numbered section, you will find a list of all the words which rhyme with your chosen word. A subsection which begins with a bullet point and the first word in bold indicates a list of words which are full or perfect rhymes for each other. Other subsections will offer near or half-rhymes for your chosen word. In practice, the further away in the text you get from your chosen word, the less 'perfectly' the words will rhyme with it.

For example, if you look up the word 'candy' in the index, it will direct you to section 4.12 where you will find several subsections. The one which begins with the word '**Andy**' is the section you want for full rhymes. There you will find 'brandy', 'dandy', and 'Gandhi' among others. In the neighbouring sections, you will find 'hardy', 'lardy', 'daddy', and 'laddie', all of which are pararhymes for 'candy'.

The notes within sections will help you to create whole new sets of rhymes, and will enable you to link different rhyming sets in the book. For instance you can make additional rhymes for words such as 'shallow' (and the other words in that section), by adding '-ness' to make 'shallowness', 'sallowness', and 'fallowness'. Also, by adding '-(r)ed' to words like 'blur' and 'deter', you can create a new set of rhyming words: 'absurd', 'overheard', and so on. The in-text notes will thus help you to make new and unexpected rhymes.

In some cases, derived words (words with suffixes such as '-ness', '-ly', '-ed' and so on) are not listed explicitly, but the notes will indicate when extra rhyming lists can be created by adding these to an existing list of words.

The poetry panels contain useful information on types of rhymes and give examples from many different styles of writing, from sonnets and songs, to nursery rhymes and limericks. Their purpose is both to illustrate technical aspects of rhyme and to inspire you to explore the possibilities for yourself. Searching for rhymes has never been more fun or enlightening. Good luck and good rhyming!

JOHN LENNARD
May 2005

List of sections

Section 1: -ar

1.1

- **aargh**, Accra, afar, ah, aha, aide-mémoire, ajar, Alcazar, are, Armagh, armoire, Artois, au revoir, baa, bah, bar, barre, bazaar, beaux-arts, Bekaa, bête noire, Bihar, bizarre, blah, Bogotá, Bonnard, bra, cafard, café noir, Calabar, car, Carr, Castlebar, catarrh, Changsha, char, charr, cigar, comme ci comme ça, commissar, coup d'état, de haut en bas, devoir, Dhofar, Directoire, Du Bois, Dumas, Dunbar, éclat, embarras de choix, escritoire, fah, famille noire, far, feu de joie, film noir, foie gras, Fra, galah, gar, guar, guitar, ha, hah, ha-ha, Halacha, hurrah, hussar, huzza, insofar, Invar, jar, je ne sais quoi, ka, kala-azar, Kandahar, Khorramshahr, knar, Krasnodar, Kwa, la-di-da, lah, Lehár, Loire, ma, mama, mamma, mar, Mardi Gras, ménage à trois, mirepoix, moire, Navarre, noir, objet d'art, pa, pah, Panama, papa, par, Pará, Paraná, pas, pâté de foie gras, peau-de-soie, pictà, Pinot Noir, pooh-bah, poult-de-soie, pya, rah, registrar, Saar, Salazar, Sana'a, sang-froid, scar, schwa, Seychellois, shah, Shangri-La, shikar, ska, sol-fa, spa, spar, star, Starr, Stranraer, ta, tahr, tar, tartare, tata, tra-la, tsar, Twa, Villa, voilà, waratah, yah

1.2

- penniä • caviar

1.3

- boyar

1.4

- Akbar • handlebar • sandbar • kasbah
- baba • rebar • heelbar • Finbar
- millibar • coolibah • minibar
- Zanzibar • sidebar • crossbar
- **crowbar**, towbar
- rollbar • Nicobar • isobar • durbar

1.5

- cha-cha

1.6

- Dada • radar • zamindar • Pindar
- chowkidar • havildar • Godard
- doodah
- **purdah**, sirdar

1.7

- Afar • Sofar

1.8

- gaga • Elgar
- **Degas**, Hagar
- budgerigar • nougat • Bulgar

1.9

- **ha-ha**, Praha
- brouhaha • Mudéjar • pakeha • Doha
- hoo-ha • Omaha

1.10

- Sharjah • nightjar

1.11

- **Dakar**, fracas
- tramcar • Shankar
- **Farquhar**, kaka, markka, taka
- railcar • cablecar • streetcar • Indycar
- Hamilcar • tricar • sidecar • stockcar
- boxcar • chukar • Issachar • motorcar
- advocaat

1.12

- verglas • Alar • Mylar • foulard
- hoopla

1.13

- Dagmar • Kalmar • grandma • Tamar
- **Valdemar**, Waldemar
- Weimar • Bislama • grandmama
- Kostroma • Fermat

1.14

- dinar • seminar • sonar • Fragonard

1.15

- grandpa • feldspar • oompah
- fluorspar • grandpapa

1.16

- Marat • rah-rah • bajra • baccarat
- Aymara • Seurat

1.17

- ahimsa • paisa • pulsar

1.18

- entrechat

1.19

- Qatar • Telstar • sitar • Ishtar • co-star
- lodestar • sunstar • megastar
- superstar • avatar • earthstar

1.20

- Cathar

1.21

- Avar • Alvar
- **bolivar**, Bolívar
- cultivar • shalwar • samovar

1.22

- Valois • chamois
- **fatwa**, patois
- wah-wah • Hardwar • memoir
- Renoir • peignoir • pissoir • Chippewa
- **François**, Françoise
- renvoi • Vaudois • boudoir
- pourboire • bourgeois • abattoir
- fille de joie • Delacroix • repertoire
- conservatoire • reservoir

1.23

- Magyar • Chechnya • Iyyar

1.24

- **César**, quasar

Section 2: **-air**

2.1

- **affair**, affaire, air, Altair, Althusser, Anvers, Apollinaire, Astaire, aware, Ayer, Ayr, bare, bear, bêche-de-mer, beware, billionaire, Blair, blare, Bonaire, cafetière, care, chair, chargé d'affaires, chemin de fer, Cher, Clair, Claire, Clare, commissionaire, compare, concessionaire, cordon sanitaire, couvert, Daguerre, dare, debonair, declare, derrière, despair, doctrinaire, éclair, e'er, elsewhere, ensnare, ere, extraordinaire, Eyre, fair, fare, fayre, Finisterre, flair, flare, Folies-Bergère, forbear, forswear, foursquare, glair, glare, hair, hare, heir, Herr, impair, jardinière, Khmer, Kildare, La Bruyère, lair, laissez-faire, legionnaire, luminaire, mal de mer, mare, mayor, meunière, mid-air, millionaire, misère, Mon-Khmer, multimillionaire, ne'er, Niger, nom de guerre, outstare, outwear, pair, pare, parterre, pear, père, pied-à-terre, Pierre, plein-air, prayer, questionnaire, rare, ready-to-wear, rivière, Rosslare, Santander, savoir faire, scare, secretaire, share, snare, solitaire, Soufrière, spare, square, stair, stare, surface-to-air, swear, Tailleferre, tare, tear, their, there, they're, vin ordinaire, Voltaire, ware, wear, Weston-super-Mare, where, yeah

2.2

- Molière • première • son et lumière • Robespierre

2.3

- threadbare • Colbert • Rambert
- **forbear**, forebear
- Flaubert • bugbear • Camembert

2.4

- armchair • deckchair • wheelchair • pushchair

2.5

- fanfare • carfare • welfare • airfare
- **Mayfair**, Playfair
- fieldfare • warfare • funfair
- thoroughfare

Rime riche (or *identical rhyme*) includes rhymes created with homophones (words which sound the same but have different meanings and spellings):

"All things thy fancy hath desired of me
Thou hast received. I have prepared for thee
Within my house a spacious chamber, where
Are delicate things to handle and to wear [...]

(Edna St Vincent Millay, 'The Suicide')

2.6

• camelhair • maidenhair • longhair
• horsehair • shorthair • mohair

2.7

• haircare • skincare • Medicare
• childcare • aftercare

2.8

• Sinclair • Baudelaire

2.9

• nightmare • commère

2.10

• **ampere**, milliampere
• compère

2.11

• confrère

2.12

• corsair

2.13

• timeshare
• ploughshare (US plowshare)

2.14

• hectare

2.15

• flatware • hardware • glassware
• neckwear • headsquare • setsquare
• delftware • menswear • shareware
• tableware • rainwear • freeware
• beachwear • T-square • creamware
• swimwear • tinware • knitwear
• giftware • kitchenware
• womenswear • anywhere
• everywhere • nightwear • software
• sportswear • nowhere • stoneware
• cookware • footwear • somewhere
• ovenware • ironware • underwear
• leisurewear • Delaware • Tupperware
• outerwear • otherwhere • silverware
• workwear • earthenware

> Try rhyming one word with a set of two: nightwear, might wear; nowhere, go there. ⓘ

2.16

• Gruyère

Section 3: **-ay**

3.1

- **affray**, agley, aka, allay, Angers, A-OK, appellation contrôlée, array, assay, astray, au fait, auto-da-fé, away, aweigh, aye, bay, belay, betray, bey, Bombay, Bordet, boulevardier, bouquet, brae, bray, café au lait, Carné, cassoulet, Cathay, chassé, chevet, chez, chiné, clay, convey, Cray, crème brûlée, crudités, cuvée, cy-pres, day, decay, deejay, dégagé, distinguée, downplay, dray, Dufay, Dushanbe, eh, embay, engagé, essay, everyday, faraway, fay, fey, flay, fray, Frey, fromage frais, gainsay, gay, Gaye, Genet, gilet, glissé, gray, grey, halfway, hay, heigh, hey, hooray, Hubei, Hué, hurray, inveigh, jay, jeunesse dorée, José, Kay, Kaye, Klee, Kray, Lae, lay, lei, Littré, Lough Neagh, lwei, Mae, maguey, Malay, Mallarmé, Mandalay, Marseilles, may, midday, midway, mislay, misplay, Monterrey, Na-Dene, nay, né, née, neigh, Ney, noway, obey, O'Dea, okay, olé, outlay, outplay, outstay, outweigh, oyez, part-way, pay, Pei, per se, pince-nez, play, portray, pray, prey, purvey, qua, Quai d'Orsay, Rae, rangé, ray, re, reflet, relevé, roman-à-clef, Santa Fé, say, sei, Shar Pei, shay, slay, sleigh, sley, spae, spay, Spey, splay, spray, stay, straightaway, straightway, strathspey, stray, Sui, survey, sway, Taipei, Tay, they, today, tokay, Torbay, Tournai, trait, tray, trey, two-way, ukiyo-e, underlay, way, waylay, Wei, weigh, wey, Whangarei, whey, yea

3.2

- **déshabillé**, plié

3.3

- **Chevalier**, Duvalier
- tablier
- **atelier**, Tortelier
- Rainier •croupier •Le Verrier •Kyrie
- Du Maurier •couturier •Cartier
- métier
- **Poitier**, Poitiers
- bustier •Olivier •Cuvier •Lavoisier
- Le Corbusier

3.4

- foyer

3.5

- **Niue**, roué

3.6

- habitué

3.7

- abbé •thebe •sickbay •yohimbe
- flambé •sorbet •rosebay

3.8

- Elche •seviche
- **Croce**, mezza voce
- Duce

3.9

- **Allende**, duende
- Wednesday
- **heyday**, mayday, payday
- bidet • weekday • Halliday • holiday
- Friday • Hobday • washday • Corday
- **magna cum laude**, summa cum laude
- **Daudet**, démodé
- noonday • Tuesday
- **Domesday**, doomsday
- Yaoundé • someday
- **Monday**, sundae, Sunday
- Muscadet • workaday • faraday
- Saturday • yesterday • workday
- birthday • Thursday

> [i] Try rhyming one word with a set of two: bidet, key day; sundae, one day.

3.10

- café • cybercafé • parfait • coryphée
- buffet

3.11

- distingué • reggae • Sergei • Tenzing Norgay • nosegay

3.12

- Piaget • negligee • protégé • Roget
- Fabergé

3.13

- popinjay

3.14

- parquet
- **appliqué**, piqué
- **Biscay**, risqué
- communiqué • tourniquet • sobriquet
- manqué

- **cloqué**, croquet
- Malplaquet

3.15

- **ballet**, Calais, chalet, Hallé, palais, pis aller
- matchplay • parlay
- **cor anglais**, franglais
- **melee**, pappardelle, Pelé
- endplay • Nestlé • airplay
- **belay**, relay
- replay • screenplay • Millais • inlay
- misplay • cantabile • roundelay
- teleplay • pipeclay • byplay • volet
- bobsleigh • foreplay • swordplay
- horseplay • outlay • paso doble
- stroke play • soufflé • bouclé
- gunplay • cabriolet • Rabelais
- underlay • Beaujolais • Charolais
- interplay • overlay • wordplay

> [i] Create extra rhymes by adding -ing or -ed to words like belay and replay.

3.16

- gamay
- **lamé**, Niamey
- Aimée • animé • consommé • Lomé
- **résumé**, resume
- gourmet • entremets

3.17

- Manet • carnet
- **nota bene**, René
- Binet • estaminet
- **gratiné**, matinée
- **cloisonné**, donnée, Dubonnet, Monet
- Mornay • panettone • Chardonnay
- Hogmanay

3.18

- frappé • jaspé
- **épée**, Pepe

- Príncipe
- **coupé**, Nupe, toupée
- agape • canapé

3.19

- Le Carré • Sierra Madre • ashtray
- **mare**, soirée
- padre • Castlereagh • beret • sempre
- X-ray • affairé • hairspray • respray
- Tigray • stingray • in-tray • émigré
- vertebrae
- **foray**, moray
- **chambray**, chambré, hombre, ombré
- André • osprey • entrée
- **con amore**, Doré, Fauré
- sucre • outré • Vouvray • bourrée
- sunray
- **Desirée**, Dies Irae
- **curé**, purée
- cabaret

3.20

- **déclassé**, glacé, laissez-passer
- passé
- **fiancé**, fiancée
- essay • naysay
- **lycée**, plissé
- pensée
- **repoussé**, retroussé
- hearsay

3.21

- **attaché**, cachet, papier-mâché, sachet, sashay
- Beaumarchais • recherché • cliché
- crochet • touché • ricochet • Pinochet

3.22

- **latte**, maté, pâté, pattée, satay
- concertante • backstay • commedia dell'arte, écarté, Jubilate
- **fouetté**, jeté, mantellette
- Deo volente • mainstay • décolleté

- cinéma-vérité • diamanté • bobstay
- **forte**, panforte, prêt-à-porter
- forestay • sauté • velouté

3.23

- Pathé

3.24

- pavé • névé • corvée • duvet
- champlevé • survey

3.25

- Kabwe • hatchway • trackway
- tramway • gangway • Yahweh
- archway • parkway • pathway
- headway • segue • expressway
- **airway**, fairway, stairway
- railway • gateway
- **freeway**, keyway, leeway, seaway
- speedway • breezeway • Midway
- ridgeway
- **shipway**, slipway
- Kitwe • alleyway • Hemingway
- anyway • carriageway • entryway
- steerageway • taxiway • passageway
- **byway**, highway, skyway
- **guideway**, tideway
- bridleway • Steinway • driveway
- Otway
- **doorway**, Norway
- Broadway • walkway
- **Galway**, hallway
- causeway • roadway • throughway
- sluiceway • footway • subway
- someway • runway • clearway
- areaway • flyaway
- **stowaway**, throwaway
- hideaway • foldaway
- **breakaway**, takeaway
- galloway • rollaway
- **colourway** (*US* colorway), mulloway
- Greenaway • Stornoway • runaway
- caraway • tearaway • castaway
- getaway • straightaway • waterway

- motorway - cutaway - Hathaway
- giveaway - companionway - sternway

3.26

- **soigné**, soignée

3.27

- blasé
- **Bizet**, Champs-Élysées, frisée
- **exposé**, rosé

Section 4: **-ee**

4.1

- **absentee**, addressee, adoptee,
agree, allottee, amputee, appellee,
appointee, appraisee, après-ski,
assignee, attendee, bailee,
bain-marie, Bangui, bargee, bawbee,
be, Bea, bee, bootee, bouquet garni,
bourgeoisie, Brie, BSc, buckshee,
Capri, cc, chimpanzee, cohabitee,
conferee, consignee, consultee, Cree,
debauchee, decree, dedicatee, Dee,
degree, deportee, dernier cri,
detainee, devisee, devotee, divorcee,
draftee, dree, Dundee, dungaree,
eau-de-vie, emcee, employee,
endorsee, en famille, ennui,
enrollee, escapee, esprit, evacuee,
examinee, expellee, fee,
fiddle-de-dee, flea, flee, fleur-de-lis,
foresee, franchisee, free, fusee
(*US* fuzee), Gardaí, garnishee, gee,
ghee, glee, goatee, grandee, Grand
Prix, grantee, Guarani, guarantee,
he, indictee, inductee, internee,
interviewee, invitee, jamboree,
Jaycee, jeu d'esprit, key, knee, Lea,
lee, legatee, Leigh, lessee, Ley,
licensee, loanee, lychee, manatee,
Manichee, maquis, Marie, marquee,
me, Midi, mortgagee, MSc, nominee,
obligee, Otomi, parolee, Parsee, parti

pris, patentee, Pawnee, payee, pea,
pee, permittee, plc, plea, pledgee,
pollee, presentee, promisee, quay,
ratatouille, referee, refugee,
releasee, repartee, retiree, returnee,
rupee, scot-free, scree, sea, secondee,
see, settee, Shanxi, Shawnee, shchi,
she, shea, si, sirree, ski, spree,
standee, suttee, tant pis, tea, tee,
tee-hee, Tennessee, testee, the, thee,
three, thuggee, Tiree, Torquay,
trainee, Tralee, transferee, tree,
Trincomalee, trustee, tutee, twee,
Twi, undersea, vestee, vis-à-vis,
wagon-lit, Waikiki, warrantee, we,
wee, whee, whoopee, ye, yippee,
Zuider Zee

4.2

- **Agnus Dei**, clayey, Pompeii

4.3

- Danae •filariae •torii •differentiae
- prima facie •facetiae •reliquiae

4.4

- **Hawaii**, skyey

A combination of *unstressed* (or *feminine*) *rhyme*, *autorhyme*, and *medial
rhyme* gives this passage a lilting and soft cadence:

Time for you and time for me,
And time yet for a hundred indecisions,
And for a hundred visions and revisions,
Before the taking of a toast and tea.

(T. S. Eliot, 'The Love Song of J. Alfred Prufrock')

> Two successive lines that rhyme are called a *rhyming couplet*; this example from a well-known Shakespeare sonnet is also a *heroic couplet* (written in iambic pentameter which means five stressed syllables: ti-TUM ti-TUM ti-TUM ti-TUM ti-TUM):
>
> So long as men can breathe or eyes can see,
> So long lives this, and this gives life to thee.
>
> (William Shakespeare, Sonnet XVIII 'Shall I Compare thee to a Summer's Day?')

4.5

- strawy

4.6

- Towy

4.7

- **blowy**, doughy, joey, showy, snowy, toey, towy, Zoë
- shadowy • meadowy • echoey
- **sallowy**, tallowy
- yellowy
- **billowy**, pillowy, willowy
- arrowy • furrowy • tomatoey

4.8

- **bluey**, chewy, chop suey, cooee, Dewey, dewy, Drambuie, feng shui, gluey, gooey, hooey, Hughie, Louie, Louis, phooey, rouille, screwy, Wanganui
- mildewy • sinewy

4.9

- Anouilh

4.10

- **abbey**, cabby, crabby, flabby, gabby, grabby, Rabbie, scabby, shabby, tabby, yabby
- namby-pamby

- **Abu Dhabi**, Babi, Darby, derby, kohlrabi, Mugabe, Punjabi, Wahhabi
- **Entebbe**, plebby
- cobwebby
- **Achebe**, baby, maybe
- Naseby • crybaby • bushbaby
- **freebie**, Hebe, phoebe
- Libby • Digby
- **astilbe**, Philby, trilby
- Dimbleby • nimby • Whitby
- **frisbee**, Thisbe
- Grimsby • renminbi • honeybee
- oribi
- **Bobbie**, bobby, Gobbi, hobby, knobby, lobby, snobby, swabbie
- Dolby • zombie • Crosby
- **corbie**, warby
- Albee • Formby • Port Moresby
- **adobe**, dhobi, dobe, Nairobi, obi, Robey
- Toynbee
- **booby**, jube, newbie, Newby, ruby
- would-be
- **chubby**, clubby, cubby, grubby, hubby, nubby, scrubby, shrubby, stubby, tubby

> Create extra rhymes by changing words like chubby to chubbiness, or to chubbier and chubbiest.

- rugby • bumblebee • brumby • busby
- Niobe • Jacobi • Lockerbie • Allenby
- Willoughby • wallaby • wannabe
- Araby • tsessebi • herby

4.11

- **Apache**, catchy, patchy, scratchy, snatchy

- **hibachi**, Karachi, Liberace, starchy, vivace
- **sketchy**, stretchy, tetchy
- squelchy •Strachey
- **caliche**, Campeche, peachy, preachy, screechy
- **bitchy**, itchy, kitschy, pitchy, Richie, titchy, twitchy
- Medici •semplice
- **blotchy**, bocce, notchy, splotchy
- **grouchy**, pouchy, slouchy
- **sotto voce**, viva voce
- **Bertolucci**, smoochy, Vespucci
- **archduchy**, duchy, touchy
- churchy

4.12

- **baddy**, caddie, caddy, daddy, faddy, kabaddi, laddie, paddy
- **alcalde**, Chaldee, Fittipaldi, Vivaldi
- **Andy**, bandy, brandy, candy, dandy, Gandhi, glissandi, handy, jim-dandy, Kandy, Mandy, modus operandi, Nandi, randy, Río Grande, sandhi, sandy, sforzandi, shandy
- **cadi**, cardy, Guardi, Hardie, hardy, jihadi, lardy, Mahdi, mardy, Saadi, samadhi, tardy, Yardie
- foolhardy •autostrade
- **already**, Eddie, eddy, Freddie, heady, neddy, oven-ready, ready, reddy, steady, teddy, thready
- **bendy**, effendi, Gassendi, modus vivendi, trendy, Wendy

- **Monteverdi**, Verdi
- **Adie**, Brady, lady, milady, Sadie, shady
- landlady •charlady •saleslady
- **beady**, greedy, needy, reedy, seedy, speedy, tweedy, weedy

> Create extra rhymes by changing words like needy to neediness, or to needier and neediest. ℹ

- wieldy
- **biddy**, diddy, giddy, kiddie, middy, midi
- higgledy-piggledy
- **Cindy**, Hindi, indie, Indy, Lindy, Rawalpindi, shindy, Sindhi, Sindy, windy
- perfidy •raggedy •tragedy •remedy
- **comedy**, tragicomedy
- Kennedy •Cassidy •accidie •subsidy
- **bona fide**, Heidi, mala fide, tidy, vide

4.13

- **body**, embody, Irrawaddy, Kirkcaldy, noddy, Passamaquoddy, shoddy, Soddy, squaddie, toddy, wadi
- **secondi**, spondee, tondi
- anybody •everybody •busybody
- dogsbody •homebody
- **bawdy**, gaudy, Geordie, Lordy

Rhyming on proper names is often used for humour, and to add topicality—Cole Porter managed to squeeze in more than most in his song 'You're the Top':

You're a melody from a symphony by Strauss,
You're a Bendel bonnet, a Shakespeare sonnet, you're Mickey Mouse.
You're the Nile, you're the Tower of Pisa,
You're the smile on the Mona Lisa,
I'm a worthless check, a total wreck, a flop,
But if, baby, I'm the bottom, you're the top! ...

You're the top, you're Mahatma Gandhi,
You're the top, you're Napoleon Brandy ...

(Cole Porter, 'You're the Top')

- **baldy**, Garibaldi, Grimaldi
- Maundy
- **cloudy**, dowdy, Gaudí, howdy, rowdy, Saudi
- **Jodie**, roadie, toady, tody
- **Goldie**, mouldy (*US* moldy), oldie
- **broody**, foodie, Judy, moody, Rudi, Trudy, Yehudi
- **goody**, hoodie, woody
- **Burundi**, Kirundi, Mappa Mundi
- Rushdie
- **bloody**, buddy, cruddy, cuddy, muddy, nuddy, ruddy, study
- **barramundi**, bassi profundi, Lundy, undy
- fuddy-duddy •understudy
- Lombardy •nobody •somebody
- organdie (*US* organdy) •burgundy
- Arcady
- **chickadee**, Picardy
- malady •melody •Lollardy
- psalmody •Normandy •threnody
- hymnody •jeopardy •chiropody
- parody •rhapsody •prosody
- bastardy •custody
- **birdie**, curdy, hurdy-gurdy, nerdy, sturdy, vinho verde, wordy
- olde worlde

4.14

- **daffy**, taffy
- Amalfi
- **Cavafy**, Gaddafi
- Effie
- **beefy**, Fifi, leafy
- **cliffy**, iffy, jiffy, Liffey, niffy, sniffy, spiffy, squiffy, stiffy, whiffy
- salsify
- **coffee**, toffee
- wharfie
- **Sophie**, strophe, trophy
- **Dufy**, goofy, Sufi
- **fluffy**, huffy, puffy, roughie, roughy, scruffy, snuffy, stuffy, toughie

> Create extra rhymes by changing words like fluffy to fluffiness. [i]

- comfy •atrophy
- **anastrophe**, catastrophe
- **calligraphy**, epigraphy, tachygraphy
- **dystrophy**, epistrophe
- **autobiography**, bibliography, biography, cardiography, cartography, chirography, choreography, chromatography, cinematography, cosmography, cryptography, demography, discography, filmography, geography, hagiography, historiography, hydrography, iconography, lexicography, lithography, oceanography, orthography, palaeography (*US* paleography), photography, pornography, radiography, reprography, stenography, topography, typography
- apostrophe
- **gymnosophy**, philosophy, theosophy
- **furphy**, murphy, scurfy, surfy, turfy

4.15

- **Aggie**, baggy, craggy, draggy, jaggy, Maggie, quaggy, saggy, scraggy, shaggy, slaggy, snaggy
- Hwange
- **dreggy**, eggy, leggy, Peggy
- dengue •plaguy
- **Carnegie**, Malpighi
- **ciggy**, piggy, spriggy
- **boggy**, cloggy, doggy, foggy, froggy, groggy, moggie, smoggy, soggy

> Create extra rhymes for words like moggie by adding -*gy* to smog etc. (see section 18.8). [i]

- demagogy
- **corgi**, porgy
- **bogey**, bogie, dogie, fogey, hoagie, stogy, yogi
- **boogie**, boogie-woogie, sastrugi
- **buggy**, druggy, fuggy, muggy, puggy
- **lungi**, sarangi
- Lalage •lurgy

4.16

- **Rajshahi**, spahi, surahi
- tarakihi • towhee • takahe

4.17

- haji • algae • Angie
- **argy-bargy**, Panaji
- **edgy**, sedgy, solfeggi, veggie, wedgie
- **cagey**, stagy
- **mangy**, rangy
- **Fiji**, gee-gee, squeegee
- **Murrumbidgee**, ridgy, squidgy
- **dingy**, fringy, mingy, stingy, whingy
- cabbagy • prodigy • effigy • villagey
- porridgy • strategy • cottagey
- **dodgy**, podgy, splodgy, stodgy
- pedagogy
- **Georgie**, orgy
- ogee • Fuji
- **bhaji**, budgie, pudgy, sludgy, smudgy
- bulgy
- **bungee**, grungy, gungy, scungy, spongy
- **allergy**, analogy, genealogy, hypallage, metallurgy, mineralogy, tetralogy
- elegy
- **antilogy**, trilogy
- aetiology (*US* etiology), amphibology, anthology, anthropology, apology, archaeology (*US* archeology), astrology, biology, campanology, cardiology, chronology, climatology, cosmology, craniology, criminology, dermatology, ecology, embryology, entomology, epidemiology, etymology, geology, gynaecology (*US* gynecology), haematology (*US* hematology), hagiology, horology, hydrology, iconology, ideology, immunology, iridology, kidology, meteorology, methodology, musicology, mythology, necrology, neurology, numerology, oncology, ontology, ophthalmology, ornithology, parasitology, pathology, pharmacology, phraseology, phrenology, physiology, psychology, radiology, reflexology, scatology, Scientology, seismology, semiology, sociology, symbology, tautology, technology, terminology, theology, topology, toxicology, urology, zoology • eulogy • energy • synergy • apogee • liturgy • lethargy
- **burgee**, clergy
- zymurgy • dramaturgy

4.18

- **ackee**, Bacchae, baccy, cracky, Jackie, lackey, tacky, wacky
- latchkey • talcy
- **cranky**, Frankie, hanky, hanky-panky, lanky, manky, swanky, wanky, Yankee
- **Askey**, Pulaski
- Polanski • Blavatsky • Stanislavsky
- ticky-tacky
- **Iraqi**, Kawasaki, khaki, larky, malarkey, menarche, Nagasaki, narky, parky, raki, saké, saki, sarky, souvlaki, sparky, sukiyaki, teriyaki
- passkey
- **matriarchy**, patriarchy
- diarchy • oligarchy • synarchy
- hierarchy
- **Becky**, recce, techie
- Elkie • Palenque
- **Esky**, pesky
- **Dostoevsky**, Paderewski
- **achy**, Blakey, flaky, quaky, shaky, snaky, wakey-wakey
- headachy
- **beaky**, cheeky, cliquey, cock-a-leekie, creaky, freaky, Geikie, Kon-Tiki, Leakey, leaky, peaky, reeky, sleeky, sneaky, squeaky, streaky, Thessaloníki, tiki, tzatziki

> Create extra rhymes by changing words like cheeky to cheekiness. [i]

4.19

- **brickie**, Dickie, hickey, icky, mickey, Nicky, picky, quickie, rickey, Rikki, sickie, sticky, tricky, Vicky
- **milky**, silky, Wilkie
- **Chinky**, dinky, Helsinki, inky, Kinki, kinky, minke, pinkie, pinky, slinky, stinky, stotinki
- **frisky**, risky, whisky
- **Dzerzhinsky**, Kandinsky, kolinsky, Nijinsky, Stravinsky
- doohickey •smart-alecky •garlicky
- colicky •gimmicky •panicky •finicky
- plasticky
- **crikey**, Nike, psyche, spiky
- **choccy**, cocky, flocky, gnocchi, hockey, jockey, oche, pocky, rocky, schlocky, stocky
- **conchae**, donkey, honky, shonky, wonky
- Brodsky
- **Malinowski**, Minkowski, Stokowski, Tchaikovsky
- Chomsky •Trotsky •droshky
- jabberwocky
- **balky**, chalky, corky, gawky, Gorky, Milwaukee, pawky, porky, talkie, walkie-talkie
- Sikorsky •Mussorgsky

4.20

- **chokey**, croaky, folkie, folky, hokey, hokey-cokey, hoki, jokey, karaoke, Loki, okey-dokey, Okie, pokey, poky, smoky, trochee
- **adzuki**, bouzouki, fluky, kabuki, kooky, pukey, saluki, spooky, Sukie, Suzuki, verrucae
- **bookie**, cookie, hookey, hooky, nooky, rookie
- netsuke
- **clucky**, ducky, happy-go-lucky, Kentucky, lucky, mucky, plucky, yucky
- **bulky**, sulky
- **chunky**, clunky, flunkey, funky, hunky, junkie, junky, monkey, punky, spunky

- **dusky**, husky, musky
- synecdoche •Malachy •hillocky
- bullocky
- **Andromache**, logomachy, theomachy
- hummocky •anarchy •monarchy
- Cherokee •tussocky
- **herky-jerky**, jerky, mirky, murky, perky, quirky, smirky, turkey
- turnkey •Albuquerque

4.21

- **Ali**, alley, Allie, Ally, bally, dally, dilly-dally, farfalle, galley, Halley, mallee, Mexicali, pally, Raleigh, rally, reveille, sally, tally, valley
- Chablis •brambly
- **badly**, Bradley, Hadlee, madly, sadly
- scraggly
- **dangly**, gangly
- crackly •Shankly •Bramley
- **Manley**, manly, Osmanli, Stanley
- slatternly
- **Langley**, tangly
- amply •Ashley
- **Attlee**, fatly, patly
- aptly •shilly-shally
- **Bali**, barley, Cali, Carly, Charlie, Dali, Diwali, finale, gnarly, Gurkhali, Kali, Kigali, Mali, Marley, marly, Pali, parley, snarly, Somali, Svengali, tamale
- **Barclay**, Berkeley, clerkly, sparkly
- Darnley •ghastly •Hartley •Barnsley
- blackguardly

4.22

- **belly**, Botticelli, casus belli, Corelli, Delhi, deli, Ellie, Grappelli, jelly, Kelly, lamellae, Machiavelli, Mahaweli, nelly, Schiaparelli, Shelley, shelly, smelly, tagliatelle, telly, Torricelli, vermicelli, welly, Zeffirelli
- trebly
- **assembly**, trembly
- **deadly**, Hedley, medley, redly
- friendly •freckly

- **cleanly**, eco-friendly, user-friendly
- heavenly •fleshly •wetly •directly
- Bentley •deathly
- **Lesley**, Leslie, Presley, Wesley
- yellow-belly •underbelly
- **bailey**, bailie, capercaillie, Cayley, ceilidh, daily, Daley, Daly, Disraeli, Eilidh, feyly, gaily, Haley, Hayley, Israeli, Rayleigh, scaly, shaly, ukulele
- ably •ungainly •maidenly •shapely
- stately •saintly •paisley •Ainsley
- comradely

4.23

- **campanile**, dele, eely, Ely, fusilli, Gigli, Ismaili, Keeley, Keneally, KwaNdebele, Lely, Matabele, mealie, mealy, Ndebele, sapele, Sindebele, steely, Swahili, wheelie
- **biweekly**, weakly, weekly
- seemly
- **cleanly**, queenly
- **beastly**, Priestley, priestly
- Keighley •measly

4.24

- **Billie**, billy, Chile, chilli (*US* chili), chilly, Dili, dilly, filly, frilly, ghillie, gillie, Gilly, hilly, Lillee, lily, Lyly, papillae, Philly, Piccadilly, piccalilli, silly, skilly, stilly, Tilly, willy, willy-nilly

> Create extra rhymes by changing words like chilly to chilliness. i

- **Ridley**, tiddly
- **Brindley**, spindly
- sniffly
- **giggly**, niggly
- **jingly**, shingly, Zwingli
- **prickly**, sickly
- **crinkly**, tinkly, twinkly, wrinkly
- dimly
- **Finlay**, inly, McKinlay
- musicianly
- **kingly**, tingly

- Shipley •pimply
- **bristly**, gristly
- princely •fitly
- **drizzly**, grisly, grizzly, Sisley
- Kingsley •Cybele •hillbilly •jubilee
- rockabilly •bodily
- **bibliophily**, cartophily, toxophily
- Galilee •family •stepfamily
- subfamily
- **Emily**, Semele
- **facsimile**, simile
- homily •contumely
- **cicely**, Sicily
- icily •volatile •Maithili •weevily

4.25

- **drily**, kylie, Riley, shyly, slyly, smiley, Smily, wily, wryly

> Create extra rhymes for words like drily by adding *-ly* to high etc. (see section 6.1). i

- idly •kindly •wifely •likely •timely
- Christly
- **knightly**, nightly, sightly, sprightly
- lively •fortnightly •housewifely
- **Barbirolli**, brolly, collie, dolly, folly, golly, holly, jolly, lolly, Mollie, molly, Ollie, polly, poly, trolley, volley, wally
- knobbly
- **Bodley**, godly, oddly
- wanly •Copley •fait accompli
- costly
- **hotly**, motley
- softly-softly
- **Bengali**, Cawley, crawly, creepy-crawly, Macaulay, Morley, Nepali, poorly, rawly, scrawly, squally
- lordly
- **courtly**, portly
- **jowly**, Pauli
- **aïoli**, coaly, coley, Foley, goalie, guacamole, holey, Holi, holy, lowly, moly, pinole, ravioli, roly-poly, Rowley, shoaly, soli
- nobly •Oakley •homely
- **lonely**, only

- ghostly •Moseley
- **coyly**, doily, oily

4.26

- **boule**, coolie, coulée, duly, Friuli, goolie, Hooley, Julie, mooli, newly, puli, schoolie, stoolie, Thule, truly, unruly
- **googly**, Hooghly
- muesli •absolutely •torulae
- **ampullae**, bullae, bully, fully, Lully, pulley, Woolley, woolly
- goodly •patchouli •nebuly
- vox populi •formulae •uvulae
- **dully**, gulley, gully, sully
- nubbly
- **crumbly**, grumbly
- **cuddly**, Dudley
- **plug-ugly**, ugly
- jungly
- **comely**, rumly
- slovenly •cousinly •crumply
- Huxley •Uttley
- **bimonthly**, monthly
- lovely

4.27

- **biyearly**, really, yearly
- Beardsley •lawyerly •immediately
- hourly •cowardly •surely •marbly
- pebbly
- neighbourly (*US* neighborly)
- **dribbly**, scribbly
- Kimberley
- **bobbly**, wobbly
- Stromboli
- **bubbly**, lubberly, rubbly, stubbly
- husbandly •hyperbole
- **creaturely**, teacherly
- Wycherley •elderly
- **fiddly**, twiddly
- orderly •puddly
- **Offaly**, waffly
- snuffly
- **straggly**, waggly
- spangly •laggardly •beggarly

- **jiggly**, squiggly, wiggly, wriggly
- niggardly •sluggardly •leisurely
- gingerly •soldierly •curmudgeonly
- rascally •treacly •tickly •broccoli
- knuckly •melancholy •sailorly
- scholarly •gentlemanly •seamanly
- anomaly •yeomanly •womanly
- mannerly •panoply •Connolly
- **Gallipoli**, ripply, tripoli
- dimply
- **monopoly**, oligopoly
- rumply •purply •matronly
- squirrelly •scoundrelly •Thessaly
- thistly •tinselly •muscly
- **Natalie**, philately, rattly
- dastardly
- **headmasterly**, masterly
- schoolmasterly •westerly •painterly
- easterly •Italy •winterly
- **sisterly**, systole
- writerly •doctorly •quarterly
- fatherly •grandfatherly •weatherly
- northerly
- **brotherly**, motherly, southerly
- grandmotherly •gravelly •Beverley
- weaselly •frizzly •wizardly •miserly
- Rosalie

4.28

- **Burghley**, Burley, burly, curly, early, girlie, hurley, hurly-burly, pearly, Shirley, surly, swirly, twirly
- worldly •Berkeley •termly •earthly

4.29

- **chamois**, clammy, gammy, Grammy, hammy, jammy, mammae, mammee, mammy, Miami, ramie, rammy, Sammy, shammy, whammy
- **acme**, drachmae
- Lakshmi
- **army**, balmy, barmy, gourami, macramé, origami, palmy, pastrami, salami, smarmy, swami, tsunami, Yanomami
- **Clemmie**, Emmy, jemmy, lemme, semi

- elmy
- **Amy**, cockamamie, flamy, gamy, Jamie, Mamie, samey
- **beamy**, creamy, dreamy, gleamy, Mimi, preemie, seamy, steamy

> Try rhyming one word with a set of two: steamy, see me. [i]

- **gimme**, shimmy, Timmy
- pygmy • filmy
- **arch-enemy**, enemy
- synonymy • Jeremy • sashimi
- **blimey**, gorblimey, grimy, limey, slimy, stymie, thymy
- **commie**, mommy, pommie, pommy, tommy
- **dormy**, stormy
- **foamy**, homey, loamy, Naomi, Salome
- polychromy

4.30

- **fumy**, gloomy, plumy, rheumy, roomie, roomy, spumy
- excuse-me • mushroomy • perfumy
- **Brummie**, chummy, crumby, crummy, dummy, gummy, lumme, mummy, plummy, rummy, scrummy, scummy, slummy, tummy, yummy
- academy • sodomy • blasphemy
- infamy
- **bigamy**, polygamy, trigamy
- **endogamy**, exogamy, heterogamy, homogamy, misogamy, monogamy
- hypergamy • alchemy • Ptolemy
- anomie • antinomy
- **agronomy**, astronomy, autonomy, bonhomie, Deuteronomy, economy, gastronomy, heteronomy, metonymy, physiognomy, taxonomy
- thingummy • Laramie • sesame
- blossomy
- **anatomy**, atomy
- **hysterectomy**, mastectomy, tonsillectomy, vasectomy
- epitome
- **dichotomy**, lobotomy, tracheotomy, trichotomy
- colostomy • bosomy

- **squirmy**, thermae, wormy
- taxidermy

4.31

- **Annie**, ca'canny, canny, cranny, Danny, fanny, granny, nanny, tranny

> Create extra rhymes by changing words like cranny to crannies. [i]

- **Ariadne**, Evadne
- daphne
- **Agni**, Cagney
- **acne**, Arachne, hackney
- hootenanny
- **Afghani**, ani, Armani, Azerbaijani, Barney, biriani, blarney, Carney, frangipani, Fulani, Galvani, Giovanni, Hindustani, Killarney, maharani, Mbabane, Modigliani, Omani, Pakistani, Rafsanjani, Rajasthani, rani, sarnie
- McCartney
- **antennae**, any, Benny, blenny, Dene, fenny, jenny, Kenny, Kilkenny, Lenny, many, penne, penny, Rennie
- catchpenny • pinchpenny
- pyrotechny
- **Bahraini**, brainy, Chaney, Eugénie, grainy, Janey, Khomeini, rainy, veiny, waney, zany
- **halfpenny**, shove-halfpenny, twopenny-halfpenny
- **Athene**, bambini, beanie, Bellini, Bernini, bikini, Boccherini, Borromini, capellini, catenae, Cellini, Cherubini, Cyrene, Fellini, fettuccine, genie, greeny, grissini, Heaney, Houdini, Jeanie, linguine, martini, Mazzini, meanie, Mussolini, Mycenae, Paganini, Panini, porcini, Puccini, queenie, Rossellini, Rossini, Santoríni, Selene, sheeny, spaghettini, Sweeney, teeny, teeny-weeny, tortellini, Toscanini, Trini, tweeny, wahine, weeny, zucchini
- monokini

4.32

- **blini**, cine, Finney, finny, Ginny, guinea, hinny, mini, Minnie, ninny, pinny, Pliny, shinny, skinny, spinney, tinny, whinny
- **kidney**, Sidney, Sydney
- chimney
- **jitney**, Whitney
- Disney
- **aborigine**, polygeny, polygyny
- **androgyny**, homogeny, misogyny, progeny
- Gemini
- **niminy-piminy**, Rimini
- **dominie**, hominy, Melpomene
- ignominy •Panini •larceny •telecine
- satiny •destiny •mountainy
- **mutiny**, scrutiny
- **briny**, Heine, liny, piny, shiny, spiny, tiny, whiny
- sunshiny
- **Bonnie**, bonny, Connie, johnny, Lonnie, Ronnie, Suwannee
- Rodney
- **Cockney**, Procne
- Romney •Novotný •Grozny
- **brawny**, corny, horny, lawny, mulligatawny, scrawny, tawny, thorny
- Orkney •Courtney
- **brownie**, browny, downy, townie

4.33

- **abalone**, Albinoni, Annigoni, Antonioni, baloney, Bodoni, boloney, bony, calzone, cannelloni, canzone, cicerone, coney, conversazione, coronae, crony, Gaborone, Giorgione, macaroni, Manzoni, Marconi, mascarpone, minestrone, Moroni, Mulroney, padrone, panettoni, pepperoni, phoney, polony, pony, rigatoni, Shoshone, Sloaney, stony, Toni, tony, zabaglione
- **cartoony**, lacunae, loony, Moonie, moony, Nguni, puny, Rooney, spoony, uni

- Sunni
- **bunny**, dunny, funny, gunny, honey, money, runny, sonny, sunny, tunny
- twopenny •chutney •beermoney

4.34

- **Léonie**, peony
- Tierney
- **Briony**, bryony, Hermione
- tourney •ebony •Albany
- chalcedony •Alderney
- **Persephone**, Stephanie, telephony
- **antiphony**, epiphany, polyphony, tiffany
- symphony
- **cacophony**, homophony, theophany, Zoffany
- euphony •agony •garganey
- Antigone
- **cosmogony**, mahogany, theogony
- balcony •Gascony •Tuscany
- calumny
- **felony**, Melanie, miscellany
- villainy •colony
- **Chamonix**, salmony, scammony, Tammany
- harmony
- **anemone**, Emeny, hegemony, lemony, Yemeni
- **alimony**, palimony
- agrimony •acrimony
- **matrimony**, patrimony
- ceremony •parsimony •antimony
- sanctimony •testimony •simony
- Romany •Germany •threepenny
- timpani •sixpenny •tuppenny
- **accompany**, company
- barony •saffrony •tyranny
- synchrony •irony •saxony •cushiony
- Anthony •betony
- **Brittany**, dittany, litany
- **botany**, cottony, monotony
- **gluttony**, muttony
- Bethany •oniony •raisiny
- **attorney**, Burney, Czerny, Ernie, ferny, gurney, journey, Verny

4.35

- **hangi**, slangy, tangy, twangy
- **clingy**, dinghy, springy, stingy, stringy, swingy, thingy, zingy
- puddingy
- **Missolonghi**, pongy

4.36

- **crappie**, crappy, flappy, gappy, happi, happy, nappy, pappy, sappy, scrappy, slap-happy, snappy, strappy, tapis, yappy, zappy

> Create extra rhymes by changing words like happy to happiness. ⓘ

- **campy**, scampi, vampy
- **harpy**, okapi, serape, sharpie
- raspy
- **Giuseppe**, peppy, preppy
- kelpie
- **kempy**, tempi
- Gillespie
- **crêpey**, kepi, scrapie
- **creepy**, sleepy, tepee, weepy
- **chippy**, clippie, dippy, drippy, grippy, hippy, Lippi, lippy, Mississippi, nippy, slippy, snippy, tippy, trippy, whippy, Xanthippe, zippy
- chickpea
- **crimpy**, gimpy, skimpy, wimpy
- **crispy**, wispy
- turnipy • recipe • praecipe • gossipy
- **pipy**, stripy
- **choppy**, copy, floppy, jalopy, moppy, poppy, sloppy, soppy, stroppy
- **Pompey**, swampy
- **waspie**, waspy
- photocopy • cowpea
- **dopey**, Hopi, Opie, ropy, soapy, topi

4.37

- **croupy**, droopy, goopy, groupie, loopy, pupae, roupy, snoopy, soupy, Tupi
- whoopee
- **duppy**, guppy, puppy, yuppie
- **gulpy**, pulpy
- **bumpy**, clumpy, dumpy, frumpy, grumpy, humpy, jumpy, lumpy, plumpy, rumpy-pumpy, scrumpy, stumpy

> Create a different rhyming set by changing words like bumpy to bumpiness. ⓘ

- hiccupy • chirrupy • calliope
- pericope • syncope
- **colonoscopy**, horoscopy, microscopy, stereoscopy
- Penelope • canopy • satrapy
- **lycanthropy**, misanthropy, philanthropy
- **aromatherapy**, chemotherapy, hypnotherapy, physiotherapy, psychotherapy, radiotherapy, therapy
- entropy • syrupy (*US* sirupy) • chirpy

4.38

- **Barry**, Carrie, carry, Cary, Clarrie, Gary, glengarry, harry, intermarry, Larry, marry, miscarry, parry, tarry
- angry • chapelry • cavalry • lamprey
- Crabtree
- **gantry**, pantry
- Langtry • polyandry
- **askari**, Bari, Cagliari, calamari, Campari, charivari, curare, Ferrari, Harare, Kalahari, Mari, Mata Hari, Qatari, Rastafari, safari, sari, Scutari, shikari, sparry, starry, Stradivari, tamari, terramare, Vasari, Zanzibari
- compadre • chantry
- **beriberi**, berry, bury, Ceri, cherry, Derry, ferry, Gerry, jerry, Kerry, merry, perry, Pondicherry, sherry, terry, very, wherry
- débris • Hendry • Geoffrey • belfry
- **devilry**, revelry
- **Henri**, henry

- peltry
- **entry**, gentry, sentry
- pedantry
- **peasantry**, pheasantry, pleasantry
- vestry •every •elderberry
- checkerberry •whortleberry
- chokecherry •daredevilry
- Londonderry •knobkerrie

4.39

- **airy**, Azeri, canary, carabinieri, Carey, Cary, chary, clary, contrary, dairy, Dari, faerie, fairy, glairy, glary, Guarneri, hairy, lairy, Mary, miserere, nary, Nyerere, prairie, Salieri, scary, Tipperary, vary, wary
- carefree •masonry •blazonry
- Aintree •pastry •masturbatory
- freemasonry •stonemasonry •Petrie

4.40

- hara-kiri •ribaldry •chivalry •Tishri
- figtree •wintry •poetry •casuistry
- Babbittry •banditry •pedigree
- punditry •verdigris •sophistry
- porphyry •gadgetry •registry
- Valkyrie
- **marquetry**, parquetry
- basketry •trinketry •daiquiri
- **coquetry**, rocketry
- circuitry •varletry •filigree
- palmistry
- **biochemistry**, chemistry, photochemistry
- **gimmickry**, mimicry
- **asymmetry**, symmetry
- **craniometry**, geometry, micrometry, optometry, psychometry, pyrometry, sociometry, trigonometry
- tenebrae •ministry •cabinetry
- tapestry •carpentry •papistry
- piripiri •puppetry
- **agroforestry**, floristry, forestry
- ancestry •corsetry •artistry
- dentistry •Nyree •rivalry •pinetree

4.41

- **Florrie**, Laurie, lorry, Macquarie, quarry, sorry, whare
- Rhodri •Godfrey •hostelry
- Coventry •quixotry
- **cacciatore**, Corey, dory, Florey, flory, furore, glory, gory, hoary, hunky-dory, lory, Maury, monsignori, Montessori, multistorey, Pori, Rory, satori, saury, storey, story, Tory, vainglory
- Aubrey •aumbry
- **Audrey**, bawdry, tawdry
- laundry
- **gallimaufry**, orphrey
- palfrey •paltry •outlawry •centaury
- clerestory (US clearstory)
- understorey
- **cowrie**, kauri, Lowry, Maori
- Cowdrey •foundry •Rowntree
- ochry (US ochery) •poultry
- coxcombry •matsuri •Kirkcudbright
- shoetree
- **Hurri**, potpourri
- kukri •century •penury •estuary
- residuary •augury •mercury

4.42

- **curry**, dhurrie, flurry, hurry, Murray, scurry, slurry, surrey, worry

> Create extra rhymes by adding -ing to words like curry. [i]

- penumbrae •sundry
- **comfrey**, Humphrey
- hungry •Cymru •sultry
- **country**, upcountry
- Guthrie •backcountry

4.43

- **beery**, bleary, cheery, dearie, dreary, Dun Laoghaire, eerie, eyrie (US aerie), Kashmiri, leery, peri, praemunire, query, smeary, teary, theory, weary
- Deirdre •incendiary •intermediary

- subsidiary
- **auxiliary**, ciliary, domiciliary
- apiary • topiary • farriery • furriery
- justiciary
- **bestiary**, vestiary
- breviary • aviary • hosiery
- **diary**, enquiry, expiry, fiery, friary, inquiry, miry, priory, spiry, wiry
- **podiatry**, psychiatry
- **dowry**, floury, flowery, loury, showery, towery
- brewery • jewellery (US jewelry)
- **curie**, de jure, fioriture, fury, houri, Jewry, jury, Manipuri, Missouri, moory, Newry, tandoori, Urey
- statuary • actuary • sanctuary
- obituary • sumptuary • voluptuary
- January • electuary • ossuary
- mortuary
- **Bradbury**, Cadbury
- **blackberry**, hackberry
- cranberry • waxberry
- **Barbary**, barberry
- Shaftesbury • raspberry
- **bayberry**, blaeberry
- Avebury • Aylesbury • Sainsbury
- **bilberry**, tilbury
- bribery
- **corroboree**, jobbery, robbery, slobbery, snobbery
- dogberry • Roddenberry • Fosbury
- strawberry • Salisbury
- **crowberry**, snowberry
- chokeberry
- **Rosebery**, Shrewsbury
- **blueberry**, dewberry
- Dewsbury • Bloomsbury • gooseberry
- **blubbery**, rubbery, shrubbery
- Sudbury • mulberry • huckleberry
- Bunbury • husbandry • loganberry
- Canterbury • Glastonbury
- **Burberry**, turbary
- hatchery • archery
- **lechery**, treachery
- **stitchery**, witchery
- debauchery • butchery • camaraderie
- **cindery**, tindery
- industry • dromedary • lapidary
- spidery • bindery • doddery
- quandary • powdery • boundary

- bouldery • embroidery
- **prudery**, rudery
- do-goodery • shuddery • thundery
- prebendary • legendary • secondary
- amphorae • wafery
- **midwifery**, periphery
- infantry • housewifery • spoofery
- puffery • sulphury (US sulfury)
- Calgary
- **beggary**, Gregory
- vagary
- **piggery**, priggery, whiggery
- brigandry • bigotry • allegory
- vinegary • category • subcategory
- **hoggery**, toggery
- pettifoggery • demagoguery
- roguery • sugary
- **buggery**, skulduggery, snuggery, thuggery
- Hungary • humbuggery
- ironmongery • lingerie • treasury
- usury • menagerie • pageantry
- Marjorie • kedgeree • gingery
- imagery • orangery • savagery
- forgery • soldiery • drudgery
- **perjury**, surgery
- microsurgery
- **hackery**, quackery, Thackeray, Zachary
- mountebankery • knick-knackery
- gimcrackery • peccary • grotesquerie
- **bakery**, fakery, jacquerie
- **chickaree**, chicory, hickory, Terpsichore, trickery
- whiskery • apothecary
- **crockery**, mockery, rockery
- falconry • jiggery-pokery
- **cookery**, crookery, rookery
- brusquerie
- **puckery**, succory
- cuckoldry
- **calorie**, gallery, Malory, salary, Valerie
- saddlery • balladry • gallantry
- kilocalorie • diablerie • chandlery
- harlotry • celery • pedlary
- exemplary
- **helotry**, zealotry
- **nailery**, raillery
- Tuileries

- **ancillary**, artillery, capillary, codicillary, distillery, fibrillary, fritillary, Hilary, maxillary, pillory
- mamillary •tutelary •corollary
- **bardolatry**, hagiolatry, iconolatry, idolatry
- **cajolery**, drollery
- **foolery**, tomfoolery
- **constabulary**, vocabulary
- scapulary •capitulary •formulary
- scullery •jugglery •cutlery
- chancellery •epistolary •burglary
- mammary •fragmentary
- passementerie •flimflammery
- **armory**, armoury, gendarmerie
- almonry
- **emery**, memory
- creamery •shimmery •primary
- rosemary •yeomanry
- **parfumerie**, perfumery
- **flummery**, Montgomery, mummery, summary, summery
- gossamery •customary •infirmary
- **cannery**, granary, tannery
- canonry
- **antennary**, bimillenary, millenary, venery
- tenantry •chicanery
- **beanery**, bicentenary, catenary, centenary, deanery, greenery, machinery, plenary, scenery, senary, septenary
- **disciplinary**, interdisciplinary
- hymnary •missionary
- **ordinary**, subordinary
- valetudinary •imaginary •millinery
- culinary •seminary •preliminary
- luminary •urinary •veterinary
- mercenary •sanguinary
- **binary**, finery, pinery, quinary, vinery, winery
- Connery •Conakry •ornery •joinery
- **buffoonery**, poltroonery, sublunary, superlunary
- **gunnery**, nunnery
- consuetudinary •visionary
- exclusionary •legionary •pulmonary
- coronary •reactionary •expansionary
- **concessionary**, confessionary,

discretionary
- **confectionery**, insurrectionary, lectionary
- **deflationary**, inflationary, probationary, stationary, stationery
- **expeditionary**, petitionary, prohibitionary, traditionary, transitionary
- dictionary •cautionary
- **ablutionary**, counter-revolutionary, devolutionary, elocutionary, evolutionary, revolutionary, substitutionary
- functionary
- **diversionary**, reversionary
- **fernery**, quaternary, ternary
- peppery •extempore •weaponry
- **apery**, drapery, japery, napery, papery, vapoury (*US* vapory)
- **frippery**, slippery
- **coppery**, foppery
- popery •dupery •trumpery
- February •heraldry •knight-errantry
- arbitrary •registrary •library
- contrary •horary •supernumerary
- itinerary •honorary •funerary
- **contemporary**, extemporary, temporary
- literary •brasserie •chancery
- **accessory**, intercessory, pessary, possessory, tesserae
- **dispensary**, incensory, ostensory, sensory, suspensory
- tracery
- **pâtisserie**, rotisserie
- emissary •dimissory
- **commissary**, promissory
- janissary •necessary •derisory
- glossary •responsory •sorcery
- grocery •greengrocery
- **delusory**, illusory
- compulsory •vavasory •adversary
- **anniversary**, bursary, cursory, mercery, nursery
- haberdashery
- **evidentiary**, penitentiary, plenipotentiary, residentiary
- **beneficiary**, fishery, judiciary
- noshery •gaucherie •fiduciary

- luxury •tertiary
- **battery**, cattery, chattery, flattery, tattery
- **factory**, manufactory, olfactory, phylactery, refractory, satisfactory
- **artery**, martyry, Tartary
- **mastery**, plastery
- **directory**, ex-directory, interjectory, rectory, refectory, trajectory
- peremptory
- **alimentary**, complementary, complimentary, documentary, elementary, parliamentary, rudimentary, sedimentary, supplementary, testamentary
- investigatory
- **adulatory**, aleatory, approbatory, celebratory, clarificatory, classificatory, commendatory, congratulatory, consecratory, denigratory, elevatory, gyratory, incantatory, incubatory, intimidatory, modificatory, participatory, placatory, pulsatory, purificatory, reificatory, revelatory, rotatory
- natatory •elucidatory •castigatory
- mitigatory •justificatory
- imprecatory •equivocatory
- flagellatory •execratory •innovatory
- **eatery**, excretory
- **glittery**, jittery, skittery, twittery
- **benedictory**, contradictory, maledictory, valedictory, victory
- **printery**, splintery
- **consistory**, history, mystery
- presbytery
- **inhibitory**, prohibitory
- hereditary •auditory •budgetary
- **military**, paramilitary
- solitary •cemetery •limitary
- vomitory •dormitory •fumitory
- **interplanetary**, planetary, sanitary
- primogenitary •dignitary
- **admonitory**, monitory
- unitary •monetary •territory
- secretary •undersecretary
- plebiscitary •repository •baptistery
- transitory
- **depositary**, depository, expository,

suppository
- niterie
- **Godwottery**, lottery, pottery, tottery
- bottomry •watery •psaltery
- **coterie**, notary, protonotary, rotary, votary
- upholstery
- **bijouterie**, charcuterie, circumlocutory
- persecutory •statutory •salutary
- executory
- **contributory**, retributory, tributary
- interlocutory
- **buttery**, fluttery
- introductory •adultery •effrontery
- perfunctory •blustery •mediatory
- retaliatory •conciliatory •expiatory
- **denunciatory**, renunciatory
- **appreciatory**, depreciatory
- **initiatory**, propitiatory
- **dietary**, proprietary
- extenuatory
- **mandatary**, mandatory
- predatory •sedentary •laudatory
- prefatory •offertory •negatory
- obligatory
- **derogatory**, interrogatory, supererogatory
- nugatory
- **expurgatory**, objurgatory, purgatory
- precatory
- **explicatory**, indicatory, vindicatory
- **confiscatory**, piscatory
- dedicatory •judicatory
- qualificatory •pacificatory
- supplicatory
- **communicatory**, excommunicatory
- masticatory •prognosticatory
- invocatory •obfuscatory
- revocatory •charlatanry
- **depilatory**, dilatory, oscillatory
- assimilatory •consolatory
- voluntary •emasculatory
- ejaculatory
- **ambulatory**, circumambulatory, perambulatory
- regulatory
- **articulatory**, gesticulatory
- manipulatory •copulatory

- expostulatory •circulatory
- **amatory**, declamatory, defamatory, exclamatory, inflammatory, proclamatory
- crematory •segmentary
- lachrymatory
- **commentary**, promontory
- **informatory**, reformatory
- momentary
- **affirmatory**, confirmatory
- explanatory •damnatory
- condemnatory
- **cosignatory**, signatory
- combinatory
- **discriminatory**, eliminatory, incriminatory, recriminatory
- comminatory •exterminatory
- hallucinatory •procrastinatory
- monastery •repertory
- emancipatory •anticipatory
- **exculpatory**, inculpatory
- **declaratory**, preparatory
- respiratory •perspiratory
- vibratory
- **migratory**, transmigratory
- **exploratory**, laboratory, oratory
- inauguratory •adjuratory
- corroboratory •reverberatory
- refrigeratory •compensatory
- desultory •dysentery
- **exhortatory**, hortatory
- salutatory •gustatory •lavatory
- inventory
- **conservatory**, observatory
- improvisatory
- **accusatory**, excusatory
- lathery
- **feathery**, heathery, leathery
- **dithery**, slithery
- carvery
- **reverie**, severy
- **Avery**, bravery, knavery, quavery, Savery, savory, savoury, slavery, wavery
- thievery
- **livery**, quivery, shivery
- silvery
- **ivory**, salivary
- ovary
- **discovery**, recovery

- servery •equerry •reliquary
- antiquary •cassowary •stipendiary
- colliery •pecuniary •chinoiserie
- misery •wizardry •citizenry
- **advisory**, provisory, revisory, supervisory
- **causerie**, rosary

- **blurry**, firry, furry

4.45

- **bassi**, Brassey, brassie, chassis, gassy, Haile Selassie, lassie, Malagasy, Manasseh, massé, massy, sassy, Tallahassee
- **Cotopaxi**, maxi, taxi, waxy
- Anglesey
- **antsy**, Clancy, fancy, Nancy
- **paparazzi**, patsy
- Yangtze •necromancy •cartomancy
- geomancy •bibliomancy
- chiromancy •ataraxy
- **Adivasi**, brassy, classy, dalasi, Darcy, farcy, Farsi, glassy, grassy
- chancy •ardency •Nazi
- **Bessie**, Crécy, dressy, Jessie, messy, Nessie, tressy
- **prexy**, sexy
- **Chelsea**, Elsie
- Dempsey •Montmorency
- discrepancy •incessancy
- **Betsy**, tsetse
- epilepsy •narcolepsy •nympholepsy
- apoplexy •catalepsy
- **Basie**, Casey, Gracie, lacy, O'Casey, pace, pacy, precis, racy, spacey, Stacey, Sulawesi, Tracy
- cadency •complacency
- **blatancy**, patency
- **Assisi**, fleecy, greasy, Tbilisi
- decency

4.46

- **Chrissie**, Cissy, kissy, missy, prissy, sissy

- **dixie**, pixie, tricksy, Trixie
- **chintzy**, De Quincey, wincey
- **efficiency**, proficiency, sufficiency
- **Gypsy**, tipsy
- **ditzy**, glitzy, itsy-bitsy, Mitzi, ritzy, Uffizi
- Eurydice
- **odyssey**, theodicy
- sub judice •prophecy •anglice
- chaplaincy •policy •baronetcy
- governessy •Pharisee •actressy
- **clerisy**, heresy
- secrecy • statice • captaincy
- courtesy
- **dicey**, icy, pricey, spicy, vice

> Try rhyming one word with a set of two: dicey, high sea. ⓘ

- stridency •sightsee
- **bossy**, Flossie, flossy, glossy, mossy, posse
- **boxy**, doxy, epoxy, foxy, moxie, poxy, proxy
- bonxie
- **poncey**, sonsy
- **dropsy**, popsy
- biopsy •heterodoxy •orthodoxy
- autopsy

4.47

- **gorsy**, horsey, saucy
- normalcy •schmaltzy
- **discordancy**, mordancy
- Orczy •mousy •bouncy •viscountcy
- paramountcy •folksy •potency
- **Debussy**, goosey, juicy, Lucy, Senussi, Watusi
- **lucency**, translucency
- **cutesy**, rootsy
- pussy
- **booksy**, look-see
- **Abruzzi**, footsie, tootsie, Tutsi
- Sadducee
- **fussy**, hussy, mussy
- fubsy •Dulcie •gutsy •bankruptcy

4.48

- radiancy
- **immediacy**, intermediacy

- expediency •idiocy •saliency
- resiliency •leniency
- **incipiency**, recipiency
- recreancy •pruriency •deviancy
- subserviency •transiency •pliancy
- **buoyancy**, flamboyancy
- **fluency**, truancy
- constituency •abbacy •embassy
- celibacy •absorbency
- **incumbency**, recumbency
- **ascendancy**, intendancy, interdependency, pendency, resplendency, superintendency, tendency, transcendency
- candidacy
- **presidency**, residency
- despondency •redundancy •infancy
- sycophancy •argosy •legacy
- profligacy •surrogacy
- extravagancy •plangency •agency
- regency
- **astringency**, contingency, stringency
- intransigency •exigency •cogency
- pungency
- **convergency**, emergency, insurgency, urgency
- vacancy •piquancy •fricassee
- mendicancy •efficacy •prolificacy
- insignificancy •delicacy •intricacy
- advocacy •fallacy •galaxy
- **jealousy**, prelacy
- repellency •valency •Wallasey
- articulacy •corpulency •inviolacy
- excellency •equivalency •pharmacy
- supremacy •clemency •Christmassy
- **illegitimacy**, legitimacy
- intimacy •ultimacy •primacy
- dormancy •diplomacy •contumacy
- stagnancy
- **lieutenancy**, subtenancy, tenancy
- pregnancy
- **benignancy**, malignancy
- effeminacy •prominency
- obstinacy •pertinency •lunacy
- immanency
- **impermanency**, permanency
- rampancy •papacy •flippancy
- occupancy
- **archiepiscopacy**, episcopacy
- transparency •leprosy •inerrancy
- **flagrancy**, fragrancy, vagrancy

- conspiracy •idiosyncrasy
- minstrelsy •magistracy •piracy
- vibrancy
- **adhocracy**, aristocracy, autocracy, bureaucracy, democracy, gerontocracy, gynaecocracy (*US* gynecocracy), hierocracy, hypocrisy, meritocracy, mobocracy, monocracy, plutocracy, technocracy, theocracy
- accuracy •obduracy •currency
- **curacy**, pleurisy
- confederacy •numeracy
- degeneracy •itinerancy •inveteracy
- **illiteracy**, literacy
- innocency •trenchancy •deficiency
- **fantasy**, phantasy
- intestacy •ecstasy •expectancy
- latency •chieftaincy •intermittency
- **consistency**, insistency, persistency
- instancy •militancy •impenitency
- precipitancy •competency
- hesitancy •apostasy •constancy
- accountancy •adjutancy
- **consultancy**, exultancy
- impotency •discourtesy
- inadvertency •privacy
- **irrelevancy**, relevancy
- solvency •frequency •delinquency
- adequacy •poignancy

4.49

- **arsy-versy**, Circe, mercy, Percy, pursy
- colonelcy •verdancy •conversancy
- **conservancy**, fervency
- curtsy •controversy

4.50

- **ashy**, flashy, Lubumbashi, mashie, plashy, splashy, trashy
- Gramsci
- **banshee**, Comanche
- **marshy**, Ustashe
- **branchy**, Ranchi
- **Bangladeshi**, fleshy
- Frenchy •chichi
- **dishy**, fishy, maharishi, squishy, swishy, Vichy

> Create extra rhymes by changing words like dishy to dishiness.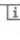

- rubbishy
- **sloshy**, squashy, washy
- bolshie •conchie •wishy-washy
- **paunchy**, raunchy
- sushi •munshi
- **bushy**, cushy, pushy
- **brushy**, gushy, mushy, plushy, rushy, slushy
- **bunchy**, crunchy, punchy

4.51

- **batty**, bratty, catty, chatty, Cincinnati, Dolcelatte, fatty, flattie, Hattie, natty, patty, ratty, Satie, Scarlatti, scatty, Tati, tattie, tatty

> Create extra rhymes by changing words like batty to battiness.

- faculty
- **Alicante**, andante, ante, anti, Ashanti, Bramante, Chianti, Dante, dilettante, Fante, Ferranti, infante, scanty, shanty (*US* chanty), spumante, vigilante, Zante
- **Asti**, pasty
- pederasty
- **Amati**, arty, Astarte, castrati, chapatti, clarty, coati, ex parte, Frascati, glitterati, Gujarati, hearty, illuminati, karate, Kiribati, lathi, literati, Marathi, obbligati (*US* obligati), party, tarty
- **crafty**, draughty (*US* drafty)
- auntie •nasty •contrasty
- **amaretti**, amoretti, Betti, Betty, confetti, cornetti, Donizetti, Getty, Giacometti, Hettie, jetty, machete, Marinetti, Nettie, petit, petty, Rossetti, Serengeti, spaghetti, sweaty, vaporetti, yeti
- **hefty**, lefty
- **felty**, sheltie
- penalty •specialty •empty
- **al dente**, aplenty, cognoscenti,

divertimenti, lisente, plenty,
portamenti, sente, twenty,
twenty-twenty
• seventy • peasanty
• **chesty**, testy, zesty
• Ghiberti

4.52

• **Albacete**, eighty, Haiti, Katy,
Kuwaiti, Leyte, matey, pratie, slaty,
weighty
• safety • frailty
• **dainty**, painty
• **hasty**, pastie, pasty, tasty
• suzerainty
• **Beatty**, entreaty, graffiti, meaty,
Nefertiti, peaty, sleety, sweetie,
Tahiti, titi, treaty
• **beastie**, yeasty

4.53

• **banditti**, bitty, chitty, city,
committee, ditty, gritty, intercity,
kitty, nitty-gritty, Pitti, pity, pretty,
shitty, slitty, smriti, spitty, titty,
vittae, witty

> Create extra rhymes by   [i]
> changing words like bitty to
> bittiness.

• **fifty**, fifty-fifty, nifty, shifty, swiftie,
thrifty
• **guilty**, kiltie, silty
• **flinty**, linty, minty, shinty
• **ballistae**, Christie, Corpus Christi,
misty, twisty, wristy
• sixty
• **deity**, gaiety (*US* gayety), laity,
simultaneity, spontaneity
• **contemporaneity**, corporeity,
femineity, heterogeneity,
homogeneity
• **anxiety**, contrariety, dubiety,
impiety, impropriety, inebriety,
notoriety, piety, satiety, sobriety,
ubiety, variety
• moiety
• **acuity**, ambiguity, annuity,

assiduity, congruity, contiguity,
continuity, exiguity, fatuity,
fortuity, gratuity, ingenuity,
perpetuity, perspicuity, promiscuity,
suety, superfluity, tenuity, vacuity
• rabbity
• **improbity**, probity
• acerbity • witchetty • crotchety
• heredity
• **acidity**, acridity, aridity, avidity,
cupidity, flaccidity, fluidity,
frigidity, humidity, hybridity,
insipidity, intrepidity, limpidity,
liquidity, lividity, lucidity,
morbidity, placidity, putridity,
quiddity, rabidity, rancidity,
rapidity, rigidity, solidity, stolidity,
stupidity, tepidity, timidity,
torpidity, torridity, turgidity,
validity, vapidity
• **commodity**, oddity
• **immodesty**, modesty
• **crudity**, nudity
• **fecundity**, jocundity, moribundity,
profundity, rotundity, rubicundity
• absurdity • difficulty • gadgety
• majesty • fidgety • rackety
• **pernickety**, rickety
• biscuity
• **banality**, duality, fatality, finality,
ideality, legality, locality, modality,
morality, natality, orality, reality,
regality, rurality, tonality, totality,
venality, vitality, vocality
• fidelity
• **ability**, agility, civility, debility,
docility, edibility, facility, fertility,
flexility, fragility, futility, gentility,
hostility, humility, imbecility,
infantility, juvenility, liability,
mobility, nihility, nobility, nubility,
puerility, senility, servility, stability,
sterility, tactility, tranquillity
(*US* tranquility), usability, utility,
versatility, viability, virility,
volatility
• ringlety
• **equality**, frivolity, jollity, polity,
quality

- **credulity**, garrulity, sedulity
- nullity
- **amity**, calamity
- extremity •enmity
- **anonymity**, dimity, equanimity, magnanimity, proximity, pseudonymity, pusillanimity, unanimity
- comity
- **conformity**, deformity, enormity, multiformity, uniformity
- subcommittee •pepperminty
- infirmity
- **Christianity**, humanity, inanity, profanity, sanity, urbanity, vanity
- amnesty
- **lenity**, obscenity, serenity
- **indemnity**, solemnity
- mundanity •amenity
- **affinity**, asininity, clandestinity, divinity, femininity, infinity, masculinity, salinity, trinity, vicinity, virginity
- **benignity**, dignity, malignity
- honesty
- **community**, immunity, importunity, impunity, opportunity, unity

> Create extra rhymes by changing words like community to communities. [i]

- **confraternity**, eternity, fraternity, maternity, modernity, paternity, taciturnity
- **serendipity**, snippety
- uppity
- **angularity**, barbarity, bipolarity, charity, circularity, clarity, complementarity, familiarity, granularity, hilarity, insularity, irregularity, jocularity, linearity, parity, particularity, peculiarity, polarity, popularity, regularity, secularity, similarity, singularity, solidarity, subsidiarity, unitarity, vernacularity, vulgarity
- alacrity •sacristy
- **ambidexterity**, asperity, austerity, celerity, dexterity, ferrety, posterity, prosperity, severity, sincerity,

temerity, verity
- celebrity •integrity •rarity
- **authority**, inferiority, juniority, majority, minority, priority, seniority, sonority, sorority, superiority
- mediocrity •sovereignty •salubrity
- entirety
- **futurity**, immaturity, impurity, maturity, obscurity, purity, security, surety
- touristy
- **audacity**, capacity, fugacity, loquacity, mendacity, opacity, perspicacity, pertinacity, pugnacity, rapacity, sagacity, sequacity, tenacity, veracity, vivacity, voracity
- laxity
- **sparsity**, varsity
- necessity
- **complexity**, perplexity
- **density**, immensity, propensity, tensity
- scarcity •obesity
- **felicity**, toxicity
- **fixity**, prolixity
- **benedicite**, nicety
- **anfractuosity**, animosity, atrocity, bellicosity, curiosity, fabulosity, ferocity, generosity, grandiosity, impecuniosity, impetuosity, jocosity, luminosity, monstrosity, nebulosity, pomposity, ponderosity, porosity, preciosity, precocity, reciprocity, religiosity, scrupulosity, sinuosity, sumptuosity, velocity, verbosity, virtuosity, viscosity
- paucity •falsity •caducity •russety
- **adversity**, biodiversity, diversity, perversity, university
- **sacrosanctity**, sanctity
- chastity
- **entity**, identity
- quantity •certainty
- **cavity**, concavity, depravity, gravity
- travesty •suavity
- **brevity**, levity, longevity
- velvety •naivety
- **activity**, nativity
- equity

- **antiquity**, iniquity, obliquity, ubiquity
- propinquity

4.54

- **almighty**, Aphrodite, Blighty, flighty, mighty, nightie, whitey
- ninety •feisty
- **dotty**, grotty, hottie, knotty, Lanzarote, Lottie, Pavarotti, potty, Scottie, snotty, spotty, totty, yachtie, zloty

> Create extra rhymes by changing words like dotty to dottiness. [i]

- **lofty**, softie
- Solti •novelty
- **Brontë**, démenti, Monte, Monty, Visconti
- frosty
- **forty**, haughty, naughty, pianoforte, rorty, shorty, sortie, sporty, UB40, warty
- **balti**, faulty, salty
- **flaunty**, jaunty
- **doughty**, outie, pouty, snouty
- **bounty**, county, Mountie
- frowsty •viscounty
- **Capote**, coatee, coyote, dhoti, floaty, goaty, oaty, peyote, roti, throaty
- jolty
- **postie**, toastie, toasty
- hoity-toity •pointy
- **agouti**, beauty, booty, cootie, cutie, Djibouti, duty, fluty, fruity, rooty, snooty, tutti-frutti

4.55

- **footy**, putti, sooty, tutti
- shufti •casualty •deputy
- **butty**, cutty, gutty, nutty, puttee, putty, rutty, smutty
- **mufti**, tufty
- bhakti •subtlety •humpty-dumpty
- **Bunty**, runty
- **bustee**, busty, crusty, dusty, fusty, gusty, lusty, musty, rusty, trusty

- fealty •realty
- **propriety**, society
- **loyalty**, royalty
- cruelty
- **Krishnamurti**, Trimurti
- liberty •puberty
- **faggoty**, maggoty
- Hecate •chocolatey •Cromarty
- commonalty •personalty •property
- carroty •guaranty •mayoralty
- warranty •admiralty •severalty
- poverty
- **Alberti**, Bertie, dirty, flirty, shirty, thirty
- uncertainty
- **Kirstie**, thirsty
- bloodthirsty

4.56

- Cathy
- **Iolanthe**, Xanthe
- McCarthy •breathy
- **healthy**, stealthy, wealthy
- lengthy
- **heathy**, Lethe
- pithy •filthy
- **bothy**, frothy, mothy, wrathy
- toothy
- **polymathy**, timothy
- apathy •telepathy •empathy
- antipathy •sympathy
- **encephalopathy**, homeopathy, osteopathy
- Dorothy •earthy

4.57

- **prithee**, smithy, withy
- swarthy
- **mouthy**, Southey
- smoothie •worthy •airworthy
- blameworthy •praiseworthy
- seaworthy •Galsworthy
- roadworthy •noteworthy
- newsworthy •trustworthy

4.58

- **navvy**, savvy
- **ave**, Garvey, Harvey, larvae, Mojave

- **bevvy**, bevy, Chevy, heavy, levee, Levi, levy, top-heavy
- envy
- **cavy**, Davy, Devi, gravy, navy, slavey, venae cavae, wavy
- **bivvy**, chivvy, civvy, divvy, Livy, privy, skivvy, spivvy
- Sylvie • ivy • grovy
- **groovy**, movie
- **covey**, lovey, lovey-dovey, luvvy
- anchovy • Muscovy • Pahlavi
- **curvy**, Nervi, nervy, scurvy, topsy-turvy

4.59

- Myfanwy • Malawi • Zimbabwe
- Anhui • Dewi
- **kiwi**, peewee, weewee
- **Conwy**, Goronwy
- **soliloquy**, ventriloquy
- colloquy • obloquy

4.60

- Mascagni • Daubigny • bouilli

4.61

- **jazzy**, snazzy
- palsy-walsy • Ramsay
- **pansy**, tansy
- **Anasazi**, Ashkenazi, Ashkenazy, Benghazi, Ghazi, kamikaze, khazi, Stasi, Swazi
- prezzie
- **frenzy**, Mackenzie

- **Bel Paese**, Buthelezi, crazy, daisy, Farnese, glazy, hazy, lazy, Maisie, mazy, oops-a-daisy, Piranesi, upsy-daisy, Veronese
- stir-crazy

> Create extra rhymes by changing words like crazy to craziness. [i]

- **breezy**, cheesy, easy, easy-peasy, Kesey, Parcheesi, queasy, sleazy, wheezy, Zambezi
- teensy • speakeasy
- **busy**, dizzy, fizzy, frizzy, Izzy, Lizzie, tizzy
- **flimsy**, whimsy
- **Kinsey**, Lindsay, Lynsey
- poesy
- **Aussie**, cossie, mossie
- Swansea • gauzy • causey
- **ballsy**, palsy
- **blowsy**, Dalhousie, drowsy, frowzy, housey-housey, lousy
- cosy (*US* cozy), dozy, Josie, mafiosi, mosey, nosy, posey, posy, prosy, Rosie, rosy
- **Boise**, noisy

4.62

- **bluesy**, boozy, choosy, doozy, floozie, jacuzzi, medusae, newsy, oozy, Pusey, snoozy, Susie, Uzi, woozy
- woodsy • Wolsey • jalousie
- **fuzzy**, muzzy, scuzzy
- sudsy • clumsy • klutzy
- **durzi**, furzy, jersey, kersey, Mersey
- Guernsey

Section 5: **-i**

Section 6: -iy

- **ally**, Altai, apply, assai, awry, ay, aye, Baha'i, belie, bi, Bligh, buy, by, bye, bye-bye, chi, Chiangmai, Ciskei, comply, cry, Cy, Dai, defy, deny, Di, die, do-or-die, dry, Dubai, dye, espy, eye, fie, fly, forbye, fry, Frye, goodbye (*US* goodby), guy, hereby, hi, hie, high, I, imply, I-spy, July, kai, lie, lye, Mackay, misapply, my, nearby, nigh, Nye, outfly, passer-by, phi, pi, pie, ply, pry, psi, Qinghai, rai, rely, rocaille, rye, scry, serai, shanghai, shy, sigh, sky, Skye, sky-high, sly, spin-dry, spry, spy, sty, Sukhotai, supply, Tai, Thai, thereby, thigh, thy, tie, Transkei, try, tumble-dry, underlie, Versailles, Vi, vie, whereby, why, wry, Wye, xi, Xingtai, Yantai

- genii • Sinai • denarii • caducei
- minutiae • sestertii

- aye-aye

- rabbi • standby • lay-by • nimbi • alibi
- rhombi • go-by • incubi • succubi
- syllabi • lullaby • hushaby

- **deadeye**, red-eye
- Sendai • solidi
- **nidi**, tie-dye
- eisteddfodau • Bondi • fundi

6.2

- uraei

6.3

- leylandii • radii • bindi-eye • nuclei

6.7

- Delphi
- **deify**, reify
- **preachify**, speechify
- edify • ladyfy
- **acidify**, humidify, rigidify, solidify
- **commodify**, modify
- codify • amplify • jellify • exemplify
- vilify • simplify

Cross-rhyme is a rhyme pattern with alternating end rhymes (in the pattern *abab*):

Drink and dance and laugh and lie,
    Love, the reeling midnight through,
For tomorrow we shall die!
    (But, alas, we never do.)

(Dorothy Parker, 'The Flaw in Paganism')

- **mollify**, qualify
- nullify • uglify • ramify
- **humify**, tumefy
- mummify • magnify • damnify
- **dignify**, signify
- personify • unify • typify • stupefy
- yuppify
- **clarify**, scarify
- **terrify**, verify
- petrify • electrify • gentrify • rarefy
- vitrify • horrify • transmogrify
- glorify • putrefy • purify
- **classify**, pacify
- calcify • Nazify • specify • intensify
- ossify • detoxify • falsify • crucify
- **dulcify**, emulsify
- **diversify**, versify
- **beatify**, gratify, ratify, stratify
- sanctify • satisfy
- **objectify**, rectify
- **identify**, misidentify
- testify • prettify • mystify • quantify
- **fortify**, mortify
- notify • beautify • fructify • stultify
- justify • certify • liquefy
- **hi-fi**, sci-fi

> Create extra rhymes by [i]
> changing word endings from *-fy*
> to *-fying*, *-fies*, or *-fied*.

6.8

- Haggai • Belgae • gilgai • fungi
- sarcophagi • mamaguy • assegai

6.9

- magi

6.10

- pink-eye • Mordecai • sockeye
- **croci**, foci
- buckeye • Diadochi • Malachi

6.11

- **ally**, phalli

- Adlai • gadfly • blackfly • damselfly
- sandfly • barfly • mayfly
- **Eli**, Ely
- greenfly • bacilli • multiply • styli
- whitefly • wall eye • horsefly
- housefly
- **alveoli**, E. coli, gladioli
- blowfly • lapis lazuli • reguli • stimuli
- flocculi • ranunculi • firefly
- discoboli • astragali • dragonfly
- alkali • Lorelei • Naphtali • butterfly
- hoverfly

6.12

- rami • calami

6.13

- decani • Iceni • Gemini • Anno Domini • termini • acini
- **personae**, tostone
- Brunei • alumni • goldeneye

6.14

- magpie • Philippi • sweetie-pie
- occupy

6.15

- panfry • certiorari • spray-dry • papyri
- **a fortiori**, a posteriori, a priori, memento mori, sori, thesauri, tori
- outcry • blow-dry • samurai
- caravanserai • stir-fry

6.16

- Masai • narcissi • prophesy • nisi
- colossi • flocci • bonsai • loci • fuci
- thyrsi

6.17

- gun-shy • work-shy

6.18

- cacti • necktie
- **aqua vitae**, curriculum vitae
- pigsty • hogtie • crosstie • shut-eye
- conducti • tongue-tie

6.19

- lecythi • mythi

6.20

- Levi

6.21

- lapsus linguae • Paraguay • Uruguay

6.22

- banzai • tiger's-eye • bird's-eye

Section 7: **-or**

7.1

- **abhor**, adore, afore, anymore, ashore, awe, bandore, Bangalore, before, boar, Boer, bore, caw, chore, claw, cocksure, comprador, cor, core, corps, craw, Delors, deplore, door, draw, drawer, evermore, explore, flaw, floor, for, forbore, fore, foresaw, forevermore, forswore, four, fourscore, furthermore, Gábor, galore, gnaw, gore, grantor, guarantor, guffaw, hard-core, Haugh, haw, hoar, ignore, implore, Indore, interwar, jaw, Johor, Lahore, law, lessor, lor, lore, macaw, man-o'-war, maw, mirador, mor, more, mortgagor, Mysore, nevermore, nor, oar, obligor, offshore, onshore, or, ore, outdoor, outwore, paw, poor, pore, pour, rapport, raw, roar, saw, scaur, score, senhor, señor, shaw, ship-to-shore, shop-floor, shore, signor, Singapore, snore, soar, softcore, sore, spore, squaw, store, straw, swore, Tagore, tau, taw, thaw, Thor, threescore, tor, tore, torr, trapdoor, tug-of-war, two-by-four, underfloor, underscore, war, warrantor, Waugh, whore, withdraw, wore, yaw, yore, your

7.2

- Dior

7.3

- Melchior •Gwalior •excelsior

7.4

- hellebore •usquebaugh •Tombaugh

7.5

- jackdaw •battledore
- **landau**, Landor
- chador •vendor •humidor •lobster thermidor •cuspidor •corridor
- stevedore •Isidore •condor
- stormdoor •Sodor •Theodore
- toreador •troubadour •picador
- commodore •parador •Labrador
- matador •conquistador •Salvador
- Ecuador

The use of *rime riche* (or *identical rhyme*) underlines the fear in the voice of the narrator and makes it appear that he is trying to convince himself that nothing untoward is happening by chanting a comforting refrain:

Once upon a midnight dreary, while I pondered weak and weary,
Over many a quaint and curious volume of forgotten lore,
While I nodded, nearly napping, suddenly there came a tapping,
As of some one gently rapping, rapping at my chamber door.
'Tis some visitor,' I muttered, 'tapping at my chamber door -
Only this, and nothing more.'

(Edgar Allan Poe, 'The Raven')

Rhyme schemes are referred to by letters indicating the rhyming words for each line, so the rhyme scheme *abab* (known as *cross-rhyme*) is one in which the first and third, and second and fourth lines rhyme:

I don't go to parties. Well, what are they for,
If you don't need to find a new lover?
You drink and you listen and drink a bit more
And you take the next day to recover.

(Wendy Cope, 'Being Boring')

7.6

- **therefore**, wherefore
- Roquefort •semaphore •ctenophore
- pinafore

7.7

- Igor •rigor •gewgaw

7.8

- hee-haw

7.9

- lockjaw

7.10

- Angkor •hardcore •décor •Agincourt
- manticore •ichor •encore
- kwashiorkor •underscore

7.11

- Danelaw •in-law •son-in-law
- sister-in-law •by-law •outlaw
- folklore •coleslaw •subfloor

7.12

- Blackmore •Sedgemoor •claymore

- **Seymour**, Timor
- Brynmor •Barrymore •Baltimore
- Broadmoor •Growmore •sophomore
- sagamore •blackamoor •sycamore
- Tullamore

7.13

- mackinaw •Elsinore

7.14

- millepore
- **forepaw**, pawpaw
- downpour •southpaw

7.15

- jackstraw •bedstraw •uproar
- wire-draw

7.16

- Nassau •hacksaw •heartsore
- bedsore •Ensor •fretsaw •chainsaw
- **Esau**, seesaw
- jigsaw
- **ripsaw**, whipsaw
- eyesore •Warsaw •bowsaw
- footsore •Luxor •plesiosaur
- stegosaur •Arkansas •Chickasaw
- dinosaur •brontosaur

7.17

- Bradshaw •seashore

- **kickshaw**, rickshaw
- scrimshaw • trishaw • dogshore
- **alongshore**, longshore
- foreshore

7.18

- cantor • lector • caveat emptor
- **centaur**, mentor, stentor
- Wichita • Choctaw • coldstore • Utah
- drugstore • megastore • Minotaur
- superstore

7.19

- Hathor

7.20

- Ifor • Gwynfor • herbivore • carnivore
- omnivore • insectivore

7.21

- bezoar

Section 8: **-ow**

8.1

- **allow**, avow, Bilbao, Bissau, bough, bow, bow-wow, brow, cacao, chow, ciao, cow, dhow, Dow, endow, Foochow, Frau, Hangzhou, Hough, how, Howe, kowtow, Lao, Liao, Macao, Macau, miaow, Mindanao, mow, now, ow, Palau, plough (*US* plow), pow, prow, row, scow, Slough, sough, sow, Tao, thou, vow, wow, Yangshao

8.2

- luau

8.3

- Moldau

> *Stressed* (or *masculine*) *rhymes* can be created with single and multi-syllable words where the stress is on the last syllable. In 'When We Two Parted', Byron alternates double and single syllable words, and *stressed* and *unstressed* rhymes:
>
> The dew of the morning
>   Sunk chill on my brow—
> It felt like the warning
>   Of what I feel now.
> Thy vows are all broken,
>   And light is thy fame:
> I hear thy name spoken,
>   And share in its shame.
>
> (Lord Byron, 'When We Two Parted')

8.4

- hoosegow • Oberammergau

8.5

- anyhow
- **know-how**, nohow
- somehow

8.6

- **Dachau**, Kraków

8.7

- Breslau
- snowplough (*US* snowplow)
- Tokelau

8.8

- Mau Mau

8.9

- Donau • Lucknow

8.10

- middlebrow
- **eyebrow**, highbrow
- Hausfrau • lowbrow • Jungfrau

8.11

- Nassau • Dessau

8.12

- **bow-wow**, powwow

Section 9: **-oh**

9.1

- **aglow**, ago, alow, although, apropos, art nouveau, Bamako, Bardot, beau, Beaujolais Nouveau, below, bestow, blow, bo, Boileau, bons mots, Bordeaux, Bow, bravo, bro, cachepot, cheerio, Coe, crow, Defoe, de trop, doe, doh, dos-à-dos, do-si-do, dough, dzo, Flo, floe, flow, foe, foreknow, foreshow, forgo, Foucault, froe, glow, go, good-oh, go-slow, grow, gung-ho, Heathrow, heave-ho, heigh-ho, hello, ho, hoe, ho-ho, jo, Joe, kayo, know, lo, low, maillot, malapropos, Marceau, mho, Miró, mo, Mohs, Monroe, mot, mow, Munro, no, Noh, no-show, oh, oho, outgo, outgrow, owe, Perrault, po, Poe, pro, quid pro quo, righto, roe, Rouault, row, Rowe, sew, shew, show, sloe, slow, snow, so, soh, sow, status quo, stow, Stowe, strow, tally-ho, though, throw, tic-tac-toe, to-and-fro, toe, touch-and-go, tow, trow, undergo, undersow, voe, whacko, whoa, wo, woe, Xuzhou, yo, yo-ho-ho, Zhengzhou, Zhou

> The combination of *terminal* (or
> *end*) rhymes and *medial* (or
> *internal*) rhymes helps give this
> Nursery Rhyme its typical bounce:
>
> Mary, Mary, quite contrary,
> How does your garden grow?
> With silver bells and cockleshells,
> And pretty maids all in a row.

9.2

- **Bulawayo**, Galileo, Mayo, Montevideo

9.3

- **brio**, Clio, Krio, Leo, Milhaud, Rio, Theo, trio

9.4

- Cleo • Carpaccio • Boccaccio
- capriccio • braggadocio • Palladio
- cardio • radio • video • audio • rodeo
- studio
- **Caravaggio**, DiMaggio
- adagio
- **arpeggio**, Correggio
- Sergio • radicchio • Tokyo • intaglio
- seraglio
- **billy-o**, punctilio
- **folio**, imbroglio, olio, polio, portfolio
- cameo • Romeo
- **Borneo**, Tornio
- Antonio • Scipio • Scorpio
- **barrio**, Mario
- **impresario**, Lothario, Polisario, Rosario, scenario
- stereo • embryo
- **Blériot**, Ontario
- vireo • Florio
- **oratorio**, Oreo
- curio • Ajaccio • Lazio • nuncio
- pistachio
- **fellatio**, Horatio, ratio
- **ab initio**, ex officio
- patio • Subbuteo • physio

9.5

• **bio**, Cetshwayo, Io, ngaio, Ohio

9.6

• **arroyo**, boyo

9.7

• **duo**, Luo

9.8

• in vacuo • moto perpetuo • continuo

9.9

• **jabot**, sabot
• **ambo**, flambeau, mambo, Rambo, Rimbaud, Tambo
• **Gabo**, Garbo, lavabo
• elbow • Strabo • rainbow
• **gazebo**, grebo, placebo
• Igbo • bilbo
• **akimbo**, bimbo, limbo
• Maracaibo • yobbo
• **combo**, Negombo
• longbow • crossbow • oxbow
• **hobo**, lobo, oboe
• **Colombo**, dumbo, gumbo, jumbo, mumbo-jumbo, umbo
• Malabo • Mirabeau • turbo

9.10

• **gazpacho**, macho
• nacho • pasticcio • honcho • gaucho
• Ayacucho

9.11

• **foreshadow**, shadow
• Faldo
• **accelerando**, bandeau, Brando, glissando, Orlando
• eyeshadow

• **aficionado**, amontillado, avocado, Bardo, Barnardo, bastinado, bravado, Colorado, desperado, Dorado, eldorado, incommunicado, Leonardo, Mikado, muscovado, Prado, renegado, Ricardo, stifado
• commando
• **eddo**, Edo, meadow
• **crescendo**, diminuendo, innuendo, kendo
• **carbonado**, dado, Feydeau, gambado, Oviedo, Toledo, tornado
• **aikido**, bushido, credo, Guido, Ido, libido, lido, speedo, teredo, torpedo, tuxedo
• widow • dildo • window
• **Dido**, Fido, Hokkaido
• **condo**, rondeau, rondo, secondo, tondo
• Waldo
• **dodo**, Komodo, Quasimodo
• **escudo**, judo, ludo, pseudo, testudo, Trudeau
• weirdo • sourdough • fricandeau
• tournedos • Murdo

9.12

• Sappho • nympho • info • boffo
• Castel Gandolfo
• **buffo**, Truffaut

9.13

• Hidalgo
• **charango**, Durango, fandango, mango, Okavango, quango, Sango, tango
• Glasgow
• **Argo**, argot, cargo, Chicago, embargo, escargot, farrago, largo, Margot, Otago, Santiago, virago
• Lego • Marengo
• **Diego**, galago, Jago, lumbago, sago, Tierra del Fuego, Tobago, Winnebago
• **amigo**, ego, Vigo
• **bingo**, dingo, Domingo, flamingo, gringo, jingo, lingo
• Bendigo • indigo • archipelago

- vertigo • Sligo
- **doggo**, logo
- **bongo**, Congo, drongo, Kongo, pongo
- **a-gogo**, go-go, pogo, Togo
- Hugo
- **fungo**, mungo
- **ergo**, Virgo

9.14

- Tajo
- **boho**, coho, Moho, Soho
- Idaho • Arapaho • Navajo

9.15

- banjo • Gorgio
- **dojo**, mojo, Tojo

9.16

- **tacho**, taco, tobacco, wacko
- **blanco**, Franco
- **churrasco**, fiasco, Tabasco
- **Arco**, Gran Chaco, mako
- **art deco**, dekko, echo, Eco, El Greco, gecko, secco
- **flamenco**, Lysenko, Yevtushenko
- **alfresco**, fresco, Ionesco
- **Draco**, shako
- **Biko**, Gromyko, pekoe, picot, Puerto Rico, Tampico
- **sicko**, thicko, tricot, Vico
- **ginkgo**, pinko, stinko
- **cisco**, disco, Disko, Morisco, pisco, San Francisco
- zydeco • magnifico • calico • Jellicoe
- haricot • Jericho • Mexico • simpatico
- politico • portico
- **psycho**, Tycho
- **Morocco**, Rocco, sirocco, socko
- bronco
- **Moscow**, roscoe
- Rothko
- **coco**, cocoa, loco, moko, Orinoco, poco, rococo
- osso buco • Acapulco
- **Cuzco**, Lambrusco

- **bucko**, stucco
- **bunco**, junco, unco
- guanaco • Monaco • turaco • Turco

9.17

- **aloe**, callow, fallow, hallow, mallow, marshmallow, sallow, shallow, tallow

> Create extra rhymes by adding -*ness* to words like callow. ⓘ

- **Pablo**, tableau
- cashflow • Anglo • matelot
- **Carlo**, Harlow, Marlowe
- **Bargello**, bellow, bordello, cello, Donatello, fellow, jello, martello, mellow, morello, niello, Novello, Pirandello, Portobello, Punchinello, Uccello, violoncello, yellow
- pueblo • bedfellow • playfellow
- Oddfellow • Longfellow
- schoolfellow • Robin Goodfellow
- airflow • halo • Day-Glo
- **filo**, kilo
- **armadillo**, billow, cigarillo, Murillo, Negrillo, peccadillo, pillow, tamarillo, Utrillo, willow
- inflow • Wicklow • furbelow • Angelo
- pomelo • uniflow
- **kyloe**, lilo, milo, silo
- **Apollo**, follow, hollow, Rollo, swallow, wallow
- Oslo • São Paulo • outflow
- **bolo**, criollo, polo, solo, tombolo
- rouleau • regulo • modulo • mudflow
- diabolo • bibelot • pedalo • underflow
- buffalo
- **brigalow**, gigolo
- bungalow
- **Michelangelo**, tangelo
- piccolo • tremolo • alpenglow • tupelo
- contraflow • afterglow • overflow
- furlough • workflow

9.18

- **ammo**, Gamow
- Rameau • Malmö
- **demo**, memo

- Elmo • Palermo
- **emo**, primo, supremo
- limo
- **gizmo**, gran turismo, machismo, verismo
- Eskimo • Geronimo
- **duodecimo**, octodecimo, sextodecimo
- **altissimo**, fortissimo, generalissimo, pianissimo
- proximo • centimo • ultimo • Cosmo
- Pontormo
- **chromo**, duomo, Homo, majordomo, Nkomo, promo, slo-mo
- **Profumo**, sumo
- Alamo • dynamo • paramo

9.19

- **Mano**, piano
- **Arno**, boliviano, Bolzano, Carnot, chicano, guano, Kano, llano, Locarno, Lugano, Marciano, Marrano, meccano, oregano, Pisano, poblano, Romano, siciliano, soprano, Sukarno
- **Renault**, steno, tenno
- techno • Fresno • Pernod
- **ripieno**, volcano
- **albino**, bambino, beano, Borodino, Borsalino, cappuccino, casino, chino, Comino, concertino, Filipino, fino, Gino, keno, Ladino, Latino, Leno, maraschino, merino, Monte Cassino, Navarino, neutrino, Pacino, palomino, pecorino, Reno, San Marino, Sansovino, Torino, Trevino, Valentino, vino, Zeno
- **minnow**, winnow
- Llandudno • Gobineau • domino
- Martineau
- **lino**, rhino, wino
- tonneau • Grodno
- **Livorno**, porno
- Mezzogiorno
- **cui bono?**, kimono, Mono, no-no, phono
- **Bruno**, Gounod, Juneau, Juno, Uno
- Huguenot • pompano
- **Brno**, inferno, journo, Salerno, Sterno

9.20

- capo • Gestapo
- **Aleppo**, depot
- **downtempo**, tempo, uptempo
- Expo
- **cheapo**, Ipoh, peep-bo, repo
- hippo
- **hypo**, typo
- **oppo**, topo, troppo
- compo • Limpopo

9.21

- **arrow**, barrow, farrow, harrow, Jarrow, marrow, narrow, sparrow, taro, tarot, Varro, yarrow

> Create extra rhymes by adding -s to words like arrow. [i]

- gabbro • Avogadro • Afro • aggro
- macro • cilantro • Castro
- wheelbarrow
- **Faro**, Kilimanjaro, Pissarro, Pizarro, Tupamaro
- Pedro • allegro • hedgerow • velcro
- escrow
- **metro**, retro
- electro • Jethro
- **bolero**, caballero, dinero, Faeroe, pharaoh, ranchero, sombrero, torero
- scarecrow • Ebro
- **Montenegro**, Negro
- repro • in vitro • Pyrrho • synchro
- windrow • impro • intro • bistro
- Babygro • McEnroe
- **biro**, Cairo, giro, gyro, tyro
- fibro • micro • maestro
- **borrow**, Corot, morrow, sorrow, tomorrow
- cockcrow • cointreau
- **Moro**, Sapporo, Thoreau
- Mindoro • Yamoussoukro
- Woodrow
- **burro**, burrow, furrow
- upthrow
- **De Niro**, hero, Nero, Pierrot, Pinero, Rio de Janeiro, sub-zero, zero
- **bureau**, chiaroscuro, Douro, enduro, euro, Ishiguro, Oruro, Truro

- Politburo •guacharo •Diderot
- vigoro •Prospero •Cicero •in utero
- Devereux •Jivaro •overthrow

9.22

- **basso**, El Paso, Picasso, Sargasso, Tasso
- **fatso**, paparazzo, terrazzo
- Brasso
- **espresso**, gesso
- **intermezzo**, mezzo
- scherzo
- **peso**, say-so
- **calypso**, dipso
- schizo •Mato Grosso •torso •also
- **amoroso**, capriccioso, oloroso, so-so
- **Caruso**, Robinson Crusoe, Rousseau, trousseau
- so-and-so
- **Curaçao**, curassow
- **Thurso**, verso

9.23

- basho •Sancho •chat show
- peep show •sideshow •poncho
- roadshow •dumbshow

9.24

- **bateau**, chateau, gateau, gelato, mulatto, plateau
- **de facto**, ipso facto
- alto
- **canto**, Esperanto, manteau, panto, portmanteau
- **antipasto**, impasto -
- **agitato**, Ambato, castrato, esparto, inamorato, legato, moderato, obbligato (*US* obligato), ostinato, pizzicato, rubato, staccato, tomato, vibrato, Waikato
- contralto
- **allegretto**, amaretto, amoretto, Canaletto, cornetto, falsetto, ghetto, larghetto, libretto, Loreto, Orvieto,

Soweto, stiletto, Tintoretto, vaporetto, zucchetto
- **perfecto**, recto
- **cento**, cinquecento, divertimento, lento, memento, pimiento, portamento, Risorgimento, Sacramento, Sorrento, Trento
- **manifesto**, pesto, presto
- concerto
- **Cato**, Plato, potato
- **Benito**, bonito, burrito, coquito, graffito, Hirohito, incognito, Ito, magneto, Miskito, mosquito, Quito, Tito, veto
- ditto •in flagrante delicto •mistletoe
- **pinto**, Shinto
- tiptoe
- **Callisto**, fritto misto
- cogito •Felixstowe •Sillitoe

9.25

- **blotto**, Giotto, grotto, lotto, motto, Otto, risotto, Watteau
- Cocteau
- **molto**, Sholto
- **pronto**, Toronto
- Ariosto
- **auto**, Oporto, Porto, quarto
- **in toto**, koto, Kumamoto, Kyoto, photo, Sesotho, Yamamoto
- **Bhutto**, Maputo, Pluto, prosciutto, ritenuto, sostenuto, tenuto
- Cousteau •putto •gusto •Pashto
- undertow •Erato

9.26

- litho
- **Clotho**, Otho

9.27

- salvo
- **arvo**, bravo, centavo, multum in parvo, octavo
- Sarajevo
- **in vivo**, relievo

- **ab ovo**, de novo, Denovo, Porto Novo, Provo
- Kosovo • servo

- bagnio
- **dal segno**, jalapeño
- **cursillo**, Trujillo
- caudillo • El Niño • yo-yo

9.29

- garbanzo • Chimborazo
- Lorenzo • whizzo
- **proviso**, Valparaiso
- **Alfonso**, Alonzo, gonzo
- **arioso**, bozo, Gozo, mafioso, virtuoso
- **muso**, ouzo

Section 10: -oy

10.1

- **ahoy**, alloy, Amoy, annoy, boy, buoy, cloy, coy, destroy, employ, enjoy, Hanoi, hoi polloi, hoy, Illinois, joy, koi, oi, ploy, poi, Roy, savoy, soy, toy, trompe l'œil, troy

10.2

- **naoi**, pronaoi

10.3

- sandboy •bellboy •rentboy •playboy
- pageboy •lifebuoy •tomboy
- **ballboy**, tallboy
- cowboy •houseboy
- **doughboy**, hautboy, lowboy
- homeboy •toyboy •schoolboy
- bootboy •newsboy •busboy
- choirboy •paperboy •attaboy

10.4

- hobbledehoy

10.5

- killjoy

10.6

- decoy •didicoi •Khoikhoi

10.7

- alloy •saveloy

10.8

- dromoi

10.9

- tannoy

10.10

- charpoy
- **sepoy**, teapoy
- topoi

10.11

- Elroy •Leroy
- **Gilroy**, Kilroy
- Fitzroy •viceroy •Norroy •corduroy
- Fauntleroy

10.12

- Tolstoy

10.13

- **envoi**, envoy
- convoy

10.14

- Iroquois

10.15

• Yayoi

10.16

• borzoi

Section 11: -oo

11.1

- **accrue**, adieu, ado, anew, Anjou, aperçu, askew, ballyhoo, bamboo, bedew, bestrew, billet-doux, blew, blue, boo, boohoo, brew, buckaroo, canoe, chew, clew, clou, clue, cock-a-doodle-doo, cockatoo, construe, coo, Corfu, coup, crew, Crewe, cru, cue, déjà vu, derring-do, dew, didgeridoo, do, drew, due, endue, ensue, eschew, feu, few, flew, flu, flue, foreknew, glue, gnu, goo, grew, halloo, hereto, hew, Hindu, hitherto, how-do-you-do, hue, Hugh, hullabaloo, imbrue, imbue, jackaroo, Jew, kangaroo, Karroo, Kathmandu, kazoo, Kiangsu, knew, Kru, K2, kung fu, Lahu, Lanzhou, Lao-tzu, lasso, lieu, loo, Lou, Manchu, mangetout, mew, misconstrue, miscue, moo, moue, mu, nardoo, new, non-U, nu, ooh, outdo, outflew, outgrew, peekaboo, Peru, pew, plew, Poitou, pooh, pooh-pooh, potoroo, pursue, queue, revue, roo, roux, rue, screw, Selous, set-to, shampoo, shih-tzu, shoe, shoo, shrew, Sioux, skean dhu, skew, skidoo, slew, smew, snafu, sou, spew, sprue, stew, strew, subdue, sue, switcheroo, taboo, tattoo, thereto, thew, threw, thro, through, thru, tickety-boo, Timbuktu, tiramisu, to, to-do, too, toodle-oo, true, true-blue, tu-whit tu-whoo, two, vendue, view, vindaloo, virtu, wahoo, wallaroo, Waterloo, well-to-do, whereto, whew, who, withdrew, woo, Wu, yew, you, zoo

11.2

- leu

11.3

- bayou

11.4

- babu •Malibu •caribou •booboo • **marabou**, marabout

11.5

- statue •Machu Picchu •virtue

11.6

- **sadhu**, Tamil Nadu

Medial (or *internal*) *rhyme* is used here to emphasize and summarize the main idea of the first stanza of this poem; this is also a good example of rhyming used in free verse:

Your clear eye is the one absolutely beautiful thing.
I want to fill it with colour and ducks,
The zoo of the new …

(Sylvia Plath, 'Child')

• hairdo •Pompidou •fondue
• **hoodoo**, kudu, voodoo
• Urdu •amadou •Xanadu

11.7

• samfu •tofu •Khufu

11.8

• ragout
• **fugu**, Ouagadougou
• Telugu •burgoo

11.9

• bijou

11.10

• **Oahu**, yahoo
• yoo-hoo

11.11

• juju •carcajou •kinkajou

11.12

• **Baku**, raku
• haiku •Shikoku •cuckoo

11.13

• Yalu •igloo •Oulu
• **Honolulu**, KwaZulu, lulu, Zulu
• Pagalu •Angelou •ormolu
• superglue •curlew

11.14

• **Camus**, Jammu
• rimu •muumuu •tinamou

11.15

• Manu •Vishnu •Ainu •ingénue
• parvenu

11.16

• tapu •quipu •coypu •hoopoe

11.17

• Andrew
• **Maseru**, Nehru
• aircrew •écru •breakthrough
• Hebrew •see-through •corkscrew
• walk-through
• **Nakuru**, Nauru
• froufrou •guru •woodscrew
• thumbscrew •run-through •Timaru

11.18

• shiatsu •keiretsu •ju-jitsu
• Clarenceux

11.19

• **cachou**, cashew
• sandshoe •fichu
• **issue**, Mogadishu, tissue
• Honshu •horseshoe •snowshoe
• Kyushu •gumshoe •overshoe

11.20

• **Bantu**, stand-to
• **Manawatu**, Vanuatu
• passe-partout •gentoo •lean-to
• pistou
• **into**, thereinto
• manitou •onto •Motu
• **Basotho**, Hutu, Lesotho, Mobutu, Sotho, tutu
• **hereunto**, thereunto, unto
• surtout

11.21

- rendezvous

11.22

- Askew
- **undervalue**, value
- Matthew • countervalue • argue
- début • nephew • Pegu • ecu • rescue
- Verdelho
- **menu**, venue
- ague • Jehu • emu • preview • Jesu
- mildew • miscue

- **continue**, sinew
- in situ • barbecue • curlicue
- honeydew • clerihew • retinue
- avenue • residue • impromptu • shoyu
- Autocue • Kikuyu • Bartholomew
- interview • Montague • overview
- curfew • purlieu • purview

> Try rhyming one word with a
> set of two: menu, when you;
> preview, sea view.

11.23

- kudzu

Section 12: -ə ('-uh')

12.1

- **huh**, ugh, uh-huh

12.2

- **abaya**, betrayer, conveyor, Eritrea, flayer, Freya, gainsayer, layer, Malaya, Marbella, Maya, Mayer, Nouméa, obeyer, payer, player, portrayer, prayer, preyer, purveyor, slayer, sprayer, stayer, strayer, surveyor, waylayer, weigher
- tracklayer • bricklayer • minelayer
- record-player • taxpayer • ratepayer
- naysayer • soothsayer • crocheter

12.3

- **Achaea**, aliyah, Almería, Apia, Bahía, Caesarea, Cassiopeia, Chaldea, Cytherea, Euboea, foreseer, freer, galleria, gynaecea, Iphigenia, Kampuchea, kea, keyer, Latakia, Leah, Lucia, Nicaea, Nicosia, onomatopoeia, Oriya, Pangaea, Pantelleria, pharmacopoeia, pizzeria, ria, rupiah, sangría, seer, sharia, Shia, skier, spiraea (*US* spirea), Tanzania, taqueria, Tarpeia, Thea, trachea, trattoria, urea
- sightseer

12.4

- **adhere**, Agadir, appear, arrear, auctioneer, austere, balladeer, bandolier, Bashkir, beer, besmear, bier, blear, bombardier, brigadier, buccaneer, cameleer, career, cashier, cavalier, chandelier, charioteer, cheer, chevalier, chiffonier, clavier, clear, Coetzee, cohere, commandeer, conventioneer, Cordelier, corsetière, Crimea, dear, deer, diarrhoea (*US* diarrhea), domineer, Dorothea, drear, ear, electioneer, emir, endear, engineer, fear, fleer, Freer, fusilier, gadgeteer, Galatea, gazetteer, gear, gondolier, gonorrhoea (*US* gonorrhea), Greer, grenadier, hear, here, Hosea, idea, interfere, Izmir, jeer, Judaea, Kashmir, Keir, kir, Korea, Lear, leer, Maria, marketeer, Medea, Meir, Melilla, mere, Mia, Mir, mishear, mountaineer, muleteer, musketeer, mutineer, near, orienteer, pamphleteer, panacea, paneer, peer, persevere, pier, Pierre, pioneer, pistoleer, privateer, profiteer, puppeteer, queer, racketeer, ratafia, rear, revere, rhea, rocketeer, Sapir, scrutineer, sear, seer, sere, severe, Shamir, shear, sheer, sincere, smear, sneer, sonneteer, souvenir, spear, sphere, steer, stere, summiteer, Tangier, tear, tier, Trier, Tyr, veer, veneer, Vere, Vermeer, vizier, volunteer, Wear, weir, we're, year, Zaïre

12.5

- **Gambia**, Zambia
- **Arabia**, labia, Swabia
- **Libya**, Namibia, tibia
- euphorbia
- **agoraphobia**, claustrophobia, homophobia, hydrophobia, phobia, technophobia, xenophobia, Zenobia
- Nubia • rootbeer • cumbia
- **Colombia**, Columbia
- **exurbia**, Serbia, suburbia

> In this well-known poem Robert Frost uses an interesting *rhyme pattern* called *chain rhyme*, in which the rhyme-sound is echoed from stanza to stanza, with the third line signalling the main rhyme of the following stanza ('here' with 'queer/near/year'):
>
> Whose woods these are I think I know.
> His house is in the village, though;
> He will not see me stopping here
> To watch his woods fill up with snow.
>
> My little horse must think it queer
> To stop without a farmhouse near
> Between the woods and frozen lake
> The darkest evening of the year.
>
> (Robert Frost 'Stopping by Woods on a Snowy Evening')

- Wiltshire •Flintshire
- **gaillardia**, Nadia, tachycardia
- steadier •compendia
- **Acadia**, Arcadia, nadir, stadia
- reindeer
- **acedia**, encyclopedia, media, multimedia
- **Lydia**, Numidia
- India •belvedere •Claudia
- **Cambodia**, odea, plasmodia, podia, roe-deer
- **Mafia**, raffia, tafia
- Philadelphia •hemisphere
- planisphere •Montgolfier •Sofia
- ecosphere •biosphere •atmosphere
- thermosphere •ionosphere
- stratosphere •headgear •switchgear
- logia •nemesia •menhir

12.6

- **myalgia**, nostalgia
- sporangia
- **florilegia**, quadriplegia
- Phrygia •Thuringia •loggia •Borgia
- **apologia**, eulogia
- Perugia
- **Czechoslovakia**, Slovakia
- Saskia
- **clarkia**, souvlakia
- rudbeckia
- **fakir**, Wallachia
- Ischia
- **Antalya**, espalier, pallia, rallier

- shilly-shallyer •Somalia
- **hotelier**, Montpellier, sommelier, St Helier
- **Australia**, azalea, bacchanalia, Castalia, dahlia, echolalia, genitalia, inter alia, Lupercalia, Mahalia, marginalia, paraphernalia, regalia, Saturnalia, Thalia, Westphalia
- **Amelia**, camellia, Celia, Cordelia, Cornelia, Delia, Elia, epithelia, Karelia, Montpelier, Ophelia, psychedelia
- **bougainvillea**, Brasília, cilia, conciliar, familiar, haemophilia (*US* hemophilia), Hillier, juvenilia, memorabilia, necrophilia, paedophilia (*US* pedophilia), sedilia
- chanticleer
- **collier**, volleyer
- cochlea •haulier
- **Anatolia**, magnolia, melancholia, Mongolia
- **Apulia**, dulia, Julia, peculiar
- **nuclear**, sub-nuclear, thermonuclear
- buddleia

12.7

- Grasmere •cashmere
- **Emyr**, premier
- **macadamia**, Mesopotamia
- **academia**, anaemia (*US* anemia), Bohemia, Euphemia, hypoglycaemia, leukaemia (*US* leukemia),

septicaemia (*US* septicemia), uraemia
- **bulimia**, Ymir
- arrhythmia •Vladimir •encomia
- costumier •Windermere
- **Hermia**, hyperthermia, hypothermia

12.8

- **Campania**, Catania, pannier
- apnoea
- **Oceania**, Tanya, Titania
- **biennia**, denier, quadrennia, quinquennia, septennia, triennia
- **Albania**, balletomania, bibliomania, crania, dipsomania, egomania, erotomania, kleptomania, Lithuania, Lusitania, mania, Mauritania, megalomania, miscellanea, monomania, nymphomania, Pennsylvania, Pomerania, pyromania, Rainier, Romania, Ruritania, Tasmania, Transylvania, Urania
- **Armenia**, bergenia, gardenia, neurasthenia, proscenia, schizophrenia, senior, Slovenia
- **Abyssinia**, Bithynia, curvilinear, Gdynia, gloxinia, interlinear, Lavinia, linear, rectilinear, Sardinia, triclinia, Virginia, zinnia
- insignia •Sonia •insomnia •Bosnia
- **California**, cornea
- **Amazonia**, ammonia, Antonia, Babylonia, begonia, bonier, Catalonia, catatonia, Cephalonia, Estonia, Ionia, Laconia, Livonia, Macedonia, mahonia, Patagonia, pneumonia, Rondônia, sinfonia, Snowdonia, valonia, zirconia
- **junior**, petunia
- **hernia**, journeyer

12.9

- Dampier
- **Napier**, rapier, tapir
- Shakespeare •sepia •Olympia
- copier •compeer •photocopier

- **cornucopia**, dystopia, Ethiopia, myopia, subtopia, Utopia

12.10

- **barrier**, carrier, farrier, harrier, tarrier
- **Calabria**, Cantabria
- Andrea •Kshatriya •Bactria
- **Amu Darya**, aria, Zaria
- Alexandria
- **Ferrier**, terrier
- destrier
- **aquaria**, area, armamentaria, Bavaria, Bulgaria, caldaria, cineraria, columbaria, filaria, frigidaria, Gran Canaria, herbaria, honoraria, malaria, pulmonaria, rosaria, sacraria, Samaria, solaria, tepidaria, terraria
- **atria**, gematria
- **Assyria**, Illyria, Styria, Syria
- **Laurier**, warrior
- **hypochondria**, mitochondria
- Austria
- **auditoria**, ciboria, conservatoria, crematoria, emporia, euphoria, Gloria, moratoria, phantasmagoria, Pretoria, sanatoria, scriptoria, sudatoria, victoria, Vitoria, vomitoria
- Maurya
- **courier**, Fourier
- **currier**, furrier, spurrier, worrier
- **Cumbria**, Northumbria, Umbria
- **Algeria**, anterior, bacteria, Bashkiria, cafeteria, criteria, cryptomeria, diphtheria, exterior, hysteria, Iberia, inferior, interior, Liberia, listeria, Nigeria, posterior, Siberia, superior, ulterior, wisteria
- **Etruria**, Liguria, Manchuria, Surya

12.11

- **cassia**, glacier
- **apraxia**, dyspraxia
- banksia •eclampsia
- **estancia**, fancier, financier, Landseer

- **intarsia**, mahseer, Marcia, tarsier
- **bartsia**, bilharzia
- **anorexia**, dyslexia
- intelligentsia • dyspepsia
- **Dacia**, fascia
- **Felicia**, Galicia, indicia, Lycia, Mysia
- **asphyxia**, elixir, ixia
- dossier • nausea
- **Andalusia**, Lucia
- overseer • Mercia • Hampshire
- Berkshire • Caernarvonshire
- Cheshire • differentia • Breconshire
- Devonshire • Ayrshire
- **Galatia**, Hypatia, solatia
- **alopecia**, godetia, Helvetia
- **Alicia**, Leticia
- Derbyshire • Berwickshire
- Cambridgeshire • Warwickshire
- Argyllshire • quassia • Shropshire
- Yorkshire • Staffordshire
- Hertfordshire • Bedfordshire
- Herefordshire • Oxfordshire
- Forfarshire • Lancashire
- Lincolnshire • Monmouthshire
- Buckinghamshire • Nottinghamshire
- Northamptonshire • Leicestershire
- Wigtownshire • Worcestershire

12.12

- astrantia • Bastia
- **Dei gratia**, hamartia
- poinsettia
- **in absentia**, Parmentier
- Izvestia
- **meteor**, wheatear
- Whittier • cottier • Ostia
- **consortia**, courtier
- protea • Yakutia • frontier • Althea
- Anthea • Parthia
- **Pythia**, stichomythia
- **Carinthia**, Cynthia
- forsythia • Scythia • clothier • salvia
- Latvia • Yugoslavia • envier
- **Flavia**, Moldavia, Moravia, Octavia, paviour (US pavior), Scandinavia, Xavier
- **Bolivia**, Livia, Olivia, trivia
- Sylvia • Guinevere • Elzevir
- **Monrovia**, Segovia
- Retrovir • effluvia • colloquia

- Goodyear • yesteryear • brassiere
- Abkhazia
- **Anastasia**, aphasia, brazier, dysphasia, dysplasia, euthanasia, fantasia, Frazier, glazier, grazier, gymnasia, Malaysia
- **amnesia**, anaesthesia (US anesthesia), analgesia, freesia, Indonesia, Silesia, synaesthesia
- **artemisia**, Kirghizia, Tunisia
- **ambrosia**, crozier, hosier, osier, symposia

12.13

- **acquire**, admire, afire, applier, aspire, attire, ayah, backfire, barbwire, bemire, briar, buyer, byre, choir, conspire, crier, cryer, defier, denier, desire, dire, drier, dryer, dyer, enquire, entire, esquire, expire, fire, flyer, friar, fryer, Gaia, gyre, hellfire, hire, hiya, ire, Isaiah, jambalaya, Jeremiah, Josiah, Kintyre, latria, liar, lyre, Maia, Maya, Mayer, messiah, mire, misfire, Nehemiah, Obadiah, papaya, pariah, peripeteia, perspire, playa, Praia, prior, pyre, quire, replier, scryer, shire, shyer, sire, skyer, Sophia, spire, squire, supplier, Surabaya, suspire, tier, tire, transpire, trier, tumble-dryer, tyre, Uriah, via, wire, Zechariah, Zedekiah, Zephaniah

> Create extra rhymes by changing words like acquire to acquiring. [i]

- homebuyer

12.14

- sapphire • backfire • campfire
- shellfire • ceasefire • misfire • spitfire
- speechifier
- **humidifier**, solidifier
- modifier • codifier • amplifier
- vilifier
- **mollifier**, qualifier
- nullifier • magnifier • indemnifier

- signifier •personifier •unifier
- typifier •stupefier
- **clarifier**, scarifier
- **terrifier**, verifier
- gentrifier •glorifier •purifier
- **classifier**, pacifier
- specifier •intensifier •crucifier
- emulsifier •versifier
- **gratifier**, ratifier
- sanctifier •identifier •testifier
- prettifier •quantifier •fortifier
- beautifier •stultifier •justifier
- liquefier •wildfire •watchfire
- bonfire •crossfire •bushfire •gunfire
- surefire •lammergeier •multiplier
- outlier •Niemeyer •quagmire
- vampire •empire •occupier •umpire
- hairdryer •prophesier •satire
- Blantyre •saltire •haywire •tripwire
- retrochoir •underwire

12.15

- **drawer**, tawer

12.16

- **bower**, cower, devour, dower,
  embower, empower, endower, flour,
  flower, gaur, Glendower, glower,
  hour, lour, lower, our, plougher
  (*US* plower), power, scour, shower,
  sour, Stour, sweet-and-sour, tower
- Beckenbauer •Eisenhower
- Schopenhauer •safflower
- passion flower •bellflower
- mayflower •cauliflower •wallflower
- **cornflour**, cornflower
- sunflower •elderflower •man-hour
- Adenauer •manpower •brainpower
- willpower •horsepower •firepower
- water power •rush hour
- watchtower

12.17

- **anoa**, Balboa, blower, boa, foregoer,
  goer, grower, hoer, jerboa, knower,
  Krakatoa, Lebowa, lower, moa,
  mower, Mururoa, Noah, o'er, proa,
  protozoa, rower, Samoa, sewer,
  Shenandoah, shower, sower,
  spermatozoa, Stour, thrower, tower
- shadower •widower •racegoer
- **theatregoer** (*US* theatergoer)
- churchgoer •echoer
- **follower**, swallower
- snowblower •lawnmower •genoa
- winnower •harrower •winegrower
- borrower •burrower •vetoer

12.18

- **annoyer**, Boyer, destroyer,
  employer, enjoyer, Goya, hoya,
  lawyer, Nagoya, paranoia, sequoia,
  soya

12.19

- **Amur**, brewer, chewer, Dewar, doer,
  ewer, hewer, Kahlua, lassoer, Nuer,
  pursuer, renewer, screwer, sewer,
  skewer, skua, spewer, strewer, suer,
  tattooer, viewer, who're, wooer
- evil-doer •wrongdoer •issuer
- snowshoer •rescuer •interviewer

12.20

- **abjure**, adjure, allure, amour,
  assure, Bahawalpur, boor,
  Borobudur, Cavour, coiffure,
  conjure, couture, cure, dastur,
  de nos jours, doublure, dour,
  embouchure, endure, ensure, enure,
  gravure, immature, immure, impure,
  inure, Jaipur, Koh-i-noor, Kultur,
  liqueur, lure, manure, mature, moor,
  Moore, Muir, mure, Nagpur, Namur,
  obscure, photogravure, plat du jour,
  Pompadour, procure, pure,
  rotogravure, Ruhr, Saussure, secure,
  simon-pure, spoor, Stour, sure, tour,
  Tours, velour, Yom Kippur, you're

> Create extra rhymes by   [i]
> adding *-ing* or *-(e)d* to words like
> abjure.

• tambour •prefecture •caricature
• armature
• **tamandua**, tandoor
• Dartmoor •Exmoor •Hawksmoor
• paramour •Papua •Jabalpur
• Manipur •Jodhpur •Kuala Lumpur
• Kolhapur •Karlsruhe •Joshua
• cynosure •Fraktur •détour •contour
• Padua
• **jaguar**, Managua, Nicaragua
• vacua •valuer •Langmuir •mantua
• arguer •residua
• **continua**, continuer
• pedicure •manicure •sinecure
• epicure •conure
• **bordure**, ordure
• Saumur •nunciature •overture
• couverture •coverture •purpure

12.21

• **abba**, blabber, dabber, grabber,
  jabber, stabber, yabber
• **Alba**, Galba
• **amber**, camber, caramba, clamber,
  Cochabamba, gamba, mamba,
  Maramba, samba, timbre
• **Annaba**, arbor, arbour, barber,
  Barbour, harbour (*US* harbor),
  indaba, Kaaba, Lualaba, Pearl
  Harbor, Saba, Sabah, Shaba
• **sambar**, sambhar
• **rebbe**, Weber
• Elba
• **Bemba**, December, ember, member,
  November, Pemba, September
• **belabour** (*US* belabor), caber,
  labour (*US* labor), neighbour
  (*US* neighbor), sabre (*US* saber),
  tabor
• chamber •bedchamber
• antechamber
• **amoeba** (*US* ameba), Bathsheba,
  Bourguiba, Geber, Sheba, zariba
• **cribber**, dibber, fibber, gibber, jibba,
  jibber, libber, ribber
• Wilbur
• **limber**, marimba, timber
• winebibber
• **calibre** (*US* caliber), Excalibur
• **briber**, fibre (*US* fiber), scriber,
  subscriber, Tiber, transcriber
• **clobber**, cobber, jobber, mobber,

robber, slobber
• **ombre**, sombre (*US* somber)
• **carnauba**, catawba, dauber,
  Micawber
• **jojoba**, Manitoba, October, sober
• **Aruba**, Cuba, Nuba, scuba, tuba,
  tuber
• Drouzhba •Toowoomba •Yoruba
• Hecuba

12.22

• **blubber**, clubber, grubber, lubber,
  rubber, scrubber, snubber
• **Columba**, cumber, encumber,
  Humber, lumbar, lumber, number,
  outnumber, rumba, slumber, umber
• cucumber •landlubber
• Addis Ababa •Córdoba
• Aqaba •djellaba •mastaba
• **Berber**, disturber, Djerba, Thurber

12.23

• **catcher**, dacha, focaccia, patcher,
  scratcher, snatcher, stature, thatcher
• **facture**, fracture, manufacture
• **capture**, enrapture, rapture
• flycatcher •oystercatcher
• **archer**, departure, kwacha, marcher,
  starcher, viscacha
• pasture
• **etcher**, fetcher, fletcher, lecher,
  sketcher, stretcher
• **conjecture**, lecture
• sepulture
• **denture**, misadventure,
  peradventure
• **divesture**, gesture, vesture
• texture •architecture •nature
• magistrature
• **bleacher**, creature, feature,
  headteacher, Katowice, Nietzsche,
  preacher, screecher, teacher
• schoolteacher
• **ditcher**, hitcher, pitcher, stitcher,
  twitcher
• Chibcha
• **picture**, stricture
• filcher •simcha

- **cincture**, tincture
- scripture
- **admixture**, commixture, fixture, intermixture, mixture
- expenditure • forfeiture
- discomfiture • garniture
- **primogeniture**, progeniture
- miniature • furniture • temperature
- portraiture • literature
- **divestiture**, vestiture

12.24

- **botcher**, gotcha, top-notcher, watcher, wotcha
- **imposture**, posture
- firewatcher • birdwatcher
- **debaucher**, scorcher, torture
- **Boucher**, voucher
- **cloture**, encroacher, poacher, reproacher
- jointure • moisture
- **cachucha**, future, moocher, smoocher, suture
- butcher
- **kuccha**, scutcher, toucher
- structure
- **culture**, vulture
- **conjuncture**, juncture, puncture
- rupture • sculpture • viniculture
- agriculture • sericulture
- arboriculture • pisciculture
- horticulture • silviculture
- subculture • counterculture
- aquaculture • acupuncture
- substructure • infrastructure
- candidature • ligature • judicature
- implicature
- **entablature**, tablature
- prelature • nomenclature • filature
- legislature • musculature
- premature • signature • aperture
- curvature
- **lurcher**, nurture, percher, searcher

12.25

- **adder**, bladder, khaddar, ladder, madder
- **Esmeralda**, Valda

- scaffolder • lambda
- **Amanda**, Aranda, Baganda, Banda, brander, candour (*US* candor), coriander, dander, expander, gander, germander, goosander, jacaranda, Leander, Luanda, Lysander, meander, memoranda, Menander, Miranda, oleander, panda, pander, philander, propaganda, Rwanda, sander, Skanda, stander, Uganda, understander, Vanda, veranda, withstander, zander
- backhander • Laplander • stepladder
- inlander • outlander • Netherlander
- overlander • gerrymander
- pomander
- **calamander**, salamander
- bystander
- **ardour** (*US* ardor), armada, Bader, cadre, carder, cicada, Dalriada, enchilada, Garda, gelada, Granada, Haggadah, Hamada, intifada, lambada, larder, Masada, Nevada, panada, piña colada, pousada, promenader, retarder, Scheherazade, Theravada, Torquemada, tostada
- **Alexander**, commander, demander, Lahnda, slander
- Pravda • autostrada

12.26

- **bedder**, cheddar, Edda, Enzedder, header, Kedah, shedder, shredder, spreader, tedder, threader, treader, Vedda
- **elder**, Griselda, welder, Zelda
- **addenda**, agenda, amender, ascender, attender, bender, blender, Brenda, contender, corrigenda, descender, engender, extender, fazenda, fender, gender, Glenda, Gwenda, hacienda, Länder, lender, mender, offender, pudenda, recommender, referenda, render, sender, slender, spender, splendour (*US* splendor), surrender, suspender, tender, Venda, weekender, Wenda
- parascender • bartender
- homesteader • newsvendor
- spot-welder

- **abrader**, Ada, blockader, crusader, dissuader, evader, fader, grader, Grenada, invader, masquerader, Nader, parader, persuader, raider, Rigveda, Seder, serenader, trader, upgrader, Veda, wader
- **attainder**, remainder
- rollerblader
- **Aïda**, bleeder, Breda, breeder, cedar, conceder, corrida, Derrida, Elfreda, Etheldreda, feeder, follow-my-leader, interceder, interpleader, kneader, leader, Leda, Lieder, misleader, pleader, reader, seceder, seeder, speeder, stampeder, succeeder, weeder
- **fielder**, midfielder, wielder, yielder
- outfielder •bandleader •ringleader
- cheerleader •copyreader
- mind-reader •sight-reader
- stockbreeder •proofreader
- newsreader

12.27

- **bidder**, consider, Jiddah, kidder, whydah
- **bewilder**, builder, guilder, Hilda, Matilda, St Kilda, Tilda, tilde
- **Belinda**, Cabinda, cinder, Clarinda, Dorinda, hinder, Kinder, Linda, Lucinda, Melinda, tinder
- Drogheda •shipbuilder •bodybuilder
- coachbuilder •boatbuilder •Candida
- spina bifida
- **calendar**, calender
- Phillida •cylinder •Phasmida
- Andromeda •Mérida •Florida
- Cressida •lavender •provender
- **chider**, cider, divider, eider, glider, Guider, Haida, hider, Ida, insider, Oneida, outsider, provider, rider, Ryder, Saida, slider, spider, strider, stridor
- Wilder
- **binder**, blinder, finder, grinder, kinda, minder, ringbinder, winder
- Fassbinder •spellbinder •highbinder
- bookbinder •pathfinder
- rangefinder •viewfinder •backslider

- paraglider •childminder •outrider
- joyrider •roughrider •ringsider
- Tynesider •sidewinder

12.28

- **dodder**, fodder, plodder, prodder
- **Isolde**, solder
- **absconder**, anaconda, Fonda, Golconda, Honda, nonda, ponder, responder, squander, Wanda, wander, yonder
- hot-rodder
- **awarder**, boarder, border, defrauder, hoarder, Korda, marauder, order, recorder, sordor, warder
- **alder**, Balder, Calder
- **launder**, maunder
- sailboarder •skateboarder
- keyboarder •snowboarder
- camcorder •video recorder
- **chowder**, Gouda, howdah, Lauda, powder
- **bounder**, compounder, expounder, flounder, founder, grounder, impounder, pounder, propounder, rounder, sounder
- gunpowder
- **Clodagh**, coda, coder, exploder, loader, Oder, odour (US odor), pagoda, Rhoda, Sargodha, Schroder, soda, vocoder
- **beholder**, boulder, folder, holder, moulder (US molder), polder, scolder, shoulder, smoulder (US smolder), upholder, withholder

> Try rhyming one word with a set of two: shoulder, told her; smoulder, hold her.   [i]

- cardholder •shareholder
- stakeholder
- **freeholder**, keyholder
- leaseholder •copyholder
- policyholder •stockholder
- **smallholder**, stallholder
- householder •freeloader
- **avoider**, embroider
- joinder •Schadenfreude

12.29

- **Barbuda**, barracuda, Bermuda, brooder, Buxtehude, colluder, deluder, excluder, intruder, Judah, Luda, Neruda, obtruder, Tudor
- mouthbrooder
- **Buddha**, do-gooder
- **Kaunda**, Munda
- **judder**, rudder, shudder, udder
- numdah
- **asunder**, blunder, chunder, hereunder, plunder, rotunda, sunder, thereunder, thunder, under, up-and-under, wonder
- husbander • seconder • Shetlander
- mainlander • Greenlander
- Queenslander • midlander
- Little Englander
- **Highlander**, islander
- Icelander • Hollander • lowlander
- Newfoundlander • woodlander
- colander • Canada • Kannada
- ambassador • forwarder
- **birder**, Gerda, girder, herder, murder

12.30

- **chaffer**, gaffer, Jaffa, kafir, Staffa
- **alfalfa**, alpha, Balfour, Wadi Halfa
- **camphor**, chamfer
- Luftwaffe
- **laugher**, staffer
- **heifer**, zephyr
- **chafer**, trefa, wafer
- cockchafer
- **feoffor**, reefer
- **differ**, sniffer
- pilfer • titfer • umbellifer • Jennifer
- conifer • apocrypha • thurifer
- **crucifer**, Lucifer
- Potiphar • aquifer
- **cipher**, encipher, fifer, Haifa, knifer, lifer

> Try rhyming one word with a　i
> set of two: lifer, knife her.

- **coffer**, cougher, Offa, offer, proffer, quaffer, scoffer

- golfer • phosphor • Forfar • Altdorfer
- **chauffeur**, gofer, goffer, gopher, loafer, Nuku'alofa, Ophir, shofar, sofa
- Fraunhofer
- **hoofer**, loofah, opera buffa, roofer, spoofer, tufa, woofer
- waterproofer
- **bluffer**, buffer, duffer, puffer, snuffer, suffer

> Create extra rhymes for　i
> words like bluffer by adding -er
> to gruff etc. (see section 17.15).

- **sulphur** (*US* sulfur) • telegrapher
- **calligrapher**, serigrapher
- **autobiographer**, bibliographer, biographer, cartographer, choreographer, cinematographer, crystallographer, geographer, Hagiographa, hagiographer, iconographer, lexicographer, lithographer, oceanographer, palaeographer (*US* paleographer), photographer, pornographer, radiographer, stenographer, topographer, typographer
- **philosopher**, theosopher
- metaphor • Christopher • surfer
- Bonhoeffer • windsurfer

12.31

- **blagger**, bragger, dagger, flagger, Jagger, lagger, nagger, quagga, saggar, shagger, stagger, swagger
- **alga**, realgar, Trafalgar
- **anger**, clangour (*US* clangor), Katanga, languor, manga, panga, sangar, tanga, Tauranga, Zamboanga
- sandbagger • carpetbagger • Erlanger
- **Aga**, Braga, dagga, dargah, laager, lager, naga, Onondaga, raga, saga
- **beggar**, eggar, Gregor, mega, Megger
- Edgar • Helga • Heidegger
- bootlegger
- **Jaeger**, maigre, Meleager, Noriega, Ortega, rutabaga, Sagar
- **Antigua**, beleaguer, bodega, eager,

intriguer, leaguer, meagre
(*US* meager), reneger, Riga, Seeger,
Vega
- **chigger**, configure, digger, figure,
Frigga, jigger, ligger, rigger, rigor,
rigour, snigger, swigger, transfigure,
trigger, vigour (*US* vigor)
- **churinga**, finger, linger, malinger
- gravedigger • ladyfinger • forefinger
- omega • vinegar • Honegger
- outrigger • Minnesinger
- **Auriga**, Eiger, liger, saiga, taiga,
tiger

12.32

- **dogger**, flogger, Hoggar, hogger,
jogger, logger, slogger, Wagga
Wagga
- **brolga**, Olga, Volga
- **conga**, conger, donga, Rarotonga
- pettifogger • footslogger
- **cataloguer** (*US* cataloger)
- **auger**, augur
- **ogre**, Saratoga, toga, yoga
- **beluga**, cougar, Kaluga, Kruger,
Luger
- **sugar**, Zeebrugge
- **bugger**, hugger, lugger, mugger,
plugger, rugger, slugger, Srinagar,
tugger
- **mulga**, vulgar
- **hunger**, sangha, Younger
- scandalmonger • scaremonger
- fishmonger
- **warmonger**, whoremonger
- ironmonger • hugger-mugger
- costermonger • Málaga
- **Berger**, burger, burgher
- hamburger • beefburger
- cheeseburger • Limburger
- Vegeburger • Erzgebirge
- Luxembourger

12.33

- azure
- **leisure**, made-to-measure, measure,
pleasure, treasure
- countermeasure

- **Australasia**, embrasure
- seizure
- **closure**, composure, enclosure,
exposure, foreclosure
- Hoosier

12.34

- Brahe • Fatiha • aloha

12.35

- **badger**, cadger
- **Alger**, neuralgia
- **ganja**, grandeur, phalanger
- **charger**, enlarger, maharaja, raja
- slàinte • turbocharger
- **dredger**, edger, hedger, ledger,
pledger, St Leger

> Create extra rhymes for
> words like dredger by adding *-er*
> to hedge etc. (see section 20.3).   ⓘ

- **avenger**, revenger
- **gauger**, golden-ager, major,
old-stager, pager, rampager,
sergeant major, stager, wager
- **arranger**, changer, danger,
endanger, exchanger, Grainger,
hydrangea, manger, ranger, stranger
- moneychanger • teenager
- bushranger
- **besieger**, paraplegia, procedure
- abridger
- **cringer**, ginger, impinger, infringer,
injure, ninja, whinger, winger
- dowager • voyager • harbinger
- bondager • wharfinger • packager
- Scaliger
- **challenger**, Salinger
- **pillager**, villager
- armiger • scrimmager
- **rummager**, scrummager
- manager • derringer • forager
- porringer • encourager
- **Massinger**, passenger
- presager • messenger • Kissinger
- **integer**, vintager
- cottager • frontager • ravager
- salvager • scavenger

- **Elijah**, Niger, obliger
- **codger**, dodger, lodger, roger, todger
- **forger**, Georgia, gorger
- gouger
- **lounger**, scrounger
- sunlounger •soldier
- **Abuja**, puja

12.36

- **bludger**, grudger, nudger, trudger
- indulger
- **blunger**, conjure, expunger, plunger, sponger
- **astrologer**, mythologer
- tanager •onager •massager •potager
- **merger**, perjure, purger, scourger, urger, verdure, verger

12.37

- **alpaca**, attacker, backer, clacker, claqueur, cracker, Dhaka, hacker, Hakka, knacker, lacquer, maraca, paca, packer, sifaka, slacker, smacker, stacker, tacker, tracker, whacker, yakka
- Kafka
- **anchor**, banker, Bianca, canker, Casablanca, Costa Blanca, flanker, franker, hanker, lingua franca, Lubyanka, rancour (US rancor), ranker, Salamanca, spanker, Sri Lanka, tanka, tanker, up-anchor, wanker

> Try rhyming one word with a set of two: hanker, thank her. ⓘ

- **Alaska**, lascar, Madagascar, Nebraska
- Kamchatka •linebacker •outbacker
- **hijacker**, skyjacker
- Schumacher •backpacker
- safecracker •wisecracker
- nutcracker •firecracker •ransacker
- scrimshanker •bushwhacker
- **barker**, haka, Kabaka, Lusaka, marker, moussaka, nosy parker, Oaxaca, Osaka, parka, Shaka, Zarqa

- **asker**, masker
- backmarker •waymarker
- **Becker**, checker, Cheka, chequer, Dekker, exchequer, Flecker, mecca, Neckar, Necker, pecker, Quebecker, Rebecca, Rijeka, trekker, weka, wrecker
- **sepulchre** (US sepulcher) •Cuenca
- **burlesquer**, Francesca, Wesker
- woodpecker

12.38

- **acre**, baker, breaker, Chandrasekhar, faker, forsaker, Jamaica, Laker, maker, nacre, partaker, Quaker, raker, saker, shaker, staker, taker, undertaker, waker
- bellyacher •matchmaker •bedmaker
- dressmaker
- **haymaker**, playmaker
- sailmaker •rainmaker
- **lacemaker**, pacemaker
- peacemaker •filmmaker •kingmaker
- printmaker •holidaymaker
- cabinetmaker •moneymaker
- merrymaker •watchmaker
- clockmaker •lawmaker •homemaker
- bookmaker •troublemaker
- boilermaker •heartbreaker
- safebreaker •Windbreaker
- tie-breaker •strikebreaker
- icebreaker •jawbreaker
- housebreaker •muckraker
- boneshaker •caretaker •piss-taker
- stavesacre •wiseacre
- **beaker**, Costa Rica, Dominica, eureka, Frederica, Griqua, leaker, loudspeaker, seeker, shrieker, sika, sneaker, speaker, squeaker, streaker, Tanganyika, theca, tikka, Topeka, wreaker

12.39

- **bicker**, clicker, dicker, flicker, kicker, liquor, nicker, picker, pricker, shicker, slicker, snicker, sticker, ticker, tricker, vicar, whicker, Wicca, wicker

- **bilker**, milker, Rilke
- **blinker**, clinker, drinker, finca, freethinker, Glinka, Inca, inker, jinker, shrinker, sinker, Soyinka, stinker, stotinka, thinker, tinker, Treblinka, winker
- **frisker**, whisker
- **kibitka**, Sitka
- Cyrenaica • Bandaranaike
- perestroika • Baedeker • melodica
- Boudicca • trafficker • angelica
- replica
- **basilica**, silica
- **frolicker**, maiolica, majolica
- bootlicker • res publica • mimicker
- Anneka • arnica • Seneca • Lineker
- picnicker
- **electronica**, harmonica, Honecker, japonica, Monica, moniker, Salonica, santonica, veronica
- Guernica • Africa • paprika
- **America**, erica
- headshrinker • Armorica • brassica
- Jessica • lip-syncer • fossicker
- Corsica
- **Attica**, hepatica, sciatica, viatica
- Antarctica • billsticker
- **erotica**, exotica
- swastika

12.40

- **balalaika**, biker, duiker, Formica, hiker, mica, pica, pika, piker, striker
- **blocker**, chocker, docker, Fokker, interlocker, knocker, locker, mocha, mocker, ocker, quokka, rocker, saltimbocca, shocker, soccer, stocker
- vodka • polka
- **concha**, conker, conquer, Dzongkha, plonker, stonker
- Oscar • Kotka • Knickerbocker
- footlocker
- **caulker** (US calker), corker, hawker, Lorca, Majorca, Minorca, orca, porker, squawker, stalker, talker, walker, yorker
- deerstalker • jaywalker • sleepwalker
- streetwalker • hillwalker
- shopwalker
- **Asoka**, broker, carioca, choker, coca, croaker, evoker, invoker, joker, mediocre, ochre (US ocher), poker, provoker, revoker, Rioja, smoker, soaker, soca, Stoker, tapioca
- judoka • shipbroker • stockbroker
- pawnbroker • troika

12.41

- **bazooka**, euchre, farruca, lucre, palooka, pooka, rebuker, snooker, Stuka, verruca
- babushka
- **booker**, cooker, hookah, hooker, looker, Sukkur
- Junker • onlooker • yarmulke
- Hanukkah • manuka
- **chukka** (US chukker), ducker, felucca, fucker, mucker, plucker, pucker, pukka, shucker, succour (US succor), sucker, trucker, tucker, yucca
- **skulker**, sulker
- **bunker**, hunker, lunker, punkah, spelunker
- **busker**, tusker
- latke • motherfucker • bloodsucker
- seersucker • abaca • stomacher
- **Linacre**, spinnaker
- massacre
- **Jataka**, Karnataka
- Tripitaka • Ithaca
- **burka**, circa, Gurkha, jerker, lurker, mazurka, shirker, smirker, worker
- tearjerker • craftworker
- metalworker • networker
- caseworker • fieldworker
- teleworker • shopworker • outworker
- homeworker • stoneworker
- woodworker

12.42

- **Allah**, calla, Caracalla, Haller, inshallah, pallor, Valhalla, valour (US valor), Whyalla
- **gabbler**, tabla
- **ambler**, gambler, rambler, scrambler
- **Adler**, saddler

- handler
- **angler**, dangler, strangler, wrangler
- tackler • trampler • antler • dazzler
- **Carla**, challah, Douala, gala, Guatemala, Gujranwala, impala, kabbala, Kampala, koala, La Scala, Lingala, Mahler, Marsala, masala, nyala, parlour (*US* parlor), Sinhala, snarler, tala, tambala, Uppsala
- garbler • chandler • sparkler
- sampler
- **a cappella**, Arabella, Bella, bestseller, Capella, cellar, Cinderella, citronella, Clarabella, corella, Daniela, Della, dispeller, dweller, Ella, expeller, favela, fella, fellah, feller, Fenella, Floella, foreteller, Heller, impeller, interstellar, Keller, Louella, Mandela, mortadella, mozzarella, Nigella, novella, paella, panatella, patella, predella, propeller, queller, quinella, repeller, rosella, rubella, salmonella, Santiago de Compostela, seller, smeller, speller, Stella, stellar, tarantella, teller, umbrella, Viyella
- Puebla
- **assembler**, dissembler, trembler
- **medlar**, pedlar
- ländler
- **fin de siècle**, Hekla
- Kepler
- **exempla**, exemplar, Templar
- **tesla**, wrestler
- embezzler • Rockefeller
- knee-trembler • saltcellar
- bookseller • storyteller

12.43

- **Adela**, bailer, bailor, baler, Benguela, bewailer, derailleur, hailer, inhaler, jailer, loudhailer, mailer, nailer, railer, retailer, sailer, sailor, scaler, Scheele, shillelagh, tailor, Taylor, trailer, Venezuela, wailer, whaler
- fabler • Daimler • blackmailer
- abseiler • wassailer • boardsailor
- wholesaler
- **appealer**, candela, Coahuila,

concealer, dealer, feeler, healer, Keeler, kneeler, Leila, peeler, Philomela, reeler, revealer, Schiele, sealer, sheila, Shelagh, spieler, squealer, stealer, tequila, velar, Vila, wheeler, wheeler-dealer
- enfant terrible
- **Anguilla**, Aquila, Attila, Camilla, cedilla, chiller, chinchilla, driller, Drusilla, fibrillar, filler, flotilla, fulfiller, Godzilla, gorilla, griller, guerrilla, killer, Manila, manilla, mantilla, miller, pillar, Priscilla, sapodilla, sarsaparilla, Schiller, scilla, scintilla, spiller, swiller, thriller, tiller, vanilla, vexilla, villa, Willa, willer, zorilla

> Try rhyming one word with a set of two: chiller, kill her.

- kiblah • fiddler
- **kindler**, swindler
- sniffler • sigla • stickler
- **sprinkler**, twinkler, winkler
- **Himmler**, Simla
- crippler
- **Hitler**, Littler, Mitla
- grizzler • Polyfilla • drosophila
- downhiller • Angela • painkiller
- weedkiller • ladykiller • Pamela
- **similar**, verisimilar
- propyla • caterpillar • canceller
- **councillor** (*US* councilor), counsellor (*US* counselor)

12.44

- **beguiler**, compiler, Delilah, filer, Isla, miler, reviler, smiler, styler, tiler, Tyler
- idler
- **stifler**, trifler
- recycler • Kreisler • profiler
- stockpiler • freestyler • Rottweiler
- **ayatollah**, choler, collar, corolla, dollar, dolour (*US* dolor), Hezbollah, holler, scholar, squalor, wallah, Waller, white-collar
- **cobbler**, gobbler
- **Doppler**, poplar
- ostler

- **brawler**, caller, crawler, drawler, faller, forestaller, hauler, installer, mauler, Paula, stonewaller, trawler
- warbler •dawdler •footballer
- reed-warbler
- **fowler**, growler, howler, prowler, scowler
- **Angola**, barbola, bipolar, bowler, bronchiolar, canola, carambola, circumpolar, coaler, Coca-Cola, cola, comptroller, consoler, controller, Ebola, eidola, extoller, Finola, Gorgonzola, granola, Hispaniola, kola, Lola, lunisolar, mandola, molar, multipolar, Ndola, patroller, payola, pianola, polar, roller, Savonarola, scagliola, scroller, sola, solar, stroller, tombola, Tortola, troller, Vignola, viola, Zola
- ogler
- **teetotaller** (*US* teetotaler)
- potholer •steamroller •logroller
- roadroller
- **boiler**, broiler, Euler, oiler, spoiler, toiler
- potboiler

12.45

- **cooler**, hula, moolah, Petula, ruler, Shula, Tallulah, Tula
- bugler •pre-schooler

12.46

- **ampulla**, bulla, fuller, Müller, pula, puller
- titular •Weissmuller •wirepuller
- **incunabula**, tabular
- preambular •glandular •coagula
- **angular**, quadrangular, rectangular, triangular
- **Dracula**, facula, oracular, spectacular, vernacular
- **cardiovascular**, vascular
- **annular**, granular
- scapula •capsular •spatula
- tarantula •nebula •scheduler
- calendula
- **irregular**, regular

- **Benbecula**, molecular, secular, specular
- cellular •fibula •Caligula •singular
- **auricular**, curricula, curricular, diverticula, funicular, lenticular, navicular, particular, perpendicular, testicular, vehicular, vermicular
- primula
- **insular**, peninsula
- **fistula**, Vistula
- globular
- **modular**, nodular
- **binocular**, jocular, ocular
- oscular
- **copula**, popular
- consular •formula •tubular •uvula
- jugular
- **avuncular**, carbuncular
- **crepuscular**, majuscular, minuscular, muscular
- pustular
- **circular**, semicircular, tubercular
- Ursula

12.47

- **colour** (*US* color), cruller, culler, medulla, mullah, Muller, nullah, sculler, Sulla
- **doubler**, troubler
- **bumbler**, grumbler, stumbler, tumbler
- bundler •muffler •juggler •bungler
- suckler •coupler
- **hustler**, rustler
- **butler**, cutler
- puzzler •swashbuckler •technicolor
- **multicolour** (*US* multicolor)
- **watercolour** (*US* watercolor)

12.48

- **areola**, rubeola
- Viola
- **dueller** (*US* dueler), jeweller (*US* jeweler)
- **babbler**, dabbler, parabola
- **labeller** (*US* labeler)
- **dribbler**, nibbler, quibbler, scribbler
- **libeller** (*US* libeler)
- **hobbler**, nobbler, squabbler, wobbler

- bubbler
- **fumbler**, mumbler, rumbler
- **burbler**, hyperbola
- bachelor
- **paddler**, straddler
- mandala •panhandler •meddler
- ladler •wheedler
- **diddler**, piddler, riddler, tiddler, twiddler
- **coddler**, modeller (US modeler), toddler, twaddler, waddler
- **fondler**, gondola
- **yodeller** (US yodeler)
- doodler
- **muddler**, puddler
- hurdler •waffler
- **shuffler**, snuffler
- **haggler**, straggler
- **mangler**, wangler
- finagler
- **giggler**, wiggler, wriggler
- **smuggler**, struggler
- pergola •heckler
- **Agricola**, Nicola, pickler, tickler, tricolour (US tricolor)
- chronicler
- **snorkeller** (US snorkeler)
- chuckler
- **enameller** (US enameler)
- **signaller** (US signaler)
- **tunneller** (US tunneler)
- grappler •stapler
- **stippler**, tippler
- Coppola
- **gospeller** (US gospeler)
- cupola
- **caroller** (US caroler)
- Kerala
- **quarreller** (US quarreler)
- chancellor
- **penciller** (US penciler)
- whistler
- **battler**, prattler, rattler, tattler
- dismantler •startler
- **fettler**, settler, settlor
- **belittler**, victualler (US victualer)
- **hospitaller** (US hospitaler)
- **bottler**, throttler
- **hosteller** (US hosteler)
- **caviller** (US caviler), traveller (US traveler)
- **marveller** (US marveler)

- **leveller** (US leveler), reveller (US reveler)
- **driveller** (US driveler), sniveller (US sniveler)
- **groveller** (US groveler)
- **shoveller**, shoveler
- chiseller (US chiseler), sizzler
- **bamboozler**, methuselah
- guzzler

12.49

- **curler**, pearler, purler, twirler, whirler
- curdler •burglar •Koestler

12.50

- **Alabama**, clamour (US clamor), crammer, gamma, glamour (US glamor), gnamma, grammar, hammer, jammer, lamber, mamma, rammer, shammer, slammer, stammer, yammer
- Padma •magma •drachma
- **Alma**, halma, Palma
- Cranmer •asthma •mahatma
- **miasma**, plasma
- jackhammer •sledgehammer
- yellowhammer •windjammer
- flimflammer •programmer
- **amah**, armour (US armor), Atacama, Brahma, Bramah, charmer, cyclorama, dharma, diorama, disarmer, drama, embalmer, farmer, Kama, karma, lama, llama, Matsuyama, panorama, Parma, pranayama, Rama, Samar, Surinamer, Vasco da Gama, Yama, Yokohama
- snake-charmer •docudrama
- melodrama
- **contemner**, dilemma, Emma, emmer, Jemma, lemma, maremma, stemma, tremor
- **Elmer**, Selma, Thelma, Velma
- Mesmer
- **claimer**, defamer, framer, proclaimer, Shema, tamer

12.51

- **beamer**, blasphemer, Colima, creamer, dreamer, emphysema, femur, Iwo Jima, Kagoshima, lemur, Lima, oedema (*US* edema), ottava rima, Pima, reamer, redeemer, schema, schemer, screamer, seamer, Selima, steamer, streamer, terza rima, Tsushima
- daydreamer
- **dimmer**, glimmer, limber, limner, shimmer, simmer, skimmer, slimmer, strimmer, swimmer, trimmer, zimmer
- **enigma**, sigma, stigma
- **Wilma**, Wilmer
- charisma • Gordimer • polymer
- ulema • anima • enema
- **cinema**, minima
- maxima • Bessemer • eczema
- dulcimer • Hiroshima
- **Fatima**, Latimer
- optima • Mortimer • anathema
- **climber**, Jemima, mimer, old-timer, part-timer, primer, rhymer, timer
- Oppenheimer • two-timer
- **bomber**, comma, momma, prommer
- dogma • dolma

12.52

- **dormer**, former, korma, Norma, performer, pro-forma, stormer, transformer, trauma, warmer
- sixth-former • barnstormer
- **aroma**, carcinoma, chroma, coma, comber, diploma, glaucoma, Homer, lymphoma, melanoma, misnomer, Oklahoma, Omagh, roamer, Roma, romer, sarcoma, soma
- beachcomber
- **bloomer**, boomer, consumer, Duma, humour (*US* humor), Nkrumah, perfumer, puma, roomer, rumour (*US* rumor), satsuma, stumer, Sumer, tumour (*US* tumor)
- zeugma • fulmar
- **bummer**, comer, drummer, hummer, midsummer, mummer,

plumber, rummer, strummer, summa, summer
- latecomer • newcomer • agama
- welcomer
- **astronomer**, monomer
- ashrama • isomer • gossamer
- customer
- **affirmer**, Burma, derma, Irma, murmur, squirmer, terra firma, wormer

12.53

- **Alana**, Anna, bandanna, banner, Branagh, canna, canner, Diana, fanner, Fermanagh, Guyana, Hannah, Havana, hosanna, Indiana, Joanna, lanner, Louisiana, manna, manner, manor, Montana, nana, planner, Pollyanna, Rosanna, savannah, scanner, spanner, Susanna, tanner
- Abner • Jaffna • Patna • caravanner
- **Africana**, Afrikaner, Americana, ana, banana, Botswana, bwana, cabana, caragana, Christiana, Dana, darner, Edwardiana, garner, Georgiana, Ghana, Gloriana, Guiana, gymkhana, Haryana, iguana, Lana, lantana, liana, Lipizzaner, Ljubljana, Mahayana, mana, mañana, marijuana, nirvana, Oriana, pacarana, piranha, prana, Purana, Rosh Hashana, Santayana, Setswana, sultana, Tatiana, Tijuana, Tirana, tramontana, Tswana, varna, Victoriana, zenana
- Gardner • partner
- **antenna**, Avicenna, duenna, henna, Jenna, Jenner, Morwenna, Ravenna, senna, Siena, sienna, tenner, tenor, Vienna
- Edna • interregna • Etna • Pevsner

12.54

- **abstainer**, arcana, campaigner, Cana, caner, cantilena, complainer, container, detainer, drainer, entertainer, explainer, Gaenor,

gainer, Gaynor, grainer, Jena, Lena,
maintainer, Marlene, N'Djamena,
obtainer, ordainer, planar, planer,
profaner, Rayner, retainer, scena,
seiner, Sinn Feiner, strainer,
sustainer, trainer, uniplanar
• straightener
• **Adelina**, Angelina, arena,
Argentina, ballerina, Ballymena,
Bettina, Bukovina, Burkina, cantina,
Cartagena, casuarina, catena,
Christina, cleaner, concertina,
congener, contravener, convener,
Cortina, demeanour (*US* demeanor),
deus ex machina, duodena, Edwina,
Ena, farina, Filipina, galena,
Georgina, Gina, gleaner, hyena, Ina,
intervener, kachina, kina,
Magdalena, marina, Martina,
Medina, Messalina, Messina,
misdemeanour (*US* misdemeanor),
Nina, novena, ocarina, Palestrina,
Pasadena, Philomena, piscina,
retsina, Rowena, Sabrina, scarlatina,
screener, Selina, semolina,
Seraphina, Serena, Sheena,
signorina, sonatina, subpoena,
Taormina, tsarina, verbena, vina,
weaner, wiener, Wilhelmina, Zena
• sweetener • pipecleaner

12.55

• **beginner**, Berliner, Corinna, dinner,
grinner, inner, Jinnah, sinner,
skinner, spinner, thinner, winner
• echidna
• **Krishna**, Mishnah, Ramakrishna
• vintner • prisoner • Pilsner
• Kitchener • Modena • bargainer
• imaginer
• **Elinor**, Helena
• milliner
• **examiner**, stamina
• **epiphenomena**, phenomena,
prolegomena
• **alumina**, noumena, numina
• determiner

• **mariner**, submariner
• foreigner • larcener • Porsena
• patina • retina • Pristina
• Herzegovina • breadwinner
• prizewinner
• **angina**, assigner, china, consignor,
decliner, definer, Dinah, diner,
diviner, forty-niner, hardliner,
incliner, Indo-China, liner, maligner,
Medina, miner, minor, mynah,
recliner, refiner, Regina, Salina,
Shekinah, shiner, signer, South
Carolina, Steiner, twiner, vagina,
whiner
• headliner • jetliner • airliner
• mainliner • eyeliner • moonshiner
• Landsteiner • Niersteiner
• Liechtensteiner

12.56

• **belladonna**, Connor, donna, goner,
gonna, honour (*US* honor),
Maradona, Mashona, O'Connor,
Shona, wanna
• **corner**, fauna, forewarner, Lorna,
Morna, mourner, sauna, scorner,
suborner, warner
• softener • Faulkner
• **downer**, uptowner
• sundowner
• **Arizona**, Barcelona, boner,
condoner, corona, Cremona,
Desdemona, donor, Fiona, groaner,
Iona, Jonah, kroner, Leona, loaner,
loner, moaner, Mona, owner,
Pamplona, persona, postponer,
Ramona, stoner, toner, Valona,
Verona, Winona
• landowner • homeowner • shipowner
• **coiner**, joiner, purloiner
• **crooner**, harpooner, lacuna, lacunar,
lampooner, Luna, lunar, mizuna,
Oona, oppugner, Poona, pruner,
puna, schooner, spooner, Tristan da
Cunha, tuna, tuner, Una, vicuña,
yokozuna
• honeymooner • Sunna • Brookner
• koruna

12.57

- **Corunna**, front-runner, gunner, oner, punner, runner, scunner, stunner
- columnar • guv'nor • forerunner
- roadrunner • gunrunner

12.58

- Catriona • ironer • questioner
- **gardener**, hardener, pardoner
- deadener • widener • Londoner
- stiffener • toughener • wagoner
- tobogganer • provisioner • sojourner
- jacana • darkener • reckoner
- weakener
- **sickener**, thickener
- falconer • Eleanor
- **almoner**, Brahmana
- commoner • summoner • dampener
- sharpener • tympana • opener
- coroner • fastener • chastener
- **christener**, listener
- loosener • fashioner • confectioner
- **pensioner**, tensioner
- **probationer**, stationer, vacationer
- **commissioner**, conditioner, exhibitioner, missioner, munitioner, parishioner, partitioner, petitioner, positioner, practitioner, requisitioner
- extortioner • executioner • flattener
- **Smetana**, threatener
- westerner • easterner
- **enlightener**, frightener, whitener
- **lengthener**, strengthener
- marathoner • northerner
- southerner • Taverner • scrivener
- enlivener • governor • Ramayana
- reasoner • poisoner

12.59

- **Annapurna**, burner, discerner, earner, learner, Myrna, Smyrna, spurner, taverna, turner, Verner, Werner, yearner
- woodturner

12.60

- **banger**, clanger, ganger, hangar, hanger, haranguer, Sanger, Stavanger
- headbanger • doppelgänger
- straphanger • cliffhanger
- paperhanger
- **bringer**, clinger, flinger, humdinger, pinger, ringer, singer, slinger, springer, stinger, stringer, swinger, winger, wringer, zinger
- Schrödinger • mud-slinger
- gunslinger • bell-ringer • klipspringer
- Helsingor
- **prolonger**, tonga, wronger
- ponga

12.61

- **clapper**, crapper, dapper, flapper, grappa, kappa, knapper, mapper, nappa, napper, rapper, sapper, scrapper, snapper, strapper, tapper, trapper, wrapper, yapper, Zappa
- **catalpa**, scalper
- **camper**, damper, hamper, pamper, scamper, stamper, Tampa, tamper, tramper
- **Caspar**, jasper
- handicapper • kidnapper
- whippersnapper
- **carper**, harper, scarper, sharper
- **clasper**, gasper, grasper, rasper
- **leper**, pepper, salt-and-pepper
- **helper**, yelper
- temper
- **Vespa**, vesper
- Culpeper • sidestepper
- **caper**, draper, escaper, gaper, paper, raper, scraper, shaper, taper, vapour (US vapor)
- sandpaper • endpaper • flypaper
- wallpaper • notepaper • newspaper
- skyscraper
- **Arequipa**, beeper, bleeper, creeper, Dnieper, keeper, leaper, peeper, reaper, sleeper, sweeper, weeper
- gamekeeper • gatekeeper
- **greenkeeper** (US greenskeeper)

• peacekeeper • innkeeper
• wicketkeeper • timekeeper
• shopkeeper • storekeeper
• housekeeper • goalkeeper
• zookeeper • bookkeeper • treecreeper
• minesweeper

12.62

• **Agrippa**, chipper, clipper, dipper, equipper, flipper, gripper, hipper, kipper, nipper, Pippa, ripper, shipper, sipper, skipper, slipper, stripper, tipper, tripper, whipper, zipper
• **crimper**, shrimper, simper, whimper, Whymper
• **crisper**, whisper
• mudskipper • caliper • Philippa
• juniper • gossiper
• **worshipper** (*US* worshiper)
• **griper**, piper, sniper, swiper, viper, wiper
• bagpiper • sandpiper
• **bopper**, chopper, copper, cropper, Dopper, dropper, hopper, improper, Joppa, poppa, popper, proper, shopper, stopper, swapper, topper, whopper
• stomper • prosper • bebopper
• teenybopper • grasshopper
• clodhopper • sharecropper
• name-dropper • eavesdropper
• window-shopper • doorstopper
• show-stopper
• **gawper**, pauper, torpor, warper

12.63

• **coper**, doper, eloper, Europa, groper, hoper, L-dopa, moper, no-hoper, opah, toper
• interloper
• **blooper**, cooper, Cowper, duper, grouper, Hooper, looper, pea-souper, pupa, scooper, snooper, stupa, stupor, super, trooper, trouper, whooper
• pooper-scooper • party-pooper
• paratrooper • mea culpa • chutzpah

• **crupper**, cuppa, scupper, supper, upper
• **gulper**, kalpa, pulper
• **bumper**, dumper, gazumper, jumper, lumper, stumper, thumper
• showjumper • diaper • galloper
• developer
• **scalloper**, walloper
• **chirper**, sherpa, usurper

12.64

• **jarrah**, para, Tara
• **abracadabra**, Aldabra
• Alhambra • Vanbrugh
• **Cassandra**, Sandra
• **Aphra**, Biafra
• **Niagara**, pellagra, Viagra
• **bhangra**, Ingres
• Capra • Cleopatra
• **mantra**, tantra, yantra
• Basra
• **Asmara**, Bukhara, carbonara, Carrara, cascara, Connemara, Damara, Ferrara, Gemara, Guadalajara, Guevara, Honiara, Lara, marinara, mascara, Nara, Sahara, Samara, samsara, samskara, shikara, Tamara, tiara, Varah, Zara
• **candelabra**, macabre, sabra
• Alexandra • Agra • fiacre
• **Chartres**, Montmartre, Sartre, Sinatra, Sumatra
• Shastra • Maharashtra • Le Havre
• gurdwara
• **Berra**, error, Ferrer, sierra, terror
• zebra • ephedra • Porto Alegre
• **belles-lettres**, Petra, raison d'être, tetra
• **Electra**, plectra, spectra
• Clytemnestra • extra
• **chèvre**, Sèvres
• Ezra

12.65

• **airer**, bearer, carer, Clara, darer, declarer, Demerara, Éire, habanera, Halmahera, parer, Perak, primavera, repairer, Rivera, Riviera, Sarah,

scarer, sharer, snarer, sparer,
squarer, starer, swearer, tearer,
wearer
- cause célèbre •torch-bearer
- swordbearer •pallbearer •wayfarer
- seafarer •capoeira •Phaedra
- **sacra**, simulacra
- **Libra**, vers libre
- ex cathedra
- **chypre**, Ypres
- **palaestra** (*US* palestra) •urethra
- joie de vivre
- **mirror**, sirrah
- Coimbra •Middlesbrough •Indra
- Sintra
- **aspidistra**, sistra
- algebra •orchestra •vertebra
- **Beira**, Fujairah, Hegira, Lyra, Myra,
naira, palmyra, spirogyra
- Hydra •Lycra
- **begorra**, Gomorrah, horror
- double entendre •genre •amour
propre •Le Nôtre •contra
- **Cosa Nostra**, rostra

12.66

- **abhorrer**, adorer, Andorra, angora,
aura, aurora, bora, Bora-Bora, borer,
Camorra, Cora, corer, Dora,
Eleonora, Eudora, explorer, fedora,
flora, fora, ignorer, Isadora, Kia-Ora,
Laura, Leonora, Maura, menorah,
Nora, pakora, Pandora, pourer,
roarer, scorer, senhora, señora,
signora, snorer, soarer, Sonora, sora,
storer, Theodora, Torah, Tuscarora,
Vlorë
- goalscorer •cobra •okra •Oprah
- Socotra •Moira •Sudra
- chaulmoogra •supra
- **Brahmaputra**, sutra
- Zarathustra •Louvre •fulcra
- Tripura
- **borough**, burgh, Burra, curragh,
demurrer, thorough
- Rubbra
- **penumbra**, umbra
- tundra •chakra •ultra •kookaburra

12.67

- **Altamira**, chimera, clearer, Elvira,
era, hearer, Hera, hetaera,
interferer, lempira, lira, lire,
Madeira, Megaera, monstera,
rangatira, rearer, scorzonera, sera,
shearer, smearer, sneerer, steerer,
Thera, Utsire, Vera

> Create extra rhymes for
> words like clearer by adding -*er*
> to dear and near etc. (see
> section 12.4).   **i**

- **acquirer**, admirer, enquirer, firer,
hirer, inquirer, requirer, wirer
- **devourer**, flowerer, scourer
- **Angostura**, Bonaventura, bravura,
Bujumbura, caesura, camera obscura,
coloratura, curer, Dürer, durra,
Estremadura, figura, fioritura,
Führer, insurer, Jura, juror, Madura,
nomenklatura, procurer, sura, surah,
tamboura, tempura, tourer
- **labourer** (*US* laborer) •Canberra
- Attenborough
- **Barbara**, Scarborough
- Marlborough •Farnborough
- Deborah •rememberer
- Gainsborough •Edinburgh
- Aldeburgh •blubberer
- Loughborough
- **lumberer**, slumberer
- Peterborough
- **Berbera**, gerbera
- manufacturer •capturer •lecturer
- posturer •torturer •nurturer
- philanderer •gerrymanderer
- slanderer
- **renderer**, tenderer
- dodderer
- **squanderer**, wanderer
- borderer •launderer •flounderer
- embroiderer •Kundera
- **blunderer**, plunderer, thunderer,
wonderer
- murderer •amphora •pilferer
- offerer •sufferer
- **staggerer**, swaggerer

- sniggerer
- **lingerer**, malingerer
- treasurer • usurer • injurer • conjuror
- perjurer • lacquerer
- **Ankara**, hankerer
- **bickerer**, dickerer
- tinkerer • conqueror • heuchera
- cellarer • cholera
- **camera**, stammerer
- **armourer** (*US* armorer)
- **ephemera**, remora
- kumara • woomera • murmurer
- Tanagra • genera • gunnera
- **Tampere**, tamperer
- Diaspora
- **emperor**, Klemperer, tempera, temperer
- **caperer**, paperer
- whimperer • whisperer • opera
- corpora • tessera • viscera • sorcerer
- **adventurer**, venturer
- **batterer**, chatterer, flatterer, natterer, scatterer, shatterer
- banterer
- **barterer**, charterer
- plasterer • shelterer • pesterer
- et cetera • caterer
- **titterer**, twitterer
- **potterer**, totterer
- fosterer
- **slaughterer**, waterer
- **falterer**, palterer
- saunterer • poulterer
- **bolsterer**, upholsterer
- loiterer • roisterer • fruiterer
- **flutterer**, mutterer, splutterer, stutterer, utterer
- adulterer • musterer • plethora
- gatherer • ditherer • furtherer
- **favourer** (*US* favorer), waverer
- **deliverer**, shiverer
- hoverer
- **manoeuvrer** (*US* maneuverer)
- **discoverer**, recoverer

12.68

- **deferrer**, demurrer, referrer, stirrer, transferor, transferrer
- chef-d'œuvre, oeuvre

12.69

- **amasser**, gasser, macassar, Makassar, Mombasa, Nasser
- **relaxer**, waxer
- salsa
- **cancer**, romancer
- piazza • necromancer • madrasa
- **Kinshasa**, Lhasa, passer, Tarrasa, Vaasa
- **advancer**, answer, chancer, dancer, enhancer, lancer, prancer
- tazza
- **addresser**, aggressor, assessor, compressor, confessor, contessa, depressor, digresser, dresser, guesser, intercessor, lesser, Odessa, oppressor, possessor, professor, represser, successor, transgressor, Vanessa
- **Alexa**, flexor, vexer
- **Elsa**, Kielce
- **censer**, censor, dispenser, fencer, Mensa, sensor, Spenser
- seltzer
- **Faenza**, Henze
- indexer • hairdresser • predecessor
- **microprocessor**, processor
- **acer**, bracer, chaser, debaser, embracer, facer, macer, mesa, pacer, placer, racer, spacer, tracer
- Ailsa • steeplechaser
- **greaser**, Lisa, Nerissa, piecer, Raisa, releaser
- pizza

12.70

- **Alissa**, Clarissa, kisser, Larissa, Marisa, Melissa, Orissa, reminiscer
- **fixer**, mixer, sixer
- **convincer**, mincer, pincer, rinser, wincer
- **Amritsar**, Maritsa, spritzer
- howitzer • kibitzer • purchaser
- artificer • officer • surfacer • Pulitzer
- Wurlitzer • promiser • harnesser
- menacer
- **practiser** (*US* practicer)
- **de-icer**, dicer, enticer, gricer, paise,

pricer, ricer, slicer, splicer
• Schweitzer
• **Barbarossa**, dosser, embosser, fossa, glosser, josser, Ossa, Saragossa, tosser
• boxer • sponsor • matzo • bobbysoxer
• **Chaucer**, courser, endorser (US indorser), enforcer, forcer, reinforcer, saucer, Xhosa
• **balsa**, waltzer
• **dowser**, grouser, Hausa, mouser, Scouser
• **announcer**, bouncer, denouncer, pouncer, pronouncer, renouncer, trouncer
• schnauzer

12.71

• **anorexia nervosa**, bulimia nervosa, curiosa, Formosa, grocer, samosa, Via Dolorosa
• **coaxer**, hoaxer
• greengrocer
• **rejoicer**, voicer
• **Abu Musa**, Appaloosa, babirusa, inducer, introducer, juicer, producer, reducer, rusa, seducer, sprucer, traducer
• **discusser**, fusser, trusser
• **propulsor**, Tulsa, ulcer
• oncer • conveyancer • piercer
• influencer • Odense • balancer
• silencer • grimacer • trespasser
• harasser • remembrancer
• **licenser**, licensor
• traverser • canvasser • sequencer
• **bursar**, converser, curser, cursor, disburser, mercer, purser, rehearser, reverser, vice versa

12.72

• **Asher**, clasher, Falasha, flasher, lasher, masher, Natasha, pasha, rasher, Sasha, slasher, smasher, thrasher
• haberdasher • gatecrasher • Marsha
• rancher
• **flesher**, fresher, pressure, thresher

• welsher
• **adventure**, bencher, censure, dementia, front-bencher, trencher, venture, wencher
• backbencher • acupressure
• **acacia**, Asia, Croatia, Dalmatia, ex gratia, geisha
• **Lucretia**, magnesia, Rhodesia, Venetia
• **Fischer**, fisher, fissure, justiciar, Laetitia, militia, Patricia, Phoenicia, Tricia
• **clincher**, flincher, lyncher, wincher
• Frobisher • furbisher • brandisher
• Yiddisher • kingfisher • establisher
• embellisher
• **abolisher**, demolisher, polisher
• publisher • skirmisher • replenisher
• finisher • punisher
• **burnisher**, furnisher
• perisher
• **flourisher**, nourisher
• Britisher • ravisher • languisher
• vanquisher • well-wisher
• extinguisher • Elisha

12.73

• **josher**, washer
• moksha • tonsure • dishwasher
• whitewasher • Portia • launcher
• **brochure**, kosher, Scotia
• fuchsia • pusher • penpusher
• **blusher**, crusher, flusher, gusher, Prussia, rusher, Russia, usher
• **cruncher**, luncher, puncher
• cowpuncher • Udmurtia
• **inertia**, Persia

12.74

• **attar**, batter, bespatter, chatter, clatter, flatter, hatter, Kenyatta, latter, matamata, matter, natter, patter, platter, ratter, regatta, satyr, scatter, shatter, smatter, spatter, splatter, yatter
• **abstractor**, actor, attractor, compactor, contractor, enactor,

exactor, extractor, factor, infractor, protractor, redactor, refractor, tractor, transactor
- **Atlanta**, banter, canter, infanta, levanter, manta, ranter, Santa, tam-o'-shanter
- **adaptor**, captor, chapter, raptor
- **Antofagasta**, aster, Astor, canasta, Jocasta, oleaster, pasta, piastre (*US* piaster), pilaster, poetaster, Rasta, Zoroaster
- **dragster**, gagster
- Baxter •prankster •hamster
- **gangsta**, gangster
- malefactor •benefactor
- pitter-patter •subcontractor
- chiropractor

12.75

- **barter**, Bata, cantata, carter, cassata, charter, chipolata, ciabatta, darter, desiderata, errata, garter, imprimatur, Inkatha, Jakarta, Magna Carta, Maratha, martyr, Odonata, passata, persona non grata, rata, Renata, Río de la Plata, serenata, sonata, Sparta, starter, strata, taramasalata, tartar, Tatar, Zapata
- **after**, drafter, grafter, hereafter, laughter, rafter, thereafter, whereafter
- **chanter**, enchanter, granter, planter, supplanter, transplanter, Vedanta
- **blaster**, caster, castor, faster, grandmaster, headmaster, master, pastor, plaster
- alabaster •telecaster •forecaster
- broadcaster •sportscaster
- newscaster •sandblaster
- bandmaster •taskmaster
- pastmaster •paymaster •ringmaster
- quizmaster •spymaster
- housemaster •Scoutmaster
- toastmaster •schoolmaster
- harbourmaster (*US* harbormaster)
- quartermaster •substrata
- sought-after

12.76

- **abetter**, begetter, better, bettor, biretta, bruschetta, carburettor (*US* carburetor), debtor, feta, fetter, forgetter, getter, go-getter, Greta, Henrietta, letter, Loretta, mantelletta, operetta, petter, Quetta, setter, sinfonietta, sweater, upsetter, Valletta, vendetta, whetter
- **bisector**, collector, connector, convector, corrector, defector, deflector, detector, director, ejector, elector, erector, hector, injector, inspector, nectar, objector, perfecter, projector, prospector, protector, rector, reflector, rejector, respecter, sector, selector, Spector, spectre (*US* specter), vector
- **belter**, delta, helter-skelter, melter, pelta, Shelta, shelter, swelter, welter
- **pre-emptor**, tempter
- **assenter**, cementer, centre (*US* center), concentre (*US* concenter), dissenter, enter, eventer, fermenter (*US* fermentor), fomenter, frequenter, inventor, lamenter, magenta, placenta, polenta, precentor, presenter, preventer, renter, repenter, tenter, tormentor
- **inceptor**, preceptor, receptor, sceptre (*US* scepter)
- **arrester**, Avesta, Chester, contester, ester, Esther, fester, fiesta, Hester, investor, jester, Leicester, Lester, molester, Nestor, pester, polyester, protester, quester, semester, sequester, siesta, sou'wester, suggester, tester, trimester, vesta, zester
- Webster •dexter •Leinster
- Dorchester •Poindexter •newsletter
- genuflector •implementer
- experimenter •trendsetter
- **epicentre** (*US* epicenter)
- typesetter •jobcentre •photosetter
- Cirencester •interceptor •Sylvester

12.77

- **cater**, crater, creator, curator, data, debater, delator, dumbwaiter, equator, freighter, frustrater, gaiter, grater, gyrator, hater, later, legator, mater, negator, pater, peseta, plater, rotator, skater, slater, stater, tater, traitor, ultimata, understater, upstater, waiter

> Create extra rhymes for words like crater by adding -er to collate etc. (see section 30.7). [i]

- painter
- **taster**, waster
- gamester •aviator •tailgater
- hesitater •shirtwaister
- **Akita**, Anita, arboreta, beater, beta, Bhagavadgita, cheater, cheetah, Demeter, Dieter, dolce vita, eater, eta, Evita, excreta, fetor, granita, greeter, heater, Juanita, litre (US liter), Lolita, maltreater, margarita, meter, metre, Peta, peter, praetor (US pretor), repeater, Rita, saltpetre (US saltpeter), secretor, Senhorita, señorita, Sita, skeeter, teeter, terra incognita, theta, treater, tweeter, ureter, veleta, zeta
- **Batista**, Dniester, Easter, feaster, keister, leister, quaestor
- speedster
- **deemster**, teamster
- scenester •browbeater •windcheater
- beefeater
- **millilitre** (US milliliter)
- **decilitre** (US deciliter)
- **centilitre** (US centiliter)
- **kilolitre** (US kiloliter)
- ammeter •Machmeter
- **millimetre** (US millimeter)
- **decimetre** (US decimeter)
- altimeter
- **centimetre** (US centimeter)
- **nanometre** (US nanometer)
- **micrometer**, micrometre
- **decametre** (US dekameter)
- **kilometre** (US kilometer) •autopista
- anteater

12.78

- **bitter**, committer, critter, embitter, emitter, fitter, flitter, fritter, glitter, gritter, hitter, jitter, knitter, litter, permitter, pitta, quitter, remitter, sitter, skitter, slitter, spitter, splitter, submitter, titter, transmitter, twitter, witter
- **drifter**, grifter, lifter, shifter, sifter, snifter, uplifter
- **constrictor**, contradictor, depicter, dicta, evictor, inflicter, predictor, victor
- **filter**, kilter, philtre (US philter), quilter, tilter
- **Jacinta**, midwinter, Minter, Pinta, Pinter, printer, splinter, sprinter, tinter, winter
- sphincter
- **assister**, ballista, bistre (US bister), blister, enlister, glister, lister, mister, resistor, Sandinista, sister, transistor, tryster, twister, vista
- trickster
- **minster**, spinster
- **hipster**, quipster, tipster
- cohabiter •arbiter •presbyter
- **exhibitor**, inhibitor, prohibiter
- Manchester •Chichester •Silchester
- Rochester •Colchester
- **creditor**, editor, subeditor
- auditor •Perdita •taffeta •shopfitter
- forfeiter •outfitter •counterfeiter
- register •marketer
- **cricketer**, picketer
- Alistair •weightlifter •filleter
- fillister •shoplifter
- **diameter**, heptameter, hexameter, parameter, pentameter, tetrameter
- Axminster •Westminster
- **limiter**, perimeter, scimitar, velocimeter
- **accelerometer**, anemometer, barometer, gasometer, geometer, manometer, micrometer, milometer, olfactometer, optometer, pedometer, photometer, pyrometer, speedometer, swingometer, tachometer, thermometer

- Kidderminster •janitor
- **banister**, canister
- **primogenitor**, progenitor, senator
- **administer**, maladminister, minister, sinister
- monitor •per capita •carpenter
- spanakopita •Jupiter •trumpeter
- character •barrister •ferreter
- teleprinter
- **chorister**, forester
- **interpreter**, misinterpreter
- capacitor •ancestor •Exeter
- stepsister
- **elicitor**, solicitor
- babysitter •house-sitter •bullshitter
- competitor •catheter •harvester
- riveter •banqueter •non sequitur
- loquitur
- **inquisitor**, visitor
- **compositor**, expositor

[**12.79**]

- **all-nighter**, biter, blighter, fighter, igniter, inciter, indicter, inviter, lighter, mitre (*US* miter), overnighter, reciter, righter, sighter, smiter, writer

> Create extra rhymes for   [i]
> words like writer by adding -er to
> bright and tight etc. (see
> section 30.26).

- shyster •rhymester •backbiter
- expediter •prizefighter •dogfighter
- bullfighter •gunfighter •lamplighter
- highlighter •downlighter
- moonlighter •uplighter •firelighter
- screenwriter •scriptwriter
- copywriter •signwriter •typewriter
- songwriter •ghostwriter
- underwriter
- **blotter**, cotta, cottar, dotter, gotta, hotter, jotter, knotter, otter, pelota, plotter, potter, ricotta, rotter, spotter, squatter, terracotta, totter, trotter
- crofter
- **concocter**, doctor, proctor

- Volta •prompter •wanter
- **adopter**, dioptre
- **Costa**, coster, defroster, foster, Gloucester, impostor, paternoster, roster
- **lobster**, mobster
- oxter •monster •songster
- witchdoctor •helicopter
- teleprompter •globetrotter

[**12.80**]

- **aorta**, daughter, exhorter, exporter, extorter, Horta, importer, mortar, porter, quarter, slaughter, snorter, sorter, sporter, supporter, three-quarter, torte, transporter, underwater, water
- **altar**, alter, assaulter, defaulter, falter, Gibraltar, halter, Malta, palter, psalter, salter, vaulter, Walter
- **flaunter**, haunter, saunter, taunter, vaunter
- **exhauster**, Forster
- fraudster •granddaughter
- stepdaughter •manslaughter
- ripsnorter •pole-vaulter •backwater
- headquarter •freshwater
- breakwater •rainwater •seawater
- dishwater •tidewater •Whitewater
- saltwater •rosewater •shearwater
- firewater
- **doubter**, grouter, outer, pouter, scouter, shouter, spouter, touter
- **counter**, encounter, mounter
- **jouster**, ouster
- revcounter
- **bloater**, boater, Botha, Dakota, doter, emoter, floater, gloater, iota, Kota, Minnesota, motor, promoter, quota, rota, rotor, scoter, voter
- **bolter**, coulter (*US* colter), Volta
- **boaster**, coaster, poster, roaster, toaster
- roadster •oldster
- **bolster**, holster, pollster, soulster, upholster
- billposter

12.81

- **exploiter**, goitre (*US* goiter), loiter, reconnoitre (*US* reconnoiter), Reuter
- **anointer**, appointer, jointer, pointer
- **cloister**, hoister, oyster, roister
- **accoutre** (*US* accouter), commuter, computer, disputer, hooter, looter, neuter, pewter, polluter, recruiter, refuter, rooter, saluter, scooter, shooter, souter, suitor, tooter, transmuter, tutor, uprooter
- **booster**, rooster
- doomster • freebooter • sharpshooter
- peashooter • six-shooter
- troubleshooter • prosecutor
- persecutor • prostitutor
- telecommuter
- **footer**, putter
- Gupta • Worcester • Münster
- pussyfooter • executor
- **contributor**, distributor
- **collocutor**, interlocutor
- **abutter**, aflutter, butter, Calcutta, clutter, constructor, cutter, flutter, gutter, mutter, nutter, scutter, shutter, splutter, sputter, strutter, stutter, utter
- **abductor**, conductor, destructor, instructor, obstructor
- insulter
- **Arunta**, Bunter, chunter, Grantha, grunter, Gunter, hunter, junta, punter, shunter
- **corrupter**, disrupter, interrupter
- sculptor
- **adjuster**, Augusta, bluster, buster, cluster, Custer, duster, fluster, lustre (*US* luster), muster, thruster, truster
- huckster • Ulster • dumpster
- **funster**, Munster, punster
- **funkster**, youngster
- gangbuster • filibuster • blockbuster
- semiconductor • headhunter
- woodcutter
- **lacklustre** (*US* lackluster)

12.82

- **theatre** (*US* theater)
- realtor

- **amphitheatre** (*US* amphitheater)
- **proprietor**, rioter
- breakfaster • comforter • Lancaster
- Doncaster
- **Alasdair**, baluster
- **bardolater**, idolater
- **amateur**, shamateur
- schemata • stigmata • automata
- traumata • covenanter
- Mahabharata • orator • warranter
- **Alberta**, asserter, Bizerta, converter, deserter, Goethe, inserter, kurta, perverter, reverter, subverter
- frankfurter

12.83

- Cather • naphtha
- **anther**, panther, Samantha
- **Arthur**, MacArthur, Martha
- **ether**, Ibiza
- Tabitha • Hiawatha • author • Gotha
- Luther • Gunther • Agatha • Golgotha
- **Bertha**, Jugurtha

12.84

- **blather**, foregather, gather, slather
- **farther**, father, lather, rather
- grandfather • stepfather • godfather
- forefather
- **altogether**, feather, heather, leather, nether, tether, together, weather, wether, whether

> Create extra rhymes by adding *-ing* to words like feather.   ℹ

- bather • sunbather
- **bequeather**, breather
- **dither**, hither, slither, swither, thither, whither, wither, zither
- **either**, neither
- **bother**, pother
- Rhondda • mouther • loather
- **smoother**, soother
- **another**, brother, mother, other, smother, t'other
- grandmother • stepmother
- godmother • housemother
- stepbrother • further

12.85

- **cadaver**, slaver
- **halva**, salver, salvor
- **balaclava**, Bratislava, carver, cassava, Costa Brava, guava, Java, kava, larva, lava, palaver
- woodcarver
- **clever**, endeavour (*US* endeavor), ever, forever, however, howsoever, never, never-never, sever, Trevor, whatever, whatsoever, whenever, whensoever, wheresoever, wherever, whichever, whichsoever, whoever, whomever, whomsoever, whosoever
- **delver**, elver
- Denver
- **Ava**, caver, craver, deva, engraver, enslaver, favour (*US* favor), flavour (*US* flavor), graver, haver, laver, paver, quaver, raver, saver, savour (*US* savor), shaver, vena cava, waiver, waver
- lifesaver •semiquaver
- **achiever**, beaver, believer, cleaver, deceiver, diva, Eva, fever, Geneva, griever, heaver, leaver, lever, Neva, perceiver, receiver, reiver, reliever, retriever, Shiva, underachiever, viva, weaver, weever
- cantilever

12.86

- **aquiver**, downriver, forgiver, giver, quiver, river, shiver, sliver, upriver
- silver •mitzvah •lawgiver •Oliver
- **miniver**, Nineveh
- quicksilver
- **conniver**, contriver, diver, driver, fiver, Godiva, Ivor, jiver, Liver, reviver, saliva, skiver, striver, survivor, viva
- skydiver •slave-driver •piledriver
- screwdriver
- **bovver**, hover
- Moskva
- **revolver**, solver
- windhover
- **Canova**, Casanova, clover, Dover, drover, Grsbover, Jehovah, left-over,

Markova, Moldova, moreover, Navrátilová, nova, ova, over, Pavlova, rover, trover, up-and-over
- layover •flyover •handover
- changeover
- **makeover**, takeover
- walkover •spillover •pullover
- Hanover •turnover •hangover
- wingover •sleepover •slipover
- **popover**, stopover
- Passover •crossover •once-over
- pushover •leftover

12.87

- **disapprover**, hoover, improver, louvre (*US* louver), manoeuvre (*US* maneuver), mover, outmanoeuvre (*US* outmaneuver), reprover, Suva, Tuva, Vancouver
- **cover**, Glover, hardcover, lover, plover, undercover
- vulva •triumvir •slipcover •Cordova
- baklava •helluva •Ulanova •Genova
- Vaishnava •Ostrava •Vltava
- **fervour** (*US* fervor), Minerva, Nerva, observer, server, swerver
- time-server

12.88

- Aconcagua
- **aqua**, sub-aqua
- **Chihuahua**, Kurosawa, Massawa, Okinawa, Tokugawa
- Qwaqwa •Quechua
- **Chichewa**, rewarewa
- Ojibwa •Interlingua •siliqua •Iowa
- Medawar •Te Kanawa •Ottawa

12.89

- Antakya
- **Britannia**, lasagne
- Katya •Vanya
- **Kenya**, Mantegna, Sardegna, tenure
- failure •Montagna
- **behaviour** (*US* behavior), misbehaviour (*US* misbehavior),

saviour (*US* savior)
- **seguidilla**, tortilla
- Monsignor
- **Melanesia**, Micronesia, Polynesia
- Tigrinya • De Falla • Vaisya
- Lockyer • Bologna • sawyer • bowyer
- **alleluia**, hallelujah
- La Coruña
- **bunya**, gunyah

12.90

- **Balthazar**, Belshazzar, jazzer
- **bonanza**, Braganza, Constanza, extravaganza, kwanza, organza, Panzer, stanza
- **parser**, plaza, tabula rasa
- Shevardnadze • dopiaza
- Nebuchadnezzar • Demelza
- **cadenza**, cleanser, credenza, influenza, Penza
- **appraiser**, blazer, eraser, Fraser, gazer, glazer, grazer, laser, mazer, praiser, razor, salmanazar, Weser
- stargazer • trailblazer • hellraiser
- **appeaser**, Caesar, easer, Ebenezer, El Giza, freezer, geezer, geyser, Louisa, Pisa, seizer, squeezer, teaser, Teresa, Theresa, visa, wheezer
- crowd-pleaser • stripteaser
- **fizzer**, quizzer, scissor
- Windsor

12.91

- **adviser**, chastiser, coryza, despiser, deviser, divisor, Dreiser, Eliza, incisor, Kaiser, Liza, miser, Mount Isa, provisor, reviser, riser, sizer, visor
- aggrandizer • subsidizer
- merchandiser • standardizer
- methodizer • philosophizer
- mythologizer • catechizer

- **immobilizer**, mobilizer
- utilizer • idealizer • verbalizer
- idolizer • evangelizer
- **nationalizer**, rationalizer
- monopolizer • moralizer • neutralizer
- liberalizer • generalizer • catalyser
- tantalizer • totalizer • Breathalyzer
- civilizer • minimizer • maximizer
- victimizer • systemizer • itemizer
- economizer • compromiser
- atomizer • mechanizer
- homogenizer • scrutinizer
- immunizer • lionizer • modernizer
- organizer • recognizer • colonizer
- womanizer • sermonizer • patronizer
- synchronizer • westernizer
- theorizer • plagiarizer • tenderizer
- deodorizer • popularizer • memorizer
- mesmerizer • summarizer
- temporizer • terrorizer • enterpriser
- pulverizer • criticizer • exerciser
- franchiser • proselytizer • sanitizer
- sensitizer • privatizer • systematizer
- advertiser • sympathizer • improviser
- rozzer • bonzer
- **causer**, hawser

12.92

- **bowser**, browser, carouser, dowser, espouser, Mauser, rouser, trouser, wowser
- rabble-rouser
- **composer**, discloser, dozer, exposer, Mendoza, mimosa, opposer, ponderosa, poser, proposer, proser, Rosa, Somoza, Spinoza
- bulldozer • Tannhäuser
- **abuser**, accuser, boozer, bruiser, chooser, cruiser, diffuser, infuser, lollapalooza, loser, Marcuse, medusa, mezuzah, misuser, peruser, refuser, snoozer, Sousa, user, yakuza
- battlecruiser • buzzer

Section 13: **-er**

Section 14: -b

14.1

- **blab**, cab, confab, crab, Crabbe, dab, drab, fab, flab, gab, grab, jab, kebab, lab, nab, scab, slab, smash-and-grab, stab, tab

> Create extra rhymes by adding -(b)y to words like fab. ℹ

- Moab ● baobab ● rehab ● pedicab
- minicab ● taxicab ● Skylab

14.2

- **barb**, carb, garb, hijab, nawab, Punjab, sahib
- rhubarb ● mihrab

14.3

- **Aurangzeb**, bleb, celeb, deb, ebb, pleb, reb, web, Webb
- Caleb ● Deneb ● Zagreb ● cobweb

14.4

- **fines herbes**, Malherbe

14.5

- **Abe**, babe
- astrolabe

14.6

- **Antibes**, Beeb, Delibes, dweeb, glebe, grebe, Maghrib, plebe

14.7

- **bib**, crib, dib, fib, glib, jib, lib, nib, rib, sib, snib, squib
- memsahib ● Carib ● sparerib
- Sennacherib

14.8

- **ascribe**, bribe, gybe, imbibe, jibe, proscribe, scribe, subscribe, transcribe, tribe, vibe
- diatribe ● circumscribe

14.9

- **blob**, bob, cob, dob, fob, glob, gob, hob, job, knob, lob, mob, nob, rob, slob, snob, sob, squab, stob, swab, throb, yob

> Create extra rhymes by changing words like bob to bobbing. ℹ

- nabob ● skibob ● thingamabob
- corncob ● hobnob ● doorknob
- heartthrob

14.10

- **absorb**, bedaub, daub, orb, sorb

14.11

- **daube**, enrobe, globe, Job, lobe, probe, robe, strobe
- Anglophobe ● technophobe
- homophobe ● xenophobe ● earlobe
- bathrobe ● microbe ● wardrobe

14.12

- **boob**, cube, droob, j'adoube, jube, lube, rube, tube
- jujube • Danube

14.13

- **blub**, bub, chub, Chubb, club, cub, drub, dub, flub, grub, hub, nub, pub, rub, scrub, shrub, slub, snub, stub, sub, tub
- Beelzebub • hubbub • syllabub
- wolfcub • nightclub • bathtub
- twintub • washtub

14.14

- Jacob
- **Arab**, carob, scarab, Shatt al-Arab
- cherub

14.15

- **acerb**, blurb, curb, disturb, herb, kerb, perturb, Serb, superb, verb
- suburb • potherb • willowherb
- exurb • adverb • proverb

14.16

- alb • Elbe • stilb • bulb • flashbulb

Section 15: -ch

15.1

- **attach**, batch, catch, crosshatch, detach, hatch, latch, match, mismatch, natch, outmatch, patch, scratch, snatch, thatch
- Lukács •eyepatch •crosspatch
- sasquatch

15.2

- **arch**, larch, march, parch, starch
- frogmarch •cornstarch

15.3

- **etch**, fetch, ketch, kvetch, lech, outstretch, retch, sketch, stretch, vetch, wretch
- backstretch

15.4

- **mph**, pH, Rh

15.5

- **beach**, beech, beseech, bleach, breach, breech, each, impeach, leach, leech, outreach, peach, pleach, preach, reach, screech, speech, teach

> Create extra rhymes by
> adding -*ing* to words like
> beseech. ⓘ

- horseleech

15.6

- **bewitch**, bitch, ditch, enrich, fitch, flitch, glitch, hitch, itch, kitsch, Mitch, pitch, quitch, rich, snitch, stitch, switch, titch, twitch, which, witch

> Create extra rhymes by
> adding -*ed* to words like bewitch. ⓘ

- Redditch •Greenwich •eldritch
- ostrich •backstitch •hemstitch
- topstitch •Shostakovich •tsarevich
- Sandwich
- **dipswitch**, Ipswich

In the opening stanzas of this nonsense poem, Lewis Carroll invents words to rhyme with each other. It is one way to ensure you get a perfect rhyme!

'Twas brillig, and the slithy toves
    Did gyre and gimble in the wabe:
All mimsy were the borogoves,
    And the mome raths outgrabe.

''Beware the Jabberwock, my son!
    The jaws that bite, the claws that catch!
Beware the Jubjub bird, and shun
    The frumious Bandersnatch!''

(Lewis Carroll, 'Jabberwocky')

15.7

- **blotch**, botch, crotch, notch, outwatch, scotch, splotch, swatch, topnotch, watch
- hopscotch • butterscotch
- hotchpotch • wristwatch • skywatch
- fobwatch • dogwatch • stopwatch

15.8

- **debauch**, nautch, porch, scorch, torch
- blowtorch

15.9

- **avouch**, couch, crouch, debouch, grouch, ouch, pouch, slouch, vouch

15.10

- **approach**, broach, brooch, coach, encroach, loach, poach, reproach, roach
- stagecoach • slowcoach • cockroach

15.11

- **hooch**, mooch, pooch, smooch

15.12

- **butch**, putsch

15.13

- **clutch**, crutch, Dutch, hutch, inasmuch, insomuch, much, mutch, scutch, such, thrutch, touch
- nonesuch

15.14

- **besmirch**, birch, church, lurch, perch, search, smirch
- Christchurch • pikeperch
- wordsearch

15.15

- **belch**, squelch
- **filch**, zilch
- gulch

Section 16: **-d**

16.1

- **ad**, add, Allahabad, bad, Baghdad, bedad, begad, cad, Chad, clad, dad, egad, fad, forbade, gad, glad, grad, had, jihad, lad, mad, pad, plaid, rad, Riyadh, sad, scad, shad, Strad, tad, trad
- chiliad • oread
- **dryad**, dyad, naiad, triad
- Sinbad • Ahmadabad • Jalalabad
- Faisalabad • Islamabad • Hyderabad
- grandad • Soledad • Trinidad
- doodad • Galahad • Akkad • ecad
- **cycad**, nicad
- ironclad • nomad • maenad
- **monad**, trichomonad
- gonad • scratch pad • sketch pad
- keypad • helipad • launch pad
- notepad • footpad • touch pad • farad
- tetrad • Stalingrad • Leningrad
- Conrad • Titograd • undergrad
- Volgograd • Petrograd • hexad
- Mossad • Upanishad • pentad
- heptad • octad

16.2

- **Assad**, aubade, avant-garde, backyard, ballade, bard, Bernard, bombard, canard, card, charade, chard, couvade, croustade, Cunard, facade, glissade, guard, hard, ill-starred, interlard, lard, Montagnard, nard, pard, petard, pomade, promenade, regard, retard, rodomontade, roulade, saccade, Sade, salade, sard, shard, unmarred, unscarred, yard

> Create extra rhymes for [i] words like bard by adding -(r)ed to words like mar and star etc. (see section 1.1)

- Bayard • galliard • Savoyard
- Svalbard
- **bombarde**, Lombard
- Goddard • blackguard • vanguard
- Asgard • safeguard • Midgard
- bodyguard • lifeguard • Bogarde
- coastguard • mudguard • rearguard
- fireguard • Kierkegaard • diehard
- blowhard
- **Jacquard**, placard
- flashcard • railcard • racecard • Picard
- scorecard • showcard • phonecard
- **Ballard**, mallard
- Willard • Abelard • bollard • Barnard
- **Maynard**, reynard
- communard • Oudenarde • Stoppard
- Gerard • Everard • brassard
- **Hansard**, mansard
- Trenchard • Ostade • leotard
- boulevard • scrapyard • farmyard
- barnyard • graveyard • brickyard
- shipyard
- **dockyard**, stockyard
- foreyard • courtyard • boatyard
- woodyard • junkyard • churchyard

16.3

- **abed**, ahead, bed, behead, Birkenhead, bled, bread, bred, coed, cred, crossbred, dead, dread, Ed, embed, Enzed, fed, fled, Fred, gainsaid, head, infrared, ked, lead, led, Med, misled, misread, Ned, outspread, premed, pure-bred, read, red, redd, said, samoyed, shed, shred, sked, sled, sped, Spithead, spread, stead, ted, thread, tread, underbred, underfed, wed
- trackbed • flatbed • deathbed
- airbed • daybed • seabed

- **reed bed**, seedbed
- sickbed •childbed •hotbed •roadbed
- footbed •sunbed •sofa bed
- waterbed •feather bed •breastfed
- dripfed •spoonfed •Szeged
- blackhead
- **cathead**, fathead, Flathead
- masthead
- **bedhead**, deadhead, redhead
- egghead
- **airhead**, stairhead
- railhead •maidenhead •Gateshead
- beachhead •greenhead •meathead
- bighead •bridgehead
- **dickhead**, thickhead
- **pinhead**, skinhead
- pithead •Holyhead •sleepyhead
- fountainhead •whitehead •godhead
- blockhead
- **drophead**, hophead, mophead
- hothead •hogshead
- **sorehead**, warhead
- Roundhead •bonehead •arrowhead
- bullhead •wooden-head •sub-head
- bulkhead
- **chucklehead**, knucklehead
- drumhead •muttonhead •spearhead
- go-ahead •dunderhead •figurehead
- loggerhead •hammerhead
- letterhead •bobsled •cirriped •biped
- moped •quadruped

16.4

- flatbread •bedspread •teabread
- sweetbread •retread •crispbread
- wingspread •widespread •cornbread
- shortbread •sowbread •proofread
- pure-bred •gingerbread
- thoroughbred •aforesaid •Holinshed
- cowshed •woodshed •woolshed
- bloodshed •watershed •Stansted
- farmstead •bedstead •Hemel

Hempstead •roadstead •homestead
- newly-wed

16.5

- **Baird**, laird, shit-scared, undeclared, underprepared, unimpaired, unpaired, unprepared, unshared

> Create extra rhymes for
> words like laird by adding -d to
> care etc. (see section 2.1).

16.6

- **abrade**, afraid, aid, aide, ambuscade, arcade, balustrade, barricade, Belgrade, blade, blockade, braid, brigade, brocade, cannonade, carronade, cascade, cavalcade, cockade, colonnade, crusade, dissuade, downgrade, enfilade, esplanade, evade, fade, fusillade, glade, grade, grenade, grillade, handmade, harlequinade, homemade, invade, jade, lade, laid, lemonade, limeade, made, maid, man-made, marinade, masquerade, newlaid, orangeade, paid, palisade, parade, pasquinade, persuade, pervade, raid, serenade, shade, Sinéad, spade, staid, stockade, stock-in-trade, suede, tailor-made, they'd, tirade, trade, Ubaid, underpaid, undismayed, unplayed, unsprayed, unswayed, upbraid, upgrade, wade

> Create extra rhymes for
> words like abrade by adding -ed
> to array etc. (see section 3.1).

> **Unstressed** (or *feminine*) **rhymes** have at least one unstressed syllable following the final stress of the rhyme-word:
>
> Christians have burned each other, quite persuaded
> That all the Apostles would have done as they did.
>
> (Lord Byron, 'Don Juan')

- nightshade • renegade • decade
- Medicaid • motorcade • switchblade
- Adelaide • accolade • rollerblade
- marmalade • razor blade • handmaid
- barmaid • Teasmade • milkmaid
- dairymaid • bridesmaid • housemaid
- chambermaid
- parlourmaid (*US* parlormaid)
- mermaid • nursemaid • escapade
- ram raid • centigrade • multigrade
- comrade • retrograde • lampshade
- eyeshade • sunshade

16.7

- **accede**, bead, Bede, bleed, breed, cede, concede, creed, deed, Eid, exceed, feed, Gide, God speed, greed, he'd, heed, impede, interbreed, intercede, Jamshid, knead, lead, mead, Mede, meed, misdeed, mislead, misread, need, plead, proceed, read, rede, reed, Reid, retrocede, screed, secede, seed, she'd, speed, stampede, steed, succeed, supersede, Swede, tweed, weak-kneed, we'd, weed

> Create extra rhymes for [i]
> words like accede by adding -*d* to
> agree etc. (see section 4.1).

- breastfeed • greenfeed • dripfeed
- chickenfeed • spoonfeed • nosebleed
- Nibelungenlied • invalid • Ganymede
- Runnymede • airspeed • millipede
- velocipede • centipede • Siegfried
- filigreed • copyread • crossbreed
- proofread • flaxseed • hayseed
- rapeseed • linseed • pumpkinseed
- aniseed • oilseed • birdseed • ragweed
- knapweed • seaweed • chickweed
- stinkweed • blanket weed • bindweed
- pondweed • duckweed • tumbleweed
- fireweed • waterweed • silverweed

16.8

- **amid**, backslid, bid, did, forbid, grid, hid, id, kid, Kidd, lid, Madrid, mid, outbid, outdid, quid, rid, skid, slid, squid, underbid, yid
- scarabaeid • Aeneid • nereid
- spermatozoid
- **Clwyd**, Druid, fluid
- noctuid • rabid • carabid • ibid
- morbid • turbid • wretched

16.9

- **plaided**, unpadded
- **backhanded**, candid, candied, heavy-handed, high-handed, offhanded, red-handed, short-handed, unbranded, underhanded
- **retarded**, unregarded
- **bareheaded**, boneheaded, fatheaded, hard-headed, hot-headed, light-headed, pig-headed, pinheaded, thickheaded, unleaded, unwedded, wooden-headed, wrong-headed
- **intended**, splendid, unamended, unapprehended, unattended, unblended, undefended, untended
- **gadid**, unaided, unpersuaded, unshaded
- **reeded**, unheeded, unimpeded, unneeded, unseeded
- unshielded • katydid
- **lopsided**, misguided, one-sided, undecided, undivided, unguided, unprovided
- **broadminded**, like-minded, simple-minded, single-minded, small-minded, tough-minded
- disembodied
- **sordid**, unrecorded, unrewarded
- **unclouded**, uncrowded
- **unbounded**, unfounded, ungrounded
- **outmoded**, spring-loaded, unexploded
- unwounded
- **unhooded**, wooded
- **cold-blooded**, hot-blooded, red-blooded, unstudied, warm-blooded
- **underfunded**, unfunded
- unheralded • aphid • triffid
- **jagged**, ragged

- **cross-legged**, legged
- dogged •rugged

16.10

- carangid •alleged •aged
- **frigid**, rigid
- turgid •naked •wicked •whizz-kid
- orchid •crooked
- **pallid**, valid
- gelid •skidlid •eyelid
- **solid**, squalid, stolid
- Euclid •unsullied •annelid
- chrysalid •Ozalid •desmid •timid
- Fatimid
- **humid**, tumid
- pyramid •MacDiarmid •crannied
- arachnid •Enid •hominid •honied
- **Leonid**, Oceanid
- salmonid •Achaemenid
- unaccompanied •Sassanid •learned
- winged
- **rapid**, sapid, vapid
- **intrepid**, tepid
- **insipid**, lipid
- limpid •poppied •torpid
- **Cupid**, stupid
- canopied

16.11

- **arid**, married
- Alfred •Manfred •acrid •Astrid
- **serried**, unburied, viverrid
- varied •sacred •hatred •mirid
- Mildred •kindred •Wilfred •Ingrid
- Winifred •hybrid
- **florid**, forehead, horrid, torrid
- storied •Mordred •putrid
- **hurried**, unworried
- unwearied •lurid •ascarid
- unsalaried •liveried
- **Abbasid**, acid, antacid, flaccid, Hasid, placid
- alcid
- **rancid**, unfancied
- **deuced**, lucid, pellucid, Seleucid
- cussed •cursed

16.12

- **caryatid**, cravatted, dratted, fatted, matted
- **distracted**, protracted
- unadapted •Hampstead
- **downhearted**, good-hearted, hard-hearted, heavy-hearted, kind-hearted, light-hearted, lion-hearted, overparted, tender-hearted, uncharted, warm-hearted, wholehearted
- unplanted
- **fetid**, indebted, minareted, rosetted
- **aspected**, disaffected, disconnected, invected, unaffected, uncollected, unconnected, uncorrected, undetected, undirected, unelected, unexpected, uninflected, unprotected, unselected, unsuspected
- unmelted
- **discontented**, malcontented, unaccented, undented, under-represented, unfermented, unfrequented, unlamented, unrepresented, unscented
- **indigested**, predigested, Quested, uncontested, undigested, unmolested, unrequested, untested
- unprecedented •undocumented
- unornamented
- **belated**, elated, mismated, outdated, overinflated, striated, unabated, undated, unrated, unrelated, unstated, X-rated
- **sainted**, unacquainted, unpainted, untainted
- untasted •unmediated
- **ciliated**, unaffiliated
- fimbriated
- **historiated**, storiated
- unappropriated •glaciated
- unsubstantiated •undifferentiated
- unappreciated
- **uninitiated**, unvitiated
- unassociated •unalleviated
- unpunctuated •unsegregated
- uninvestigated •unmitigated
- unexpurgated •dedicated
- uncomplicated •elasticated

- undomesticated • unsophisticated
- **self-educated**, undereducated, uneducated
- unreciprocated • unassimilated
- pixilated • castellated • unventilated
- unregulated • uninsulated
- unarticulated • unmodulated
- **underpopulated**, unpopulated
- unformulated • mentholated
- unconsummated • uncoordinated
- unhyphenated • uncontaminated
- unilluminated • opinionated
- unanticipated • uncelebrated
- unconsecrated • unsaturated
- unliberated • uncorroborated
- undecorated • unillustrated
- unseparated • unincorporated
- unadulterated • uncompensated
- unpremeditated
- **self-motivated**, unmotivated
- uncultivated • antiquated
- **conceited**, uncompleted, undefeated, unheated, untreated
- **half-witted**, nitwitted, quick-witted, uncommitted, unfitted
- ungifted
- **self-inflicted**, unconstricted, unpredicted, unrestricted
- stilted
- **unprinted**, unstinted
- unscripted
- **limp-wristed**, tight-fisted, unassisted, unlisted, unresisted
- uninhabited • uninhibited
- **uncredited**, unedited
- ringletted • limited • uncarpeted
- unmerited
- **self-interested**, uninterested
- multifaceted • unsolicited • unvisited
- **benighted**, clearsighted, shortsighted, uninvited, unlighted, unrequited, unsighted
- foresighted
- **besotted**, carotid, unspotted
- unprompted • unwanted • unadopted
- **undistorted**, unescorted, unreported, unsorted, unsupported
- unsalted • undaunted • undoubted
- **unaccounted**, uncounted, unmounted

- sugarcoated • wonted • unexploited
- **self-appointed**, unpointed
- **undiluted**, undisputed, unpolluted, unsuited, voluted
- convoluted • unexecuted
- **barefooted**, club-footed, light-footed, splay-footed, sure-footed, wrong-footed
- worsted
- **unattributed**, undistributed
- **uninstructed**, unobstructed, unreconstructed
- **uncorrupted**, uninterrupted
- maladjusted • untalented
- uncovenanted • propertied
- unwarranted • unpatented
- **concerted**, uncontroverted, unconverted
- extroverted • introverted

16.13

- avid • unenvied • David
- **livid**, vivid
- ivied • Ovid • bovid
- **beloved**, Dyfed
- **fervid**, perfervid
- languid • equid
- **illiquid**, liquid
- frenzied • palsied

16.14

- **abide**, applied, aside, astride, backslide, beside, bestride, betide, bide, bride, chide, Clyde, cockeyed, coincide, collide, confide, cried, decide, divide, dried, elide, five-a-side, glide, guide, hide, hollow-eyed, I'd, implied, lied, misguide, nationwide, nide, offside, onside, outride, outside, pan-fried, pied, pie-eyed, popeyed, pride, provide, ride, Said, shied, side, slide, sloe-eyed, snide, square-eyed, starry-eyed, statewide, Strathclyde, stride, subdivide, subside, tide, tried, undyed, wall-eyed, wide, worldwide

> Create extra rhymes for words like abide by changing comply etc. to complied (see section 6.1). ⓘ

- carbide • unmodified
- **overqualified**, unqualified
- **dignified**, signified
- unverified • countrified
- unpurified • unclassified
- unspecified • sissified • unsanctified
- **self-satisfied**, unsatisfied
- unidentified • unquantified
- unfortified • unjustified • uncertified
- formaldehyde • oxhide • rawhide
- cowhide • allied • landslide • bolide
- paraglide • polyamide • bromide
- thalidomide • selenide • cyanide
- unoccupied

16.15

- hayride • chloride • joyride • telluride
- sun-dried • fluoride • saccharide

16.16

- **backside**, trackside
- bedside • airside
- **Tayside**, wayside
- lakeside • stateside • graveside
- **quayside**, seaside, Teesside
- beachside • hillside • ringside
- suicide • herbicide • regicide
- fungicide • filicide • Barmecide
- homicide
- **germicide**, spermicide
- tyrannicide • parricide
- **fratricide**, matricide, patricide
- uxoricide • countryside • infanticide
- insecticide • pesticide • parasiticide
- mountainside • Merseyside
- Tyneside
- **dioxide**, dockside, hydroxide, monoxide, oxide, peroxide
- alongside
- **diopside**, topside
- broadside • downside • roadside
- poolside • upside • nearside

- fireside • Humberside • underside
- genocide • waterside • riverside
- silverside • overside
- kerbside (*US* curbside) • Burnside

16.17

- peptide • eventide • Whitsuntide
- springtide • riptide • Shrovetide
- Yuletide • noontide • nucleotide

16.18

- **bod**, clod, cod, god, hod, mod, nod, od, odd, plod, pod, prod, quad, quod, rod, scrod, shod, sod, squad, tod, Todd, trod, wad
- demigod • amphipod • unipod
- tripod • isopod • myriapod • decapod
- cephalopod • monopod • macropod
- gastropod • arthropod • sauropod
- ramrod • Nimrod • hotrod • pushrod
- goldenrod • Novgorod • slipshod
- roughshod • eisteddfod • tightwad

16.19

- **aboard**, abroad, accord, afford, applaud, award, bawd, board, broad, chord, Claude, cord, ford, fraud, gaud, Gawd, hoard, horde, laud, lord, maraud, milord, sward, sword, toward, unawed, unexplored, unrestored, ward

> Create extra rhymes for words like applaud by adding -*ed* to soar and thaw etc. (see section 7.1). ⓘ

- fjord

16.20

- scratchboard
- **backboard**, blackboard
- gangboard • clapboard • dashboard
- **cardboard**, hardboard
- draughtboard • bargeboard

- dartboard
- **breadboard**, headboard
- pegboard (*US* Peg-board)
- chessboard • fretboard
- **sailboard**, tailboard
- drainboard
- **baseboard**, pasteboard
- skateboard
- **freeboard**, keyboard, seaboard
- cheeseboard • switchboard
- billboard
- **springboard**, stringboard
- **chipboard**, clipboard, shipboard
- running board • storyboard
- noticeboard • diving board
- sandwich board • sideboard
- signboard • whiteboard • washboard
- **floorboard**, scoreboard, strawboard
- chalkboard • soundboard • outboard
- snowboard
- mouldboard (*US* moldboard)
- **buckboard**, duckboard
- shuffleboard • shovelboard
- fibreboard (*US* fiberboard)
- smorgasbord
- chequerboard (*US* checkerboard)
- clapperboard • scraperboard
- plasterboard
- centreboard (*US* centerboard)
- mortar board • weatherboard
- motherboard • surfboard

16.21

- record • telerecord • needlecord
- **ripcord**, whipcord
- discord • tape-record • misericord
- harpsichord • clavichord
- **concord**, Concorde
- drawcord • monochord • pentachord
- landlord • warlord • slumlord
- overlord • broadsword • greensward

16.22

- **aloud**, becloud, cloud, crowd,
  enshroud, loud, Macleod, proud,
  shroud, Stroud, unavowed,
  unbowed, unendowed, unploughed
  (*US* unplowed)

- thundercloud

> Create extra rhymes for [i]
> words like cloud by adding -*ed* to
> allow etc. (see section 8.1).

16.23

- **abode**, bestrode, bode, code,
  commode, corrode, download,
  encode, erode, explode, forebode,
  goad, implode, load, lode,
  middle-of-the-road, mode, node, ode,
  offload, outrode, road, rode, sarod,
  Spode, strode, toad, upload, woad

> Create extra rhymes for [i]
> words like abode by adding -*ed*
> to bestow etc. (see section 9.1).

- geode
- **diode**, triode
- barcode • zip code • unhallowed
- carload • cartload • payload
- trainload • caseload • freeload
- peakload • shipload • coachload
- boatload • truckload • wagonload
- workload • anode • internode
- epode • antipode • electrode
- railroad
- **byroad**, highroad
- rhapsode • episode • cestode
- **nematode**, trematode
- cathode

16.24

- **avoid**, Boyd, Coed, droid, Floyd,
  Freud, Lloyd, overjoyed,
  self-employed, unalloyed,
  underemployed, unemployed, void

> Create extra rhymes for [i]
> words like avoid by adding -*ed* to
> alloy etc. (see section 10.1).

- geoid • amoeboid (*US* ameboid)
- globoid • cuboid • gadoid • typhoid
- fungoid • discoid • tabloid • colloid
- celluloid • mongoloid • alkaloid
- coralloid • crystalloid • prismoid
- arachnoid • sphenoid • hominoid

- **crinoid**, echinoid
- solenoid • humanoid • paranoid
- hypoid • anthropoid • gabbroid
- android • steroid • thyroid • hydroid
- spheroid • meteoroid • Murgatroyd
- Polaroid
- haemorrhoid (*US* hemorrhoid)
- asteroid • schizoid • factoid • mastoid
- deltoid • planetoid • ovoid • trapezoid
- rhizoid

16.25

- **allude**, brood, collude, conclude, crude, delude, dude, elude, étude, exclude, extrude, exude, feud, food, illude, include, intrude, Jude, lewd, mood, nude, obtrude, occlude, Oudh, preclude, protrude, prude, pseud, pultrude, rood, rude, seclude, shrewd, snood, transude, unglued, unsubdued, who'd, you'd
- habitude

> Create extra rhymes for words like allude by adding -(e)*d* to chew etc. (see section 11.1). i

- magnitude • seafood • wholefood
- Quaalude • postlude • interlude
- Ermintrude • Gertrude • unvalued
- prelude • quietude • hebetude
- longitude • amplitude
- **similitude**, verisimilitude
- solitude • plenitude • finitude
- decrepitude • turpitude • pulchritude
- **crassitude**, lassitude
- **solicitude**, vicissitude
- **attitude**, beatitude, gratitude, latitude, platitude
- exactitude • sanctitude • aptitude
- rectitude • ineptitude • promptitude
- fortitude • multitude • certitude
- servitude • consuetude

16.26

- **could**, good, hood, Likud, misunderstood, pud, should, stood, understood, withstood, wood, would

- Gielgud • manhood • maidenhood
- nationhood • statehood • sainthood
- priesthood • kinghood • babyhood
- likelihood • livelihood • puppyhood
- childhood • wifehood • knighthood
- falsehood • widowhood • boyhood
- cousinhood • adulthood
- neighbourhood (*US* neighborhood)
- husbandhood • bachelorhood
- toddlerhood • womanhood
- parenthood • sisterhood
- spinsterhood • fatherhood
- **brotherhood**, motherhood
- girlhood • Talmud • Malamud
- matchwood • Dagwood • Blackwood
- sandalwood • sapwood • basswood
- Atwood
- **Harewood**, Larwood
- hardwood • lancewood • heartwood
- redwood • Wedgwood • Elmwood
- bentwood • Hailwood • lacewood
- beechwood • greenwood • Eastwood
- cheesewood • driftwood • stinkwood
- Littlewood • giltwood • Hollywood
- satinwood • plywood • wildwood
- pinewood • whitewood • softwood
- **dogwood**, logwood
- cottonwood • coachwood • rosewood
- fruitwood • Goodwood • brushwood
- firewood • ironwood • underwood
- Isherwood • wormwood

16.27

- **blood**, bud, crud, cud, dud, flood, Judd, mud, rudd, scud, spud, stud, sudd, thud
- redbud • lifeblood
- stick-in-the-mud

16.28

- multi-layered
- **beard**, weird
- greybeard (*US* graybeard)
- bluebeard • Iliad • Olympiad • myriad
- period
- **hamadryad**, jeremiad, semi-retired, underwired, undesired, unexpired, uninspired

One of the most popular types of poem in English is the *limerick*, a five-line humorous poem with the rhyme scheme *aabba*, which uses a three-beat metre (made up of two unstressed and one stressed beats, ti-ti-TUM, called *anapaestic*):

There was an Old Man with a beard,
Who said, 'It is just as I feared!
Two Owls and a Hen,
Four Larks and a Wren,
Have all built their nests in my beard!'

(Edward Lear, 'There was an Old Man with a beard')

- **coward**, Howard, underpowered, unpowered
- froward
- **leeward**, steward
- **gourd**, Lourdes, self-assured, uncured, uninsured, unobscured, unsecured
- **scabbard**, tabard
- halberd ·starboard
- unremembered ·tribade ·cupboard
- **unencumbered**, unnumbered
- **good-natured**, ill-natured
- Richard ·pilchard ·pochard ·orchard
- unstructured ·uncultured
- **standard**, sub-standard
- unconsidered ·unhindered
- unordered ·Stafford ·Bradford
- **Sandford**, Sanford, Stanford
- **Hartford**, Hertford
- **Bedford**, Redford
- Telford ·Wexford ·Chelmsford
- Clifford ·Pickford ·Guildford
- Linford ·Mitford ·Hereford
- Longford ·Oxford ·Watford
- Crawford ·Salford ·Rutherford
- **haggard**, laggard
- niggard ·unsugared ·sluggard
- unmeasured ·uninjured ·tankard
- becard ·bewhiskered ·unconquered
- drunkard

16.29

- **ballad**, salad

- **collard**, Lollard, pollard
- bicoloured (*US* bicolored), dullard, multicoloured (*US* multicolored), particoloured (*US* particolored), self-coloured (*US* self-colored), uncoloured (*US* uncolored), varicoloured (*US* varicolored), versicoloured (*US* versicolored)
- **enamored**, Muhammad
- ill-humoured (*US* ill-humored)
- **Seanad**, unmannered
- Leonard ·synod ·unhonoured
- **Bernard**, gurnard
- unhampered
- **leopard**, shepherd
- untempered
- **Angharad**, Harrod
- Herod ·hundred ·unanswered
- uncensored ·unsponsored
- Blanchard ·dastard ·unchartered
- bastard ·unlettered ·unsheltered
- self-centred (*US* self-centered) ·it'd
- unfiltered ·unregistered ·unwatered
- unaltered ·dotard ·untutored
- **uncluttered**, unuttered
- **bustard**, custard, mustard
- method ·unbothered ·Harvard
- unflavoured (*US* unflavored)
- **lily-livered**, undelivered
- undiscovered

16.30

- landward ·backward
- **Edward**, headward
- hellward ·heavenward ·leftward
- **northwestward**, southwestward, westward
- wayward
- **leeward**, seaward
- **eastward**, northeastward, southeastward
- windward ·inward ·cityward
- skyward ·sideward ·rightward
- onward
- **forward**, henceforward, shoreward, straightforward, thenceforward
- awkward ·northward
- **downward**, townward

- outward • southward • poleward
- homeward • oceanward • Woodward
- sunward • upward • frontward
- rearward • afterward • earthward
- halyard
- **lanyard**, Spaniard
- untenured • steelyard • vineyard
- poniard
- **haphazard**, hazard, mazzard
- **blizzard**, gizzard, izard, lizard, vizard, wizard
- buzzard

16.31

- **absurd**, bird, Byrd, curd, engird, gird, Heard, herd, Kurd, misheard, nerd, overheard, reheard, third, turd, undergird, undeterred, unheard, unstirred, word

> Create extra rhymes for $\boxed{i}$
> words like absurd by adding -(e)d
> to blur etc. (see section 13.1).

- blackbird • yardbird • cage bird
- jailbird • seabird • ladybird
- dickybird • mockingbird • whirlybird
- hummingbird • nightbird • songbird
- shorebird • bluebird • lovebird
- lyrebird • bowerbird • thunderbird
- waterbird • weaverbird • Sigurd
- swineherd • cowherd • goatherd
- potsherd • catchword • password
- headword • swear word • keyword
- byword • watchword • crossword

> **This poem shows how effective**
> *delayed rhyme* **can be. The rhyme**
> **scheme is** *abbcac,* **and the very**
> **delayed a-rhyme**
> **('blurred/absurd') stands out:**
>
> Side by side, their faces blurred,
> The earl and countess lie in stone,
> Their proper habits vaguely shown
> As jointed armour, stiffened pleat,
> And that faint hint of the absurd—
> The little dogs under their feet.
>
> (Philip Larkin, 'An Arundel Tomb')

- foreword • loanword • buzzword
- afterword

16.32

- undersubscribed • self-absorbed
- **undisturbed**, unperturbed

16.33

- jagged • gatelegged
- **bewigged**, ship-rigged, square-rigged
- outrigged • waterlogged

16.34

- **uncharged**, undischarged
- **gilt-edged**, unfledged, unhedged
- **aged**, unassuaged, unengaged, unwaged
- unabridged
- **privileged**, underprivileged
- unacknowledged • undamaged
- unmanaged • unchanged • untinged
- unchallenged

16.35

- Schwarzwald • Buchenwald
- **beheld**, eld, geld, held, meld, self-propelled, upheld, weld, withheld
- Ziegfeld • unparalleled • spot-weld
- unscaled
- **afield**, field, midfield, misfield, shield, unaneled, unconcealed, unhealed, unpeeled, unrevealed, unsealed, wield, yield

> Create extra rhymes for $\boxed{i}$
> afield by adding -ed to conceal
> etc. (see section 23.7).

- backfield • battlefield • Mansfield
- Garfield • Sheffield • Lee-Enfield
- airfield • Wakefield • Masefield
- Greenfield • Lichfield • brickfield
- Springfield • Smithfield • minefield

- cornfield • brownfield • outfield
- snowfield
- **coalfield**, goldfield, Sutton Coldfield
- oilfield • Bloomfield • Nuffield
- upfield • Huddersfield • Sellafield
- chesterfield • windshield
- gumshield
- **build**, deskilled, gild, guild, self-willed, sild, unfilled, unfulfilled, unskilled, untilled, upbuild

> Create extra rhymes for [i] words like build by adding -ed to words like grill etc. (see Section 23.8).

- Brunhild • Roskilde

16.36

- **child**, Childe, mild, self-styled, undefiled, wild, Wilde
- grandchild • stepchild • brainchild
- godchild • Rothschild • schoolchild
- love child • unreconciled
- **bald**, scald, so-called, uncalled, unwalled
- Archibald • piebald • skewbald
- Theobald • Cumbernauld

16.37

- **behold**, bold, cold, enfold, fold, foretold, gold, hold, mould (US mold), old, outsold, scold, self-controlled, sold, told, uncontrolled, undersold, unpolled, uphold, withhold, wold

> Create extra rhymes for [i] words like behold by adding -(e)d to bowl and console etc. (see section 23.17).

- scaffold • tenfold
- **elevenfold**, sevenfold
- twelvefold
- **eightfold**, gatefold
- threefold • sheepfold • billfold
- pinfold • sixfold • manifold
- manyfold • twentyfold
- **blindfold**, ninefold

- fivefold • fourfold • thousandfold
- twofold • hundredfold
- centrefold (US centerfold)
- millionfold • mangold • marigold
- handhold • stranglehold • threshold
- freehold • leasehold • copyhold
- stronghold • shorthold • household
- toehold • foothold • commonhold
- cuckold • Leopold • Courtauld
- Cotswold
- **unoiled**, unsoiled, unspoiled
- shopsoiled
- **Gould**, unschooled
- unscheduled • thick-skulled

16.38

- Roald • unlabelled (US unlabeled)
- ribald • untroubled • unruffled
- newfangled • unwrinkled
- bespectacled
- untrammelled (US untrammeled)
- Arnold • Reginald
- **Donald**, Macdonald, Ronald
- unexampled • unprincipled
- uncrumpled • Harold
- **Fitzgerald**, Gerald, herald
- emerald • embattled • unmetalled
- untitled • disgruntled
- untravelled (US untraveled)
- unrivalled (US unrivaled) • Tynwald
- Ostwald • Oswald • sozzled • world
- dreamworld • underworld
- afterworld • netherworld

16.39

- **unarmed**, unharmed
- **ashamed**, self-proclaimed, unclaimed, unframed, unnamed, unreclaimed, untamed
- **undreamed**, unredeemed
- **undimmed**, unskimmed, untrimmed
- **unclimbed**, unprimed, unrhymed
- **malformed**, unformed, uninformed, unreformed, untransformed
- uncombed • unconsumed
- unplumbed • unaccustomed
- unfathomed • unconfirmed

> This poem by Tennyson begins in a powerful and striking way with a mixture of alliteration in the first line and *stressed* (or *masculine*) *rhyme*:
>
> He clasps the crag with crooked hands;
> Close to the sun in lonely lands,
> Ring'd with the azure world, he stands.
>
> (Alfred Lord Tennyson, 'The Eagle')

16.40

- **and**, band, bland, brand, expand, firsthand, gland, grand, hand, land, manned, misunderstand, offhand, rand, righthand, Samarkand, sand, stand, strand, thirdhand, underhand, undermanned, understand, unplanned, untanned, withstand

> **i** Create extra rhymes for words like and by adding -(n)ed to ban etc. (see section 25.1).

- graduand • hatband • armband
- headband • neckband • sweatband
- waistband • waveband • wristband
- broadband • showband • noseband
- saraband • backhand • chargehand
- farmhand • deckhand • stagehand
- freehand • millhand • behindhand
- longhand
- **beforehand**, forehand
- shorthand • gangland • Lapland
- flatland • no-man's-land • Saarland
- farmland • grassland • marshland
- fenland • wetland • Sudetenland
- wasteland • dreamland • peatland
- Matabeleland • Ngamiland
- fairyland • Dixieland • Swaziland
- Thailand • Rhineland • swampland
- washland • homeland • Heligoland
- Basutoland
- **clubland**, scrubland
- timberland • borderland
- wonderland • Nagaland • Helgoland
- **Bechuanaland**, Gondwanaland
- Mashonaland • Damaraland
- Nyasaland • platteland • hinterland
- fatherland • motherland

- Namaqualand • Öland • allemande
- confirmand • ordinand • Ferdinand
- Talleyrand • firebrand • Krugerrand
- honorand • Witwatersrand
- greensand • quicksand • analysand
- Streisand • ampersand
- **bandstand**, grandstand, handstand
- hatstand • kickstand • inkstand
- washstand • hallstand • news-stand

16.41

- **command**, demand, remand
- reprimand • countermand
- **amend**, append, apprehend, ascend, attend, befriend, bend, blend, blende, commend, comprehend, condescend, contend, depend, emend, end, expend, extend, fend, forfend, friend, impend, interdepend, lend, mend, misapprehend, misspend, offend, Oostende, Ostend, perpend, portend, rend, reprehend, scrag-end, send, spend, subtend, suspend, tail end, tend, transcend, trend, underspend, upend, vend, weekend, wend
- U-bend • dividend • bookend
- ill-omened • bin-end • stipend
- penfriend • boyfriend • girlfriend
- godsend • parascend • repetend
- **ingrained**, self-contained, self-restrained, self-sustained, unascertained, unconstrained, undertrained, undrained, unexplained, unfeigned, unrestrained, unstained, unstrained, unsustained, untrained
- crackbrained • harebrained

- featherbrained • tearstained
- **fiend**, unscreened, unweaned

- dewpond • Trebizond
- **unadorned**, unmourned, unwarned

16.42

- **downwind**, Lind, prescind, rescind, Sind, upwind, wind

> Create extra rhymes for words like downwind by changing grin etc. to grinned (see section 25.13). [i]

- Wedekind • wunderkind • Rosalind
- unexamined • undetermined
- tamarind • uncurtained • headwind
- tradewind • tailwind • crosswind
- woodwind • whirlwind
- **affined**, behind, bind, blind, find, grind, hind, humankind, interwind, kind, mankind, mind, nonaligned, resigned, rind, unaligned, unassigned, unconfined, undefined, undersigned, undesigned, unlined, unrefined, unsigned, wynd

> Create extra rhymes for words like affined by adding -(e)d to assign etc. (see section 25.21). [i]

- spellbind • womankind • snowblind
- sunblind • colourblind • purblind
- mastermind
- **abscond**, beau monde, beyond, blonde, bond, correspond, demi-monde, despond, fond, frond, Gironde, haut monde, pond, respond, ronde, second, wand
- Eurobond • vagabond • millpond

16.43

- **abound**, aground, around, astound, bound, compound, confound, dumbfound, expound, found, ground, hound, impound, interwound, mound, pound, profound, propound, redound, round, sound, stoneground, surround, theatre-in-the-round (*US* theater-in-the-round), underground, wound

> Create extra rhymes for words like abound by adding -ed to clown etc. (see section 25.29). [i]

- spellbound • westbound • casebound
- eastbound • windbound • hidebound
- fogbound • stormbound
- northbound • housebound
- outbound • southbound • snowbound
- weatherbound • earthbound
- hellhound • greyhound • foxhound
- newshound • wolfhound
- bloodhound • background
- battleground • campground
- fairground • playground
- whip-round • foreground
- showground • merry-go-round
- runaround • turnaround • ultrasound
- **pre-owned**, unowned
- unchaperoned • poind • untuned
- Lund

> An unusual rhyming device is to rhyme a word with itself: this is called *autorhyme* (or *identical* or *null rhyme*), and can have a slowing or deadening effect:
>
> We paused before a House that seemed
> A Swelling of the Ground—
> The Roof was scarcely visible—
> The Cornice—in the Ground—
>
> (Emily Dickinson, 'Because I could not stop for Death')

16.44

- **bund**, fund, Lund, rotund
- moribund • cummerbund
- Rosamund • orotund

16.45

- **unironed**, viand
- prebend
- **beribboned**, riband
- husband • house husband
- unquestioned • escutcheoned
- **brigand**, ligand
- legend
- **fecund**, second, split-second
- millisecond • nanosecond
- microsecond • rubicund • jocund
- Langland • garland • parkland
- **Cartland**, heartland
- headland • Shetland • Lakeland
- mainland
- **eland**, Leland, Wieland, Zealand, Zeeland
- Greenland • heathland • Cleveland
- Friesland • Queensland • midland
- England • Finland • Maryland
- **dryland**, highland, island
- Iceland • Holland • dockland
- Scotland
- **foreland**, Westmorland
- **Auckland**, Falkland
- Portland • Northland
- **lowland**, Poland, Roland
- Oakland • Copland • Newfoundland
- woodland • Buckland • upland
- **Jutland**, Rutland
- Ireland • moorland
- **Cumberland**, Northumberland
- Sunderland • Switzerland
- Sutherland • Hammond
- **almond**, Armand
- **Edmund**, Redmond
- **Desmond**, Esmond
- Raymond • Grimond • Richmond
- Sigmund • Sigismund • Osmond
- Dortmund • unsummoned
- diamond • gourmand • unopened
- **errand**, gerund
- reverend • Bertrand • dachshund

- unchastened
- **old-fashioned**, unimpassioned
- unsanctioned
- **aforementioned**, undermentioned, unmentioned
- unconditioned • unsweetened
- unenlightened • unleavened
- self-governed • unseasoned
- wizened • thousand

16.46

- **learned**, unearned, unreturned, unturned, upturned

16.47

- winged • smooth-tongued

16.48

- unscathed
- **loudmouthed**, mealy-mouthed

16.49

- **unpaved**, unsaved, unshaved
- **broadleaved**, unrelieved
- uncontrived
- **unapproved**, unimproved, unmoved
- **ungloved**, unloved
- **undeserved**, unobserved
- **undissolved**, uninvolved, unresolved, unsolved

16.50

- **unfazed**, unglazed
- unappeased
- **undersized**, undisguised, unrevised, unsized, unsurprised
- unanalysed (*US* unanalyzed)
- unspecialized • pearlized • satinized
- unmodernized • unpressurized
- unpublicized • uncircumcised
- unadvertised • unsupervised

- **self-imposed**, undisclosed, unenclosed, unexposed, unopposed, unposed

- toffee-nosed • undiagnosed
- **unamused**, unbruised, underused, used

Section 17: **-f**

17.1

- **caff**, carafe, faff, gaff, gaffe, naff, Najaf, piaffe, Taff
- Piaf • chiffchaff • decaf • pilaf • Olaf
- paraph • riffraff • Asaph

17.2

- **barf**, behalf, calf, chaff, coif, giraffe, Graf, graph, half, laugh, scarf, scrum half, staff, strafe, wing half
- headscarf • mooncalf • bar graph
- telegraph • polygraph • epigraph
- serigraph • cardiograph • radiograph
- spectrograph • micrograph
- lithograph • heliograph
- choreograph • tachograph
- stylograph • holograph • seismograph
- **chronograph**, monograph
- phonograph • paragraph
- cinematograph • pictograph
- autograph • photograph • flagstaff
- jackstaff • distaff • tipstaff • epitaph
- pikestaff • cenotaph

17.3

- **chef**, clef, deaf, def, eff, Geoff, Jeff, Kiev, ref, teff, tone-deaf
- Nureyev • Prokofiev • Ipatieff
- Kislev • Diaghilev • Turgenev

17.4

- **chafe**, Rafe, safe, vouchsafe, waif

17.5

- **aperitif**, beef, belief, brief, chief, enfeoff, fief, grief, interleaf, leaf, Leif, lief, Mazar-e-Sharif, misbelief, motif, naif, O'Keeffe, reef, seif, Sharif, sheaf, shereef, sportif, Tenerife, thief
- tea leaf • fig leaf • bas-relief • flyleaf
- drop-leaf • broadleaf • cloverleaf
- massif • leitmotif

17.6

- **biff**, cliff, glyph, if, kif, miff, niff, quiff, riff, skew-whiff, skiff, sniff, spliff, stiff, tiff, whiff
- mischief • handkerchief
- neckerchief • kerchief • Cardiff
- Radcliffe
- **bailiff**, calif, caliph
- Wyclif • Northcliffe • anaglyph
- hieroglyph • tariff
- **serif**, sheriff
- midriff • hippogriff • mastiff • caitiff
- plaintiff • pontiff • Joseph

17.7

- **fife**, Fyfe, knife, life, pro-life, rife, still-life, strife, wife
- shelf-life • midlife • wildlife
- nightlife • lowlife • afterlife
- jackknife • penknife • paperknife
- spaewife • alewife • midwife
- fishwife • housewife • goodwife

17.8

- **boff**, cough, doff, far-off, off, quaff, roll-on roll-off, scoff, telling-off, toff, trough
- lay-off, payoff, playoff
- show-off • Khrushchev • Gorbachev

- stand-off • Meyerhof • Cracow
- Schwarzkopf • Chekhov • Cherenkov
- take-off • kick-off • Kalashnikov
- Baryshnikov • Rimsky-Korsakov
- Kirchhoff • Karloff • Wolof • spin-off
- Rachmaninov • Ustinov • Godunov
- Stroganoff • Romanov • rip-off
- eavestrough • Sakharov • cut-off
- Molotov

17.9

- **corf**, dwarf, morph, orfe, Orff, swarf, wharf, Whorf
- Ludendorff • Düsseldorf • biomorph
- pseudomorph

17.10

- langlauf

17.11

- **loaf**, oaf
- Lagerlöf • sugarloaf

17.12

- **coif**, Cruyff

17.13

- **aloof**, behoof, goof, hoof, pouffe, proof, roof, shadoof, spoof, Tartuffe, underproof, woof
- flameproof • rainproof • greaseproof
- heatproof • windproof • bulletproof
- childproof • shockproof • mothproof
- stormproof • soundproof • foolproof
- sunroof • ovenproof • rustproof
- fireproof • showerproof
- shatterproof • waterproof
- weatherproof

17.14

- **pouffe**, woof

17.15

- **bluff**, buff, chough, chuff, cuff, duff, enough, fluff, gruff, guff, huff, luff, muff, puff, rough, ruff, scruff, scuff, slough, snuff, stuff, Tough, tuff
- handcuff • earmuff • powder puff
- dandruff • woodruff • feedstuff
- greenstuff • foodstuff

17.16

- seraph

17.17

- **scurf**, serf, soixante-neuf, surf, turf
- windsurf • Astroturf

17.18

- Ralph
- **elf**, herself, himself, itself, myself, oneself, ourself, self, shelf, themself, thyself, yourself
- mantelshelf • bookshelf • sylph
- **golf**, Rolf, Wolf
- Randolph • Rudolph
- **Wolfe**, Woolf
- aardwolf • werewolf • Beowulf
- **engulf**, gulf
- Ranulf

17.19

- Kulturkampf
- **lymph**, nymph
- Arc de Triomphe • oomph
- **bumf**, galumph, harrumph, humph
- triumph

Section 18: **-g**

18.1

- **bag**, blag, brag, Bragg, crag, dag, drag, fag, flag, gag, hag, jag, lag, mag, nag, quag, rag, sag, scrag, shag, slag, snag, sprag, stag, swag, tag, wag, zag

> Create extra rhymes by changing words like brag to bragging. [i]

- ragbag •saddlebag
- **handbag**, sandbag
- gasbag •ratbag •air bag •mailbag
- **fleabag**, tea bag
- beanbag •windbag •kitbag •dillybag
- carpet bag •washbag •growbag
- nosebag
- **bumbag**, scumbag
- punchbag •Stalag •jetlag •greylag
- gulag •dishrag •bullyrag •Morag
- ragtag •dog tag •Sontag •wigwag
- chinwag
- scallywag (*US* scallawag) •zigzag

18.2

- **Camargue**, Den Haag, Prague
- Reichstag •Bundestag

18.3

- **beg**, cleg, egg, Eigg, Greg, keg, leg, Meg, peg, skeg, teg, yegg
- filibeg •blackleg •peg-leg •dogleg
- foreleg •Oleg •bootleg •nutmeg
- Winnipeg •clothes peg •thalweg

18.4

- **Craig**, Hague, Haig, plague, taig, vague

18.5

- **fatigue**, Grieg, intrigue, league, renege
- colleague
- **Blitzkrieg**, Sitzkrieg

18.6

- **big**, brig, dig, fig, frig, gig, grig, jig, lig, pig, prig, rig, snig, sprig, swig, tig, trig, twig, Whig, wig
- Liebig •shindig •whirligig
- thingamajig •Pfennig •Gehrig
- thimblerig •Meurig •oilrig •Leipzig
- Schleswig •bigwig •periwig •Ludwig
- earwig •Danzig •Zagazig

18.7

- Braunschweig

18.8

- **agog**, befog, blog, bog, clog, cog, dog, flog, fog, frog, grog, hog, Hogg, hotdog, jog, log, nog, prog, slog, smog, snog, sprog, tautog, tog, trog, wog
- hangdog •lapdog •seadog •sheepdog
- watchdog •bulldog •gundog •firedog
- underdog •pettifog •pedagogue
- demagogue •synagogue •sandhog
- hedgehog •warthog •groundhog
- roadhog •backlog •Kellogg •weblog
- eclogue
- epilogue (*US* epilog)
- prologue (*US* prolog) •footslog
- ideologue
- dialogue (*US* dialog) •duologue
- Decalogue

- **analog**, analogue (*US* analog)
- monologue • apologue
- catalogue (*US* catalog) • travelogue
- eggnog • leapfrog • bullfrog
- Taganrog
- **golliwog**, polliwog
- phizog • Herzog

18.9

- **Borg**, morgue
- Aalborg • Swedenborg • Helsingborg
- cyborg • Cherbourg

18.10

- **brogue**, disembogue, drogue, pirog, pirogue, prorogue, rogue, vogue

18.11

- fugue

18.12

- **bug**, chug, Doug, drug, dug, fug, glug, hug, jug, lug, mug, plug, pug, rug, shrug, slug, smug, snug, thug, trug, tug

> Create extra rhymes by changing words like bug to bugging. **i**

- bedbug • ladybug • doodlebug
- humbug • firebug • thunderbug
- **jitterbug**, litterbug
- shutterbug • Rawlplug • earplug
- fireplug • hearthrug

18.13

- **Berg**, burg, erg, exergue
- Hamburg • Battenberg • Strasberg
- Habsburg • Salzburg • Strasbourg
- Pressburg • Spielberg • Tilburg
- **Lindbergh**, Strindberg
- Wittenberg • Vicksburg • Pittsburgh
- Ginsberg • Johannesburg
- Königsberg • Gettysburg • Freiburg
- Heidelberg • Heisenberg • iceberg
- **Bromberg**, homburg, Romberg
- Gothenburg • Warburg • Jo'burg
- Gutenberg • Duisburg • Magdeburg
- Brandenburg • Hindenburg
- Mecklenburg • Wallenberg
- Orenburg • Nuremberg
- Luxembourg • St Petersburg
- Williamsburg • Schoenberg
- Würzburg • Esbjerg

Section 19: **-zh**

19.1

- **décolletage**, découpage, Lesage, maquillage, paysage, plage, potage, vernissage
- triage • persiflage • fuselage • collage
- ménage • badinage
- counter-espionage • mirage
- entourage • corsage • repêchage
- frottage
- **montage**, photomontage
- cabotage

19.2

- Courrèges

19.3

- **auberge**, barège
- concierge

19.4

- **beige**, cortège, Liège, manège

19.5

- **Limoges**, loge, Vosges

19.6

- **Bruges**, rouge

19.7

- mélange

Section 20: **-ge**

20.1

- **badge**, cadge, hajj, Madge

20.2

- **barge**, charge, enlarge, large, marge, raj, reportage, sarge, sparge, Swaraj, taj, undercharge

> Create extra rhymes by changing words like barge to barging. [i]

- turbocharge •countercharge
- cover charge •surcharge
- camouflage •espionage
- **barrage**, garage
- massage •dressage •sabotage

20.3

- **allege**, dredge, edge, fledge, hedge, kedge, ledge, pledge, reg, sedge, sledge, veg, wedge
- straight edge

20.4

- **age**, assuage, backstage, cage, downstage, engage, enrage, gage, gauge, mage, multistage, offstage, onstage, Osage, page, Paige, rage, rampage, sage, stage, swage, under-age, upstage, wage
- greengage •ribcage •birdcage
- teenage •saxifrage •outrage
- space-age

20.5

- **besiege**, liege, prestige, siege

20.6

- **abridge**, bridge, fridge, frig, midge, ridge
- quayage •verbiage •foliage •lineage
- ferriage
- **stowage**, towage
- **buoyage**, voyage
- sewage
- **Babbage**, cabbage
- garbage •cribbage
- **Burbage**, herbage
- adage •bandage •yardage •headage
- appendage •windage •bondage
- vagabondage •cordage •poundage
- wordage •staffage •roughage
- baggage •mortgage •luggage
- **package**, trackage
- tankage •wreckage •breakage
- leakage
- **linkage**, shrinkage, sinkage
- **blockage**, dockage, lockage
- boscage •corkage •soakage
- truckage •tallage •assemblage
- railage
- **grillage**, pillage, spillage, stillage, tillage, village
- pupillage (*US* pupilage) •sacrilege
- ensilage •mucilage •cartilage
- sortilege •tutelage •curtilage
- privilege
- **mileage**, silage
- **acknowledge**, college, foreknowledge, knowledge
- **haulage**, stallage
- spoilage •Coolidge

20.7

- damage
- **image**, scrimmage
- pilgrimage

- **homage**, West Bromwich
- plumage
- **rummage**, scrummage
- **manage**, mismanage, pannage, stage-manage
- carnage
- **cranage**, drainage
- spinach •concubinage •libertinage
- linage •nonage •coinage
- **dunnage**, tonnage
- orphanage •baronage •patronage
- parsonage •personage •Stevenage
- cozenage •seepage •slippage
- equipage •stoppage •warpage
- groupage

20.8

- **carriage**, disparage, Harwich, intermarriage, marriage, miscarriage
- undercarriage
- **cartridge**, partridge
- Selfridge •Cambridge •Bainbridge
- Knightsbridge •umpirage
- **borage**, forage, Norwich, porridge
- Oxbridge •storage •drawbridge
- Trowbridge •tollbridge •footbridge
- **courage**, demurrage, encourage
- umbrage •suffrage
- **peerage**, steerage
- sewerage •moorage
- harbourage (*US* harborage)
- pasturage •pilferage •anchorage
- acreage •vicarage •brokerage
- cellarage •Coleridge
- **haemorrhage** (*US* hemorrhage)
- amperage •factorage •hectarage
- **litreage** (*US* literage), metreage (*US* meterage) •fosterage
- **porterage**, quarterage
- tutorage •average
- **beverage**, Beveridge
- leverage •overage •coverage

20.9

- passage
- **message**, presage
- sausage •dosage
- **misusage**, usage

- cartage
- **advantage**, vantage
- curettage •percentage •vestige
- freightage •wastage
- **mintage**, vintage
- hermitage •baronetage •heritage
- **cottage**, pottage, wattage
- hostage
- **portage**, shortage
- outage •dotage •voltage •postage
- anecdotage •footage •frontage
- pilotage •parentage •Carthage
- **ravage**, savage
- salvage •selvedge •pavage •cleavage
- lovage •language •sandwich
- **envisage**, visage

20.10

- oblige

20.11

- **bodge**, dodge, Hodge, lodge, splodge, stodge, wodge
- horologe •hodgepodge

20.12

- **engorge**, forge, George, gorge

20.13

- gouge

20.14

- doge

20.15

- **huge**, kludge, luge, scrooge, smoodge, stooge
- refuge •centrifuge •subterfuge

20.16

- **adjudge**, begrudge, bludge, budge,

drudge, fudge, grudge, judge, misjudge, nudge, pudge, sludge, smudge, trudge

> Create extra rhymes by changing words like adjudge to adjudging. ⓘ

20.17

- **converge**, dirge, diverge, emerge, merge, purge, scourge, serge, splurge, spurge, submerge, surge, urge, verge
- demiurge ● upsurge ● dramaturge
- thaumaturge

20.18

- bilge
- **bulge**, divulge, indulge, promulge

20.19

- **Falange**, flange
- **avenge**, henge, revenge, Stonehenge
- **arrange**, change, counterchange, estrange, exchange, grange, interchange, Lagrange, mange, part-exchange, range, short-change, strange
- **binge**, cringe, fringe, hinge, impinge, singe, springe, swinge, syringe, tinge, twinge, whinge

> Create extra rhymes by changing words like binge to bingeing. ⓘ

- challenge ● orange ● scavenge
- lozenge ● blancmange
- **lounge**, scrounge
- **blunge**, expunge, grunge, gunge, lunge, plunge, scunge, sponge

---

'Orange' is a word which famously has no full rhyme. Here the poet uses a device called *eye rhyme* (words that look the same when printed but which sound different) to play on this rhyming fact:

Most Saturday afternoons
At the local Hippodrome
Saw the Pathe-News rooster,
Then the recurring dream

Of a lonesome drifter
Through uninterrupted range.
Will Hunter, so gifted
He could peel an orange

In a single fluent gesture,
Was the leader of our gang.

(Paul Muldoon, 'The Weepies')

Section 21: -k

21.1

- **aback**, alack, attack, back, black, brack, clack, claque, crack, Dirac, drack, flack, flak, hack, jack, Kazakh, knack, lack, lakh, mac, mach, Nagorno-Karabakh, pack, pitchblack, plaque, quack, rack, sac, sack, shack, shellac, slack, smack, snack, stack, tach, tack, thwack, track, vac, wack, whack, wrack, yak, Zack
- cardiac • zodiac
- **haemophiliac** (*US* hemophiliac), necrophiliac, sacroiliac
- umiak
- **bibliomaniac**, dipsomaniac, egomaniac, kleptomaniac, maniac, megalomaniac, monomaniac, nymphomaniac, pyromaniac
- insomniac • celeriac • Syriac
- hypochondriac • Mauriac • theriac
- amnesiac
- **aphrodisiac**, Dionysiac
- **Dayak**, kayak
- Kerouac • bivouac

21.2

- hatchback • saddleback • camelback
- **flashback**, splashback
- fatback • hardback • halfback
- fastback • redback • shellback
- **setback**, wetback
- bareback
- **payback**, playback
- **tailback**, whaleback
- zwieback • feedback • greenback
- sweepback • leaseback • switchback
- kickback • stickleback
- **slingback**, wingback
- piggyback
- **dieback**, tieback
- **fightback**, right-back

- softback
- **clawback**, drawback
- talkback
- **callback**, fallback
- horseback • outback
- **blowback**, throwback
- rollback • yellowback • crookback
- fullback • touchback • comeback
- humpback • hunchback • cutback
- fireback • pickaback • huckaback
- Blumenbach • diamondback
- cornerback • paperback • quarterback
- razorback

21.3

- blackjack • applejack • flapjack
- steeplejack • cheapjack • skipjack
- **hijack**, skyjack
- bootjack • lumberjack • crackerjack
- ack-ack • click-clack • eyeblack
- kulak • shoeblack • bootblack
- yashmak • Tarmac • Cormac
- Potomac • sumac
- **Karnak**, Nanak, Pontianak
- knick-knack • almanac • Pasternak
- backpack • woolpack • mudpack
- power pack • Mubarak • backtrack
- **amtrac**, Amtrak
- half-track • serac • racetrack
- rickrack • gimcrack • tribrach
- wisecrack • sidetrack • soundtrack
- bladderwrack • sandarac • Skagerrak
- Bergerac • Bacharach • bric-à-brac
- tamarack • anorak

21.4

- ransack • knapsack • Barsac • Cossack
- Husák • woolsack • rucksack
- cul-de-sac • haversack • hard tack

- haystack • tic-tac • chimney stack
- smokestack • Blu-Tack • thumbtack
- counter-attack • Medevac
- **Czechoslovak**, Slovak
- Sarawak • bushwhack • Arawak
- cognac • Armagnac • Balzac • Anzac
- Prozac • Muzak

21.5

- **arc**, ark, Bach, bark, barque, Braque, Clark, clerk, dark, embark, hark, impark, Iraq, Ladakh, Lamarck, lark, macaque, marc, mark, marque, narc, nark, Newark, park, quark, sark, shark, snark, spark, stark, Vlach
- **matriarch**, patriarch
- tanbark • ringbark • stringy-bark
- Offenbach • ironbark • oligarch
- salesclerk • titlark • skylark
- meadowlark • woodlark • mudlark
- landmark • checkmark • Denmark
- benchmark • waymark • trademark
- seamark • Bismarck • telemark
- tidemark • Kitemark • pockmark
- Ostmark • hallmark • Goldmark
- Deutschmark • bookmark • footmark
- earmark • watermark • birthmark
- anarch • car park • skatepark
- ballpark
- **Petrarch**, tetrarch
- **hierarch**, squirearch
- exarch • Pesach • loan shark
- Plutarch • aardvark

21.6

- **beck**, bedeck, check, cheque, Chiang Kai-shek, crosscheck, Czech, deck, dreck, exec, fleck, heck, hitech, keck, lek, neck, peck, Québec, rec, reck, sec, sneck, spec, speck, spot-check, tec, tech, Toulouse-Lautrec, trek, wreck

> Create extra rhymes by   [i]
> adding -ing to words like check.

- Hayek • Baalbek • pinchbeck
- Steinbeck • Warbeck
- **Brubeck**, Lübeck

- Uzbek • Beiderbecke • hacek
- soundcheck • Dubcek • foredeck
- sundeck • afterdeck • quarterdeck
- **Dalek**, Palekh
- fartlek • Chichimec • Olmec • redneck
- breakneck • V-neck • bottleneck
- swan-neck • roughneck • rubberneck
- halterneck • leatherneck • turtleneck
- henpeck • kopek • shipwreck • Hasek
- Aztec • Mixtec • Toltec • infotech
- discothèque • Zapotec

21.7

- **ache**, awake, bake, betake, Blake, brake, break, cake, crake, drake, fake, flake, forsake, hake, Jake, lake, make, mistake, opaque, partake, quake, rake, sake, shake, sheikh, slake, snake, splake, stake, steak, strake, take, undertake, wake, wideawake
- bellyache • clambake • headache
- backache • pancake • teacake
- seedcake • beefcake • cheesecake
- fishcake • johnnycake • tipsy cake
- rock cake • shortcake • oatcake
- oilcake • fruitcake • cupcake
- pat-a-cake • cornflake • snowflake
- rattlesnake • handbrake • mandrake
- heartbreak • airbrake • daybreak
- jailbreak • canebrake • windbreak
- tiebreak • corncrake • outbreak
- footbrake • muckrake • earache
- firebreak • namesake • keepsake
- handshake • milkshake • heartache
- beefsteak • sweepstake • stocktake
- out-take • uptake • grubstake
- wapentake • toothache • seaquake
- kittiwake • moonquake • earthquake

21.8

- **antique**, batik, beak, bespeak, bezique, bleak, boutique, cacique, caïque, cheek, chic, clique, creak, creek, critique, Dominique, eke, freak, geek, Greek, hide-and-seek, keek, Lalique, leak, leek, Martinique, meek, midweek, Mozambique, Mustique, mystique, oblique, opéra comique, ortanique, peak, Peake, peek, physique, pique, pratique, reek, seek, shriek, Sikh, sleek, sneak, speak, Speke, squeak, streak, teak, technique, tongue-in-cheek, tweak, unique, veronique, weak, week, wreak

> Create extra rhymes by adding -*ly* to words like bleak. [i]

- stickybeak • grosbeak • houseleek
- forepeak • technospeak • newspeak
- doublespeak • hairstreak • tugrik
- fenugreek • Realpolitik • Ostpolitik
- pipsqueak • workweek

21.9

- **artic**, brick, chick, click, crick, dick, flick, hand-pick, hic, hick, kick, lick, mick, miskick, nick, pic, pick, prick, quick, rick, shtick, sic, sick, slick, snick, spic, stick, thick, tic, tick, trick, Vic, wick
- **alcaic**, algebraic, Aramaic, archaic, choleraic, Cyrenaic, deltaic, formulaic, Hebraic, Judaic, Mishnaic, Mithraic, mosaic, Pharisaic, prosaic, Ptolemaic, Romaic, spondaic, stanzaic, trochaic
- **logorrhoeic** (*US* logorrheic), mythopoeic, onomatopoeic
- **echoic**, heroic, Mesozoic, Palaeozoic (*US* Paleozoic), Stoic
- Bewick
- **disyllabic**, monosyllabic, polysyllabic, syllabic
- **choriambic**, dithyrambic, iambic
- alembic
- amoebic (*US* amebic)
- **aerobic**, agoraphobic, claustrophobic, homophobic, hydrophobic, phobic, technophobic, xenophobic
- **cherubic**, cubic, pubic
- **Arabic**, Mozarabic
- acerbic • apparatchik • dabchick
- peachick

21.10

- **Chadic**, Cycladic, Helladic, maenadic, nomadic, sporadic, triadic
- heraldic • Icelandic • asdic
- **bardic**, Haggadic, Lombardic, Sephardic
- **medic**, paramedic, Samoyedic
- Wendic • Vedic
- **comedic**, cyclopedic, encyclopedic, medick, orthopaedic (*US* orthopedic)
- **acidic**, Druidic, hasidic
- dik-dik
- **Indic**, syndic
- **aperiodic**, episodic, geodic, melodic, methodic, monodic, parodic, periodic, prosodic, psalmodic, rhapsodic, Roddick, spasmodic, threnodic
- Nordic
- **ludic**, pudic
- Talmudic
- **autobiographic**, autographic, bibliographic, biographic, calligraphic, cartographic, choreographic, cinematographic, cryptographic, demographic, geographic, graphic, hagiographic, historiographic, holographic, hydrographic, iconographic, lithographic, monographic, orthographic, palaeographic (*US* paleographic), photographic, pictographic, pornographic, reprographic, Sapphic, seraphic, stenographic, telegraphic, traffic, typographic, xerographic

> Create extra rhymes by adding -*al* to words like autobiographic.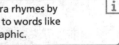

- **Efik**, malefic
- **Delphic**, Guelphic
- **anaglyphic**, beatific, calorific, colorific, hieroglyphic, honorific, horrific, Indo-Pacific, pacific, prolific, scientific, soporific, specific, terrific, transpacific, triglyphic
- **catastrophic**, dystrophic,

philosophic, strophic, theosophic, trophic
- **anamorphic**, biomorphic, metamorphic, Orphic, polymorphic, zoomorphic
- **Kufic**, Sufic
- demagogic • yogic

21.11

- **bathypelagic**, magic, tragic
- **neuralgic**, nostalgic
- **lethargic**, Tajik
- Belgic
- **paraplegic**, quadriplegic, strategic
- **dialogic**, ethnologic, hydrologic, isagogic, logic, monologic, mythologic, pathologic, pedagogic, teleologic
- georgic • muzhik
- **allergic**, dramaturgic
- **anarchic**, heptarchic, hierarchic, monarchic, oligarchic
- psychic • sidekick • dropkick
- synecdochic • Turkic
- **Alec**, cephalic, encephalic, Gallic, intervallic, italic, medallic, mesocephalic, metallic, phallic, Salic, tantalic, Uralic, Vandalic
- catlick • garlic
- **angelic**, archangelic, evangelic, melic, melick, philatelic, psychedelic, relic
- Ehrlich • Gaelic
- **acrylic**, bibliophilic, Cyrillic, dactylic, exilic, idyllic, imbecilic, necrophilic
- niblick • skinflick
- **acyclic**, cyclic, polycyclic
- **alcoholic**, anabolic, apostolic, bucolic, carbolic, chocoholic, colic, diabolic, embolic, frolic, hydraulic, hyperbolic, melancholic, metabolic, parabolic, rollick, shambolic, shopaholic, symbolic, vitriolic, workaholic
- saltlick • cowlick • souslik • gemütlich
- public • Catholic

21.12

- **aerodynamic**, balsamic, ceramic, cryptogamic, cycloramic, dynamic, hydrodynamic, Islamic, panoramic, psychodynamic, thermodynamic
- **Kalmyk**, ophthalmic
- **chasmic**, cytoplasmic, ectoplasmic, miasmic, orgasmic, phantasmic
- **karmic**, psalmic
- **academic**, alchemic, endemic, epidemic, pandemic, polemic, totemic
- **anaemic** (*US* anemic), epistemic, systemic
- **bulimic**, gimmick, metronymic, mimic, pantomimic, patronymic
- **filmic**
- **eurhythmic**, logarithmic, rhythmic
- cataclysmic • seismic
- **agronomic**, astronomic, atomic, comic, economic, ergonomic, gastronomic, metronomic, palindromic, physiognomic, subatomic, taxonomic, tragicomic
- **cosmic**, macrocosmic, microcosmic
- **gnomic**, monochromic, ohmic, photochromic
- humic
- **hypodermic**, taxidermic, thermic

21.13

- **aldermanic**, botanic, Brahmanic, Britannic, epiphanic, galvanic, Germanic, Hispanic, interoceanic, Koranic, manganic, manic, mechanic, messianic, oceanic, organic, panic, Puranic, Romanic, satanic, shamanic, talismanic, titanic, transoceanic, tympanic, volcanic
- **anthropogenic**, arsenic, autogenic, callisthenic (*US* calisthenic), carcinogenic, cariogenic, cryogenic, erotogenic, eugenic, fennec, hallucinogenic, Hellenic, hypo-allergenic, photogenic,

pyrogenic, radiogenic, schizophrenic, telegenic
- **polytechnic**, pyrotechnic, technic
- Chetnik
- **ethnic**, multi-ethnic
- Selznick
- **hygienic**, scenic
- peacenik • beatnik
- **actinic**, clinic, cynic, Finnic, Jacobinic, rabbinic
- **picnic**, pyknic
- hymnic • Iznik • Dominic
- **anachronic**, animatronic, bionic, Brythonic, bubonic, Byronic, canonic, carbonic, catatonic, chalcedonic, chronic, colonic, conic, cyclonic, daemonic, demonic, diatonic, draconic, electronic, embryonic, euphonic, harmonic, hegemonic, histrionic, homophonic, hypersonic, iconic, ionic, ironic, isotonic, laconic, macaronic, Masonic, Miltonic, mnemonic, monotonic, moronic, Napoleonic, philharmonic, phonic, Platonic, Plutonic, polyphonic, quadraphonic, sardonic, saxophonic, siphonic, Slavonic, sonic, stereophonic, subsonic, subtonic, symphonic, tectonic, Teutonic, thermionic, tonic, transonic, ultrasonic
- Dubrovnik
- **Munich**, Punic, runic, tunic
- refusenik • nudnik • kibbutznik
- sputnik • Metternich

21.14

- priapic • aspic • epic
- **philippic**, prototypic, stereotypic
- Olympic • nitpick
- **ectopic**, gyroscopic, heliotropic, horoscopic, isotopic, isotropic, kaleidoscopic, macroscopic, microscopic, misanthropic, myopic, philanthropic, phototropic, telescopic, topic, tropic
- Ethiopic • biopic
- **Inupik**, Yupik
- toothpick

21.15

- **Amharic**, barbaric, Garrick, Pindaric, samsaric
- fabric • cambric • Aelfric • chivalric
- **geriatric**, paediatric (*US* pediatric), Patrick, psychiatric, theatric
- tantric
- **epigastric**, gastric
- **alphanumeric**, atmospheric, chimeric, cleric, climacteric, congeneric, Derek, derrick, Eric, esoteric, exoteric, ferric, generic, hemispheric, Herrick, Homeric, hysteric, mesmeric, numeric, skerrick, spheric, stratospheric

> Create extra rhymes by [i]
> adding -al to words like
> atmospheric.

- red-brick • Cedric
- **calendric**, Kendrick
- **anthropometric**, asymmetric, diametric, geometric, isometric, kilometric, metric, obstetric, psychometric, pyrometric, sociometric
- **electric**, hydroelectric, photoelectric
- **androcentric**, centric, concentric, eccentric, egocentric, ethnocentric, Eurocentric, geocentric, phallocentric, theocentric
- airbrick • hayrick • Friedrich
- Dietrich
- **empiric**, lyric, panegyric, Pyrrhic, satiric, satyric, vampiric
- pinprick • citric • oneiric • hydric
- nitric
- **aleatoric**, allegoric, anaphoric, camphoric, categoric, choric, Doric, euphoric, historic, metaphoric, meteoric, phantasmagoric, phosphoric, pyrophoric, semaphoric, sophomoric, theophoric, Warwick, Yorick
- con trick
- **auric**, boric, folkloric
- **Kubrick**, rubric
- Ugric • Cymric • xeric • firebrick

- **Rurik**, sulphuric (*US* sulfuric), telluric, Zürich
- Frederick • Roderick • undertrick
- agaric • Alaric • choleric • limerick
- turmeric
- **archbishopric**, bishopric
- rhetoric • maverick • overtrick
- Masaryk

21.16

- **boracic**, classic, Jurassic, neoclassic, potassic, thoracic, Triassic
- ataraxic • carsick • heartsick
- geodesic
- **anorexic**, dyslexic
- airsick • basic • seasick
- **extrinsic**, intrinsic
- **fossick**, virtuosic
- toxic • homesick • lovesick

21.17

- **achromatic**, acrobatic, Adriatic, aerobatic, anagrammatic, aquatic, aristocratic, aromatic, Asiatic, asthmatic, athematic, attic, autocratic, automatic, axiomatic, bureaucratic, charismatic, chromatic, cinematic, climatic, dalmatic, democratic, diagrammatic, diaphragmatic, diplomatic, dogmatic, dramatic, ecstatic, emblematic, emphatic, enigmatic, epigrammatic, erratic, fanatic, hepatic, hieratic, hydrostatic, hypostatic, idiomatic, idiosyncratic, isochromatic, lymphatic, melodramatic, meritocratic, miasmatic, monochromatic, monocratic, monogrammatic, numismatic, operatic, panchromatic, pancreatic, paradigmatic, phlegmatic, photostatic, piratic, plutocratic, pneumatic, polychromatic, pragmatic, prelatic, prismatic, problematic, programmatic, psychosomatic, quadratic, rheumatic, schematic, schismatic, sciatic, semi-automatic, Socratic, somatic, static, stigmatic, sub-aquatic, sylvatic, symptomatic, systematic, technocratic, thematic, theocratic, thermostatic, traumatic
- **anaphylactic**, ataractic, autodidactic, chiropractic, climactic, didactic, galactic, lactic, prophylactic, syntactic, tactic
- asphaltic
- **antic**, Atlantic, corybantic, frantic, geomantic, gigantic, mantic, necromantic, pedantic, romantic, semantic, sycophantic, transatlantic
- synaptic
- **bombastic**, drastic, dynastic, ecclesiastic, elastic, encomiastic, enthusiastic, fantastic, gymnastic, iconoclastic, mastic, monastic, neoplastic, orgastic, orgiastic, pederastic, periphrastic, plastic, pleonastic, sarcastic, scholastic, scholiastic, spastic
- matchstick • candlestick • panstick
- slapstick • cathartic
- **Antarctic**, arctic, subantarctic, subarctic
- Vedantic • yardstick
- **aesthetic** (*US* esthetic), alphabetic, anaesthetic (*US* anesthetic), antithetic, apathetic, apologetic, arithmetic, ascetic, athletic, balletic, bathetic, cosmetic, cybernetic, diabetic, dietetic, diuretic, electromagnetic, emetic, energetic, exegetic, frenetic, genetic, Helvetic, hermetic, homiletic, kinetic, magnetic, metic, mimetic, parenthetic, pathetic, peripatetic, phonetic, photosynthetic, poetic, prophetic, prothetic, psychokinetic, splenetic, sympathetic, syncretic, syndetic, synthetic, telekinetic, theoretic, zetetic
- **apoplectic**, catalectic, dialectic, eclectic, hectic
- Celtic
- **authentic**, crescentic
- **aseptic**, dyspeptic, epileptic, nympholeptic, peptic, proleptic, sceptic (*US* skeptic), septic
- **domestic**, majestic

- cretic
- **analytic**, anchoritic, anthracitic, arthritic, bauxitic, calcitic, catalytic, critic, cryptanalytic, Cushitic, dendritic, diacritic, dioritic, dolomitic, enclitic, eremitic, hermitic, lignitic, mephitic, paralytic, parasitic, psychoanalytic, pyritic, Sanskritic, saprophytic, Semitic, sybaritic, syenitic, syphilitic, troglodytic
- **apocalyptic**, cryptic, diptych, elliptic, glyptic, styptic, triptych
- **aoristic**, artistic, autistic, cystic, deistic, distich, egoistic, fistic, holistic, juristic, logistic, monistic, mystic, puristic, sadistic, Taoistic, theistic, truistic, veristic
- fiddlestick
- **dipstick**, lipstick
- **impolitic**, politic
- polyptych ● hemistich ● heretic
- nightstick
- **abiotic**, amniotic, antibiotic, autoerotic, chaotic, demotic, despotic, erotic, exotic, homoerotic, hypnotic, idiotic, macrobiotic, meiotic, narcotic, neurotic, osmotic, patriotic, psychotic, quixotic, robotic, sclerotic, semiotic, symbiotic, zygotic, zymotic
- **Coptic**, optic, panoptic, synoptic
- **acrostic**, agnostic, diagnostic, gnostic, prognostic
- knobstick ● chopstick ● aeronautic
- **Baltic**, basaltic, cobaltic
- caustic ● swordstick ● photic ● joystick
- **psychotherapeutic**, therapeutic
- acoustic ● broomstick ● cultic
- **fustic**, rustic
- drumstick ● gearstick ● lunatic

21.18

- **homeopathic**, polymathic, psychopathic, telepathic
- ethic
- **Eolithic**, megalithic, Mesolithic, monolithic, mythic, neolithic, Palaeolithic (*US* Paleolithic)

- **Gothic**, Visigothic
- Sothic ● anacoluthic
- **Narvik**, Slavic
- pelvic ● civic ● Bolshevik ● Ludovic
- Keflavik ● Menshevik ● Reykjavik
- Chadwick ● candlewick ● Gatwick
- Sedgwick ● Prestwick ● bailiwick
- Warwick ● Brunswick ● Lerwick
- Herdwick ● Ashkenazic ● Keswick
- forensic
- **aphasic**, phasic
- **amnesic**, analgesic, mesic
- metaphysic ● music

21.19

- **alike**, bike, dyke, haik, hike, kike, like, mic, mike, mislike, pike, psych, psyche, shrike, spike, strike, trike, tyke, Van Dyck, vandyke

> Create extra rhymes by changing words like bike to biking. ⓘ

- pushbike ● motorbike ● Klondike
- Thorndike ● Updike ● hitchhike
- crablike ● lamblike
- **fanlike**, manlike, panlike
- trap-like ● catlike ● starlike ● calf-like
- **glass-like**, grass-like
- branch-like ● plant-like ● thread-like
- gem-like ● deathlike ● waiflike
- vein-like ● wraithlike ● fiendlike
- leaf-like ● dreamlike ● queen-like
- sheeplike ● witchlike ● sylphlike
- piglike
- **springlike**, string-like, wing-like
- lip-like ● princelike ● ladylike
- businesslike ● lifelike ● childlike
- **Christlike**, vice-like
- knob-like
- **godlike**, rod-like
- doglike ● rock-like ● swanlike
- foxlike ● warlike ● lord-like
- horselike ● globe-like
- **dome-like**, homelike
- ghostlike ● rose-like ● toylike
- root-like ● tooth-like ● hood-like
- wolf-like ● hook-like

Try rhyming one word with a set of two: hooklike, look like. ⓘ

- wool-like • suchlike • sponge-like
- **nunlike**, sunlike
- dovelike • lion-like • flower-like
- soundalike • lookalike
- statesmanlike • seamanlike
- sportsmanlike • womanlike
- workmanlike • fatherlike • worm-like
- handspike • garpike • marlinspike
- turnpike

21.20

- **ad hoc**, amok, Bangkok, baroque, belle époque, bloc, block, bock, brock, chock, chock-a-block, clock, cock, crock, doc, dock, floc, flock, frock, hock, hough, interlock, jock, knock, langue d'oc, lock, Locke, Médoc, mock, nock, o'clock, pock, post hoc, roc, rock, schlock, shock, smock, sock, Spock, stock, wok, yapok
- manioc • Antioch • sjambok
- gemsbok • rhebok • steenbok
- springbok • grysbok • Lombok
- Zadok • Languedoc
- **burdock**, Murdoch
- hollyhock • forehock • spatchcock
- blackcock • Hancock • petcock
- haycock • gamecock
- **Leacock**, peacock, seacock
- Hickok • Hitchcock • poppycock
- stopcock • gorcock
- **Alcock**, ballcock
- monocoque • woodcock • shuttlecock
- moorcock • weathercock

21.21

- matchlock • padlock • armlock
- Belloc
- **deadlock**, headlock, wedlock
- hemlock • fetlock • airlock
- breeze block • gridlock • ziplock
- flintlock • Shylock
- **forelock**, oarlock, warlock
- roadblock • woodblock • sunblock

- gunlock • lovelock • firelock
- hammerlock • fetterlock • interlock
- Enoch • kapok • epoch • shamrock
- bedrock • pibroch • Sheetrock
- Ragnarök • bedsock • windsock
- shell shock • aftershock • fatstock
- Bartók
- **deadstock**, headstock
- penstock • tailstock • feedstock
- tick-tock • laughing stock • livestock
- **nostoc**, Rostock, Vladivostok, Vostok
- rootstock • Woodstock • bloodstock
- gunstock

21.22

- **auk**, baulk, Bork, caulk (US calk), chalk, cork, dork, Dundalk, Falk, fork, gawk, hawk, Hawke, nork, orc, outwalk, pork, squawk, stalk, stork, talk, torc, torque, walk, york
- pitchfork • nighthawk • goshawk
- mohawk • sparrowhawk • tomahawk
- back talk • peptalk • beanstalk
- sweet-talk • crosstalk • small talk
- smooth-talk • catwalk • jaywalk
- cakewalk • space walk
- **sheep walk**, sleepwalk
- skywalk • sidewalk • crosswalk
- boardwalk • rope-walk

21.23

- gowk

21.24

- **awoke**, bespoke, bloke, broke, choke, cloak, Coke, convoke, croak, evoke, folk, invoke, joke, Koch, moke, oak, okey-doke, poke, provoke, revoke, roque, smoke, soak, soke, spoke, stoke, stony-broke (US stone-broke), stroke, toke, toque, woke, yoke, yolk
- Holyoake • artichoke • gentlefolk
- menfolk • kinsfolk • womenfolk
- townsfolk • fisherfolk • holmoak

• woodsmoke •cowpoke •slowpoke
• backstroke •breaststroke •keystroke
• heatstroke •sidestroke •downstroke
• sunstroke •upstroke •masterstroke
• counterstroke •equivoque

21.25

• **hoick**, oik

21.26

• guestbook

21.27

• **archduke**, chibouk, duke, Farouk,
fluke, gook, kook, Luke, nuke,
peruke, puke, rebuke, Seljuk, snook,
souk, spook, spruik, stook, tuque,
zouk
• gobbledegook •sail-fluke
• Marmaduke •Pentateuch

21.28

• **betook**, book, brook, Brooke,
Chinook, chook, Coke, cook, Cooke,
crook, forsook, Gluck, hook, look,
mistook, nook, partook, rook,
schnook, schtuck, Shilluk, shook,
Tobruk, took, undercook, undertook
• handbook
• **chapbook**, scrapbook
• cash book •passbook •sketchbook
• chequebook •textbook
• **daybook**, playbook
• casebook •phrase book •dybbuk
• pocketbook •copybook •storybook
• guidebook •logbook •songbook
• scorebook •hornbook •sourcebook
• notebook •cookbook •yearbook
• picture book •wordbook •workbook
• caoutchouc •Windhoek •billhook
• fishhook •skyhook •buttonhook
• tenterhook •wet look •outlook
• Inuk •inglenook •Sihanouk

• Pembroke •Innsbruck •donnybrook
• Uruk •Osnabrück •Beaverbrook
• nainsook

21.29

• **buck**, Canuck, chuck, cluck, cruck,
duck, fuck, luck, muck, pluck, puck,
ruck, schmuck, shuck, struck, stuck,
suck, truck, tuck, upchuck, yuck
• blackbuck •reedbuck •sawbuck
• roebuck •bushbuck •megabuck
• woodchuck •shelduck •Habakkuk
• stagestruck •awestruck •moonstruck
• dumbstruck •thunderstruck

21.30

• elegiac •Newark •Lubbock
• **Caradoc**, haddock, paddock,
shaddock
• Marduk •piddock •Norfolk •Suffolk
• charlock
• **hillock**, pillock
• lilac
• **ballock**, pollack, pollock, rowlock
• bullock •hammock
• **hummock**, slummock, stomach
• **bannock**, Zanuck
• Kilmarnock •Greenock •monarch
• eunuch
• **arrack**, barrack, Baruch, carrack
• **cassock**, hassock
• tussock •Taoiseach •mattock
• **buttock**, futtock
• havoc •bulwark •wazzock •Isaac

21.31

• **berk**, berserk, Burke, cirque, dirk,
Dunkirk, erk, irk, jerk, kirk, lurk,
mirk, murk, outwork, perk, quirk,
shirk, smirk, stirk, Turk, work
• Selkirk •Falkirk •Atatürk
• patchwork •handwork •waxwork
• **artwork**, part-work
• craftwork •headwork •legwork
• metalwork •guesswork
• **fretwork**, network

- breastwork • daywork • spadework

> Try rhyming one word with a set of two: spadework, made work. | i |

- framework • brainwork
- **casework**, lacework
- paintwork • beadwork • fieldwork
- needlework • teamwork • piecework
- brickwork • handiwork • bodywork
- basketwork • donkeywork • telework
- clockwork • knotwork • formwork
- coursework • falsework
- groundwork • housework
- coachwork • roadwork • homework
- stonework • woodwork • bookwork
- footwork • brushwork • firework
- ironwork • underwork • wickerwork
- paperwork • openwork • camerawork
- **masterwork**, plasterwork
- earthwork

21.32

- **calque**, talc
- catafalque
- **elk**, whelk
- **bilk**, ilk, milk, silk
- Liebfraumilch • buttermilk • volk
- **bulk**, hulk, skulk, sulk

21.33

- **ankh**, bank, blank, clank, crank, dank, drank, embank, flank, franc, frank, hank, lank, outflank, outrank, Planck, plank, point-blank, prank, rank, sank, shank, shrank, spank, stank, swank, tank, thank, wank, yank

> Create extra rhymes by adding -ing to words like bank. | i |

- sandbank • piggy bank • mountebank
- fog bank • mudbank • Bundesbank
- databank • riverbank • Burbank
- gangplank • Poulenc • redshank

- greenshank • sheepshank
- scrimshank • Cruikshank
- think tank • Franck • Eysenck
- **bethink**, blink, brink, chink, cinque, clink, dink, drink, fink, Frink, gink, ink, interlink, jink, kink, link, mink, pink, plink, prink, rink, shrink, sink, skink, slink, stink, sync, think, wink, zinc
- rinky-dink • Humperdinck • iceblink
- cufflink • bobolink • Maeterlinck
- lip-sync • countersink • doublethink
- kiddiewink
- tiddlywink (*US* tiddledywink)
- hoodwink

21.34

- **bonk**, clonk, conk, cronk, honk, Leblanc, pétanque, plonk, tronc, zonk
- honky-tonk • oink • Munch
- **bunk**, chunk, clunk, drunk, dunk, flunk, funk, gunk, hunk, junk, Monck, monk, plunk, punk, shrunk, skunk, slunk, spunk, stunk, sunk, thunk, trunk
- chipmunk • quidnunc • cyberpunk
- punch-drunk • countersunk

21.35

- **Basque**, Monégasque
- **ask**, bask, cask, flask, Krasnoyarsk, mask, masque, task
- facemask
- **arabesque**, burlesque, Dantesque, desk, grotesque, humoresque, Junoesque, Kafkaesque, Moresque, picaresque, picturesque, plateresque, Pythonesque, Romanesque, sculpturesque, statuesque
- **bisque**, brisk, disc, disk, fisc, frisk, risk, whisk
- laserdisc • obelisk • basilisk
- odalisque • tamarisk • asterisk
- **mosque**, Tosk
- kiosk • Nynorsk • brusque

- **busk**, dusk, husk, musk, rusk, tusk
- subfusc • Novosibirsk
- mollusc (*US* mollusk) • damask
- Vitebsk
- **Aleksandrovsk**, Sverdlovsk
- Khabarovsk • Komsomolsk

- **Omsk**, Tomsk
- **Gdansk**, Murmansk, Saransk
- Smolensk
- **Chelyabinsk**, Minsk
- **Donetsk**, Novokuznetsk
- **Irkutsk**, Yakutsk

Section 22: **-kh**

22.1

- Sassenach

22.2

- quaich

22.3

- Reich

22.4

- **Bloch**, Clough, loch, lough, och
- torgoch

22.5

- Tough

22.6

- Harlech •cromlech •coronach
- Rhydderch

Section 23: -l

23.1

- **Al**, bacchanal, cabal, canal, Chagall, Chantal, chaparral, gal, grand mal, Guadalcanál, Hal, La Salle, mall, Natal, pal, pall-mall, petit mal, sal, shall, Val
- Iqbal • Parsifal • mescal • decal
- caracal • Amytal • Nembutal
- Pentothal

23.2

- **Amal**, Arles, banal, Barisal, Basle, Bhopal, Carl, chorale, corral, dhal, entente cordiale, Escorial, farl, femme fatale, Funchal, gayal, gnarl, halal, Karl, kraal, locale, marl, morale, musicale, Pascal, pastorale, procès-verbal, Provençal, rationale, real, rial, riyal, snarl, Taal, Taj Mahal, timbale, toile, Vaal, Vidal, Waal
- Stendhal • Heyerdahl • housecarl
- cantal • hartal • Wiesenthal
- Lilienthal • neanderthal • Emmental
- Hofmannsthal • Wuppertal
- Transvaal • Roncesvalles • Kursaal

23.3

- **Adele**, Aix-la-Chapelle, aquarelle, artel, au naturel, bagatelle, béchamel, befell, bell, belle, boatel, Brunel, Cadell, carousel, cartel, cell, Chanel, chanterelle, clientele, Clonmel, compel, Cornell, crime passionnel, dell, demoiselle, dispel, dwell, el, ell, Estelle, excel, expel, farewell, fell, Fidel, fontanelle, foretell, Gabrielle, gazelle, gel, Giselle, hell, hotel, impel, knell, lapel, mademoiselle, maître d'hôtel, Manuel, marcel, matériel, mesdemoiselles, Michel, Michelle, Miguel, misspell, morel, moschatel, Moselle, motel, muscatel, nacelle, Nell, Nobel, Noel, organelle, outsell, Parnell, pell-mell, personnel, propel, quell, quenelle, rappel, Raquel, Ravel, rebel, repel, Rochelle, Sahel, sardelle, sell, shell, show-and-tell, smell, Snell, spell, spinel, swell, tell, undersell, vielle, villanelle, well, yell

> Create extra rhymes by changing words like compel to compelling. [i]

- Buñuel • Pachelbel • handbell
- barbell • harebell • decibel • doorbell
- cowbell • bluebell • Annabel
- mirabelle • Christabel • Jezebel
- **Isabel**, Isobel
- nutshell • infidel • asphodel
- zinfandel • Grenfell • Hillel • parallel
- Cozumel • caramel • Fresnel
- pimpernel • pipistrelle • Tricel
- filoselle

23.4

- clamshell • eggshell • seashell
- cockleshell • bombshell
- tortoiseshell • razorshell • Oftel
- caravel • Maxwell • Cherwell
- stairwell • Bakewell • speedwell
- inkwell • Sitwell • wishing well
- bridewell • Sizewell • Rockwell
- Cromwell • Bothwell
- **Boswell**, Roswell
- Orwell • Caldwell • groundswell
- ne'er-do-well

23.5

- **ail**, ale, assail, avail, bail, bale, bewail, brail, Braille, chain mail, countervail, curtail, dale, downscale, drail, dwale, entail, exhale, fail, faille, flail, frail, Gael, Gail, gale, Grail, grisaille, hail, hale, impale, jail, kale, mail, male, nail, nonpareil, outsail, pail, pale, quail, rail, sail, sale, sangrail, scale, shale, snail, stale, swale, tail, tale, they'll, trail, upscale, vail, vale, veil, wail, wale, whale, Yale

> Create extra rhymes by adding -s or -(e)d to words like ail.

- Passchendaele • Airedale
- Wensleydale • Clydesdale
- Chippendale • Coverdale • Abigail
- galingale • martingale • nightingale
- farthingale • Windscale • timescale
- blackmail • airmail
- **email**, female
- Ishmael • voicemail • vermeil

23.6

- hangnail • treenail • hobnail
- doornail • toenail • thumbnail
- fingernail
- **handrail**, landrail
- cantrail • guard rail • Israel • contrail
- monorail • abseil • headsail • resale
- skysail • wassail • topsail • foresail
- wholesale • lugsail • wagtail
- tattletale • fantail • bangtail
- rat's-tail • telltale
- **detail**, retail
- pigtail • bristletail • pintail
- **ringtail**, springtail
- fishtail • ponytail • hightail • bobtail
- cocktail • cottontail

- **foxtail**, oxtail
- horsetail • folktale • swallowtail
- dovetail • shirt tail • travail

23.7

- **allele**, anele, anneal, appeal, Bastille, Beale, Castile, chenille, cochineal, cockatiel, conceal, congeal, creel, deal, eel, Emile, feel, freewheel, genteel, Guayaquil, heal, heel, he'll, keel, Kiel, kneel, leal, Lille, Lucille, manchineel, meal, misdeal, Neil, O'Neill, ordeal, peal, peel, reel, schlemiel, seal, seel, she'll, spiel, squeal, steal, steel, Steele, teal, underseal, veal, weal, we'll, wheel, zeal
- airmobile • Dormobile • snowmobile
- Popemobile • bookmobile
- automobile • piecemeal
- **sweetmeal**, wheatmeal
- fishmeal • inchmeal • cornmeal
- wholemeal • bonemeal • oatmeal
- kriegspiel • bonspiel • Glockenspiel
- newsreel • imbecile • Jugendstil
- cartwheel • treadwheel • millwheel
- pinwheel • flywheel • gearwheel
- waterwheel

23.8

- **bill**, Brazil, brill, Camille, chill, cookchill, dill, distil (US distill), downhill, drill, Edgehill, Estoril, fill, freewill, frill, fulfil (US fulfill), Gill, goodwill, grill, grille, hill, ill, instil, kill, krill, mil, mill, nil, Phil, pill,

---

The juxtaposition of simple *stressed* (or *masculine*) *rhymes* ('chill/will') with more complex *unstressed* (or *feminine*) *rhymes* ('vision/indecision') underpins the statement of death's inevitability in this passage:

And so it stays just on the edge of vision,
A small unfocused blur, a standing chill
That slows each impulse down to indecision.
Most things may never happen; this one will

(Philip Larkin, 'Aubade')

quadrille, quill, rill, Seville, shill, shrill, sill, skill, spadille, spill, squill, still, stock-still, swill, thill, thrill, till, trill, twill, until, uphill, will
- hwyl • bank bill • handbill • waxbill
- **playbill**, waybill
- cranesbill • sibyl • crossbill • sawbill
- hornbill • storksbill • shoebill
- spoonbill • duckbill • razorbill
- gerbil • wind chill • Churchill • idyll
- daffodil • back-fill • landfill • monofil
- fibrefill (*US* fiberfill) • chlorophyll
- bluegill

23.9

- anthill • Edgehill • sidehill • molehill
- foothill • dunghill
- **sigil**, strigil, vigil
- strongyle • Virgil • Gaitskell • orchil
- roadkill • Danakil • overkill
- **amyl**, Tamil
- treadmill • windmill • gristmill
- sawmill • watermill • vinyl • mini-pill
- overspill • Caryl
- **mandrel**, mandrill
- Avril
- **beryl**, Cheryl, chrysoberyl, imperil, Merrill, peril, Sheryl
- tendril • April • Cyril • fibril • nombril
- nostril • Bovril • tumbril • escadrille
- espadrille • gracile • Cecil • utensil
- codicil • windowsill
- **dactyl**, pterodactyl
- pastille • standstill
- **dentil**, lentil, ventil
- quintile • pistil • postil • tormentil
- ethyl

23.10

- **anvil**, Granville
- Jacksonville • Nashville
- **Greville**, Neville
- Melville • Grenville • weevil
- Merthyr Tydfil • Louisville
- Mandeville • Stanleyville • Knoxville
- Orville • Townsville • Léopoldville
- Huntsville • Elisabethville
- vaudeville • Bougainville

- Brazzaville • chervil • tranquil
- Anwyl • pigswill • jonquil
- whippoorwill • frazil • fusil

23.11

- **aisle**, Argyle, awhile, beguile, bile, Carlisle, Carlyle, compile, De Stijl, ensile, file, guile, I'll, interfile, isle, Kabyle, kyle, lisle, Lyle, Mikhail, mile, Nile, pile, rank-and-file, resile, rile, Ryle, Sieg Heil, smile, spile, stile, style, tile, vile, Weil, while, wile, worthwhile
- **labile**, stabile
- **immobile**, mobile
- nubile • aedile • crocodile • cinephile
- profile • audiophile • bibliophile
- Francophile • Anglophile
- technophile • necrophile
- Russophile
- paedophile (*US* pedophile)
- **agile**, fragile
- chamomile
- **penile**, senile
- juvenile • stockpile • isopropyl
- woodpile • sterile • febrile • virile
- puerile • facile • decile • flexile
- **extensile**, prehensile, tensile
- **fissile**, missile
- domicile • docile • reconcile

23.12

- tactile • pantile
- **erectile**, insectile, projectile
- **gentile**, percentile
- reptile
- **sextile**, textile
- hairstyle • freestyle • fictile • epistyle
- peristyle • acetyl • lifestyle • hostile
- homestyle
- **butyl**, futile, rutile, utile
- ductile • fluviatile • infantile
- decastyle • mercantile • cyclostyle
- volatile • hypostyle • tetrastyle
- hexastyle • versatile • fertile
- turnstile • servile • meanwhile
- erstwhile • exile

23.13

- **boll**, Chabrol, Coll, doll, Guignol, haute école, loll, moll, pol, poll, skol, sol, troll, vol
- obol • aldol • Panadol • Algol • argol
- Gogol • googol • alcohol • glycol
- protocol • paracetamol
- **ethanol**, methanol
- Sebastopol • Interpol • folderol
- cholesterol • Lysol • Limassol
- parasol • aerosol • girasol • entresol
- atoll
- **Dettol**, metol
- sorbitol • capitol • Athol • menthol
- benzol

23.14

- **all**, appal (*US* appall), awl, Bacall, ball, bawl, befall, Bengal, brawl, call, caul, crawl, Donegal, drawl, drywall, enthral (*US* enthrall), fall, forestall, gall, Galle, Gaul, hall, haul, maul, miaul, miscall, Montreal, Naipaul, Nepal, orle, pall, Paul, pawl, Saul, schorl, scrawl, seawall, Senegal, shawl, small, sprawl, squall, stall, stonewall, tall, thrall, trawl, wall, waul, wherewithal, withal, yawl
- carryall • blackball • handball
- patball • hardball • netball • baseball
- paintball • speedball • heelball
- meatball • stickball • pinball • spitball
- racquetball • basketball • volleyball
- **eyeball**, highball
- oddball • softball • mothball
- korfball • cornball
- **lowball**, no-ball, snowball
- goalball
- **cueball**, screwball
- goofball • stoolball • football
- puffball • punchball • fireball
- rollerball • cannonball • butterball
- catchall • bradawl • holdall • Goodall

23.15

- landfall • pratfall • deadfall

- rainfall • windfall • pitfall • icefall
- nightfall • rockfall • shortfall
- downfall • outfall • snowfall • dewfall
- footfall • waterfall • overfall
- keelhaul • guildhall • Whitehall
- shorthaul • overhaul • catcall • recall
- Rockall • rollcall • photocall • overcall
- Bokmål • pub crawl • overall
- coverall • Walsall • tattersall
- headstall • bookstall • fingerstall
- **therewithal**, wherewithal
- gadwall • whitewall • Cornwall
- firewall • caterwaul • Kirkwall

23.16

- **afoul**, befoul, cowl, foul, fowl, growl, howl, jowl, owl, prowl, Rabaul, scowl, yowl
- gamefowl • peafowl • wildfowl
- moorfowl • waterfowl

23.17

- **barcarole**, bole, bowl, cajole, coal, Cole, condole, console, control, dhole, dole, droll, enrol (*US* enroll), extol, foal, goal, hole, Joel, knoll, kohl, mol, mole, Nicole, parol, parole, patrol, pole, poll, prole, rôle, roll, scroll, Seoul, shoal, skoal, sole, soul, stole, stroll, thole, Tirol, toad-in-the-hole, toll, troll, vole, whole
- Creole
- **carriole**, dariole
- cabriole • capriole
- **aureole**, gloriole, oriole
- wassail-bowl • fishbowl • dustbowl
- punchbowl • rocambole • farandole
- girandole • manhole • rathole
- armhole • arsehole • hellhole
- **keyhole**, kneehole
- peephole

> Try rhyming one word with a set of two: peephole, keep whole.

- sinkhole • pinhole • cubbyhole
- hidey-hole • pigeonhole

- **eyehole**, spyhole
- foxhole
- **knothole**, pothole
- **borehole**, Warhol
- porthole •soundhole •blowhole
- stokehole •bolthole •loophole
- **lughole**, plughole
- chuckhole •buttonhole •bunghole
- earhole •waterhole •wormhole
- charcoal •caracole •Seminole
- pinole

23.18

- tadpole •flagpole •bargepole
- redpoll •maypole •beanpole
- ridgepole •Walpole •bibliopole
- Monopole •quadrupole •Metropole
- bankroll •bedroll •payroll
- banderole •rigmarole •fumarole
- casserole •profiterole •rissole
- insole •camisole •console •oversoul
- turnsole •citole •pistole

23.19

- **boil**, Boyle, broil, coil, Dáil, Doyle, embroil, Fianna Fáil, foil, Hoyle, moil, noil, oil, roil, Royle, soil, spoil, toil, voile
- parboil •trefoil •jetfoil •airfoil
- cinquefoil •milfoil •tinfoil
  •multifoil •aerofoil •hydrofoil
- counterfoil •gargoyle •turmoil
- charbroil •topsoil •subsoil

23.20

- **Banjul**, befool, Boole, boule, boules, boulle, cagoule, cool, drool, fool, ghoul, Joule, mewl, misrule, mule, O'Toole, pool, Poole, pul, pule, Raoul, rule, school, shul, sool, spool, Stamboul, stool, Thule, tomfool, tool, tulle, you'll, yule
- mutule •kilojoule •playschool
- intercool •Blackpool
- ampoule (*US* ampule) •cesspool
- Hartlepool •Liverpool •whirlpool

- **ferrule**, ferule
- curule •cucking-stool •faldstool
- toadstool •footstool •animalcule
- granule •capsule •ridicule •molecule
- minuscule •fascicule •graticule
- vestibule •reticule •globule
- **module**, nodule
- floccule •noctule •opuscule
- pustule •majuscule •virgule

23.21

- **bull**, full, Istanbul, pull, push-pull, wool
- Kabul •bagful
- **manful**, panful
- **capful**, lapful
- hatful •carful •armful •artful
- wilful (*US* willful) •sinful •fitful
- eyeful •boxful •potful
- **awful**, lawful
- woeful •joyful •rueful •useful
- tubful
- **jugful**, mugful
- cupful •earful •ring pull •lambswool
- schedule •residual

23.22

- **annul**, cull, dull, gull, hull, lull, mull, null, scull, skull, Solihull, trull, Tull
- seagull •multihull •monohull
- numbskull •Elul

23.23

- **Baal**, betrayal, defrayal, portrayal
- Raphael
- **empyreal**, genial, hymeneal, peritoneal

23.24

- beau idéal, ideal, real, surreal
- labial •microbial •connubial
- **adverbial**, proverbial
- prandial •radial •medial •mondial
- **cordial**, exordial, primordial

- **custodial**, plasmodial
- preludial ● collegial ● vestigial
- monarchial ● Ezekiel ● bronchial
- parochial ● pallial ● Belial
- **familial**, filial
- proemial ● binomial ● Nathaniel
- **bicentennial**, biennial, centennial, decennial, millennial, perennial, Tenniel, triennial
- cranial
- **congenial**, genial, menial, venial
- **finial**, lineal, matrilineal, patrilineal
- corneal
- **baronial**, ceremonial, colonial, matrimonial, monial, neocolonial, patrimonial, testimonial
- participial ● marsupial
- **burial**, Meriel
- terrestrial
- **actuarial**, adversarial, aerial, areal, bursarial, commissarial, filarial, malarial, notarial, secretarial, vicarial
- Gabriel
- **atrial**, patrial
- vitriol
- **accessorial**, accusatorial, advertorial, ambassadorial, arboreal, armorial, auditorial, authorial, boreal, censorial, combinatorial, consistorial, conspiratorial, corporeal, curatorial, dictatorial, directorial, editorial, equatorial, executorial, gladiatorial, gubernatorial, immemorial, imperatorial, janitorial, lavatorial, manorial, marmoreal, memorial, monitorial, natatorial, oratorial, oriel, pictorial, piscatorial, prefectorial, professorial, proprietorial, rectorial, reportorial, sartorial, scriptorial, sectorial, senatorial, territorial, tonsorial, tutorial, uxorial, vectorial, visitorial
- Umbriel ● industrial
- **arterial**, bacterial, cereal, criterial, ethereal, ferial, funereal, immaterial, imperial, magisterial, managerial, material, ministerial, presbyterial, serial, sidereal, venereal

- **mercurial**, Muriel, seigneurial, tenurial, Uriel
- entrepreneurial
- **axial**, biaxial, coaxial, triaxial
- uncial ● lacteal
- **bestial**, celestial
- gluteal
- **convivial**, trivial
- **jovial**, synovial
- **alluvial**, diluvial, fluvial, pluvial
- **colloquial**, ventriloquial
- gymnasial ● ecclesial ● ambrosial

23.25

- **denial**, dial, espial, Lyall, mistrial, myall, Niall, phial, trial, vial, viol
- sundial
- **knawel**, withdrawal
- **avowal**, Baden-Powell, bowel, disembowel, dowel, Howell, Powell, rowel, towel, trowel, vowel
- semivowel
- **bestowal**, koel, Lowell, Noel
- **loyal**, royal, viceroyal
- **accrual**, construal, crewel, cruel, dual, duel, fuel, gruel, jewel, newel, renewal, reviewal
- eschewal
- artefactual (*US* artifactual), contractual, factual, tactual
- perpetual
- **aspectual**, effectual, intellectual
- **conceptual**, perceptual
- **contextual**, textual
- **habitual**, ritual
- conflictual ● instinctual ● spiritual
- mutual ● punctual ● virtual ● casual
- **audio-visual**, televisual, visual
- usual ● gradual ● individual
- menstrual ● actual
- **asexual**, bisexual, heterosexual, homosexual, psychosexual, sexual, transsexual, unisexual
- **accentual**, conventual, eventual
- Samuel
- **annual**, biannual, Emanuel, Emmanuel, manual
- Lemuel
- **consensual**, sensual
- continual

23.26

- **babble**, bedabble, dabble, drabble, gabble, grabble, rabble, scrabble
- **amble**, bramble, Campbell, gamble, gambol, ramble, scramble, shamble
- psychobabble •technobabble
- **barbel**, garble, marble
- **pebble**, rebel, treble
- **assemble**, dissemble, Kemble, resemble, tremble
- **Abel**, able, Babel, cable, enable, fable, gable, label, Mabel, sable, stable, table
- **enfeeble**, feeble, Keble
- **dibble**, dribble, fribble, Gribble, kibble, nibble, quibble, scribble
- **Abu Simbel**, cymbal, gimbal, nimble, symbol, thimble, timbal
- mandible
- **credible**, edible
- **descendible**, extendible, vendible
- audible
- **frangible**, tangible
- **illegible**, legible
- **eligible**, intelligible
- negligible •dirigible •corrigible
- submergible •fallible •indelible
- gullible
- **cannibal**, Hannibal
- discernible •terrible •horrible
- thurible
- **irascible**, passible
- expansible •collapsible •impassible
- **accessible**, compressible, impressible, inexpressible, irrepressible, repressible
- flexible
- **apprehensible**, comprehensible, defensible, distensible, extensible, ostensible, reprehensible, sensible
- indexible
- **admissible**, dismissible, immiscible, impermissible, irremissible, miscible, omissible, permissible, remissible, transmissible
- **convincible**, vincible
- **compossible**, impossible, possible
- **irresponsible**, responsible
- forcible
- **adducible**, crucible, deducible,

- inducible, irreducible, producible, reducible, seducible
- **coercible**, irreversible, reversible, submersible
- **biocompatible**, compatible
- contractible •partible
- **indefectible**, perfectible
- contemptible
- **imperceptible**, perceptible, susceptible
- **comestible**, digestible, suggestible
- **irresistible**, resistible
- exhaustible
- **conductible**, deductible, destructible, tax-deductible
- **corruptible**, interruptible
- combustible
- **controvertible**, convertible, invertible
- discerptible •persuasible •feasible
- **divisible**, risible, visible
- **implausible**, plausible
- fusible
- **Bible**, intertribal, libel, scribal, tribal
- **bobble**, Chernobyl, cobble, gobble, hobble, knobble, nobble, squabble, wobble
- ensemble
- **bauble**, corbel, warble
- **coble**, ennoble, Froebel, global, Grenoble, ignoble, noble
- foible •rouble •Hasdrubal •chasuble
- **soluble**, voluble
- **bubble**, double, Hubble, nubble, rubble, stubble, trouble
- **bumble**, crumble, fumble, grumble, humble, jumble, mumble, rough-and-tumble, rumble, scumble, stumble, tumble, umbel

> Create extra rhymes by changing words like bumble to bumbling.   [i]

- **payable**, sayable
- **seeable**, skiable
- amiable
- **dyeable**, flyable, friable, liable, pliable, triable, viable
- towable
- **doable**, suable, wooable
- affable •effable •exigible •cascabel
- takable •likable •salable •tenable

- tunable • capable • dupable
- **arable**, parable
- **curable**, durable
- taxable
- **fixable**, mixable
- actable • collectible
- **datable**, hatable
- eatable
- **notable**, potable
- mutable • savable • livable • movable
- lovable • equable • sizable • usable
- **burble**, herbal, verbal

23.27

- satchel • Rachel • Mitchell

23.28

- **addle**, paddle, saddle, skedaddle, staddle, straddle
- **candle**, Coromandel, dandle, Handel, handle, mishandle, Randall, sandal, scandal, vandal
- **manhandle**, panhandle
- packsaddle • side-saddle
- **backpedal**, heddle, medal, meddle, pedal, peddle, treadle
- **Grendel**, Kendall, Lendl, Mendel, Rendell, sendal, Wendell
- **cradle**, ladle
- **beadle**, bipedal, credal, needle, wheedle
- **diddle**, fiddle, griddle, kiddle, Liddell, middle, piddle, riddle, twiddle
- **brindle**, dwindle, kindle, spindle, swindle, Tyndale
- **paradiddle**, taradiddle
- pyramidal • apsidal
- **bridal**, bridle, fratricidal, genocidal, germicidal, homicidal, idle, idol, infanticidal, insecticidal, intertidal, matricidal, parricidal, patricidal, pesticidal, regicidal, sidle, suicidal, tidal, tyrannicidal, uxoricidal
- **coddle**, doddle, model, noddle, swaddle, toddle, twaddle, waddle
- **fondle**, rondel
- mollycoddle

- **caudal**, chordal, dawdle
- **poundal**, roundel
- **Gödel**, modal, yodel
- crinoidal
- **boodle**, caboodle, canoodle, doodle, feudal, noodle, poodle, strudel, udal
- **befuddle**, cuddle, fuddle, huddle, muddle, puddle, ruddle
- **bundle**, trundle
- prebendal • synodal
- **antipodal**, tripodal
- citadel
- **curdle**, engirdle, girdle, hurdle
- dirndl

23.29

- **baffle**, raffle, snaffle
- falafel
- **piffle**, riffle, skiffle, sniffle, whiffle
- nymphal • apocryphal
- **Eiffel**, rifle, stifle, trifle
- **coffle**, offal, waffle
- **duffel**, kerfuffle, muffle, ruffle, scuffle, shuffle, snuffle, truffle
- triumphal

23.30

- **draggle**, gaggle, haggle, raggle-taggle, straggle, waggle
- algal
- **angle**, bangle, bespangle, dangle, entangle, fandangle, jangle, mangel, mangle, spangle, strangle, tangle, wangle, wide-angle, wrangle
- triangle • quadrangle • rectangle
- pentangle • right angle • gargle
- **bagel**, finagle, Hegel, inveigle, Schlegel
- **beagle**, eagle, illegal, legal, paralegal, regal, spread eagle, viceregal
- porbeagle
- **giggle**, higgle, jiggle, niggle, sniggle, squiggle, wiggle, wriggle

> Create extra rhymes by [i]
> changing words like giggle to
> giggling.

- **commingle**, cringle, dingle, Fingal, intermingle, jingle, mingle, shingle, single, swingle, tingle
- prodigal •madrigal •warrigal
- surcingle •Christingle
- **boggle**, goggle, joggle, synagogal, toggle, woggle
- **diphthongal**, Mongol, pongal
- hornswoggle
- **bogle**, mogul, ogle
- Bruegel
- **bugle**, frugal, fugal, google
- **Dougal**, Mughal
- Portugal •conjugal
- **juggle**, smuggle, snuggle, struggle
- **bungle**, fungal, jungle
- McGonagall •astragal
- **burghal**, burgle, Fergal, gurgle

23.31

- Tintagel •evangel •angel •archangel
- brinjal •Nigel •cudgel

23.32

- **cackle**, crackle, grackle, hackle, jackal, mackle, shackle, tackle
- **ankle**, rankle
- **Gaskell**, mascle, paschal
- tabernacle •ramshackle
- **débâcle**, diarchal, matriarchal, monarchal, patriarchal, sparkle
- rascal
- **deckle**, freckle, heckle, Jekyll, shekel, speckle
- faecal (*US* fecal), treacle
- **chicle**, fickle, mickle, nickel, pickle, prickle, sickle, strickle, tickle, trickle
- **besprinkle**, crinkle, sprinkle, tinkle, twinkle, winkle, wrinkle
- fiscal
- **laical**, Pharisaical
- vehicle •stoical •cubicle •radical
- **medical**, paramedical
- **Druidical**, juridical, veridical
- syndical
- **methodical**, periodical, rhapsodical, synodical
- Talmudical •graphical •pontifical

- **magical**, tragical
- strategical
- **alogical**, illogical, logical
- **dramaturgical**, liturgical, metallurgical, surgical
- **anarchical**, hierarchical, monarchical, oligarchical
- psychical
- **angelical**, evangelical, helical
- umbilical •biblical •encyclical
- **diabolical**, follicle, hyperbolical, symbolical
- **dynamical**, hydrodynamical
- **academical**, agrochemical, alchemical, biochemical, chemical, petrochemical, photochemical, polemical
- inimical •rhythmical •seismical
- **agronomical**, anatomical, astronomical, comical, economical, gastronomical, physiognomical
- **botanical**, Brahmanical, mechanical, puritanical, sanicle, tyrannical
- ecumenical
- **geotechnical**, pyrotechnical, technical
- **clinical**, cynical, dominical, finical, Jacobinical, pinnacle, rabbinical
- **canonical**, chronicle, conical, ironical
- tunicle •pumpernickel •vernicle
- apical •epical
- **atypical**, prototypical, stereotypical, typical
- **misanthropical**, semi-tropical, subtropical, topical, tropical
- theatrical
- **chimerical**, clerical, hemispherical, hysterical, numerical, spherical
- calendrical
- **asymmetrical**, diametrical, geometrical, metrical, symmetrical, trimetrical
- electrical •ventricle
- **empirical**, lyrical, miracle, panegyrical, satirical
- cylindrical
- **ahistorical**, allegorical, categorical, historical, metaphorical, oratorical, phantasmagorical, rhetorical
- auricle •rubrical •curricle

- **classical**, fascicle, neoclassical
- farcical •vesicle
- **indexical**, lexical
- **commonsensical**, nonsensical
- **bicycle**, icicle, tricycle
- paradoxical • Popsicle • versicle
- **anagrammatical**, apostatical, emblematical, enigmatical, fanatical, grammatical, mathematical, piratical, prelatical, problematical, sabbatical
- **impractical**, practical, syntactical, tactical
- canticle
- **ecclesiastical**, fantastical
- **article**, particle
- **alphabetical**, arithmetical, heretical, hypothetical, metathetical, metical, parenthetical, poetical, prophetical, reticle, synthetical, theoretical
- dialectical
- **conventicle**, identical
- sceptical (*US* skeptical) •testicle
- **analytical**, apolitical, critical, cryptanalytical, diacritical, eremitical, geopolitical, hypercritical, hypocritical, political, socio-political, subcritical
- **deistical**, egoistical, logistical, mystical, papistical
- **optical**, synoptical
- **aeronautical**, nautical, vortical
- **cuticle**, pharmaceutical, therapeutical
- vertical •ethical •mythical •clavicle
- periwinkle •lackadaisical

- **metaphysical**, physical, quizzical
- whimsical •musical
- **Carmichael**, cervical, cycle, Michael
- unicycle •monocycle •motorcycle
- **cockle**, grockle
- corncockle •snorkel
- **bifocal**, focal, local, univocal, varifocal, vocal, yokel
- **archducal**, coucal, ducal, pentateuchal
- **buckle**, chuckle, knuckle, muckle, ruckle, suckle, truckle
- **peduncle**, uncle
- parbuckle •carbuncle •turnbuckle
- pinochle •furuncle •honeysuckle
- **demoniacal**, maniacal, megalomaniacal, paradisiacal, zodiacal
- manacle •barnacle •cenacle
- binnacle •monocle •epochal
- reciprocal
- **coracle**, oracle
- spectacle
- **pentacle**, tentacle
- receptacle •obstacle •equivocal
- **circle**, encircle
- semicircle

23.33

- sewellel
- **camel**, enamel, entrammel, mammal, trammel
- **miasmal**, phantasmal
- Carmel
- **abysmal**, baptismal, catechismal, dismal, paroxysmal

More unusual— and trickier— rhymes often include *unstressed* (or *feminine*) *rhymes* involving words with multiple syllables. Lord Byron used many of these, typically for comic effect:

And there are dresses splendid, but fantastical,
Masks of all times and nations, Turks and Jews,
And harlequins and clowns, with feats gymnastical,
Greeks, Romans, Yankee-doodles, and Hindoos;
All kinds of dress, except the ecclesiastical,
All people, as their fancies hit, may choose

(Lord Byron, '*Beppo*')

- animal •minimal •lachrymal
- maximal
- **decimal**, infinitesimal
- septimal •optimal •primal •Rommel
- **abnormal**, conformal, formal, normal, paranormal, subnormal
- chromosomal •Kümmel
- **Brummell**, pommel, pummel
- **epidermal**, geothermal, isothermal, pachydermal, taxidermal, thermal

23.34

- **annal**, channel, flannel, impanel, multichannel, panel
- cracknel
- **grapnel**, shrapnel
- carnal
- **antennal**, crenel, fennel, kennel
- regnal
- **anal**, decanal
- **adrenal**, officinal, penal, renal, venal
- **signal**, spignel
- hymnal •cardinal •libidinal •ordinal
- **attitudinal**, latitudinal, longitudinal
- altitudinal
- **imaginal**, paginal
- **marginal**, submarginal
- aboriginal •virginal •disciplinal
- seminal
- **criminal**, liminal, subliminal
- **abdominal**, nominal, phenomenal, pronominal
- noumenal
- **germinal**, terminal
- **vaticinal**, vicinal
- sentinel •intestinal •Juvenal
- **doctrinal**, final, semi-final, spinal, urinal, vaginal
- quarterfinal
- **cantonal**, O'Connell
- cornel •nounal
- **atonal**, Donal, hormonal, Monel, patronal, polytonal, tonal, zonal
- motional
- **lagoonal**, monsoonal, tribunal
- communal
- **Chunnel**, funnel, gunnel, gunwale, runnel, tunnel

- autumnal •meridional
- **embryonal**, Lionel
- **diagonal**, heptagonal, hexagonal, octagonal, tetragonal
- trigonal •orthogonal •occasional
- **divisional**, provisional, visional
- **delusional**, fusional, illusional
- regional •original •coronal •arsenal
- medicinal
- **impersonal**, interpersonal, personal, transpersonal
- **irrational**, national, passional, rational
- **factional**, fractional, redactional, transactional
- **confessional**, congressional, expressional, impressional, obsessional, processional, professional, progressional, recessional, secessional, sessional, successional
- **connectional**, correctional, directional, interjectional, intersectional, sectional, unidirectional
- **ascensional**, attentional, conventional, declensional, intentional, tensional, three-dimensional, two-dimensional
- **conceptional**, exceptional, perceptional
- **durational**, locational, oblational, relational, vocational
- rotational
- **additional**, positional, tuitional, volitional
- **fictional**, jurisdictional
- inscriptional •optional •proportional
- **devotional**, emotional, notional, promotional
- **constitutional**, evolutional, institutional, substitutional
- **constructional**, fluxional, instructional
- **conjunctional**, dysfunctional, functional, multifunctional
- versional •seasonal
- **colonel**, diurnal, eternal, external, fraternal, infernal, internal, journal, kernel, maternal, nocturnal, paternal, supernal, vernal

23.35

- **apple**, chapel, chappal, Chappell, dapple, grapple, scrapple
- scalpel
- **ample**, trample
- pineapple
- **carpal**, carpel
- **example**, sample
- sepal
- **stemple**, temple
- **maple**, papal, staple
- **peepul**, people, steeple
- tradespeople • sportspeople
- townspeople • workpeople
- **cripple**, fipple, nipple, ripple, stipple, tipple, triple
- **dimple**, pimple, simple, wimple
- Oedipal • maniple • manciple
- municipal
- **principal**, principle
- participle • multiple
- **archetypal**, disciple, typal
- prototypal
- **hopple**, popple, stopple, topple
- gospel
- **Constantinople**, copal, nopal, opal, Opel
- **duple**, pupal, pupil, scruple
- quadruple • septuple • sextuple
- quintuple • octuple
- **couple**, supple
- **crumple**, rumple, scrumple
- syncopal • episcopal • purple

23.36

- **apparel**, barrel, carol, Carole, carrel, Carroll, Darrell, Darryl, Farrell
- gambrel • spandrel
- **astral**, plastral
- cracker-barrel
- **Errol**, feral
- **petrel**, petrol
- spectral
- **central**, epicentral, ventral
- **ancestral**, kestrel, orchestral
- dextral • Sacheverell • mayoral
- sacral • wastrel • cerebral
- **anhedral**, cathedral, dihedral,

tetrahedral
- hypaethral (US hypethral), urethral
- **squirrel**, Tyrol, Wirral
- **timbrel**, whimbrel
- minstrel • arbitral • sinistral • integral
- triumviral
- **spiral**, viral
- **amoral**, Balmoral, coral, immoral, laurel, moral, quarrel, sorel, sorrel
- **cockerel**, Cockerell
- dotterel • rostral
- **aboral**, aural, choral, floral, goral, oral
- **austral**, claustral
- scoundrel • cloistral • neutral • figural
- augural
- **demurral**, Durrell
- mongrel • sepulchral • lustral
- spheral • retiral
- **crural**, jural, mural, neural, plural, rural
- **illiberal**, liberal
- natural • federal • peripheral
- doggerel • mackerel • pickerel
- **bicameral**, unicameral
- admiral
- **ephemeral**, femoral
- **humeral**, numeral
- general • mineral • funeral
- **spatio-temporal**, temporal
- corporal • tesseral • visceral
- **bilateral**, collateral, equilateral, lateral, multilateral, quadrilateral, trilateral, unilateral
- pastoral
- **electoral**, pectoral, prefectoral, protectoral
- **clitoral**, literal, littoral, presbyteral
- **dipteral**, peripteral
- doctoral • several • behavioural
- **conferral**, deferral, referral, transferral

23.37

- **hassle**, Kassel, passel, tassel, vassal
- **axel**, axle
- **cancel**, hansel, Hänsel, Mansell
- transaxle
- **castle**, metatarsal, parcel, tarsal
- chancel • sandcastle • Newcastle

- **Bessel**, nestle, pestle, redressal, trestle, vessel, wrestle
- Edsel •Texel
- **intercensal**, pencil, stencil
- pretzel •staysail •mainsail •Wiesel
- **abyssal**, bristle, epistle, gristle, missal, scissel, thistle, whistle
- pixel •plimsoll
- **tinsel**, windsail
- **schnitzel**, spritsail
- Birtwistle
- **paradisal**, sisal, trysail
- **apostle**, colossal, dossal, fossil, glossal, jostle, throstle
- **consul**, proconsul, tonsil
- **dorsal**, morsel
- **council**, counsel, groundsel
- Mosul •fo'c's'le, forecastle
- **bustle**, hustle, muscle, mussel, Russell, rustle, tussle
- gunsel •corpuscle
- **disbursal**, dispersal, Purcell, rehearsal, reversal, succursal, tercel, transversal, traversal, universal
- Herzl

23.38

- **circumstantial**, financial, substantial
- **court-martial**, impartial, marshal, martial, partial
- **especial**, special
- **cadential**, confidential, consequential, credential, deferential, differential, essential, evidential, existential, experiential, exponential, influential, intelligential, irreverential, jurisprudential, penitential, pestilential, potential, preferential, presidential, providential, prudential, quintessential, referential, residential, reverential, sapiential, sciential, sentential, sequential, tangential, torrential
- **abbatial**, facial, fascial, glacial, interracial, multiracial, palatial, primatial, racial, spatial
- **artificial**, beneficial, initial, interstitial, judicial, official,

sacrificial, solstitial, superficial
- provincial •seneschal •equinoctial
- **asocial**, precocial, psychosocial, social
- **crucial**, fiducial
- bushel
- **antenuptial**, nuptial
- **commercial**, controversial, Herschel, inertial, infomercial

23.39

- **battle**, cattle, chattel, embattle, prattle, rattle, Seattle, tattle
- fractal
- **cantle**, covenantal, mantel, mantle, Prandtl
- pastel •Fremantle •tittle-tattle
- **startle**, stratal
- Nahuatl
- **fettle**, kettle, metal, mettle, nettle, petal, Popocatépetl, settle
- **dialectal**, rectal
- **dental**, gentle, mental, Oriental, parental, rental
- transeptal
- **festal**, vestal
- gunmetal
- **antenatal**, fatal, hiatal, natal, neonatal, ratel
- **beetle**, betel, chital, decretal, fetal
- blackbeetle
- **acquittal**, belittle, brittle, committal, embrittle, it'll, kittle, little, remittal, skittle, spittle, tittle, victual, whittle
- **edictal**, rictal
- **lintel**, pintle, quintal
- **Bristol**, Chrystal, crystal, pistol
- varietal •coital •phenobarbital
- orbital •pedestal •sagittal •vegetal
- digital •skeletal •Doolittle
- **congenital**, genital, primogenital, urogenital
- capital •lickspittle •hospital •marital
- **entitle**, mistitle, recital, requital, title, vital
- subtitle •surtitle
- **axolotl**, bottle, dottle, glottal, mottle, pottle, throttle, wattle
- **fontal**, horizontal

- **hostel**, intercostal, Pentecostal
- **greenbottle** •bluebottle •Aristotle
- **chortle**, immortal, mortal, portal
- **Borstal**
- **anecdotal**, sacerdotal, teetotal, total
- **coastal**, postal
- subtotal
- **brutal**, footle, pootle, refutal, rootle, tootle
- **buttle**, cuttle, rebuttal, scuttle, shuttle, subtle, surrebuttal
- **buntal**, contrapuntal, frontal
- crustal •societal •pivotal
- **hurtle**, kirtle, myrtle, turtle

23.40

- Ethel •lethal •brothel •betrothal
- **Cavell**, cavil, gavel, gravel, ravel, travel
- **Havel**, larval, marvel, Marvell, rondavel
- **bedevil**, bevel, devil, dishevel, kevel, level, revel, split-level
- daredevil •she-devil •eye level
- **naval**, navel
- **coeval**, evil, Khedival, medieval, primeval, retrieval, shrieval, upheaval
- **civil**, drivel, shrivel, snivel, swivel
- carnival •Percival •perspectival
- **festival** •aestival (*US* estival)
- **adjectival**, arrival, deprival, genitival, imperatival, infinitival, outrival, relatival, revival, rival, substantival, survival
- archival
- **grovel**, hovel, novel
- oval
- **approval**, removal
- **Lovell**, shovel
- interval •serval •narwhal

- **coequal**, equal, prequel, sequel
- **bilingual**, lingual, monolingual, multilingual
- rorqual •Hywel
- **Daniel**, spaniel

23.41

- **basil**, bedazzle, dazzle, frazzle, razzle
- damsel •razzle-dazzle •Basel
- **bezel**, embezzle
- Denzil
- **appraisal**, hazel, nasal, phrasal
- wych hazel
- **diesel**, easel, teasel, weasel
- **chisel**, drizzle, fizzle, frizzle, grizzle, mizzle, pizzle, sizzle, swizzle, twizzle
- **reprisal**, revisal
- **nozzle**, shemozzle
- **acausal**, causal, clausal, menopausal, monocausal
- **arousal**, carousal, espousal, spousal, tousle
- **disposal**, proposal
- **accusal**, bamboozle, foozle, ouzel, perusal, refusal
- **guzzle**, muzzle, nuzzle, puzzle
- mangel-wurzel

23.42

- **birl**, burl, churl, curl, earl, Erle, furl, girl, herl, hurl, knurl, merle, pas seul, pearl, purl, Searle, skirl, squirl, swirl, twirl, whirl, whorl
- salesgirl
- **ballgirl**, call girl
- cowgirl •showgirl •schoolgirl
- choirgirl •weathergirl •Husserl

Section 24: -m

24.1

- **am**, Amsterdam, Assam, Bram, cam, cham, cheongsam, clam, cram, dam, damn, drachm, dram, exam, femme, flam, gam, glam, gram, ham, jam, jamb, lam, lamb, mam, mesdames, Omar Khayyám, Pam, pram, pro-am, ram, Sam, scam, scram, sham, Siam, slam, Spam, swam, tam, tram, Vietnam, wham, yam
- in memoriam • ad nauseam
- **iamb**, Priam
- grandam • Edam • goddam
- quondam • Potsdam • cofferdam
- Rotterdam • Oxfam • Birmingham
- Abraham • logjam • CAD-CAM
- minicam • Nicam
- **Eelam**, Elam
- flimflam • oriflamme • Suriname
- ad personam • diazepam • tangram
- ashram • telegram • milligram
- epigram • centigram • dithyramb
- **program**, programme

- cardiogram • radiogram • echogram
- mammogram
- aerogramme (US aerogram)
- microgram • dirham
- electrocardiogram • ideogram
- heliogram • diaphragm • diagram
- parallelogram • kilogram • hologram
- encephalogram • anagram
- monogram • sonogram • kissogram
- pentagram • cryptogram • photogram
- tam-tam • wigwam • whim-wham

24.2

- **alarm**, arm, Bairam, balm, barm, becalm, calm, charm, embalm, farm, forearm, Guam, harm, imam, ma'am, malm, Montcalm, Notre-Dame, palm, psalm, qualm, salaam, smarm

> Create extra rhymes by adding -ed to words like alarm. ⓘ

- yardarm • sidearm • gendarme
- wind farm • Islam • schoolmarm

It is well known that rap depends on rhyming for its structure and power; this example includes *medial* (*internal*) *rhyme*, *stressed* (*masculine*) *rhyme*, *unstressed* (*feminine*) *rhyme*, and *half-rhyme*:

Don't u call this a regular jam
I'm gonna rock this land
I'm gonna take this itty bitty world by storm
And I'm just gettin warm

[...]

Listen to my gear shift
I'm blastin, outlastin
Kinda like Shaft, so u could say I'm shaftin
Old English filled my mind
And I came up with a funky rhyme

(LL Cool J, 'Mama said knock you out')

- tonearm • napalm • firearm
- underarm • short-arm

24.3

- **ahem**, Belém, Clem, condemn,
  contemn, crème de la crème, em,
  gem, hem, Jem, LibDem, phlegm,
  pro tem, rem, Shem, stem, them
- **carpe diem**, per diem
- proem • idem • modem • diadem
- mayhem • Bethlehem • ad hominem
- ad valorem • brainstem
- apophthegm (*US* apothegm)

24.4

- **acclaim**, aflame, aim, became,
  blame, came, claim, dame, exclaim,
  fame, flame, frame, game, lame,
  maim, misname, name, proclaim,
  same, shame, tame
- endgame • counterclaim • nickname
- byname • filename • forename
- surname • airframe • mainframe
- Ephraim • doorframe • subframe
- underframe • aspartame

24.5

- **abeam**, agleam, beam, blaspheme,
  bream, cream, deem, deme,
  downstream, dream, esteem,
  extreme, gleam, hakim, kilim, meme,
  midstream, Nîmes, ream, régime,
  scheme, scream, seam, seem, steam,
  stream, supreme, team, teem, theme,
  upstream

> Create extra rhymes by i
> adding -*ing* to words like beam.

- cross-beam • hornbeam • moonbeam
- sunbeam • academe • morpheme
- phoneme • jet stream • airstream
- daydream • mainstream • Brylcreem
- millstream • slipstream
- bloodstream • monotreme
- buttercream • raceme • septime
- centime

24.6

- **bedim**, brim, crim, dim, glim, grim,
  Grimm, gym, him, hymn, Jim, Kim,
  limb, limn, nim, prim, quim, rim,
  scrim, shim, Sim, skim, slim, swim,
  Tim, trim, vim, whim

> Create extra rhymes by i
> changing words like bedim to
> bedims or bedimmed.

- poem • goyim • cherubim • Hasidim
- **seraphim**, teraphim
- Elohim • Sikkim • Joachim • prelim
- forelimb • Muslim • Blenheim
- paynim • minim • pseudonym
- homonym • anonym • synonym
- eponym • acronym • antonym
- metonym • Antrim • megrim
- Leitrim • pilgrim • Purim • interim
- passim • maxim • kibbutzim
- Midrashim • literatim
- **seriatim**, verbatim
- victim

> Try rhyming one word with a i
> set of two: victim, picked him.

- system • ecosystem • subsystem
- item • Ashkenazim

24.7

- **begrime**, Chaim, chime, climb,
  clime, crime, dime, grime, half-time,
  I'm, lime, mime, mistime, part-time,
  prime, rhyme, rime, slime, sublime,
  thyme, time
- paradigm • Mannheim • Waldheim
- Sondheim • Trondheim
- Guggenheim • Anaheim • Durkheim
- quicklime • brooklime • birdlime
- pantomime • ragtime • pastime
- bedtime • airtime
- **daytime**, playtime
- teatime • mealtime • dreamtime
- meantime • peacetime • springtime
- anytime • maritime • flexitime
- lifetime • nighttime • wartime
- downtime • noontime • sometime
- one-time • lunchtime • summertime
- wintertime • enzyme

24.8

- **aplomb**, bomb, bombe, CD-ROM, dom, from, glom, mom, pom, prom, Rom, shalom, Somme, therefrom, Thom, tom, wherefrom
- stink bomb • firebomb • sitcom
- Telecom • non-com • intercom
- coulomb • pompom • tomtom

24.9

- **conform**, corm, dorm, form, forme, haulm, lukewarm, Maugham, misinform, norm, outperform, perform, shawm, storm, swarm, transform, underperform, warm

> Create extra rhymes by adding -ing to words like conform. [i]

- landform • platform • cubiform
- **fungiform**, spongiform
- aliform • bacilliform
- **cuneiform**, uniform
- variform • vitriform • cruciform
- unciform • retiform • multiform
- oviform • triform • microform
- chloroform • cairngorm • sandstorm
- barnstorm
- **brainstorm**, rainstorm
- windstorm • snowstorm • firestorm
- thunderstorm

24.10

- Lebensraum

24.11

- **brome**, chrome, comb, Crome, dome, foam, gnome, holm, Holme, hom, home, Jerome, loam, Nome, ohm, om, roam, Rome, tome
- Guillaume • biome • Beerbohm
- radome • astrodome • Styrofoam
- megohm • Stockholm • Bornholm
- motorhome • backcomb • honeycomb
- **cockscomb**, coxcomb

- toothcomb • genome • gastronome
- metronome • syndrome • palindrome
- polychrome • Nichrome
- monochrome • velodrome
- hippodrome • aerodrome
- cyclostome • rhizome

24.12

- **abloom**, assume, backroom, bloom, Blum, boom, broom, brume, combe, consume, doom, entomb, exhume, flume, foredoom, fume, gloom, groom, Hume, illume, inhume, Khartoum, khoum, loom, neume, perfume, plume, presume, resume, rheum, room, spume, subsume, tomb, vroom, whom, womb, zoom
- catacomb • heirloom • broadloom
- taproom • guardroom • staffroom
- darkroom • classroom • bathroom
- **bedroom**, headroom
- legroom • restroom
- **dayroom**, playroom
- saleroom • stateroom • salesroom
- tearoom • green room • sickroom
- anteroom • bridegroom • stockroom
- strongroom • box room • washroom
- storeroom • boardroom • ballroom
- courtroom • houseroom • showroom
- cloakroom • elbow room
- **poolroom**, schoolroom
- newsroom
- **gunroom**, sunroom
- mushroom • common room
- workroom • hecatomb • vacuum
- legume • volume • costume
- Leverhulme

24.13

- **Qum**, stum
- Aksum

24.14

- **become**, benumb, Brum, bum, chum, come, crumb, cum, drum,

dumb, glum, gum, ho-hum, hum, Kara Kum, lum, mum, numb, plum, plumb, Rhum, rhumb, rum, scrum, scum, slum, some, strum, stum, succumb, sum, swum, thrum, thumb, tum, yum-yum
• natatorium

> Create extra rhymes by adding -*ly* to words like come and crumb. 🛈

• stumblebum •dumdum •bubblegum
• outcome •sugarplum •lanthanum
• kettledrum •breadcrumb •humdrum
• eardrum

24.15

• um
• **Graeme**, graham
• **athenaeum**, atheneum, coliseum, Liam, lyceum, mausoleum, museum, peritoneum, propylaeum, Te Deum
• Rijksmuseum

24.16

• columbium
• **erbium**, terbium, ytterbium
• scandium •compendium
• **palladium**, radium, stadium, vanadium
• **medium**, tedium
• **cryptosporidium**, cymbidium, idiom, iridium, rubidium
• indium
• **exordium**, Gordium, rutherfordium
• **odeum**, odium, plasmodium, podium, sodium
• **allium**, gallium, pallium, thallium, valium
• **berkelium**, epithelium, helium, nobelium, Sealyham
• **beryllium**, cilium, psyllium, trillium
• **linoleum**, petroleum
• thulium •cadmium
• **epithalamium**, prothalamium
• **gelsemium**, premium
• **chromium**, encomium
• holmium •fermium

• **biennium**, millennium
• **cranium**, geranium, germanium, Herculaneum, titanium, uranium
• **helenium**, proscenium, rhenium, ruthenium, selenium
• **actinium**, aluminium, condominium, delphinium
• **ammonium**, euphonium, harmonium, pandemonium, pelargonium, plutonium, polonium, zirconium
• neptunium
• **europium**, opium
• **aquarium**, armamentarium, barium, caldarium, cinerarium, columbarium, dolphinarium, frigidarium, herbarium, honorarium, planetarium, rosarium, sanitarium, solarium, sudarium, tepidarium, terrarium, vivarium
• atrium
• **delirium**, Miriam
• **equilibrium**, Librium
• yttrium
• **auditorium**, ciborium, conservatorium, crematorium, emporium, moratorium, sanatorium, scriptorium, sudatorium, vomitorium
• opprobrium
• **cerium**, imperium, magisterium
• **curium**, tellurium
• potassium •axiom •calcium
• francium •lawrencium •americium
• **Latium**, solatium
• **lutetium**, technetium
• Byzantium •strontium •consortium
• protium •promethium •lithium
• **alluvium**, effluvium
• requiem •colloquium •gymnasium
• **caesium** (*US* cesium), magnesium, trapezium
• Elysium •symposium

24.17

• **jeroboam**, Noam, Siloam
• brougham
• **residuum**, triduum
• continuum •Brabham •album
• sachem •Beecham •Mitchum

- **Adam**, macadam, madam, Madame
- **avizandum**, fandom, memorandum, nil desperandum, random, tandem
- tarmacadam
- **shahdom**, stardom, tsardom
- **beldam**, seldom
- **addendum**, corrigendum, referendum
- heirdom • sheikhdom • Gaeldom
- thanedom • saintdom
- **Edom**, freedom, Needham
- **chiefdom**, fiefdom
- queendom • heathendom
- crippledom • officialdom • Wyndham
- Christendom • kingdom • princedom
- wisdom • fogeydom • yuppiedom
- **rodham**, Sodom
- condom
- **boredom**, whoredom
- thraldom • Oldham • popedom
- dukedom
- **Carborundum**, corundum
- poppadom • pauperdom • martyrdom
- reductio ad absurdum • serfdom
- earldom

24.18

- amalgam • Targum • begum
- Brigham • lingam • ogham • sorghum
- Nahum • Belgium • dodgem
- Brummagem • stratagem • Rackham
- Malcolm • Ascham • Beckham
- welcome • vade mecum • stickum
- dinkum • modicum • hypericum
- capsicum • viaticum • practicum
- Occam
- **hokum**, locum, oakum
- bunkum
- **alum**, Calum, mallam, vallum
- Pablum
- **Haarlem**, Harlem, Malayalam, slalom
- **antebellum**, cerebellum, elm, helm, overwhelm, pelham, realm, underwhelm, vellum
- emblem • bedlam • peplum
- exemplum • wychelm • Kenelm
- Salem • velum
- **aspergillum**, chillum, film, vexillum

- Whitlam • clingfilm • telefilm
- microfilm
- **asylum**, hilum, phylum, whilom
- **column**, olm, solemn
- problem • golem • hoodlum • Ulm
- **incunabulum**, pabulum
- coagulum • pendulum • speculum
- curriculum • cimbalom • paspalum
- Absalom • Jerusalem • tantalum

24.19

- minimum • maximum • optimum
- **chrysanthemum**, helianthemum
- cardamom • Pergamum • sesamum
- per annum • magnum • damnum
- **Arnhem**, Barnum
- **envenom**, venom
- interregnum • Cheltenham • arcanum
- **duodenum**, plenum
- platinum • antirrhinum • Bonham
- summum bonum • Puttnam
- ladanum • molybdenum • laudanum
- **origanum**, polygonum
- organum • tympanum
- **laburnum**, sternum
- gingham • Gillingham • Birmingham
- Cunningham • Walsingham
- Nottingham • wampum • carom
- Abram • panjandrum • tantrum
- angstrom • alarum • candelabrum
- **plectrum**, spectrum
- **arum**, harem, harum-scarum, Sarum
- **sacrum**, simulacrum
- maelstrom • cerebrum • pyrethrum
- Ingram
- **sistrum**, Tristram
- Hiram
- **grogram**, pogrom
- **nostrum**, rostrum
- **cockalorum**, decorum, forum, jorum, Karakoram, Karakorum, Mizoram, pons asinorum, quorum
- wolfram • fulcrum • Durham
- conundrum • buckram • lustrum
- **serum**, theorem
- labarum • marjoram • pittosporum
- Rotherham • Bertram

24.20

- **hansom**, ransom, Ransome, transom
- Wrexham • sensum • Epsom • jetsam
- lissom • winsome • gypsum • alyssum
- **blossom**, opossum, possum
- flotsam • awesome • balsam • Folsom
- noisome • twosome

> Try rhyming one word with a i
> set of two: twosome, lose some.

- fulsome • buxom • Hilversum
- irksome • Gresham • meerschaum
- petersham • nasturtium
- **atom**, Euratom
- factum
- **bantam**, phantom
- sanctum
- **desideratum**, erratum, post-partum, stratum
- substratum • rectum • momentum
- septum
- **datum**, petrolatum, pomatum, Tatum, ultimatum
- arboretum • dictum • symptom
- ad infinitum
- **bottom**, rock-bottom
- quantum
- **autumn**, postmortem
- **factotum**, Gotham, scrotum, teetotum, totem
- sputum
- **accustom**, custom
- diatom • anthem • Bentham • Botham
- fathom • rhythm • biorhythm
- algorithm • logarithm • sempervivum
- ovum • William

24.21

- **chasm**, spasm
- enthusiasm • orgasm • sarcasm
- ectoplasm • cytoplasm • iconoclasm
- cataplasm • pleonasm • phantasm
- besom • dirigisme
- **abysm**, arrivisme, chrism, chrisom, ism, prism, schism
- **Shiism**, theism
- **Maoism**, Taoism
- egoism • truism • Babism • cubism
- sadism • nudism • Sufism • ageism
- holism • cataclysm • monism • papism
- verism • aneurysm • purism • Nazism
- sexism • racism • paroxysm • autism
- macrocosm • microcosm • bosom

24.22

- **affirm**, berm, confirm, firm, germ, herm, midterm, perm, sperm, squirm, term, therm, worm
- pachyderm • echinoderm
- wheatgerm • endosperm
- gymnosperm • isogeotherm
- ragworm • flatworm • threadworm
- tapeworm
- **eelworm**, mealworm
- silkworm • ringworm • inchworm
- blindworm • lobworm • roundworm
- slow-worm • screw worm
- woodworm
- **bookworm**, hookworm
- bloodworm • lugworm • lungworm
- earthworm

Section 25: **-n**

25.1

- **Aberfan**, Adrianne, an, Anne, artisan, astrakhan, ban, began, Belmopan, bipartisan, bran, can, Cannes, Cézanne, Cheyenne, clan, courtesan, cran, dan, Dayan, Diane, divan, élan, Elan, fan, flan, foreran, Fran, Friedan, Gell-Mann, gran, Han, Hunan, Ivan, Jan, Japan, Jinan, Joanne, Kazan, Klan, Kordofan, Lacan, Lausanne, Leanne, Limousin, Louvain, man, Mann, Marianne, Milan, Moran, nan, Oran, outran, outspan, Pan, panne, parmesan, partisan, pavane, pecan, Pétain, plan, Pusan, ran, rataplan, rattan, Rosanne, Sagan, Saipan, saran, scan, scran, sedan, span, spick-and-span, Spokane, Suzanne, Tainan, tan, than, tisane, trepan, van, vin, Wuhan, Xian, Yerevan, Yunnan, Zhongshan
- koan • kanban • Seremban
- **Cardin**, Teilhard de Chardin
- Rodin • Ramadan • dauphin
- turbofan • Afghan • Gauguin
- Callaghan

25.2

- cancan
- **ashcan**, trash can
- billycan • jerrycan • oilcan
- Leninakan • gamelan • Ameslan
- Acrilan • Catalan • adman
- **bagman**, ragman, swagman
- **packman**, Pac-man
- sandman • gasman • taxman • Batman
- jazzman • yardman • legman
- chessman • repairman • mailman
- apeman • spaceman • caveman
- he-man • freedman • linkman

- middleman • Winckelmann
- wingman • hitman • handyman
- bogeyman • everyman • iceman
- conman • strongman
- **lawman**, strawman
- snowman • patrolman • oilman
- schoolman • newsman
- **frontman**, stuntman
- wireman • anchorman • Telemann
- newspaperman • Superman
- cameraman • motorman
- weatherman • merman • Poznan

25.3

- sampan • tarpan
- **bedpan**, deadpan
- skidpan • inspan • wingspan
- marzipan
- **frypan**, taipan
- lifespan • Chopin • saltpan • outspan
- dustpan • tragopan • Perrin
- trimaran • catamaran • Poussin
- Anshan • gratin • kaftan • suntan
- Chambertin • orang-utan • minivan
- Ativan • caravan • banyan

25.4

- **Abadan**, Abidjan, Amman, Antoine, Arne, Aswan, Avon, Azerbaijan, Baltistan, Baluchistan, Bantustan, barn, Bhutan, Dagestan, darn, dewan, Farne, guan, Hahn, Hanuman, Hindustan, Huascarán, Iban, Iran, Isfahan, Juan, Kazakhstan, khan, Koran, Kurdistan, Kurgan, Kyrgyzstan, macédoine, Mahon, maidan, Marne, Michoacán, Oman, Pakistan, pan, Pathan, Qumran, Rajasthan, Shan, Siân, Sichuan, skarn, soutane, Sudan,

Tai'an, t'ai chi ch'uan, Taiwan,
Tajikistan, Taklimakan, tarn,
Tatarstan, Tehran, Tenochtitlán,
Turkestan, Turkmenistan, tzigane,
Uzbekistan, Vientiane, yarn,
Yinchuan, yuan, Yucatán
• Autobahn • Lindisfarne
• Bildungsroman • Nisan • Khoisan
• Afghanistan • bhagwan • Karajan

25.5

• **Adrienne**, again, amen, Ardennes,
Behn, Ben, Benn, Bren, cayenne,
Cévennes, Dairen, den, en, fen, gen,
glen, Glenn, Guyenne, Gwen, hen,
julienne, Karen, ken, Len, Loren,
men, Nene, Ogaden, paren, pen,
Penn, Phnom Penh, Rennes,
Shenzhen, Sun Yat-sen, ten, then,
Tlemcen, when, wren, yen, zazen,
Zen
• Chechen • Nurofen • peahen
• moorhen • Origen • allergen • admen
• **bagmen**, ragmen, swagmen
• packmen • gasmen • taxmen
• jazzmen • ramen • yardmen • legmen
• chessmen • repairmen • flamen
• mailmen • cavemen • he-men
• freedmen • milkmen • linkmen
• middlemen • wingmen • hitmen
• handymen • bogeymen • hymen
• icemen • conmen • strongmen
• **lawmen**, strawmen
• **cognomen**, nomen, praenomen,
snowmen
• patrolmen • oilmen • Shumen
• newsmen
• **frontmen**, stuntmen
• **firemen**, wiremen
• anchormen • newspapermen
• cameramen • motormen
• weathermen • mermen • playpen
• pigpen • fountain pen • bullpen
• samisen • Leuven • Ceinwen
• somewhen

25.6

• **Auvergne**, bairn, cairn

25.7

• **abstain**, appertain, arcane, arraign,
ascertain, attain, Bahrain, bane,
blain, brain, Braine, Cain, Caine,
campaign, cane, chain, champagne,
champaign, Champlain, Charmaine,
chicane, chow mein, cocaine,
Coleraine, Coltrane, complain,
constrain, contain, crane, Dane,
deign, demesne, demi-mondaine,
detain, disdain, domain, domaine,
drain, Duane, Dwane, Elaine,
entertain, entrain, explain, fain,
fane, feign, gain, Germaine,
germane, grain, humane, Hussein,
inane, Jain, Jane, Jermaine, Kane,
La Fontaine, lain, lane, legerdemain,
Lorraine, main, Maine, maintain,
mane, mise en scène, Montaigne,
moraine, mundane, obtain, ordain,
pain, Paine, pane, pertain, plain,
plane, Port-of-Spain, profane, rain,
Raine, refrain, reign, rein, retain,
romaine, sane, Seine, Shane, Sinn
Fein, skein, slain, Spain, Spillane,
sprain, stain, strain, sustain, swain,
terrain, thane, train, twain, Ujjain,
Ukraine, underlain, urbane, vain,
vane, vein, Verlaine, vicereine, wain,
wane, Wayne
• watch chain • mondaine • Haldane
• ultramundane • Cellophane
• novocaine • sugar cane • marocain

25.8

• **airplane**, terreplein
• **sailplane**, tailplane
• mainplane
• **seaplane**, ski-plane
• chilblain
• **biplane**, triplane
• warplane • towplane • Tamerlane
• monoplane • aeroplane • gyroplane
• hydroplane • châtelaine • aquaplane
• balletomane • Moulmein
• Charlemagne • frangipane • propane
• windowpane • counterpane
• membrane • checkrein • lamebrain

• migraine •ingrain •quatrain
• grosgrain •wholegrain •scatterbrain
• suzerain •birdbrain •sixain
• elastane •Beltane •Aquitaine
• octane
• **Fonteyn**, montane
• Holstein •Bloemfontein •butane
• bloodstain •chevrotain
• **ethane**, methane
• polyurethane •Alfvén •paravane
• weathervane •vervain •Gawain

25.9

• **Aberdeen**, Amin, aquamarine,
baleen, bean, been, beguine, Benin,
between, canteen, careen, Claudine,
clean, contravene, convene, cuisine,
dean, Dene, e'en, eighteen, fascine,
fedayeen, fifteen, figurine, foreseen,
fourteen, Francine, gean, gene,
glean, gombeen, green, Greene,
Halloween, intervene, Janine, Jean,
Jeannine, Jolene, Kean, keen, Keene,
Ladin, langoustine, latrine, lean,
limousine, machine, Maclean,
magazine, Malines, margarine,
marine, Mascarene, Massine,
Maxine, mean, Medellín, mesne,
mien, Moline, moreen, mujahedin,
Nadine, nankeen, Nazarene, Nene,
nineteen, nougatine, obscene,
palanquin, peen, poteen, preen,
quean, queen, Rabin, Racine, ramin,
ravine, routine, Sabine, saltine,
sardine, sarin, sateen, scene, screen,
seen, serene, seventeen, shagreen,
shebeen, sheen, sixteen, spleen,
spring-clean, squireen, Steen,
submarine, supervene, tambourine,
tangerine, teen, terrine, thirteen,
transmarine, treen, tureen,
Tyrrhene, ultramarine, umpteen,
velveteen, wean, ween, Wheen, yean

> Try rhyming one word with a ⓘ
> set of two or more: foreseen, one
> more scene.

• soybean •buckbean

25.10

• gradine •sanidine
• **codeine**, Roedean
• undine •iodine
• **Aberdeen**, gaberdine
• almandine •grenadine •Geraldine
• caffeine •Delphine •Josephine
• morphine •carrageen •aubergine
• indigene •hygiene •phosgene
• Eugene •Tolkien •Kathleen
• **Arlene**, Charlene, Darlene, Marlene,
praline
• **Hellene**, philhellene
• **Aileen**, Raelene, scalene
• spring-clean •crimplene •Abilene
• Ghibelline •Cymbeline •terylene
• vaseline •acetylene •Mytilene
• Eileen •colleen •Pauline
• mousseline •Hölderlin •nepheline
• Evangeline
• **Jacqueline**, Sakhalin
• Emmeline •tourmaline •trampoline
• gasoline •naphthalene •Rosaleen
• rosaline

25.11

• gamine •bromine •thiamine
• dopamine •amphetamine •histamine
• quinine •strychnine •mezzanine
• spalpeen •Philippine •lycopene
• gangrene •terrene •silkscreen
• windscreen •citrine •Dexedrine
• putting green •Benzedrine
• **Irene**, polystyrene
• widescreen •sight screen
• **chlorine**, chorine, Doreen, Maureen,
Noreen, taurine
• smokescreen •rood screen
• sunscreen •fluorine •helleborine
• Gadarene •Hippocrene
• **glycerine** (*US* glycerin),
nitroglycerine (*US* nitroglycerin)
• nectarine •wintergreen •Methedrine
• evergreen •wolverine •vaccine
• glassine •Essene •Rexine •piscine
• epicene •glycine •pyroxene

- **Palaeocene** (*US* Paleocene)
- Pliocene •Miocene •Holocene
- damascene •kerosene •Plasticine
- Pleistocene

25.12

- diamantine •dentine •Benedictine
- **Christine**, pristine, Sistine
- Springsteen •tontine •protein
- Justine •libertine •mangosteen
- brigantine •Augustine •nicotine
- galantine •guillotine •carotene
- quarantine •astatine •travertine
- brilliantine •ethene •polythene
- hypersthene •olivine •Slovene
- go-between •fanzine
- **benzene**, benzine
- bombazine •organzine

25.13

- **agin**, akin, begin, Berlin, bin, Boleyn, Bryn, chin, chin-chin, Corinne, din, fin, Finn, Flynn, gaijin, gin, Glyn, grin, Gwyn, herein, Ho Chi Minh, in, inn, Jin, jinn, kin, Kweilin, linn, Lynn, mandolin, mandoline, Min, no-win, pin, Pinyin, quin, shin, sin, skin, spin, therein, thin, Tientsin, tin, Tonkin, Turin, twin, underpin, Vietminh, violin, wherein, whin, whipper-in, win, within, Wynne, yin
- weigh-in •lutein •lie-in •Samhain
- **Bowen**, Cohen, Owen, throw-in
- **heroin**, heroine
- benzoin
- **bruin**, ruin, shoo-in
- Bedouin •Islwyn
- **genuine**, Menuhin
- **cabin**, Scriabin
- Portakabin •sin bin •swingbin
- **bobbin**, dobbin, robin
- **haemoglobin** (*US* hemoglobin)
- Reuben •dubbin •dustbin •Jacobin
- **kitchen**, lichen
- Cochin •urchin

25.14

- Aladdin •stand-in
- **Dunedin**, lead-in
- **Blondin**, Girondin
- Odin
- **paladin**, Saladin
- Borodin •Baffin •elfin
- **biffin**, griffin, tiffin
- **boffin**, coffin
- dolphin •endorphin •bowfin
- yellowfin
- **muffin**, puffin
- ragamuffin •paraffin •perfin
- bargain •Begin •Kosygin
- **hoggin**, noggin
- imagine •margin •engine
- **pidgin**, pigeon, smidgen, wigeon
- stool pigeon •wood pigeon •origin
- Pugin •virgin

25.15

- grimalkin •lambkin •napkin •gaskin
- lambskin •catkin
- **Larkin**, parkin
- calfskin •sharkskin •welkin
- Potemkin •Jenkin •redskin
- bearskin •snakeskin •Deakin
- sealskin •sheepskin •chicken
- limpkin •pipkin
- **griskin**, siskin
- pigskin •spillikin •ramekin
- **manikin**, mannequin, pannikin
- minikin •larrikin •Zworykin
- wineskin •bodkin •Hodgkin
- Donkin
- **Algonquin**, Tonkin
- Hopkin
- **Kropotkin**, Watkin
- walk-in •foreskin •doeskin
- moleskin •goatskin •oilskin
- coonskin •wolfskin •Pushkin
- **bumpkin**, pumpkin
- **buskin**, Ruskin
- buckskin •deerskin •baldachin
- manakin

- **firkin**, gherkin, jerkin, merkin, Perkin

25.16

- **Alun**, Malin, Tallinn
- Jacklin •franklin
- **chaplain**, Chaplin
- ratline
- **Carlin**, marlin, marline, Stalin
- **Helen**, Llewelyn
- Mechlin
- **Emlyn**, gremlin, Kremlin
- Galen •capelin •kylin •Evelyn
- **Enniskillen**, penicillin, villein
- Hamelin •Marilyn •discipline
- **Colin**, Dolin
- **goblin**, hobgoblin
- Loughlin
- **Joplin**, poplin
- compline •tarpaulin
- **Magdalen**, maudlin
- **bowline**, pangolin
- Ventolin •moulin •Lublin •Brooklyn
- masculine •insulin •globulin
- mullein •Dublin •dunlin •muslin
- kaolin •chamberlain •Michelin
- madeleine •Mary Magdalene
- Gwendolen •francolin •mescaline
- formalin •lanolin
- **adrenalin**, noradrenalin
- crinoline •zeppelin •cipolin
- Carolyn •Jocelyn •porcelain •Ritalin
- Ottoline
- **javelin**, ravelin
- Rosalyn
- **merlin**, purlin
- Dunfermline •purslane

25.17

- **examine**, famine, gamin
- admin •jasmine •Yasmin •Brahmin
- women •specimen •madwomen
- clanswomen •charwomen
- craftswomen •draughtswomen
- gentlewomen •Welshwomen
- Frenchwomen
- **airwomen**, chairwomen
- laywomen •stateswomen

- saleswomen •policewomen
- kinswomen •Englishwomen
- businesswomen •Irishwomen
- congresswomen •countrywomen
- jurywomen •servicewomen
- tribeswomen
- **Scotswomen**, yachtswomen
- forewomen •horsewomen
- sportswomen •oarswomen
- councilwomen •townswomen
- noblewomen •spokeswomen
- frontierswomen •alderwomen
- anchorwomen •washerwomen
- Ulsterwomen •churchwomen
- **catechumen**, illumine, lumen
- bitumen
- **albumen**, albumin
- Duralumin •cumin •Benjamin
- theremin •vitamin
- **determine**, ermine, vermin

25.18

- tannin
- **antivenin**, Lenin
- Kalinin •linen •bedlinen
- underlinen •feminine
- **Cronin**, phone-in, ronin, serotonin
- Bakunin •run-in •melanin •santonin
- crankpin •backspin •hatpin
- tenpin •hairpin •tailspin •wheelspin
- **Crippen**, pippin
- stickpin •kingpin •Crispin •linchpin
- tiepin •topspin •clothespin
- **lupin**, lupine
- pushpin •terrapin •Turpin •Karin
- chagrin •aspirin •Catrin •Kathryn
- Gagarin
- **Erin**, Perrin, serin
- Sanhedrin •epinephrine •dextrin
- brethren •Montenegrin •pyrethrin
- peregrine
- **Corin**, florin, foreign
- doctrine •sovereign •Aldrin
- Paludrine •murrain
- **Kirin**, stearin
- Lohengrin
- **burin**, urine
- tambourin •mandarin •warfarin
- **saccharin**, saccharine

- tamarin •Catherine
- **navarin**, savarin
- culverin •Mazarin

25.19

- assassin •Yeltsin •sasine
- Solzhenitsyn •rebbetzin
- **biomedicine**, medicine
- ceresin
- **ricin**, Terramycin
- **tocsin**, toxin
- Wisconsin •oxytocin •niacin
- moccasin •characin •Capuchin
- **Latin**, satin
- plantain •captain
- **marten**, martin
- cretin
- **pecten**, pectin
- Quentin
- **clandestine**, destine, intestine
- sit-in •quintain •bulletin •chitin
- **Austen**, Mostyn
- **fountain**, mountain
- **gluten**, highfalutin, Rasputin
- **Dustin**, Justin
- biotin •legatine •gelatin •keratin
- **certain**, Curtin
- Kirsten •Gethin •lecithin •Bleddyn
- **Gavin**, ravin, ravine, savin, spavin
- **Alvin**, Calvin
- Marvin
- **Bevin**, Kevin, levin, Previn, replevin
- **kelvin**, Melvin
- riboflavin •covin •Mervyn

25.20

- Gladwin
- **anguine**, sanguine
- Alcuin •Darwin •Tarquin
- **Cledwyn**, Edwin
- penguin
- **Delwyn**, Selwyn
- sequin •Chindwin •Dilwyn
- harlequin
- **Blodwen**, Godwin
- Olwen •Baldwin •Alwyn •Goldwyn
- Goodwin •Irwin •Gershwin

- **muezzin**, resin
- seisin •rosin

25.21

- **align**, assign, benign, brine, chine, cline, combine, condign, confine, consign, dine, divine, dyne, enshrine, entwine, fine, frontline, hardline, interline, intertwine, kine, Klein, line, Main, malign, mine, moline, nine, on-line, opine, outshine, pine, Rhein, Rhine, shine, shrine, sign, sine, spine, spline, stein, Strine, swine, syne, thine, tine, trine, twine, Tyne, underline, undermine, vine, whine, wine
- Sabine •carbine •Holbein •woodbine
- concubine •columbine •turbine
- sardine •Aldine •muscadine
- celandine •anodyne •androgyne

25.22

- catchline •dragline •tramline
- landline •strapline •chatline
- carline
- **breadline**, deadline, headline, redline
- neckline •hemline •helpline
- **airline**, hairline
- saline •mainline
- **baseline**, bassline, waistline
- dateline
- **beeline**, feline, treeline
- streamline •slimline •sibylline
- Adeline •bodyline •storyline
- Catiline •aquiline
- **byline**, skyline
- **guideline**, sideline, tideline
- lifeline •pipeline •sight line •hotline
- **jawline**, Pauline, shoreline
- outline
- **snowline**, towline
- coastline •clothesline •microcline
- Fräulein •Ursuline •touchline
- bloodline •plumb line •punchline
- buntline •timberline •borderline
- underline •alkaline •opaline
- Caroline •coralline •crystalline

- waterline • landmine • carmine
- goldmine

> Try rhyming one word with a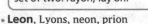
> set of two: goldmine, sold mine.

- calamine • melamine

25.23

- canine • asinine • leonine • saturnine
- Antonine • pavonine • rapine
- **alpine**, cisalpine
- pitchpine • orpine
- **lupine**, supine
- porcupine • vulpine • salamandrine
- alexandrine • sapphirine • taurine
- endocrine • aventurine • vulturine
- colubrine • lacustrine • estuarine
- viperine • passerine • catarrhine
- **intrauterine**, uterine
- adulterine • riverine • ensign
- **internecine**, V-sign
- piscine • porcine • cosine • thylacine
- countersign
- **hircine**, ursine
- shoeshine • moonshine • sunshine
- earthshine
- **adamantine**, Byzantine, elephantine
- Tridentine • Levantine • Bechstein
- Epstein • amethystine • Rubinstein
- Frankenstein • Palestine • Philistine
- turpentine • Einstein • Eisenstein
- **cispontine**, transpontine
- serotine • infantine • Wittgenstein
- Argentine • Palatine
- **Ballantyne**, valentine
- eglantine • Hammerstein
- clementine • vespertine • serpentine
- Florentine
- **Lichtenstein**, Liechtenstein
- Constantine • nemertine • Bernstein
- **hyacinthine**, labyrinthine
- Jugurthine • grapevine • bovine
- Glühwein • cervine • equine

25.24

- **aide-de-camp**, aides-de-camp, anon,

Asunción, au courant, begone, Bonn, bon vivant, Caen, Canton, Carcassonne, Ceylon, chaconne, chateaubriand, ci-devant, Colón, colon, Concepción, con (*US* conn), cretonne, don, Duchamp, Evonne, foregone, fromage blanc, Gabon, Garonne, gone, guenon, hereupon, Inchon, Jean, john, Jon, Le Mans, León, Luzon, Mont Blanc, Narbonne, odds-on, on, outgone, outshone, Perón, phon, piñon, Pinot Blanc, plafond, Ramón, Saigon, Saint-Saëns, Sand, Schwann, scone, shone, side-on, sine qua non, Sorbonne, spot-on, swan, thereon, thereupon, ton, Toulon, undergone, upon, Villon, wan, whereon, whereupon, won, wonton, yon, Yvonne
- **crayon**, rayon

> Try rhyming one word with a [i]
> set of two: rayon, lay on.

- **Leon**, Lyons, neon, prion
- Ceredigion • Mabinogion • nucleon
- Amiens • dupion • parathion
- Laocoon
- **gluon**, Rouen
- bon-bon • Audubon

25.25

- radon • Chalcedon • Proudhon
- Mogadon • pteranodon • iguanodon
- mastodon • chiffon • Ctesiphon
- bouffant • balafon • Xenophon
- Bellerophon
- **argon**, Sargon
- Dagon • woebegone • bygone
- **doggone**, logon
- dodecagon • Dijon • demijohn • ancon
- archon • racon • Comecon • emoticon
- stereopticon • icon • walk-on • neocon
- Yukon • zircon • salon • Fablon
- decathlon • Teflon • Dralon • Simplon
- Babylon • papillon • propylon
- epsilon • nylon • Orlon
- **eidolon**, roll-on, Solon
- mouflon • Ascalon • Ashqelon

- echelon • Avalon
- **gnomon**, Jomon

25.26

- **Agamemnon**, Memnon
- **ninon**, xenon
- noumenon • Trianon • xoanon
- organon • Simenon • Maintenon
- **crampon**, kampong, tampon
- Nippon • coupon
- **Akron**, Dacron, macron
- electron • natron • Hebron • positron
- Heilbronn • micron
- **boron**, moron, oxymoron
- neutron • interferon
- **fleuron**, Huron, neuron
- Oberon • mellotron • aileron
- cyclotron • Percheron • Mitterrand
- vigneron • croissant • Maupassant
- garçon • Cartier-Bresson • exon
- frisson • Oxon • chanson • Tucson
- soupçon • Aubusson • Besançon
- penchant • torchon • cabochon
- **Anton**, canton, Danton
- lepton
- **piton**, Teton
- krypton • feuilleton • magneton
- chiton
- **photon**, proton
- **croûton**, futon
- eschaton • peloton • contretemps
- telethon
- **talkathon**, walkathon
- Avon • tableau vivant • vol-au-vent

25.27

- par avion • Messiaen
- **chignon**, filet mignon
- Avignon • Sauvignon • Semillon
- Roussillon • sabayon
- **demi-pension**, pension
- **bouillon**, court-bouillon
- K-meson • soi-disant • blouson

25.28

- **adorn**, born, borne, bourn, Braun,
brawn, corn, dawn, drawn, faun,
fawn, forborne, forewarn, forlorn,
freeborn, horn, lawn, lorn, morn,
mourn, newborn, Norn, outworn,
pawn, porn, prawn, Quorn, sawn,
scorn, Sean, shorn, spawn, suborn,
sworn, thorn, thrawn, torn,
Vaughan, warn, withdrawn, worn,
yawn

> Create extra rhymes by   ⓘ
> adding -ing to words like dawn
> and fawn.

- airborne • Ayckbourn • seaborne
- Eastbourne • stillborn • highborn
- Osborne • winterbourne
- waterborne • firstborn • Apeldoorn
- althorn • hartshorn • leghorn
- greenhorn • bighorn • inkhorn
- tinhorn • foghorn • longhorn
- shorthorn • shoehorn • Flügelhorn
- bullhorn • alpenhorn • Matterhorn
- acorn • seedcorn • sweetcorn
- barleycorn • unicorn • Capricorn
- leprechaun • tricorne • einkorn
- popcorn • Runcorn • peppercorn
- lovelorn • frogspawn • wire-drawn
- wartorn • blackthorn • hawthorn
- careworn • time-worn • shopworn
- toilworn

25.29

- **brown**, Browne, clown, crown,
down, downtown, drown, frown,
gown, low-down, noun, renown,
run-down, town, upside-down,
uptown
- crackdown • clampdown • Ashdown
- markdown • letdown • meltdown
- **breakdown**, shakedown, takedown
- kick-down • thistledown • sit-down
- climbdown • countdown
- Southdown
- **godown**, hoedown, showdown,
slowdown
- put-down • touchdown • tumbledown
- comedown
- **rundown**, sundown
- shutdown • eiderdown • nightgown

When a rhyme is formed using words within a line rather than at the end of lines, it is called a *medial* (or *internal*) *rhyme*. The particular kind shown here is known as a *leonine rhyme*, a type of *medial rhyme* in which the rhymes occur between the mid- and end-words of the same line; it can, as in this poem by Blake, have a dramatic linking effect:

And Priests in black gowns were walking their rounds,
And binding with briars my joys and desires.

(William Blake, 'The Garden of Love')

- pronoun - Jamestown - Freetown
- midtown - Bridgetown - Kingstown
- shanty town - Georgetown - Motown
- hometown - toytown - Newtown
- Charlottetown - Chinatown

25.30

- **alone**, atone, Beaune, bemoan, blown, bone, Capone, clone, Cohn, Cologne, condone, cone, co-own, crone, drone, enthrone, flown, foreknown, foreshown, groan, grown, half-tone, home-grown, hone, Joan, known, leone, loan, lone, moan, Mon, mown, ochone, outflown, outgrown, own, phone, pone, prone, Rhône, roan, rone, sewn, shown, Simone, Sloane, Soane, sone, sown, stone, strown, throne, thrown, tone, trombone, Tyrone, unbeknown, undersown, zone

> **i**
> Create extra rhymes for words like alone by adding -n to words like blow and sew (see section 9.1).

- Dione - backbone - hambone
- breastbone - aitchbone
- **tail bone**, whalebone
- cheekbone - shin bone - hip bone
- wishbone - splint bone - herringbone
- thigh bone - jawbone - marrowbone
- knuckle bone - collarbone
- methadone - headphone - cellphone
- heckelphone - payphone - Freefone
- **radio-telephone**, telephone
- videophone - francophone
- megaphone - speakerphone

- allophone - Anglophone - xylophone
- gramophone - homophone
- vibraphone - microphone
- saxophone - answerphone
- dictaphone
- **sarrusophone**, sousaphone
- silicone - pine cone - snow cone
- flyblown - cyclone - violone
- hormone - pheromone - Oenone
- chaperone - progesterone
- testosterone

25.31

- **flagstone**, ragstone
- **Blackstone**, jackstone
- sandstone - capstone - hearthstone
- headstone - gemstone - whetstone
- hailstone - gravestone
- **freestone**, keystone
- greenstone - Wheatstone
- Tinseltown - ringtone - pitchstone
- millstone - whinstone - siltstone
- holystone - semitone
- stepping stone - coping stone
- baritone - acetone - dulcitone
- tritone - drystone - milestone
- limestone
- **grindstone**, rhinestone
- cobblestone - gallstone - brownstone
- lodestone - soapstone - duotone
- microtone - bluestone - tombstone
- moonstone - touchstone
- **bloodstone**, mudstone
- sunstone - ironstone - undertone
- monotone - cornerstone
- Silverstone - overtone
- **kerbstone** (*US* curbstone)
- turnstone

- birthstone • flavone • endzone
- cortisone • ozone

25.32

- **adjoin**, Boulogne, coign, coin, conjoin, Des Moines, Dordogne, enjoin, groin, groyne, join, loin, purloin, quoin, subjoin
- Burgoyne • Gascogne • tenderloin
- sirloin • talapoin

25.33

- **afternoon**, attune, autoimmune, baboon, balloon, bassoon, bestrewn, boon, Boone, bridoon, buffoon, Cameroon, Cancún, cardoon, cartoon, Changchun, cocoon, commune, croon, doubloon, dragoon, dune, festoon, galloon, goon, harpoon, hoon, immune, importune, impugn, Irgun, jejune, June, Kowloon, lagoon, lampoon, loon, macaroon, maroon, monsoon, moon, Muldoon, noon, oppugn, picayune, platoon, poltroon, pontoon, poon, prune, puccoon, raccoon, Rangoon, ratoon, rigadoon, rune, saloon, Saskatoon, Sassoon, Scone, soon, spittoon, spoon, swoon, Troon, tune, tycoon, typhoon, Walloon
- **fortune**, misfortune
- vodun • veldskoen • honeymoon
- forenoon • tablespoon • teaspoon
- soupspoon • dessertspoon • Neptune
- tribune • triune • opportune

25.34

- Gudrun

25.35

- **begun**, bun, done, Donne, dun, fine-spun, forerun, fun, gun, Gunn, hon, Hun, none, nun, one, one-to-one, outdone, outgun, outrun, pun, run, shun, son, spun, stun, sun, ton, tonne, tun, underdone, Verdun, won

> Create extra rhymes by changing words like gun to gunning. [i]

- honeybun • handgun • flashgun
- air gun • sixgun • popgun • shotgun
- **blowgun**, shogun
- speargun • scattergun • homespun
- endrun • sheep run • grandson
- stepson • godson • kiloton • megaton
- anyone • everyone • someone

> Try rhyming one word with a set of two: someone, become one. [i]

25.36

- **Eritrean**, Ghanaian, Himalayan, Malayan, Tigrayan
- **Actaeon**, Aegean, aeon (*US* eon), Augean, Behan, Cadmean, Caribbean, Carolean, Chaldean, Cyclopean, empyrean, epicurean,

---

The use of past participles in an *aaaa...* pattern at the end of each line in this sonnet lends it an odd relentlessness. This is an example of *wrenched monorhyme*:

WILD, wild the storm, and the sea high running,
Steady the roar of the gale, with incessant undertone muttering,
Shouts of demoniac laughter fitfully piercing and pealing,
Waves, air, midnight, their savagest trinity lashing,

(Walt Whitman, 'Patroling Barnegat')

These four lines from John Donne's poem 'The Sun Rising' use a *rhyming pattern* (or rhyme scheme) known as *arch-rhyme* (*abba*):

> BUSY old fool, unruly Sun,
>   Why dost thou thus,
> Through windows, and through curtains, call on us?
> Must to thy motions lovers' seasons run?

(John Donne, 'The Sun Rising')

European, Fijian, Galilean, Hasmonean, Hebridean, Herculean, Ian, Jacobean, Kampuchean, Laodicean, lien, Linnaean (*US* Linnean), Maccabean, Mandaean (*US* Mandean), Medicean, monogenean, Nabataean (*US* Nabatean), Orphean, paean, paeon, pean, peon, Periclean, piscean, plebeian, Pyrenean, Pythagorean, Sabaean, Sadducean, Sisyphean, skean, Tanzanian, Tennesseean, Terpsichorean, theodicean, Tyrolean

25.37

- **antipodean**, Crimean, Judaean, Korean
- Albion
- **Gambian**, Zambian
- lesbian
- **Arabian**, Bessarabian, Fabian, gabion, Sabian, Swabian
- **amphibian**, Libyan, Namibian
- Sorbian
- **Danubian**, Nubian
- Colombian • Serbian • Nietzschean
- **Chadian**, Trinidadian
- **Andean**, Kandyan
- guardian
- **Acadian**, Akkadian, Arcadian, Barbadian, Canadian, circadian, Grenadian, Hadean, Orcadian, Palladian, radian, steradian
- **Archimedean**, comedian, epicedian, median, tragedian
- **ascidian**, Derridean, Dravidian, enchiridion, Euclidean, Floridian, Gideon, Lydian, meridian, Numidian,

obsidian, Pisidian, quotidian, viridian
- **Amerindian**, Indian
- **accordion**, Edwardian
- **Cambodian**, collodion, custodian, melodeon, nickelodeon, Odeon
- Freudian • Bermudian • Burundian
- Burgundian
- **Falstaffian**, Halafian
- **Christadelphian**, Delphian, Philadelphian
- nymphean • ruffian • Brobdingnagian
- Carolingian • Swedenborgian
- **logion**, Muskogean
- Jungian
- **magian**, Pelagian
- collegian
- **callipygian**, Cantabrigian, Phrygian, Stygian
- Merovingian • philologian • Fujian
- Czechoslovakian • Pickwickian
- Algonquian • Chomskian
- Kentuckian
- **battalion**, galleon, medallion, rapscallion, scallion
- **Anglian**, ganglion
- Heraklion
- **Dalian**, Malian, Somalian
- **Chellean**, Machiavellian, Orwellian, Sabellian, Trevelyan, triskelion
- Wesleyan
- **alien**, Australian, bacchanalian, Castalian, Deucalion, episcopalian, Hegelian, madrigalian, mammalian, Pygmalion, Salian, saturnalian, sesquipedalian, tatterdemalion, Thessalian, Westphalian
- **anthelion**, Aristotelian, Aurelian, carnelian, chameleon, Karelian, Mendelian, Mephistophelian, Pelion, Sahelian

- **Abbevillian**, Azilian, Brazilian, caecilian, Castilian, Chilean, Churchillian, civilian, cotillion, crocodilian, epyllion, Gillian, Lilian, Maximilian, Pamphylian, pavilion, postilion, Quintilian, reptilian, Sicilian, Tamilian, vaudevillian, vermilion, Virgilian
- **Aeolian**, Anatolian, Eolian, Jolyon, Mongolian, napoleon, simoleon
- **Acheulian**, Boolean, cerulean, Friulian, Julian, Julien
- bullion
- **mullion**, scullion, Tertullian
- Liverpudlian
- **Bahamian**, Bamian, Damian, Mesopotamian, Samian
- **anthemion**, Bohemian
- **Endymion**, prosimian, Simeon, simian
- isthmian • antinomian
- **Permian**, vermian
- Oceanian
- **Albanian**, Azanian, Iranian, Jordanian, Lithuanian, Mauritanian, Mediterranean, Panamanian, Pennsylvanian, Pomeranian, Romanian, Ruritanian, Sassanian, subterranean, Tasmanian, Transylvanian, Tripolitanian, Turanian, Ukrainian, Vulcanian
- **Armenian**, Athenian, Fenian, Magdalenian, Mycenaean (US Mycenean), Slovenian, Tyrrhenian
- **Argentinian**, Arminian, Augustinian, Carthaginian, Darwinian, dominion, Guinean, Justinian, Ninian, Palestinian, Sardinian, Virginian
- **epilimnion**, hypolimnion
- Bosnian
- **Bornean**, Californian, Capricornian
- **Aberdonian**, Amazonian, Apollonian, Babylonian, Baconian, Bostonian, Caledonian, Catalonian, Chalcedonian, Ciceronian, Devonian, draconian, Estonian, Etonian, gorgonian, Ionian, Johnsonian, Laconian, Macedonian, Miltonian, Newtonian, Oregonian, Oxonian, Patagonian, Plutonian, Tennysonian, Tobagonian, Washingtonian
- **Cameroonian**, communion, Mancunian, Neptunian, Réunion, union
- **Hibernian**, Saturnian
- **Campion**, champion, Grampian, rampion, tampion
- thespian • Mississippian • Olympian
- Crispian
- **Scorpian**, scorpion
- **cornucopian**, dystopian, Ethiopian, Salopian, subtopian, Utopian
- Guadeloupian
- **Carian**, carrion, clarion, Marian
- **Calabrian**, Cantabrian
- Cambrian • Bactrian
- **Lancastrian**, Zoroastrian
- Alexandrian • Maharashtrian
- **equestrian**, pedestrian
- **agrarian**, antiquarian, apiarian, Aquarian, Arian, Aryan, authoritarian, barbarian, Bavarian, Bulgarian, Caesarean (US Cesarean), centenarian, communitarian, contrarian, Darien, disciplinarian, egalitarian, equalitarian, establishmentarian, fruitarian, Gibraltarian, grammarian, Hanoverian, humanitarian, Hungarian, latitudinarian, libertarian, librarian, majoritarian, millenarian, necessarian, necessitarian, nonagenarian, octogenarian, ovarian, Parian, parliamentarian, planarian, predestinarian, prelapsarian, proletarian, quadragenarian, quinquagenarian, quodlibetarian, Rastafarian, riparian, rosarian, Rotarian, sabbatarian, Sagittarian, sanitarian, Sauveterrian, sectarian, seminarian, septuagenarian, sexagenarian, topiarian, totalitarian, Trinitarian, ubiquitarian, Unitarian, utilitarian, valetudinarian, vegetarian, veterinarian, vulgarian
- **Adrian**, Hadrian
- **Assyrian**, Illyrian, Syrian, Tyrian
- morion • Austrian

- **Dorian**, Ecuadorean, historian, Hyperborean, Nestorian, oratorian, praetorian (*US* pretorian), salutatorian, Salvadorean, Singaporean, stentorian, Taurean, valedictorian, Victorian
- Ugrian • Zarathustrian
- **Cumbrian**, Northumbrian, Umbrian
- **Algerian**, Cancerian, Chaucerian, Cimmerian, criterion, Hesperian, Hitlerian, Hyperion, Iberian, Liberian, Nigerian, Presbyterian, Shakespearean, Siberian, Spenserian, Sumerian, valerian, Wagnerian, Zairean
- **Arthurian**, Ben-Gurion, centurion, durian, holothurian, Khachaturian, Ligurian, Missourian, Silurian, tellurian
- **Circassian**, Parnassian
- halcyon • Capsian • Hessian
- **Albigensian**, Waldensian
- Dacian • Keatsian
- **Cilician**, Galician, Lycian, Mysian, Odyssean
- Leibnizian • Piscean • Ossian
- Gaussian • Joycean • Andalusian
- Mercian • Appalachian • Decian
- **Ordovician**, Priscian
- Lucian
- **himation**, Montserratian
- **Atlantean**, Dantean, Kantian
- **bastion**, Erastian, Sebastian
- Mozartian • Brechtian • Thyestean
- Fortean • Faustian • protean
- Djiboutian
- **fustian**, Procrustean
- **Gilbertian**, Goethean, nemertean
- pantheon
- **Hogarthian**, Parthian
- **Lethean**, Promethean
- Pythian • Corinthian • Scythian
- **Lothian**, Midlothian
- Latvian • Yugoslavian
- **avian**, Batavian, Flavian, Moldavian, Moravian, Octavian, Scandinavian, Shavian
- **Bolivian**, Maldivian, oblivion, Vivian
- **Chekhovian**, Harrovian, Jovian, Pavlovian

- **alluvion**, antediluvian, diluvian, Peruvian
- Servian • Malawian • Zimbabwean
- Abkhazian • Dickensian
- **Caucasian**, Malaysian, Rabelaisian
- Keynesian
- **Belizean**, Cartesian, Indonesian, Milesian, Salesian, Silesian
- **Elysian**, Frisian, Parisian, Tunisian
- Holmesian
- **Carthusian**, Malthusian, Venusian

25.38

- **Brian**, cyan, Gaian, Geminian, Hawaiian, ion, iron, Ixion, lion, Lyon, Mayan, Narayan, O'Brien, Orion, Paraguayan, prion, Ryan, scion, Uruguayan, Zion
- andiron
- **gridiron**, midiron
- dandelion • anion • Bruneian
- **cation**, flatiron
- **gowan**, Palawan, rowen
- **anthozoan**, bryozoan, Goan, hydrozoan, Minoan, protozoan, protozoon, rowan, Samoan, spermatozoon
- Ohioan • Chicagoan • Virgoan
- Idahoan
- **doyen**, Illinoisan, Iroquoian
- **Ewan**, Labuan, McEwan, McLuhan, Siouan
- Saskatchewan • Papuan • Paduan
- Nicaraguan • gargantuan
- **carbon**, chlorofluorocarbon, graben, hydrocarbon, Laban, radiocarbon
- ebon • Melbourne • Theban
- **gibbon**, ribbon
- **Brisbane**, Lisbon
- Tyburn
- **auburn**, Bourbon
- Alban • Manitoban • Cuban
- stubborn
- **Durban**, exurban, suburban, turban, urban

25.39

- **congestion**, digestion, ingestion,

question, suggestion
- richen •Chibchan
- **Christian**, unchristian
- exhaustion
- **escutcheon**, scutcheon
- combustion •birchen

25.40

- **Abaddon**, gladden, gladdon, Ibadan, madden, sadden
- **abandon**, Brandon, Rwandan, Ugandan
- **Baden**, Baden-Baden, Coloradan, garden, harden, lardon, Nevadan, pardon
- Wiesbaden •bear garden
- tea garden
- **Armageddon**, deaden, leaden, redden
- **Eldon**, Sheldon
- **Brendan**, tendon
- Dresden
- **Aden**, Aidan, Haydn, laden, maiden
- handmaiden
- **cedarn**, cotyledon, dicotyledon, Eden, monocotyledon, Sweden
- wealden
- **bestridden**, forbidden, hidden, midden, outridden, ridden, stridden, unbidden
- Wimbledon
- **linden**, Lindon, Swindon
- Wisden •Mohammedan •Myrmidon
- harridan •hagridden •Sheridan
- bedridden •Macedon •Huntingdon
- **Dryden**, guidon, Leiden, Poseidon, Sidon, widen
- **Culloden**, hodden, modern, sodden, trodden
- Cobden •downtrodden
- **Auden**, broaden, cordon, Gordon, Hordern, Jordan, warden
- churchwarden •louden •bounden
- **loden**, Snowdon
- **beholden**, embolden, golden, olden
- hoyden •Bermudan •wooden
- Mukden •gulden •sudden
- **Blunden**, London
- Riordan •bourdon •bombardon

- celadon •Clarendon
- **burden**, guerdon

25.41

- deafen
- **griffon**, stiffen
- antiphon
- **hyphen**, siphon
- **often**, soften
- orphan •ibuprofen
- **roughen**, toughen
- colophon
- **dragon**, flagon, lagan, pendragon, wagon
- snapdragon •bandwagon •jargon
- Megan
- **Copenhagen**, pagan, Reagan
- Nijmegen
- **Antiguan**, Egan, Keegan, Regan, vegan
- Wigan •cardigan •Milligan •polygon
- hooligan •mulligan •ptarmigan
- Branigan •Oregon •Michigan
- Rattigan
- **tigon**, trigon
- toboggan
- **Glamorgan**, gorgon, Morgan, morgen, organ
- **Brogan**, hogan, Logan, slogan
- Cadogan •decagon
- **Aragon**, paragon, tarragon
- hexagon •pentagon •heptagon
- octagon •Bergen •Spitsbergen

25.42

- **abrasion**, Australasian, equation, Eurasian, evasion, invasion, occasion, persuasion, pervasion, suasion, Vespasian
- **adhesion**, cohesion, Friesian, lesion
- **circumcision**, collision, concision, decision, derision, division, elision, envision, excision, imprecision, incision, misprision, precisian, precision, provision, scission, vision
- subdivision •television •Eurovision

- LaserVision
- **corrosion**, eclosion, erosion, explosion, implosion
- **allusion**, collusion, conclusion, confusion, contusion, delusion, diffusion, effusion, exclusion, extrusion, fusion, illusion, inclusion, interfusion, intrusion, obtrusion, occlusion, preclusion, profusion, prolusion, protrusion, reclusion, seclusion, suffusion, transfusion
- Monaghan • Belgian
- **Bajan**, Cajun, contagion, Trajan
- **Glaswegian**, legion, Norwegian, region
- **irreligion**, religion
- Injun • Harijan • oxygen • antigen
- sojourn • donjon • Georgian
- **theologian**, Trojan
- Rügen
- **bludgeon**, curmudgeon, dudgeon, gudgeon, trudgen
- dungeon • glycogen • halogen
- collagen • Imogen • carcinogen
- hallucinogen • androgen
- **oestrogen** (US estrogen)
- hydrogen • nitrogen
- **burgeon**, sturgeon, surgeon

25.43

- **blacken**, bracken, slacken
- Sri Lankan
- **Alaskan**, Gascon, Madagascan, Nebraskan
- **Aachen**, darken, hearken, kraken, Marcan, Petrarchan
- Interlaken
- **beckon**, Deccan, pekan, reckon
- Mencken
- **awaken**, bacon, betaken, forsaken, Jamaican, mistaken, partaken, shaken, taken, waken
- godforsaken
- **archdeacon**, beacon, Costa Rican, deacon, Dominican, Mohican, Mozambican, Puerto Rican, weaken
- **quicken**, sicken, stricken, thicken, Wiccan
- silken
- **Incan**, Lincoln

- **brisken**, Franciscan
- barbican • Rubicon • Gallican
- Anglican
- **Helicon**, pelican
- **basilican**, Millikan, silicon
- publican • pantechnicon • Copernican
- African • American • hurricane
- **lexicon**, Mexican
- Corsican • Vatican • liken
- **Brocken**, Moroccan
- **falcon**, Lorcan, Majorcan, Minorcan
- **Balcon**, Balkan
- gyrfalcon
- **awoken**, bespoken, betoken, broken, foretoken, oaken, outspoken, plain-spoken, ryokan, spoken, token, woken
- heartbroken
- **Lucan**, toucan
- Saarbrücken • Buchan • Vulcan
- **drunken**, Duncan, shrunken, sunken
- **Etruscan**, molluscan (US molluskan), Tuscan
- Ardnamurchan • lochan

25.44

- **Alan**, gallon, talon
- raglan
- **biathlon**, heptathlon, pentathlon, tetrathlon, triathlon
- **Guatemalan**, Marlon
- **Ellen**, felon, Magellan, Mellon, melon
- Veblen • Declan • watermelon
- Venezuelan • Elan
- **Anguillan**, Dillon, Dylan, kiln, Macmillan, Milne, villain
- limekiln • abutilon
- **pylon**, upsilon
- **Hohenzollern**, pollan, pollen, Stollen
- Lachlan
- **befallen**, fallen
- chapfallen • crestfallen
- **Angolan**, colon, Nolan, semicolon, stolen, swollen
- kulan
- **woollen** (US woolen)

- sullen • myrobalan • gonfalon
- castellan
- **ortolan**, portolan
- **Köln**, merlon

25.45

- **Alabaman**, Amman, Ammon, Drammen, gammon, Mammon, salmon
- **Bradman**, Caedmon, madman, madmen
- **flagman**, flagmen
- **trackman**, trackmen
- **hangman**, hangmen
- **chapman**, chapmen
- **cragsman**, cragsmen
- **cracksman**, cracksmen, Flaxman
- **batsman**, batsmen
- **batman**, batmen
- Tasman
- **clansman**, clansmen, Klansman, Klansmen, landsman, landsmen
- backgammon
- **barman**, barmen, Brahman, Carman, Carmen, shaman, Sharman, Tutankhamen
- **craftsman**, craftsmen, draftsman, draftsmen, draughtsman, draughtsmen, raftsman, raftsmen
- **marksman**, marksmen
- atman
- **guardsman**, guardsmen
- **leman**, Lemmon, lemon, Yemen
- **headman**, headmen, Stedman
- Beckmann
- **bellman**, bellmen, Hellman
- **gentleman**, gentlemen
- **penman**, penmen
- Helpmann
- **pressman**, pressmen
- **freshman**, freshmen
- **Welshman**, Welshmen
- **Frenchman**, Frenchmen, henchman, henchmen
- desman
- **headsman**, headsmen
- **helmsman**, helmsmen
- **lensman**, lensmen
- **airman**, airmen, chairman, chairmen
- **Bremen**, caiman, Damon, Eamon, layman, laymen, stamen

- **railman**, railmen
- **brakesman**, brakesmen
- **statesman**, statesmen
- **tradesman**, tradesmen
- **salesman**, salesmen
- **gamesman**, gamesmen
- **plainsman**, plainsmen
- **railwayman**, railwaymen
- **highwayman**, highwaymen
- **cacodemon**, daemon, demon, Freeman, freemen, Philemon, Riemann, Schliemann, seaman, seamen, semen
- Friedman
- **liegeman**, liegemen
- **Eastman**, policeman, policemen
- **beadsman**, beadsmen, seedsman, seedsmen
- **fieldsman**, fieldsmen
- **wheelsman**, wheelsmen
- **persimmon**, Rimmon
- **pitchman**, pitchmen
- Bridgman • milkman • Hillman
- **signalman**, signalmen
- Lippmann
- **pitman**, pitmen, Whitman
- **guildsman**, guildsmen
- **kinsman**, kinsmen
- Betjeman • regimen
- **clergyman**, clergymen
- **tallyman**, tallymen
- talisman
- **Englishman**, Englishmen
- **businessman**, businessmen
- **Cornishman**, Cornishmen
- **journeyman**, journeymen
- **cavalryman**, cavalrymen
- **ferryman**, ferrymen
- **vestryman**, vestrymen
- **dairyman**, dairymen
- **Irishman**, Irishmen
- **quarryman**, quarrymen
- **Orangeman**, Orangemen
- **congressman**, congressmen
- **countryman**, countrymen
- **infantryman**, infantrymen
- **nurseryman**, nurserymen
- **liveryman**, liverymen
- **midshipman**, midshipmen
- **harvestman**, harvestmen
- **serviceman**, servicemen

- **Hyman**, Simon
- Eichmann
- **rifleman**, riflemen
- **Feynman**, lineman, linemen
- Weismann •Wiseman
- **tribesman**, tribesmen
- **linesman**, linesmen
- **exciseman**, excisemen
- **common**, Roscommon
- **watchman**, watchmen
- **Godman**, hodman, hodmen
- Hoffman
- **frogman**, frogmen
- **stockman**, stockmen
- **dolman**, dolmen
- **Scotsman**, Scotsmen, yachtsman, yachtsmen
- Boltzmann •Cotman
- **bondsman**, bondsmen
- **Bormann**, doorman, doormen, foreman, foremen, Mormon, Norman, storeman, storemen
- Kauffmann •Walkman
- **horseman**, horsemen, Norseman, Norsemen
- **sportsman**, sportsmen
- **oarsman**, oarsmen, outdoorsman, outdoorsmen
- swordsman
- **longshoreman**, longshoremen
- **bowmen**, cowman, cowmen, ploughman (*US* plowman), ploughmen (*US* plowmen)
- **councilman**, councilmen
- Hauptmann •Housman
- **groundsman**, groundsmen, roundsman, roundsmen, townsman, townsmen
- **warehouseman**, warehousemen
- **Bowman**, Oklahoman, Oman, omen, Roman, showman, showmen, yeoman, yeomen
- **coachman**, coachmen
- **Coleman**, Goldman
- **nobleman**, noblemen
- **postman**, postmen
- **spokesman**, spokesmen
- **boatman**, boatmen
- **lifeboatman**, lifeboatmen
- dragoman
- **crewman**, crewmen, energumen,

human, ichneumon, Newman, numen, Schumann, subhuman, Trueman
- woman
- **woodman**, woodmen
- **bookman**, bookmen
- Pullman
- **Bushman**, Bushmen
- **footman**, footmen
- **woodsman**, woodsmen
- **ombudsman**, ombudsmen
- clanswoman
- **backwoodsman**, backwoodsmen
- charwoman
- **craftswoman**, draughtswoman
- gentlewoman •Welshwoman
- Frenchwoman
- **airwoman**, chairwoman
- laywoman •stateswoman
- saleswoman •policewoman
- kinswoman •Englishwoman
- businesswoman •Irishwoman
- congresswoman •countrywoman
- jurywoman •servicewoman
- tribeswoman
- **Scotswoman**, yachtswoman
- forewoman •horsewoman
- sportswoman •oarswoman
- townswoman •spokeswoman
- Dutchwoman •frontierswoman
- alderwoman •anchorwoman
- washerwoman •Ulsterwoman
- churchwoman •acumen •summon
- **Dutchman**, Dutchmen
- **gunman**, gunmen
- **busman**, busmen, dustman, dustmen
- **huntsman**, huntsmen
- Newcomen •Layamon
- **privateersman**, privateersmen, steersman, steersmen
- **frontiersman**, frontiersmen
- fireman •Dobermann •lumbermen
- abdomen •Omdurman
- **alderman**, aldermen
- Turkoman
- **cellarman**, cellarmen, telamon
- cyclamen
- **Highlandman**, Highlandmen
- Solomon •trawlerman •cinnamon
- **Chinaman**, Chinamen

> **The tension between *full rhymes*
> and *half-rhymes* offers scope to
> play with language and
> pronunciation. In 'It Ain't
> Necessarily So', achieving a *full
> rhyme* depends on distorting the
> pronunciation of the second
> word, called a *wrenched rhyme*:**
>
> Oh Jonah, he lived in de whale
> Fo' he made his home in
> Dat fish's abdomen
> Oh Jonah, he lived in de whale
>
> (George and Ira Gershwin, 'It Ain't
> Necessarily So')

- **trencherman**, trenchermen
- **fisherman**, fishermen, militiaman, militiamen
- **washerman**, washermen
- ottoman
- **waterman**, watermen
- **Ulsterman**, Ulstermen
- **Burman**, firman, German, Herman, sermon, Sherman
- **churchman**, churchmen
- **turfman**, turfmen
- Bergman
- **kirkman**, kirkmen, workman, workmen
- Perelman
- **herdsman**, herdsmen

25.46

- **Buchanan**, cannon, canon, colcannon, Louisianan, Montanan, Rhiannon, Shannon
- Botswanan
- **Lennon**, pennon, tenon
- Canaan
- **Burkinan**, Henan
- finnan
- **phenomenon**, prolegomenon
- Parthenon
- **Arizonan**, Conan, Ronan
- Lebanon • Algernon • Vernon
- Groningen • Vlissingen
- **Tongan**, wrong'un

- cap'n, happen
- **dampen**, lampern
- aspen
- **parpen**, sharpen, tarpon
- weapon • hempen
- **capon**, misshapen
- **cheapen**, deepen, steepen
- tympan • ripen • saucepan • open
- lumpen

25.47

- **Aran**, Arran, baron, barren, Darren, Karen, Sharon, yarran
- **Biafran**, saffron
- plastron • Saharan • Sumatran
- **heron**, perron
- rhododendron • chevron
- **Aaron**, Charon, Dáil Eireann
- apron
- **matron**, patron
- Libran
- **decahedron**, dodecahedron, octahedron, polyhedron, tetrahedron
- children • citron • grandchildren
- stepchildren • godchildren
- schoolchildren
- **Byron**, Chiron, environ, Myron, siren
- **sporran**, warren
- squadron • Cochran
- **Andorran**, Doran, Lauren, loran
- cauldron
- **Kieran**, Madeiran, schlieren
- **Honduran**, Van Buren
- Aldebaran • Auberon • Acheron
- **Cameron**, Decameron
- **cateran**, Lateran
- veteran
- **dipteran**, hemipteran
- lepidopteran • Lutheran

25.48

- Masson
- **flaxen**, Jackson, klaxon, Sachsen, Saxon, waxen
- Samson
- **Branson**, Jansen, Manson, Nansen

- **arson**, Carson, fasten, parson, sarsen
- **Bresson**, delicatessen, Essen, lessen, lesson
- Texan
- **Belsen**, keelson, Nelson
- Mendelssohn • Empson
- **Benson**, ensign
- Stetson
- **basin**, caisson, chasten, diapason, hasten, Jason, mason
- Bateson • handbasin • washbasin
- Freemason • stonemason • Nielsen
- Stevenson
- **christen**, glisten, listen
- **Gibson**, Ibsen
- **Blixen**, Nixon, vixen
- **Nilsson**, Stillson, Wilson
- Nicholson • Simpson • Whitsun
- Robinson • Acheson
- **Addison**, Madison
- Edison

> Try rhyming one word with a [i] set of two or more: Edison, fed his son.

- Atkinson • Dickinson • Alison
- **Tennyson**, venison
- unison
- **caparison**, comparison, garrison, Harrison
- Ericsson • Morrison
- **archdiocesan**, diocesan
- jettison • Davisson
- **bison**, Meissen, Tyson
- Michelson • Robson
- **coxswain**, oxen
- **Mommsen**, Thompson
- **Johnson**, Jonson, sponson, Swanson
- Watson
- **coarsen**, hoarsen, Orson
- **boatswain**, bosun
- Robeson • Jolson • moisten • loosen
- Wolfson • Cookson • Hudson
- Bunsen • tutsan
- **Grierson**, Pearson
- Culbertson • Richardson • Anderson
- Jefferson • Ferguson • Rowlandson
- Amundsen • Emerson • Jespersen
- Saracen • Peterson • Williamson
- **person**, worsen
- Bergson • chairperson • layperson
- salesperson • sportsperson
- spokesperson

25.49

- **ashen**, fashion, passion, ration
- **abstraction**, action, attraction, benefaction, compaction, contraction, counteraction, diffraction, enaction, exaction, extraction, faction, fraction, interaction, liquefaction, malefaction, petrifaction, proaction, protraction, putrefaction, redaction, retroaction, satisfaction, stupefaction, subtraction, traction, transaction, tumefaction, vitrifaction
- **expansion**, mansion, scansion, stanchion
- sanction
- **caption**, contraption
- **harshen**, Martian
- **cession**, discretion, freshen, session
- **abjection**, affection, circumspection, collection, complexion, confection, connection, convection, correction, defection, deflection, dejection, detection, direction, ejection, election, erection, genuflection, imperfection, infection, inflection, injection, inspection, insurrection, interconnection, interjection, intersection, introspection, lection, misdirection, objection, perfection, predilection, projection, protection, refection, reflection, rejection, resurrection, retrospection, section, selection, subjection, transection, vivisection
- **exemption**, pre-emption, redemption
- **abstention**, apprehension, ascension, attention, circumvention, comprehension, condescension, contention, contravention, convention, declension, detention, dimension, dissension, extension, gentian, hypertension, hypotension,

intention, intervention, invention,
mention, misapprehension,
obtention, pension, prehension,
prevention, recension, retention,
subvention, supervention,
suspension, tension
- **conception**, contraception,
deception, exception, inception,
interception, misconception,
perception, reception
- Übermenschen ●subsection
- **ablation**, aeration, agnation,
Alsatian, Amerasian, Asian, aviation,
cetacean, citation, conation,
creation, Croatian, crustacean,
curation, Dalmatian, delation,
dilation, donation, duration, elation,
fixation, Galatian, gyration, Haitian,
halation, Horatian, ideation, illation,
lavation, legation, libation, location,
lunation, mutation, natation, nation,
negation, notation, nutation,
oblation, oration, ovation, potation,
relation, rogation, rotation,
Sarmatian, sedation, Serbo-Croatian,
station, taxation, Thracian, vacation,
vexation, vocation, zonation
- **accretion**, Capetian, completion,
concretion, deletion, depletion,
Diocletian, excretion, Grecian,
Helvetian, repletion, Rhodesian,
secretion, suppletion, Tahitian,
venetian
- **academician**, addition, aesthetician
(*US* esthetician), ambition, audition,
beautician, clinician, coition,
cosmetician, diagnostician,
dialectician, dietitian, Domitian,
edition, electrician, emission,
fission, fruition, Hermitian, ignition,
linguistician, logician, magician,
mathematician, Mauritian,
mechanician, metaphysician,
mission, monition, mortician,
munition, musician, obstetrician,
omission, optician, paediatrician
(*US* pediatrician), patrician, petition,
Phoenician, physician, politician,
position, rhetorician, sedition,
statistician, suspicion, tactician,
technician, theoretician, Titian,

tuition, volition
- **addiction**, affliction, benediction,
constriction, conviction, crucifixion,
depiction, dereliction, diction,
eviction, fiction, friction, infliction,
interdiction, jurisdiction,
malediction, restriction, transfixion,
valediction
- **distinction**, extinction, intinction
- **ascription**, circumscription,
conscription, decryption,
description, Egyptian, encryption,
inscription, misdescription,
prescription, subscription,
superscription, transcription
- proscription
- **concoction**, decoction
- **adoption**, option
- **abortion**, apportion, caution,
contortion, distortion, extortion,
portion, proportion, retortion,
torsion
- auction
- **absorption**, sorption
- **commotion**, devotion, emotion,
groschen, Laotian, locomotion,
lotion, motion, notion, Nova Scotian,
ocean, potion, promotion
- **ablution**, absolution, allocution,
attribution, circumlocution,
circumvolution, Confucian,
constitution, contribution,
convolution, counter-revolution,
destitution, dilution, diminution,
distribution, electrocution,
elocution, evolution, execution,
institution, interlocution,
irresolution, Lilliputian, locution,
perlocution, persecution, pollution,
prosecution, prostitution,
restitution, retribution, Rosicrucian,
solution, substitution, volution
- cushion ●resumption ●München
- pincushion
- **Belorussian**, Prussian, Russian
- **abduction**, conduction,
construction, deduction, destruction,
eduction, effluxion, induction,
instruction, introduction,
misconstruction, obstruction,
production, reduction, ruction,

seduction, suction, underproduction
- **avulsion**, compulsion, convulsion, emulsion, expulsion, impulsion, propulsion, repulsion, revulsion
- **assumption**, consumption, gumption, presumption
- **luncheon**, scuncheon, truncheon
- **compunction**, conjunction, dysfunction, expunction, function, junction, malfunction, multifunction, unction
- **abruption**, corruption, disruption, eruption, interruption
- T-junction •liposuction
- **animadversion**, aspersion, assertion, aversion, Cistercian, coercion, conversion, desertion, disconcertion, dispersion, diversion, emersion, excursion, exertion, extroversion, immersion, incursion, insertion, interspersion, introversion, Persian, perversion, submersion, subversion, tertian, version
- excerption

25.50

- **baton**, batten, fatten, flatten, harmattan, Manhattan, Mountbatten, paten, patten, pattern, platen, Saturn, slattern

> | i |
> Create extra rhymes by adding -*ing* to words like batten.

- Shackleton •Appleton
- **Hampton**, Northampton, Rockhampton, Southampton, Wolverhampton
- **Canton**, lantern, Scranton
- **Langton**, plankton
- Clapton
- **Aston**, pastern
- Gladstone
- **Caxton**, Paxton
- capstan •Ashton •phytoplankton
- **Akhenaten**, Akhetaten, Aten, Barton, carton, Dumbarton, hearten, Parton, smarten, spartan, tartan
- Grafton
- **Carlton**, Charlton
- Charleston •kindergarten
- Aldermaston
- **Breton**, jetton, Sowetan, threaten, Tibetan
- lectern
- **Elton**, melton, Skelton
- **Denton**, Fenton, Kenton, Lenten, Trenton
- Repton
- **Avestan**, Midwestern, northwestern, Preston, southwestern, western
- sexton
- **Clayton**, Deighton, Leighton, Paton, phaeton, Satan, straighten, straiten
- Paignton •Maidstone
- **beaten**, Beaton, Beeton, Cretan, Keaton, neaten, Nuneaton, overeaten, sweeten, uneaten, wheaten
- chieftain
- **eastern**, northeastern, southeastern
- browbeaten •weatherbeaten
- **bitten**, bittern, Britain, Briton, Britten, handwritten, hardbitten, kitten, Lytton, mitten, smitten, underwritten, witan, written
- Clifton

This poem by Robert Burns uses dialect to create vibrant rhymes:

O wad some Power the giftie gie us
To see oursels as ithers see us!
It wad frae monie a blunder free us
An' foolish notion:
What airs in dress an' gait wad lea'e us,
An' ev'n devotion!

(Robert Burns, 'To a Louse')

In this poem by Stevie Smith, the use of *pararhymes* throughout (the words Singleton/Edmonton appear to be *stressed* but in fact, both words have initial stress, SIN and ED, making them *pararhymes*) creates an unconvincing feel which undermines the meaning of the words:

Come, wed me, Lady Singleton,
And we will have a baby soon
And we will live in Edmonton
Where all the friendly people run.

(Stevie Smith, 'Lady "Rogue" Singleton')

- **Milton**, Shilton, Stilton, Wilton
- Middleton • singleton • simpleton
- **Clinton**, Linton, Minton, Quinton, Winton
- **cistern**, Liston, piston, Wystan
- brimstone • Winston • Kingston
- Addington • Eddington
- Workington
- **Arlington**, Darlington
- skeleton
- **Ellington**, wellington
- exoskeleton
- **cosmopolitan**, megalopolitan, metropolitan, Neapolitan
- Burlington • Hamilton • badminton
- lamington • Germiston • Penistone
- Bonington • Orpington • Samaritan
- **Carrington**, Harrington
- sacristan • Festschriften
- Sherrington • typewritten

- Warrington • puritan • Fredericton
- Lexington • Occitan • Washington
- Whittington • Huntington
- Galveston • Livingstone
- Kensington
- **Blyton**, brighten, Brighton, Crichton, enlighten, frighten, heighten, lighten, righten, tighten, titan, triton, whiten

Create extra rhymes by adding *-ing* to words like brighten.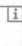

- **begotten**, cotton, forgotten, ill-gotten, misbegotten, rotten
- **Compton**, Crompton
- wanton • Longton
- **Boston**, postern
- **boughten**, chorten, foreshorten, Laughton, Morton, Naughton, Orton, quartan, quartern, shorten, tauten, torten, Wharton
- **Alton**, Dalton, Galton, saltern, Walton
- Taunton • Allston • Launceston
- **croton**, Dakotan, Minnesotan, oaten, verboten
- **Bolton**, Doulton, molten
- Folkestone • Royston
- **Luton**, newton, rambutan, Teuton
- Houston • Fulton
- **button**, glutton, Hutton, mutton
- sultan
- **doubleton**, subaltern
- fronton • Augustan • Dunstan
- tungsten • quieten • Pinkerton
- charlatan • Wollaston • Palmerston
- Edmonton • automaton • Sheraton

The *unstressed rhymes* in this song partly depend on accent and knowledge of local pronunciation which underlines the strong link between the authors and their subject (the Beastie Boys and their city).

Brooklyn, Bronx, Queens and Staten
From the Battery to the top of Manhattan
Asian, Middle-Eastern and Latin
Black, White, New York you make it happen

(Beastie Boys, 'An Open Letter to NYC')

- Geraldton •Chatterton •Betterton
- Chesterton •Athelstan
- **burton**, curtain, uncertain
- Hurston

25.51

- Melanchthon
- **lengthen**, strengthen
- Nathan
- **Elizabethan**, Ethan
- Phaethon •python •leviathan
- Jonathan •marathon •earthen
- Carmarthen •leathern •heathen
- northern •southern •burthen
- **Avon**, Cavan, cavern, raven, tavern
- **Caernarfon**, Dungarvan, Javan
- Wilhelmshaven •Tórshavn
- **Bevan**, Devon, eleven, Evan, heaven, leaven, Pleven, seven, Severn
- Hesvan
- **craven**, graven, haven, maven, shaven, Stratford-upon-Avon
- **even**, Sivan, Steven
- **driven**, forgiven, given, misgiven, Niven, riven, shriven, thriven
- **silvern**, sylvan
- Godgiven •Sullivan
- **enliven**, Ivan, liven
- **cloven**, interwoven, woven
- Beethoven •Eindhoven •proven
- **coven**, govern, misgovern, oven, sloven
- cordovan •Donovan •Quechuan
- Bronwen •Iowan

25.52

- **Italian**, stallion
- **cañon**, canyon, companion
- **hellion**, rebellion
- Kenyan

- **Melanesian**, Micronesian, Polynesian
- **billion**, jillion, million, modillion, multimillion, pillion, septillion, sextillion, squillion, trillion, zillion
- **minion**, opinion, pinion
- carillon •slumgullion
- **bunion**, Bunyan, grunion, onion, Runyon
- roentgen •damson •Kansan •Tarzan
- **blazon**, brazen, emblazon, liaison, raisin
- Spätlesen
- **reason**, season, treason
- **arisen**, grison, imprison, mizzen, prison, risen, uprisen
- Pilsen •crimson •malison
- **benison**, denizen
- orison •citizen
- **bedizen**, greisen, horizon, kaizen
- Stockhausen
- **chosen**, frozen
- Lederhosen •poison •Susan
- **cousin**, cozen, dozen
- Amazon

25.53

- **adjourn**, astern, Berne, burn, churn, concern, discern, earn, fern, fohn, kern, learn, Lucerne, quern, Sauternes, spurn, stern, Sterne, tern, terne, Traherne, turn, urn, Verne, yearn

> Create extra rhymes by [i]
> adding -ed to words like adjourn.

- Bayern •Blackburn •heartburn
- Hepburn •Raeburn •Swinburne
- **Gisborne**, Lisburn
- sideburn •sunburn •Bannockburn
- lady-fern •Vättern •extern
- **cittern**, gittern
- Comintern •taciturn
- **nocturn**, nocturne
- U-turn •upturn

Section 26: -ng

26.1

- **bang**, Battambang, bhang, clang, Da Nang, dang, fang, gang, hang, harangue, kiang, Kuomintang, Kweiyang, Laing, Luang Prabang, meringue, Nanchang, Pahang, pang, parang, Penang, prang, Pyongyang, rang, sang, satang, Shang, shebang, Shenyang, slambang, slang, spang, sprang, Sturm und Drang, tang, thang, trepang, twang, vang, whang, Xizang, yang, Zaozhuang

> Create extra rhymes by adding -ing to words like bang. ⓘ

- **Xinjiang**, Zhanjiang, Zhenjiang
- Palembang • whiz-bang • charabanc
- pressgang • chaingang • Wolfgang
- strap-hang • ylang-ylang • boomslang
- Semarang • boomerang • linsang
- Sittang • mustang

26.2

- **Kaifeng**, Yancheng
- ginseng

26.3

- **Beijing**, bing, bring, Chungking, cling, ding, dingaling, fling, I Ching, king, Kunming, ling, Ming, Nanjing, Peking, ping, ring, sing, Singh, sling, spring, sting, string, swing, Synge, thing, ting, wing, wring, Xining, zing
- **saying**, slaying
- bricklaying • minelaying
- **being**, far-seeing, unseeing
- sightseeing • well-being
- blackberrying

- **dairying**, unvarying
- unwearying
- **self-pitying**, unpitying
- **belying**, dying, lying, self-denying, tying, vying
- unedifying • unsatisfying • outlying
- drawing • underdrawing
- **easygoing**, flowing, going, knowing, mowing, outgoing, showing, sowing, thoroughgoing, toing and froing
- seagoing • ongoing • foregoing
- theatregoing • churchgoing
- following • borrowing • annoying
- **bluing**, doing, misdoing
- evil-doing • wrongdoing

26.4

- stabbing • ribbing • winebibbing
- zorbing • probing • tubing • rubbing
- hatching • backscratching • etching
- **preaching**, teaching
- schoolteaching • firewatching
- birdwatching • heartsearching

26.5

- scaffolding
- **freestanding**, hardstanding, landing, misunderstanding, notwithstanding, outstanding, standing, stranding, understanding, upstanding
- **Harding**, self-regarding
- undemanding
- **heading**, Reading, steading, wedding
- gelding
- **ending**, impending, uncomprehending, unoffending, unpretending

- sub-heading •heartrending
- goaltending
- **arcading**, grading, lading, shading, unfading, upbraiding
- **exceeding**, leading, misleading, pleading, reeding, self-feeding, sheading, unheeding
- **Fielding**, yielding
- inbreeding •stockbreeding
- **forbidding**, Ridding
- building •wingding •shipbuilding
- bodybuilding •outbuilding
- **confiding**, hiding, riding, siding
- wilding
- **binding**, finding
- paragliding •wadding
- corresponding •hot-rodding
- **according**, hoarding, recording, unrewarding
- sailboarding •snowboarding
- telerecording •videorecording
- Dowding
- **grounding**, sounding, surrounding
- **foreboding**, loading
- **Golding**, holding, moulding (*US* molding), scolding
- landholding •shareholding
- smallholding •roadholding
- wounding
- **peasepudding**, pudding
- underfunding •wording

26.6

- **strafing**, understaffing
- debriefing •spiffing •offing
- morphing •roofing •stuffing
- **lagging**, unflagging
- legging
- **digging**, rigging, wigging
- Vereeniging
- **frogging**, nogging
- mugging •turbocharging •edging
- **aging**, engaging, staging
- unchanging •unchallenging
- managing •discouraging •cottaging
- obliging •lodging •ungrudging
- urging

26.7

- **backing**, blacking, packing, sacking, tracking, whacking
- **ranking**, spanking
- nerve-racking
- **marking**, sarking
- **making**, taking, undertaking
- matchmaking •dressmaking
- haymaking
- **lacemaking**, pacemaking
- peacemaking •filmmaking
- printmaking •cabinetmaking
- moneymaking •merrymaking
- winemaking •home-making
- shoemaking •toolmaking
- bookmaking •troublemaking
- backbreaking •heartbreaking
- strikebreaking •housebreaking
- breathtaking •painstaking
- piss-taking •stocktaking
- **self-seeking**, unspeaking
- **licking**, ticking
- **freethinking**, shrinking, sinking, unblinking, unthinking, unwinking
- Mafeking •finicking •politicking
- **liking**, Viking
- **self-cocking**, self-mocking, shocking, stocking
- stonking •bluestocking •Hawking
- sleepwalking •streetwalking
- hillwalking •firewalking
- **soaking**, Woking
- pawnbroking •thought-provoking
- **booking**, Brooking
- onlooking
- **spelunking**, trunking
- motherfucking •bloodsucking
- bollocking
- **hardworking**, working
- erl-king •tear-jerking •metalworking
- outworking

26.8

- **brambling**, rambling
- hatchling •brandling
- **gangling**, wrangling
- crackling •sapling
- **fatling**, Gatling
- **mantling**, scantling
- **darling**, sparling, starling
- sampling •starveling
- **dwelling**, misspelling,

self-propelling, spelling, swelling,
telling, upwelling
• trembling • vetchling • fledgling
• **nestling**, wrestling
• storytelling
• **failing**, grayling, mailing, paling,
railing, sailing, tailing, unavailing,
veiling, wailing
• changeling • boardsailing
• parasailing
• **appealing**, ceiling, Darjeeling,
dealing, feeling, Keeling, peeling,
revealing, self-sealing, shieling,
wheeler-dealing, wheeling
• **reedling**, seedling
• weakling • Riesling
• **deskilling**, filling, grilling, killing,
Pilling, quilling, Schilling,
self-fulfilling, shilling, Trilling,
unfulfilling, willing
• sibling • kindling • piffling
• **inkling**, sprinkling, tinkling
• **Kipling**, stripling
• princeling • witling
• **brisling**, quisling
• painkilling
• **filing**, piling, reviling, tiling,
unsmiling
• motorcycling • hairstyling • rockling
• gosling
• **calling**, Pauling
• lordling • porkling
• **cowling**, fowling
• **foundling**, groundling
• **ruling**, schooling
• intercooling • wirepulling
• grumbling
• **buckling**, duckling, Suckling
• youngling • coupling • dumpling
• puzzling • swashbuckling
• **shearling**, yearling
• hireling
• **towelling** (US toweling)
• **gruelling** (US grueling)
• **babbling**, dabbling
• marbling • scribbling
• **mumbling**, rumbling
• sanderling • middling • doodling
• underling • rifling • shuffling
• strangling • fingerling

• **enamelling** (US enameling)
• rustling • rattling
• **bitterling**, chitterling
• titling
• **sterling**, Stirling
• **nurseling**, nursling
• earthling

26.9

• **charming**, disarming
• **Fleming**, lemming
• **Deeming**, scheming, steaming
• trimming • timing • heartwarming
• house-warming
• **coaming**, gloaming, homing,
Wyoming
• assuming
• **becoming**, coming, forthcoming,
mumming, up-and-coming
• oncoming • shortcoming
• homecoming • upcoming
• mind-numbing
• **Canning**, Manning, undermanning
• **Denning**, kenning
• **caning**, entertaining,
self-sustaining, uncomplaining
• **greening**, leaning, meaning,
overweening, screening,
spring-cleaning
• sweetening • evening
• **beginning**, inning, thinning,
twinning, underpinning, winning
• prizewinning
• **lining**, signing, Twining, vining
• lightning
• **aborning**, awning, dawning,
morning, mourning, spawning,
warning
• **Browning**, Downing, drowning
• landowning • tuning • cunning
• gunrunning • unquestioning
• widening • stiffening • reckoning
• thickening • happening • sharpening
• opening • fastening • christening
• unthreatening
• **lightening**, unenlightening
• self-governing
• **reasoning**, seasoning
• poisoning

- **discerning**, Herning, turning, yearning
- woodturning

26.10

- hanging • headbanging
- straphanging • cliffhanging
- mud-slinging • gunslinging
- bell-ringing • upbringing • longing
- tonguing
- **tapping**, wrapping
- camping • kneecapping
- backslapping
- **kidnapping** (*US* kidnaping)
- helping
- **scraping**, shaping
- **safekeeping**, sweeping, unsleeping
- gamekeeping • station-keeping
- greenkeeping • peacekeeping
- wicketkeeping • timekeeping
- shopkeeping • housekeeping
- goalkeeping • bookkeeping
- minesweeping
- **chipping**, clipping, dripping, snipping, whipping
- **dropping**, sopping, stopping, topping
- clodhopping • show-stopping
- wife-swapping
- **coping**, roping
- grouping • showjumping

26.11

- handspring • hamstring • herring
- headspring • wellspring
- **airing**, ballbearing, bearing, Behring, Bering, caring, daring, fairing, hardwearing, pairing, paring, raring, sparing, Waring, wearing
- talebearing • childbearing
- wayfaring • seafaring • cheeseparing
- time-sharing • mainspring • keyring
- gee-string • watch spring • offspring
- **boring**, flooring, Goring, riproaring, roaring, scoring, shoring
- drawstring • goalscoring
- outpouring • bowstring • shoestring
- bullring

- **auctioneering**, clearing, earring, electioneering, engineering, gearing, orienteering, privateering, shearing

> Create extra rhymes for
> words like auctioneering by
> adding -*ing* to appear etc. (see
> section 12.4).

- God-fearing • puppeteering
- **firing**, retiring, uninspiring, untiring, wiring
- **during**, mooring, reassuring, Turing
- posturing • restructuring
- meandering • rendering
- **pondering**, wandering
- ordering • maundering
- **plundering**, thundering, wondering
- offering • suffering • fingering
- scaremongering • hankering
- **flickering**, Pickering
- tinkering • hammering • glimmering
- unmurmuring • tampering
- whimpering • whispering
- **smattering**, unflattering
- earthshattering • schoolmastering
- Kettering • self-catering • wittering
- **quartering**, watering
- faltering • roistering • muttering
- gathering • woolgathering
- blithering
- **flavouring** (*US* flavoring), unwavering
- quivering
- **manoeuvring** (*US* maneuvering)
- covering • wallcovering
- **Goering**, stirring, unerring

26.12

- waxing
- **passing**, surpassing
- **Lancing**, Lansing
- **blessing**, distressing, dressing, Lessing, pressing, unprepossessing
- hairdressing
- **bracing**, casing, facing, lacing, placing, self-effacing, spacing, tracing

> Try rhyming one word with a
> set of two: bracing, may sing.

- steeplechasing •interfacing
- unceasing •Gissing •unconvincing
- unpromising
- **enticing**, icing
- self-sacrificing •crossing
- kick-boxing
- **rejoicing**, voicing
- conveyancing •embarrassing
- videoconferencing
- **dashing**, flashing, lashing, thrashing
- square-bashing •tongue-lashing
- **lynching**, unflinching
- garnishing •furnishing •ravishing
- Cushing
- **Flushing**, gushing, unblushing
- inrushing •onrushing

26.13

- matting •exacting
- **Banting**, ranting
- parting
- **enchanting**, planting
- **everlasting**, fasting, lasting
- narrowcasting
- **letting**, setting, wetting
- **self-respecting**, self-selecting, unreflecting, unsuspecting
- tempting
- **unconsenting**, unrelenting
- excepting
- **arresting**, unprotesting, unresting, westing
- bloodletting •trendsetting
- pace-setting •typesetting
- photosetting
- **grating**, plating, rating, slating, uprating, weighting
- painting
- **pasting**, tasting
- undeviating •self-perpetuating
- unaccommodating •self-deprecating
- suffocating •self-regulating
- undiscriminating •underpainting
- unhesitating
- **beating**, fleeting, greeting, Keating, meeting, self-defeating, sweeting
- easting
- **fitting**, sitting, unbefitting, unremitting, witting

- **printing**, unstinting
- **listing**, twisting, unresisting
- shopfitting •marketing
- telemarketing •pickpocketing
- weightlifting •side-splitting
- carpeting •trumpeting
- uninteresting •visiting
- **backlighting**, lighting, self-righting, sighting, unexciting, uninviting, whiting, writing
- infighting •prizefighting
- dogfighting •bullfighting
- handwriting •screenwriting
- scriptwriting •copywriting
- skywriting •signwriting
- typewriting •songwriting •knotting
- prompting
- **costing**, frosting
- **self-supporting**, unsporting
- **malting**, salting
- ripsnorting •outing
- **accounting**, mounting
- coating
- **Boulting**, revolting
- **posting**, roasting
- billposting •disappointing
- **shooting**, suiting, Tooting
- sharpshooting •footing
- off-putting
- **cutting**, Nutting
- bunting
- **disgusting**, self-adjusting, trusting
- blockbusting •linocutting
- woodcutting •disquieting
- **disconcerting**, shirting, skirting

26.14

- pennyfarthing •plaything
- silversmithing •anything
- everything •northing •nothing
- something •rebirthing •farthing
- scathing •sheathing
- **tithing**, writhing
- southing •clothing •underclothing
- Worthing •carving •woodcarving
- delving
- **craving**, engraving, paving, raving, saving, shaving
- **self-deceiving**, unbelieving, weaving

- **living**, misgiving, thanksgiving, unforgiving
- skydiving •piledriving •coving
- **approving**, reproving, unmoving
- unloving
- **Irving**, serving, unswerving
- time-serving •lapwing •waxwing
- batwing •redwing •lacewing
- beeswing •forewing •downswing
- outswing •viewing •upswing
- underwing •phrasing •stargazing
- trailblazing •hellraising •unpleasing
- **rising**, surprising
- self-aggrandizing •uncompromising
- unpatronizing •uprising
- enterprising •appetizing
- **Dowsing**, housing
- unimposing
- **amusing**, confusing, musing

26.15

- **along**, belong, bong, chaise longue, dong, Geelong, gong, Guangdong, Haiphong, Heilong, Hong Kong, Jong, King Kong, long, mah-jong, Mao Zedong, Mekong, nong, pong, prolong, prong, sarong, Shillong, song, souchong, strong, thong, throng, tong, Vietcong, wrong

> Create extra rhymes by [i]
> adding -ing to words like belong.

- billabong •dingdong •Wollongong
- Chittagong •headlong •livelong
- sidelong •lifelong •oblong •oolong
- singalong •furlong •pingpong
- Armstrong •headstrong •part song
- plainsong •evensong •singsong
- swansong •birdsong •biltong
- diphthong

26.16

- boing

26.17

- **Jung**, Kung, Taichung
- Bandung •Nibelung •Hornung

26.18

- **among**, bung, clung, dung, flung, hung, lung, outflung, rung, shantung, slung, sprung, strung, stung, sung, swung, tongue, underslung, wrung, young
- aqualung •hamstrung •ox tongue

26.19

- vingt-et-un

Section 27: -p

27.1

- **bap**, cap, chap, clap, crap, dap, entrap, enwrap, flap, frap, gap, giftwrap, hap, Jap, knap, lap, Lapp, map, nap, nappe, pap, rap, sap, schappe, scrap, slap, snap, strap, tap, trap, wrap, yap, zap
- stopgap •mayhap •mishap •madcap
- blackcap •redcap •kneecap
- handicap
- **nightcap**, whitecap
- **snowcap**, toecap
- foolscap •hubcap •skullcap
- dunce cap •handclap •dewlap
- mudflap •thunderclap •burlap
- bitmap •catnap •kidnap •Saranwrap
- mantrap •claptrap •deathtrap
- chinstrap •jockstrap •mousetrap
- bootstrap •suntrap •firetrap
- heeltap

27.2

- **Arp**, carp, harp, scarp, sharp, tarp
- cardsharp

27.3

- **cep**, Dieppe, hep, misstep, outstep, pep, prep, rep, schlepp, skep, step, steppe, strep
- quickstep •sidestep •doorstep
- goosestep •footstep •one-step

27.4

- **agape**, ape, cape, chape, crape, crêpe, drape, escape, gape, grape, jape, misshape, nape, rape, scrape, shape, tape
- landscape •seascape •cityscape
- skyscape •townscape •snowscape
- roofscape •moonscape •broomrape
- shipshape •videotape •sellotape
- ticker tape

27.5

- **asleep**, beep, bleep, cheap, cheep, creep, deep, heap, Jeep, keep, leap, neap, neep, peep, reap, seep, sheep, skin-deep, sleep, steep, Streep, sweep, veep, weep

> Create extra rhymes by adding -ing to words like beep. ⓘ

- slagheap •scrapheap •antheap
- housekeep •upkeep •chimney sweep

A *pararhyme* (one kind of *half-rhyme*) is one in which the final consonant of the stressed syllable matches but the stressed vowel does not, as in cape/keep. Wilfred Owen made frequent use of it:

It seemed that out of the battle I escaped
Down some profound dull tunnel, long since scooped
Through granites which Titanic wars had groined.
Yet also there encumbered sleepers groaned ...

(Wilfred Owen, 'Strange Meeting')

27.6

- **blip**, chip, clip, dip, drip, equip, flip, grip, gyp, harelip, hip, kip, lip, nip, outstrip, pip, quip, rip, scrip, ship, sip, skip, slip, snip, strip, tip, toodle-pip, trip, whip, yip, zip
- biochip • microchip • woodchip
- sheepdip • skinny-dip • rosehip
- landslip • payslip
- **fillip**, Philip
- gymslip • side-slip • polyp • oxlip
- cowslip • pillowslip
- **julep**, tulip
- Cudlipp • paperclip • catnip • parsnip
- turnip • handgrip • cantrip • hairgrip
- airstrip • filmstrip • kirby grip
- weatherstrip • gossip • airship
- midship • kinship • godship • warship
- gunship • worship • wingtip
- fingertip • horsewhip • bullwhip
- bunyip

27.7

- **gripe**, hype, mistype, pipe, ripe, sipe, slype, snipe, stripe, swipe, tripe, type, wipe

> Create extra rhymes by changing words like grip to gripping. [i]

- guttersnipe • bagpipe • standpipe
- tailpipe • drainpipe • pitchpipe
- windpipe • hornpipe • blowpipe
- stovepipe • hosepipe • soilpipe
- pinstripe • archetype • logotype
- phenotype • linotype • Monotype
- electrotype • daguerreotype
- subtype • stereotype • collotype
- **genotype**, stenotype
- prototype • sideswipe

27.8

- **atop**, bop, chop, clop, cop, crop, dop, drop, Dunlop, estop, flop, fop, glop, hop, intercrop, knop, kop, lop, mop, op, plop, pop, prop, screw-top, shop, slop, sop, stop, strop, swap, tiptop, top, underprop, whop, wop
- co-op • bebop • sweatshop • carhop
- hedgehop • bellhop • hiphop • flipflop
- clip-clop • bellyflop • megaflop
- gigaflop • teraflop • rollmop • coin-op
- lollipop • backdrop • airdrop
- sharecrop • namedrop • raindrop
- eavesdrop • Ribbentrop • Winthrop
- agitprop • outcrop • snowdrop
- stonecrop • turboprop • dewdrop
- gumdrop • teardrop • malaprop
- Aesop • sweetsop • milksop
- pawnshop • window-shop • toyshop
- **bookshop**, cookshop
- barbershop • workshop • ragtop
- blacktop • tanktop • laptop • backstop
- flat-top • hardtop • palmtop • desktop
- tabletop • maintop • treetop • hilltop
- whistle-stop • ripstop • longstop
- foretop • doorstop • shortstop
- screwtop • rooftop • worktop

27.9

- **dorp**, gawp, scaup, scorp, Thorpe, warp, whaup, yawp
- Klerksdorp • Scunthorpe

27.10

- **aslope**, cope, dope, elope, grope, hope, interlope, lope, mope, nope, ope, pope, rope, scope, slope, soap, taupe, tope, trope
- myope • telescope • periscope
- stereoscope • bioscope • stroboscope
- kaleidoscope • CinemaScope
- gyroscope • microscope • horoscope
- stethoscope • antelope • envelope
- zoetrope • skipping-rope • tightrope
- towrope • heliotrope • lycanthrope
- philanthrope • thaumatrope
- misanthrope
- **isotope**, radioisotope

27.11

- **bloop**, cock-a-hoop, coop, croup, droop, drupe, dupe, goop, group,

Guadeloupe, hoop, loop, poop, recoup, roup, scoop, sloop, snoop, soup, stoep, stoop, stoup, stupe, swoop, troop, troupe, whoop

> Create extra rhymes by adding -*ing* to words like droop.   [i]

- hula-hoop • cantaloupe • nincompoop
- playgroup • subgroup • peer group

27.12

- Krupp

27.13

- **cup**, grown up, pup, scup, straight-up, stuck-up, summing-up, sup, totting-up, tup, two-up, up, washing-up
- pick-me-up • fry-up • wind-up
- round-up • hold-up • backup • markup
- check-up
- **break-up**, make-up, shake-up, take-up

> Try rhyming one word with a set of two: makeup, wake up.   [i]

- teacup
- **hiccup**, pickup, stick-up
- link-up
- **cock-up**, lock-up
- walk-up
- **hook-up**, lookup
- buttercup • snarl-up • pile-up
- pull-up • warm-up • clean-up • pin-up
- line-up • grown-up
- **run-up**, sun-up, ton-up
- turn-up • hang-up • slap-up • zip-up
- top-up • chirrup • press-up • piss-up
- toss-up
- **nosh-up**, wash-up
- punch-up • start-up
- **let-up**, set-up
- sit-up • cut-up • rave-up

27.14

- ketchup
- **callop**, escallop, escalope, gallop,

galop, Salop, shallop
- **develop**, envelop
- **collop**, dollop, gollop, lollop, scallop, scollop, trollop, Trollope, wallop
- codswallop • Stanhope • larrup
- satrap • caltrop
- **stirrup**, syrup (*US* sirup)
- Europe
- **archbishop**, bishop
- tittup

27.15

- **burp**, chirp, Earp, slurp, twerp, usurp
- Antwerp

27.16

- **alp**, scalp
- **help**, kelp, whelp, yelp
- **gulp**, pulp

27.17

- **amp**, camp, champ, clamp, cramp, damp, encamp, gamp, lamp, ramp, samp, scamp, stamp, tamp, tramp, vamp
- firedamp • headlamp • wheel clamp
- sidelamp • spotlamp • blowlamp
- sunlamp
- **hemp**, kemp, temp
- **blimp**, chimp, crimp, gimp, imp, limp, pimp, primp, scrimp, shrimp, simp, skimp, wimp
- **chomp**, clomp, comp, pomp, romp, stomp, swamp, tromp, whomp, yomp
- **bump**, chump, clump, crump, dump, flump, frump, gazump, grump, hump, jump, lump, outjump, plump, pump, rump, scrump, slump, stump, sump, thump, trump, tump, ump, whump

> Create extra rhymes by adding -*ing* to words like bump.   [i]

- ski-jump • showjump • handpump
- mugwump

27.18

- asp

- **clasp**, gasp, grasp, hasp, rasp
- **crisp**, lisp, will-o'-the-wisp, wisp
- wasp • woodwasp • cusp

Section 28: -s

28.1

- **alas**, Alsace, amass, ass, Bass, chasse, crass, crevasse, en masse, gas, Hamas, lass, mass, morass, sass, tarantass, tass, wrasse
- Díaz •Phidias •palliasse
- **materfamilias**, paterfamilias
- Asturias •Aphrodisias •Trias
- Donbas •Vargas •Ofgas •biogas
- teargas •jackass •Hellas •Ulfilas
- Stanislas •Candlemas •landmass
- Martinmas •biomass •Childermas
- Esdras •Mithras •hippocras
- sassafras •demitasse •gravitas

28.2

- **arse**, baas, brass, carse, class, coup de grâce, farce, glass, grass, Grasse, impasse, Kars, kick-ass, kvass, Laplace, Maas, Madras, outclass, pass, sparse, stained glass, surpass, upper class, volte-face
- badass •lardass •sandglass
- **eyeglass**, spyglass
- wine glass •tooth glass •subclass
- hourglass
- fibreglass (US fiberglass) •underclass
- masterclass •weather glass •bypass
- underpass •wheatgrass •ryegrass
- knotgrass •sawgrass •bluegrass
- goosegrass •smart-arse

28.3

- **acquiesce**, address, assess, Bess, bless, bouillabaisse, caress, cess, chess, coalesce, compress, confess, convalesce, cress, deliquesce, digress, dress, duchesse, duress, effervesce, effloresce, evanesce, excess, express, fess, finesse, fluoresce, guess, Hesse, impress, incandesce, intumesce, jess, largesse, less, manageress, mess, ness, noblesse, obsess, oppress, outguess, phosphoresce, politesse, possess, press, priestess, princess, process, profess, progress, prophetess, regress, retrogress, stress, success, suppress, tendresse, top-dress, transgress, tress, tristesse, underdress, vicomtesse, yes
- Jewess •shepherdess •Borges
- battledress •Mudéjares •headdress
- protectress •egress •ingress
- minidress •nightdress •congress
- sundress •procuress •murderess
- letterpress •watercress •shirtdress
- access

28.4

- scarce

28.5

- **abase**, ace, apace, backspace, base, bass, brace, case, chase, dace, efface, embrace, encase, enchase, enlace, face, grace, interlace, interspace, in-your-face, lace, mace, misplace, outface, outpace, pace, place, plaice, race, space, Thrace, trace, upper case
- airbase •freebase •wheelbase
- database •steeplechase •paperchase
- paleface •typeface •whiteface
- boldface •coalface •interface
- staircase •briefcase •slipcase
- packing case •doorcase •showcase

• notecase •pillowcase •suitcase
• bookcase •nutcase •marketplace
• anyplace •everyplace •showplace
• shoelace •bootlace •someplace
• Lovelace •fireplace •commonplace
• workplace •birthplace •tenace
• airspace •aerospace •hyperspace
• carapace •workspace •ratrace
• millrace •Fuentes •rosace

28.6

• **anis**, apiece, Berenice, caprice,
cassis, cease, coulisse, crease,
Dumfries, fils, fleece, geese, grease,
Greece, kris, lease, Lucrece,
MacNeice, Matisse, McAleese, Nice,
niece, obese, peace, pelisse, piece,
police, Rees, Rhys, set piece,
sublease, surcease, two-piece,
underlease
• mantelpiece •headpiece •hairpiece
• tailpiece •Greenpeace
• chimney piece •frontispiece
• timepiece •codpiece •crosspiece
• mouthpiece •showpiece •earpiece
• masterpiece
• centrepiece (*US* centerpiece)
• altarpiece •workpiece •ambergris
• calabrese

28.7

• **abyss**, amiss, bis, bliss, Chris, Diss,
hiss, kiss, Majlis, miss, piss,
reminisce, sis, Swiss, this, vis
• dais
• **Powys**, prowess
• **loess**, Lois
• **Lewes**, lewis
• abbess •ibis
• **Anubis**, pubis
• cannabis •arabis •duchess •purchase
• **caddis**, Gladys
• Candice
• **Sardis**, Tardis
• vendace •Charybdis
• **bodice**, goddess
• demigoddess •Aldiss •jaundice
• de profundis •prejudice •hendiadys
• cowardice •stewardess •preface
• Memphis •aphis •edifice •benefice
• orifice •artifice •office
• **surface**, surface-to-surface
• undersurface •haggis •aegis
• burgess
• **clerkess**, Theodorákis
• Colchis

28.8

• **Alice**, chalice, challis, malice, palace,
Tallis

Monorhyme describes a poem or part of a poem in which all the lines have
the same *end rhyme*; the rhyme pattern is *aaaa* (or as part of a larger stanza,
it could also be *bbbb* or *cccc* etc.). Shakespeare sometimes makes use of it as
in this section from *The Merchant of Venice*:

ARAGON: The fire seven times tried this;
Seven times tried that judgement is
That did never choose amiss.
Some there be that shadows kiss;
There be fools alive, iwis,
Silvered o'er; and so was this.
Take what wife you will to bed,
I will ever be your head.
So be gone; you are sped.

(William Shakespeare, *The Merchant of Venice*, 2.9.62-71)

- aurora australis
- **Ellis**, trellis
- necklace
- **aurora borealis**, Baylis, digitalis, Fidelis, rayless
- ageless • aimless • keyless
- **amaryllis**, cilice, Dilys, fillis, Phyllis
- ribless • lidless • rimless
- **kinless**, sinless, winless
- lipless • witless • annus mirabilis
- annus horribilis • syphilis
- **eyeless**, skyless, tieless
- **polis**, solace, Wallace
- joyless
- **Dulles**, portcullis
- accomplice
- **Annapolis**, Indianapolis, Minneapolis
- Persepolis
- **acropolis**, cosmopolis, Heliopolis, megalopolis, metropolis, necropolis
- chrysalis • surplice • amice • premise
- airmiss • Amis • in extremis • Artemis
- promise
- **pomace**, pumice
- Salamis
- **dermis**, epidermis, kermis

28.9

- **anise**, Janice
- Daphnis • Agnes
- **harness**, Kiwanis
- **Dennis**, Ennis, Glenys, menace, tennis, Venice
- **feyness**, gayness, greyness (*US* grayness)
- **finis**, penis
- **Glynis**, Innes, pinnace
- Widnes • bigness • lychnis • illness
- dimness • hipness
- **fitness**, witness
- Erinys • iciness
- **dryness**, flyness, shyness, slyness, wryness
- cornice
- **Adonis**, Clones, Issigonis
- coyness
- **Eunice**, Tunis
- **Bernice**, furnace

- Thespis • precipice • coppice • hospice
- auspice • Serapis

28.10

- **arris**, Clarice, Harries, Harris, Paris
- mattress • actress • benefactress
- Polaris • enchantress
- **derris**, Nerys, terrace
- Emrys • empress
- **directress**, Electress
- temptress • sempstress
- **Apollinaris**, heiress
- waitress • seamstress • ex libris
- **headmistress**, mistress
- housemistress • toastmistress
- schoolmistress • ancestress
- dentifrice
- **iris**, Osiris
- **tigress**, Tigris
- cypress
- **Boris**, doch-an-dorris, Doris, Horace, Maurice, Norris, orris
- **cantoris**, Dolores, loris
- laundress • fortress • jointress
- hubris • buttress
- **conductress**, instructress, seductress
- huntress • peeress • Beatrice
- arbitress • berberis • anchoress
- ephemeris • ambassadress
- adventuress • clitoris • authoress
- avarice

28.11

- **glacis**, Onassis
- abscess
- **anaphylaxis**, axis, praxis, taxis
- Chalcis • Jancis • synapsis • catharsis
- **Frances**, Francis
- thesis • Alexis • amanuensis
- **prolepsis**, sepsis, syllepsis
- **basis**, oasis, stasis
- **amniocentesis**, anamnesis, ascesis, catechesis, exegesis, mimesis, prosthesis, psychokinesis, telekinesis
- **ellipsis**, paralipsis
- Lachesis

- **analysis**, catalysis, dialysis, paralysis, psychoanalysis
- electrolysis •nemesis
- **genesis**, parthenogenesis, pathogenesis
- diaeresis (*US* dieresis) •metathesis
- parenthesis
- **photosynthesis**, synthesis
- **hypothesis**, prothesis
- **crisis**, Isis
- proboscis •synopsis
- **apotheosis**, chlorosis, cirrhosis, diagnosis, halitosis, hypnosis, kenosis, meiosis, metempsychosis, misdiagnosis, mononucleosis, myxomatosis, necrosis, neurosis, osmosis, osteoporosis, prognosis, psittacosis, psychosis, sclerosis, symbiosis, thrombosis, toxoplasmosis, trichinosis, tuberculosis
- **archdiocese**, diocese, elephantiasis, psoriasis
- anabasis •apodosis
- **emphasis**, underemphasis
- **anamorphosis**, metamorphosis
- periphrasis •entasis •protasis
- **hypostasis**, iconostasis

28.12

- **Attis**, gratis, lattice
- **malpractice**, practice, practise
- **Atlantis**, mantis
- pastis
- **Lettice**, lettuce, Thetis
- **apprentice**, compos mentis, in loco parentis, prentice
- **Alcestis**, testis
- poetess •armistice
- **appendicitis**, arthritis, bronchitis, cellulitis, colitis, conjunctivitis, cystitis, dermatitis, encephalitis, gastroenteritis, gingivitis, hepatitis, laryngitis, lymphangitis, meningitis, nephritis, neuritis, osteoarthritis, pericarditis, peritonitis, pharyngitis, sinusitis, tonsillitis
- **epiglottis**, glottis
- solstice

- **mortise**, rigor mortis
- countess •viscountess
- **myosotis**, notice, Otis
- poultice •justice •giantess •clematis
- Curtis •interstice •Tethys
- Glenrothes •Travis
- **Jarvis**, parvis
- **clevis**, crevice, Nevis
- **Elvis**, pelvis
- **Avis**, Davies, mavis
- Leavis •Divis •novice •Clovis
- **Jervis**, service
- **marquess**, marquis

28.13

- **advice**, bice, Brice, choc ice, concise, dice, entice, gneiss, ice, imprecise, lice, mice, nice, precise, price, rice, sice, slice, speiss, spice, splice, suffice, syce, thrice, trice, twice, underprice, vice, Zeiss
- merchandise •paradise •sacrifice
- packice •woodlice •fieldmice
- titmice •dormice •allspice
- cockatrice •edelweiss

28.14

- **across**, boss, Bros, cos, cross, crosse, doss, dross, emboss, en brosse, floss, fosse, gloss, Goss, joss, Kos, lacrosse, loss, moss, MS-DOS, Ross, toss
- Laos
- **Áyios Nikólaos**, chaos
- Eos •Helios
- **Chios**, Khíos
- Lesbos •straw boss •Phobos •rooibos
- extrados •kudos •reredos •intrados
- Calvados •Argos •Lagos •logos
- Marcos •telos
- **Delos**, Melos
- Byblos •candyfloss
- **tholos**, Vólos
- bugloss •omphalos •Pátmos
- **Amos**, Deimos, Sámos
- Demos •peatmoss •cosmos •Los Alamos •Lemnos •Hypnos •Minos
- Mykonos •tripos •topos •Atropos
- **Ballesteros**, pharos, Saros
- Imbros •criss-cross •rallycross •Eros

- albatross - monopteros - Dos Passos
- Náxos - Hyksos - Knossos - Santos
- benthos
- **bathos**, pathos
- ethos - Kórinthos

28.15

- **coarse**, corse, course, divorce, endorse (*US* indorse), enforce, force, gorse, hoarse, horse, morse, Norse, perforce, reinforce, sauce, source, torse
- Wilberforce - workforce - packhorse
- carthorse - racehorse - sea horse
- hobby horse - Whitehorse
- **sawhorse**, warhorse
- clothes horse - shire horse
- workhorse - racecourse - concourse
- intercourse - watercourse
- outsource

28.16

- **douse**, dowse, Gauss, grouse, house, Klaus, louse, Manaus, mouse, nous, Rouse, souse, spouse, Strauss
- Windaus - madhouse - cathouse
- Gasthaus - guardhouse - farmhouse
- glasshouse - bathhouse - almshouse
- penthouse - guesthouse - warehouse
- playhouse
- **bakehouse**, steakhouse
- **alehouse**, jailhouse
- **gatehouse**, statehouse
- treehouse - wheelhouse - greenhouse
- clearing house - meeting house
- counting house - ice house
- **lighthouse**, White House
- doghouse - dollhouse
- **chophouse**, flophouse
- dosshouse
- **hothouse**, pothouse
- **poorhouse**, storehouse, whorehouse
- courthouse - malthouse - Bauhaus
- town house - outhouse - coach house
- roadhouse - smokehouse - boathouse
- oast house - schoolhouse

- Wodehouse - cookhouse - clubhouse
- nuthouse - beerhouse - powerhouse
- summerhouse - barrelhouse
- **porterhouse**, slaughterhouse, Waterhouse
- workhouse - lobscouse - woodlouse
- field mouse - titmouse - dormouse

28.17

- **adiós**, chausses, Close, Davos, dose, engross, gross, Grosz, jocose, morose, Rhos, verbose
- grandiose - religiose - otiose
- globose - viscose - bellicose - varicose
- vorticose - cellulose - lachrymose
- lactose - comatose - siliquose

28.18

- **bourgeois**, Boyce, choice, Joyce, pro-choice, rejoice, Royce, voice

28.19

- **abstruse**, abuse, adduce, Ballets Russes, Belarus, Bruce, burnous, caboose, charlotte russe, conduce, deduce, deuce, diffuse, douce, educe, excuse, goose, induce, introduce, juice, Larousse, loose, luce, misuse, moose, mousse, noose, obtuse, Palouse, papoose, produce, profuse, puce, recluse, reduce, Rousse, seduce, sluice, Sousse, spruce, traduce, truce, use, vamoose, Zeus
- cayuse - calaboose - mongoose
- Aarhus - verjuice - couscous
- footloose - ventouse - refuse
- Odysseus - Idomeneus - hypotenuse
- Syracuse

28.20

- **puss**, schuss, wuss
- Anschluss - sourpuss

28.21

- **bus**, buss, concuss, cuss, fuss, Gus, huss, muss, plus, pus, Russ, sus, suss, thus, truss, us

> Create extra rhymes by adding -*ing* to words like fuss. ⓘ

- trolleybus •minibus •blunderbuss

28.22

- **Andreas**, Antaeus, Laius, Menelaus
- **Aeneas**, Apuleius, Judas Maccabaeus, Linnaeus, Piraeus, uraeus

28.23

- **Bierce**, fierce, Pearce, Peirce, pierce, tierce
- **Fabius**, scabious
- Eusebius
- **amphibious**, Polybius
- dubious •Thaddeus •compendious
- radius •tedious
- **fastidious**, hideous, insidious, invidious, perfidious

> Create extra rhymes by adding -*ly* to words like fastidious. ⓘ

- Claudius
- **commodious**, melodious, odious
- studious •Cepheus
- **Morpheus**, Orpheus

> *Unstressed* (or *feminine*) *rhymes* are rhymes with a stressed syllable followed by one or more unstressed syllables; here the rhyme is spread over two words at the end of each line:
>
> "No," said Lizzie, "no, no, no;
> Their offers should not charm us,
> Their evil gifts would harm us."
>
> (Christina Rossetti, 'Goblin Market')

- Pelagius •callipygous •Vitellius
- **alias**, Sibelius, Vesalius
- **Aurelius**, Berzelius, contumelious, Cornelius, Delius
- **bilious**, punctilious, supercilious
- coleus •Julius •nucleus •Equuleus
- abstemious
- **Ennius**, Nennius
- **contemporaneous**, cutaneous, extemporaneous, extraneous, instantaneous, miscellaneous, Pausanias, porcellaneous, simultaneous, spontaneous, subcutaneous
- **genius**, heterogeneous, homogeneous, ingenious
- **consanguineous**, ignominious, Phineas, sanguineous
- **igneous**, ligneous
- Vilnius
- **acrimonious**, antimonious, ceremonious, erroneous, euphonious, felonious, harmonious, parsimonious, Petronius, sanctimonious, Suetonius
- Apollonius •impecunious
- calumnious •Asclepius •impious
- Scorpius
- **copious**, Gropius, Procopius
- Marius •pancreas •retiarius
- **Aquarius**, calcareous, Darius, denarius, gregarious, hilarious, multifarious, nefarious, omnifarious, precarious, Sagittarius, senarius, Stradivarius, temerarious, various, vicarious
- Atreus
- **delirious**, Sirius
- vitreous
- **censorious**, glorious, laborious, meritorious, notorious, uproarious, uxorious, vainglorious, victorious
- opprobrious
- **lugubrious**, salubrious
- **illustrious**, industrious
- **cinereous**, deleterious, imperious, mysterious, Nereus, serious, Tiberius
- **curious**, furious, injurious, luxurious, penurious, perjurious,

spurious, sulphureous
(*US* sulfureous), usurious
- **Cassius**, gaseous
- Alcaeus •Celsius
- **Theseus**, Tiresias
- **osseous**, Roscius
- nauseous
- **caduceus**, Lucius
- Perseus •Statius •Propertius
- Deo gratias •plenteous •piteous
- bounteous
- **Grotius**, Photius, Proteus
- **beauteous**, duteous
- **courteous**, sestertius
- **Boethius**, Prometheus
- envious •Octavius
- **devious**, previous
- **lascivious**, niveous, oblivious
- obvious
- **Vesuvius**, Vitruvius
- **impervious**, pervious
- aqueous •subaqueous •obsequious
- Dionysius

28.24

- **Ananias**, bias, Darius, dryas, Elias,
  eyas, Gaius, hamadryas, Lias,
  Mathias, pious, Tobias
- joyous •Shavuoth •tempestuous
- spirituous •tortuous •sumptuous
- voluptuous •virtuous •mellifluous
- superfluous •congruous •vacuous
- fatuous •anfractuous •arduous
- **ingenuous**, strenuous, tenuous
- flexuous •sensuous •impetuous
- contemptuous •incestuous
- **assiduous**, deciduous
- **ambiguous**, contiguous, exiguous
- **inconspicuous**, perspicuous
- promiscuous
- **continuous**, sinuous
- nocuous •fructuous •tumultuous
- unctuous
- **Abbas**, shabbos
- **choriambus**, iambus
- Arbus
- **Phoebus**, rebus
- gibbous
- **cumulonimbus**, nimbus

- omnibus •ceteris paribus •Erebus
- rhombus •incubus •succubus
- bulbous •Columbus •syllabus
- colobus •Barnabas •righteous
- rumbustious

28.25

- **horrendous**, stupendous,
  tremendous
- Barbados •Indus •solidus •Lepidus
- **Midas**, nidus
- Aldous •Judas •Enceladus •exodus
- hazardous •Dreyfus •Josephus
- Sisyphus •typhus •Dollfuss
- **amorphous**, anthropomorphous,
  polymorphous
- **rufous**, Rufus
- Angus •Argus
- **Las Vegas**, magus, Tagus
- negus
- **anilingus**, cunnilingus, dingus,
  Mingus
- bogus
- **fungous**, fungus, humongous
- **anthropophagous**, oesophagus (*US*
  esophagus), sarcophagus
- analogous
- **homologous**, tautologous
- Areopagus •asparagus
- **Burgas**, Fergus, Lycurgus
- Carajás •frabjous
- **advantageous**, contagious,
  courageous, outrageous, rampageous
- egregious
- **irreligious**, litigious, prestigious,
  prodigious, religious, sacrilegious
- umbrageous •gorgeous

28.26

- **Bacchus**, Caracas, Gracchus
- Damascus
- **Aristarchus**, carcass, Hipparchus,
  Marcus
- **discus**, hibiscus, meniscus, viscous
- umbilicus •Copernicus
- Ecclesiasticus •Leviticus •floccus

- **caucus**, Dorcas, glaucous, raucous
- **Archilochus**, Cocos, crocus, focus, hocus, hocus-pocus, locus
- autofocus
- **fucus**, Lucas, mucous, mucus, Ophiuchus, soukous
- ruckus • fuscous • abacus
- diplodocus • Telemachus
- Callimachus • Caratacus • Spartacus
- circus

28.27

- **Callas**, callous, callus, Dallas, Pallas, phallus
- Nablus • manless
- **hapless**, mapless
- **atlas**, fatless, hatless
- **braless**, parlous
- armless • artless
- **jealous**, zealous
- endless • legless • sexless • airless
- talus • bacillus • windlass • Nicklaus
- obelus • strobilus
- **acidophilus**, Theophilus
- angelus • Aeschylus • perilous
- scurrilous • Wenceslas • nautilus
- **Silas**, stylus
- jobless
- **godless**, rodless
- Patroclus • topless • coxless
- **lawless**, oarless
- **Aeolus**, alveolus, bolas, bolus, gladiolus, holus-bolus, solus, toeless
- Troilus • Douglas • useless • Tibullus
- garrulous • querulous • fabulous
- miraculous • calculus • famulus
- crapulous • patulous • nebulous
- **credulous**, sedulous
- pendulous • regulus
- **emulous**, tremulous
- bibulous • acidulous
- **meticulous**, ridiculous
- **mimulus**, stimulus
- scrofulous • flocculus • Romulus
- **populace**, populous
- convolvulus
- **altocumulus**, cirrocumulus, cumulus, stratocumulus, tumulus
- scrupulous

- **furunculous**, homunculus, ranunculus
- Catullus • troublous
- **gunless**, sunless
- **cutlass**, gutless
- earless • Heliogabalus
- libellous (US libelous) • discobolus
- scandalous • Daedalus • astragalus
- Nicholas • anomalous • Sardanapalus
- tantalus
- marvellous (US marvelous)
- frivolous • furless • surplus

28.28

- Lammas • Cadmus • Las Palmas
- **chiasmus**, Erasmus
- Nostradamus
- **famous**, ignoramus, Seamus, shamus
- **Polyphemus**, Remus
- grimace • Michaelmas
- **Christmas**, isthmus
- litmus
- **animus**, equanimous, magnanimous, pusillanimous, unanimous
- **anonymous**, eponymous, Hieronymus, pseudonymous, synonymous
- Septimus
- **Mimas**, primus, thymus, timeous
- Thomas
- **enormous**, ginormous
- **brumous**, hummus, humous, humus, spumous, strumous
- blasphemous
- **bigamous**, polygamous, trigamous
- **endogamous**, monogamous
- **calamus**, hypothalamus, thalamus
- venomous
- **autonomous**, bonhomous, heteronomous
- Pyramus
- **dichotomous**, hippopotamus, trichotomous
- Thermos

28.29

- pandanus

- **badness**, madness, sadness
- Magnus • aptness
- **fatness**, patness
- redness • wetness
- **anus**, Coriolanus, heinous, Janus, Punta Arenas, Silvanus
- **genus**, intravenous, Maecenas, Malvinas, Salinas, venous, Venus
- Cygnus • proteinous • ruinous
- libidinous
- **multitudinous**, platitudinous, pulchritudinous, vicissitudinous
- **cartilaginous**, farraginous, oleaginous
- **fuliginous**, indigenous, oxygenous, polygynous, rubiginous, vertiginous
- **androgynous**, autogenous, endogenous, erogenous, exogenous, homogenous, hydrogenous, misogynous
- ferruginous • ominous
- **bituminous**, leguminous, luminous, numinous, voluminous
- **conterminous**, coterminous, terminus, verminous
- larcenous • gelatinous • cretinous
- mountainous
- **glutinous**, mutinous
- resinous
- **Aquinas**, Delphinus, echinus, Linus, Longinus, minus, Plotinus, sinus, vinous
- oddness • wanness • hotness
- **Faunus**, rawness
- Kaunas
- **bonus**, Cronus, Jonas, lowness, onus, Tithonus

> Try rhyming one word with a set of two: onus, phone us.   ⓘ

- oldness
- **newness**, twoness
- fulness
- **alumnus**, rumness
- oneness • Oceanus • Eridanus
- diaphanous • polyphonous
- **cacophonous**, homophonous
- porcellanous • villainous
- membranous • tyrannous
- synchronous • Uranus • tetanus
- monotonous • gluttonous

- **cavernous**, ravenous
- treasonous • poisonous • Avernus

28.30

- **Chiapas**, tapas
- **campus**, grampus, hippocampus, pampas
- **metacarpus**, streptocarpus
- trespass • Priapus • Lepus
- **Aristippus**, Lysippus
- Olympus • Oedipus • platypus
- pompous
- **corpus**, porpoise
- **Canopus**, opus
- **lupus**, upas
- **compass**, encompass, rumpus
- octopus
- **multipurpose**, purpose

28.31

- **Arras**, embarrass, harass
- **gynandrous**, polyandrous
- Pancras • charas • Tatras • disastrous
- ferrous • leprous • ambidextrous
- **Carreras**, mayoress
- scabrous
- **cirrus**, Pyrrhus
- chivalrous
- **citrous**, citrus
- ludicrous • tenebrous
- **Cyrus**, Epirus, papyrus, virus
- fibrous • hydrous • Cyprus
- retrovirus • monstrous
- **brachiosaurus**, brontosaurus, canorous, chorus, Epidaurus, Horus, megalosaurus, pelorus, porous, sorus, stegosaurus, Taurus, thesaurus, torus, tyrannosaurus
- walrus
- ochrous (*US* ocherous)
- cumbrous • wondrous • lustrous
- **Algeciras**, Severus
- desirous
- **Arcturus**, Epicurus, Honduras
- barbarous • tuberous • slumberous
- Cerberus • rapturous
- **lecherous**, treacherous
- torturous • vulturous • Pandarus
- slanderous • ponderous

- **malodorous**, odorous
- thunderous • murderous
- **carboniferous**, coniferous, cruciferous, melliferous, odoriferous, pestiferous, somniferous, splendiferous, umbelliferous, vociferous
- **phosphorous**, phosphorus
- sulphurous (*US* sulfurous)
- **Anaxagoras**, Pythagoras
- **clangorous**, languorous
- **rigorous**, vigorous
- dangerous • verdurous
- **cankerous**, cantankerous, rancorous
- decorous • Icarus • valorous
- dolorous • idolatrous
- **amorous**, clamorous, glamorous
- timorous
- **humerus**, humorous, numerous
- murmurous • generous • sonorous
- onerous • obstreperous • Hesperus
- vaporous • viviparous • viperous
- **Bosporus**, prosperous
- stuporous • cancerous
- **Monoceros**, rhinoceros
- sorcerous • adventurous • Tartarus
- nectarous • dexterous • traitorous
- preposterous • slaughterous
- **boisterous**, roisterous
- uterus • adulterous • stertorous
- cadaverous • feverous
- **carnivorous**, herbivorous, insectivorous, omnivorous
- Lazarus

28.32

- **Crassus**, Halicarnassus, Lassus
- tarsus
- **nexus**, plexus, Texas
- Paracelsus
- **census**, consensus
- Croesus • narcissus • Ephesus
- Dionysus • colossus • Pegasus
- Caucasus • petasus
- **excursus**, thyrsus, versus

28.33

- **factious**, fractious

- anxious • captious
- **precious**, semi-precious
- infectious
- **conscientious**, contentious, licentious, pretentious, sententious, tendentious
- **Athanasius**, audacious, bodacious, cactaceous, capacious, carbonaceous, contumacious, Cretaceous, curvaceous, disputatious, edacious, efficacious, fallacious, farinaceous, flirtatious, foliaceous, fugacious, gracious, hellacious, herbaceous, Ignatius, loquacious, mendacious, mordacious, ostentatious, perspicacious, pertinacious, pugnacious, rapacious, sagacious, salacious, saponaceous, sebaceous, sequacious, setaceous, spacious, tenacious, veracious, vexatious, vivacious, voracious
- **facetious**, Lucretius, specious
- **adventitious**, Aloysius, ambitious, auspicious, avaricious, capricious, conspicuous, delicious, expeditious, factitious, fictitious, flagitious, judicious, lubricious, malicious, Mauritius, meretricious, nutritious, officious, pernicious, propitious, repetitious, seditious, siliceous, superstitious, supposititious, surreptitious, suspicious, vicious

> Create extra rhymes by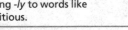
> adding -*ly* to words like
> ambitious.

- **noxious**, obnoxious
- **conscious**, subconscious, unselfconscious
- **cautious**, tortious
- **atrocious**, ferocious, precocious
- Confucius • luscious
- **bumptious**, scrumptious
- **compunctious**, rambunctious

28.34

- cactus • saltus • Diophantus • Sanctus
- **Rastus**, Theophrastus
- **altostratus**, cirrostratus

nimbostratus, stratus
- **conspectus**, prospectus
- **momentous**, portentous
- **asbestos**, Festus
- **apparatus**, Donatus, hiatus, status
- **acetous**, boletus, Cetus, Epictetus, fetus, Miletus, quietus
- Hephaestus
- **Benedictus**, ictus, rictus
- Quintus •linctus •eucalyptus •cistus
- coitus
- **circuitous**, fortuitous, gratuitous
- Hippolytus •calamitous •tinnitus
- Iapetus •crepitus
- **precipitous**, serendipitous
- impetus •emeritus •spiritous
- **Democritus**, Theocritus
- Tacitus •necessitous
- **duplicitous**, felicitous, solicitous
- covetous
- **iniquitous**, ubiquitous
- **detritus**, Heraclitus, Polyclitus, Titus, Vitus
- **Pocahontas**, Pontus
- **Plautus**, tortoise
- cobaltous
- **Duns Scotus**, lotus
- hostess
- **arbutus**, Brutus
- Eustace •conductus •cultus
- coitus interruptus •Augustus
- riotous •Herodotus •Oireachtas

28.35

- Malthus
- **acanthus**, agapanthus, clianthus, dianthus, helianthus, polyanthus
- Hyacinthus •Aegisthus •traverse
- **canvas**, canvass
- Selvas •grievous •mischievous
- redivivus •fulvous •nervous
- **Peleus**, rebellious
- Kansas •Jesus

28.36

- **amerce**, asperse, averse, burse, coerce, converse, curse, diverse, Erse, hearse, immerse, intersperse, nurse, perse, perverse, purse, reimburse, submerse, terce, terse, transverse, verse, worse
- commerce •wet nurse •sesterce
- adverse •universe •obverse

28.37

- handkerchiefs •fisticuffs

28.38

- **axe** (*US* ax), Backs, Bax, fax, flax, lax, max, pax, Sachs, sax, saxe, tax, wax

> Create extra rhymes for axe by adding -*s* to attack etc. (see section 21.1).   ⓘ

- co-ax •addax •Fairfax •Ceefax
- Halifax •Telefax •Filofax •banjax
- Ajax
- pickaxe (*US* pickax) •gravlax
- gravadlax •poleaxe •toadflax
- parallax
- battleaxe (*US* battleax)
- minimax •climax •Betamax •anthrax
- hyrax
- **borax**, storax, thorax
- syntax •surtax •beeswax •earwax
- **Berks**, Lourenço Marques, Marks, Marx, Parks, Sparks
- **annex**, convex, ex, flex, hex, perplex, Rex, sex, specs, Tex, Tex-Mex, vex
- ibex •index •codex •tubifex
- spinifex •pontifex •Telex •triplex
- simplex •multiplex
- **ilex**, silex
- complex •duplex •circumflex •Amex
- annexe •Kleenex •apex •Tipp-Ex
- haruspex •perspex •Pyrex
- **Durex**, Lurex, murex
- Middlesex •unisex •Semtex •latex
- **cortex**, Gore-tex, vortex
- vertex •Jacques
- **breeks**, idée fixe, maxixe, Weeks

28.39

- **admix**, affix, commix, fix, Hicks,

intermix, MI6, mix, nix, Nyx, pix, Pnyx, prix fixe, pyx, Ricks, six, Styx, transfix, Wicks

> Create extra rhymes for affix by adding -s to brick etc. (see section 21.9). [i]

- Aquarobics •radix •appendix
- crucifix •suffix •Alex •calyx
- **Felix**, helix
- kylix •Horlicks •prolix •spondulicks
- hydromechanics •phoenix
- **Ebonics**, onyx
- mechatronics •sardonyx
- Paralympics •semi-tropics
- subtropics •Hendrix
- **dominatrix**, matrix
- administratrix •oryx •tortrix
- executrix •Beatrix •cicatrix
- **Essex**, Wessex
- kinesics •coccyx •Sussex
- **informatics**, mathematics
- Dianetics •geopolitics •bioethics
- cervix •astrophysics •yikes

28.40

- **box**, cox, detox, fox, Foxe, Knox, lox, outfox, ox, phlox, pox, Stocks

> Create extra rhymes for cox by adding -s to block etc. (see section 21.20). [i]

- matchbox
- **bandbox**, sandbox
- hatbox •haybox •mailbox •brainbox
- paintbox •squeezebox •pillbox
- icebox •strongbox •horsebox
- saltbox •soundbox •soapbox
- shadow-box •shoebox •jukebox
- toolbox •snuffbox •gearbox •firebox
- tinderbox •thunderbox •pillar box
- pepperbox •chatterbox •letter box
- workbox •paradox •heterodox
- orthodox •dementia praecox
- Wilcox •backblocks •dreadlocks
- Goldilocks •Magnox •equinox
- chickenpox •smallpox •cowpox
- aurochs •xerox •volvox
- **Faux**, Fawkes

- **Boaks**, coax, hoax, Oaks, stokes
- yoicks
- **Fuchs**, gadzooks, Jukes
- **Brooks**, Crookes

28.41

- **crux**, dux, flux, lux, luxe, tux
- afflux •efflux •Benelux •conflux
- **bollocks**, Pollux
- **flummox**, lummox
- Lennox •barracks •Trossachs
- **circs**, Merckx, Perks
- gasworks •steelworks •printworks
- waterworks •calx
- **Franks**, Hanks, Manx, Shanks
- Fairbanks •phalanx •Gollancz
- spindleshanks
- **jinks**, jinx, lynx, methinks, minx, sphinx

> Create extra rhymes for jinx by adding -s to blink etc. (see section 21.33). [i]

- **larynx**, pharynx
- **Bronx**, Tonks, yonks
- Monks •quincunx

28.42

- Hals •rinkhals •valse •else •grilse
- **false**, waltz
- **convulse**, dulse, pulse
- impulse

28.43

- glimpse

28.44

- **askance**, expanse, finance, Hans, Hanse, manse, nance, Penzance, Romance
- underpants •happenstance
- **advance**, Afrikaans, à outrance, chance, dance, enhance, entrance, faience, France, glance, lance,

mischance, outdance, perchance, prance, Provence, stance, trance
- nuance •tap-dance •square dance
- freelance •convenance
- **cense**, commence, common sense, condense, dense, dispense, expense, fence, hence, Hortense, immense, offence (*US* offense), pence, prepense, pretence (*US* pretense), sense, spence, suspense, tense, thence, whence
- ring-fence •recompense
- frankincense
- **chintz**, convince, evince, Linz, mince, Port-au-Prince, prince, quince, rinse, since, Vince, wince
- province
- **bonce**, ensconce, nonce, ponce, response, sconce
- séance •pièce de résistance
- **announce**, bounce, denounce, flounce, fluid ounce, jounce, mispronounce, ounce, pounce, pronounce, renounce, trounce
- **dunce**, once

28.45

- **abeyance**, conveyance, purveyance
- creance •ambience
- **irradiance**, radiance
- **expedience**, obedience
- audience
- **dalliance**, mésalliance
- salience
- **consilience**, resilience
- emollience •ebullience
- **convenience**, lenience, provenience
- **impercipience**, incipience, percipience
- variance •experience
- **luxuriance**, prurience
- nescience •omniscience
- insouciance •deviance
- subservience •transience
- **alliance**, appliance, compliance, defiance, misalliance, neuroscience, reliance, science
- allowance

- **annoyance**, clairvoyance, flamboyance
- **fluence**, pursuance
- perpetuance •affluence •effluence
- mellifluence •confluence
- congruence •issuance •continuance
- disturbance
- **attendance**, dependence, interdependence, resplendence, superintendence, tendance, transcendence
- cadence
- **antecedence**, credence, impedance
- riddance •diffidence •confidence
- accidence •precedence •dissidence
- **coincidence**, incidence
- evidence
- **improvidence**, providence
- residence
- **abidance**, guidance, misguidance, subsidence
- **correspondence**, despondence
- **accordance**, concordance, discordance
- **avoidance**, voidance
- **imprudence**, jurisprudence, prudence
- impudence •abundance •elegance
- arrogance •extravagance
- allegiance •indigence
- **counter-intelligence**, intelligence
- negligence •diligence •intransigence
- exigence
- **divulgence**, effulgence, indulgence, refulgence
- **convergence**, divergence, emergence, insurgence, resurgence, submergence
- significance
- **balance**, counterbalance, imbalance, outbalance, valance
- parlance •repellence •semblance
- **bivalence**, covalence, surveillance, valence
- sibilance •jubilance •vigilance
- pestilence •silence •condolence
- virulence •ambulance •crapulence
- flatulence •feculence •petulance
- opulence •fraudulence •corpulence
- **succulence**, truculence
- turbulence •violence •redolence

- indolence •somnolence •excellence
- insolence •nonchalance
- **benevolence**, malevolence
- **ambivalence**, equivalence
- Clemence •vehemence
- **conformance**, outperformance, performance
- adamance •penance •ordinance
- eminence •imminence
- **dominance**, prominence
- abstinence •maintenance
- continence •countenance
- sustenance
- **appurtenance**, impertinence, pertinence
- provenance •ordnance •repugnance
- ordonnance •immanence
- **impermanence**, permanence
- assonance •dissonance •consonance
- governance •resonance •threepence
- halfpence •sixpence
- **comeuppance**, tuppence, twopence
- **clarence**, transparence
- **aberrance**, deterrence, inherence, Terence
- remembrance •entrance
- **Behrens**, forbearance
- fragrance •hindrance •recalcitrance
- **abhorrence**, Florence, Lawrence, Lorentz
- monstrance
- **concurrence**, co-occurrence, occurrence, recurrence
- encumbrance
- **adherence**, appearance, clearance, coherence, interference, perseverance
- **assurance**, durance, endurance, insurance
- **exuberance**, protuberance
- preponderance •transference
- **deference**, preference, reference
- difference •inference •conference
- sufferance •circumference
- belligerence •tolerance •ignorance
- temperance •utterance •furtherance
- **irreverence**, reverence, severance
- deliverance •renascence •absence
- **acquiescence**, adolescence, arborescence, coalescence, convalescence, deliquescence,

effervescence, essence, evanescence, excrescence, florescence, fluorescence, incandescence, iridescence, juvenescence, luminescence, obsolescence, opalescence, phosphorescence, pubescence, putrescence, quiescence, quintessence, tumescence
- **obeisance**, Renaissance
- puissance
- **impuissance**, reminiscence
- **beneficence**, maleficence
- **magnificence**, munificence
- reconnaissance •concupiscence
- reticence
- **licence**, license
- nonsense
- **nuisance**, translucence
- innocence •conversance •sentience
- **impatience**, patience
- conscience
- **repentance**, sentence
- acceptance •acquaintance
- **acquittance**, admittance, intermittence, pittance, quittance, remittance
- **assistance**, coexistence, consistence, distance, existence, insistence, outdistance, persistence, resistance, subsistence
- instance •exorbitance
- concomitance
- **impenitence**, penitence
- appetence
- **competence**, omnicompetence
- inheritance •capacitance •hesitance
- Constance •importance •potence
- **conductance**, inductance, reluctance
- substance •circumstance
- omnipotence •impotence
- inadvertence •grievance
- **irrelevance**, relevance
- **connivance**, contrivance
- observance •sequence •consequence
- subsequence •eloquence
- **grandiloquence**, magniloquence
- brilliance •poignance
- **omnipresence**, pleasance, presence
- complaisance •malfeasance

- **incognizance**, recognizance
- usance • recusance

28.46

- **apse**, collapse, craps, elapse, lapse, perhaps, schnapps

> Create extra rhymes for apse ⓘ
> by adding -s to tap etc. (see
> section 27.1).

- prolapse • synapse • Lesseps
- quadriceps
- **biceps**, triceps
- forceps
- **traipse**, trapes
- jackanapes • Pepys
- **Chips**, eclipse, ellipse, thrips
- Phillips • apocalypse
- **amidships**, midships
- **cripes**, Stars and Stripes
- copse • Cheops • Pelops • Cyclops
- triceratops • corpse • Stopes
- **oops**, whoops
- turps • mumps • goosebumps

28.47

- **congrats**, stats
- ersatz • Graz
- **godets**, Metz, pantalettes
  (*US* pantalets)
- Odets
- **Bates**, Fates, Gates, Trucial States, United States, Yeats

- annates
- **eats**, Keats
- foresheets
- **Biarritz**, blitz, Fritz, glitz, it's, its, Ritz, spitz, spritz, St Kitts
- blewits • Colditz • rickets • giblets
- Austerlitz • Chemnitz • Leibniz
- Massachusetts • slivovitz
- Clausewitz • Auschwitz • Horowitz
- Golan Heights • house lights
- footlights
- **Scots**, Watts
- **Cinque Ports**, orts, quartz
- undershorts
- **thereabouts**, whereabouts
- **Coats**, John o'Groats, Oates
- Hakenkreuz
- **cahoots**, Schütz
- slyboots
- **kibbutz**, Lutz, Perutz, putz
- **futz**, klutz, Smuts
- Roberts • polyunsaturates
- **deserts**, Hertz
- megahertz • kilohertz • outskirts
- Weltschmerz
- draughts (*US* drafts)
- Helmholtz • schmaltz
- Schulz
- **Hants**, Northants, pants
- sweatpants • smarty-pants
- shin splints • Mainz • Y-fronts
- arrondissements • Barents

28.48

- maths • meths • cloths

Section 29: -sh

29.1

- **abash**, ash, Ashe, bash, brash, cache, calash, cash, clash, crash, dash, encash, flash, gash, gnash, hash, lash, mash, Nash, panache, pash, plash, rash, sash, slash, smash, soutache, splash, stash, thrash, trash

> Create extra rhymes by adding -ing to words like cash. ⓘ

- earbash • kurbash • calabash
- slapdash • pebbledash • balderdash
- spatterdash • backlash • backslash
- whiplash • eyelash • goulash
- newsflash • thunderflash • mishmash
- gatecrash • Midrash • potash
- succotash

29.2

- **démarche**, gouache, harsh, marsh, moustache (*US* mustache)
- Saltmarsh

29.3

- **afresh**, Andhra Pradesh, Bangladesh, crème fraîche, enmesh, flesh, fresh, intermesh, Kesh, Madhya Pradesh, Marrakesh, mesh, nesh, thresh, Uttar Pradesh
- parfleche • horseflesh • gooseflesh
- micromesh • Gilgamesh
- synchromesh

29.4

- **crèche**, flèche, kesh

29.5

- **babiche**, Dalglish, fiche, Laois, leash, niche, nouveau riche, pastiche, quiche, Rajneesh, schottische
- microfiche • corniche • hashish
- baksheesh

29.6

- **bish**, dish, fish, Frisch, Gish, knish, pish, squish, swish, wish

> Create extra rhymes by adding -ing to words like fish. ⓘ

- **clayish**, greyish (*US* grayish)
- puppyish • babyish
- **dandyish**, sandyish
- toadyish • fogeyish • monkeyish
- sissyish • Gypsyish • prettyish
- heavyish • dryish
- **lowish**, slowish
- sallowish • yellowish • narrowish
- boyish • tomboyish
- **bluish**, Jewish, newish, shrewish
- Pollyannaish • prima donna-ish
- nebbish
- **slobbish**, snobbish, yobbish
- rubbish • furbish
- **baddish**, caddish, faddish, kaddish, laddish, radish, saddish
- **blandish**, brandish, outlandish, Standish
- Cavendish • Netherlandish
- horseradish • hardish • reddish
- Wendish • old-maidish • Swedish
- fiendish • Yiddish • widish
- **childish**, mildish, wildish
- **cloddish**, oddish

- baldish • roundish
- **modish**, toadish
- **coldish**, oldish
- prudish • goodish • Kurdish

29.7

- raffish • damselfish
- **catfish**, flatfish
- **garfish**, starfish
- redfish
- **elfish**, selfish, shellfish
- devilfish
- **crayfish**, waifish
- stiffish • kingfish • jellyfish
- killifish • filefish • pipefish
- white fish
- **offish**, standoffish
- codfish • dogfish • rockfish • crawfish
- swordfish
- **blowfish**, oafish
- goldfish

> Try rhyming one word with a
> set of two: goldfish, cold fish.   🛈

- **bonefish**, stonefish
- wolfish
- **huffish**, roughish, toughish
- mudfish • monkfish • cuttlefish
- lungfish • lumpfish • spearfish
- angelfish • parrotfish • silverfish
- **haggish**, waggish
- vaguish
- **biggish**, piggish, priggish, whiggish
- **doggish**, hoggish
- **roguish**, voguish
- **puggish**, sluggish, thuggish
- largish

29.8

- **blackish**, brackish, quackish
- **Frankish**, prankish
- **clerkish**, darkish, sparkish
- peckish • rakish
- **cliquish**, freakish, weakish
- **sickish**, thickish
- pinkish
- **hawkish**, mawkish
- folkish • bookish • textbookish

- puckish
- **monkish**, punkish
- **quirkish**, Turkish
- **establish**, stablish
- Spanglish
- **embellish**, hellish, relish
- **palish**, Salish
- English • stylish
- **abolish**, demolish, spit-and-polish
- **Gaulish**, smallish, tallish
- owlish • Polish
- **coolish**, foolish, ghoulish, mulish
- bullish • dullish • publish
- accomplish • ticklish • purplish
- devilish
- **churlish**, girlish
- famish • Amish • schoolmarmish
- **blemish**, Flemish
- Hamish • squeamish • dimmish
- warmish • gnomish • Carchemish
- skirmish

29.9

- **banish**, clannish, mannish, Spanish, tannish, vanish
- **garnish**, tarnish, varnish
- **replenish**, Rhenish
- Danish
- **cleanish**, greenish
- **diminish**, finish, Finnish, thinnish
- swinish
- **admonish**, astonish, donnish
- Cornish
- **brownish**, clownish, townish
- **buffoonish**, cartoonish, soonish
- **Hunnish**, nunnish, punish
- maidenish • hoydenish • paganish
- womanish • vixenish • kittenish
- heathenish
- **burnish**, furnish
- **longish**, strongish
- youngish
- **Lappish**, snappish
- **dampish**, scampish, trampish, vampish
- sharpish • apish
- **cheapish**, sheepish, steepish
- **blimpish**, impish, wimpish
- foppish • waspish • uppish

- **frumpish**, grumpish, lumpish, plumpish
- parish
- **cherish**, perish
- **bearish**, fairish, garish, squarish
- nightmarish • Irish
- **moreish**, whorish
- **flourish**, nourish
- **nearish**, queerish
- sourish
- **boorish**, Moorish
- gibberish • Micawberish • vulturish
- spiderish • vigorish • vinegarish
- tigerish • ogreish • Quakerish
- **lickerish**, liquorice (*US* licorice)
- ochreish (*US* ocherish)
- vapourish (*US* vaporish) • viperish
- spinsterish • Pooterish • amateurish
- feverish • liverish • impoverish
- minxish • niceish • coarsish • closish

29.10

- **cattish**, fattish, flattish
- smartish
- **coquettish**, fetish, pettish, wettish
- leftish • Kentish
- **latish**, straightish
- sweetish
- **British**, skittish, twittish
- Pictish
- **brightish**, lightish, rightish, slightish, whitish
- **hottish**, Scottish, sottish
- softish • shortish • saltish
- **loutish**, stoutish
- goatish
- **coltish**, doltish
- **brutish**, Jutish
- sluttish • smoothish
- **lavish**, ravish
- elvish
- **knavish**, slavish
- **peevish**, thievish
- spivvish • dervish
- **anguish**, languish
- vanquish
- **distinguish**, extinguish
- relinquish

29.11

- **awash**, Boche, Bosch, bosh, brioche, cloche, cohosh, cosh, dosh, Foch, galosh, gosh, josh, mosh, nosh, posh, quash, slosh, splosh, squash, swash, tosh, wash
- kibosh
- **mackintosh**, McIntosh
- backwash • car wash • brainwash
- wish-wash
- **eyewash**, Siwash
- limewash • whitewash • hogwash
- mouthwash • musquash

29.12

- Porsche

29.13

- **gauche**, guilloche

29.14

- **barouche**, cartouche, douche, farouche, louche, ruche, sloosh, swoosh, tarboosh
- scaramouch

29.15

- **bush**, Hindu Kush, kurus, mush, push, whoosh, woosh
- shadbush • ambush • spicebush
- saltbush • kiddush • cush-cush
- bell push

29.16

- **ablush**, blush, brush, crush, flush, gush, hush, hush-hush, lush, mush, plush, rush, shush, slush, thrush, tush

i
Create extra rhymes by adding *-ing* to words like blush.

- **airbrush**, hairbrush
- sagebrush • paintbrush • onrush
- song thrush • outrush • toothbrush
- woodrush • bulrush • uprush

- kirsch

29.18

- Smersh

29.19

- welsh • milch • Walsh • mulch

29.20

- Romansh

- **blanch**, Blanche, branch, ranch, tranche
- avalanche
- **backbench**, bench, blench, clench, Dench, drench, entrench, French, frontbench, quench, stench, tench, trench, wench, wrench
- crossbench • workbench
- **cinch**, clinch, finch, flinch, inch, lynch, Minch, pinch, squinch, winch
- chaffinch • greenfinch • hawfinch
- goldfinch • bullfinch
- **carte blanche**, conch
- **graunch**, haunch, launch, paunch, raunch, staunch
- **brunch**, bunch, crunch, hunch, lunch, munch, punch, scrunch

> Create extra rhymes by
> adding -*ing* to words like bunch. | i |

- honeybunch • keypunch

Section 30: -t

30.1

- **at**, bat, brat, cat, chat, cravat, drat, expat, fat, flat, frat, gat, gnat, hat, hereat, high-hat, howzat, lat, mat, matt, matte, Montserrat, Nat, outsat, pat, pit-a-pat, plait, plat, prat, Rabat, rat, rat-tat, Sadat, sat, scat, Sebat, shabbat, shat, skat, slat, spat, splat, sprat, stat, Surat, tat, that, thereat, tit-for-tat, vat, whereat

> Create extra rhymes by changing words like bat to batting. [i]

- fiat • floreat • exeat • caveat
- **Croat**, Serbo-Croat
- Nanga Parbat • brickbat • dingbat
- **combat**, wombat
- fruitbat • numbat • acrobat • backchat
- whinchat • chitchat • samizdat
- concordat • Arafat • Jehoshaphat
- butterfat • Kattegat • hard hat
- sun hat • fat cat • hellcat • requiescat
- scaredy-cat • Magnificat • copycat
- pussycat • wildcat • bobcat • tomcat
- Sno-Cat • polecat • muscat • meerkat
- mudflat • cervelat
- **doormat**, format
- diplomat • laundromat • Zermatt
- Donat • cowpat

30.2

- Eurocrat • ziggurat • muskrat
- theocrat • jurat • Ballarat • democrat
- technocrat • bureaucrat • aristocrat
- autocrat • plutocrat • babysat
- Comsat • Randstad • Darmstadt
- diktat • habitat • Eisenstadt
- Kronstadt • cryostat • aerostat
- aegrotat • rheostat • haemostat
- thermostat • photostat

30.3

- **apart**, apparat, art, baht, Bart, Barthes, cart, carte, chart, clart, dart, Eilat, fart, ghat, Gujarat, Gujrat, hart, Harte, heart, heart-to-heart, impart, Jat, kart, kyat, Maat, Mansart, mart, outsmart, part, quarte, salat, savate, Scart, smart, start, tart, zakat

> Create extra rhymes by adding -ed or -ing to words like chart. [i]

- Hobart • wallchart • flow chart
- Bogart • Stuttgart • Earhart
- greenheart • sweetheart • Leichhardt
- Reinhardt • Bernhardt • handcart
- Descartes • dogcart • go-kart
- pushcart • dustcart • rampart
- forepart • underpart • Bonaparte
- counterpart • Bundesrat • Robsart
- Mozart • Hallstatt • kick-start
- push-start • upstart

30.4

- **abet**, aiguillette, anisette, Annette, Antoinette, arête, Arlette, ate, baguette, banquette, barbette, barrette, basinet, bassinet, beget, Bernadette, beset, bet, Bette, blanquette, Brett, briquette, brochette, brunette (*US* brunet), Burnett, cadet, caravanette, cassette, castanet, cigarette (*US* cigaret), clarinet, Claudette, Colette, coquette, corvette, couchette, courgette, croquette, curette, curvet,

Debrett, debt, dinette, diskette, duet, epaulette (*US* epaulet), flageolet, flannelette, forget, fret, galette, gazette, Georgette, get, godet, grisette, heavyset, Jeanette, jet, kitchenette, La Fayette, landaulet, launderette, layette, lazaret, leatherette, let, Lett, lorgnette, luncheonette, lunette, Lynette, maisonette, majorette, maquette, Marie-Antoinette, marionette, Marquette, marquisette, martinet, met, minaret, minuet, moquette, motet, musette, Nanette, net, noisette, nonet, novelette, nymphet, octet, Odette, on-set, oubliette, Paulette, pet, Phuket, picquet, pillaret, pincette, pipette, piquet, pirouette, planchette, pochette, quartet, quickset, quintet, regret, ret, Rhett, roomette, rosette, roulette, satinette, septet, serviette, sestet, set, sett, sextet, silhouette, soubrette, spinet, spinneret, statuette, stet, stockinet, sublet, suffragette, Suzette, sweat, thickset, threat, Tibet, toilette, tret, underlet, upset, usherette, vedette, vet, vignette, vinaigrette, wagonette, wet, whet, winceyette, yet, Yvette
- quodlibet • alphabet
- **ramjet**, scramjet
- propjet • turbojet • etiquette • outlet
- triolet • calumet • cermet

30.5

- dragnet • Fastnet • telnet • hairnet
- keepnet • driftnet • fishnet • jaconet
- alkanet • Intranet • Ethernet
- aigrette • asset • handset • headset
- **hic jacet**, placet
- **preset**, teaset
- filmset
- **inset**, twinset
- videlicet • scilicet • mindset • typeset
- offset • onset • outset • photoset
- moonset • subset • sunset • upset
- Somerset • Exocet • avocet
- trebuchet • epithet • Tevet
- marmoset

30.6

- **famille verte**, terre-verte

30.7

- **abate**, ablate, aerate, ait, await, backdate, bait, bate, berate, castrate, collate, conflate, crate, create, cremate, date, deflate, dictate, dilate, distraite, donate, downstate, eight, elate, equate, estate, fate, fellate, fête, fixate, freight, frustrate, gait, gate, gestate, gradate, grate, great, gyrate, hate, hydrate, inflate, innate, interrelate, interstate, irate, Kate, Kuwait, lactate, late, locate, lustrate, mandate, mate, migrate, misdate, misstate, mistranslate, mutate, narrate, negate, notate, orate, ornate, Pate, placate, plate, prate, prorate, prostrate, pulsate, pupate, quadrate, rate, rotate, sate, sedate, serrate, short weight, skate, slate, spate, spectate, spruit, stagnate, state, straight, strait, Tate, tête-à-tête, Thwaite, translate, translocate, transmigrate, truncate, underrate, understate, underweight, update, uprate, upstate, up-to-date, vacate, vibrate, wait, weight

30.8

- labiate
- **irradiate**, radiate
- mediate • ideate • repudiate
- **palliate**, retaliate
- **affiliate**, ciliate, conciliate, humiliate
- **exfoliate**, foliate
- nucleate • permeate • delineate
- calumniate • expiate
- **expatriate**, repatriate
- recreate • inebriate
- **aureate**, excoriate
- procreate
- **appropriate**, expropriate, impropriate, misappropriate

- **infuriate**, luxuriate
- asphyxiate •nauseate

> Try rhyming one word with a set of two or more: nauseate, because we ate. ⓘ

- **annunciate**, enunciate
- **instantiate**, substantiate, transubstantiate
- **differentiate**, potentiate
- **expatiate**, ingratiate, satiate
- **appreciate**, depreciate
- **initiate**, officiate, propitiate, vitiate
- **associate**, dissociate, negotiate
- excruciate •aviate
- **abbreviate**, alleviate, deviate
- obviate •exuviate •inchoate
- actuate •perpetuate •effectuate
- habituate •fluctuate •punctuate
- graduate •individuate •menstruate
- **accentuate**, eventuate
- evacuate
- **evaluate**, valuate
- superannuate •infatuate
- **attenuate**, extenuate
- insinuate •situate

30.9

- jailbait •rebate •whitebait •probate
- stereobate •approbate •incubate
- stylobate •exacerbate •masturbate
- mandate •candidate •validate
- consolidate •intimidate •dilapidate
- cuspidate •fluoridate •elucidate
- antedate •liquidate •chordate
- update •inundate •fecundate
- accommodate •caliphate •phosphate
- Margate •Irangate •tailgate
- lychgate •Lydgate
- **delegate**, relegate
- Billingsgate •obligate •fumigate
- abnegate •aggregate •segregate
- irrigate •congregate •castigate
- investigate
- **litigate**, mitigate
- instigate
- **circumnavigate**, navigate
- promulgate •elongate •toll gate
- Newgate •sluice gate •conjugate

- subjugate •floodgate •vulgate
- objurgate •expurgate •propagate
- arrogate •abrogate
- **derogate**, interrogate
- corrugate •subrogate •watergate

30.10

- defalcate •demarcate •cheapskate
- eradicate •abdicate
- **dedicate**, medicate, predicate
- **indicate**, syndicate, vindicate
- adjudicate •defecate
- **certificate**, pontificate
- confiscate •replicate •explicate
- spifflicate •triplicate •implicate
- complicate
- **duplicate**, quadruplicate, quintuplicate
- supplicate •fornicate
- **communicate**, excommunicate, intercommunicate, tunicate
- **divaricate**, prevaricate
- fabricate •deprecate •metricate
- extricate
- **lubricate**, rubricate
- desiccate •intoxicate •masticate
- authenticate •domesticate
- sophisticate •prognosticate
- rusticate •hypothecate •manducate
- educate •obfuscate •inculcate
- bifurcate •suffocate •allocate
- dislocate •reciprocate •coruscate
- altercate •advocate •equivocate
- furcate

30.11

- circumvallate •bedplate •template
- breastplate •nameplate •faceplate
- chelate •fishplate •sibilate •jubilate
- flagellate •legislate •invigilate
- **assimilate**, dissimilate
- **depilate**, epilate
- fibrillate
- **correlate**, intercorrelate
- vacillate •tessellate •oscillate
- cantillate
- **hyperventilate**, ventilate
- titillate •scintillate •constellate

- mutilate •oblate •hotplate
- electroplate •bookplate •footplate
- congratulate
- **confabulate**, tabulate
- **ambulate**, circumambulate, perambulate
- adulate •coagulate
- **strangulate**, triangulate
- ejaculate
- **calculate**, miscalculate
- emasculate •granulate •encapsulate
- regulate •speculate •emulate
- infibulate •acidulate
- **articulate**, gesticulate, matriculate
- **simulate**, stimulate
- **manipulate**, stipulate
- insulate •capitulate
- discombobulate •modulate
- **flocculate**, inoculate
- osculate
- **copulate**, populate
- **expostulate**, postulate
- ovulate •formulate •ululate
- **accumulate**, cumulate
- undulate •pustulate •circulate
- lanceolate
- **annihilate**, violate
- number plate •fingerplate •escalate
- percolate •immolate
- crenellate (*US* crenelate)
- extrapolate •copperplate
- **interpellate**, interpolate
- desolate •insufflate •isolate
- apostolate •contemplate

30.12

- flatmate •classmate •checkmate
- helpmate •messmate •playmate
- stalemate •stablemate •teammate
- inmate •shipmate •acclimate
- sublimate •animate •decimate
- approximate
- **estimate**, guesstimate, underestimate
- intimate •primate •housemate
- soulmate •schoolmate •room-mate
- consummate •amalgamate
- diplomate •automate •glutamate
- workmate

30.13

- **agnate**, magnate
- **incarnate**, khanate
- impregnate
- **coordinate**, subordinate
- decaffeinate •paginate •originate
- oxygenate
- **cachinnate**, machinate
- pollinate
- **contaminate**, laminate
- **disseminate**, ingeminate, inseminate
- **discriminate**, eliminate, incriminate, recriminate
- **abominate**, dominate, nominate
- **illuminate**, ruminate
- fulminate •culminate
- **exterminate**, germinate, terminate, verminate
- marinate •peregrinate •indoctrinate
- chlorinate •urinate
- **assassinate**, deracinate, fascinate
- vaccinate •hallucinate •Latinate
- procrastinate •predestinate
- agglutinate •rejuvenate •resinate
- designate •cognate •neonate
- lunate •alienate •carbonate
- hibernate •odonate •hyphenate
- emanate
- **impersonate**, personate
- fractionate •detonate •intonate
- consternate •alternate •Italianate
- resonate

30.14

- palpate •emancipate
- **anticipate**, dissipate, participate
- constipate •cuspate •exculpate
- inculpate •syncopate •extirpate

30.15

- serrate •concentrate •airfreight
- ingrate •filtrate •arbitrate
- exfiltrate •magistrate •orchestrate
- calibrate •celebrate •emigrate
- immigrate •denigrate •penetrate

- defenestrate • administrate • aspirate
- perpetrate • decerebrate • desecrate
- execrate • consecrate • integrate
- **carbohydrate**, hydrate
- nitrate • quadrate • prostrate
- **borate**, quorate
- portrait • polyunsaturate
- acculturate • depurate • indurate
- triturate • inaugurate • suppurate
- substrate • adumbrate
- **ameliorate**, meliorate
- deteriorate
- **collaborate**, elaborate
- liberate • corroborate • reverberate
- saturate
- **confederate**, federate
- desiderate • moderate
- preponderate
- **proliferate**, vociferate
- perforate • invigorate • exaggerate
- refrigerate • decorate
- **accelerate**, decelerate
- exhilarate • illustrate • tolerate
- commemorate
- **demonstrate**, remonstrate
- **agglomerate**, conglomerate
- enumerate
- **generate**, venerate
- **incinerate**, itinerate
- exonerate • remunerate • evaporate
- exasperate • separate
- **cooperate**, operate
- incorporate
- **recuperate**, vituperate
- perorate
- **lacerate**, macerate
- incarcerate • eviscerate • expectorate
- **alliterate**, iterate, obliterate, transliterate
- adulterate • asseverate • sequestrate
- commiserate • birth rate • sensate
- condensate • decussate • compensate
- tergiversate

30.16

- **lactate**, tractate
- apartheid • peltate • edentate
- testate • dictate • meditate • agitate
- vegetate • interdigitate

- **cogitate**, excogitate
- **ingurgitate**, regurgitate
- **facilitate**, habilitate, militate
- debilitate • imitate • decapitate
- palpitate • crepitate • precipitate
- irritate
- **acetate**, capacitate, triacetate
- necessitate • felicitate • resuscitate
- gravitate • levitate • hesitate
- **apostate**, prostate
- pernoctate • potentate • annotate
- amputate • permutate • orientate
- auscultate • commentate • superstate
- devastate • salivate • elevate
- activate • captivate • titivate
- motivate • cultivate • ovate • excavate
- **enervate**, renovate
- innovate • aggravate • rotavate

30.17

- catchweight • middleweight
- pennyweight • heavyweight
- flyweight • lightweight • paperweight
- hundredweight • bantamweight
- welterweight • counterweight
- featherweight • birthweight
- solmizate

30.18

- **accrete**, beat, beet, bittersweet, bleat, cheat, cleat, clubfeet, compete, compleat, complete, conceit, Crete, deceit, delete, deplete, discreet, discrete, eat, effete, élite, entreat, escheat, estreat, excrete, feat, feet, fleet, gîte, greet, heat, leat, leet, Magritte, maltreat, marguerite, meat, meet, mesquite, mete, mistreat, neat, outcompete, peat, Pete, petite, pleat, receipt, replete, seat, secrete, sheet, skeet, sleet, splay-feet, street, suite, sweet, teat, treat, tweet, wheat

> Create extra rhymes by adding -ing to words like bleat. 🛈

- backbeat • heartbeat • deadbeat
- breakbeat • offbeat • browbeat

- downbeat •drumbeat •upbeat
- sugar beet • Blackfeet •flatfeet
- forefeet •exegete •polychaete
- lorikeet •parakeet
- **athlete**, biathlete, decathlete, heptathlete, pentathlete, triathlete
- kick-pleat •paraclete •obsolete
- gamete •crabmeat •sweetmeat
- mincemeat •forcemeat •backstreet
- concrete •window seat

30.19

- spreadsheet •mainsheet •flysheet
- time sheet •broadsheet
- groundsheet •flowsheet •news-sheet
- dust sheet •worksheet
- aesthete (US esthete) •wholewheat
- meadowsweet •buckwheat
- bittersweet

30.20

- **acquit**, admit, backlit, bedsit, befit, bit, Brit, Britt, chit, commit, demit, dit, emit, fit, flit, frit, git, grit, hit, intermit, it, kit, knit, legit, lickety-split, lit, manumit, mishit, mitt, nit, omit, outsit, outwit, permit, pit, Pitt, pretermit, quit, remit, retrofit, shit, sit, skit, slit, snit, spit, split, sprit, squit, submit, tit, transmit, twit, whit, wit, writ, zit
- **albeit**, howbeit
- poet
- **bluet**, cruet, intuit, suet, Yuit
- Inuit •floruit •Jesuit
- **Babbitt**, cohabit, habit, rabbet, rabbit
- **ambit**, gambit
- jackrabbit •barbet •Nesbit •rarebit
- **adhibit**, exhibit, gibbet, inhibit, prohibit
- titbit (US tidbit) •flibbertigibbet
- **Cobbett**, gobbet, hobbit, obit, probit
- orbit •Tobit
- **cubit**, two-bit
- **hatchet**, latchet, ratchet
- Pritchett
- **crotchet**, rochet

30.21

- adit
- **bandit**, pandit
- **accredit**, credit, edit, subedit
- Chindit •conduit
- **audit**, plaudit
- pundit •refit •misfit •benefit
- **profit**, prophet, soffit
- forfeit •outfit •Tophet •photofit
- **buffet**, tuffet
- comfit •counterfeit •surfeit •agate
- **margate**, target
- frigate •Tlingit •hogget
- **drugget**, nugget
- Brigitte •gadget •eejit
- **Bridget**, digit, fidget, midget, widget
- budget
- **Blackett**, bracket, jacket, packet, placket, racket
- blanket •gasket •bedjacket
- straitjacket •lifejacket •leatherjacket
- **downmarket**, market, upmarket
- **basket**, casket
- breadbasket •Euromarket
- Newmarket •hypermarket
- **Becket**, Beckett
- **cricket**, midwicket, picket, picquet, piquet, pricket, snicket, thicket, ticket, wicket

> Try rhyming one word with a set of two: ticket, stick it.

- trinket
- **biscuit**, brisket, frisket
- identikit
- **brocket**, crocket, Crockett, docket, locket, pocket, rocket, socket, sprocket

> Try rhyming one word with a set of two: socket, shock it.

- airpocket •pickpocket •skyrocket
- toolkit
- **bucket**, Nantucket, tucket
- **Blunkett**, junket
- musket •rust bucket
- **circuit**, short-circuit

30.22

- **mallet**, palette, pallet, valet
- tablet •pamphlet •aglet •anklet
- candlelit •hamlet
- **Caplet**, chaplet
- lamplit •flatlet •mantlet
- **haslet**, Hazlitt
- **scarlet**, Scarlett, starlet, starlit, varlet
- armlet •lancelet •branchlet
- **martlet**, tartlet
- plantlet •pellet •reglet •necklet
- playlet •lakelet •bracelet
- **platelet**, statelet
- wavelet •leaflet •eaglet •streamlet
- **billet**, filet, fillet, millet, skillet, willet
- **driblet**, triblet
- piglet •singlet •gimlet •inlet
- **kinglet**, ringlet, springlet, winglet
- **ripplet**, triplet
- wristlet
- **eyelet**, islet, stylet, twilit
- pikelet
- **collet**, Smollett, wallet
- goblet •rodlet
- omelette (*US* omelet) •droplet
- torchlit
- **corselet**, corselette
- gauntlet (*US* gantlet) •owlet
- townlet •toadlet •notelet •toilet
- moonlit •sextuplet •fruitlet
- **bullet**, pullet
- **booklet**, brooklet, hooklet
- quadruplet •annulet •septuplet
- rivulet •quintuplet
- **gullet**, mullet
- doublet •floodlit
- **runlet**, sunlit
- couplet •cutlet •frontlet •violet
- coverlet •circlet •verselet

30.23

- **dammit**, Hammett, Mamet
- **emmet**, semmit
- **helmet**, pelmet
- remit •limit •kismet •climate
- **comet**, grommet, vomit

- Goldschmidt
- **plummet**, summit
- Hindemith
- **hermit**, Kermit, permit
- **gannet**, granite, Janet, planet
- magnet •Hamnett •pomegranate
- **Barnet**, garnet
- **Bennett**, genet, jennet, rennet, senate, sennet, sennit, tenet
- **innit**, linnet, minute, sinnet
- **cygnet**, signet
- cabinet •definite •Plantagenet
- **bonnet**, sonnet
- **cornet**, hornet
- unit
- **punnet**, whodunnit (*US* whodunit)
- bayonet •dragonet •falconet
- baronet •coronet
- **alternate**, burnet
- sandpit •carpet •armpit •decrepit
- cesspit •bear pit •fleapit
- **pipit**, sippet, skippet, snippet, tippet, Tippett, whippet
- limpet •incipit •limepit
- **moppet**, poppet
- cockpit •cuckoo-spit •pulpit •puppet
- **crumpet**, strumpet, trumpet
- parapet •turnspit

30.24

- caret •Sanskrit •Prakrit
- **ferret**, inherit, merit
- egret •secret
- **dispirit**, skirret, spirit
- floret •pomfret •bowsprit
- barbiturate
- **turret**, worrit
- culprit •floweret •Margaret
- cellaret (*US* cellarette)
- **banneret**, lanneret
- hypocrite •preterite (*US* preterit)
- **Everett**, leveret
- favourite (*US* favorite)
- **interpret**, misinterpret
- **basset**, facet, tacet, tacit
- **Narragansett**, transit
- lancet
- **cresset**, Knesset
- exit •resit

- **complicit**, elicit, explicit, illicit, implicit, licit, solicit
- Tilsit • plebiscite • babysit • deficit
- **cosset**, posset
- Quonset • whatsit
- **corset**, Dorset, faucet
- **gusset**, russet
- dulcet
- **tercet**, verset
- ashet • planchet • bullshit • Bastet
- tomtit • bluetit

30.25

- davit • brevet • velvet • affidavit
- **civet**, privet, rivet, trivet
- private • covet • aquavit • banquet
- halfwit • peewit • dimwit • nitwit
- **exquisite**, visit
- requisite • perquisite
- **closet**, posit
- apposite • opposite • composite

30.26

- **affright**, alight, alright, aright, bedight, bight, bite, blight, bright, byte, cite, dight, Dwight, excite, fight, flight, fright, goodnight, height, ignite, impolite, indict, indite, invite, kite, knight, light, lite, might, mite, night, nite, outfight,

outright, plight, polite, quite, right, rite, shite, sight, site, skintight, skite, sleight, slight, smite, Snow-white, spite, sprite, tight, tonight, trite, twite, underwrite, unite, uptight, white, wight, wright, write
- Shiite • Trotskyite • McCarthyite
- Vishnuite • Sivaite • albite
- snakebite • frostbite • soundbite
- kilobyte • columbite • love bite
- Moabite • megabyte • gigabyte
- Jacobite • Rechabite • jadeite
- lyddite • expedite • cordite • erudite
- Luddite • recondite • troglodyte
- hermaphrodite • extradite

30.27

- graphite • prizefight • dogfight
- cockfight • neophyte • saprophyte
- bullfight • gunfight • firefight
- gesundheit • Fahrenheit • malachite
- blatherskite

30.28

- halite • candlelight • fanlight
- lamplight • gaslight • flashlight
- starlight • headlight • penlight
- daylight • tail light
- **Peelite**, pelite
- street light • phyllite • rubellite
- Carmelite • proselyte • Monothelite
- **highlight**, skylight, stylite, twilight
- sidelight • limelight • night light
- spotlight • torchlight • lowlight
- cryolite • microlight • moonlight

> Try rhyming one word with a
> set of two: moonlight, soon light.

- cellulite • floodlight • sunlight
- rushlight • Pre-Raphaelite • firelight
- acolyte • Bakelite • Armalite
- Ishmaelite • phonolite • cosmopolite
- electrolyte • Israelite • corallite
- heteroclite • chrysolite • socialite
- satellite • tantalite • overflight
- **pearlite**, perlite
- searchlight

> The use of *stressed* (or *masculine*) *rhyme* followed by *wrenched* *rhyme* (where the last vowel is mis-stressed—eye/symmetry) can have a dramatic deadening effect if one chooses not to force the word to rhyme: here, it practically halts the flow which the stanza has built up:
>
> Tyger Tyger, burning bright,
> In the forests of the night;
> What immortal hand or eye,
> Could frame thy fearful symmetry?
>
> (William Blake, 'The Tyger')

30.29

- **Hamite**, samite
- marmite •Semite •Vegemite
- eremite •Hashemite •Fatimite
- chromite •Edomite •sodomite
- stalagmite •Elamite •dolomite
- Adullamite •dynamite •catamite
- Benthamite
- **termite**, thermite
- Samnite •sennight •midnight
- lignite •selenite •gelignite
- kaolinite •Leninite
- **finite**, transfinite
- watchnight •fortnight •Sunnite
- **exurbanite**, suburbanite, urbanite
- manganite •ammonite •Mennonite
- Canaanite •Maronite •bentonite
- Irvingite •respite •alexandrite
- Arkwright •cartwright •nephrite
- playwright •wainwright
- wheelwright •millwright
- shipwright •copyright •Nazirite
- pyrite •eyebright •nitrite •contrite
- chlorite •forthright •downright
- Fulbright •upright •meteorite
- diorite •fluorite
- Labourite (*US* Laborite) •sybarite
- Thatcherite •phosphorite •azurite
- anchorite •Hitlerite •dolerite
- Amorite •Minorite •laterite
- Hutterite •birthright

30.30

- calcite •campsite

> Try rhyming one word with a [i]
> set of two: campsite, damp site.

- website •dacite •insight
- Monophysite •magnesite •eyesight
- hindsight •bombsight •foresight
- bauxite •quartzite •leucocyte
- Hussite •gunsight •phagocyte
- marcasite •parasite •anthracite
- oversight •worksite
- **bipartite**, multipartite, partite, quadripartite, sexpartite, tripartite
- transvestite •airtight •Hittite
- magnetite •appetite •stalactite
- watertight •Levite •Muscovite
- Hepplewhite •bobwhite

30.31

- **allot**, begot, Bernadotte, blot, bot, capot, clot, cocotte, cot, culotte, dot, forgot, garrotte (*US* garrote), gavotte, got, grot, hot, jot, knot, lot, Mayotte, motte, not, Ott, outshot, plot, pot, rot, sans-culotte, Scot, Scott, shallot, shot, slot, snot, sot, spot, squat, stot, swat, swot, tot, trot, twat, undershot, Wat, Watt, what, wot, yacht

> Create extra rhymes by [i]
> adding -(*t*)*ing* to words like blot.

- robot •hotshot •peridot •microdot
- Wyandot •polka dot •fylfot •mascot
- Caldecott •carrycot •apricot
- boycott •dovecote •sandlot •melilot
- polyglot •Camelot •ocelot
- monoglot •sub-plot •Lancelot
- cachalot •counterplot •Wilmot
- guillemot •motmot •bergamot

30.32

- cannot •slip knot •forget-me-not
- touch-me-not •topknot •whatnot
- **crackpot**, jackpot
- blackspot •dashpot •sexpot •despot
- fleshpot •teapot •stinkpot •tinpot
- **gallipot**, talipot
- chimney pot •nightspot •stockpot
- tosspot •hotspot •hotpot •stewpot
- fusspot •sunspot •flowerpot
- pepperpot •lobster pot •tommyrot
- **dogtrot**, jogtrot
- foxtrot
- **slapshot**, snapshot
- mailshot •grapeshot •slingshot
- eyeshot •potshot •bloodshot
- mugshot •buckshot •troubleshot
- gunshot •upshot •earshot
- Aldershot •Hottentot •aliquot
- diddly-squat •Ofwat •loquat
- kumquat •somewhat •megawatt
- kilowatt •paraquat •terawatt

30.33

- **abort**, apport, assort, athwart, aught, besought, bethought, bort, bought, brought, caught, cavort, comport, consort, contort, Cort, court, distraught, escort, exhort, export, extort, fort, fought, fraught, import, methought, misreport, mort, naught, nought, Oort, ought, outfought, port, Porte, purport, quart, rort, short, snort, sort, sought, sport, support, swart, taught, taut, thought, thwart, tort, transport, wart, wrought

> Create extra rhymes by adding -*ing* to words like contort. ⓘ

- cohort ● backcourt ● Port Harcourt
- forecourt ● onslaught ● dreadnought
- Connacht ● aeronaut ● Argonaut
- juggernaut ● cosmonaut ● astronaut
- aquanaut ● davenport ● carport
- passport ● airport
- **Freeport**, seaport
- Shreveport
- **heliport**, teleport
- Stockport ● outport ● Coalport
- spoilsport
- **Newport**, viewport
- hoverport
- **forethought**, malice aforethought
- afterthought ● worrywart

30.34

- **about**, bout, clout, devout, doubt, down-and-out, drought, flout, gout, grout, knout, Kraut, lout, mahout, misdoubt, nowt, out, out-and-out, owt, pout, Prout, right about, rout, scout, shout, snout, spout, sprout, stout, thereabout, thereout, throughout, timeout, tout, trout, way-out, without
- **layout**, payout
- buyout ● blowout ● layabout
- gadabout ● roundabout ● knockabout
- walkabout ● runabout ● turnabout
- hereabout ● roustabout

- **handout**, standout
- readout ● hideout ● dugout ● blackout
- checkout
- **breakout**, stakeout, takeout
- strikeout
- **knockout**, lockout
- walkout
- **cookout**, lookout
- workout ● sell-out ● fallout ● pull-out
- umlaut ● litter lout ● spin-out
- **burnout**, turnout
- hangout ● wipeout
- **copout**, dropout
- waterspout ● beansprout ● clearout
- sauerkraut ● washout ● printout
- white-out ● shoot-out
- **cut-out**, shut-out

30.35

- **afloat**, bloat, boat, capote, coat, connote, cote, dote, emote, float, gloat, goat, groat, misquote, moat, mote, note, oat, outvote, promote, quote, rote, shoat, smote, stoat, Succoth, table d'hôte, Terre Haute, throat, tote, vote, wrote

> Create extra rhymes by changing words like float and note to floating and noting. ⓘ

- flatboat
- **mailboat**, sailboat, whaleboat
- speedboat ● keelboat
- **dreamboat**, steamboat
- lifeboat ● iceboat ● longboat
- sauceboat ● houseboat
- **rowboat**, showboat
- U-boat ● tugboat ● gunboat
- powerboat ● motorboat ● riverboat
- workboat ● Haggadoth ● anecdote
- scapegoat ● redingote ● nanny goat
- zygote ● redcoat ● tailcoat ● raincoat
- waistcoat ● greatcoat ● petticoat
- topcoat ● housecoat ● undercoat
- entrecôte ● surcoat ● turncoat
- matelote ● banknote ● headnote
- endnote ● keynote ● woodnote
- footnote ● compote ● whitethroat

• shofroth • bluethroat • cut-throat
• creosote • mitzvoth • mezuzoth

30.36

• **adroit**, dacoit, Detroit, doit, droit,
  exploit, maladroit, quoit
• introit • Bayreuth

30.37

• **acute**, argute, astute, beaut, Beirut,
  boot, bruit, brut, brute, Bute, butte,
  Canute, cheroot, chute, commute,
  compute, confute, coot, cute, depute,
  dilute, dispute, flute, fruit, galoot,
  hoot, impute, jute, loot, lute,
  minute, moot, mute, newt, outshoot,
  permute, pollute, pursuit, recruit,
  refute, repute, root, route, salute,
  Salyut, scoot, shoot, Shute, sloot,
  snoot, subacute, suit, telecommute,
  Tonton Macoute, toot, transmute,
  undershoot, uproot, Ute, volute
• Paiute • jackboot • freeboot • top boot
• snow boot • gumboot • marabout
• statute • bandicoot • Hakluyt
• archlute • absolute • dissolute
• **irresolute**, resolute
• jackfruit • passion fruit • breadfruit
• grapefruit • snakeroot • beetroot
• arrowroot • autoroute

30.38

• tracksuit • catsuit • pantsuit
• Hatshepsut
• **sweatsuit**, wetsuit
• playsuit • spacesuit • swimsuit
• bodysuit • drysuit • lawsuit
• jumpsuit • offshoot • troubleshoot
• parachute • Aleut
• **attribute**, contribute, tribute
• execute • prosecute • persecute
• destitute • institute • prostitute
• constitute • substitute • malamute
• electrocute • hirsute

> Try rhyming one word with a [i]
> set of two: hirsute, fur suit.

30.39

• **afoot**, clubfoot, foot, hotfoot, kaput,
  put, soot, splay-foot, underfoot,
  wrong-foot, Yakut
• Blackfoot • flatfoot • barefoot
• pussyfoot • forefoot • crowfoot
• coltsfoot • goosefoot • tenderfoot
• per caput • Rajput • output
• throughput • Inuktitut

30.40

• **abut**, but, butt, cut, glut, gut, hut,
  intercut, jut, Mut, mutt, nut, phut,
  putt, rut, scut, shortcut, shut, slut,
  smut, strut, tut, undercut

> Create extra rhymes by [i]
> changing words like cut to
> cutting.

• sackbut • scuttlebutt • catgut
• midgut • Vonnegut • rotgut • haircut
• offcut • cross-cut • linocut • crew cut
• woodcut • uppercut • chestnut
• hazelnut • peanut • wing nut • cobnut
• locknut • walnut • groundnut
• doughnut (*US* donut) • coconut
• butternut

30.41

• peart
• **immediate**, intermediate
• idiot
• **collegiate**, intercollegiate
• orgeat • Eliot • affiliate
• **foliate**, trifoliate
• **aculeate**, Juliet
• Uniate • opiate
• **chariot**, Harriet, Judas Iscariot,
  lariat, Marryat
• **compatriot**, expatriate, patriot
• **heriot**, Herriot
• **commissariat**, lumpenproletariat,
  proletariat, salariat, secretariat,
  vicariate
• inebriate • Cypriot
• **baccalaureate**, laureate,
  professoriate

- appropriate •licentiate •satiate
- **initiate**, novitiate, patriciate
- associate •cruciate •Cheviot •soviet
- roseate
- **Byatt**, diet, quiet, riot, ryot, Wyatt
- inchoate
- **Ewart**, Stewart
- Verwoerd
- **graduate**, undergraduate
- attenuate •situate
- **abbot**, Cabot
- Albert •lambert •Egbert •Delbert
- **filbert**, Gilbert
- halibut •celibate •Robert •Osbert
- Norbert
- **Hubert**, Schubert
- Humbert •Cuthbert
- **burbot**, Herbert, sherbet, turbot
- Frankfort •effort •comfort

30.42

- **braggart**, faggot (US fagot), maggot
- legate
- **bigot**, gigot, Piggott, spigot
- ingot •profligate •aggregate •yogurt
- conjugate •abrogate •surrogate
- **ergot**, virgate
- Bagehot •patriarchate •wainscot
- Sickert •predicate •syndicate
- **certificate**, pontificate
- Calicut •delicate •silicate •triplicate
- **duplicate**, quadruplicate
- intricate •Connecticut •Alcott
- ducat •advocate
- **ballot**, palate
- **charlotte**, harlot
- **appellate**, Helot, prelate, zealot
- flagellate •distillate
- **Pilate**, pilot
- copilot •gyropilot •autopilot
- triangulate
- **ejaculate**, immaculate
- amulet •spatulate
- **articulate**, denticulate
- **consulate**, proconsulate
- postulate •ungulate
- **inviolate**, ultraviolet
- chocolate •cardinalate •desolate
- isolate •disconsolate •Merlot

30.43

- gamut
- **imamate**, marmot
- animate
- **approximate**, proximate
- **estimate**, guesstimate, underestimate
- **illegitimate**, legitimate
- intimate
- **penultimate**, ultimate
- primate •foumart •consummate
- Dermot
- **discarnate**, incarnate
- impregnate •rabbinate
- **coordinate**, inordinate, subordinate, superordinate
- infinite •laminate •effeminate
- discriminate •innominate
- determinate •Palatinate •pectinate
- obstinate •agglutinate •designate
- tribunate •importunate •Arbuthnot
- bicarbonate •umbonate •fortunate
- pulmonate
- **compassionate**, passionate
- affectionate
- **extortionate**, proportionate
- sultanate •companionate
- principate •Rupert •episcopate
- **carat**, carrot, claret, garret, karat, parrot
- emirate •aspirate •vertebrate
- levirate
- **duumvirate**, triumvirate
- pirate •quadrat •accurate •indurate
- obdurate
- **Meerut**, vizierate
- priorate •curate •elaborate
- deliberate •confederate
- **considerate**, desiderate
- **immoderate**, moderate
- ephorate
- **imperforate**, perforate
- **agglomerate**, conglomerate
- numerate
- **degenerate**, regenerate
- separate •temperate •desperate
- disparate •corporate •professorate
- commensurate •pastorate
- inveterate
- **directorate**, electorate,

inspectorate, protectorate, rectorate
- **illiterate**, literate, presbyterate
- doctorate • Don Quixote • marquisate
- concert • cushat • precipitate

30.44

- Evert • sievert
- **divot**, pivot
- **covert**, lovat
- culvert • adequate • stalwart • desert

30.45

- **advert**, alert, animadvert, assert,
  avert, Bert, blurt, Burt, cert, chert,
  concert, controvert, convert, curt,
  desert, dessert, dirt, divert, exert,
  flirt, girt, hurt, inert, insert,
  introvert, Kurt, malapert, overt,
  pert, pervert, quirt, shirt, skirt, spirt,
  spurt, squirt, Sturt, subvert, vert,
  wort, yurt
  - Engelbert • Colbert • sweatshirt
  - nightshirt • pay dirt • Frankfurt
  - miniskirt • underskirt • expert
  - Blackshirt • redshirt • T-shirt
  - Brownshirt • undershirt • extrovert
  - ragwort • milkwort • pillwort
  - nipplewort • lungwort • bladderwort
  - liverwort

30.46

- **semi-detached**, unattached,
  unhatched, unmatched
- **farfetched**, outstretched
- unwatched • untouched

30.47

- Taft
- **abaft**, aft, craft, daft, draft, draught,
  engraft, graft, haft, kraft, raft, shaft,
  understaffed, unstaffed, waft

> Create extra rhymes for   i
> words like abaft by adding -ed to
> laugh etc. (see section 17.2).

- backdraft • handcraft • aircraft
- stagecraft • spacecraft • statecraft
- needlecraft • priestcraft • witchcraft
- kingcraft • handicraft • woodcraft
- Wollstonecraft • bushcraft
- watercraft • hovercraft • crankshaft
- camshaft • layshaft • driveshaft
- turboshaft • countershaft
- **bereft**, cleft, deft, eft, heft, klepht,
  left, reft, theft, weft
- **adrift**, drift, gift, grift, lift, rift,
  shift, shrift, sift, squiffed, swift,
  thrift, uplift
- **airlift**, chairlift, stairlift
- facelift • skilift • shoplift • Festschrift
- spendthrift • spindrift • snowdrift
- makeshift • downshift • upshift
- **aloft**, croft, loft, oft, soft, toft

> Create extra rhymes for   i
> words like aloft by adding -ed to
> cough etc. (see section 17.8).

- hayloft • Ashcroft • Cockcroft
- undercroft • Lowestoft
- **tuft**, unstuffed
- Delft

30.48

- **abreact**, abstract, act, attract, bract,
  compact, contract, counteract,
  diffract, enact, exact, extract, fact,
  humpbacked, hunchbacked, impact,
  interact, matter-of-fact, pact,
  protract, redact, refract, retroact,
  subcontract, subtract, tact, tract,
  transact, unbacked, underact,
  untracked

> Create extra rhymes for   i
> words like abstract by adding -ed
> to crack etc. (see section 21.1).

- play-act • autodidact
- artefact (US artifact) • cataract
- contact
- **marked**, unremarked
- Wehrmacht
- **affect**, bisect, bull-necked, collect,
  confect, connect, correct, defect,
  deflect, deject, detect, direct, effect,

eject, elect, erect, expect, infect, inflect, inject, inspect, interconnect, interject, intersect, misdirect, neglect, object, perfect, project, prospect, protect, reflect, reject, respect, resurrect, sect, select, subject, suspect, transect, unchecked, Utrecht
- prefect • abject • retroject • intellect
- genuflect • idiolect • dialect • aspect
- circumspect • retrospect • Dordrecht
- vivisect • architect • unbaked
- sun-baked

30.49

- **addict**, afflict, conflict, constrict, contradict, convict, delict, depict, evict, hand-picked, inflict, interdict, Pict, predict, strict
- edict

> Create new rhymes for words like addict by adding -ed to lick etc. (see section 21.9). [i]

- Benedict • verdict
- **imperfect**, perfect, pluperfect, word-perfect
- object • subject • relict • district
- **concoct**, decoct
- landlocked • dreadlocked
- **unprovoked**, unsmoked
- **uncooked**, unlooked
- **abduct**, adduct, conduct, construct, destruct, duct, instruct, misconduct, obstruct
- ventiduct • aqueduct • product
- safe-conduct • viaduct
- **handworked**, unworked
- mulct • unthanked • sacrosanct
- **distinct**, extinct, succinct
- precinct • instinct
- **conjunct**, defunct, disjunct, injunct
- adjunct • unasked

30.50

- Kristallnacht • Gaeltacht
- **Brecht**, echt
- Fichte • Maastricht

30.51

- gestalt • asphalt
- **belt**, Celt, dealt, dwelt, felt, gelt, knelt, melt, misdealt, pelt, Scheldt, smelt, spelt, svelte, veld, welt
- fan belt • seat belt • lifebelt • sunbelt
- rust belt • Copperbelt • heartfelt
- underfelt • backveld • bushveld
- Roosevelt
- **atilt**, built, gilt, guilt, hilt, jilt, kilt, lilt, quilt, silt, spilt, stilt, tilt, upbuilt, wilt
- Vanderbilt • volte
- **assault**, Balt, exalt, fault, halt, malt, salt, smalt, vault
- cobalt • stringhalt • basalt
- somersault • polevault
- **bolt**, colt, dolt, holt, jolt, moult (*US* molt), poult, smolt, volt
- deadbolt • Humboldt • thunderbolt
- megavolt • spoilt • Iseult
- **consult**, cult, exult, indult, insult, penult, result, ult
- adult • occult • tumult • catapult
- difficult • Hasselt

30.52

- unstamped
- **attempt**, contempt, dreamt, exempt, kempt, pre-empt, tempt
- Klimt • prompt

30.53

- **ant**, Brabant, Brandt, brant, cant, enceinte, extant, gallant, Kant, levant, pant, pointe, pointes, rant, scant
- confidant • commandant • hierophant
- Rembrandt • Amirante
- gallivant
- **aren't**, aslant, aunt, can't, chant, courante, détente, enchant, entente, grant, implant, Nantes, plant, shan't, slant, supplant, transplant, underplant
- plainchant • ashplant • eggplant
- house plant • restaurant

- **debutant**, debutante
- **absent**, accent, anent, ascent, assent, augment, bent, cement, cent, circumvent, consent, content, dent, event, extent, ferment, foment, forewent, forwent, frequent, gent, Ghent, Gwent, lament, leant, lent, meant, misrepresent, misspent, outwent, pent, percent, pigment, rent, scent, segment, sent, spent, stent, Stoke-on-Trent, Tashkent, tent, torment, Trent, underspent, underwent, vent, went

> **i** Create extra rhymes by adding *-ing* to words like absent.

- orient •comment •portent
- malcontent

30.54

- **acquaint**, ain't, attaint, complaint, constraint, distraint, faint, feint, paint, plaint, quaint, restraint, saint, taint
- spray-paint •greasepaint •warpaint
- **asquint**, bint, clint, dint, flint, glint, hint, imprint, lint, mint, misprint, print, quint, skint, splint, sprint, squint, stint, tint

> **i** Create extra rhymes by adding *-ing* to words like glint.

- Septuagint •skinflint •catmint
- varmint •spearmint •calamint
- peppermint •enprint •screen print
- offprint •blueprint •newsprint
- footprint •thumbprint •fingerprint
- monotint •mezzotint •aquatint
- pint •Geraint
- **Comte**, conte, font, fount, pont, quant, Vermont, want
- Delfont •vicomte •Frémont
- piedmont •Beaumont •Hellespont
- passant •poste restante
- **avaunt**, daunt, flaunt, gaunt, haunt, jaunt, taunt, vaunt

> **i** Create extra rhymes by adding *-ed* to words like daunt.

30.55

- **account**, amount, count, fount, miscount, mount, no-account, surmount
- headcount •viscount •paramount
- tantamount
- **don't**, won't, wont
- **anoint**, appoint, conjoint, joint, outpoint, point, point-to-point
- standpoint
- **cashpoint**, flashpoint
- checkpoint •endpoint •breakpoint
- needlepoint •midpoint •pinpoint
- vantage point •knifepoint
- strongpoint •viewpoint •gunpoint
- counterpoint •punt
- **affront**, blunt, brunt, bunt, confront, cunt, front, Granth, grunt, hunt, mahant, runt, shunt, stunt, up-front
- exeunt •manhunt •headhunt
- witch-hunt •seafront •beachfront
- shopfront
- **forefront**, storefront

> **i** Try rhyming one word with a set of two: forefront, more front.

- waterfront

30.56

- **abeyant**, mayn't
- **ambient**, circumambient
- **gradient**, irradiant, radiant
- **expedient**, ingredient, mediant, obedient
- valiant •salient •resilient •emollient
- defoliant •ebullient •suppliant
- **convenient**, intervenient, lenient, prevenient
- sapient
- **impercipient**, incipient, percipient, recipient
- recreant •variant •miscreant
- Orient •nutrient
- **esurient**, luxuriant, parturient, prurient
- **nescient**, prescient
- omniscient •insouciant •renunciant

- officiant •negotiant •deviant
- subservient •transient
- **affiant**, Bryant, client, compliant, defiant, giant, pliant, reliant
- **buoyant**, clairvoyant, flamboyant
- **fluent**, pursuant, truant
- affluent •effluent •mellifluent
- confluent •circumfluent •congruent
- issuant •continuant •constituent
- lambent •absorbent
- **incumbent**, recumbent
- couchant •merchant •hadn't
- **ardent**, guardant, regardant
- pedant
- **appendant**, ascendant, attendant, codependent, defendant, descendant, descendent, intendant, interdependent, pendant, pendent, splendent, superintendent, transcendent
- **antecedent**, decedent, needn't, precedent
- didn't •diffident •confident
- accident •dissident
- **coincident**, incident
- oxidant •evident
- **improvident**, provident
- **president**, resident
- **strident**, trident
- **co-respondent**, correspondent, despondent, fondant, respondent
- **accordant**, concordant, discordant, mordant, mordent
- rodent
- **imprudent**, jurisprudent, prudent, student
- **couldn't**, shouldn't, wouldn't
- impudent
- **abundant**, redundant
- decadent •verdant •infant •elephant
- triumphant •sycophant •elegant
- fumigant •congregant •litigant
- termagant •arrogant •extravagant
- pageant
- **cotangent**, plangent, tangent
- **argent**, Sargent, sergeant
- agent •newsagent •regent
- **astringent**, contingent, stringent
- indigent •intelligent •negligent
- diligent •intransigent •exigent
- cogent

- **effulgent**, fulgent, indulgent
- pungent
- **convergent**, detergent, divergent, emergent, insurgent, resurgent, urgent
- bacchant •peccant •vacant •piquant
- predicant •mendicant •significant
- applicant •supplicant •communicant
- lubricant •desiccant •intoxicant
- **gallant**, talent
- **appellant**, propellant, propellent, repellent, water-repellent
- resemblant
- **assailant**, inhalant
- sealant •sibilant •jubilant
- flagellant •vigilant •pestilent
- silent
- **Solent**, volant
- coolant •virulent •purulent
- **ambulant**, somnambulant
- coagulant •crapulent •flatulent
- feculent •esculent •petulant
- stimulant •flocculent •opulent
- postulant •fraudulent •corpulent
- undulant
- **succulent**, truculent
- turbulent •violent •redolent
- indolent •somnolent •excellent
- insolent •nonchalant
- **benevolent**, malevolent, prevalent
- **ambivalent**, equivalent
- garment •clement •segment
- **claimant**, clamant, payment, raiment
- ailment
- **figment**, pigment
- fitment •aliment •clement
- oddment
- **dormant**, informant
- moment •adamant •stagnant
- **lieutenant**, pennant, subtenant, tenant
- **pregnant**, regnant
- remnant •complainant
- **benignant**, indignant, malignant
- recombinant •contaminant
- eminent
- **discriminant**, imminent
- **dominant**, prominent
- **illuminant**, ruminant
- determinant •abstinent

- **continent**, subcontinent
- **appurtenant**, impertinent, pertinent
- revenant
- **component**, deponent, exponent, opponent, proponent
- **oppugnant**, repugnant
- immanent
- **impermanent**, permanent
- dissonant •consonant •alternant
- covenant •resonant •rampant
- discrepant •flippant •participant
- occupant •serpent
- **apparent**, arrant, transparent
- Arendt
- **aberrant**, deterrent, errant, inherent, knight-errant
- entrant
- **declarant**, parent
- grandparent •step-parent
- godparent
- **flagrant**, fragrant, vagrant
- registrant •celebrant •emigrant
- immigrant •ministrant •aspirant
- antiperspirant •recalcitrant
- integrant •tyrant •vibrant •hydrant
- **migrant**, transmigrant
- **abhorrent**, torrent, warrant
- quadrant •figurant •obscurant
- **blackcurrant**, concurrent, currant, current, occurrent, redcurrant
- white currant •cross-current
- undercurrent
- **adherent**, coherent, sederunt
- **exuberant**, protuberant
- reverberant •denaturant
- preponderant •deodorant
- **different**, vociferant
- **belligerent**, refrigerant
- accelerant •tolerant •cormorant
- itinerant •ignorant •cooperant
- expectorant •adulterant
- **irreverent**, reverent
- **nascent**, passant
- absent
- **accent**, relaxant
- **acquiescent**, adolescent, albescent, Besant, coalescent, confessant, convalescent, crescent, depressant, effervescent, erubescent, evanescent, excrescent, flavescent, fluorescent, immunosuppressant, incandescent, incessant, iridescent,

juvenescent, lactescent, liquescent, luminescent, nigrescent, obsolescent, opalescent, pearlescent, phosphorescent, pubescent, putrescent, quiescent, suppressant, tumescent, turgescent, virescent, viridescent
- **adjacent**, complacent, obeisant
- **decent**, recent
- **impuissant**, reminiscent
- Vincent •puissant
- **beneficent**, maleficent
- **magnificent**, munificent
- Millicent •concupiscent •reticent
- docent
- **lucent**, translucent
- **discussant**, mustn't
- innocent
- **conversant**, versant
- **consentient**, sentient, trenchant
- **impatient**, patient
- ancient •outpatient
- **coefficient**, deficient, efficient, proficient, sufficient
- quotient •patent
- **interactant**, reactant
- **disinfectant**, expectant, protectant
- repentant •acceptant
- **contestant**, decongestant
- sextant
- **blatant**, latent
- intermittent
- **assistant**, coexistent, consistent, distant, equidistant, existent, insistent, persistent, resistant, subsistent, water-resistant

> Create extra rhymes by adding -*ly* to words like consistent. ⓘ

- instant
- **cohabitant**, habitant
- exorbitant •militant •concomitant
- **impenitent**, penitent
- palpitant •crepitant •precipitant
- **competent**, omnicompetent
- irritant •incapacitant •Protestant
- hesitant •visitant •mightn't •octant
- remontant •constant
- **important**, oughtn't
- accountant •potent
- **mutant**, pollutant
- adjutant •executant •disputant

- reluctant
- **consultant**, exultant, resultant
- combatant • omnipotent • impotent
- inadvertent
- **Havant**, haven't, savant, savante
- advent
- **irrelevant**, relevant
- pursuivant • solvent • convent
- adjuvant
- **fervent**, observant, servant
- manservant • maidservant
- **frequent**, sequent
- delinquent • consequent
- subsequent • unguent • eloquent
- **grandiloquent**, magniloquent
- brilliant • poignant • hasn't
- **bezant**, omnipresent, peasant, pheasant, pleasant, present
- complaisant • malfeasant • isn't
- cognizant • wasn't • recusant
- doesn't

30.57

- **burnt**, learnt, weren't
- sunburnt

30.58

- **adapt**, apt, enrapt, rapt, unmapped, untapped
- periapt • snow-capped
- **accept**, crept, except, incept, inept, intercept, kept, leapt, overleaped, sept, slept, swept, upswept, wept, yclept

> Create extra rhymes for   **i**
> words like accept by adding
> -(p)ed to step etc. (see
> section 27.3).

- adept • housekept • transept
- precept • concept • percept
- rainswept • windswept • undraped
- pearshaped
- **conscript**, crypt, encrypt, harelipped, hipped, script, unequipped, unwhipped
- Egypt • eucalypt • transcript
- nondescript • typescript • manuscript
- subscript
- **adopt**, co-opt, Copt, opt
- unhoped
- **abrupt**, corrupt, disrupt, erupt, interrupt, irrupt

> Create new rhymes for words   **i**
> like abrupt by adding -(p)ed to
> cup etc. (see section 27.13).

- bankrupt
- **underdeveloped**, undeveloped
- excerpt • sculpt

30.59

- **unabashed**, uncashed
- unfleshed • whisht • unestablished
- unembellished • unpolished
- unpublished • unaccomplished
- unblemished
- **untarnished**, unvarnished
- **undiminished**, unfinished
- unpunished • unfurnished
- **malnourished**, undernourished
- undistinguished • unwashed
- stonewashed • borscht • unquenched

30.60

- **sawtoothed**, snaggle-toothed

Section 31: -st

31.1

- bast •cineaste •encomiast
- symposiast •enthusiast •bombast
- oblast •chloroplast •iconoclast
- gymnast •pederast •fantast

31.2

- **aghast**, avast, Belfast, blast, cast, caste, contrast, fast, last, mast, miscast, outlast, past, rat-arsed, unsurpassed, vast

> Create extra rhymes for words like aghast by adding -ed to class etc. (see section 28.2). [i]

- steadfast •lightfast •holdfast
- sunfast •colourfast •flabbergast
- simulcast •telecast •typecast
- forecast •broadcast •sportscast
- downcast
- **outcast**, outcaste
- newscast •roughcast •upcast
- opencast •worm cast •sandblast
- Elastoplast •counterblast •mainmast
- mizzenmast •topmast •foremast
- fly-past

31.3

- **abreast**, arrest, attest, beau geste, behest, bequest, best, blessed, blest, breast, Brest, Bucharest, Budapest, celeste, chest, contest, crest, digest, divest, guest, hest, infest, ingest, jest, lest, Midwest, molest, nest, northwest, pest, prestressed, protest, quest, rest, self-addressed, self-confessed, self-possessed, southwest, suggest, test, Trieste, unaddressed, unexpressed, unimpressed, unpressed, unstressed, vest, west, wrest, zest

> Create extra rhymes for words like abreast by adding -ed to address etc. (see section 28.3). [i]

- manifest •talkfest •Hammerfest
- Almagest •backrest •armrest
- redbreast •headrest •imprest
- chimney breast •footrest •firecrest
- incest •palimpsest •unprocessed
- road test •undervest •conquest

31.4

- **barefaced**, baste, boldfaced, chaste, haste, lambaste, paste, po-faced, red-faced, self-faced, shamefaced, smooth-faced, strait-laced, taste, unplaced, untraced, waist, waste

> Create extra rhymes for words like barefaced by adding -d to base etc. (see section 28.5). [i]

- toothpaste •foretaste •aftertaste
- shirtwaist

31.5

- **arriviste**, artiste, batiste, beast, dirigiste, east, feast, least, Mideast, modiste, northeast, piste, priest, southeast, uncreased, unreleased, yeast
- wildebeest •hartebeest •beanfeast
- **anapaest** (*US* anapest)

31.6

- **assist**, cist, coexist, consist, cyst, desist, enlist, exist, fist, gist, grist,

hist, insist, list, Liszt, mist, persist,
resist, schist, subsist, tryst, twist,
whist, wist, wrist
- Dadaist • deist • fideist • Hebraist
- Mithraist • essayist • prosaist
- **hobbyist**, lobbyist
- Trotskyist • boniest • copyist • veriest
- pantheist • atheist • polytheist
- monotheist
- **Maoist**, Taoist
- oboist • egoist • jingoist • banjoist
- soloist • Titoist • Shintoist
- **canoeist**, tattooist, Uist
- voodooist • altruist • casuist
- euphuist • Lamaist • vibist • cubist
- Arabist • faddist • propagandist
- contrabandist • avant-gardist • eldest
- sadist • encyclopedist
- **immodest**, modest
- Girondist • keyboardist
- harpsichordist • nudist • Buddhist
- unprejudiced • Talmudist
- psalmodist • threnodist • hymnodist
- monodist • chiropodist • parodist
- heraldist • rhapsodist • prosodist
- Methodist • absurdist

31.7

- pacifist • sophist
- **calligraphist**, epigraphist
- monographist • theosophist
- unsurfaced • druggist • collagist
- **Falangist**, phalangist
- ageist • elegist • imagist • strategist
- theurgist
- **genealogist**, metallurgist,
mineralogist
- **apologist**, biologist, ecologist,
geologist, ideologist, oncologist,
ontologist, pedologist, sexologist,
theologist, zoologist
- eulogist • suffragist • liturgist
- thaumaturgist • catechist • stockist
- Yorkist • anarchist • monarchist
- **masochist**, sadomasochist

31.8

- **backlist**, blacklist

- handlist • cabbalist • cellist • checklist
- playlist • wish-list
- **cartophilist**, necrophilist,
oenophilist (*US* enophilist)
- nihilist • pugilist • homilist
- **bicyclist**, tricyclist
- stylist • cyclist • unicyclist
- motorcyclist • hairstylist • shortlist
- **Gaullist**, holist
- spiritualist • fabulist
- **funambulist**, noctambulist,
somnambulist
- oculist • populist
- **idealist**, realist, surrealist
- millennialist
- **ceremonialist**, colonialist,
neocolonialist
- aerialist
- **editorialist**, memorialist
- industrialist
- **immaterialist**, imperialist,
materialist, serialist
- **trialist**, violist
- **loyalist**, royalist
- **dualist**, duellist (*US* duelist)
- intellectualist • conceptualist
- textualist • mutualist • individualist
- sensualist • contextualist
- **diabolist**, kabbalist
- **cymbalist**, symbolist
- tribalist
- **herbalist**, verbalist
- **medallist** (*US* medalist)
- feudalist • triumphalist • legalist
- **evangelist**, televangelist
- syndicalist • clericalist • physicalist
- vocalist • animalist • maximalist
- formalist • minimalist
- **analyst**, annalist, cryptanalyst,
panellist (*US* panelist),
psychoanalyst
- **nominalist**, phenomenalist
- **finalist**, semi-finalist
- communalist • regionalist
- **internationalist**, nationalist,
rationalist
- sectionalist • conventionalist
- **Congregationalist**,
conversationalist, educationalist,
representationalist, sensationalist

- traditionalist • emotionalist
- constitutionalist • functionalist
- **journalist**, paternalist, photojournalist
- papalist
- **monopolist**, oligopolist
- centralist
- **amoralist**, moralist
- oralist • neutralist
- **muralist**, pluralist, ruralist
- liberalist • naturalist • structuralist
- **agriculturalist**, horticulturalist, multiculturalist
- federalist • generalist
- **multilateralist**, unilateralist
- literalist • universalist
- substantialist • specialist
- **consequentialist**, essentialist, existentialist
- racialist • provincialist • socialist
- controversialist
- **catalyst**, philatelist
- **documentalist**, environmentalist, experimentalist, fundamentalist, instrumentalist, mentalist, orientalist, ornamentalist, sentimentalist, transcendentalist
- fatalist • capitalist
- **recitalist**, vitalist
- Pentecostalist • anecdotalist
- brutalist • medievalist
- **revivalist**, survivalist
- novelist

31.9

- **alarmist**, palmist, psalmist
- **biochemist**, chemist
- extremist • animist • pessimist
- legitimist • optimist • rhymist
- **conformist**, reformist
- **bigamist**, polygamist
- misogamist • alchemist • Islamist
- columnist • dynamist
- **agronomist**, autonomist, economist, ergonomist, physiognomist
- palindromist
- **anatomist**, atomist
- epitomist • totemist • taxidermist

31.10

- Hispanist • Zenist • pyrotechnist
- Jainist • liberationist
- **machinist**, tambourinist
- hygienist • trampolinist
- **mandolinist**, violinist
- unwitnessed
- **misogynist**, philogynist
- Stalinist • Hellenist • feminist
- illuminist • determinist • Leninist
- alpinist • larcenist • Latinist
- Byzantinist • Calvinist • chauvinist
- Darwinist
- **honest**, monist
- **corniced**, hornist
- trombonist • vibraphonist
- sousaphonist
- **balloonist**, bassoonist, cartoonist, lampoonist
- opportunist • communist • pianist
- Fabianist • accordionist • alienist
- unionist • Zionist • urbanist
- hedonist • modernist • telephonist
- symphonist
- **saxophonist**, xylophonist
- **agonist**, antagonist, protagonist
- tobogganist • organist • revisionist
- **diffusionist**, exclusionist, fusionist, illusionist
- religionist • tobacconist • mechanist
- Africanist • Vaticanist • colonist
- Mammonist
- **harmonist**, shamanist
- humanist • Germanist • canonist
- expansionist • onanist • timpanist
- accompanist • ironist • Saxonist
- Jansenist • arsonist • abstractionist
- **expressionist**, impressionist, progressionist, secessionist
- **insurrectionist**, perfectionist, projectionist, protectionist, rejectionist, vivisectionist
- interventionist • receptionist
- **accommodationist**, associationist, collaborationist, conservationist, creationist, deviationist, educationist, federationist, isolationist, preservationist, representationist, restorationist, revelationist, salvationist,

situationist, vacationist
- **abolitionist**, coalitionist, demolitionist, exhibitionist, intuitionist, nutritionist, partitionist, prohibitionist, requisitionist, traditionist
- **fictionist**, restrictionist
- **abortionist**, contortionist, extortionist
- **Confucianist**, devolutionist, elocutionist, evolutionist, revolutionist
- **constructionist**, percussionist
- **obstructionist**, reductionist
- excursionist
- **Neoplatonist**, Platonist, satanist
- botanist
- **earnest**, Ernest

31.11

- Trappist • harpist • tempest
- **escapist**, papist, rapist
- landscapist • typist
- **misanthropist**, philanthropist
- **aromatherapist**, physiotherapist, psychotherapist, therapist

31.12

- tantrist
- **guitarist**, scenarist, tsarist
- sitarist • memoirist • belletrist
- centrist • Marist • sacrist
- **lyrist**, panegyrist
- equilibrist • interest
- **optometrist**, psychometrist, sociometrist
- satirist
- **afforest**, florist, forest, Forrest
- rainforest • folklorist
- **careerist**, querist, theorist
- plagiarist • meliorist • apiarist
- topiarist • diarist • psychiatrist
- **jurist**, purist, tourist
- obituarist • caricaturist • pedicurist
- manicurist • sinecurist • naturist
- miniaturist • futurist
- **agriculturist**, apiculturist, arboriculturist, horticulturist,

pisciculturist, sericulturist, silviculturist, viniculturist, viticulturist
- acupuncturist • welfarist • allegorist
- Eucharist • artillerist • secularist
- particularist
- **colourist** (*US* colorist)
- amorist • ephemerist • mesmerist
- **consumerist**, humorist
- mannerist • tenorist • seminarist
- terrorist • adventurist • detectorist
- documentarist • militarist
- monetarist • lepidopterist
- **motorist**, votarist
- scooterist • voluntarist • zitherist
- Everest • aquarist • auteurist

31.13

- saxist • classist • Marxist
- **heterosexist**, sexist
- **bassist**, racist
- solipsist • publicist
- **ceramicist**, dynamicist
- polemicist • Hispanicist • eugenicist
- technicist • esotericist
- **empiricist**, lyricist
- historicist
- **classicist**, neoclassicist
- narcissist • romanticist • geneticist
- vorticist
- **bioethicist**, ethicist
- mythicist • synthesist • physicist
- exorcist • pharmacist • supremacist
- fantasist • fascist • fetishist

31.14

- fattist
- **unpractised** (*US* unpracticed)
- **Esperantist**, obscurantist
- **Anabaptist**, Baptist
- **artist**, Chartist
- **clarinettist** (*US* clarinetist), cornetist, duettist, librettist, vignettist
- leftist • dentist • transvestist • statist
- **completist**, defeatist, Docetist, élitist, graffitist
- **pietist**, quietist, varietist

- Semitist •Sanskritist •spiritist
- syncretist •portraitist
- **anaesthetist** (*US* anesthetist)
- rightist •finitist •orthodontist
- synoptist •flautist
- **protist**, unnoticed
- **chutist**, flutist, therapeutist
- absolutist •parachutist •cultist
- contrapuntist •occultist •scientist
- egotist
- **dramatist**, epigrammatist, melodramatist
- pragmatist •stigmatist •numismatist
- systematist •dogmatist •diplomatist
- hypnotist •immanentist •nepotist
- comparatist •indifferentist
- separatist •corporatist •Adventist
- Baathist •amethyst •telepathist
- homeopathist •farthest •furthest

31.15

- harvest •recidivist •archivist
- progressivist •Bolshevist •activist
- **collectivist**, objectivist, subjectivist
- nativist •prescriptivist •primitivist
- positivist •constructivist •negativist
- relativist
- **fauvist**, Jehovist
- reservist •linguist
- **soliloquist**, ventriloquist
- pointillist

31.16

- **Christ**, heist, underpriced, unsliced
- Zeitgeist •poltergeist •Antichrist

31.17

- **accost**, cost, frost, lost, Prost, riposte

> Create extra rhymes for [i] words like accost by adding -*ed* to cross etc. (see section 28.14).

- teleost •Pentecost •oncost •glasnost
- compost •star-crossed •hoar frost
- permafrost

31.18

- **exhaust**, under-resourced, unforced
- hypocaust •holocaust

31.19

- **Faust**, frowst, joust, oust, roust

31.20

- **boast**, coast, ghost, host, most, oast, post, roast, toast

> Create extra rhymes by [i] adding -*ing* to words like boast.

- backmost •headmost •leftmost
- endmost •midmost •hindmost
- rightmost •topmost •foremost
- almost •northernmost •downmost
- outmost •southernmost •upmost
- utmost •rearmost •lowermost
- undermost •innermost •uppermost
- aftermost
- **centremost** (*US* centermost)
- westernmost •easternmost
- bottommost •outermost •uttermost
- nethermost •furthermost
- lamp post •bedpost •gatepost
- Freepost •impost •guidepost
- milepost •signpost •doorpost
- outpost •goalpost •newel post
- fingerpost •sternpost

31.21

- **foist**, hoist, joist, moist, unvoiced

31.22

- **boost**, langouste, mot juste, Proust, roost, self-induced, used

31.23

- August

31.24

- **adjust**, august, bust, combust, crust, dust, encrust, entrust, gust, just, lust, mistrust, must, robust, rust, thrust, trust, undiscussed

> Create extra rhymes for [i] words like adjust by adding -ed to fuss etc. (see section 28.21).

- stardust • sawdust • angel dust
- bloodlust • wanderlust • upthrust

31.25

- unbiased • breakfast • August
- **locust**, unfocused
- **ballast**, Sallust
- dynast • unembarrassed • provost

31.26

- **accursed**, burst, curst, erst, first, headfirst, Hurst, thirst, under-rehearsed, unrehearsed, unversed, verst, worst, wurst
- starburst • airburst • cloudburst
- outburst • sunburst • Sandhurst
- Pankhurst • Bathurst • knackwurst
- bratwurst

31.27

- **amidst**, midst
- wouldst

31.28

- **Bakst**, unrelaxed
- **next**, oversexed, sext, text, undersexed
- teletext • context • subtext
- hypertext
- **betwixt**, unmixed
- suffix

31.29

- discalced • whilst • Holst

31.30

- **against**, unfenced
- Ernst • unconvinced • unlicensed
- unannounced • uninfluenced
- valanced • fragranced • Nernst

31.31

- angst • amongst

Section 32: -θ ('-th')

32.1

- **Kath**, math, Plath, strath
- polymath • aftermath • telepath
- sociopath • homeopath • osteopath
- psychopath

32.2

- **Barth**, bath, garth, hearth, lath, path
- sand bath • hip bath • eyebath
- **bloodbath**, mudbath
- Hogarth • warpath • towpath
- footpath

32.3

- **Beth**, breath, death, Jerez, Macbeth, Seth
- megadeath • Japheth • shibboleth

32.4

- **faith**, Galbraith, inter-faith, wraith

32.5

- **beneath**, buck teeth, Hadith, heath, Keith, neath, Reith, sheath, teeth, underneath, Westmeath, wreath
- eye teeth • dog-teeth

32.6

- **myth**, outwith, pith, smith
- twentieth • seventieth • eightieth
- fiftieth • sixtieth • ninetieth
- fortieth • thirtieth • Edith • Judith
- Meredith • Griffith • Hesketh
- tallith • Delyth • Lilith • megalith
- monolith • blacksmith • Nasmyth
- tinsmith • Ladysmith • locksmith
- songsmith • goldsmith • gunsmith
- coppersmith • silversmith
- wordsmith
- **Kenneth**, zenith
- Gwyneth • Lapith • Hollerith
- Asquith • Sopwith

32.7

- Forsyth

32.8

- **broth**, cloth, froth, Goth, moth, Roth, wrath
- Sabaoth • Visigoth

This poem gives a good example of *semantic* (or, in this case, *counter-semantic*) *rhyme*. 'Breath' and 'death' rhyme but emphasize opposite concepts:

I am sick of singing: the bays burn deep and chafe: I am fain
To rest a little from praise and grievous pleasure and pain.
For the Gods we know not of, who give us our daily breath,
We know they are cruel as love or life, and lovely as death.

(Algernon C. Swinburne, 'Hymn to Proserpine')

- **backcloth**, sackcloth
- saddlecloth •waxcloth •grasscloth
- haircloth •J-cloth •sailcloth
- tablecloth •facecloth •cheesecloth
- dishcloth •washcloth •oilcloth
- loincloth •hawkmoth

32.9

- **forth**, fourth, henceforth, north, thenceforth

32.10

- **Louth**, mouth, mouth-to-mouth, south
- bad-mouth •bigmouth •loudmouth
- goalmouth •blabbermouth
- motormouth

32.11

- **both**, growth, loath, oath, quoth, sloth, Thoth, troth
- outgrowth •upgrowth
- undergrowth

32.12

- **buck tooth**, couth, Duluth, forsooth, Maynooth, ruth, sleuth, sooth, strewth, tooth, truth, youth
- eye tooth •dog-tooth •sawtooth
- houndstooth •sabretooth

32.13

- Goliath •Haworth •sabbath
- Elizabeth •mammoth •Dartmouth
- Weymouth •behemoth •Plymouth
- Sidmouth •bismuth •azimuth
- Monmouth •Bournemouth
- Portsmouth •vermouth
- pennyworth •Elspeth •ha'p'orth
- Morpeth •Gareth •Nazareth
- Tamworth •Hayworth •Woolworth
- Wordsworth

32.14

- **berth**, birth, dearth, earth, firth, girth, mirth, Perth, worth
- stillbirth •childbirth •afterbirth
- Edgeworth •Hepworth •Ellsworth
- Whitworth •halfpennyworth
- Bosworth •jobsworth •Iorwerth

32.15

- breadth •width •bandwidth
- hundredth

32.16

- fifth •twelfth

32.17

- **health**, stealth, wealth
- commonwealth
- **filth**, tilth
- coolth

32.18

- warmth

32.19

- amaranth
- **nth**, tenth
- **eighteenth**, fifteenth, fourteenth, nineteenth, seventeenth, sixteenth, thirteenth, umpteenth
- **plinth**, synth
- Corinth •labyrinth •jacinth
- absinthe •hyacinth •ninth
- crème de menthe •month
- twelvemonth
- **billionth**, millionth, trillionth, zillionth
- **eleventh**, seventh
- thousandth •dozenth

32.20

• **length**, strength
• wavelength

32.21

• depth

32.22

• sixth

32.23

• eighth

Section 33: -ð ('-th')

33.1

- eth • Gorsedd

33.2

- **bathe**, lathe, rathe, scathe, spathe, swathe
- sunbathe

33.3

- **bequeath**, breathe, enwreathe, Meath, seethe, sheathe, teethe, wreathe

> Create extra rhymes by [i] changing words like breathe to breathing.

33.4

- **forthwith**, herewith, therewith, wherewith, with
- Dafydd

33.5

- **blithe**, lithe, scythe, tithe, writhe

33.6

- mouth

33.7

- **betroth**, clothe, loathe

33.8

- **booth**, smooth, soothe
- tollbooth (*US* tolbooth)

33.9

- Gwynedd

Section 34: -v

34.1

- **have**, lav
- satnav

34.2

- **Algarve**, calve, carve, grave, Graves, halve, Slav, starve, suave, Zouave
- Wroclaw
- **Jugoslav**, Yugoslav
- moshav • Gustave

34.3

- rev • Mendeleev • Negev • maglev
- Brezhnev

34.4

- **behave**, brave, Cave, clave, concave, crave, Dave, deprave, engrave, enslave, fave, forgave, gave, grave, knave, lave, Maeve, misbehave, misgave, nave, outbrave, pave, rave, save, shave, shortwave, slave, stave, they've, waive, wave

> Create extra rhymes by changing words like behave to behaving. [i]

- enclave • exclave • conclave
- Redgrave • architrave • Wargrave
- Palgrave • palsgrave • aftershave
- brainwave • heatwave • microwave

34.5

- **achieve**, believe, breve, cleave, conceive, deceive, eve, greave, grieve, heave, interleave, interweave, khedive, leave, misconceive, naive, Neve, peeve, perceive, reave, receive, reive, relieve, reprieve, retrieve, sheave, sleeve, steeve, Steve, Tananarive, Tel Aviv, thieve, underachieve, upheave, weave, we've, Yves

> Create extra rhymes by changing words like achieve to achieving. [i]

- make-believe • shirtsleeve
- semibreve • Congreve

34.6

- **forgive**, give, live, misgive, outlive, shiv, sieve, spiv, Viv
- endive • gerundive • olive

34.7

- **impassive**, massive, passive
- expansive
- **aggressive**, compressive, concessive, degressive, depressive, digressive, excessive, expressive, impressive, obsessive, oppressive, possessive, progressive, recessive, regressive, repressive, retrogressive, successive, transgressive

> Create extra rhymes by adding -ly to words like aggressive. [i]

- reflexive
- **apprehensive**, coextensive, comprehensive, defensive, expensive, extensive, intensive, offensive, ostensive, pensive, suspensive

- counteroffensive
- **abrasive**, evasive, invasive, persuasive, pervasive
- **adhesive**, cohesive
- **missive**, omissive, permissive, submissive
- **decisive**, derisive, divisive, incisive
- **irresponsive**, responsive
- **corrosive**, explosive, implosive, plosive
- **abusive**, allusive, collusive, conclusive, conducive, delusive, diffusive, effusive, elusive, exclusive, illusive, inclusive, intrusive, obtrusive, preclusive, reclusive, seclusive
- percussive
- **compulsive**, convulsive, impulsive, propulsive, repulsive
- purposive
- **coercive**, cursive, excursive, subversive

34.8

- active • captive
- **festive**, restive
- **dative**, native, stative
- fictive • unitive • octave • costive
- **emotive**, motive, votive
- furtive • appraisive

34.9

- **alive**, arrive, chive, Clive, connive, contrive, deprive, dive, drive, five, gyve, hive, I've, jive, live, MI5,

revive, rive, shrive, skive, strive, survive, swive, thrive
- skydive • swan dive • nosedive
- swallow dive • scuba-dive • Argive
- beehive • archive

34.10

- **hereof**, of, thereof, whereof
- Zhukov • Nabokov • Pavlov • Asimov
- Zhdanov • Karpov • improv • Kirov
- Kasparov

34.11

- **behove**, clove, cove, dove, drove, fauve, grove, interwove, Jove, mauve, rove, shrove, stove, strove, trove, wove
- alcove • mangrove

34.12

- **approve**, groove, improve, move, prove, you've
- countermove

34.13

- **above**, dove, glove, guv, love, shove, tug-of-love
- ringdove • turtle dove • foxglove

34.14

- **conserve**, curve, Deneuve, derv,

Some rhymes look like *full rhymes* on paper but in fact the sounds are not the same. In poetry from the past one reason for this may be because pronunciation of the words has changed over time—as with 'move' and 'love' in this example:

So let us melt, and make no noise,
    No teare-floods, nor sigh-tempests move,
'Twere prophanation of our joyes
    To tell the layetie our love.

(John Donne, 'A Valediction: forbidding mourning')

hors d'oeuvre, nerve, observe, perv, roman-fleuve, serve, subserve, swerve, verve

34.15

- **multivalve**, salve, valve
- lipsalve •check valve •univalve

- bivalve
- **delve**, helve, shelve, twelve
- **absolve**, devolve, evolve, exsolve, involve, revolve, solve

> Create extra rhymes by changing words like absolve to absolving. ⓘ

Section 35: **-z**

35.1

- **Abkhaz**, as, Baz, has, jazz, pizzazz, razz, whereas
- **Boas**, Boaz
- topaz •Shiraz •Alcatraz •razzmatazz

35.2

- **aides-mémoires**, Lamaze, Lars, Mars, parse, Paz, Stars and Bars, vase, vichyssoise

35.3

- **Fès**, fez, fraise, Kes, Les, Montez, says, sez, Varèse
- Baez •Jabez •Boulez
- **Alvarez**, Juárez
- Peres •Gutiérrez
- **Cortés**, Cortes

35.4

- **backstairs**, chargés d'affaires, downstairs, Pears, theirs, unawares, understairs, upstairs

> Create extra rhymes for [i]
> words like backstairs by adding -s
> to affair etc. (see section 2.1).

35.5

- **ablaze**, amaze, appraise, baize, Blaise, blaze, braise, broderie anglaise, chaise, craze, daze, écossaise, erase, faze, gaze, glaze, graze, Hayes, Hays, haze, laze, liaise, lyonnaise, maize, malaise, Marseillaise, mayonnaise, Mays, maze, phase, phrase, polonaise, praise, prase, raise, raze, upraise

> Create extra rhymes for [i]
> words like ablaze by adding -s to
> allay and fray etc. (see
> section 3.1).

- nowadays •polyphase •multiphase
- stargaze •amylase •periclase
- underglaze •manes •lipase
- catchphrase
- **conquistadores**, mores, señores
- polymerase •paraphrase
- chrysoprase •lactase •equites
- Gervaise •endways •edgeways
- eques •breadthways •lengthways
- leastways •widthways •anyways
- sideways •longways •crossways
- always

35.6

- **Achinese**, Ambonese, appease, Assamese, Balinese, Belize, Beninese, Bernese, bêtise, Bhutanese, breeze, Burmese, Cantonese, Castries, cerise, cheese, chemise, Chinese, Cingalese, Cleese, Congolese, Denise, Dodecanese, ease, éminence grise, expertise, Faroese, freeze, Fries, frieze, Gabonese, Genoese, Goanese, Guyanese, he's, Japanese, Javanese, jeez, journalese, Kanarese, Keys, Lebanese, lees, legalese, Louise, Macanese, Madurese, Maltese, marquise, Milanese, Nepalese, Nipponese, officialese, overseas, pease, Pekinese, Peloponnese, Piedmontese, please, Portuguese, Pyrenees, reprise, Rwandese, seise, seize, Senegalese, she's, Siamese, Sienese, Sikkimese, Sinhalese,

sleaze, sneeze, squeeze,
Stockton-on-Tees, Sudanese,
Sundanese, Surinamese, Tabriz,
Taiwanese, tease, Tees,
telegraphese, these, Timorese,
Togolese, trapeze, valise, Viennese,
Vietnamese, vocalese, wheeze

> Create extra rhymes for words like appease by adding -s to agree etc. (see section 4.1). 🛈

- superficies • Héloïse • Averroës
- rabies • pubes • Maccabees
- headcheese

35.7

- Andes
- **Hades**, Mercedes
- Archimedes • Thucydides • aphides
- **Eumenides**, Parmenides
- **Maimonides**, Simonides
- Euripides • cantharides • Hesperides
- Hebrides
- **Aristides**, bona fides
- Culdees
- **Alcibiades**, Hyades, Pleiades
- Cyclades • antipodes • Sporades
- Ganges • Apelles
- **tales**, Thales
- **Achilles**, Antilles
- Los Angeles • Ramillies • Pericles
- isosceles • Praxiteles • Hercules
- Empedocles • Sophocles • Damocles
- Androcles • Heracles • Themistocles
- Hermes • Menes • testudines
- Diogenes • Cleisthenes
- Demosthenes
- **Aristophanes**, Xenophanes
- manganese • Holofernes • editiones principes • herpes
- **lares**, primus inter pares
- **Antares**, Ares, Aries, caries
- antifreeze • Ceres • Buenos Aires

35.8

- fasces • calces • heartsease
- **Albigenses**, amanuenses, menses, Waldenses

- syllepses
- **oases**, parabases
- **aposiopeses**, exegeses, faeces (*US* feces), theses
- radices • appendices • indices
- codices • pontifices
- **analyses** (*US* analyzes), paralyses
- helices • Ulysses • nemeses • apices
- haruspices
- **administratrices**, dominatrices, matrices, testatrices
- tortrices • executrices • diaereses
- **cortices**, vortices
- vertices • parentheses • syntheses
- **hypotheses**, protheses
- cervices
- **Anchises**, Cambyses, cicatrices, crises, Pisces
- synopses
- **apotheoses**, diagnoses, misdiagnoses, neuroses, prognoses, psychoses, scleroses, symbioses
- **anacruses**, cruces
- anabases • apodoses • emphases
- anamorphoses • periphrases
- thoraces • entases • protases
- iconostases

35.9

- **atlantes**, Cervantes
- Ecclesiastes • penates • gentes
- **Orestes**, testes, Thyestes
- **Achates**, Euphrates
- diabetes • striptease
- **pyrites**, Stylites, troglodytes
- Orontes • Boötes • Procrustes
- **Harpocrates**, Hippocrates, Isocrates, Socrates
- litotes • Surtees • Dives

35.10

- **biz**, Cadíz, Cadiz, fizz, frizz, gee-whiz, his, is, jizz, Liz, Ms, phiz, quiz, squiz, swizz, tizz, viz, whizz, wiz, zizz
- **louis**, Suez
- scabies
- **Celebes**, heebie-jeebies

- showbiz • laches • Marches • breeches
- Indies • undies • hafiz • Kyrgyz
- Hedges • Bridges • Hodges • Judges
- Rockies • walkies
- **Gillies**, Scillies
- pennies • Benares
- **Jefferies**, Jeffreys
- Canaries
- **Delores**, Flores, furores
- series • miniseries • Furies
- congeries • Potteries • molasses
- glasses • sunglasses • missus • suffix
- falsies • fracases • galluses
- Pontine Marshes • species
- subspecies • conches • munchies
- treatise
- **civvies**, Skivvies
- Velázquez • exequies • obsequies
- Menzies • elevenses
- **cosies** (US cozies), Moses
- Joneses

35.11

- **advise**, apprise, apprize, arise, assize, capsize, chastise, comprise, demise, despise, devise, downsize, excise, flies, guise, incise, low-rise, misprize, outsize, previse, prise, prize, remise, revise, rise, size, surmise, surprise, uprise, wise

> Create extra rhymes for words like advise by changing apply etc. to applies (see section 6.1).   [i]

- archaize • heroize • ghettoize
- Judaize • bye-byes • disenfranchise
- propagandize • periodize • iodize
- merchandise • melodize
- gourmandize • methodize
- anthropomorphize • apostrophize
- elegize • analogize • syllogize
- **anthologize**, mythologize, psychologize, tautologize, theologize
- hierarchize

35.12

- underutilize

- **tranquillize** (US tranquilize)
- spiritualize • capsulize • memorialize
- imperialize • bestialize • dialyse
- dualize • ritualize • sexualize
- sensualize • contextualize
- detribalize • feudalize • radicalize
- theatricalize • verticalize • musicalize
- **delocalize**, focalize, vocalise
- animalize
- **analyse** (US analyze), channelize, psychoanalyse (US psychoanalyze)
- signalize • criminalize
- **phenomenalize**, pronominalize
- communalize • regionalize
- depersonalize • renationalize
- **factionalize**, fractionalize
- professionalize • conventionalize
- sectionalize
- **operationalize**, vocationalize
- emotionalize • constitutionalize
- **eternalize**, journalize, vernalize
- municipalize • paralyse • mongrelize
- ruralize • denaturalize • federalize
- overgeneralize • mineralize
- literalize • substantialize
- overspecialize • spatialize • initialize
- **catalyse** (US catalyze)
- cartelize
- **metallize** (US metalize)
- **departmentalize**, monumentalize, occidentalize, orientalize, segmentalize, transcendentalize
- devitalize • totalize • palatalize
- **breathalyse** (US breathalyze)
- medievalize • novelize • unequalize
- dieselize

35.13

- euphemize • systemize • randomize
- sodomize • alchemize • dynamize
- compromise • anatomize
- **dichotomize**, lobotomize
- routinize • platitudinize • indigenize
- masculinize • vitaminize • gelatinize
- divinize • cognize • communize
- **proletarianize**, sectarianize
- suburbanize • euphonize • jargonize
- paganize • disorganize
- **decolonize**, recolonize
- ironize • satanize • cosmopolitanize

- gluttonize • civilianize
- philanthropize • panegyrize
- high-rise • low-rise • moonrise
- sunrise • denuclearize • linearize
- **exteriorize**, interiorize
- diarize • barbarize • rubberize
- texturize • slenderize • aphorize
- allegorize • subcategorize • cicatrize
- solarize • vernacularize • secularize
- singularize • formularize • circularize
- glamorize • containerize • pauperize
- mercerize • depressurize • martyrize
- vectorize • enterprise • winterize
- **motorize**, notarize
- etherize

35.14

- excise • queen-size • laicize
- **Anglicise**, Anglicize
- polemicize • classicize • fanaticize
- elasticize • poeticize • parenthesize
- mythicize
- **photosynthesize**, synthesize
- synopsize • apotheosize • emphasize
- circumcise • exercise • metastasize
- hypostasize
- **affranchise**, enfranchise, franchise
- fetishize • alphabetize • concretize
- poetize • palletize • pelletize
- unitize • remonetize • syncretize
- securitize • synthetize • robotize
- narcotize
- **anagrammatize**, epigrammatize, melodramatize, overdramatize
- **emblematize**, lemmatize
- legitimatize • dogmatize • aromatize
- problematize • automatize
- bureaucratize • advertise
- telepathize • televise
- **collectivize**, objectivize
- relativize • supervise • improvise

35.15

- crabwise • slantwise • stepwise
- lengthwise • streetwise • anywise
- contrariwise • sidewise • likewise
- **clockwise**, counterclockwise

- crosswise • nowise • coastwise
- **soliloquize**, ventriloquize
- cornerwise • otherwise

35.16

- **because**, Boz, cos, Oz, Ros, Roz, schnozz, was

35.17

- **applause**, Azores, cause, clause, Dors, drawers, gauze, hawse, indoors, Laws, outdoors, pause, plus-fours, quatorze, Santa Claus, taws, tawse, yaws, yours

> Create extra rhymes for words like applause by adding -s to adore etc. (see section 7.1). [i]

- menopause

35.18

- **arouse**, blouse, browse, carouse, Cowes, dowse, drowse, espouse, house, Howes, rouse

> Create extra rhymes for words like arouse by adding -s to brow and endow etc. (see section 8.1). [i]

35.19

- **appose**, arose, Bose, brose, chose, close, compose, diagnose, doze, enclose, expose, foreclose, froze, hose, impose, interpose, juxtapose, Montrose, noes, nose, oppose, plainclothes, pose, propose, prose, rose, suppose, those, transpose, underexpose, uprose

> Create extra rhymes for words like arose by adding -s to blow etc. (see section 9.1). [i]

- Berlioz • flambeaux • thrombose

- bandeaux •bulldoze •fricandeaux
- metamorphose •pantyhose •glucose
- **gallows**, Hallowes
- tableaux •parclose •Fellows
- bedclothes •nightclothes •rouleaux
- underclothes •misdiagnose
- Ambrose •dextrose •Faeroes
- primrose •cornrows •sucrose
- Burroughs •tuberose
- **bateaux**, gateaux, plateaux
- portmanteaux •fructose

35.20

- **avoirdupois**, noise, poise

> Create extra rhymes for [i]
> words like noise and poise by
> adding -s to boy etc. (see
> section 10.1).

- Anglepoise •equipoise
- counterpoise •turquoise

35.21

- **abuse**, accuse, adieux, amuse,
  bemuse, billets-doux, blues, booze,
  bruise, choose, Clews, confuse,
  contuse, cruise, cruse, Cruz, diffuse,
  do's, Druze, effuse, enthuse, excuse,
  fuse (*US* fuze), Hughes, incuse,
  interfuse, lose, Mahfouz, mews,
  misuse, muse, news, ooze, Ouse,
  perfuse, peruse, rhythm-and-blues,
  ruse, schmooze, snooze, suffuse,
  Toulouse, transfuse, trews, use,
  Vaduz, Veracruz, who's, whose,
  youse

- Andrews

> Create extra rhymes for [i]
> words like abuse by adding -s to
> accrue and brew etc. (see
> section 11.1).

- Matthews •circumfuse •Syracuse
- purlieux

35.22

- Hormuz •Thammuz •Soyuz

35.23

- **abuzz**, buzz, coz, does, fuzz, outdoes

35.24

- has •Sayers
- **Algiers**, cheers, Pamirs, Pears, Piers,
  Sears, Spears
- Teniers
- **Blackfriars**, Briers, pliers
- Greyfriars
- **Bowers**, Flowers, ours, Powers,
  Towers
- bejabers •Chambers •Sobers
- Scriptures •weight-watchers
- **glanders**, Landers, Randers, sanders
- **alexanders**, Flanders
- Enders •Childers •flinders
- Saunders •Bermudas •butterfingers
- Tigers •Rodgers •starkers
- Chequers •Snickers •camiknickers
- bonkers •bluchers •Moluccas
- Sellers •binoculars •Bahamas
- Summers •Marianas •Connors
- **champers**, Pampers

A standard rhyming pair is based on two single words; a *mosaic rhyme* on
the other hand uses one word with several syllables to rhyme with two or
more words, or rhymes phrases, as in the words of this song from Gilbert and
Sullivan's *Pirates of Penzance*:

About binomial theorem I'm learning a lot o' news
With interesting facts about the square of the hypotenuse

(W. S. Gilbert, 'The Modern Major-General')

- jeepers • jodhpurs • Messrs • Masters
- Peters • squitters • Winters
- **headquarters**, hindquarters, Waters
- Klosters • Butters
- **Smithers**, withers
- **Carothers**, druthers
- Travers • Havers • cleavers • Rivers
- vivers • estovers • Marquesas

35.25

- **agents provocateurs**, berceuse, chanteuse, charmeuse, chartreuse, chauffeuse, coiffeurs, danseuse, diseuse, furze, hers, messieurs, Meuse, secateurs, vendeuse
- Betelgeuse • divers

35.26

- **Babs**, dribs and drabs
- Thebes
- **Gibbs**, Hibs
- vibes • Hobbs • Forbes • Stubbs
- Jacobs • Proverbs

35.27

- **adze** (*US* adz)
- Everglades • Palisades
- Leeds • proceeds • Perseids
- Geminids
- **besides**, ides
- upsides • Mods • towards • Rhodes
- crossroads • Lloyd's • adenoids
- **goods**, Woods
- backwoods • suds • soapsuds
- Richards • innards • backwards
- Edwards • inwards • forwards
- downwards • outwards • afterwards
- **Fields**, Shields
- Bluefields • Reynolds • Sands
- badlands • odds and ends • calends
- zounds • Falklands

35.28

- moneybags • daddy-long-legs
- yellowlegs • sheer legs

- **Briggs**, Higgs
- Joe Bloggs

35.29

- Casals • Charles
- **Dardanelles**, Seychelles, Wells
- **Hales**, Swales, Wales
- entrails • telesales • cat-o'-nine-tails
- **Hills**, Mills, Sills, Wills
- **Giles**, Miles, Smiles, Stiles
- hols • consols
- **balls**, Rawls, Walls
- Fowles
- **Bowles**, Coles, Rolls
- **gules**, Jules
- collywobbles • Gorbals • Mumbles
- Goebbels • Needles • oodles • Raffles
- Engels • Gleneagles • Eccles • Pickles
- Naples • Brussels • battels • Beatles
- bristols • measles

35.30

- Abrahams • jimjams
- **alms**, Brahms, man-at-arms
- Thames
- **hames**, James
- Reims • Sims
- **betimes**, Grimes, Times
- Maritimes • oftentimes • sometimes
- Toms • telecoms • Cairngorms
- Holmes
- **Coombes**, Tombs
- Adams • diddums • Helms • doldrums
- Williams • Worms

35.31

- **banns**, glans, Prestonpans, sans
- Octans
- **Benz**, cleanse, Fens, gens, lens
- Homo sapiens • impatiens • nolens volens • delirium tremens • Serpens
- vas deferens • Cairns • Keynes
- **Jeans**, means, Queens, smithereens
- Owens • Robbins • Rubens • gubbins
- Hitchens • O'Higgins
- **Huggins**, juggins, muggins

- imagines •Jenkins •Eakins •Dickens
- Wilkins •Hopkins
- **Dawkins**, Hawkins
- Collins •Gobelins •widdershins
- matins •Martens •Athens •avens
- Heinz •confines •Apennines
- **bonze**, bronze, Johns, mod cons, Mons, St John's
- **Downs**, grounds, hash-browns, Townes
- **Jones**, nones
- lazybones •sawbones •fivestones
- **New Orleans**, Orléans
- **Lions**, Lyons
- Gibbons •St Albans •Siddons
- shenanigans •Huygens •vengeance
- goujons •St Helens •Hollands
- Newlands •Brooklands •Netherlands
- Siemens •Symons •commons
- summons •Lorenz •Parsons
- Goossens
- **Lamentations**, United Nations
- Colossians •Sextans •Buttons
- Evans •Stevens •Ovens •Onions
- Lutyens
- **Cousins**, Cozens
- Burns

35.32

- Springs •proceedings •tidings
- pickings •feelings •filings
- Cummings •gleanings •imaginings
- earnings •belongings •trappings
- fixings •furnishings •Hastings

- beestings •hustings •underthings
- leavings •Livings •water wings
- arisings

35.33

- Stieglitz

35.34

- clothes

35.35

- haves
- **calves**, scarves
- headscarves •mooncalves •Graves
- **beeves**, eaves, Greaves, Jeeves, leaves, Reeves, thieves
- tea leaves •fig leaves •flyleaves
- Hargreaves •lives
- **Ives**, knives, wives
- jackknives •penknives •paperknives
- spaewives •alewives •midwives
- fishwives •housewives •goodwives
- **corves**, dwarves, wharves
- **Groves**, loaves
- hooves •turves
- **elves**, ourselves, selves, shelves, theirselves, themselves, yourselves
- mantelshelves •bookshelves
- wolves •aardwolves •werewolves

A *heroic couplet* is a rhyming couplet written in iambic pentameter (five pairs of unstressed and stressed beats: ti-TUM ti-TUM ti-TUM ti-TUM ti-TUM); they were often used by Chaucer and by Restoration and eighteenth-century poets, especially John Dryden and Alexander Pope:

What dire offence from am'rous causes springs,
What mighty contests rise from trivial things

(Alexander Pope, 'The Rape of the Lock')

Index

accompany 4.34
accomplice 28.8
accomplish 29.8
accord 16.19
accordance 28.45
accordant 30.56
according 26.5
accordion 25.37
accordionist 31.10
accost 31.17
account 30.55
accountancy 4.48
accountant 30.56
accounting 26.13
accouter 12.81
accoutre 12.81
Accra 1.1
accredit 30.21
accrete 30.18
accretion 25.49
accrual 23.25
accrue 11.1
acculturate 30.15
accumulate 30.11
accuracy 4.48
accurate 30.43
accursed 31.26
accusal 23.41
accusatorial 23.24
accusatory 4.43
accuse 35.21
accuser 12.92
accustom 24.20
ace 28.5
acedia 12.5
acer 12.69
acerb 14.15
acerbic 21.9
acerbity 4.53
acetate 30.16
acetone 25.31
acetous 28.34
acetyl 23.12
acetylene 25.10
Achaea 12.3
Achaemenid 16.10
Achates 35.9
ache 21.7
Achebe 4.10
Acheron 25.47
Acheson 25.48
Acheulian 25.37
achieve 34.5
achiever 12.85
Achilles 35.7
Achinese 35.6
achromatic 21.17
achy 4.18
acid 16.11
acidic 21.10
acidify 6.7

acidity 4.53
acidophilus 28.27
acidulate 30.11
acidulous 28.27
acini 6.13
ack-ack 21.3
ackee 4.18
acknowledge 20.6
acme 4.29
acne 4.31
acolyte 30.28
Aconcagua 12.88
acorn 25.28
acoustic 21.17
acquaint 30.54
acquaintance 28.45
acquiesce 28.3
acquiescence 28.45
acquiescent 30.56
acquire 12.13
acquirer 12.67
acquit 30.20
acquittal 23.39
acquittance 28.45
acre 12.38
acreage 20.8
acrid 16.11
acridity 4.53
Acrilan 25.2
acrimonious 28.23
acrimony 4.34
acrobat 30.1
acrobatic 21.17
acronym 24.6
acropolis 28.8
across 28.14
acrostic 21.17
acrylic 21.11
act 30.48
actable 23.26
Actaeon 25.36
actinic 21.13
actinium 24.16
action 25.49
activate 30.16
active 34.8
activist 31.15
activity 4.53
actor 12.74
actress 28.10
actressy 4.46
actual 23.25
actuarial 23.24
actuary 4.43
actuate 30.8
acuity 4.53
aculeate 30.41
acumen 25.45
acupressure 12.72
acupuncture 12.24
acupuncturist 31.12

acute 30.37
acyclic 21.11
ad 16.1
Ada 12.26
adage 20.6
adagio 9.4
Adam 24.17
adamance 28.45
adamant 30.56
adamantine 25.23
Adams 35.30
adapt 30.58
adaptor 12.74
add 16.1
addax 28.38
addenda 12.26
addendum 24.17
adder 12.25
addict 30.49
addiction 25.49
Addington 25.50
Addis Ababa 12.22
Addison 25.48
addition 25.49
additional 23.34
addle 23.28
address 28.3
addressee 4.1
addresser 12.69
adduce 28.19
adducible 23.26
adduct 30.49
Adela 12.43
Adelaide 16.6
Adele 23.3
Adelina 12.54
Adeline 25.22
Aden 25.40
Adenauer 12.16
adenoids 35.27
adept 30.58
adequary 4.48
adequate 30.44
à deux 13.1
adhere 12.4
adherence 28.45
adherent 30.56
adhesion 25.42
adhesive 34.7
adhibit 30.20
ad hoc 21.20
adhocracy 4.48
ad hominem 24.3
Adie 4.12
adieu 11.1
adieux 35.21
ad infinitum 24.20
adiós 28.17
adit 30.21
Adivasi 4.45
adjacent 30.56

adjectival 23.40
adjoin 25.32
adjourn 25.53
adjudge 20.16
adjudicate 30.10
adjunct 30.49
adjuratory 4.43
adjure 12.20
adjust 31.24
adjuster 12.81
adjutancy 4.48
adjutant 30.56
adjuvant 30.56
Adlai 6.11
Adler 12.42
adman 25.2
admen 25.5
admin 25.17
administer 12.78
administrate 30.15
administratrices 35.8
administratrix 28.39
admiral 23.36
admiralty 4.55
admire 12.13
admirer 12.67
admissible 23.26
admit 30.20
admittance 28.45
admix 28.39
admixture 12.23
admonish 29.9
admonitory 4.43
ad nauseam 24.1
ado 11.1
adobe 4.10
adolescence 28.45
adolescent 30.56
Adonis 28.9
adopt 30.58
adoptee 4.1
adopter 12.79
adoption 25.49
adore 7.1
adorer 12.66
adorn 25.28
ad personam 24.1
adrenal 23.34
adrenalin 25.16
Adrian 25.37
Adrianne 25.1
Adriatic 21.17
Adrienne 25.5
adrift 30.47
adroit 30.36
adulate 30.11
adulatory 4.43
Adullamite 30.29
adult 30.51
adulterant 30.56

adulterate 30.15
adulterer 12.67
adulterine 25.23
adulterous 28.31
adultery 4.43
adulthood 16.26
adumbrate 30.15
ad valorem 24.3
advance 28.44
advancer 12.69
advantage 20.9
advantageous 28.25
advent 30.56
Adventist 31.14
adventitious 28.33
adventure 12.72
adventurer 12.67
adventuress 28.10
adventurist 31.12
adventurous 28.31
adverb 14.15
adverbial 23.24
adversarial 23.24
adversary 4.43
adverse 28.36
adversity 4.53
advert 30.45
advertise 35.14
advertiser 12.91
advertorial 23.24
advice 28.13
advise 35.11
adviser 12.91
advisory 4.43
advocaat 1.11
advocacy 4.48
advocate 30.10, 30.42
adz 35.27
adze 35.27
adzuki 4.20
aedile 23.11
Aegean 25.36
aegis 28.7
Aegisthus 28.35
aegrotat 30.2
Aelfric 21.15
Aeneas 28.22
Aeneid 16.8
Aeolian 25.37
Aeolus 28.27
aeon 25.36
aerate 30.7
aeration 25.49
aerial 23.24
aerialist 31.8
aerie 4.43
aerobatic 21.17
aerobic 21.9
aerodrome 24.11
aerodynamic 21.12
aerofoil 23.19

aerogram 24.1
aerogramme 24.1
aeronaut 30.33
aeronautic 21.17
aeronautical 23.32
aeroplane 25.8
aerosol 23.13
aerospace 28.5
aerostat 30.2
Aeschylus 28.27
Aesop 27.8
aesthete 30.19
aesthetic 21.17
aesthetician 25.49
aestival 23.40
aetiology 4.17
afar 1.1
Afar 1.7
affable 23.26
affair 2.1
affairé 3.19
affaire 2.1
affect 30.48
affection 25.49
affectionate 30.43
affiant 30.56
affidavit 30.25
affiliate 30.8, 30.41
affined 16.42
affinity 4.53
affirm 24.22
affirmatory 4.43
affirmer 12.52
affix 28.39
afflict 30.49
affliction 25.49
affluence 28.45
affluent 30.56
afflux 28.41
afford 16.19
afforest 31.12
affranchise 35.14
affray 3.1
affright 30.26
affront 30.55
Afghan 25.1
Afghani 4.31
Afghanistan 25.4
aficionado 9.11
afield 16.35
afire 12.13
aflame 24.4
afloat 30.35
aflutter 12.81
afoot 30.39
afore 7.1
aforementioned
  16.45
aforesaid 16.4
a fortiori 6.15
afoul 23.16

afraid 16.6
afresh 29.3
Africa 12.39
African 25.43
Africana 12.53
Africanist 31.10
Afrikaans 28.44
Afrikaner 12.53
Afro 9.21
aft 30.47
after 12.75
afterbirth 32.14
aftercare 2.7
afterdeck 21.6
afterglow 9.17
afterlife 17.7
aftermath 32.1
aftermost 31.20
afternoon 25.33
aftershave 34.4
aftershock 21.21
aftertaste 31.4
afterthought 30.33
afterward 16.30
afterwards 35.27
afterword 16.31
afterworld 16.38
Aga 12.31
Agadir 12.4
again 25.5
against 31.30
agama 12.52
Agamemnon 25.26
agapanthus 28.35
agape 3.18, 27.4
agaric 21.15
agate 30.21
Agatha 12.83
age 20.4
aged 16.10, 16.34
ageism 24.21
ageist 31.7
ageless 28.8
agency 4.48
agenda 12.26
agent 30.56
agent provocateur
  13.1
agents
  provocateurs
  35.25
Aggie 4.15
agglomerate 30.15,
  30.43
agglutinate 30.13,
  30.43
aggrandizer 12.91
aggravate 30.16
aggregate 30.9, 30.42
aggressive 34.7
aggressor 12.69
aggro 9.21

aghast 31.2
agile 23.11
agility 4.53
agin 25.13
Agincourt 7.10
aging 26.6
agitate 30.16
agitato 9.24
agitprop 27.8
agleam 24.5
aglet 30.22
agley 3.1
aglow 9.1
agnate 30.13
agnation 25.49
Agnes 28.9
Agni 4.31
agnostic 21.17
Agnus Dei 4.2
ago 9.1
agog 18.8
a-gogo 9.13
agonist 31.10
agony 4.34
agoraphobia 12.5
agoraphobic 21.9
agouti 4.54
Agra 12.64
agrarian 25.37
agree 4.1
Agricola 12.48
agriculturalist 31.8
agriculture 12.24
agriculturist 31.12
agrimony 4.34
Agrippa 12.62
agrochemical 23.32
agroforestry 4.40
agronomic 21.12
agronomical 23.32
agronomist 31.9
agronomy 4.30
aground 16.43
ague 11.22
ah 1.1
aha 1.1
ahead 16.3
ahem 24.3
ahimsa 1.17
ahistorical 23.32
Ahmadabad 16.1
ahoy 10.1
aid 16.6
Aïda 12.26
Aidan 25.40
aide 16.6
aide-de-camp 25.24
aide-mémoire 1.1
aides-de-camp 25.24
aides-mémoires
  35.2

aigrette 30.5
aiguillette 30.4
aikido 9.11
ail 23.5
Aileen 25.10
aileron 25.26
ailment 30.56
Ailsa 12.69
aim 24.4
Aimée 3.16
aimless 28.8
Ainsley 4.22
ain't 30.54
Aintree 4.39
Ainu 11.15
aïoli 4.25
air 2.1
air bag 18.1
airbase 28.5
airbed 16.3
airborne 25.28
airbrake 21.7
airbrick 21.15
airbrush 29.16
airburst 31.26
aircraft 30.47
aircrew 11.17
airdrop 27.8
Airedale 23.5
airer 12.65
airfare 2.5
airfield 16.35
airflow 9.17
airfoil 23.19
airframe 24.4
airfreight 30.15
air gun 25.35
airhead 16.3
airing 26.11
airless 28.27
airlift 30.47
airline 25.22
airliner 12.55
airlock 21.21
airmail 23.5
airman 25.45
airmen 25.45
airmiss 28.8
airmobile 23.7
airplane 25.8
airplay 3.15
airpocket 30.21
airport 30.33
airship 27.6
airsick 21.16
airside 16.16
airspace 28.5
airspeed 16.7
airstream 24.5
airstrip 27.6
airtight 30.30

airtime 24.7
airway 3.25
airwoman 25.45
airwomen 25.17
airworthy 4.57
airy 4.39
aisle 23.11
ait 30.7
aitchbone 25.30
Aix-la-Chapelle 23.3
Ajaccio 9.4
ajar 1.1
Ajax 28.38
aka 3.1
Akbar 1.4
Akhenaten 25.50
Akhetaten 25.50
akimbo 9.9
akin 25.13
Akita 12.77
Akkad 16.1
Akkadian 25.37
Akron 25.26
Aksum 24.13
Al 23.1
Alabama 12.50
Alabaman 25.45
alabaster 12.75
alack 21.1
alacrity 4.53
Aladdin 25.14
Alamo 9.18
Alan 25.44
Alana 12.53
Alar 1.12
Alaric 21.15
alarm 24.2
alarmist 31.9
alarum 24.19
alas 28.1
Alasdair 12.82
Alaska 12.37
Alaskan 25.43
alb 14.16
Alba 12.21
Albacete 4.52
Alban 25.38
Albania 12.8
Albanian 25.37
Albany 4.34
albatross 28.14
Albee 4.10
albeit 30.20
Albert 30.41
Alberta 12.82
Alberti 4.55
albescent 30.56
Albigenses 35.8
Albigensian 25.37
albino 9.19
Albinoni 4.33

Albion 25.37
albite 30.26
album 24.17
albumen 25.17
albumin 25.17
Albuquerque 4.20
Alcaeus 28.23
alcaic 21.9
alcalde 4.12
Alcatraz 35.1
Alcestis 28.12
alchemic 21.12
alchemical 23.32
alchemist 31.9
alchemize 35.13
alchemy 4.30
Alcibiades 35.7
alcid 16.11
Alcock 21.20
alcohol 23.13
alcoholic 21.11
Alcott 30.42
alcove 34.11
Alcuin 25.20
Aldabra 12.64
Aldebaran 25.47
Aldeburgh 12.67
al dente 4.51
alder 12.28
alderman 25.45
aldermanic 21.13
Aldermaston 25.50
aldermen 25.45
Alderney 4.34
Aldershot 30.32
alderwoman 25.45
alderwomen 25.17
Aldine 25.21
Aldiss 28.7
aldol 23.13
Aldous 28.25
Aldrin 25.18
ale 23.5
aleatoric 21.15
aleatory 4.43
Alec 21.11
alehouse 28.16
Aleksandrovsk 21.35
alembic 21.9
Aleppo 9.20
alert 30.45
Aleut 30.38
alewife 17.7
alewives 35.35
Alex 28.39
Alexa 12.69
Alexander 12.25
alexanders 35.24
Alexandra 12.64

Alexandria 12.10
Alexandrian 25.37
alexandrine 25.23
alexandrite 30.29
Alexis 28.11
alfalfa 12.30
Alfonso 9.29
Alfred 16.11
alfresco 9.16
Alfvén 25.8
alga 12.31
algae 4.17
algal 23.30
Algarve 34.2
algebra 12.65
algebraic 21.9
Algeciras 28.31
Alger 12.35
Algeria 12.10
Algerian 25.37
Algernon 25.46
Algiers 35.24
Algol 23.13
Algonquian 25.37
Algonquin 25.15
algorithm 24.20
Alhambra 12.64
Ali 4.21
alias 28.23
alibi 6.5
Alicante 4.51
Alice 28.8
Alicia 12.11
alien 25.37
alienate 30.13
alienist 31.10
aliform 24.9
alight 30.26
align 25.21
alike 21.19
aliment 30.56
alimentary 4.43
alimony 4.34
aliquot 30.32
Alison 25.48
Alissa 12.70
Alistair 12.78
alive 34.9
aliyah 12.3
alkali 6.11
alkaline 25.48
alkaloid 16.24
alkanet 30.5
all 23.14
Allah 12.42
Allahabad 16.1
allay 3.1
allege 20.3
alleged 16.10
allegiance 28.45
allegoric 21.15

allegorical 23.32
allegorist 31.12
allegorize 35.13
allegory 4.43
allegretto 9.24
allegro 9.21
allele 23.7
alleluia 12.89
allemande 16.40
Allenby 4.10
Allende 3.9
allergen 25.5
allergic 21.11
allergy 4.17
alleviate 30.8
alley 4.21
alleyway 3.25
alliance 28.45
Allie 4.21
allied 16.14
alliterate 30.15
allium 24.16
all-nighter 12.79
allocate 30.10
allocution 25.49
allophone 25.30
allot 30.31
allottee 4.1
allow 8.1
allowance 28.45
alloy 10.1, 10.7
allspice 28.13
Allston 25.50
allude 16.25
allure 12.20
allusion 25.42
allusive 34.7
alluvial 23.24
alluvion 25.37
alluvium 24.16
ally 6.1, 6.11
Ally 4.21
Alma 12.50
Almagest 31.3
almanac 21.3
almandine 25.10
Almería 12.3
almighty 4.54
almond 16.45
almoner 12.58
almonry 4.43
almost 31.20
alms 35.30
almshouse 28.16
aloe 9.17
aloft 30.47
alogical 23.32
aloha 12.34
alone 25.30
along 26.15
alongshore 7.17

alongside 16.16
Alonzo 9.29
aloof 17.13
alopecia 12.11
aloud 16.22
alow 9.1
Aloysius 28.33
alp 27.16
alpaca 12.37
alpenglow 9.17
alpenhorn 25.28
alpha 12.30
alphabet 30.4
alphabetic 21.17
alphabetical 23.32
alphabetize 35.14
alphanumeric 21.15
alpine 25.23
alpinist 31.10
already 4.12
alright 30.26
Alsace 28.1
Alsatian 25.49
also 9.22
Altai 6.1
Altair 2.1
Altamira 12.67
altar 12.80
altarpiece 28.6
Altdorfer 12.30
alter 12.80
altercate 30.10
altercation 30.10
alternant 30.56
alternate 30.13, 30.23
Althea 12.12
althorn 25.28
although 9.1
Althusser 2.1
altimeter 12.77
altissimo 9.18
altitudinal 23.34
alto 9.24
altocumulus 28.27
altogether 12.84
Alton 25.50
altostratus 28.34
altruist 31.6
alum 24.18
alumina 12.55
aluminium 24.16
alumni 6.13
alumnus 28.29
Alun 25.16
Alvar 1.21
Alvarez 35.3
alveoli 6.11
alveolus 28.27
Alvin 25.19
always 35.5
Alwyn 25.20

alyssum 24.20
am 24.1
amadou 11.6
amah 12.50
Amal 23.2
Amalfi 4.14
amalgam 24.18
amalgamate 30.12
Amanda 12.25
amanuenses 35.8
amanuensis 28.11
amaranth 32.19
amaretti 4.51
amaretto 9.24
amaryllis 28.8
amass 28.1
amasser 12.69
amateur 12.82
amateurish 29.9
Amati 4.51
amatory 4.43
amaze 35.5
Amazon 25.52
Amazonia 12.8
Amazonian 25.37
ambassador 12.29
ambassadorial 23.24
ambassadress 28.10
Ambato 9.24
amber 12.21
ambergris 28.6
ambidexterity 4.53
ambidextrous 28.31
ambience 28.45
ambient 30.56
ambiguity 4.53
ambiguous 28.24
ambit 30.20
ambition 25.49
ambitious 28.33
ambivalence 28.45
ambivalent 30.56
amble 23.26
ambler 12.42
ambo 9.9
Ambonese 35.6
Ambrose 35.19
ambrosia 12.12
ambrosial 23.24
ambulance 28.45
ambulant 30.56
ambulate 30.11
ambulatory 4.43
ambuscade 16.6
ambush 29.15
ameba 12.21
amebic 21.9
ameboid 16.24
Amelia 12.6
ameliorate 30.15
amen 25.5

amend 16.41
amender 12.26
amenity 4.53
Amerasian 25.49
amerce 28.36
America 12.39
American 25.43
Americana 12.53
americium 24.16
Amerindian 25.37
Ameslan 25.2
amethyst 31.14
amethystine 25.23
Amex 28.38
Amharic 21.15
amiable 23.26
amice 28.8
amid 16.8
amidships 28.46
amidst 31.27
Amiens 25.24
amigo 9.13
Amin 25.9
Amirante 30.53
Amis 28.8
Amish 29.8
amiss 28.7
amity 4.53
Amman 25.4, 25.45
ammeter 12.77
ammo 9.18
Ammon 25.45
ammonia 12.8
ammonite 30.29
ammonium 24.16
amnesia 12.12
amnesiac 21.1
amnesic 21.18
amnesty 4.53
amniocentesis 28.11
amniotic 21.17
amoeba 12.21
amoebic 21.9
amoeboid 16.24
amok 21.20
among 26.18
amongst 31.31
amontillado 9.11
amoral 23.36
amoralist 31.8
amoretti 4.51
amoretto 9.24
amorist 31.12
Amorite 30.29
amoroso 9.22
amorous 28.31
amorphous 28.25
Amos 28.14
amount 30.55
amour 12.20
amour propre 12.65

Amoy 10.1
amp 27.17
amperage 20.8
ampere 2.10
ampersand 16.40
amphetamine 25.11
amphibian 25.37
amphibious 28.23
amphibology 4.17
amphipod 16.18
amphitheater 12.82
amphitheatre 12.82
amphora 12.67
amphorae 4.43
ample 23.35
amplifier 12.14
amplify 6.7
amplitude 16.25
amply 4.21
ampoule 23.20
ampule 23.20
ampulla 12.46
ampullae 4.26
amputate 30.16
amputee 4.1
Amritsar 12.70
Amsterdam 24.1
amtrac 21.3
Amtrak 21.3
Amu Darya 12.10
amulet 30.42
Amundsen 25.48
Amur 12.19
amuse 35.21
amusing 26.14
Amy 4.29
amyl 23.9
amylase 35.5
Amytal 23.1
an 25.1
ana 12.53
Anabaptist 31.14
anabases 35.8
anabasis 28.11
anabolic 21.11
anachronic 21.13
anacoluthic 21.18
anaconda 12.28
anacruses 35.8
anaemia 12.7
anaemic 21.12
anaesthesia 12.12
anaesthetic 21.17
anaesthetist 31.14
anaglyph 17.6
anaglyphic 21.10
anagram 24.1
anagrammatic 21.17
anagrammatical 23.32

anagrammatize 35.14
Anaheim 24.7
anal 23.34
analgesia 12.12
analgesic 21.18
analog 18.8
analogize 35.11
analogous 28.25
analogue 18.8
analogy 4.17
analysand 16.40
analyse 35.12
analyses 35.8
analysis 28.11
analyst 31.8
analytic 21.17
analytical 23.32
analyze 35.12
analyzes 35.8
anamnesis 28.11
anamorphic 21.10
anamorphoses 35.8
anamorphosis 28.11
Ananias 28.24
anapaest 31.5
anapest 31.5
anaphoric 21.15
anaphylactic 21.17
anaphylaxis 28.11
anarch 21.5
anarchic 21.11
anarchical 23.32
anarchist 31.7
anarchy 4.20
Anasazi 4.61
Anastasia 12.12
anastrophe 4.14
anathema 12.51
Anatolia 12.6
Anatolian 25.37
anatomical 23.32
anatomist 31.9
anatomize 35.13
anatomy 4.30
Anaxagoras 28.31
ancestor 12.78
ancestral 23.36
ancestress 28.10
ancestry 4.40
Anchises 35.8
anchor 12.37
anchorage 20.8
anchoress 28.10
anchorite 30.29
anchoritic 21.17
anchorman 25.2
anchormen 25.5
anchorwoman 25.45
anchorwomen 25.17
anchovy 4.58

ancient 30.56
ancillary 4.43
ancon 25.25
and 16.40
Andalusia 12.11
Andalusian 25.37
andante 4.51
Andean 25.37
Anderson 25.48
Andes 35.7
Andhra Pradesh 29.3
andiron 25.38
Andorra 12.66
Andorran 25.47
André 3.19
Andrea 12.10
Andreas 28.22
Andrew 11.17
Andrews 35.21
androcentric 21.15
Androcles 35.7
androgen 25.42
androgyne 25.21
androgynous 28.29
androgyny 4.32
android 16.24
Andromache 4.20
Andromeda 12.27
Andy 4.12
anecdotage 20.9
anecdotal 23.39
anecdotalist 31.8
anecdote 30.35
anele 23.7
anemia 12.7
anemic 21.12
anemometer 12.78
anemone 4.34
anent 30.53
anesthesia 12.12
anesthetic 21.17
anesthetist 31.14
aneurysm 24.21
anew 11.1
anfractuosity 4.53
anfractuous 28.24
angel 23.31
Angela 12.43
angel dust 31.24
angelfish 29.7
angelic 21.11
angelica 12.39
angelical 23.32
Angelina 12.54
Angelo 9.17
Angelou 11.13
angelus 28.27
anger 12.31
Angers 3.1
Angharad 16.29

Angie 4.17
angina 12.55
Angkor 7.10
angle 23.30
Anglepoise 35.20
angler 12.42
Anglesey 4.45
Anglian 25.37
Anglican 25.43
anglice 4.46
Anglicise 35.14
Anglicize 35.14
Anglo 9.17
Anglophile 23.11
Anglophobe 14.11
Anglophone 25.30
Angola 12.44
Angolan 25.44
angora 12.66
Angostura 12.67
angry 4.38
angst 31.31
angstrom 24.19
Anguilla 12.43
Anguillan 25.44
anguine 25.20
anguish 29.10
angular 12.46
angularity 4.53
Angus 28.25
anhedral 23.36
Anhui 4.59
ani 4.31
anilingus 28.25
anima 12.51
animadversion 25.49
animadvert 30.45
animal 23.33
animalcule 23.20
animalist 31.8
animalize 35.12
animate 30.12, 30.43
animatronic 21.13
animé 3.16
animist 31.9
animosity 4.53
animus 28.28
anion 25.38
anis 28.6
anise 28.9
aniseed 16.7
anisette 30.4
Anita 12.77
Anjou 11.1
Ankara 12.67
ankh 21.33
ankle 23.32
anklet 30.22
Anna 12.53
Annaba 12.21

Annabel 23.3
annal 23.34
annalist 31.8
Annapolis 28.8
Annapurna 12.59
annates 28.47
Anne 25.1
anneal 23.7
Anneka 12.39
annelid 16.10
Annette 30.4
annex 28.38
annexe 28.38
Annie 4.31
Annigoni 4.33
annihilate 30.11
anniversary 4.43
Anno Domini 6.13
annotate 30.16
announce 28.44
announcer 12.70
annoy 10.1
annoyance 28.45
annoyer 12.18
annoying 26.3
annual 23.25
annuity 4.53
annul 23.22
annular 12.46
annulet 30.22
annunciate 30.8
annus horribilis 28.8
annus mirabilis 28.8
anoa 12.17
anode 16.23
anodyne 25.21
anoint 30.55
anointer 12.81
anomalous 28.27
anomaly 4.27
anomie 4.30
anon 25.24
anonym 24.6
anonymity 4.53
anonymous 28.28
anorak 21.3
anorexia 12.11
anorexia nervosa 12.71
anorexic 21.16
another 12.84
Anouilh 4.9
Anschluss 28.20
Anshan 25.3
answer 4.17
answerphone 25.30
ant 30.53
antacid 16.11
Antaeus 28.22

antagonist 31.10
Antakya 12.89
Antalya 12.6
Antarctic 21.17
Antarctica 12.39
Antares 35.7
ante 4.51
anteater 12.77
antebellum 24.18
antecedence 28.45
antecedent 30.56
antechamber 12.21
antedate 30.9
antediluvian 25.37
antelope 27.10
antenatal 23.39
antenna 12.53
antennae 4.31
antennal 23.34
antennary 4.43
antenuptial 23.38
anterior 12.10
anteroom 24.12
Anthea 12.12
antheap 27.5
anthelion 25.37
anthem 24.20
anthemion 25.37
anther 12.83
anthill 23.9
anthologize 35.11
anthology 4.17
Anthony 4.34
anthozoan 25.38
anthracite 30.30
anthracitic 21.17
anthrax 28.38
anthropogenic 21.13
anthropoid 16.24
anthropology 4.17
anthropometric 21.15
anthropomorphize 35.11
anthropomorphous 28.25
anthropophagous 28.25
anti 4.51
Antibes 14.6
antibiotic 21.17
antic 21.17
Antichrist 31.16
anticipate 30.14
anticipatory 4.43
antifreeze 35.7
antigen 25.42
Antigone 4.34
Antigua 12.31
Antiguan 25.41
Antilles 35.7

antilogy 4.17
antimonious 28.23
antimony 4.34
antinomian 25.37
antinomy 4.30
Antioch 21.20
antipasto 9.24
antipathy 4.56
antiperspirant 30.56
antiphon 25.41
antiphony 4.34
antipodal 23.28
antipode 16.23
antipodean 25.37
antipodes 35.7
antiquarian 25.37
antiquary 4.43
antiquated 16.12
antique 21.8
antiquity 4.53
antirrhinum 24.19
antithetic 21.17
antivenin 25.18
antler 12.42
Antofagasta 12.74
Antoine 25.4
Antoinette 30.4
Anton 25.26
Antonia 12.8
Antonine 25.23
Antonio 9.4
Antonioni 4.33
antonym 24.6
Antrim 24.6
antsy 4.45
Antwerp 27.15
Anubis 28.7
anus 28.29
Anvers 2.1
anvil 23.10
Anwyl 23.10
anxiety 4.53
anxious 28.33
any 4.31
anybody 4.13
anyhow 8.5
anymore 7.1
anyone 25.35
anyplace 28.5
anything 26.14
anytime 24.7
anyway 3.25
anyways 35.5
anywhere 2.15
anywise 35.15
Anzac 21.4
A-OK 3.1
aoristic 21.17
aorta 12.80
à outrance 28.44
apace 28.5

Apache 4.11
apart 30.3
apartheid 30.16
apathetic 21.17
apathy 4.56
ape 27.4
Apeldoorn 25.28
Apelles 35.7
apeman 25.2
Apennines 35.31
aperçu 11.1
aperiodic 21.10
aperitif 17.5
aperture 12.24
apery 4.43
apex 28.38
aphasia 12.12
aphasic 21.18
aphid 16.9
aphides 35.7
aphis 28.7
aphorize 35.13
Aphra 12.64
aphrodisiac 21.1
Aphrodisias 28.1
Aphrodite 4.54
Apia 12.3
apiarian 25.37
apiarist 31.12
apiary 4.43
apical 23.32
apices 35.8
apiculturist 31.12
apiece 28.6
apish 29.9
aplenty 4.51
aplomb 24.8
apnoea 12.8
apocalypse 28.46
apocalyptic 21.17
apocrypha 12.30
apocryphal 23.29
apodoses 35.8
apodosis 28.11
apogee 4.17
apolitical 23.32
Apollinaire 2.1
Apollinaris 28.10
Apollo 9.17
Apollonian 25.37
Apollonius 28.23
apologetic 21.17
apologia 12.6
apologist 31.7
apologue 18.8
apology 4.17
apophthegm 24.3
apoplectic 21.17
apoplexy 4.45
aposiopeses 35.8
apostasy 4.48

apostate 30.16
apostatical 23.32
a posteriori 6.15
apostle 23.37
apostolate 30.11
apostolic 21.11
apostrophe 4.14
apostrophize 35.11
apothecary 4.43
apothegm 24.3
apotheoses 35.8
apotheosis 28.11
apotheosize 35.14
appal 23.14
Appalachian 25.37
appall 23.14
Appaloosa 12.71
apparat 30.3
apparatchik 21.9
apparatus 28.34
apparel 23.36
apparent 30.56
appeal 23.7
appealer 12.43
appealing 26.8
appear 12.4
appearance 28.45
appease 35.6
appeaser 12.90
appellant 30.56
appellate 30.42
appellation
   contrôlée 3.1
appellee 4.1
append 16.41
appendage 20.6
appendant 30.56
appendices 35.8
appendicitis 28.12
appendix 28.39
appertain 25.7
appetence 28.45
appetite 30.30
appetizing 26.14
applaud 16.19
applause 35.17
apple 23.35
applejack 21.3
Appleton 25.50
appliance 28.45
applicant 30.56
applied 16.14
applier 12.13
appliqué 3.14
apply 6.1
appoint 30.55
appointee 4.1
appointer 12.81
apport 30.33
apportion 25.49
appose 35.19

apposite 30.25
appraisal 23.41
appraise 35.5
appraisee 4.1
appraiser 12.90
appraisive 34.8
appreciate 30.8
appreciatory 4.43
apprehend 16.41
apprehensible 23.26
apprehension 25.49
apprehensive 34.7
apprentice 28.12
apprise 35.11
apprize 35.11
approach 15.10
approbate 30.9
approbatory 4.43
appropriate 30.8,
   30.41
approval 23.40
approve 34.12
approving 26.14
approximate 30.12,
   30.43
appurtenance 28.45
appurtenant 30.56
apraxia 12.11
après-ski 4.1
apricot 30.31
April 23.9
a priori 6.15
apron 25.47
apropos 9.1
apse 28.46
apsidal 23.28
apt 30.58
aptitude 16.25
aptly 4.21
aptness 28.29
Apuleius 28.22
Apulia 12.6
Aqaba 12.22
aqua 12.88
aquaculture 12.24
aqualung 26.18
aquamarine 25.9
aquanaut 30.33
aquaplane 25.8
aquarelle 23.3
aquaria 12.10
Aquarian 25.37
aquarist 31.12
aquarium 24.16
Aquarius 28.23
Aquarobics 28.39
aquatic 21.17
aquatint 30.54
aquavit 30.25
aqua vitae 6.18
aqueduct 30.49

aqueous 28.23
aquifer 12.30
Aquila 12.43
aquiline 25.22
Aquinas 28.29
Aquitaine 25.8
aquiver 12.86
Arab 14.14
Arabella 12.42
arabesque 21.35
Arabia 12.5
Arabian 25.37
Arabic 21.9
arabis 28.7
Arabist 31.6
arable 23.26
Araby 4.10
Arachne 4.31
arachnid 16.10
arachnoid 16.24
Arafat 30.1
Aragon 25.41
Aramaic 21.9
Aran 25.47
Aranda 12.25
Arapaho 9.14
Arawak 21.4
arbiter 12.78
arbitral 23.36
arbitrary 4.43
arbitrate 30.15
arbitress 28.10
arbor 12.21
arboreal 23.24
arborescence 28.45
arboreta 12.77
arboretum 24.20
arboriculture 12.24
arboriculturist
   31.12
arbour 12.21
Arbus 28.24
Arbuthnot 30.43
arbutus 28.34
arc 21.5
arcade 16.6
Arcadia 12.5
Arcadian 25.37
arcading 26.5
Arcady 4.13
arcana 12.54
arcane 25.7
arcanum 24.19
Arc de Triomphe
   17.19
arch 15.2
archaeology 4.17
archaic 21.9
archaize 35.11
archangel 23.31
archangelic 21.11

archbishop 27.14
archbishopric 21.15
archdeacon 25.43
archdiocesan 25.48
archdiocese 28.11
archducal 23.32
archduchy 4.11
archduke 21.27
arch-enemy 4.29
archeology 4.17
archer 12.23
archery 4.43
archetypal 23.35
archetype 27.7
Archibald 16.36
archiepiscopacy
   4.48
Archilochus 28.26
Archimedean 25.37
Archimedes 35.7
archipelago 9.13
architect 30.48
architecture 12.23
architrave 34.4
archival 23.40
archive 34.9
archivist 31.15
archlute 30.37
archon 25.25
archway 3.25
Arco 9.16
arctic 21.17
Arcturus 28.31
ardency 4.45
Ardennes 25.5
ardent 30.56
Ardnamurchan
   25.43
ardor 12.25
ardour 12.25
arduous 28.24
are 1.1
area 12.10
areal 23.24
areaway 3.25
arena 12.54
Arendt 30.56
aren't 30.53
areola 12.48
Areopagus 28.25
Arequipa 12.61
Ares 35.7
arête 30.4
argent 30.56
Argentina 12.54
Argentine 25.23
Argentinian 25.37
Argive 34.9
Argo 9.13
argol 23.13
argon 25.25

Argonaut 30.33
Argos 28.14
argosy 4.48
argot 9.13
argue 11.22
arguer 12.20
Argus 28.25
argute 30.37
argy-bargy 4.17
Argyle 23.11
Argyllshire 12.11
aria 12.10
Ariadne 4.31
Arian 25.37
arid 16.11
aridity 4.53
Aries 35.7
aright 30.26
arioso 9.29
Ariosto 9.25
arise 35.11
arisen 25.52
arisings 35.32
Aristarchus 28.26
Aristides 35.7
Aristippus 28.30
aristocracy 4.48
aristocrat 30.2
aristocratic 21.17
Aristophanes 35.7
Aristotelian 25.37
Aristotle 23.39
arithmetic 21.17
arithmetical 23.32
Arizona 12.56
Arizonan 25.46
ark 21.5
Arkansas 7.16
Arkwright 30.29
Arlene 25.10
Arles 23.2
Arlette 30.4
Arlington 25.50
arm 24.2
armada 12.25
armadillo 9.17
Armageddon 25.40
Armagh 1.1
Armagnac 21.4
Armalite 30.28
armamentaria 12.10
armamentarium 24.16
Armand 16.45
Armani 4.31
armature 12.20
armband 16.40
armchair 2.4
Armenia 12.8
Armenian 25.37
armful 23.21

armhole 23.17
armiger 12.35
Arminian 25.37
armistice 28.12
armless 28.27
armlet 30.22
armlock 21.21
armoire 1.1
armor 12.50
armorer 12.67
armorial 23.24
Armorica 12.39
armory 4.43
armour 12.50
armourer 12.67
armoury 4.43
armpit 30.23
armrest 31.3
Armstrong 26.15
army 4.29
Arne 25.4
Arnhem 24.19
arnica 12.39
Arno 9.19
Arnold 16.38
aroma 12.52
aromatherapist 31.11
aromatherapy 4.37
aromatic 21.17
aromatize 35.14
arose 35.19
around 16.43
arousal 23.41
arouse 35.18
Arp 27.2
arpeggio 9.4
arrack 21.30
arraign 25.7
Arran 25.47
arrange 20.19
arranger 12.35
arrant 30.56
Arras 28.31
array 3.1
arrear 12.4
arrest 31.3
arrester 12.76
arresting 26.13
arrhythmia 12.7
arris 28.10
arrival 23.40
arrive 34.9
arrivisme 24.21
arriviste 31.5
arrogance 28.45
arrogant 30.56
arrogate 30.9
arrondissements 28.47
arrow 9.21

arrowhead 16.3
arrowroot 30.37
arrowy 4.7
arroyo 9.6
arse 28.2
arsehole 23.17
arsenal 23.34
arsenic 21.13
arson 25.48
arsonist 31.10
arsy-versy 4.49
art 30.3
art deco 9.16
artefact 30.48
artefactual 23.25
artel 23.3
Artemis 28.8
artemisia 12.12
arterial 23.24
artery 4.43
artful 23.21
arthritic 21.17
arthritis 28.12
arthropod 16.18
Arthur 12.83
Arthurian 25.37
artic 21.9
artichoke 21.24
article 23.32
articulacy 4.48
articulate 30.11, 30.42
articulatory 4.43
artifact 30.48
artifactual 23.25
artifice 28.7
artificer 12.70
artificial 23.38
artillerist 31.12
artillery 4.43
artisan 25.1
artist 31.14
artiste 31.5
artistic 21.17
artistry 4.40
artless 28.27
art nouveau 9.1
Artois 1.1
artwork 21.31
arty 4.51
Aruba 12.21
arum 24.19
Arunta 12.81
arvo 9.27
Aryan 25.37
as 35.1
Asaph 17.1
asbestos 28.34
Ascalon 25.25
ascarid 16.11
ascend 16.41

ascendancy 4.48
ascendant 30.56
ascender 12.26
ascension 25.49
ascensional 23.34
ascent 30.53
ascertain 25.7
ascesis 28.11
ascetic 21.17
Ascham 24.18
ascidian 25.37
Asclepius 28.23
ascribe 14.8
ascription 25.49
asdic 21.10
aseptic 21.17
asexual 23.25
Asgard 16.2
ash 29.1
ashamed 16.39
Ashanti 4.51
ashcan 25.2
Ashcroft 30.47
Ashdown 25.29
Ashe 29.1
ashen 25.49
Asher 12.72
ashet 30.24
Ashkenazi 4.61
Ashkenazic 21.18
Ashkenazim 24.6
Ashkenazy 4.61
Ashley 4.21
ashore 7.1
ashplant 30.53
Ashqelon 25.25
ashram 24.1
ashrama 12.52
Ashton 25.50
ashtray 3.19
ashy 4.50
Asia 12.72
Asian 25.49
Asiatic 21.17
aside 16.14
Asimov 34.10
asinine 25.23
asininity 4.53
ask 21.35
askance 28.44
askari 4.38
asker 12.37
askew 11.1
Askew 11.22
Askey 4.18
aslant 30.53
asleep 27.5
aslope 27.10
Asmara 12.64
asocial 23.38
Asoka 12.40

babysitter 12.78
Bacall 23.14
baccalaureate 30.41
baccarat 1.16
Bacchae 4.18
bacchanal 23.1
bacchanalia 12.6
bacchanalian 25.37
bacchant 30.56
Bacchus 28.26
baccy 4.18
Bach 21.5
Bacharach 21.3
bachelor 12.48
bachelorhood 16.26
bacilli 6.11
bacilliform 24.9
bacillus 28.27
back 21.1
backache 21.7
backbeat 30.18
backbench 29.20
backbencher 12.72
backbiter 12.79
backblocks 28.40
backboard 16.20
backbone 25.30
backbreaking 26.7
backchat 30.1
backcloth 32.8
backcomb 24.11
backcountry 4.42
backcourt 30.33
backdate 30.7
backdraft 30.47
backdrop 27.8
backer 12.37
backfield 16.35
back-fill 23.8
backfire 12.13, 12.14
backgammon 25.45
background 16.43
backhand 18.40
backhanded 16.9
backhander 12.25
backing 26.7
backlash 29.1
backlighting 26.13
backlist 31.8
backlit 30.20
backlog 18.8
backmarker 12.37
backmost 31.20
backpack 21.3
backpacker 12.37
backpedal 23.28
backrest 31.3
backroom 24.12
Backs 28.38
backscratching 26.4
backside 16.16

backslapping 26.10
backslash 29.1
backslid 16.8
backslide 16.14
backslider 12.27
backspace 28.5
backspin 25.18
backstage 20.4
backstairs 35.4
backstay 3.22
backstitch 15.6
backstop 27.8
backstreet 30.18
backstretch 15.3
backstroke 21.24
back talk 21.22
backtrack 21.3
backup 27.13
backveld 30.51
backward 16.30
backwards 35.27
backwash 29.11
backwater 12.80
backwoods 35.27
backwoodsman 25.45
backwoodsmen 25.45
backyard 16.2
bacon 25.43
Baconian 25.37
bacteria 12.10
bacterial 23.24
Bactria 12.10
Bactrian 25.37
bad 16.1
badass 28.2
baddish 29.6
baddy 4.12
Baden 25.40
Baden-Baden 25.40
Baden-Powell 23.25
Bader 12.25
badge 20.1
badger 12.35
badinage 19.1
badlands 35.27
badly 4.21
badminton 25.50
bad-mouth 32.10
badness 28.29
Baedeker 12.39
Baez 35.3
Baffin 25.14
baffle 23.29
bag 18.1
Baganda 12.25
bagatelle 23.3
Bagehot 30.42
bagel 23.30
bagful 23.21

baggage 20.6
baggy 4.15
Baghdad 16.1
bagman 25.2
bagmen 25.5
bagnio 9.28
bagpipe 27.7
bagpiper 12.62
baguette 30.4
bah 1.1
Baha'i 6.1
Bahamas 35.24
Bahamian 25.37
Bahawalpur 12.20
Bahía 12.3
Bahrain 25.7
Bahraini 4.31
baht 30.3
bail 23.5
bailee 4.1
bailer 12.43
hailey 4.22
bailie 4.22
bailiff 17.6
bailiwick 21.18
bailor 12.43
Bainbridge 20.8
bain-marie 4.1
Bairam 24.2
Baird 16.5
bairn 25.6
bait 30.7
baize 35.5
Bajan 25.42
bajra 1.16
bake 21.7
bakehouse 28.16
Bakelite 30.28
baker 12.38
bakery 4.43
Bakewell 23.4
baklava 12.87
baksheesh 29.5
Bakst 31.28
Baku 11.12
Bakunin 25.18
balaclava 12.85
balafon 25.25
balalaika 12.40
balance 28.45
balancer 12.71
Balboa 12.17
Balcon 25.43
balcony 4.34
bald 16.36
baldachin 25.15
Balder 12.28
balderdash 29.1
baldish 29.6
Baldwin 25.20
baldy 4.13

bale 23.5
baleen 25.9
baler 12.43
Balfour 12.30
Bali 4.21
Balinese 35.6
Balkan 25.43
balky 4.19
ball 23.14
ballad 16.29
ballade 16.2
balladeer 12.4
balladry 4.43
Ballantyne 25.23
Ballarat 30.2
Ballard 16.2
ballast 31.25
ballbearing 26.11
ballboy 10.3
ballcock 21.20
ballerina 12.54
Ballesteros 28.14
ballet 3.15
balletic 21.17
balletomane 25.8
balletomania 12.8
Ballets Russes 28.19
ballgirl 23.42
ballista 12.78
ballistae 4.53
ballock 21.30
balloon 25.33
balloonist 31.10
ballot 30.42
ballpark 21.5
ballroom 24.12
balls 35.29
ballsy 4.61
bally 4.21
ballyhoo 11.1
Ballymena 12.54
balm 24.2
Balmoral 23.36
balmy 4.29
baloney 4.33
balsa 12.70
balsam 24.20
balsamic 21.12
Balt 30.51
Balthazar 12.90
balti 4.54
Baltic 21.17
Baltimore 7.12
Baltistan 25.4
Baluchistan 25.4
baluster 12.82
balustrade 16.6
Balzac 21.4
Bamako 9.1
bambini 4.31
bambino 9.19

bamboo 11.1
bamboozle 23.41
bamboozler 12.48
Bamian 25.37
ban 25.1
banal 23.2
banality 4.53
banana 12.53
band 16.40
Banda 12.25
bandage 20.6
bandanna 12.53
Bandaranaike 12.39
bandbox 28.40
bandeau 9.11
bandeaux 35.19
banderole 23.18
bandicoot 30.37
bandit 30.21
banditry 4.40
banditti 4.53
bandleader 12.26
bandmaster 12.75
bandolier 12.4
bandore 7.1
bandstand 16.40
Bandung 26.17
bandwagon 25.41
bandwidth 32.15
bandy 4.12
bane 25.7
bang 26.1
Bangalore 7.1
banger 12.60
Bangkok 21.20
Bangladesh 29.3
Bangladeshi 4.50
bangle 23.30
bangtail 23.6
Bangui 4.1
banish 29.9
banister 12.78
banjax 28.38
banjo 9.15
banjoist 31.6
Banjul 23.20
bank 21.33
bank bill 23.8
banker 12.37
banknote 30.35
bankroll 23.18
bankrupt 30.58
bankruptcy 4.47
banksia 12.11
banner 12.53
banneret 30.24
bannock 21.30
Bannockburn 25.53
banns 35.31
banquet 30.25
banqueter 12.78

banquette 30.4
banshee 4.50
bantam 24.20
bantamweight 30.17
banter 12.74
banterer 12.67
Banting 26.13
Bantu 11.20
Bantustan 25.4
banyan 25.3
banzai 6.22
baobab 14.1
bap 27.1
baptismal 23.33
Baptist 31.14
baptistery 4.43
bar 1.1
barb 14.2
Barbadian 25.37
Barbados 28.25
Barbara 12.67
barbarian 25.37
barbaric 21.15
barbarity 4.53
barbarize 35.13
Barbarossa 12.70
barbarous 28.31
Barbary 4.43
barbecue 11.22
barbel 23.26
barbell 23.3
barber 12.21
barberry 4.43
barbershop 27.8
barbet 30.20
barbette 30.4
barbican 25.43
Barbirolli 4.25
barbiturate 30.24
barbola 12.44
Barbour 12.21
Barbuda 12.29
barbwire 12.13
barcarole 23.17
Barcelona 12.56
Barclay 4.21
barcode 16.23
bard 16.2
bardic 21.10
Bardo 9.11
bardolater 12.82
bardolatry 4.43
Bardot 9.1
bare 2.1
bareback 21.2
barefaced 31.4
barefoot 30.39
barefooted 16.12
barège 19.3
bareheaded 16.9
Barents 28.47

barf 17.2
barfly 6.11
bargain 25.14
bargainer 12.55
barge 20.2
bargeboard 16.20
bargee 4.1
Bargello 9.17
bargepole 23.18
bar graph 17.2
Bari 4.38
Barisal 23.2
baritone 25.31
barium 24.16
bark 21.5
barker 12.37
barley 4.21
barleycorn 25.28
barm 24.2
barmaid 16.6
barman 25.45
Barmecide 16.16
barmen 25.45
barmy 4.29
barn 25.4
Barnabas 28.24
barnacle 23.32
Barnard 16.2
Barnardo 9.11
Barnet 30.23
Barney 4.31
Barnsley 4.21
barnstorm 24.9
barnstormer 12.52
Barnum 24.19
barnyard 16.2
barometer 12.78
baron 25.47
baronage 20.7
baronet 30.23
baronetage 20.9
baronetcy 4.46
baronial 23.24
barony 4.34
baroque 21.20
barouche 29.14
barque 21.5
barrack 21.30
barracks 28.41
barracuda 12.29
barrage 20.2
barramundi 4.13
barre 1.1
barrel 23.36
barrelhouse 28.16
barren 25.47
barrette 30.4
barricade 16.6
barrier 12.10
barrio 9.4
barrister 12.78

barrow 9.21
Barry 4.38
Barrymore 7.12
Barsac 21.4
Bart 30.3
bartender 12.26
barter 12.75
barterer 12.67
Barth 32.2
Barthes 30.3
Bartholomew 11.22
Bartók 21.21
Barton 25.50
bartsia 12.11
Baruch 21.30
Baryshnikov 17.8
basalt 30.51
basaltic 21.17
base 28.5
baseball 23.14
baseboard 16.20
Basel 23.41
baseline 25.22
bash 29.1
Bashkir 12.4
Bashkiria 12.10
basho 9.23
basic 21.16
Basie 4.45
basil 23.41
basilica 12.39
basilican 25.43
basilisk 21.35
basin 25.48
basinet 30.4
basis 28.11
bask 21.35
basket 30.21
basketball 23.14
basketry 4.40
basketwork 21.31
Basle 23.2
Basotho 11.20
Basque 21.35
Basra 12.64
bas-relief 17.5
Bass 28.1
bass 28.5
basset 30.24
bassi 4.45
bassinet 30.4
bassi profundi 4.13
bassist 31.13
bassline 25.22
basso 9.22
bassoon 25.33
bassoonist 31.10
basswood 16.26
bast 31.1
bastard 16.29
bastardy 4.13

baste 31.4
Bastet 30.24
Bastia 12.12
Bastille 23.7
bastinado 9.11
bastion 25.37
Basutoland 16.40
bat 30.1
Bata 12.75
Batavian 25.37
batch 15.1
bate 30.7
bateau 9.24
bateaux 35.19
Bates 28.47
Bateson 25.48
bath 32.2
bathe 33.2
bather 12.84
bathetic 21.17
bathhouse 28.16
bathos 28.14
bathrobe 14.11
bathroom 24.12
Bathsheba 12.21
bathtub 14.13
Bathurst 31.26
bathypelagic 21.11
batik 21.8
Batista 12.77
batiste 31.5
Batman 25.2
batman 25.45
batmen 25.45
baton 25.50
batsman 25.45
batsmen 25.45
battalion 25.37
Battambang 26.1
battels 35.29
batten 25.50
Battenberg 18.13
batter 12.74
batterer 12.67
battery 4.43
battle 23.39
battleax 28.38
battleaxe 28.38
battlecruiser 12.92
battledore 7.5
battledress 28.3
battlefield 16.35
battleground 16.43
battler 12.48
batty 4.51
batwing 26.14
bauble 23.26
Baudelaire 2.8
Bauhaus 28.16
baulk 21.22
bauxite 30.30

bauxitic 21.17
Bavaria 12.10
Bavarian 25.37
bawbee 4.1
bawd 16.19
bawdry 4.41
bawdy 4.13
bawl 23.14
Bax 28.38
Baxter 12.74
bay 3.1
Bayard 16.2
bayberry 4.43
Bayern 25.53
Baylis 28.8
bayonet 30.23
bayou 11.3
Bayreuth 30.36
Baz 35.1
bazaar 1.1
bazooka 12.41
be 4.1
Bea 4.1
beach 15.5
beachcomber 12.52
beachfront 30.55
beachhead 16.3
beachside 16.16
beachwear 2.15
beacon 25.43
bead 16.7
beadle 23.28
beadsman 25.45
beadsmen 25.45
beadwork 21.31
beady 4.12
beagle 23.30
beak 21.8
beaker 12.38
beaky 4.18
Beale 23.7
beam 24.5
beamer 12.51
beamy 4.29
bean 25.9
beanbag 18.1
beanery 4.43
beanfeast 31.5
beanie 4.31
beano 9.19
beanpole 23.18
beansprout 30.34
beanstalk 21.22
bear 2.1
beard 16.28
Beardsley 4.27
bearer 12.65
bear garden 25.40
bearing 26.11
bearish 29.9
bear pit 30.23

bearskin 25.15
beast 31.5
beastie 4.52
beastly 4.23
beat 30.18
beaten 25.50
beater 12.77
beatific 21.10
beatify 6.7
beating 26.13
beatitude 16.25
Beatles 35.29
beatnik 21.13
Beaton 25.50
Beatrice 28.10
Beatrix 28.39
Beatty 4.52
beau 9.1
beau geste 31.3
beau idéal 23.24
Beaujolais 3.15
Beaujolais Nouveau 9.1
Beaumarchais 3.21
beau monde 16.42
Beaumont 30.54
Beaune 25.30
beaut 30.37
beauteous 28.23
beautician 25.49
beautifier 12.14
beautify 6.7
beauty 4.54
beaux-arts 1.1
beaver 12.85
Beaverbrook 21.28
bebop 27.8
bebopper 12.62
becalm 24.2
became 24.4
becard 16.28
because 35.16
béchamel 23.3
bêche-de-mer 2.1
Bechstein 25.23
Bechuanaland 16.40
beck 21.6
Beckenbauer 12.16
Becker 12.37
Becket 30.21
Beckett 30.21
Beckham 24.18
Beckmann 25.45
beckon 25.43
Becky 4.18
becloud 16.22
become 24.14
becoming 26.9
bed 16.3
bedabble 23.26
bedad 16.1

bedaub 14.10
bedazzle 23.41
bedbug 18.12
bedchamber 12.21
bedclothes 35.19
bedder 12.26
Bede 16.7
bedeck 21.6
bedevil 23.40
bedew 11.1
bedfellow 9.17
Bedford 16.28
Bedfordshire 12.11
bedhead 16.3
bedight 30.26
bedim 24.6
bedizen 25.52
bedjacket 30.21
bedlam 24.18
bedlinen 25.18
bedmaker 12.38
Bedouin 25.13
bedpan 25.3
bedplate 30.11
bedpost 31.20
bedridden 25.40
bedrock 21.21
bedroll 23.18
bedroom 24.12
bedside 16.16
bedsit 30.20
bedsock 21.21
bedsore 7.16
bedspread 16.4
bedstead 16.4
bedstraw 7.15
bedtime 24.7
bee 4.1
Beeb 14.6
beech 15.5
Beecham 24.17
beechwood 16.26
beef 17.5
beefburger 12.32
beefcake 21.7
beefeater 12.77
beefsteak 21.7
beefy 4.14
beehive 34.9
beeline 25.22
Beelzebub 14.13
been 25.9
beep 27.5
beeper 12.61
beer 12.4
Beerbohm 24.11
beerhouse 28.16
beermoney 4.33
beery 4.43
beestings 35.32
beeswax 28.38

b

beeswing 26.14
beet 30.18
Beethoven 25.51
beetle 23.39
Beeton 25.50
beetroot 30.37
beeves 35.35
befall 23.14
befallen 25.44
befell 23.3
befit 30.20
befog 18.8
befool 23.20
before 7.1
beforehand 16.40
befoul 23.16
befriend 16.41
befuddle 23.28
beg 18.3
begad 16.1
began 25.1
beget 30.4
begetter 12.76
beggar 12.31
beggarly 4.27
beggary 4.43
begin 25.13
Begin 25.14
beginner 12.55
beginning 26.9
begone 25.24
begonia 12.8
begorra 12.65
begot 30.31
begotten 25.50
begrime 24.7
begrudge 20.16
beguile 23.11
beguiler 12.44
beguine 25.9
begum 24.18
begun 25.35
behalf 17.2
Behan 25.36
behave 34.4
behavior 12.89
behaviour 12.89
behavioural 23.36
behead 16.3
beheld 16.35
behemoth 32.13
behest 31.3
behind 16.42
behindhand 16.40
Behn 25.5
behold 16.37
beholden 25.40
beholder 12.28
behoof 17.13
behove 34.11
Behrens 28.45

Behring 26.11
Beiderbecke 21.6
beige 19.4
Beijing 26.3
being 26.3
Beira 12.65
Beirut 30.37
bejabers 35.24
Bekaa 1.1
belabor 12.21
belabour 12.21
Belarus 28.19
belated 16.12
belay 3.1, 3.15
belch 15.15
beldam 24.17
beleaguer 12.31
Belém 24.3
Belfast 31.2
belfry 4.38
Belgae 6.8
Belgian 25.42
Belgic 21.11
Belgium 24.18
Belgrade 16.6
Belial 23.24
belie 6.1
belief 17.5
believe 34.5
believer 12.85
Belinda 12.27
belittle 23.39
belittler 12.48
Belize 35.6
Belizean 25.37
bell 23.3
Bella 12.42
belladonna 12.56
bellboy 10.3
belle 23.3
belle époque 21.20
Bellerophon 25.25
belles-lettres 12.64
belletrist 31.12
bellflower 12.16
bellhop 27.8
bellicose 28.17
bellicosity 4.53
belligerence 28.45
belligerent 30.56
Bellini 4.31
bellman 25.45
bellmen 25.45
Belloc 21.21
bellow 9.17
bell push 29.15
bell-ringer 12.60
bell-ringing 26.10
belly 4.22
bellyache 21.7
bellyacher 12.38

bellyflop 27.8
Belmopan 25.1
belong 26.15
belongings 35.32
Belorussian 25.49
beloved 16.13
below 9.1
Bel Paese 4.61
Belsen 25.48
Belshazzar 12.90
belt 30.51
Beltane 25.8
belter 12.76
beluga 12.32
belvedere 12.5
belying 26.3
Bemba 12.21
bemire 12.13
bemoan 25.30
bemuse 35.21
Ben 25.5
Benares 35.10
Benbecula 12.46
bench 29.20
bencher 12.72
benchmark 21.5
bend 16.41
bender 12.26
Bendigo 9.13
bendy 4.12
beneath 32.5
benedicite 4.53
Benedict 30.49
Benedictine 25.12
benediction 25.49
benedictory 4.43
Benedictus 28.34
benefaction 25.49
benefactor 12.74
benefactress 28.10
benefice 28.7
beneficence 28.45
beneficent 30.56
beneficial 23.38
beneficiary 4.43
benefit 30.21
Benelux 28.41
benevolence 28.45
benevolent 30.56
Bengal 23.14
Bengali 4.25
Benghazi 4.61
Benguela 12.43
Ben-Gurion 25.37
benighted 16.12
benign 25.21
benignancy 4.48
benignant 30.56
benignity 4.53
Benin 25.9
Beninese 35.6

benison 25.52
Benito 9.24
Benjamin 25.17
Benn 25.5
Bennett 30.23
Benny 4.31
Benson 25.48
bent 30.53
Bentham 24.20
Benthamite 30.29
benthos 28.14
Bentley 4.22
bentonite 30.29
bentwood 16.26
benumb 24.14
Benz 35.31
Benzedrine 25.11
benzene 25.12
benzine 25.12
benzoin 25.13
benzol 23.13
Beowulf 17.18
bequeath 33.3
bequeather 12.84
bequest 31.3
berate 30.7
Berber 12.22
Berbera 12.67
berberis 28.10
berceuse 35.25
bereft 30.47
Berenice 28.6
beret 3.19
Berg 18.13
bergamot 30.31
Bergen 25.41
bergenia 12.8
Berger 12.32
Bergerac 21.3
Bergman 25.45
Bergson 25.48
beribboned 16.45
beriberi 4.38
Bering 26.11
berk 21.31
Berkeley 4.21, 4.28
berkelium 24.16
Berks 28.38
Berkshire 12.11
Berlin 25.13
Berliner 12.55
Berlioz 35.19
berm 24.22
Bermuda 12.29
Bermudan 25.40
Bermudas 35.24
Bermudian 25.37
Bernadette 30.4
Bernadotte 30.31
Bernard 16.2, 16.29
Berne 25.53

Bernese 35.6
Bernhardt 30.3
Bernice 28.9
Bernini 4.31
Bernstein 25.23
Berra 12.64
berry 4.38
berserk 21.31
Bert 30.45
berth 32.14
Bertha 12.83
Bertie 4.55
Bertolucci 4.11
Bertram 24.19
Bertrand 16.45
Berwickshire 12.11
beryl 23.9
beryllium 24.16
Berzelius 28.23
Besançon 25.26
Besant 30.56
beseech 15.5
beset 30.4
beside 16.14
besides 35.27
besiege 20.5
besieger 12.35
besmear 12.4
besmirch 15.14
besom 24.21
besotted 16.12
besought 30.33
bespangle 23.30
bespatter 12.74
bespeak 21.8
bespectacled 16.38
bespoke 21.24
bespoken 25.43
besprinkle 23.32
Bess 28.3
Bessarabian 25.37
Bessel 23.37
Bessemer 12.51
Bessie 4.45
best 31.3
bestial 23.24
bestialize 35.12
bestiary 4.43
bestir 13.1
bestow 9.1
bestowal 23.25
bestrew 11.1
bestrewn 25.33
bestridden 25.40
bestride 16.14
bestrode 16.23
bestseller 12.42
bet 30.4
beta 12.77
betake 21.7
betaken 25.43

Betamax 28.38
betel 23.39
Betelgeuse 35.25
bête noire 1.1
Beth 32.3
Bethany 4.34
bethink 21.33
Bethlehem 24.3
bethought 30.33
betide 16.14
betimes 35.30
bêtise 35.6
Betjeman 25.45
betoken 25.43
betony 4.34
betook 21.28
betray 3.1
betrayal 23.23
betrayer 12.2
betroth 33.7
betrothal 23.40
Betsy 4.45
Bette 30.4
better 12.76
Betterton 25.50
Betti 4.51
Bettina 12.54
bettor 12.76
Betty 4.51
between 25.9
betwixt 31.28
Bevan 25.51
bevel 23.40
beverage 20.8
Beveridge 20.8
Beverley 4.27
Bevin 25.19
bevvy 4.58
bevy 4.58
bewail 23.5
bewailer 12.43
beware 7.1
bewhiskered 16.28
Bewick 21.9
bewigged 16.33
bewilder 12.27
bewitch 15.6
bey 3.1
beyond 16.42
bezant 30.56
bezel 23.41
bezique 21.8
bezoar 7.21
Bhagavadgita 12.77
bhagwan 25.4
bhaji 4.17
bhakti 4.55
bhang 26.1
bhangra 12.64
Bhopal 23.2
Bhutan 25.4

Bhutanese 35.6
Bhutto 9.25
bi 6.1
Biafra 12.64
Biafran 25.47
Bianca 12.37
biannual 23.25
Biarritz 28.47
bias 28.24
biathlete 30.18
biathlon 25.44
biaxial 23.24
bib 14.7
bibelot 9.17
Bible 23.26
biblical 23.32
bibliographer 12.30
bibliographic 21.10
bibliography 4.14
bibliomancy 4.45
bibliomania 12.8
bibliomaniac 21.1
bibliophile 23.11
bibliophilic 21.11
bibliophily 4.24
bibliopole 23.18
bibulous 28.27
bicameral 23.36
bicarbonate 30.43
bice 28.13
bicentenary 4.43
bicentennial 23.24
biceps 28.46
bicker 12.39
bickerer 12.67
bicolored 16.29
bicoloured 16.29
bicycle 23.32
bicyclist 31.8
bid 16.8
bidder 12.27
biddy 4.12
bide 16.14
bidet 3.9
biennia 12.8
biennial 23.24
biennium 24.16
bier 12.4
Bierce 28.23
biff 17.6
biffin 25.14
bifocal 23.32
bifurcate 30.10
big 18.6
bigamist 31.9
bigamous 28.28
bigamy 4.30
biggish 29.7
bighead 16.3
bighorn 25.28
bight 30.26

bigmouth 32.10
bigness 28.9
bigot 30.42
bigotry 4.43
bigwig 18.6
Bihar 1.1
bijou 11.9
bijouterie 4.43
bike 21.19
biker 12.40
bikini 4.31
Biko 9.16
bilateral 23.36
Bilbao 8.1
bilberry 4.43
bilbo 9.9
Bildungsroman 25.4
bile 23.11
bilge 20.18
bilharzia 12.11
bilingual 23.40
bilious 28.23
bilk 21.32
bilker 12.39
bill 23.8
billabong 26.15
billboard 16.20
billet 30.22
billet-doux 11.1
billets-doux 35.21
billfold 16.37
billhook 21.28
Billie 4.24
Billingsgate 30.9
billion 25.52
billionaire 2.1
billionth 32.19
billow 9.17
billowy 4.7
billposter 12.80
billposting 26.13
billsticker 12.39
billy 4.24
billycan 25.2
billy-o 9.4
biltong 26.15
bimbo 9.9
bimillenary 4.43
bimonthly 4.26
bin 25.13
binary 4.43
bind 16.42
binder 12.27
bindery 4.43
bindi-eye 6.3
binding 26.5
bindweed 16.7
bin-end 16.41
Binet 3.17
bing 26.3
binge 20.19

b

bingo 9.13
binnacle 23.32
binocular 12.46
binoculars 35.24
binomial 23.24
bint 30.54
bio 9.5
biochemical 23.32
biochemist 31.9
biochemistry 4.40
biochip 27.6
biocompatible 23.26
biodiversity 4.53
bioethicist 31.13
bioethics 28.39
biogas 28.1
biographer 12.30
biographic 21.10
biography 4.14
biologist 31.7
biology 4.17
biomass 28.1
biome 24.11
biomedicine 25.19
biomorph 17.9
biomorphic 21.10
bionic 21.13
biopic 21.14
biopsy 4.46
biorhythm 24.20
bioscope 27.10
biosphere 12.5
biotin 25.19
bipartisan 25.1
bipartite 30.30
biped 16.3
bipedal 23.28
biplane 25.8
bipolar 12.44
bipolarity 4.53
birch 15.14
birchen 25.39
bird 16.31
birdbrain 25.8
birdcage 20.4
birder 12.29
birdie 4.13
birdlime 24.7
birdseed 16.7
bird's-eye 6.22
birdsong 26.15
birdwatcher 12.24
birdwatching 26.4
biretta 12.76
biriani 4.31
Birkenhead 16.3
birl 23.42
Birmingham 24.1, 24.19
biro 9.21
birth 32.14

birthday 3.9
birthmark 21.5
birthplace 28.5
birth rate 30.15
birthright 30.29
birthstone 25.31
birthweight 30.17
Birtwistle 23.37
bis 28.7
Biscay 3.14
biscuit 30.21
biscuity 4.53
bisect 30.48
bisector 12.76
bisexual 23.25
bish 29.6
bishop 27.14
bishopric 21.15
Bislama 1.13
Bismarck 21.5
bismuth 32.13
bison 25.48
bisque 21.35
Bissau 8.1
bister 12.78
bistre 12.78
bistro 9.21
bit 30.20
bitch 15.6
bitchy 4.11
bite 30.26
biter 12.79
Bithynia 12.8
bitmap 27.1
bitten 25.50
bitter 12.78
bitterling 26.8
bittern 25.50
bittersweet 30.18, 30.19
bitty 4.53
bitumen 25.17
bituminous 28.29
bivalence 28.45
bivalve 34.15
bivouac 21.1
bivvy 4.58
biweekly 4.23
biyearly 4.27
biz 35.10
bizarre 1.1
Bizerta 12.82
Bizet 3.27
blab 14.1
blabber 12.21
blabbermouth 32.10
black 21.1
blackamoor 7.12
blackball 23.14
blackbeetle 23.39
blackberry 4.43

blackberrying 26.3
blackbird 16.31
blackboard 16.20
blackbuck 21.29
Blackburn 25.53
blackcap 27.1
blackcock 21.20
blackcurrant 30.56
blacken 25.43
Blackett 30.21
Blackfeet 30.18
blackfly 6.11
Blackfoot 30.39
Blackfriars 35.24
blackguard 16.2
blackguardly 4.21
blackhead 16.3
blacking 26.7
blackish 29.8
blackjack 21.3
blackleg 18.3
blacklist 31.8
blackmail 23.5
blackmailer 12.43
Blackmore 7.12
blackout 30.34
Blackpool 23.20
Blackshirt 30.45
blacksmith 32.6
blackspot 30.32
Blackstone 25.31
blackthorn 25.28
blacktop 27.8
Blackwood 16.26
bladder 12.25
bladderwort 30.45
bladderwrack 21.3
blade 16.6
blaeberry 4.43
blag 18.1
blagger 12.31
blah 1.1
blain 25.7
Blair 2.1
Blaise 35.5
Blake 21.7
Blakey 4.18
blame 24.4
blameworthy 4.57
blanch 29.20
Blanchard 16.29
Blanche 29.20
blancmange 20.19
blanco 9.16
bland 16.40
blandish 29.6
blank 21.33
blanket 30.21
blanket weed 16.7
blanquette 30.4
Blantyre 12.14

blare 2.1
blarney 4.31
blasé 3.27
blaspheme 24.5
blasphemer 12.51
blasphemous 28.28
blasphemy 4.30
blast 31.2
blaster 12.75
blatancy 4.45
blatant 30.56
blather 12.84
blatherskite 30.27
Blavatsky 4.18
blaze 35.5
blazer 12.90
blazon 25.52
blazonry 4.39
bleach 15.5
bleacher 12.23
bleak 21.8
blear 12.4
bleary 4.43
bleat 30.18
bleb 14.3
bled 16.3
Bleddyn 25.19
bleed 16.7
bleeder 12.26
bleep 27.5
bleeper 12.61
blemish 29.8
blench 29.20
blend 16.41
blende 16.41
blender 12.26
Blenheim 24.6
blenny 4.31
Blériot 9.4
bless 28.3
blessed 31.3
blessing 26.12
blest 31.3
blew 11.1
blewits 28.47
Bligh 6.1
blight 30.26
blighter 12.79
Blighty 4.54
blimey 4.29
blimp 27.17
blimpish 29.9
blind 16.42
blinder 12.27
blindfold 16.37
blindworm 24.22
blini 4.32
blink 21.33
blinker 12.39
blip 27.6
bliss 28.7

blister 12.78
blithe 33.5
blithering 26.11
blitz 28.47
Blitzkrieg 18.5
Blixen 25.48
blizzard 16.30
bloat 30.35
bloater 12.80
blob 14.9
bloc 21.20
Bloch 22.4
block 21.20
blockade 16.6
blockader 12.26
blockage 20.6
blockbuster 12.81
blockbusting 26.13
blocker 12.40
blockhead 16.3
Blodwen 25.20
Bloemfontein 25.8
blog 18.8
bloke 21.24
blonde 16.42
Blondin 25.14
blood 16.27
bloodbath 32.2
bloodhound 16.43
bloodletting 26.13
bloodline 25.22
bloodlust 31.24
bloodshed 16.4
bloodshot 30.32
bloodstain 25.8
bloodstock 21.21
bloodstone 25.31
bloodstream 24.5
bloodsucker 12.41
bloodsucking 26.7
bloodthirsty 4.55
bloodworm 24.22
bloody 4.13
bloom 24.12
bloomer 12.52
Bloomfield 16.35
Bloomsbury 4.43
bloop 27.11
blooper 12.63
blossom 24.20
blossomy 4.30
blot 30.31
blotch 15.7
blotchy 4.11
blotter 12.79
blotto 9.25
blouse 35.18
blouson 25.27
blow 9.1
blowback 21.2
blow-dry 6.15

blower 12.17
blowfish 29.7
blowfly 6.11
blowgun 25.35
blowhard 16.2
blowhole 23.17
blowlamp 27.17
blown 25.30
blowout 30.34
blowpipe 27.7
blowsy 4.61
blowtorch 15.8
blowy 4.7
blub 14.13
blubber 12.22
blubberer 12.67
blubbery 4.43
bluchers 35.24
bludge 20.16
bludgeon 25.42
bludger 12.36
blue 11.1
bluebeard 16.28
bluebell 23.3
blueberry 4.43
bluebird 16.31
bluebottle 23.39
Bluefields 35.27
bluegill 23.8
bluegrass 28.2
blueprint 30.54
blues 35.21
bluestocking 26.7
bluestone 25.31
bluesy 4.62
bluet 30.20
bluethroat 30.35
bluetit 30.24
bluey 4.8
bluff 17.15
bluffer 12.30
bluing 26.3
bluish 29.6
Blum 24.12
Blumenbach 21.2
Blunden 25.40
blunder 12.29
blunderbuss 28.21
blunderer 12.67
blunge 20.19
blunger 12.36
Blunkett 30.21
blunt 30.55
blur 13.1
blurb 14.15
blurry 4.44
blurt 30.45
blush 29.16
blusher 12.73
bluster 12.81
blustery 4.43

Blu-Tack 21.4
Blyton 25.50
bo 9.1
boa 12.17
Boaks 28.40
boar 7.1
board 16.19
boarder 12.28
boardroom 24.12
boardsailing 26.8
boardsailor 12.43
boardwalk 21.22
Boas 35.1
boast 31.20
boaster 12.80
boat 30.35
boatbuilder 12.27
boatel 23.3
boater 12.80
boathouse 28.16
boatload 16.23
boatman 25.45
boatmen 25.45
boatswain 25.48
boatyard 16.2
Boaz 35.1
bob 14.9
Bobbie 4.10
bobbin 25.13
bobble 23.26
bobbly 4.27
bobby 4.10
bobbysoxer 12.70
bobcat 30.1
bobolink 21.33
bobsled 16.3
bobsleigh 3.15
bobstay 3.22
bobtail 23.6
bobwhite 30.30
Boccaccio 9.4
bocce 4.11
Boccherini 4.31
Boche 29.11
bock 21.20
bod 16.18
bodacious 28.33
bode 16.23
bodega 12.31
bodge 20.11
bodice 28.7
bodily 4.24
bodkin 25.15
Bodley 4.25
Bodoni 4.33
body 4.13
bodybuilder 12.27
bodybuilding 26.5
bodyguard 16.2
bodyline 25.22
bodysuit 30.38

bodywork 21.31
Boer 7.1
Boethius 28.23
boff 17.8
boffin 25.14
boffo 9.12
bog 18.8
Bogarde 16.2
Bogart 30.3
bogey 4.15
bogeyman 25.2
bogeymen 25.5
boggle 23.30
boggy 4.15
bogie 4.15
bogle 23.30
Bogotá 1.1
bogus 28.25
Bohemia 12.7
Bohemian 25.37
boho 9.14
boil 23.19
Boileau 9.1
boiler 12.44
boilermaker 12.38
boing 26.16
Boise 4.61
boisterous 28.31
Bokmål 23.15
bolas 28.27
bold 16.37
boldface 28.5
boldfaced 31.4
bole 23.17
bolero 9.21
boletus 28.34
Boleyn 25.13
bolide 16.14
bolivar 1.21
Bolívar 1.21
Bolivia 12.12
Bolivian 25.37
boliviano 9.19
boll 23.13
bollard 16.2
bollocking 26.7
bollocks 28.41
bolo 9.17
Bologna 12.89
boloney 4.33
Bolshevik 21.18
Bolshevist 31.15
bolshie 4.50
bolster 12.80
bolsterer 12.67
bolt 30.51
bolter 12.80
bolthole 23.17
Bolton 25.50
Boltzmann 25.45
bolus 28.27

b

Bolzano 9.19
bomb 24.8
bombard 16.2
bombarde 16.2
bombardier 12.4
bombardon 25.40
bombast 31.1
bombastic 21.17
Bombay 3.1
bombazine 25.12
bombe 24.8
bomber 12.51
bombshell 23.4
bombsight 30.30
bona fide 4.12
bona fides 35.7
Bonaire 2.1
bonanza 12.90
Bonaparte 30.3
Bonaventura 12.67
bon-bon 25.24
bonce 28.44
bond 16.42
bondage 20.6
bondager 12.35
Bondi 6.6
bondsman 25.45
bondsmen 25.45
bone 25.30
bonefish 29.7
bonehead 16.3
boneheaded 16.9
bonemeal 23.7
boner 12.56
boneshaker 12.38
bonfire 12.14
bong 26.15
bongo 9.13
Bonham 24.19
Bonhoeffer 12.30
bonhomie 4.30
bonhomous 28.28
bonier 12.8
boniest 31.6
Bonington 25.50
bonito 9.24
bonk 21.34
bonkers 35.24
Bonn 25.24
Bonnard 1.1
bonnet 30.23
Bonnie 4.32
bonny 4.32
bonsai 6.16
bons mots 9.1
bonspiel 23.7
bonus 28.29
bon vivant 25.24
bon viveur 13.1
bonxie 4.46
bony 4.33

bonze 35.31
bonzer 12.91
boo 11.1
boob 14.12
booboo 11.4
booby 4.10
boodle 23.28
boogie 4.15
boogie-woogie 4.15
boohoo 11.1
book 21.28
bookbinder 12.27
bookcase 28.5
bookend 16.41
booker 12.41
bookie 4.20
booking 26.7
bookish 29.8
bookkeeper 12.61
bookkeeping 26.10
booklet 30.22
bookmaker 12.38
bookmaking 26.7
bookman 25.45
bookmark 21.5
bookmen 25.45
bookmobile 23.7
bookplate 30.11
bookseller 12.42
bookshelf 17.18
bookshelves 35.35
bookshop 27.8
bookstall 23.15
booksy 4.47
bookwork 21.31
bookworm 24.22
Boole 23.20
Boolean 25.37
boom 24.12
boomer 12.52
boomerang 26.1
boomslang 26.1
boon 25.33
Boone 25.33
boor 12.20
boorish 29.9
boost 31.22
booster 12.81
boot 30.37
bootblack 21.3
bootboy 10.3
bootee 4.1
Boötes 35.9
booth 33.8
bootjack 21.3
bootlace 28.5
bootleg 18.3
bootlegger 12.31
bootlicker 12.39
bootstrap 27.1
booty 4.54

booze 35.21
boozer 12.92
boozy 4.62
bop 27.8
bopper 12.62
bora 12.66
Bora-Bora 12.66
boracic 21.16
borage 20.8
borate 30.15
borax 28.38
Bordeaux 9.1
bordello 9.17
border 12.28
borderer 12.67
borderland 16.40
borderline 25.22
Bordet 3.1
bordure 12.20
bore 7.1
boreal 23.24
boredom 24.17
borehole 23.17
borer 12.66
Borg 18.9
Borges 28.3
Borgia 12.6
boric 21.15
boring 26.11
Boris 28.10
Bork 21.22
Bormann 25.45
born 25.28
borne 25.28
Bornean 25.37
Borneo 9.4
Bornholm 24.11
Borobudur 12.20
Borodin 25.14
Borodino 9.19
boron 25.26
borough 12.66
Borromini 4.31
borrow 9.21
borrower 12.17
borrowing 26.3
Borsalino 9.19
borscht 30.59
Borstal 23.39
bort 30.33
borzoi 10.16
boscage 20.6
Bosch 29.11
Bose 35.19
bosh 29.11
Bosnia 12.8
Bosnian 25.37
bosom 24.21
bosomy 4.30
Bosporus 28.31
boss 28.14

bossy 4.46
Boston 25.50
Bostonian 25.37
bosun 25.48
Boswell 23.4
Bosworth 32.14
bot 30.31
botanic 21.13
botanical 23.32
botanist 31.10
botany 4.34
botch 15.7
botcher 12.24
both 32.11
Botha 12.80
Botham 24.20
bother 12.84
Bothwell 23.4
bothy 4.56
Botswana 12.53
Botswanan 25.46
Botticelli 4.22
bottle 23.39
bottleneck 21.6
bottler 12.48
bottom 24.20
bottommost 31.20
bottomry 4.43
Boucher 12.24
bouclé 3.15
Boudicca 12.39
boudoir 1.22
bouffant 25.25
Bougainville 23.10
bougainvillea 12.6
bough 8.1
bought 30.33
boughten 25.50
bouillabaisse 28.3
bouilli 4.60
bouillon 25.27
boulder 12.28
bouldery 4.43
boule 4.26, 23.20
boules 23.20
boulevard 16.2
boulevardier 3.1
Boulez 35.3
boulle 23.20
Boulogne 25.32
Boulting 26.13
bounce 28.44
bouncer 12.70
bouncy 4.47
bound 16.43
boundary 4.43
bounden 25.40
bounder 12.28
bounteous 28.23
bounty 4.54
bouquet 3.1

bouquet garni 4.1
Bourbon 25.38
bourdon 25.40
bourgeois 1.22,
28.18
bourgeoisie 4.1
Bourguiba 12.21
bourn 25.28
Bournemouth 32.13
bourrée 3.19
bout 30.34
boutique 21.8
bouzouki 4.20
bovid 16.13
bovine 25.23
Bovril 23.9
bovver 12.86
Bow 9.1
bow 8.1
bowel 23.25
Bowen 25.13
bower 12.16
bowerbird 16.31
Bowers 35.24
bowfin 25.14
bowl 23.17
bowler 12.44
Bowles 35.29
bowline 25.16
Bowman 25.45
bowmen 25.45
bowsaw 7.16
bowser 12.92
bowsprit 30.24
bowstring 26.11
bow-wow 8.1, 8.12
bowyer 12.89
box 28.40
boxcar 1.11
boxer 12.70
boxful 23.21
box room 24.12
boxy 4.46
boy 10.1
boyar 1.3
Boyce 28.18
boycott 30.31
Boyd 16.24
Boyer 12.18
boyfriend 16.41
boyhood 16.26
boyish 29.6
Boyle 23.19
boyo 9.6
Boz 35.16
bozo 9.29
bra 1.1
Brabant 30.53
Brabham 24.17
brace 28.5
bracelet 30.22

bracer 12.69
brachiosaurus 28.31
bracing 26.12
brack 21.1
bracken 25.43
bracket 30.21
brackish 29.8
bract 30.48
bradawl 23.14
Bradbury 4.43
Bradford 16.28
Bradley 4.21
Bradman 25.45
Bradshaw 7.17
Brady 4.12
brae 3.1
brag 18.1
Braga 12.31
Braganza 12.90
Bragg 18.1
braggadocio 9.4
braggart 30.42
bragger 12.31
Brahe 12.34
Brahma 12.50
Brahman 25.45
Brahmana 12.58
Brahmanic 21.13
Brahmanical 23.32
Brahmaputra 12.66
Brahmin 25.17
Brahms 35.30
braid 16.6
brail 23.5
Braille 23.5
brain 25.7
brainbox 28.40
brainchild 16.36
Braine 25.7
brainpower 12.16
brainstem 24.3
brainstorm 24.9
brainwash 29.11
brainwave 34.4
brainwork 21.31
brainy 4.31
braise 35.5
brake 21.7
brakesman 25.45
brakesmen 25.45
braless 28.27
Bram 24.1
Bramah 12.50
Bramante 4.51
bramble 23.26
brambling 26.8
brambly 4.21
Bramley 4.21
bran 25.1
Branagh 12.53
branch 29.20

branchlet 30.22
branch-like 21.19
branchy 4.50
brand 16.40
Brandenburg 18.13
brander 12.25
brandish 29.6
brandisher 12.72
brandling 26.8
Brando 9.11
Brandon 25.40
Brandt 30.53
brandy 4.12
Branigan 25.41
Branson 25.48
brant 30.53
Braque 21.5
brash 29.1
Brasília 12.6
brass 28.2
brassard 16.2
brasserie 4.43
Brassey 4.45
brassica 12.39
brassie 4.45
brassiere 12.12
Brasso 9.22
brassy 4.45
brat 30.1
Bratislava 12.85
bratty 4.51
bratwurst 31.28
Braun 25.28
Braunschweig 18.7
bravado 9.11
brave 34.4
bravery 4.43
bravo 9.1, 9.27
bravura 12.67
brawl 23.14
brawler 12.44
brawn 25.28
brawny 4.32
bray 3.1
brazen 25.52
brazier 12.12
Brazil 23.8
Brazilian 25.37
Brazzaville 23.10
breach 15.5
bread 16.3
breadbasket 30.21
breadboard 16.20
breadcrumb 24.14
breadfruit 30.37
breadline 25.22
breadth 32.15
breadthways 35.5
breadwinner 12.55
break 21.7
breakage 20.6

breakaway 3.25
breakbeat 30.18
breakdown 25.29
breaker 12.38
breakfast 31.25
breakfaster 12.82
breakneck 21.6
breakout 30.34
breakpoint 30.55
breakthrough 11.17
break-up 27.13
breakwater 12.80
bream 24.5
breast 31.3
breastbone 25.30
breastfed 16.3
breastfeed 16.7
breastplate 30.11
breaststroke 21.24
breastwork 21.31
breath 32.3
breathalyse 35.12
breathalyze 35.12
Breathalyzer 12.91
breathe 33.3
breather 12.84
breathtaking 26.7
breathy 4.56
Brecht 30.50
Brechtian 25.37
Breconshire 12.11
bred 16.3
Breda 12.26
breech 15.5
breeches 35.10
breed 16.7
breeder 12.26
breeks 28.38
breeze 35.6
breeze block 21.21
breezeway 3.25
breezy 4.61
Bremen 25.45
Bren 25.5
Brenda 12.26
Brendan 25.40
Breslau 8.7
Bresson 25.48
Brest 31.3
brethren 25.18
Breton 25.50
Brett 30.4
breve 34.5
brevet 30.25
breviary 4.43
brevity 4.53
brew 11.1
brewer 12.19
brewery 4.43
Brezhnev 34.3
Brian 25.38

b

briar 12.13
bribe 14.8
briber 12.21
bribery 4.43
bric-à-brac 21.3
Brice 28.13
brick 21.9
brickbat 30.1
brickfield 16.35
brickie 4.19
bricklayer 12.2
bricklaying 26.3
brickwork 21.31
brickyard 16.2
bridal 23.28
bride 16.14
bridegroom 24.12
bridesmaid 16.6
bridewell 23.4
bridge 20.6
bridgehead 16.3
Bridges 35.10
Bridget 30.21
Bridgetown 25.29
Bridgman 25.45
bridle 23.28
bridleway 3.25
bridoon 25.33
Brie 4.1
brief 17.5
briefcase 28.5
Briers 35.24
brig 18.6
brigade 16.6
brigadier 12.4
brigalow 9.17
brigand 16.45
brigandry 4.43
brigantine 25.12
Briggs 35.28
Brigham 24.18
bright 30.26
brighten 25.50
brightish 29.10
Brighton 25.50
Brigitte 30.21
brill 23.8
brilliance 28.45
brilliant 30.56
brilliantine 25.12
brim 24.6
brimstone 25.50
brindle 23.28
Brindley 4.24
brine 25.21
bring 26.3
bringer 12.60
brinjal 23.31
brink 21.33
briny 4.32
brio 9.3

brioche 29.11
Briony 4.34
briquette 30.4
Brisbane 25.38
brisk 21.35
brisken 25.43
brisket 30.21
brisling 26.8
bristle 23.37
bristletail 23.6
bristly 4.24
Bristol 23.39
bristols 35.29
Brit 30.20
Britain 25.50
Britannia 12.89
Britannic 21.13
British 29.10
Britisher 12.72
Briton 25.50
Britt 30.20
Brittany 4.34
Britten 25.50
brittle 23.39
Brno 9.19
bro 9.1
broach 15.10
broad 16.19
broadband 16.40
broadcast 31.2
broadcaster 12.75
broaden 25.40
broadleaf 17.5
broadleaved 16.49
broadloom 24.12
broadminded 16.9
Broadmoor 7.12
broadsheet 30.21
broadside 16.16
broadsword 16.21
Broadway 3.25
Brobdingnagian
  25.37
brocade 16.6
broccoli 4.27
brochette 30.4
brochure 12.73
brock 21.20
Brocken 25.43
brocket 30.21
broderie anglaise
  35.5
Brodsky 4.19
Brogan 25.41
brogue 18.10
broil 23.19
broiler 12.44
broke 21.24
broken 25.43
broker 12.40
brokerage 20.8

brolga 12.32
brolly 4.25
Bromberg 18.13
brome 24.11
bromide 16.14
bromine 25.11
bronchial 23.24
bronchiolar 12.44
bronchitis 28.12
bronco 9.16
Brontë 4.54
brontosaur 7.16
brontosaurus 28.31
Bronwen 25.51
Bronx 28.41
bronze 35.31
brooch 15.10
brood 16.25
brooder 12.29
broody 4.13
brook 21.28
Brooke 21.28
Brooking 26.7
Brooklands 35.31
brooklet 30.22
brooklime 24.7
Brooklyn 25.16
Brookner 12.56
Brooks 28.40
broom 24.12
broomrape 27.4
broomstick 21.17
Bros 28.14
brose 35.19
broth 32.8
brothel 23.40
brother 12.84
brotherhood 16.26
brotherly 4.27
brougham 24.17
brought 30.33
brouhaha 1.9
brow 8.1
browbeat 30.18
browbeaten 25.50
browbeater 12.77
brown 25.29
Browne 25.29
brownfield 16.35
brownie 4.32
Browning 26.9
brownish 29.9
Brownshirt 30.45
brownstone 25.31
browny 4.32
browse 35.18
browser 12.92
Brubeck 21.6
Bruce 28.19
Bruegel 23.30
Bruges 19.6

bruin 25.13
bruise 35.21
bruiser 12.92
bruit 30.37
Brum 24.14
brumby 4.10
brume 24.12
Brummagem 24.18
Brummell 23.33
Brummie 4.30
brumous 28.28
brunch 29.20
Brunei 6.13
Bruneian 25.38
Brunel 23.3
brunet 30.4
brunette 30.4
Brunhild 16.35
Bruno 9.19
Brunswick 21.18
brunt 30.55
bruschetta 12.76
brush 29.16
brushwood 16.26
brushwork 21.31
brushy 4.50
brusque 21.35
brusquerie 4.43
Brussels 35.29
brut 30.37
brutal 23.39
brutalist 31.8
brute 30.37
brutish 29.10
Brutus 28.34
Bryant 30.56
Brylcreem 24.5
Bryn 25.13
Brynmor 7.12
bryony 4.34
bryozoan 25.38
Brythonic 21.13
BSc 4.1
bub 14.13
bubble 23.26
bubblegum 24.14
bubbler 12.48
bubbly 4.27
bubonic 21.13
buccaneer 12.4
Buchan 25.43
Buchanan 25.46
Bucharest 31.3
Buchenwald 16.35
buck 21.29
buckaroo 11.1
buckbean 25.9
buckboard 16.20
bucket 30.21
buckeye 6.10

Buckinghamshire 12.11
Buckland 16.45
buckle 23.32
buckling 26.8
bucko 9.16
buckram 24.19
buckshee 4.1
buckshot 30.32
buckskin 25.15
buck teeth 32.5
buck tooth 32.12
buckwheat 30.19
bucolic 21.11
bud 16.27
Budapest 31.3
Buddha 12.29
Buddhist 31.6
buddleia 12.6
buddy 4.13
budge 20.16
budgerigar 1.8
budget 30.21
budgetary 4.43
budgie 4.17
Buenos Aires 35.7
buff 17.15
buffalo 9.17
buffer 12.30
buffet 3.10, 30.21
buffo 9.12
buffoon 25.33
buffoonery 4.43
buffoonish 29.9
hug 18.12
bugbear 2.3
bugger 12.32
buggery 4.43
buggy 4.15
bugle 23.30
bugler 12.45
bugloss 28.14
build 16.35
builder 12.27
building 26.5
built 30.51
Bujumbura 12.67
Bukhara 12.64
Bukovina 12.54
Bulawayo 9.2
bulb 14.16
bulbous 28.24
Bulgar 1.8
Bulgaria 12.10
Bulgarian 25.37
bulge 20.18
bulgy 4.17
bulimia 12.7
bulimia nervosa 12.71
bulimic 21.12

bulk 21.32
bulkhead 16.3
bulky 4.20
bull 23.21
bulla 12.46
bullae 4.26
bulldog 18.8
bulldoze 35.19
bulldozer 12.92
bullet 30.22
bulletin 25.19
bulletproof 17.13
bullfight 30.27
bullfighter 12.79
bullfighting 26.13
bullfinch 29.20
bullfrog 18.8
bullhead 16.3
bullhorn 25.28
bullion 25.37
bullish 29.8
bull-necked 30.48
bullock 21.30
bullocky 4.20
bullpen 25.5
bullring 26.11
bullshit 30.24
bullshitter 12.78
bullwhip 27.6
bully 4.26
bullyrag 18.1
bulrush 29.16
bulwark 21.30
bum 24.14
bumbag 18.1
bumble 23.26
bumblebee 4.10
bumbler 12.47
bumf 17.19
bummer 12.52
bump 27.17
bumper 12.63
bumpkin 25.15
bumptious 28.33
bumpy 4.37
bun 25.35
Bunbury 4.43
bunch 29.20
bunchy 4.50
bunco 9.16
bund 16.44
Bundesbank 21.33
Bundesrat 30.3
Bundestag 18.2
bundle 23.28
bundler 12.47
bung 26.18
bungalow 9.17
bungee 4.17
bunghole 23.17
bungle 23.30

bungler 12.47
bunion 25.52
bunk 21.34
bunker 12.41
bunkum 24.18
bunny 4.33
Bunsen 25.48
bunt 30.55
buntal 23.39
Bunter 12.81
bunting 26.13
buntline 25.22
Bunty 4.55
Buñuel 23.3
bunya 12.89
Bunyan 25.52
bunyip 27.6
buoy 10.1
buoyage 20.6
buoyancy 4.48
buoyant 30.56
Burbage 20.6
Burbank 21.33
Burberry 4.43
burble 23.26
burbler 12.48
burbot 30.41
burden 25.40
burdock 21.20
bureau 9.21
bureaucracy 4.48
bureaucrat 30.2
bureaucratic 21.17
bureaucratize 35.14
burg 10.13
Burgas 28.25
burgee 4.17
burgeon 25.42
burger 12.32
burgess 28.7
burgh 12.66
burghal 23.30
burgher 12.32
Burghley 4.28
burglar 12.49
burglary 4.43
burgle 23.30
burgoo 11.8
Burgoyne 25.32
Burgundian 25.37
burgundy 4.13
burial 23.24
burin 25.18
burka 12.41
Burke 21.31
Burkina 12.54
Burkinan 25.46
burl 23.42
burlap 27.1
burlesque 21.35
burlesquer 12.37

Burley 4.28
Burlington 25.50
burly 4.28
Burma 12.52
Burman 25.45
Burmese 35.6
burn 25.53
burner 12.59
burnet 30.23
Burnett 30.4
Burney 4.34
burnish 29.9
burnisher 12.72
burnous 28.19
burnout 30.34
Burns 35.31
Burnside 16.16
burnt 30.57
burp 27.15
burr 13.1
Burra 12.66
burrito 9.24
burro 9.21
Burroughs 35.19
burrow 9.21
burrower 12.17
bursar 12.71
bursarial 23.24
bursary 4.43
burse 28.36
burst 31.26
Burt 30.45
burthen 25.51
burton 25.50
Burundi 4.13
Burundian 25.37
bury 4.38
bus 28.21
busboy 10.3
busby 4.10
bush 29.15
bushbaby 4.10
bushbuck 21.29
bushcraft 30.47
bushel 23.38
bushfire 12.14
bushido 9.11
Bushman 25.45
Bushmen 25.45
bushranger 12.35
bushveld 30.51
bushwhack 21.4
bushwhacker 12.37
bushy 4.50
businesslike 21.19
businessman 25.45
businessmen 25.45
businesswoman 25.45
businesswomen 25.17

calico 9.16
Calicut 30.42
calif 17.6
California 12.8
Californian 25.37
Caligula 12.46
caliper 12.62
caliph 17.6
caliphate 30.9
calisthenic 21.13
calk 21.22
calker 12.40
call 23.14
calla 12.42
Callaghan 25.1
Callas 28.27
callback 21.2
caller 12.44
call girl 23.42
calligrapher 12.30
calligraphic 21.10
calligraphist 31.7
calligraphy 4.14
Callimachus 28.26
calling 26.8
calliope 4.37
callipygian 25.37
callipygous 28.23
callisthenic 21.13
Callisto 9.24
callop 27.14
callous 28.27
callow 9.17
callus 28.27
calm 24.2
calorie 4.43
calorific 21.10
calque 21.32
caltrop 27.14
Calum 24.18
calumet 30.4
calumniate 30.8
calumnious 28.23
calumny 4.34
Calvados 28.14
calve 34.2
calves 35.35
Calvin 25.19
Calvinist 31.10
calx 28.41
calypso 9.22
calyx 28.39
calzone 4.33
cam 24.1
camaraderie 4.43
Camargue 18.2
camber 12.21
Cambodia 12.5
Cambodian 25.37
Cambrian 25.37
cambric 21.15

Cambridge 20.8
Cambridgeshire
12.11
Cambyses 35.8
camcorder 12.28
came 24.4
camel 23.33
camelback 21.2
cameleer 12.4
camelhair 2.6
camellia 12.6
Camelot 30.31
Camembert 2.3
cameo 9.4
camera 12.67
cameraman 25.2
cameramen 25.5
camera obscura
12.67
camerawork 21.31
Cameron 25.47
Cameroon 25.33
Cameroonian 25.37
camiknickers 35.24
Camilla 12.43
Camille 23.8
camisole 23.18
Camorra 12.66
camouflage 20.2
camp 27.17
campaign 25.7
campaigner 12.54
Campania 12.8
campanile 4.23
campanology 4.17
Campari 4.38
Campbell 23.26
Campeche 4.11
camper 12.61
campfire 12.14
campground 16.43
camphor 12.30
camphoric 21.15
camping 26.10
Campion 25.37
campsite 30.30
campus 28.30
campy 4.36
camshaft 30.47
Camus 11.14
can 25.1
Cana 12.54
Canaan 25.46
Canaanite 30.29
Canada 12.29
Canadian 25.37
canaille 5.1
canal 23.1
Canaletto 9.24
canapé 3.18
canard 16.2

Canaries 35.10
canary 4.39
canasta 12.74
Canberra 12.67
cancan 25.2
cancel 23.37
canceller 12.43
cancer 12.69
Cancerian 25.37
cancerous 28.31
Cancún 25.33
candela 12.43
candelabra 12.64
candelabrum 24.19
Candice 28.7
candid 16.9
Candida 12.27
candidacy 4.48
candidate 30.9
candidature 12.24
candied 16.9
candle 23.28
candlelight 30.28
candlelit 30.22
Candlemas 28.1
candlestick 21.17
candlewick 21.18
candor 12.25
candour 12.25
candy 4.12
candyfloss 28.14
cane 25.7
canebrake 21.7
caner 12.54
canine 25.23
caning 26.9
canister 12.78
canker 12.37
cankerous 28.31
canna 12.53
cannabis 28.7
cannelloni 4.33
canner 12.53
cannery 4.43
Cannes 25.1
cannibal 23.26
Canning 26.9
cannon 25.46
cannonade 16.6
cannonball 23.14
cannot 30.32
canny 4.31
canoe 11.1
canoeist 31.6
canola 12.44
canon 25.46
cañon 25.52
canonic 21.13
canonical 23.32
canonist 31.10
canonry 4.43

canoodle 23.28
canopied 16.10
Canopus 28.30
canopy 4.37
canorous 28.31
Canova 12.86
can't 30.53
cant 30.53
cantabile 3.15
Cantabria 12.10
Cantabrian 25.37
Cantabrigian 25.37
cantal 23.2
cantaloupe 27.11
cantankerous 28.31
cantata 12.75
canteen 25.9
canter 12.74
Canterbury 4.43
cantharides 35.7
canticle 23.32
cantilena 12.54
cantilever 12.85
cantillate 30.11
cantina 12.54
cantle 23.39
canto 9.24
Canton 25.24, 25.50
canton 25.26
cantonal 23.34
Cantonese 35.6
cantor 7.18
cantoris 28.10
cantrail 23.6
cantrip 27.6
Canuck 21.29
Canute 30.37
canvas 28.35
canvass 28.35
canvasser 12.71
canyon 25.52
canzone 4.33
caoutchouc 21.28
cap 27.1
capable 23.26
capacious 28.33
capacitance 28.45
capacitate 30.16
capacitor 12.78
capacity 4.53
caparison 25.48
cape 27.4
capelin 25.16
Capella 12.42
capellini 4.31
caper 12.61
capercaillie 4.22
caperer 12.67
Capetian 25.49
capful 23.21
capillary 4.43

C

cartomancy 4.45
carton 25.50
cartoon 25.33
cartoonish 29.9
cartoonist 31.10
cartoony 4.33
cartophilist 31.8
cartophily 4.24
cartouche 29.14
cartridge 20.8
cartwheel 23.7
cartwright 30.29
Caruso 9.22
carve 34.2
carver 12.85
carvery 4.43
carving 26.14
car wash 29.11
Cary 4.38, 4.39
caryatid 16.12
Caryl 23.9
Casablanca 12.37
Casals 35.29
Casanova 12.86
cascabel 23.26
cascade 16.6
cascara 12.64
case 28.5
casebook 21.28
casebound 16.43
caseload 16.23
casework 21.31
caseworker 12.41
Casey 4.45
cash 29.1
cash book 21.28
cashew 11.19
cashflow 9.17
cashier 12.4
cashmere 12.7
cashpoint 30.55
casing 26.12
casino 9.19
cask 21.35
casket 30.21
Caspar 12.61
Cassandra 12.64
cassata 12.75
cassava 12.85
casserole 23.18
cassette 30.4
cassia 12.11
Cassidy 4.12
Cassiopeia 12.3
cassis 28.6
Cassius 28.23
cassock 21.30
cassoulet 3.1
cassowary 4.43
cast 31.2
Castalia 12.6

Castalian 25.37
castanet 30.4
castaway 3.25
caste 31.2
Castel Gandolfo 9.12
castellan 25.44
castellated 16.12
caster 12.75
castigate 30.9
castigatory 4.43
Castile 23.7
Castilian 25.37
castle 23.37
Castlebar 1.1
Castlereagh 3.19
castor 12.75
castrate 30.7
castrati 4.51
castrato 9.24
Castries 35.6
Castro 9.21
casual 23.25
casualty 4.55
casuarina 12.54
casuist 31.6
casuistry 4.40
casus belli 4.22
cat 30.1
cataclysm 24.21
cataclysmic 21.12
catacomb 24.12
catafalque 21.32
Catalan 25.2
catalectic 21.17
catalepsy 4.45
catalog 18.8
cataloger 12.32
catalogue 18.8
cataloguer 12.32
Catalonia 12.8
Catalonian 25.37
catalpa 12.61
catalyse 35.12
catalyser 12.91
catalysis 28.11
catalyst 31.8
catalytic 21.17
catalyze 35.12
catamaran 25.3
catamite 30.29
Catania 12.8
cataplasm 24.21
catapult 30.51
cataract 30.48
catarrh 1.1
catarrhine 25.23
catastrophe 4.14
catastrophic 21.10
catatonia 12.8
catatonic 21.13

catawba 12.21
catcall 23.15
catch 15.1
catchall 23.14
catcher 12.23
catchline 25.22
catchpenny 4.31
catchphrase 35.5
catchweight 30.17
catchword 16.31
catchy 4.11
catechesis 28.11
catechismal 23.33
catechist 31.7
catechizer 12.91
catechumen 25.17
categoric 21.15
categorical 23.32
category 4.43
catena 12.54
catenae 4.31
catenary 4.43
cater 12.77
cateran 25.47
caterer 12.67
caterpillar 12.43
caterwaul 23.15
catfish 29.7
catgut 30.40
Cathar 1.20
catharsis 28.11
cathartic 21.17
Cathay 3.1
cathead 16.3
cathedral 23.36
Cather 12.83
Catherine 25.18
catheter 12.78
cathode 16.23
Catholic 21.11
cathouse 28.16
Cathy 4.56
Catiline 25.22
cation 25.38
catkin 25.15
catlick 21.11
catlike 21.19
catmint 30.54
catnap 27.1
catnip 27.6
Cato 9.24
cat-o'-nine-tails 35.29
Catrin 25.18
Catriona 12.58
catsuit 30.38
cattery 4.43
cattish 29.10
cattle 23.39
catty 4.51
Catullus 28.27

catwalk 21.22
Caucasian 25.37
Caucasus 28.32
caucus 28.26
caudal 23.28
caudillo 9.28
caught 30.33
caul 23.14
cauldron 25.47
cauliflower 12.16
caulk 21.22
caulker 12.40
causal 23.41
cause 35.17
cause célèbre 12.65
causer 12.91
causerie 4.43
causeway 3.25
causey 4.61
caustic 21.17
caution 25.49
cautionary 4.43
cautious 28.33
Cavafy 4.14
cavalcade 16.6
cavalier 12.4
cavalry 4.38
cavalryman 25.45
cavalrymen 25.45
Cavan 25.51
Cave 34.4
caveat 30.1
caveat emptor 7.18
Cavell 23.40
caveman 25.2
cavemen 25.5
Cavendish 29.6
caver 12.85
cavern 25.51
cavernous 28.29
caviar 1.2
cavil 23.40
caviler 12.48
caviller 12.48
cavity 4.53
cavort 30.33
Cavour 12.20
cavy 4.58
caw 7.1
Cawley 4.25
Caxton 25.50
cayenne 25.5
Cayley 4.22
cayuse 28.19
cc 4.1
CD-ROM 24.8
cease 28.6
ceasefire 12.14
Cecil 23.9
cedar 12.26
cedarn 25.40

C

cede 16.7
cedilla 12.43
Cedric 21.15
Ceefax 28.38
ceilidh 4.22
ceiling 26.8
Ceinwen 25.5
celadon 25.40
celandine 25.21
celeb 14.3
Celebes 35.10
celebrant 30.56
celebrate 30.15
celebratory 4.43
celebrity 4.53
celeriac 21.1
celerity 4.53
celery 4.43
celeste 31.3
celestial 23.24
Celia 12.6
celibacy 4.48
celibate 30.41
cell 23.3
cellar 12.42
cellarage 20.8
cellarer 12.67
cellaret 30.24
cellarette 30.24
cellarman 25.45
cellarmen 25.45
Cellini 4.31
cellist 31.8
cello 9.17
Cellophane 25.7
cellphone 25.30
cellular 12.46
cellulite 30.28
cellulitis 28.12
celluloid 16.24
cellulose 28.17
Celsius 28.23
Celt 30.51
Celtic 21.17
cement 30.53
cementer 12.76
cemetery 4.43
cenacle 23.32
cenotaph 17.2
cense 28.44
censer 12.69
censor 12.69
censorial 23.24
censorious 28.23
censure 12.72
census 28.32
cent 30.53
centaur 7.18
centaury 4.41
centavo 9.27
centenarian 25.37

centenary 4.43
centennial 23.24
center 12.76
centerboard 16.20
centerfold 16.37
centermost 31.20
centerpiece 28.6
centigrade 16.6
centigram 24.1
centiliter 12.77
centilitre 12.77
centime 24.5
centimeter 12.77
centimetre 12.77
centimo 9.18
centipede 16.7
cento 9.24
central 23.36
centralist 31.8
centre 12.76
centreboard 16.20
centrefold 16.37
centremost 31.20
centrepiece 28.6
centric 21.15
centrifuge 20.15
centrist 31.12
centurion 25.37
century 4.41
cep 27.3
cephalic 21.11
Cephalonia 12.8
cephalopod 16.18
Cepheus 28.23
ceramic 21.12
ceramicist 31.13
Cerberus 28.31
cereal 23.24
cerebellum 24.18
cerebral 23.36
cerebrum 24.19
Ceredigion 25.24
ceremonial 23.24
ceremonialist 31.8
ceremonious 28.23
ceremony 4.34
Ceres 35.7
ceresin 25.19
Ceri 4.38
cerise 35.6
cerium 24.16
cermet 30.4
cert 30.45
certain 25.19
certainty 4.53
certificate 30.10, 30.42
certify 6.7
certiorari 6.15
certitude 16.25
cerulean 25.37

Cervantes 35.9
cervelat 30.1
cervical 23.32
cervices 35.8
cervine 25.23
cervix 28.39
César 1.24
Cesarean 25.37
cesium 24.16
cess 28.3
cession 25.49
cesspit 30.23
cesspool 23.20
cestode 16.23
cetacean 25.49
ceteris paribus 28.24
Cetshwayo 9.5
Cetus 28.34
Cévennes 25.5
Ceylon 25.24
Cézanne 25.1
Chablis 4.21
Chabrol 23.13
cha-cha 1.5
chaconne 25.24
Chad 16.1
Chadian 25.37
Chadic 21.10
chador 7.5
Chadwick 21.18
chafe 17.4
chafer 12.30
chaff 17.2
chaffer 12.30
chaffinch 29.20
Chagall 23.1
chagrin 25.18
Chaim 24.7
chain 25.7
chaingang 26.1
chain mail 23.5
chainsaw 7.16
chair 2.1
chairlift 30.47
chairman 25.45
chairmen 25.45
chairperson 25.48
chairwoman 25.45
chairwomen 25.17
chaise 35.5
chaise longue 26.15
chakra 12.66
Chalcedon 25.25
Chalcedonian 25.37
chalcedony 21.13
chalcedony 4.34
Chalcis 28.11
Chaldea 12.3
Chaldean 25.36
Chaldee 4.12

chalet 3.15
chalice 28.8
chalk 21.22
chalkboard 16.20
chalky 4.19
challah 12.42
challenge 20.19
challenger 12.35
challis 28.8
cham 24.1
chamber 12.21
chamberlain 25.16
chambermaid 16.6
Chambers 35.24
Chambertin 25.3
chambray 3.19
chambré 3.19
chameleon 25.37
chamfer 12.30
chamois 1.22, 4.29
chamomile 23.11
Chamonix 4.34
champ 27.17
champagne 25.7
champaign 25.7
champers 35.24
champion 25.37
Champlain 25.7
champlevé 3.24
Champs-Élysées 3.27
chance 28.44
chancel 23.37
chancellery 4.43
chancellor 12.48
chancer 12.69
chancery 4.43
chancy 4.45
chandelier 12.4
Chandigarh 13.1
chandler 12.42
chandlery 4.43
Chandrasekhar 12.38
Chanel 23.3
Chaney 4.31
Changchun 25.33
change 20.19
changeling 26.8
changeover 12.86
changer 12.35
Changsha 1.1
channel 23.34
channelize 35.12
chanson 25.26
chant 30.53
Chantal 23.1
chanter 12.75
chanterelle 23.3
chanteuse 35.25
chanticleer 12.6

chantry 4.38
chanty 4.51
chaos 28.14
chaotic 21.17
chap 27.1
chaparral 23.1
chapatti 4.51
chapbook 21.28
chape 27.4
chapel 23.35
chapelry 4.38
chaperone 25.30
chapfallen 25.44
chaplain 25.16
chaplaincy 4.46
chaplet 30.22
Chaplin 25.16
chapman 25.45
chapmen 25.45
chappal 23.35
Chappell 23.35
chapter 12.74
char 1.1
charabanc 26.1
characin 25.19
character 12.78
charade 16.2
charango 9.13
charas 28.31
charbroil 23.19
charcoal 23.17
charcuterie 4.43
chard 16.2
Chardonnay 3.17
charge 20.2
chargé d'affaires 2.1
chargehand 16.40
charger 12.35
chargés d'affaires 35.4
chariot 30.41
charioteer 12.4
charisma 12.51
charismatic 21.17
charity 4.53
charivari 4.38
charlady 4.12
charlatan 25.50
charlatanry 4.43
Charlemagne 25.8
Charlene 25.10
Charles 35.29
Charleston 25.50
Charlie 4.21
charlock 21.30
charlotte 30.42
charlotte russe 28.19
Charlottetown 25.29

Charlton 25.50
charm 24.2
Charmaine 25.7
charmer 12.50
charmeuse 35.25
charming 26.9
Charolais 3.15
Charon 25.47
charpoy 10.10
charr 1.1
chart 30.3
charter 12.75
charterer 12.67
Chartist 31.14
Chartres 12.64
chartreuse 35.25
charwoman 25.45
charwomen 25.17
chary 4.39
Charybdis 28.7
chase 28.5
chaser 12.69
chasm 24.21
chasmic 21.12
chasse 28.1
chassé 3.1
chassis 4.45
chaste 31.4
chasten 25.48
chastener 12.58
chastise 35.11
chastiser 12.91
chastity 4.53
chasuble 23.26
chat 30.1
chateau 9.24
chateaubriand 25.24
châtelaine 25.8
chatline 25.22
chat show 9.23
chattel 23.39
chatter 12.74
chatterbox 28.40
chatterer 12.67
Chatterton 25.50
chattery 4.43
chatty 4.51
Chaucer 12.70
Chaucerian 25.37
chauffeur 12.30
chauffeuse 35.25
chaulmoogra 12.66
chausses 28.17
chauvinist 31.10
cheap 27.5
cheapen 25.46
cheapish 29.9
cheapjack 21.3
cheapo 9.20
cheapskate 30.10
cheat 30.18

cheater 12.77
Chechen 25.5
Chechnya 1.23
check 21.6
checker 12.37
checkerberry 4.38
checkerboard 16.20
checklist 31.8
checkmark 21.5
checkmate 30.12
checkout 30.34
checkpoint 30.55
checkrein 25.8
check-up 27.13
check valve 34.15
cheddar 12.26
cheek 21.8
cheekbone 25.30
cheeky 4.18
cheep 27.5
cheer 12.4
cheerio 9.1
cheerleader 12.26
cheers 35.24
cheery 4.43
cheese 35.6
cheeseboard 16.20
cheeseburger 12.32
cheesecake 21.7
cheesecloth 32.8
cheeseparing 26.11
cheesewood 16.26
cheesy 4.61
cheetah 12.77
chef 17.3
chef-d'œuvre 12.68
Cheka 12.37
Chekhov 17.8
Chekhovian 25.37
chelate 30.11
Chellean 25.37
Chelmsford 16.28
Chelsea 4.45
Cheltenham 24.19
Chelyabinsk 21.35
chemical 23.32
chemin de fer 2.1
chemise 35.6
chemist 31.9
chemistry 4.40
Chemnitz 28.47
chemotherapy 4.37
chenille 23.7
cheongsam 24.1
Cheops 28.46
cheque 21.6
chequebook 21.28
chequer 12.37
chequerboard 16.20
Chequers 35.24
Cher 2.1

Cherbourg 18.9
Cherenkov 17.8
cherish 29.9
Chernobyl 23.26
Cherokee 4.20
cheroot 30.37
cherry 4.38
chert 30.45
cherub 14.14
cherubic 21.9
cherubim 24.6
Cherubini 4.31
chervil 23.10
Cherwell 23.4
Cheryl 23.9
Cheshire 12.11
chess 28.3
chessboard 16.20
chessman 25.2
chessmen 25.5
chest 31.3
Chester 12.76
chesterfield 16.35
Chesterton 25.50
chestnut 30.40
chesty 4.51
Chetnik 21.13
Chevalier 3.3
chevalier 12.4
chevet 3.1
Cheviot 30.41
chèvre 12.64
chevron 25.47
chevrotain 25.8
Chevy 4.58
chew 11.1
chewer 12.19
chewy 4.8
Cheyenne 25.1
chez 3.1
chi 6.1
Chiang Kai-shek 21.6
Chiangmai 6.1
Chianti 4.51
Chiapas 28.30
chiaroscuro 9.21
chiasmus 28.28
Chibcha 12.23
Chibchan 25.39
chibouk 21.27
chic 21.8
Chicago 9.13
Chicagoan 25.38
chicane 25.7
chicanery 4.43
chicano 9.19
Chichester 12.78
Chichewa 12.88
chichi 4.50
Chichimec 21.6

C

c

chick 21.9
chickadee 4.13
chickaree 4.43
Chickasaw 7.16
chicken 25.15
chickenfeed 16.7
chickenpox 28.40
chickpea 4.36
chickweed 16.7
chicle 23.32
chicory 4.43
chide 16.14
chider 12.27
chief 17.5
chiefdom 24.17
chieftain 25.50
chieftaincy 4.48
chiffchaff 17.1
chiffon 25.25
chiffonier 12.4
chigger 12.31
chignon 25.27
Chihuahua 12.88
chilblain 25.8
child 16.36
childbearing 26.11
childbed 16.3
childbirth 32.14
childcare 2.7
Childe 16.36
Childermas 28.1
Childers 35.24
childhood 16.26
childish 29.6
childlike 21.19
childminder 12.27
childproof 17.13
children 25.47
Chile 4.24
Chilean 25.37
chili 4.24
chiliad 16.1
chill 23.8
chiller 12.43
chilli 4.24
chillum 24.18
chilly 4.24
Chimborazo 9.29
chime 24.7
chimera 12.67
chimeric 21.15
chimerical 23.32
chimney 4.32
chimney breast 31.3
chimney piece 28.6
chimney pot 30.32
chimney stack 21.4
chimney sweep 27.5
chimp 27.17
chimpanzee 4.1
chin 25.13

china 12.55
Chinaman 25.45
Chinamen 25.45
Chinatown 25.29
chinchilla 12.43
chin-chin 25.13
Chindit 30.21
Chindwin 25.20
chine 25.21
chiné 3.1
Chinese 35.6
chink 21.33
Chinky 4.19
chino 9.19
chinoiserie 4.43
Chinook 21.28
chinstrap 27.1
chintz 28.44
chintzy 4.46
chinwag 18.1
Chios 28.14
chip 27.6
chipboard 16.20
chipmunk 21.34
chipolata 12.75
Chippendale 23.5
chipper 12.62
Chippewa 1.22
chipping 26.10
chippy 4.36
Chips 28.46
chirography 4.14
chiromancy 4.45
Chiron 25.47
chiropodist 31.6
chiropody 4.13
chiropractic 21.17
chiropractor 12.74
chirp 27.15
chirper 12.63
chirpy 4.37
chirrup 27.13
chirrupy 4.37
chisel 23.41
chiseler 12.48
chiseller 12.48
chit 30.20
chital 23.39
chitchat 30.1
chitin 25.19
chiton 25.26
Chittagong 26.15
chitterling 26.8
chitty 4.53
chivalric 21.15
chivalrous 28.31
chivalry 4.40
chive 34.9
chivvy 4.58
chloride 16.15
chlorinate 30.13

chlorine 25.11
chlorite 30.29
chlorofluorocarbon 25.38
chloroform 24.9
chlorophyll 23.8
chloroplast 31.1
chlorosis 28.11
choccy 4.19
choc ice 28.13
chock 21.20
chock-a-block 21.20
chocker 12.40
chocoholic 21.11
chocolate 30.42
chocolatey 4.55
Choctaw 7.18
choice 28.18
choir 12.13
choirboy 10.3
choirgirl 23.42
choke 21.24
chokeberry 4.43
chokecherry 4.38
choker 12.40
chokey 4.20
choler 12.44
cholera 12.67
choleraic 21.9
choleric 21.15
cholesterol 23.13
chomp 27.17
Chomskian 25.37
Chomsky 4.19
chook 21.28
choose 35.21
chooser 12.92
choosy 4.62
chop 27.8
chophouse 28.16
Chopin 25.3
chopper 12.62
choppy 4.36
chopstick 21.17
chop suey 4.8
choral 23.36
chorale 23.2
chord 16.19
chordal 23.28
chordate 30.9
chore 7.1
choreograph 17.2
choreographer 12.30
choreographic 21.10
choreography 4.14
choriambic 21.9
choriambus 28.24
choric 21.15
chorine 25.11
chorister 12.78

chorten 25.50
chortle 23.39
chorus 28.31
chose 35.19
chosen 25.52
chough 17.15
chow 8.1
chowder 12.28
chowkidar 1.6
chow mein 25.7
Chris 28.7
chrism 24.21
chrisom 24.21
Chrissie 4.46
Christ 31.16
Christabel 23.3
Christadelphian 25.37
Christchurch 15.14
christen 25.48
Christendom 24.17
christener 12.58
christening 26.9
Christian 25.39
Christiana 12.53
Christianity 4.53
Christie 4.53
Christina 12.54
Christine 25.12
Christingle 23.30
Christlike 21.19
Christly 4.25
Christmas 28.28
Christmassy 4.48
Christopher 12.30
chroma 12.52
chromatic 21.17
chromatography 4.14
chrome 24.11
chromite 30.29
chromium 24.16
chromo 9.18
chromosomal 23.33
chronic 21.13
chronicle 23.32
chronicler 12.48
chronograph 17.2
chronology 4.17
chrysalid 16.10
chrysalis 28.8
chrysanthemum 24.19
chrysoberyl 23.9
chrysolite 30.28
chrysoprase 35.5
Chrystal 23.39
chub 14.13
Chubb 14.13
chubby 4.10
chuck 21.29

C

chuckhole 23.17
chuckle 23.32
chucklehead 16.3
chuckler 12.48
chuff 17.15
chug 18.12
chukar 1.11
chukka 12.41
chukker 12.41
chum 24.14
chummy 4.30
chump 27.17
chunder 12.29
Chungking 26.3
chunk 21.34
chunky 4.20
Chunnel 23.34
chunter 12.81
church 15.14
churchgoer 12.17
churchgoing 26.3
Churchill 23.8
Churchillian 25.37
churchman 25.45
churchmen 25.45
churchwarden 25.40
churchwoman 25.45
churchwomen 25.17
churchy 4.11
churchyard 16.2
churinga 12.31
churl 23.42
churlish 29.8
churn 25.53
churrasco 9.16
chute 30.37
chutist 31.14
chutney 4.33
chutzpah 12.63
chypre 12.65
ciabatta 12.75
ciao 8.1
ciboria 12.10
ciborium 24.16
cicada 12.25
cicatrices 35.8
cicatrix 28.39
cicatrize 35.13
cicely 4.24
Cicero 9.21
cicerone 4.33
Ciceronian 25.37
cider 12.27
ci-devant 25.24
cigar 1.1
cigaret 30.4
cigarette 30.4
cigarillo 9.17
ciggy 4.15
cilantro 9.21
cilia 12.6

ciliary 4.43
ciliate 30.8
ciliated 16.12
cilice 28.8
Cilician 25.37
cilium 24.16
cimbalom 24.18
Cimmerian 25.37
cinch 29.20
Cincinnati 4.51
cincture 12.23
cinder 12.27
Cinderella 12.42
cindery 4.43
Cindy 4.12
cine 4.32
cineaste 31.1
cinema 12.51
CinemaScope 27.10
cinematic 21.17
cinematograph 17.2
cinematographer 12.30
cinematographic 21.10
cinematography 4.14
cinéma-vérité 3.22
cinephile 23.11
cineraria 12.10
cinerarium 24.16
cinereous 28.23
Cingalese 35.6
cinnamon 25.45
cinque 21.33
cinquecento 9.24
cinquefoil 23.19
Cinque Ports 28.47
cipher 12.30
cipolin 25.16
circa 12.41
circadian 25.37
Circassian 25.37
Circe 4.49
circle 23.32
circlet 30.22
circs 28.41
circuit 30.21
circuitous 28.34
circuitry 4.40
circular 12.46
circularity 4.53
circularize 35.13
circulate 30.11
circulatory 4.43
circumambient 30.56
circumambulate 30.11
circumambulatory 4.43

circumcise 35.14
circumcision 25.42
circumference 28.45
circumflex 28.38
circumfluent 30.56
circumfuse 35.21
circumlocution 25.49
circumlocutory 4.43
circumnavigate 30.9
circumpolar 12.44
circumscribe 14.8
circumscription 25.49
circumspect 30.48
circumspection 25.49
circumstance 28.45
circumstantial 23.38
circumvallate 30.11
circumvent 30.53
circumvention 25.49
circumvolution 25.49
circus 28.26
Cirencester 12.76
cirque 21.31
cirrhosis 28.11
cirriped 16.3
cirrocumulus 28.27
cirrostratus 28.34
cirrus 28.31
cisalpine 25.23
cisco 9.16
Ciskei 6.1
cispontine 25.23
Cissy 4.46
cist 31.6
Cistercian 25.49
cistern 25.50
cistus 28.34
citadel 23.28
citation 25.49
cite 30.26
citizen 25.52
citizenry 4.43
citole 23.18
citric 21.15
citrine 25.11
citron 25.47
citronella 12.42
citrous 28.31
citrus 28.31
cittern 25.53
city 4.53
cityscape 27.4
cityward 16.30
civet 30.25
civic 21.18
civil 23.40

civilian 25.37
civilianize 35.13
civility 4.53
civilizer 12.91
civvies 35.10
civvy 4.58
clack 21.1
clacker 12.37
clad 16.1
claim 24.4
claimant 30.56
claimer 12.50
Clair 2.1
Claire 2.1
clairvoyance 28.45
clairvoyant 30.56
clam 24.1
clamant 30.56
clambake 21.7
clamber 12.21
clammy 4.29
clamor 12.50
clamorous 28.31
clamour 12.50
clamp 27.17
clampdown 25.29
clamshell 23.4
clan 25.1
Clancy 4.45
clandestine 25.19
clandestinity 4.53
clang 26.1
clanger 12.60
clangor 12.31
clangorous 28.31
clangour 12.31
clank 21.33
clannish 29.9
clansman 25.45
clansmen 25.45
clanswoman 25.45
clanswomen 25.17
clap 27.1
clapboard 16.20
clapper 12.61
clapperboard 16.20
Clapton 25.50
claptrap 27.1
claque 21.1
claqueur 12.37
Clara 12.65
Clarabella 12.42
Clare 2.1
clarence 28.45
Clarenceux 11.18
Clarendon 25.40
claret 30.43
Clarice 28.10
clarificatory 4.43
clarifier 12.14
clarify 6.7

C

colloquial 23.24
colloquium 24.16
colloquy 4.59
collotype 27.7
collude 16.25
colluder 12.29
collusion 25.42
collusive 34.7
collywobbles 35.29
colobus 28.24
Cologne 25.30
Colombia 12.5
Colombian 25.37
Colombo 9.9
Colón 25.24
colon 25.24, 25.44
colonel 23.34
colonelcy 4.49
colonial 23.24
colonialist 31.8
colonic 21.13
colonist 31.10
colonizer 12.91
colonnade 16.6
colonoscopy 4.37
colony 4.34
colophon 25.41
color 12.47
Coloradan 25.40
Colorado 9.11
coloratura 12.67
colorific 21.10
colorist 31.12
colorway 3.25
colossal 23.37
colossi 6.16
Colossians 35.31
colossus 28.32
colostomy 4.30
colour 12.47
colourblind 16.42
colourfast 31.2
colourist 31.12
colourway 3.25
colt 30.51
colter 12.80
coltish 29.10
Coltrane 25.7
coltsfoot 30.39
colubrine 25.23
Columba 12.22
columbaria 12.10
columbarium 24.16
Columbia 12.5
columbine 25.21
columbite 30.26
columbium 24.16
Columbus 28.24
column 24.18
columnar 12.57
columnist 31.9

coma 12.52
Comanche 4.50
comatose 28.17
comb 24.11
combat 30.1
combatant 30.56
combe 24.12
comber 12.52
combinatorial 23.24
combinatory 4.43
combine 25.21
combo 9.9
combust 31.24
combustible 23.26
combustion 25.39
come 24.14
comeback 21.2
Comecon 25.25
comedian 25.37
comedic 21.10
comedown 25.29
comedy 4.12
comely 4.26
comer 12.52
comestible 23.26
comet 30.23
comeuppance 28.45
comfit 30.21
comfort 30.41
comforter 12.82
comfrey 4.42
comfy 4.14
comic 21.12
comical 23.32
coming 26.9
Comino 9.19
Comintern 25.53
comity 4.53
comma 12.51
command 16.41
commandant 30.53
commandeer 12.4
commander 12.25
commando 9.11
comme ci comme
   ça 1.1
commedia dell'arte
   3.22
commemorate 30.15
commence 28.44
commend 16.41
commendatory 4.43
commensurate
   30.43
comment 30.53
commentary 4.43
commentate 30.16
commerce 28.36
commercial 23.38
commère 2.9
commie 4.29

comminatory 4.43
commingle 23.30
commiserate 30.15
commissar 1.1
commissarial 23.24
commissariat 30.41
commissary 4.43
commissionaire 2.1
commissioner 12.58
commit 30.20
committal 23.39
committee 4.53
committer 12.78
commix 28.39
commixture 12.23
commode 16.23
commodify 6.7
commodious 28.23
commodity 4.53
commodore 7.5
common 25.45
commonalty 4.55
commoner 12.58
commonhold 16.37
commonplace 28.5
common room
   24.12
commons 35.31
common sense
   28.44
commonsensical
   23.32
commonwealth
   32.17
commotion 25.49
communal 23.34
communalist 31.8
communalize 35.12
communard 16.2
commune 25.33
communicant 30.56
communicate 30.10
communicatory
   4.43
communion 25.37
communiqué 3.14
communist 31.10
communitarian
   25.37
community 4.53
communize 35.13
commute 30.37
commuter 12.81
comp 27.17
compact 30.48
compaction 25.49
compactor 12.74
compadre 4.38
companion 25.52
companionate 30.43
companionway 3.25
company 4.34

comparatist 31.14
compare 2.1
comparison 25.48
compass 28.30
compassionate
   30.43
compatible 23.26
compatriot 30.41
compeer 12.9
compel 23.3
compendia 12.5
compendious 28.23
compendium 24.16
compensate 30.15
compensatory 4.43
compère 2.10
compete 30.18
competence 28.45
competency 4.48
competent 30.56
competitor 12.78
compile 23.11
compiler 12.44
complacency 4.45
complacent 30.56
complain 25.7
complainant 30.56
complainer 12.54
complaint 30.54
complaisance 28.45
complaisant 30.56
compleat 30.18
complementarity
   4.53
complementary
   4.43
complete 30.18
completion 25.49
completist 31.14
complex 28.38
complexion 25.49
complexity 4.53
compliance 28.45
compliant 30.56
complicate 30.10
complicit 30.24
complimentary 4.43
compline 25.16
comply 6.1
compo 9.20
component 30.56
comport 30.33
compose 35.19
composer 12.92
composite 30.25
compositor 12.78
compos mentis
   28.12
compossible 23.26
compost 31.17
composure 12.33

compote 30.35
compound 16.43
compounder 12.28
comprador 7.1
comprehend 16.41
comprehensible 23.26
comprehension 25.49
comprehensive 34.7
compress 28.3
compressible 23.26
compressive 34.7
compressor 12.69
comprise 35.11
compromise 35.13
compromiser 12.91
Compton 25.50
comptroller 12.44
compulsion 25.49
compulsive 34.7
compulsory 4.43
compunction 25.49
compunctious 28.33
compute 30.37
computer 12.81
comrade 16.6
comradely 4.22
Comsat 30.2
Comte 30.54
con 25.24
Conakry 4.43
con amore 3.19
Conan 25.46
conation 25.49
concave 34.4
concavity 4.53
conceal 23.7
concealer 12.43
concede 16.7
conceder 12.26
conceit 30.18
conceited 16.12
conceive 34.5
concenter 12.76
concentrate 30.15
concentre 12.76
concentric 21.15
Concepción 25.24
concept 30.58
conception 25.49
conceptional 23.34
conceptual 23.25
conceptualist 31.8
concern 25.53
concert 30.43, 30.45
concertante 3.22
concerted 16.12
concertina 12.54
concertino 9.19
concerto 9.24

concessionaire 2.1
concessionary 4.43
concessive 34.7
conch 29.20
concha 12.40
conchae 4.19
conches 35.10
conchie 4.50
concierge 19.3
conciliar 12.6
conciliate 30.8
conciliatory 4.43
concise 28.13
concision 25.42
conclave 34.4
conclude 16.25
conclusion 25.42
conclusive 34.7
concoct 30.49
concocter 12.79
concoction 25.49
concomitance 28.45
concomitant 30.56
concord 16.21
concordance 28.45
concordant 30.56
concordat 30.1
Concorde 16.21
concourse 28.15
concrete 30.18
concretion 25.49
concretize 35.14
concubinage 20.7
concubine 25.21
concupiscence 28.45
concupiscent 30.56
concur 13.1
concurrence 28.45
concurrent 30.56
concuss 28.21
condemn 24.3
condemnatory 4.43
condensate 30.15
condense 28.44
condescend 16.41
condescension 25.49
condign 25.21
conditioner 12.58
condo 9.11
condole 23.17
condolence 28.45
condom 24.17
condominium 24.16
condone 25.30
condoner 12.56
condor 7.5
conduce 28.19
conducive 34.7
conduct 30.49
conductance 28.45
conducti 6.18

conductible 23.26
conduction 25.49
conductor 12.81
conductress 28.10
conductus 28.34
conduit 30.21
cone 25.30
coney 4.33
confab 14.1
confabulate 30.11
confect 30.48
confection 25.49
confectioner 12.58
confectionery 4.43
confederacy 4.48
confederate 30.15, 30.43
confer 13.1
conferee 4.1
conference 28.45
conferral 23.36
confess 28.3
confessant 30.56
confessional 23.34
confessionary 4.43
confessor 12.69
confetti 4.51
confidant 30.53
confide 16.14
confidence 28.45
confident 30.56
confidential 23.38
confiding 26.5
configure 12.31
confine 25.21
confines 35.31
confirm 24.22
confirmand 16.40
confirmatory 4.43
confiscate 30.10
confiscatory 4.43
conflate 30.7
conflict 30.49
conflictual 23.25
confluence 28.45
confluent 30.56
conflux 28.41
conform 24.9
conformal 23.33
conformance 28.45
conformist 31.9
conformity 4.53
confound 16.43
confraternity 4.53
confrère 2.11
confront 30.55
Confucian 25.49
Confucianist 31.10
Confucius 28.33
confuse 35.21
confusing 26.14

confusion 25.42
confute 30.37
conga 12.32
congeal 23.7
congener 12.54
congeneric 21.15
congenial 23.24
congenital 23.39
conger 12.32
congeries 35.10
congestion 25.39
conglomerate 30.15, 30.43
Congo 9.13
Congolese 35.6
congrats 28.47
congratulate 30.11
congratulatory 4.43
congregant 30.56
congregate 30.9
Congregationalist 31.8
congress 28.3
congressional 23.34
congressman 25.45
congressmen 25.45
congresswoman 25.45
congresswomen 25.17
Congreve 34.5
congruence 28.45
congruent 30.56
congruity 4.53
congruous 28.24
conic 21.13
conical 23.32
conifer 12.30
coniferous 28.31
conjecture 12.23
conjoin 25.32
conjoint 30.55
conjugal 23.30
conjugate 30.9, 30.42
conjunct 30.49
conjunction 25.49
conjunctional 23.34
conjunctivitis 28.12
conjuncture 12.24
conjure 12.20, 12.36
conjuror 12.67
conk 21.34
conker 12.40
conman 25.2
conmen 25.5
conn 25.24
Connacht 30.33
connect 30.48
Connecticut 30.42
connection 25.49
connectional 23.34
connector 12.76

Connemara 12.64
Connery 4.43
Connie 4.32
connivance 28.45
connive 34.9
conniver 12.86
connoisseur 13.1
Connolly 4.27
Connor 12.56
Connors 35.24
connote 30.35
connubial 23.24
conquer 12.40
conqueror 12.67
conquest 31.3
conquistador 7.5
conquistadores 35.5
Conrad 16.1
consanguineous 28.23
conscience 28.45
conscientious 28.33
conscious 28.33
conscript 30.58
conscription 25.49
consecrate 30.15
consecratory 4.43
consensual 23.25
consensus 28.32
consent 30.53
consentient 30.56
consequence 28.45
consequent 30.56
consequential 23.38
consequentialist 31.8
conservancy 4.49
conservationist 31.10
conservatoire 1.22
conservatoria 12.10
conservatorium 24.16
conservatory 4.43
conserve 34.14
consider 12.27
considerate 30.43
consign 25.21
consignee 4.1
consignor 12.55
consilience 28.45
consist 31.6
consistence 28.45
consistency 4.48
consistent 30.56
consistorial 23.24
consistory 4.43
consolatory 4.43
console 23.17, 23.18
consoler 12.44
consolidate 30.9

consols 35.29
consommé 3.16
consonance 28.45
consonant 30.56
consort 30.33
consortia 12.12
consortium 24.16
conspectus 28.34
conspicuous 28.33
conspiracy 4.48
conspiratorial 23.24
conspire 12.13
constabulary 4.43
Constance 28.45
constancy 4.48
constant 30.56
Constantine 25.23
Constantinople 23.35
Constanza 12.90
constellate 30.11
consternate 30.13
constipate 30.14
constituency 4.48
constituent 30.56
constitute 30.38
constitution 25.49
constitutional 23.34
constitutionalist 31.8
constitutionalize 35.12
constrain 25.7
constraint 30.54
constrict 30.49
constriction 25.49
constrictor 12.78
construal 23.25
construct 30.49
construction 25.49
constructional 23.34
constructionist 31.10
constructivist 31.15
constructor 12.81
construe 11.1
consuetude 16.25
consuetudinary 4.43
consul 23.37
consular 12.46
consulate 30.42
consult 30.51
consultancy 4.48
consultant 30.56
consultee 4.1
consume 24.12
consumer 12.52
consumerist 31.12
consummate 30.12, 30.43
consumption 25.49

contact 30.48
contagion 25.42
contagious 28.25
contain 25.7
container 12.54
containerize 35.13
contaminant 30.56
contaminate 30.13
conte 30.54
contemn 24.3
contemner 12.50
contemplate 30.11
contemporaneity 4.53
contemporaneous 28.23
contemporary 4.43
contempt 30.52
contemptible 23.26
contemptuous 28.24
contend 16.41
contender 12.26
content 30.53
contention 25.49
contentious 28.33
conterminous 28.29
contessa 12.69
contest 31.3
contestant 30.56
contester 12.76
context 31.28
contextual 23.25
contextualist 31.8
contextualize 35.12
contiguity 4.53
contiguous 28.24
continence 28.45
continent 30.56
contingency 4.48
contingent 30.56
continua 12.20
continual 23.25
continuance 28.45
continuant 30.56
continue 11.22
continuer 12.20
continuity 4.53
continuo 9.8
continuous 28.24
continuum 24.17
contort 30.33
contortion 25.49
contortionist 31.10
contour 12.20
contra 12.65
contrabandist 31.6
contraception 25.49
contract 30.48
contractible 23.26
contraction 25.49
contractor 12.74

contractual 23.25
contradict 30.49
contradictor 12.78
contradictory 4.43
contraflow 9.17
contrail 23.6
contralto 9.24
contraption 25.49
contrapuntal 23.39
contrapuntist 31.14
contrarian 25.37
contrariety 4.53
contrariwise 35.15
contrary 4.39, 4.43
contrast 31.2
contrasty 4.51
contravene 25.9
contravener 12.54
contravention 25.49
contretemps 25.26
contribute 30.38
contribution 25.49
contributor 12.81
contributory 4.43
con trick 21.15
contrite 30.29
contrivance 28.45
contrive 34.9
contriver 12.86
control 23.17
controller 12.44
controversial 23.38
controversialist 31.8
controversy 4.49
controvert 30.45
controvertible 23.26
contumacious 28.33
contumacy 4.48
contumelious 28.23
contumely 4.24
contuse 35.21
contusion 25.42
conundrum 24.19
conure 12.20
convalesce 28.3
convalescence 28.45
convalescent 30.56
convection 25.49
convector 12.76
convenance 28.44
convene 25.9
convener 12.54
convenience 28.45
convenient 30.56
convent 30.56
conventicle 23.32
convention 25.49
conventional 23.34
conventionalist 31.8

conventionalize 35.12
conventioneer 12.4
conventual 23.25
converge 20.17
convergence 28.45
convergency 4.48
convergent 30.56
conversance 28.45
conversancy 4.49
conversant 30.56
conversationalist 31.8
conversazione 4.33
converse 28.36
converser 12.71
conversion 25.49
convert 30.45
converter 12.82
convertible 23.26
convex 28.38
convey 3.1
conveyance 28.45
conveyancer 12.71
conveyancing 26.12
conveyor 12.2
convict 30.49
conviction 25.49
convince 28.44
convincer 12.70
convincible 23.26
convivial 23.24
convoke 21.24
convoluted 16.12
convolution 25.49
convolvulus 28.27
convoy 10.13
convulse 28.42
convulsion 25.49
convulsive 34.7
Conwy 4.59
coo 11.1
co-occurrence 28.45
cooee 4.8
cook 21.28
cookbook 21.28
cookchill 23.8
Cooke 21.28
cooker 12.41
cookery 4.43
cookhouse 28.16
cookie 4.20
cookout 30.34
cookshop 27.8
Cookson 25.48
cookware 2.15
cool 23.20
coolant 30.56
cooler 12.45
coolibah 1.4
Coolidge 20.6

coolie 4.26
coolish 29.8
coolth 32.17
Coombes 35.30
coonskin 25.15
co-op 27.8
coop 27.11
cooper 12.63
cooperant 30.56
cooperate 30.15
co-opt 27.10
coordinate 30.13, 30.43
coot 30.37
cootie 4.54
co-own 25.30
cop 27.8
copal 23.35
cope 27.10
Copenhagen 25.41
coper 12.63
Copernican 25.43
Copernicus 28.26
copier 12.9
copilot 30.42
coping 26.10
coping stone 25.31
copious 28.23
Copland 16.45
Copley 4.25
copout 30.34
copper 12.62
Copperbelt 30.51
copperplate 30.11
coppersmith 32.6
coppery 4.43
coppice 28.9
Coppola 12.48
copse 28.46
Copt 30.58
Coptic 21.17
copula 12.46
copulate 30.11
copulatory 4.43
copy 4.36
copybook 21.28
copycat 30.1
copyhold 16.37
copyholder 12.28
copyist 31.6
copyread 16.7
copyreader 12.26
copyright 30.29
copywriter 12.79
copywriting 26.13
coquetry 4.40
coquette 30.4
coquettish 29.10
coquito 9.24
cor 7.1
Cora 12.66

coracle 23.32
coral 23.36
coralline 25.22
corallite 25.28
coralloid 16.24
cor anglais 3.15
corbel 23.26
corbie 4.10
cord 16.19
cordage 20.6
Corday 3.9
Cordelia 12.6
Cordelier 12.4
cordial 23.24
cordite 30.26
Córdoba 12.22
cordon 25.40
cordon-bleu 13.1
cordon sanitaire 2.1
Cordova 12.87
cordovan 25.51
corduroy 10.11
core 7.1
corella 12.42
Corelli 4.22
corer 12.66
co-respondent 30.56
Corey 4.41
corf 17.9
Corfu 11.1
corgi 4.15
coriander 12.25
Corin 25.18
Corinna 12.55
Corinne 25.13
Corinth 32.19
Corinthian 25.37
Coriolanus 28.29
cork 21.22
corkage 20.6
corker 12.40
corkscrew 11.17
corky 4.19
corm 24.9
Cormac 21.3
cormorant 30.56
corn 25.28
cornball 23.14
cornbread 16.4
corncob 14.9
corncockle 23.32
corncrake 21.7
cornea 12.8
corneal 23.24
cornel 23.34
Cornelia 12.6
Cornelius 28.23
Cornell 23.3
corner 12.56
cornerback 21.2
cornerstone 25.31

cornerwise 35.15
cornet 30.23
cornetist 31.14
cornetti 4.51
cornetto 9.24
cornfield 16.35
cornflake 21.7
cornflour 12.16
cornflower 12.16
cornice 28.9
corniced 31.10
corniche 29.5
Cornish 29.9
Cornishman 25.45
Cornishmen 25.45
cornmeal 23.7
cornrows 35.19
cornstarch 15.2
cornucopia 12.9
cornucopian 25.37
Cornwall 23.15
corny 4.32
corolla 12.44
corollary 4.43
Coromandel 23.28
corona 12.56
coronach 22.6
coronae 4.33
coronal 23.34
coronary 4.43
coroner 12.58
coronet 30.23
Corot 9.21
corpora 12.67
corporal 23.36
corporate 30.43
corporatist 31.14
corporeal 23.24
corporeity 4.53
corps 7.1
corpse 28.46
corpulence 28.45
corpulency 4.48
corpulent 30.56
corpus 28.30
Corpus Christi 4.53
corpuscle 23.37
corral 23.2
correct 30.48
correction 25.49
correctional 23.34
corrector 12.76
Correggio 9.4
correlate 30.11
correspond 16.42
correspondence 28.45
correspondent 30.56
corresponding 26.5
corrida 12.26
corridor 7.5

coverture 12.20
covet 30.25
covetous 28.34
covey 4.58
covin 25.19
coving 26.14
cow 8.1
coward 16.28
cowardice 28.7
cowardly 4.27
cowbell 23.3
cowboy 10.3
Cowdrey 4.41
cower 12.16
Cowes 35.18
cowgirl 23.42
cowherd 16.31
cowhide 16.14
cowl 23.16
cowlick 21.11
cowling 26.8
cowman 25.45
cowmen 25.45
cowpat 30.1
cowpea 4.36
Cowper 12.63
cowpoke 21.24
cowpox 28.40
cowpuncher 12.73
cowrie 4.41
cowshed 16.4
cowslip 27.6
cox 28.40
coxcomb 24.11
coxcombry 4.41
coxless 28.27
coxswain 25.48
coy 10.1
coyly 4.25
coyness 28.9
coyote 4.54
coypu 11.16
coz 35.23
cozen 25.52
cozenage 20.7
Cozens 35.31
cozies 35.10
Cozumel 23.3
cozy 4.61
crab 14.1
Crabbe 14.1
crabby 4.10
crablike 21.19
crabmeat 30.18
Crabtree 4.38
crabwise 35.15
crack 21.1
crackbrained 16.41
crackdown 25.29
cracker 12.37
cracker-barrel 23.36

crackerjack 21.3
crackle 23.32
crackling 26.8
crackly 4.21
cracknel 23.34
crackpot 30.32
cracksman 25.45
cracksmen 25.45
cracky 4.18
Cracow 17.8
cradle 23.28
craft 30.47
craftsman 25.45
craftsmen 25.45
craftswoman 25.45
craftswomen 25.17
craftwork 21.31
craftworker 12.41
crafty 4.51
crag 18.1
craggy 4.15
cragsman 25.45
cragsmen 25.45
Craig 18.4
crake 21.7
cram 24.1
crammer 12.50
cramp 27.17
crampon 25.26
cran 25.1
cranage 20.7
cranberry 4.43
crane 25.7
cranesbill 23.8
crania 12.8
cranial 23.24
craniology 4.17
craniometry 4.40
cranium 24.16
crank 21.33
crankpin 25.18
crankshaft 30.47
cranky 4.18
Cranmer 12.50
crannied 16.10
cranny 4.31
crap 27.1
crape 27.4
crapper 12.61
crappie 4.36
crappy 4.36
craps 28.46
crapulence 28.45
crapulent 30.56
crapulous 28.27
crash 29.1
crass 28.1
Crassus 28.32
crate 30.7
crater 12.77

cravat 30.1
cravatted 16.12
crave 34.4
craven 25.51
craver 12.85
craving 26.14
craw 7.1
crawfish 29.7
Crawford 16.28
crawl 23.14
crawler 12.44
crawly 4.25
Cray 3.1
crayfish 29.7
crayon 25.24
craze 35.5
crazy 4.61
creak 21.8
creaky 4.18
cream 24.5
creamer 12.51
creamery 4.43
creamware 2.15
creamy 4.29
creance 28.45
crease 28.6
create 30.7
creation 25.49
creationist 31.10
creator 12.77
creature 12.23
creaturely 4.27
crèche 29.4
Crécy 4.45
cred 16.3
credal 23.28
credence 28.45
credential 23.38
credenza 12.90
credible 23.26
credit 30.21
creditor 12.78
credo 9.11
credulity 4.53
credulous 28.27
Cree 4.1
creed 16.7
creek 21.8
creel 23.7
creep 27.5
creeper 12.61
creepy 4.36
creepy-crawly 4.25
cremate 30.7
crematoria 12.10
crematorium 24.16
crematory 4.43
crème brûlée 3.1
crème de la crème 24.3

crème de menthe 32.19
crème fraîche 29.3
Cremona 12.56
crenel 23.34
crenelate 30.11
crenellate 30.11
Creole 23.17
creosote 30.35
crêpe 27.4
crêpey 4.36
crepitant 30.56
crepitate 30.16
crepitus 28.34
crept 30.58
crepuscular 12.46
crescendo 9.11
crescent 30.56
crescentic 21.17
cress 28.3
cresset 30.24
Cressida 12.27
crest 31.3
crestfallen 25.44
Cretaceous 28.33
Cretan 25.50
Crete 30.18
cretic 21.17
cretin 25.19
cretinous 28.29
cretonne 25.24
crevasse 28.1
crevice 28.12
crew 11.1
crew cut 30.40
Crewe 11.1
crewel 23.25
crewman 25.45
crewmen 25.45
crib 14.7
cribbage 20.6
cribber 12.21
Crichton 25.50
crick 21.9
cricket 30.21
cricketer 12.78
cri de cœur 13.1
cried 16.14
crier 12.13
crikey 4.19
crim 24.6
crime 24.7
Crimea 12.4
Crimean 25.37
crime passionnel 23.3
criminal 23.34
criminalize 35.12
criminology 4.17
crimp 27.17
crimper 12.62

C

C

crimplene 25.10
crimpy 4.36
crimson 25.52
cringe 20.19
cringer 12.35
cringle 23.30
crinkle 23.32
crinkly 4.24
crinoid 16.24
crinoidal 23.28
crinoline 25.16
criollo 9.17
cripes 28.46
Crippen 25.18
cripple 23.35
crippledom 24.17
crippler 12.43
crises 35.8
crisis 28.11
crisp 27.18
crispbread 16.4
crisper 12.62
Crispian 25.37
Crispin 25.18
crispy 4.36
criss-cross 28.14
criteria 12.10
criterial 23.24
criterion 25.37
critic 21.17
critical 23.32
criticizer 12.91
critique 21.8
critter 12.78
croak 21.24
croaker 12.40
croaky 4.20
Croat 30.1
Croatia 12.72
Croatian 25.49
Croce 3.8
crochet 3.21
crocheter 12.2
croci 6.10
crock 21.20
crockery 4.43
crocket 30.21
Crockett 30.21
crocodile 23.11
crocodilian 25.37
crocus 28.26
Croesus 28.32
croft 30.47
crofter 12.79
croissant 25.26
Cromarty 4.55
Crome 24.11
cromlech 22.6
Crompton 25.50
Cromwell 23.4
crone 25.30

Cronin 25.18
cronk 21.34
Cronus 28.29
crony 4.33
crook 21.28
crookback 21.2
crooked 16.10
crookery 4.43
Crookes 28.40
croon 25.33
crooner 12.56
crop 27.8
cropper 12.62
croquet 3.14
croquette 30.4
Crosby 4.10
cross 28.14
crossbar 1.4
cross-beam 24.5
crossbench 29.20
crossbill 23.8
crossbow 9.9
crossbred 16.3
crossbreed 16.7
crosscheck 21.6
cross-current 30.56
cross-cut 30.40
crosse 28.14
crossfire 12.14
crosshatch 15.1
crossing 26.12
cross-legged 16.9
crossover 12.86
crosspatch 15.1
crosspiece 28.6
crossroads 35.27
crosstalk 21.22
crosstie 6.18
crosswalk 21.22
crossways 35.5
crosswind 16.42
crosswise 35.15
crossword 16.31
crotch 15.7
crotchet 30.20
crotchety 4.53
croton 25.50
crouch 15.9
croup 27.11
croupier 3.3
croupy 4.37
croustade 16.2
croûton 25.26
crow 9.1
crowbar 1.4
crowberry 4.43
crowd 16.22
crowd-pleaser 12.90
crowfoot 30.39
crown 25.29
crozier 12.12

cru 11.1
cruces 35.8
crucial 23.38
cruciate 30.41
crucible 23.26
crucifer 12.30
cruciferous 28.31
crucifier 12.14
crucifix 28.39
crucifixion 25.49
cruciform 24.9
crucify 6.7
cruck 21.29
crud 16.27
cruddy 4.13
crude 16.25
crudités 3.1
crudity 4.53
cruel 23.25
cruelty 4.55
cruet 30.20
Cruikshank 21.33
cruise 35.21
cruiser 12.92
cruller 12.47
crumb 24.14
crumble 23.26
crumbly 4.26
crumby 4.30
crummy 4.30
crump 27.17
crumpet 30.23
crumple 23.35
crumply 4.26
crunch 29.20
cruncher 12.73
crunchy 4.50
crupper 12.63
crural 23.36
crusade 16.6
crusader 12.26
cruse 35.21
crush 29.16
crusher 12.73
crust 31.24
crustacean 25.49
crustal 23.39
crusty 4.55
crutch 15.13
crux 28.41
Cruyff 17.12
Cruz 35.21
cry 6.1
crybaby 4.10
cryer 12.13
cryogenic 21.13
cryolite 30.28
cryostat 30.2
crypt 30.58
cryptanalyst 31.8
cryptanalytic 21.17

cryptanalytical 23.32
cryptic 21.17
cryptogamic 21.12
cryptogram 24.1
cryptographic 21.10
cryptography 4.14
cryptomeria 12.10
cryptosporidium 24.16
crystal 23.39
crystalline 25.22
crystallographer 12.30
crystalloid 16.24
ctenophore 7.6
Ctesiphon 25.25
cub 14.13
Cuba 12.21
Cuban 25.38
cubby 4.10
cubbyhole 23.17
cube 14.12
cubic 21.9
cubicle 23.32
cubiform 24.9
cubism 24.21
cubist 31.6
cubit 30.20
cuboid 16.24
cucking-stool 23.20
cuckold 16.37
cuckoldry 4.43
cuckoo 11.12
cuckoo-spit 30.23
cucumber 12.22
cud 16.27
cuddle 23.28
cuddly 4.26
cuddy 4.13
cudgel 23.31
Cudlipp 27.6
cue 11.1
cueball 23.14
Cuenca 12.37
cuff 17.15
cufflink 21.33
cui bono? 9.19
cuisine 25.9
Culbertson 25.48
Culdees 35.7
cul-de-sac 21.4
culinary 4.43
cull 23.22
culler 12.47
Culloden 25.40
culminate 30.13
culotte 30.31
Culpeper 12.61
culprit 30.24
cult 30.51

c
d

daemonic 21.13
daffodil 23.8
daffy 4.14
daft 30.47
Dafydd 33.4
dag 18.1
Dagestan 25.4
dagga 12.31
dagger 12.31
Dagmar 1.13
Dagon 25.25
Daguerre 2.1
daguerreotype 27.7
Dagwood 16.26
dahlia 12.6
Dai 6.1
Dáil 23.19
Dáil Eireann 25.47
daily 4.22
Daimler 12.43
dainty 4.52
daiquiri 4.40
Dairen 25.5
dairy 4.39
dairying 26.3
dairymaid 16.6
dairyman 25.45
dairymen 25.45
dais 28.7
daisy 4.61
Dakar 1.11
Dakota 12.80
Dakotan 25.50
dalasi 4.45
dale 23.5
Dalek 21.6
Daley 4.22
Dalglish 29.5
Dalhousie 4.61
Dali 4.21
Dalian 25.37
Dallas 28.27
dalliance 28.45
dally 4.21
Dalmatia 12.72
Dalmatian 25.49
dalmatic 21.17
Dalriada 12.25
dal segno 9.28
Dalton 25.50
Daly 4.22
dam 24.1
damage 20.7
Damara 12.64
Damaraland 16.40
damascene 25.11
Damascus 28.26
damask 21.35
dame 24.4
Damian 25.37
dammit 30.23

damn 24.1
damnatory 4.43
damnify 6.7
damnum 24.19
Damocles 35.7
Damon 25.45
damp 27.17
dampen 25.46
dampener 12.58
damper 12.61
Dampier 12.9
dampish 29.9
damsel 23.41
damselfish 29.7
damselfly 6.11
damson 25.52
dan 25.1
Dana 12.53
Danae 4.3
Danakil 23.9
Da Nang 26.1
dance 28.44
dancer 12.69
dandelion 25.38
dander 12.25
dandle 23.28
dandruff 17.15
dandy 4.12
dandyish 29.6
Dane 25.7
Danelaw 7.11
dang 26.1
danger 12.35
dangerous 28.31
dangle 23.30
dangler 12.42
dangly 4.21
Daniel 23.40
Daniela 12.42
Danish 29.9
dank 21.33
Danny 4.31
danseur 13.1
danseuse 35.25
Dante 4.51
Dantean 25.37
Dantesque 21.35
Danton 25.26
Danube 14.12
Danubian 25.37
Danzig 18.6
dap 27.1
daphne 4.31
Daphnis 28.9
dapper 12.61
dapple 23.35
Darby 4.10
Darcy 4.45
Dardanelles 35.29
dare 2.1
daredevil 23.40

daredevilry 4.38
darer 12.65
Darfur 13.1
dargah 12.31
Dari 4.39
Darien 25.37
daring 26.11
dariole 23.17
Darius 28.23, 28.24
Darjeeling 26.8
dark 21.5
darken 25.43
darkener 12.58
darkish 29.8
darkroom 24.12
Darlene 25.10
darling 26.8
Darlington 25.50
Darmstadt 30.2
darn 25.4
darner 12.53
Darnley 4.21
Darrell 23.36
Darren 25.47
Darryl 23.36
dart 30.3
dartboard 16.20
darter 12.75
Dartmoor 12.20
Dartmouth 32.13
Darwin 25.20
Darwinian 25.37
Darwinist 31.10
dash 29.1
dashboard 16.20
dashing 26.12
dashpot 30.32
dastard 16.29
dastardly 4.27
dastur 12.20
data 12.77
databank 21.33
database 28.5
datable 23.26
date 30.7
dateline 25.22
dative 34.8
datum 24.20
daub 14.10
daube 14.11
dauber 12.21
Daubigny 4.60
Daudet 3.9
daughter 12.80
daunt 30.54
dauphin 25.1
Dave 34.4
davenport 30.33
David 16.13
Davies 28.12
Davisson 25.48

davit 30.25
Davos 28.17
Davy 4.58
dawdle 23.28
dawdler 12.44
Dawkins 35.31
dawn 25.28
dawning 26.9
day 3.1
Dayak 21.1
Dayan 25.1
daybed 16.3
daybook 21.28
daybreak 21.7
daydream 24.5
daydreamer 12.51
Day-Glo 9.17
daylight 30.28
dayroom 24.12
daytime 24.7
daywork 21.31
daze 35.5
dazzle 23.41
dazzler 12.42
deacon 25.43
dead 16.3
deadbeat 30.18
deadbolt 30.51
deaden 25.40
deadener 12.58
deadeye 6.6
deadfall 23.15
deadhead 16.3
deadline 25.22
deadlock 21.21
deadly 4.22
deadpan 25.3
deadstock 21.21
deaf 17.3
deafen 25.41
Deakin 25.15
deal 23.7
dealer 12.43
dealing 26.8
dealt 30.51
dean 25.9
deanery 4.43
dear 12.4
dearie 4.43
dearth 32.14
death 32.3
deathbed 16.3
deathlike 21.19
deathly 4.22
deathtrap 27.1
deb 14.3
débâcle 23.32
debaser 12.69
debater 12.77
debauch 15.8
debauchee 4.1

debaucher 12.24
debauchery 4.43
debilitate 30.16
debility 4.53
debonair 2.1
Deborah 12.67
debouch 15.9
Debrett 30.4
debriefing 26.6
débris 4.38
debt 30.4
debtor 12.76
Debussy 4.47
début 11.22
debutant 30.53
debutante 30.53
decade 16.6
decadent 30.56
decaf 17.1
decaffeinate 30.13
decagon 25.41
decahedron 25.47
decal 23.1
Decalogue 18.8
Decameron 25.47
decametre 12.77
decanal 23.34
decani 6.13
decapitate 30.16
decapod 16.18
decastyle 23.12
decathlete 30.18
decathlon 25.25
decay 3.1
Deccan 25.43
decedent 30.56
deceit 30.18
deceive 34.5
deceiver 12.85
decelerate 30.15
December 12.21
decency 4.45
decennial 23.24
decent 30.56
deception 25.49
decerebrate 30.15
Decian 25.37
decibel 23.3
decide 16.14
deciduous 28.24
decile 23.11
deciliter 12.77
decilitre 12.77
decimal 23.33
decimate 30.12
decimeter 12.77
decimetre 12.77
decision 25.42
decisive 34.7
deck 21.6
deckchair 2.4

deckhand 16.40
deckle 23.32
declamatory 4.43
Declan 25.44
declarant 30.56
declaratory 4.43
declare 2.1
declarer 12.65
déclassé 3.20
declension 25.49
declensional 23.34
decliner 12.55
decoct 30.49
decoction 25.49
décolletage 19.1
décolleté 3.22
decolonize 35.13
decongestant 30.56
décor 7.10
decorate 30.15
decorous 28.31
decorum 24.19
découpage 19.1
decoy 10.6
decree 4.1
decrepit 30.23
decrepitude 16.25
decretal 23.39
decryption 25.49
decussate 30.15
dedicate 30.10
dedicated 16.12
dedicatee 4.1
dedicatory 4.43
deduce 28.19
deducible 23.26
deductible 23.26
deduction 25.49
Dee 4.1
deed 16.7
deejay 3.1
deem 24.5
Deeming 26.9
deemster 12.77
deep 27.5
deepen 25.46
deer 12.4
deerskin 25.15
deerstalker 12.40
def 17.3
de facto 9.24
defalcate 30.10
De Falla 12.89
defamatory 4.43
defamer 12.50
defaulter 12.80
defeatist 31.14
defecate 30.10
defect 30.48
defection 25.49
defector 12.76

defendant 30.56
defenestrate 30.15
defensible 23.26
defensive 34.7
defer 13.1
deference 28.45
deferential 23.38
deferral 23.36
deferrer 12.68
defiance 28.45
defiant 30.56
deficiency 4.48
deficient 30.56
deficit 30.24
defier 12.13
definer 12.55
definite 30.23
deflate 30.7
deflationary 4.43
deflect 30.48
deflection 25.49
deflector 12.76
Defoe 9.1
defoliant 30.56
deformity 4.53
defrauder 12.28
defrayal 23.23
defroster 12.79
deft 30.47
defunct 30.49
defy 6.1
dégagé 3.1
Degas 1.8
degeneracy 4.48
degenerate 30.43
degree 4.1
degressive 34.7
de haut en bas 1.1
de-icer 12.70
deify 6.7
Deighton 25.50
deign 25.7
Dei gratia 12.12
Deimos 28.14
Deirdre 4.43
deist 31.6
deistic 21.17
deistical 23.32
deity 4.53
déjà vu 11.1
deject 30.48
dejection 25.49
de jure 4.43
dekameter 12.77
Dekker 12.37
dekko 9.16
Delacroix 1.22
delation 25.49
delator 12.77
Delaware 2.15
Delbert 30.41

dele 4.23
delegate 30.9
delete 30.18
deleterious 28.23
deletion 25.49
Delfont 30.54
Delft 30.47
delftware 2.15
Delhi 4.22
deli 4.22
Delia 12.6
deliberate 30.43
Delibes 14.6
delicacy 4.48
delicate 30.42
delicatessen 25.48
delicious 28.33
delict 30.49
Delilah 12.44
delineate 30.8
delinquency 4.48
delinquent 30.56
deliquesce 28.3
deliquescence 28.45
delirious 28.23
delirium 24.16
delirium tremens 35.31
Delius 28.23
deliverance 28.45
deliverer 12.67
delocalize 35.12
Delores 35.10
Delors 7.1
Delos 28.14
Delphi 6.7
Delphian 25.37
Delphic 21.10
Delphine 25.10
delphinium 24.16
Delphinus 28.29
delta 12.76
deltaic 21.9
deltoid 16.24
delude 16.25
deluder 12.29
delusion 25.42
delusional 23.34
delusive 34.7
delusory 4.43
delve 34.15
delver 12.85
delving 26.14
Delwyn 25.20
Delyth 32.6
demagogic 21.10
demagogue 18.8
demagoguery 4.43
demagogy 4.15

d

d

demand 16.41
demander 12.25
demarcate 30.10
démarche 29.2
deme 24.5
demeanor 12.54
demeanour 12.54
Demelza 12.90
démenti 4.54
dementia 12.72
dementia praecox 28.40
Demerara 12.65
demesne 25.7
Demeter 12.77
demigod 16.18
demigoddess 28.7
demijohn 25.25
demi-mondaine 25.7
demi-monde 16.42
demi-pension 25.27
demise 35.11
demit 30.20
demitasse 28.1
demiurge 20.17
demo 9.18
democracy 4.48
democrat 30.2
democratic 21.17
Democritus 28.34
démodé 3.9
demographic 21.10
demography 4.14
demoiselle 23.3
demolish 29.8
demolisher 12.72
demolitionist 31.10
demon 25.45
demoniacal 23.32
demonic 21.13
demonstrate 30.15
Demos 28.14
Demosthenes 35.7
demotic 21.17
Dempsey 4.45
demur 13.1
demurrage 20.8
demurral 23.36
demurrer 12.66, 12.68
den 25.5
denarii 6.3
denarius 28.23
denaturalize 35.12
denaturant 30.56
Dench 29.20
dendritic 21.17
Dene 4.31, 25.9
Deneb 14.3
Deneuve 34.14

dengue 4.15
Den Haag 18.2
denial 23.25
denier 12.8, 12.13
denigrate 30.15
denigratory 4.43
De Niro 9.21
Denise 35.6
denizen 25.52
Denmark 21.5
Denning 26.9
Dennis 28.9
de nos jours 12.20
denounce 28.44
denouncer 12.70
de novo 9.27
Denovo 9.27
dense 28.44
density 4.53
dent 30.53
dental 23.39
denticulate 30.42
dentifrice 28.10
dentil 23.9
dentine 25.12
dentist 31.14
dentistry 4.40
Denton 25.50
denture 12.23
denuclearize 35.13
denunciatory 4.43
Denver 12.85
deny 6.1
Denzil 23.41
deodorant 30.56
deodorizer 12.91
Deo gratias 28.23
Deo volente 3.22
departmentalize 35.12
departure 12.23
depend 16.41
dependence 28.45
depersonalize 35.12
depict 30.49
depicter 12.78
depiction 25.49
depilate 30.11
depilatory 4.43
deplete 30.18
depletion 25.49
deplore 7.1
deponent 30.56
deportee 4.1
depositary 4.43
depository 4.43
depot 9.20
deprave 34.4
depravity 4.53
deprecate 30.10
depreciate 30.8

depreciatory 4.43
depressant 30.56
depressive 34.7
depressor 12.69
depressurize 35.13
deprival 23.40
deprive 34.9
de profundis 28.7
depth 32.21
depurate 30.15
depute 30.37
deputy 4.55
De Quincey 4.46
deracinate 30.13
derailleur 12.43
derby 4.10
Derbyshire 12.11
Derek 21.15
dereliction 25.49
de rigueur 13.1
derision 25.42
derisive 34.7
derisory 4.43
derma 12.52
dermatitis 28.12
dermatology 4.17
dermis 28.8
Dermot 30.43
dernier cri 4.1
derogate 30.9
derogatory 4.43
derrick 21.15
Derrida 12.26
Derridean 25.37
derrière 2.1
derring-do 11.1
derringer 12.35
derris 28.10
Derry 4.38
derv 34.14
dervish 29.10
Descartes 30.3
descendant 30.56
descendent 30.56
descender 12.26
descendible 23.26
description 25.49
Desdemona 12.56
desecrate 30.15
desert 30.44, 30.45
deserter 12.82
desertion 25.49
deserts 28.47
déshabillé 3.2
desiccant 30.56
desiccate 30.10
desiderata 12.75
desiderate 30.15, 30.43
desideratum 24.20

designate 30.13, 30.43
desire 12.13
Desirée 3.19
desirous 28.31
desist 31.6
desk 21.35
deskilled 16.35
deskilling 26.8
desktop 27.8
desman 25.45
desmid 16.10
Des Moines 25.32
Desmond 16.45
desolate 30.11, 30.42
despair 2.1
desperado 9.11
desperate 30.43
despise 35.11
despiser 12.91
despond 16.42
despondence 28.45
despondency 4.48
despondent 30.56
despot 30.32
despotic 21.17
Dessau 8.11
dessert 30.45
dessertspoon 25.33
De Stijl 23.11
destine 25.19
destiny 4.32
destitute 30.38
destitution 25.49
destrier 12.10
destroy 10.1
destroyer 12.18
destruct 30.49
destructible 23.26
destruction 25.49
destructor 12.81
desultory 4.43
detach 15.1
detail 23.6
detain 25.7
detainee 4.1
detainer 12.54
detect 30.48
detection 25.49
detector 12.76
detectorist 31.12
détente 30.53
detention 25.49
deter 13.1
detergent 30.56
deteriorate 30.15
determinant 30.56
determinate 30.43
determine 25.17
determiner 12.55
determinist 31.10

deterrence 28.45
deterrent 30.56
detonate 30.13
détour 12.20
detox 28.40
detoxify 6.7
detribalize 35.12
detritus 28.34
Detroit 30.36
de trop 9.1
Dettol 23.13
Deucalion 25.37
deuce 28.19
deuced 16.11
deus ex machina 12.54
Deuteronomy 4.30
Deutschmark 21.5
deva 12.85
devastate 30.16
develop 27.14
developer 12.63
Devereux 9.21
Devi 4.58
deviance 28.45
deviancy 4.48
deviant 30.56
deviate 30.8
deviationist 31.10
devil 23.40
devilfish 29.7
devilish 29.8
devilry 4.38
devious 28.23
devise 35.11
devisee 4.1
deviser 12.91
devitalize 35.12
devoir 1.1
devolutionary 4.43
devolutionist 31.10
devolve 34.15
Devon 25.51
Devonian 25.37
Devonshire 12.11
devotee 4.1
devotion 25.49
devotional 23.34
devour 12.16
devourer 12.67
devout 30.34
dew 11.1
dewan 25.4
Dewar 12.19
dewberry 4.43
dewdrop 27.8
Dewey 4.8
dewfall 23.15
Dewi 4.59
dewlap 27.1
dewpond 16.42

Dewsbury 4.43
dewy 4.8
Dexedrine 25.11
dexter 12.76
dexterity 4.53
dexterous 28.31
dextral 23.36
dextrin 25.18
dextrose 35.19
Dhaka 12.37
dhal 23.2
dharma 12.50
dhobi 4.10
Dhofar 1.1
dhole 23.17
dhoti 4.54
dhow 8.1
dhurrie 4.42
Di 6.1
diabetes 35.9
diabetic 21.17
diablerie 4.43
diabolic 21.11
diabolical 23.32
diabolist 31.8
diabolo 9.17
diacritic 21.17
diacritical 23.32
dIadem 24.3
Diadochi 6.10
diaereses 35.8
diaeresis 28.11
Diaghilev 17.3
diagnose 35.19
diagnoses 35.8
diagnosis 28.11
diagnostic 21.17
diagnostician 25.49
diagonal 23.34
diagram 24.1
diagrammatic 21.17
dial 23.25
dialect 30.48
dialectal 23.39
dialectic 21.17
dialectical 23.32
dialectician 25.49
dialog 18.8
dialogic 21.11
dialogue 18.8
dialyse 35.12
dialysis 28.11
diamanté 3.22
diamantine 25.12
diameter 12.78
diametric 21.15
diametrical 23.32
diamond 16.45
diamondback 21.2
Diana 12.53
Diane 25.1

Dianetics 28.39
dianthus 28.35
diapason 25.48
diaper 12.63
diaphanous 28.29
diaphragm 24.1
diaphragmatic 21.17
diarchal 23.32
diarchy 4.18
diarist 31.12
diarize 35.13
diarrhea 12.4
diarrhoea 12.4
diary 4.43
Diaspora 12.67
diatom 24.20
diatonic 21.13
diatribe 14.8
Díaz 28.1
diazepam 24.1
dib 14.7
dibber 12.21
dibble 23.26
dice 28.13
dicer 12.70
dicey 4.46
dichotomize 35.13
dichotomous 28.28
dichotomy 4.30
dick 21.9
Dickens 35.31
Dickensian 25.37
dicker 12.39
dickerer 12.67
dickhead 16.3
Dickie 4.19
Dickinson 25.48
dickybird 16.31
dicotyledon 25.40
dicta 12.78
dictaphone 25.30
dictate 30.7, 30.16
dictatorial 23.24
diction 25.49
dictionary 4.43
dictum 24.20
did 16.8
didactic 21.17
diddle 23.28
diddler 12.48
diddly-squat 30.32
diddums 35.30
diddy 4.12
Diderot 9.21
didgeridoo 11.1
didicoi 10.6
didn't 30.56
Dido 9.11
die 6.1
dieback 21.2
Diego 9.13

diehard 16.2
Dieppe 27.3
dieresis 28.11
diesel 23.41
dieselize 35.12
Dies Irae 3.19
diet 30.41
dietary 4.43
Dieter 12.77
dietetic 21.17
dietitian 25.49
Dietrich 21.15
differ 12.30
difference 28.45
different 30.56
differentia 12.11
differentiae 4.3
differential 23.38
differentiate 30.8
difficult 30.51
difficulty 4.53
diffidence 28.45
diffident 30.56
diffract 30.48
diffraction 25.49
diffuse 28.19, 35.21
diffuser 12.92
diffusion 25.42
diffusionist 31.10
diffusive 34.7
dig 18.6
Digby 4.10
digest 31.3
digestible 23.26
digestion 25.39
digger 12.31
digging 26.6
dight 30.26
digit 30.21
digital 23.39
digitalis 28.8
dignified 16.14
dignify 6.7
dignitary 4.43
dignity 4.53
digress 28.3
digresser 12.69
digressive 34.7
dihedral 23.36
Dijon 25.25
dik-dik 21.10
diktat 30.2
dilapidate 30.9
dilate 30.7
dilation 25.49
dilatory 4.43
dildo 9.11
dilemma 12.50
dilettante 4.51
Dili 4.24
diligence 28.45

d

d

donnish 29.9
donnybrook 21.28
donor 12.56
Donovan 25.51
Don Quixote 30.43
don't 30.55
donut 30.40
doodad 16.1
doodah 1.6
doodle 23.28
doodlebug 18.12
doodler 12.48
doodling 26.8
doohickey 4.19
Doolittle 23.39
doom 24.12
doomsday 3.9
doomster 12.81
door 7.1
doorbell 23.3
doorcase 28.5
do-or-die 6.1
doorframe 24.4
doorknob 14.9
doorman 25.45
doormat 30.1
doormen 25.45
doornail 23.6
doorpost 31.20
doorstep 27.3
doorstop 27.8
doorstopper 12.62
doorway 3.25
doozy 4.62
dop 27.8
dopamine 25.11
dope 27.10
doper 12.63
dopey 4.36
dopiaza 12.90
doppelgänger 12.60
Dopper 12.62
Doppler 12.44
Dora 12.66
Dorado 9.11
Doran 25.47
Dorcas 28.26
Dorchester 12.76
Dordogne 25.32
Dordrecht 30.48
Doré 3.19
Doreen 25.11
Dorian 25.37
Doric 21.15
Dorinda 12.27
Doris 28.10
dork 21.22
dorm 24.9
dormancy 4.48
dormant 30.56
dormer 12.52

dormice 28.13
dormitory 4.43
Dormobile 23.7
dormouse 28.16
dormy 4.29
Dorothea 12.4
Dorothy 4.56
dorp 27.9
Dors 35.17
dorsal 23.37
Dorset 30.24
Dortmund 16.45
dory 4.41
do's 35.21
dos-à-dos 9.1
dosage 20.9
dose 28.17
dosh 29.11
do-si-do 9.1
Dos Passos 28.14
doss 28.14
dossal 23.37
dosser 12.70
dosshouse 28.16
dossier 12.11
Dostoevsky 4.18
dot 30.31
dotage 20.9
dotard 16.29
dote 30.35
doter 12.80
dotter 12.79
dotterel 23.36
dottle 23.39
dotty 4.54
Douala 12.42
double 23.26
double entendre
    12.65
doubler 12.47
doublespeak 21.8
doublet 30.22
doublethink 21.33
doubleton 25.50
doubloon 25.33
doublure 12.20
doubt 30.34
doubter 12.80
douce 28.19
douche 29.14
Doug 18.12
Dougal 23.30
dough 9.1
doughboy 10.3
doughnut 30.40
doughty 4.54
doughy 4.7
Douglas 28.27
Doulton 25.50
dour 12.20
Douro 9.21

douse 28.16
dove 34.11, 34.13
dovecote 30.31
dovelike 21.19
Dover 12.86
dovetail 23.6
Dow 8.1
dowager 12.35
Dowding 26.5
dowdy 4.13
dowel 23.25
dower 12.16
down 25.29
down-and-out 30.34
downbeat 30.18
downcast 31.2
downer 12.56
downfall 23.15
downgrade 16.6
downhearted 16.12
downhill 23.8
downhiller 12.43
Downing 26.9
downlighter 12.79
download 16.23
downmarket 30.21
downmost 31.20
downplay 3.1
downpour 7.14
downright 30.29
downriver 12.86
Downs 35.31
downscale 23.5
downshift 30.47
downside 16.16
downsize 35.11
downstage 20.4
downstairs 35.4
downstate 30.7
downstream 24.5
downstroke 21.24
downswing 26.14
downtempo 9.20
downtime 24.7
downtown 25.29
downtrodden 25.40
downward 16.30
downwards 35.27
downwind 16.42
downy 4.32
dowry 4.43
dowse 28.16, 35.18
dowser 12.70, 12.92
Dowsing 26.14
doxy 4.46
doyen 25.38
Doyle 23.19
doze 35.19
dozen 25.52
dozenth 32.19
dozer 12.92

dozy 4.61
drab 14.1
drabble 23.26
drachm 24.1
drachma 12.50
drachmae 4.29
drack 21.1
Draco 9.16
draconian 25.37
draconic 21.13
Dracula 12.46
draft 30.47
draftee 4.1
drafter 12.75
drafts 28.47
draftsman 25.45
draftsmen 25.45
drafty 4.51
drag 18.1
draggle 23.30
draggy 4.15
dragline 25.22
dragnet 30.5
dragoman 25.45
dragon 25.41
dragonet 30.23
dragonfly 6.11
dragoon 25.33
dragster 12.74
drail 23.5
drain 25.7
drainage 20.7
drainboard 16.20
drainer 12.54
drainpipe 27.7
drake 21.7
Dralon 25.25
dram 24.1
drama 12.50
dramatic 21.17
dramatist 31.14
dramaturge 20.17
dramaturgic 21.11
dramaturgical 23.32
dramaturgy 4.17
Drambuie 4.8
Drammen 25.45
drank 21.33
drape 27.4
draper 12.61
drapery 4.43
drastic 21.17
drat 30.1
dratted 16.12
draught 30.47
draughtboard 16.20
draughts 28.47
draughtsman 25.45
draughtsmen 25.45
draughtswoman
    25.45

ecology 4.17
economic 21.12
economical 23.32
economist 31.9
economizer 12.91
economy 4.30
ecosphere 12.5
écossaise 35.5
ecosystem 24.6
écru 11.17
ecstasy 4.48
ecstatic 21.17
ectopic 21.14
ectoplasm 24.21
ectoplasmic 21.12
ecu 11.22
Ecuador 7.5
Ecuadorean 25.37
ecumenical 23.32
eczema 12.51
Ed 16.3
edacious 28.33
Edam 24.1
Edda 12.26
Eddie 4.12
Eddington 25.50
eddo 9.11
eddy 4.12
edelweiss 28.13
edema 12.51
Eden 25.40
edentate 30.16
Edgar 12.31
edge 20.3
Edgehill 23.8, 23.9
edger 12.35
edgeways 35.5
Edgeworth 32.14
edging 26.6
edgy 4.17
edibility 4.53
edible 23.26
edict 30.49
edictal 23.39
edifice 28.7
edify 6.7
Edinburgh 12.67
Edison 25.48
edit 30.21
Edith 32.6
edition 25.49
editiones principes 35.7
editor 12.78
editorial 23.24
editorialist 31.8
Edmonton 25.50
Edmund 16.45
Edna 12.53
Edo 9.11
Edom 24.17

Edomite 30.29
Edsel 23.37
educate 30.10
educationalist 31.8
educationist 31.10
educe 28.19
eduction 25.49
Edward 16.30
Edwardian 25.37
Edwardiana 12.53
Edwards 35.27
Edwin 25.20
Edwina 12.54
eejit 30.21
eel 23.7
Eelam 24.1
eelworm 24.22
eely 4.23
e'en 25.9
e'er 2.1
eerie 4.43
eff 17.3
effable 23.26
efface 28.5
effect 30.48
effectual 23.25
effectuate 30.8
effeminacy 4.48
effeminate 30.43
effendi 4.12
effervesce 28.3
effervescence 28.45
effervescent 30.56
effete 30.18
efficacious 28.33
efficacy 4.48
efficiency 4.46
efficient 30.56
Effie 4.14
effigy 4.17
effloresce 28.3
effluence 28.45
effluent 30.56
effluvia 12.12
effluvium 24.16
efflux 28.41
effluxion 25.49
effort 30.41
effrontery 4.43
effulgence 28.45
effulgent 30.56
effuse 35.21
effusion 25.42
effusive 34.7
Efik 21.10
eft 30.47
egad 16.1
egalitarian 25.37
Egan 25.41
Egbert 30.41
egg 18.3

eggar 12.31
egghead 16.3
eggnog 18.8
eggplant 30.53
eggshell 23.4
eggy 4.15
eglantine 25.23
ego 9.13
egocentric 21.15
egoism 24.21
egoist 31.6
egoistic 21.17
egoistical 23.32
egomania 12.8
egomaniac 21.1
egotist 31.14
egregious 28.25
egress 28.3
egret 30.24
Egypt 30.58
Egyptian 25.49
eh 3.1
Ehrlich 21.11
Eichmann 25.45
Eid 16.7
eider 12.27
eiderdown 25.29
eidola 12.44
eidolon 25.25
Eiffel 23.29
Eiger 12.31
Eigg 18.3
eight 30.7
eighteen 25.9
eighteenth 32.19
eightfold 16.37
eighth 32.23
eightieth 32.6
eighty 4.52
Eilat 30.3
Eileen 25.10
Eilidh 4.22
Eindhoven 25.51
einkorn 25.28
Einstein 25.23
Éire 12.65
Eisenhower 12.16
Eisenstadt 30.2
Eisenstein 25.23
eisteddfod 16.18
eisteddfodau 6.6
either 12.84
ejaculate 30.11, 30.42
ejaculatory 4.43
eject 30.48
ejection 25.49
ejector 12.76
eke 21.8
el 23.3

elaborate 30.15, 30.43
Elaine 25.7
Elam 24.1
Elamite 30.29
élan 25.1
Elan 25.1, 25.44
eland 16.45
elapse 28.46
elastane 25.8
elastic 21.17
elasticated 16.12
elasticize 35.14
Elastoplast 31.2
elate 30.7
elated 16.12
elation 25.49
Elba 12.21
Elbe 14.16
elbow 9.9
elbow room 24.12
Elche 3.8
eld 16.35
elder 12.26
elderberry 4.38
elderflower 12.16
elderly 4.27
eldest 31.6
Eldon 25.40
eldorado 9.11
eldritch 15.6
Eleanor 12.58
elect 30.48
election 25.49
electioneer 12.4
electioneering 26.11
elector 12.76
electoral 23.36
electorate 30.43
Electra 12.64
Electress 28.10
electric 21.15
electrical 23.32
electrician 25.49
electrify 6.7
electro 9.21
electrocardiogram 24.1
electrocute 30.38
electrocution 25.49
electrode 16.23
electrolysis 28.11
electrolyte 30.28
electromagnetic 21.17
electron 25.26
electronic 21.13
electronica 12.39
electroplate 30.11
electrotype 27.7
electuary 4.43

elegance 28.45
elegant 30.56
elegiac 21.30
elegist 31.7
elegize 35.11
elegy 4.17
element 30.56
elementary 4.43
Eleonora 12.66
elephant 30.56
elephantiasis 28.11
elephantine 25.23
elevate 30.16
elevatory 4.43
eleven 25.51
elevenfold 16.37
elevenses 35.10
eleventh 32.19
elf 17.18
elfin 25.14
elfish 29.7
Elfreda 12.26
Elgar 1.8
El Giza 12.90
El Greco 9.16
Eli 6.11
Elia 12.6
Elias 28.24
elicit 30.24
elicitor 12.78
elide 16.14
eligible 23.26
Elijah 12.35
eliminate 30.13
eliminatory 4.43
Elinor 12.55
Eliot 30.41
Elisabethville 23.10
Elisha 12.72
elision 25.42
élite 30.18
élitist 31.14
elixir 12.11
Eliza 12.91
Elizabeth 32.13
Elizabethan 25.51
elk 21.32
Elkie 4.18
ell 23.3
Ella 12.42
Ellen 25.44
Ellie 4.22
Ellington 25.50
ellipse 28.46
ellipsis 28.11
elliptic 21.17
Ellis 28.8
Ellsworth 32.14
elm 24.18
Elmer 12.50
Elmo 9.18

Elmwood 16.26
elmy 4.29
El Niño 9.28
elocution 25.49
elocutionary 4.43
elocutionist 31.10
Elohim 24.6
elongate 30.9
elope 27.10
eloper 12.63
eloquence 28.45
eloquent 30.56
El Paso 9.22
Elroy 10.11
Elsa 12.69
else 28.42
elsewhere 2.1
Elsie 4.45
Elsinore 7.13
Elspeth 32.13
Elton 25.50
elucidate 30.9
elucidatory 4.43
elude 16.25
Elul 23.22
elusive 34.7
elver 12.85
elves 35.35
Elvira 12.67
Elvis 28.12
elvish 29.10
Ely 4.23, 6.11
Elysian 25.37
Elysium 24.16
Elzevir 12.12
em 24.3
email 23.5
emanate 30.13
emancipate 30.14
emancipatory 4.43
Emanuel 23.25
emasculate 30.11
emasculatory 4.43
embalm 24.2
embalmer 12.50
embank 21.33
embargo 9.13
embark 21.5
embarras de choix 1.1
embarrass 28.31
embarrassing 26.12
embassy 4.48
embattle 23.39
embattled 16.38
embay 3.1
embed 16.3
embellish 29.8
embellisher 12.72
ember 12.21
embezzle 23.41

embezzler 12.42
embitter 12.78
emblazon 25.52
emblem 24.18
emblematic 21.17
emblematical 23.32
emblematize 35.14
embody 4.13
embolden 25.40
embolic 21.11
emboss 28.14
embosser 12.70
embouchure 12.20
embower 12.16
embrace 28.5
embracer 12.69
embrasure 12.33
embrittle 23.39
embroider 12.28
embroiderer 12.67
embroidery 4.43
embroil 23.19
embryo 9.4
embryology 4.17
embryonal 23.34
embryonic 21.13
emcee 4.1
emend 16.41
Emeny 4.34
emerald 16.38
emerge 20.17
emergence 28.45
emergency 4.48
emergent 30.56
emeritus 28.34
emersion 25.49
Emerson 25.48
emery 4.43
emetic 21.17
emigrant 30.56
emigrate 30.15
émigré 3.19
Emile 23.7
Emily 4.24
eminence 28.45
éminence grise 35.6
eminent 30.56
emir 12.4
emirate 30.43
emissary 4.43
emission 25.49
emit 30.20
emitter 12.78
Emlyn 25.16
Emma 12.50
Emmanuel 23.25
Emmeline 25.10
Emmental 23.2
emmer 12.50
emmet 30.23
Emmy 4.29

emo 9.18
emollience 28.45
emollient 30.56
emote 30.35
emoter 12.80
emoticon 25.25
emotion 25.49
emotional 23.34
emotionalist 31.8
emotionalize 35.12
emotive 34.8
empathy 4.56
Empedocles 35.7
emperor 12.67
emphases 35.8
emphasis 28.11
emphasize 35.14
emphatic 21.17
emphysema 12.51
empire 12.14
empiric 21.15
empirical 23.32
empiricist 31.13
employ 10.1
employee 4.1
employer 12.18
emporia 12.10
emporium 24.16
empower 12.16
empress 28.10
Empson 25.48
empty 4.51
empyreal 23.23
empyrean 25.36
Emrys 28.10
emu 11.22
emulate 30.11
emulous 28.27
emulsifier 12.14
emulsify 6.7
emulsion 25.49
Emyr 12.7
en 25.5
Ena 12.54
enable 23.26
enact 30.48
enaction 25.49
enactor 12.74
enamel 23.33
enameler 12.48
enameling 26.8
enameller 12.48
enamelling 26.8
enamored 16.29
en brosse 28.14
encamp 27.17
encapsulate 30.11
encase 28.5
encash 29.1
enceinte 30.53
Enceladus 28.25

encephalic 21.11
encephalitis 28.12
encephalogram 24.1
encephalopathy 4.56
enchant 30.53
enchanter 12.75
enchanting 26.13
enchantress 28.10
enchase 28.5
enchilada 12.25
enchiridion 25.37
encipher 12.30
encircle 23.32
enclave 34.4
enclitic 21.17
enclose 35.19
enclosure 12.33
encode 16.23
encomia 12.7
encomiast 31.1
encomiastic 21.17
encomium 24.16
encompass 28.30
encore 7.10
encounter 12.80
encourage 20.8
encourager 12.35
encroach 15.10
encroacher 12.24
encrust 31.24
encrypt 30.58
encryption 25.49
encumber 12.22
encumbrance 28.45
encyclical 23.32
encyclopedia 12.5
encyclopedic 21.10
encyclopedist 31.6
end 16.41
endanger 12.35
endear 12.4
endeavor 12.85
endeavour 12.85
endemic 21.12
Enders 35.24
endgame 24.4
ending 26.5
endive 34.6
endless 28.27
endmost 31.20
endnote 30.35
endocrine 25.23
endogamous 28.28
endogamy 4.30
endogenous 28.29
endorphin 25.14
endorse 28.15
endorsee 4.1
endorser 12.70
endosperm 24.22

endow 8.1
endower 12.16
endpaper 12.61
endplay 3.15
endpoint 30.55
endrun 25.35
endue 11.1
endurance 28.45
endure 12.20
enduro 9.21
endways 35.5
Endymion 25.37
endzone 25.31
enema 12.51
enemy 4.29
energetic 21.17
energumen 25.45
energy 4.17
enervate 30.16
en famille 4.1
enfant terrible 12.43
enfeeble 23.26
enfeoff 17.5
enfilade 16.6
enfold 16.37
enforce 28.15
enforcer 12.70
enfranchise 35.14
engage 20.4
engagé 3.1
engaging 26.6
Engelbert 30.45
Engels 35.29
engender 12.26
engine 25.14
engineer 12.4
engineering 26.11
engird 16.31
engirdle 23.28
England 16.45
English 29.8
Englishman 25.45
Englishmen 25.45
Englishwoman 25.45
Englishwomen 25.17
engorge 20.12
engraft 30.47
engrave 34.4
engraver 12.85
engraving 26.14
engross 28.17
engulf 17.18
enhance 28.44
enhancer 12.69
Enid 16.10
enigma 12.51
enigmatic 21.17
enigmatical 23.32

enjoin 25.32
enjoy 10.1
enjoyer 12.18
enlace 28.5
enlarge 20.2
enlarger 12.35
enlighten 25.50
enlightener 12.58
enlist 31.6
enlister 12.78
enliven 25.51
enlivener 12.58
en masse 28.1
enmesh 29.3
enmity 4.53
Ennis 28.9
Enniskillen 25.16
Ennius 28.23
ennoble 23.26
ennui 4.1
Enoch 21.21
enophilist 31.8
enormity 4.53
enormous 28.28
enough 17.15
enprint 30.54
enquire 12.13
enquirer 12.67
enquiry 4.43
enrage 20.4
enrapt 30.58
enrapture 12.23
enrich 15.6
enrobe 14.11
enrol 23.17
enroll 23.17
enrollee 4.1
ensconce 28.44
ensemble 23.26
enshrine 25.21
enshroud 16.22
ensign 25.23, 25.48
ensilage 20.6
ensile 23.11
enslave 34.4
enslaver 12.85
ensnare 2.1
Ensor 7.16
ensue 11.1
ensure 12.20
entablature 12.24
entail 23.5
entangle 23.30
entases 35.8
entasis 28.11
Entebbe 4.10
entente 30.53
entente cordiale 23.2
enter 12.76
enterprise 35.13

enterpriser 12.91
enterprising 26.14
entertain 25.7
entertainer 12.54
entertaining 26.9
enthral 23.14
enthrall 23.14
enthrone 25.30
enthuse 35.21
enthusiasm 24.21
enthusiast 31.1
enthusiastic 21.17
entice 28.13
enticer 12.70
enticing 26.12
entire 12.13
entirety 4.53
entitle 23.39
entity 4.53
entomb 24.12
entomology 4.17
entourage 19.1
entrails 35.29
entrain 25.7
entrammel 23.33
entrance 28.44, 28.45
entrant 30.56
entrap 27.1
entreat 30.18
entreaty 4.52
entrechat 1.18
entrecôte 30.35
entrée 3.19
entremets 3.16
entrench 29.20
entrepreneur 13.1
entrepreneurial 23.24
entresol 23.13
entropy 4.37
entrust 31.24
entry 4.38
entryway 3.25
entwine 25.21
enumerate 30.15
enunciate 30.8
enure 12.20
envelop 27.14
envelope 27.10
envenom 24.19
envier 12.12
envious 28.23
environ 25.47
environmentalist 31.8
envisage 20.9
envision 25.42
envoi 10.13
envoy 10.13
envy 4.58
enwrap 27.1

establisher 12.72
establishmentarian 25.37
estaminet 3.17
estancia 12.11
estate 30.7
esteem 24.5
Estelle 23.3
ester 12.76
Esther 12.76
esthete 30.19
esthetic 21.17
esthetician 25.49
estimate 30.12, 30.43
estival 23.40
Estonia 12.8
Estonian 25.37
estop 27.8
Estoril 23.8
estovers 35.24
estrange 20.19
estreat 30.18
Estremadura 12.67
estrogen 25.42
estuarine 25.23
estuary 4.41
esurient 30.56
eta 12.77
et cetera 12.67
etch 15.3
etcher 12.23
etching 26.4
eternal 23.34
eternalize 35.12
eternity 4.53
eth 33.1
Ethan 25.51
ethane 25.8
ethanol 23.13
Ethel 23.40
Etheldreda 12.26
ethene 25.12
ether 12.83
ethereal 23.24
etherize 35.13
Ethernet 30.5
ethic 21.18
ethical 23.32
ethicist 31.13
Ethiopia 12.9
Ethiopian 25.37
Ethiopic 21.14
ethnic 21.13
ethnocentric 21.15
ethnologic 21.11
ethos 28.14
ethyl 23.9
etiology 4.17
etiquette 30.4
Etna 12.53
Etonian 25.37

Etruria 12.10
Etruscan 25.43
étude 16.25
etymology 4.17
Euboea 12.3
eucalypt 30.58
eucalyptus 28.34
Eucharist 31.12
euchre 12.41
Euclid 16.10
Euclidean 25.37
Eudora 12.66
Eugene 25.10
eugenic 21.13
eugenicist 31.13
Eugénie 4.31
Euler 12.44
eulogia 12.6
eulogist 31.7
eulogy 4.17
Eumenides 35.7
Eunice 28.9
eunuch 21.30
Euphemia 12.7
euphemize 35.13
euphonic 21.13
euphonious 28.23
euphonium 24.16
euphonize 35.13
euphony 4.34
euphorbia 12.5
euphoria 12.10
euphoric 21.15
Euphrates 35.9
euphuist 31.6
Eurasian 25.42
Euratom 24.20
eureka 12.38
eurhythmic 21.12
Euripides 35.7
euro 9.21
Eurobond 16.42
Eurocentric 21.15
Eurocrat 30.2
Euromarket 30.21
Europa 12.63
Europe 27.14
European 25.36
europium 24.16
Eurovision 25.42
Eurydice 4.46
Eusebius 28.23
Eustace 28.34
euthanasia 12.12
Eva 12.85
evacuate 30.8
evacuee 4.1
evade 16.6
evader 12.26
Evadne 4.31
evaluate 30.8

Evan 25.51
evanesce 28.3
evanescence 28.45
evanescent 30.56
evangel 23.31
evangelic 21.11
evangelical 23.32
Evangeline 25.10
evangelist 31.8
evangelizer 12.91
Evans 35.31
evaporate 30.15
evasion 25.42
evasive 34.7
eve 34.5
Evelyn 25.16
even 25.51
evening 26.9
evensong 26.15
event 30.53
eventer 12.76
eventide 16.17
eventual 23.25
eventuate 30.8
ever 12.85
Everard 16.2
Everest 31.12
Everett 30.24
Everglades 35.27
evergreen 25.11
everlasting 26.13
evermore 7.1
Evert 30.44
every 4.38
everybody 4.13
everyday 3.1
everyman 25.2
everyone 25.35
everyplace 28.5
everything 26.14
everywhere 2.15
evict 30.49
eviction 25.49
evictor 12.78
evidence 28.45
evident 30.56
evidential 23.38
evidentiary 4.43
evil 23.40
evil-doer 12.19
evil-doing 26.3
evince 28.44
eviscerate 30.15
Evita 12.77
evoke 21.24
evoker 12.40
evolution 25.49
evolutional 23.34
evolutionary 4.43
evolutionist 31.10
evolve 34.15

Evonne 25.24
Ewan 25.38
Ewart 30.41
ewer 12.19
ex 28.38
exacerbate 30.9
exact 30.48
exacting 26.13
exaction 25.49
exactitude 16.25
exactor 12.74
exaggerate 30.15
exalt 30.51
exam 24.1
examine 25.17
examinee 4.1
examiner 12.55
example 23.35
exarch 21.5
exasperate 30.15
Excalibur 12.21
ex cathedra 12.65
excavate 30.16
exceed 16.7
exceeding 26.5
excel 23.3
excellence 28.45
excellency 4.48
excellent 30.56
excelsior 7.3
except 30.58
excepting 26.13
exception 25.49
exceptional 23.34
excerpt 30.58
excerption 25.49
excess 28.3
excessive 34.7
exchange 20.19
exchanger 12.35
exchequer 12.37
excise 35.11, 35.14
exciseman 25.45
excisemen 25.45
excision 25.42
excite 30.26
exclaim 24.4
exclamatory 4.43
exclave 34.4
exclude 16.25
excluder 12.29
exclusion 25.42
exclusionary 4.43
exclusionist 31.10
exclusive 34.7
excogitate 30.16
excommunicate 30.10
excommunicatory 4.43
excoriate 30.8

excrescence 28.45
excrescent 30.56
excreta 12.77
excrete 30.18
excretion 25.49
excretory 4.43
excruciate 30.8
exculpate 30.14
exculpatory 4.43
excursion 25.49
excursionist 31.10
excursive 34.7
excursus 28.32
excusatory 4.43
excuse 28.19, 35.21
excuse-me 4.30
ex-directory 4.43
exeat 30.1
exec 21.6
execrate 30.15
execratory 4.43
executant 30.56
execute 30.38
execution 25.49
executioner 12.58
executor 12.81
executorial 23.24
executory 4.43
executrices 35.8
executrix 28.39
exegeses 35.8
exegesis 28.11
exegete 30.18
exegetic 21.17
exempla 12.42
exemplar 12.42
exemplary 4.43
exemplify 6.7
exemplum 24.18
exempt 30.52
exemption 25.49
exequies 35.10
exercise 35.14
exerciser 12.91
exergue 18.13
exert 30.45
exertion 25.49
Exeter 12.78
exeunt 30.55
exfiltrate 30.15
exfoliate 30.8
ex gratia 12.72
exhale 23.5
exhaust 31.18
exhauster 12.80
exhaustible 23.26
exhaustion 25.39
exhibit 30.20
exhibitioner 12.58
exhibitionist 31.10
exhibitor 12.78

exhilarate 30.15
exhort 30.33
exhortatory 4.43
exhorter 12.80
exhume 24.12
exigence 28.45
exigency 4.48
exigent 30.56
exigible 23.26
exiguity 4.53
exiguous 28.24
exile 23.12
exilic 21.11
exist 31.6
existence 28.45
existent 30.56
existential 23.38
existentialist 31.8
exit 30.24
ex libris 28.10
Exmoor 12.20
Exocet 30.5
exodus 28.25
ex officio 9.4
exogamy 4.30
exogenous 28.29
exon 25.26
exonerate 30.15
exorbitance 28.45
exorbitant 30.56
exorcist 31.13
exordial 23.24
exordium 24.16
exoskeleton 25.50
exoteric 21.15
exotic 21.17
exotica 12.39
expand 16.40
expander 12.25
expanse 28.44
expansible 23.26
expansion 25.49
expansionary 4.43
expansionist 31.10
expansive 34.7
ex parte 4.51
expat 30.1
expatiate 30.8
expatriate 30.8,
   30.41
expect 30.48
expectancy 4.48
expectant 30.56
expectorant 30.56
expectorate 30.15
expedience 28.45
expediency 4.48
expedient 30.56
expedite 30.26
expediter 12.79
expeditionary 4.43

expeditious 28.33
expel 23.3
expellee 4.1
expeller 12.42
expend 16.41
expenditure 12.23
expense 28.44
expensive 34.7
experience 28.45
experiential 23.38
experimentalist
   31.8
experimenter 12.76
expert 30.45
expertise 35.6
expiate 30.8
expiatory 4.43
expire 12.13
expiry 4.43
explain 25.7
explainer 12.54
explanatory 4.43
explicate 30.10
explicatory 4.43
explicit 30.24
explode 16.23
exploder 12.28
exploit 30.36
exploiter 12.81
exploratory 4.43
explore 7.1
explorer 12.66
explosion 25.42
explosive 34.7
Expo 9.20
exponent 30.56
exponential 23.38
export 30.33
exporter 12.80
expose 35.19
exposé 3.27
exposer 12.92
expositor 12.78
expository 4.43
expostulate 30.11
expostulatory 4.43
exposure 12.33
expound 16.43
expounder 12.28
express 28.3
expressional 23.34
expressionist
   31.10
expressive 34.7
expressway 3.25
expropriate 30.8
expulsion 25.49
expunction 25.49
expunge 20.19
expunger 12.36
expurgate 30.9

expurgatory 4.43
exquisite 30.25
exsolve 34.15
extant 30.53
extemporaneous
   28.23
extemporary 4.43
extempore 4.43
extend 16.41
extender 12.26
extendible 23.26
extensible 23.26
extensile 23.11
extension 25.49
extensive 34.7
extent 30.53
extenuate 30.8
extenuatory 4.43
exterior 12.10
exteriorize 35.13
exterminate 30.13
exterminatory
   4.43
extern 25.53
external 23.34
extinct 30.49
extinction 25.49
extinguish 29.10
extinguisher 12.72
extirpate 30.14
extol 23.17
extoller 12.44
extort 30.33
extorter 12.80
extortion 25.49
extortionate 30.43
extortioner 12.58
extortionist 31.10
extra 12.64
extract 30.48
extraction 25.49
extractor 12.74
extradite 30.26
extrados 28.14
extraneous 28.23
extraordinaire 2.1
extrapolate 30.11
extravagance
   28.45
extravagancy 4.48
extravagant 30.56
extravaganza 12.90
extreme 24.5
extremist 31.9
extremity 4.53
extricate 30.10
extrinsic 21.16
extroversion
   25.49
extrovert 30.45
extroverted 16.12
extrude 16.25

extrusion 25.42
exuberance 28.45
exuberant 30.56
exude 16.25
exult 30.51
exultancy 4.48
exultant 30.56
exurb 14.15
exurban 25.38
exurbanite 30.29
exurbia 12.5
exuviate 30.8
eyas 28.24
eye 6.1
eyeball 23.14
eyebath 32.2
eyeblack 21.3
eyebright 30.29
eyebrow 8.10
eyeful 23.21
eyeglass 28.2
eyehole 23.17
eyelash 29.1
eyeless 28.8
eyelet 30.22
eye level 23.40
eyelid 16.10
eyeliner 12.55
eyepatch 15.1
eyeshade 16.6
eyeshadow 9.11
eyeshot 30.32
eyesight 30.30
eyesore 7.16
eye teeth 32.5
eye tooth 32.12
eyewash 29.11
Eyre 2.1
eyrie 4.43
Eysenck 21.33
Ezekiel 23.24
Ezra 12.64

F

fab 14.1
Fabergé 3.12
Fabian 25.37
Fabianist 31.10
Fabius 28.23
fable 23.26
fabler 12.43
Fablon 25.25
fabric 21.15
fabricate 30.10
fabulist 31.8
fabulosity 4.53
fabulous 28.27
facade 16.2
face 28.5

facecloth 32.8
facelift 30.47
facemask 21.35
faceplate 30.11
facer 12.69
facet 30.24
facetiae 4.3
facetious 28.33
facial 23.38
facile 23.11
facilitate 30.16
facility 4.53
facing 26.12
facsimile 4.24
fact 30.48
faction 25.49
factional 23.34
factionalize 35.12
factious 28.33
factitious 28.33
factoid 16.24
factor 12.74
factorage 20.8
factory 4.43
factotum 24.20
factual 23.25
factum 24.20
facture 12.23
facula 12.46
faculty 4.51
fad 16.1
faddish 29.6
faddist 31.6
faddy 4.12
fade 16.6
fader 12.26
faecal 23.32
faeces 35.8
Faenza 12.69
faerie 4.39
Faeroe 9.21
Faeroes 35.19
faff 17.1
fag 18.1
faggot 30.42
faggoty 4.55
fagot 30.42
fah 1.1
Fahrenheit 30.27
faience 28.44
fail 23.5
failing 26.8
faille 23.5
failure 12.89
fain 25.7
faint 30.54
fair 2.1
Fairbanks 28.41
Fairfax 28.38
fairground 16.43
fairing 26.11

fairish 29.9
fairway 3.25
fairy 4.39
fairyland 16.40
Faisalabad 16.1
fait accompli 4.25
faith 32.4
fake 21.7
faker 12.38
fakery 4.43
fakir 12.6
falafel 23.29
Falange 20.19
Falangist 31.7
Falasha 12.72
falcon 25.43
falconer 12.58
falconet 30.23
falconry 4.43
Faldo 9.11
faldstool 23.20
Falk 21.22
Falkirk 21.31
Falkland 16.45
Falklands 35.27
fall 23.14
fallacious 28.33
fallacy 4.48
fallback 21.2
fallen 25.44
faller 12.44
fallible 23.26
fallout 30.34
fallow 9.17
false 28.42
falsehood 16.26
falsetto 9.24
falsework 21.31
falsies 35.10
falsify 6.7
falsity 4.53
Falstaffian 25.37
falter 12.80
falterer 12.67
faltering 26.11
fame 24.4
familial 23.24
familiar 12.6
familiarity 4.53
famille noire 1.1
famille verte 30.6
family 4.24
famine 25.17
famish 29.8
famous 28.28
famulus 28.27
fan 25.1
fanatic 21.17
fanatical 23.32
fanaticize 35.14
fan belt 30.51

fancier 12.11
fancy 4.45
fandangle 23.30
fandango 9.13
fandom 24.17
fane 25.7
fanfare 2.5
fang 26.1
fanlight 30.28
fanlike 21.19
fanner 12.53
fanny 4.31
fantail 23.6
fantasia 12.12
fantasist 31.13
fantast 31.1
fantastic 21.17
fantastical 23.32
fantasy 4.48
Fante 4.51
fanzine 25.12
far 1.1
farad 16.1
faraday 3.9
farandole 23.17
faraway 3.1
farce 28.2
farceur 13.1
farcical 23.32
farcy 4.45
fare 2.1
farewell 23.3
farfalle 4.21
farfetched 30.46
farina 12.54
farinaceous 28.33
farl 23.2
farm 24.2
farmer 12.50
farmhand 16.40
farmhouse 28.16
farmland 16.40
farmstead 16.4
farmyard 16.2
Farnborough 12.67
Farne 25.4
Farnese 4.61
Faro 9.21
Faroese 35.6
far-off 17.8
farouche 29.14
Farouk 21.27
Farquhar 1.11
farraginous 28.29
farrago 9.13
Farrell 23.36
farrier 12.10
farriery 4.43
farrow 9.21
farruca 12.41
far-seeing 26.3

Farsi 4.45
fart 30.3
farther 12.84
farthest 31.14
farthing 26.14
farthingale 23.5
fartlek 21.6
fasces 35.8
fascia 12.11
fascial 23.38
fascicle 23.32
fascicule 23.20
fascinate 30.13
fascine 25.9
fascist 31.13
fashion 25.49
fashioner 12.58
Fassbinder 12.27
fast 31.2
fastback 21.2
fasten 25.48
fastener 12.58
fastening 26.9
faster 12.75
fastidious 28.23
fasting 26.13
Fastnet 30.5
fat 30.1
fatal 23.39
fatalist 31.8
fatality 4.53
fatback 21.2
fat cat 30.1
fate 30.7
Fates 28.47
fathead 16.3
fatheaded 16.9
father 12.84
fatherhood 16.26
fatherland 16.40
fatherlike 21.19
fatherly 4.27
fathom 24.20
fatigue 18.5
Fatiha 12.34
Fatima 12.51
Fatimid 16.10
Fatimite 30.29
fatless 28.27
fatling 26.8
fatly 4.21
fatness 28.29
fatso 9.22
fatstock 21.21
fatted 16.12
fatten 25.50
fattish 29.10
fattist 31.14
fatty 4.51
fatuity 4.53
fatuous 28.24

fatwa 1.22
faucet 30.24
Faulkner 12.56
fault 30.51
faulty 4.54
faun 25.28
fauna 12.56
Fauntleroy 10.11
Faunus 28.29
Fauré 3.19
Faust 31.19
Faustian 25.37
faute de mieux 13.1
fauteuil 5.3
fauve 34.11
fauvist 31.15
Faux 28.40
fave 34.4
favela 12.42
favor 12.85
favorer 12.67
favorite 30.24
favour 12.85
favourer 12.67
favourite 30.24
Fawkes 28.40
fawn 25.28
fax 28.38
fay 3.1
fayre 2.1
faze 35.5
fazenda 12.26
fealty 4.55
fear 12.4
feasible 23.26
feast 31.5
feaster 12.77
feat 30.18
feather 12.84
feather bed 16.3
featherbrained
    16.41
featherweight 30.17
feathery 4.43
feature 12.23
febrile 23.11
February 4.43
fecal 23.32
feces 35.8
feculence 28.45
feculent 30.56
fecund 16.45
fecundate 30.9
fecundity 4.53
fed 16.3
fedayeen 25.9
federal 23.36
federalist 31.8
federalize 35.12
federate 30.15
federationist 31.10

fedora 12.66
fee 4.1
feeble 23.26
feed 16.7
feedback 21.2
feeder 12.26
feedstock 21.21
feedstuff 17.15
feel 23.7
feeler 12.43
feeling 26.8
feelings 35.32
feet 30.18
feign 25.7
feint 30.54
feisty 4.54
feldspar 1.15
Felicia 12.11
felicitate 30.16
felicitous 28.34
felicity 4.53
feline 25.22
Felix 28.39
Felixstowe 9.24
fell 23.3
fella 12.42
fellah 12.42
fellate 30.7
fellatio 9.4
feller 12.42
Fellini 4.31
fellow 9.17
Fellows 35.19
felon 25.44
felonious 28.23
felony 4.34
felt 30.51
felty 4.51
felucca 12.41
female 23.5
femineity 4.53
feminine 25.18
femininity 4.53
feminist 31.10
femme 24.1
femme fatale 23.2
femoral 23.36
femur 12.51
fen 25.5
fence 28.44
fencer 12.69
fend 16.41
fender 12.26
Fenella 12.42
feng shui 4.8
Fenian 25.37
fenland 16.40
fennec 21.13
fennel 23.34
fenny 4.31
Fens 35.31

Fenton 25.50
fenugreek 21.8
feoffor 12.30
feral 23.36
Ferdinand 16.40
Fergal 23.30
Fergus 28.25
Ferguson 25.48
ferial 23.24
Fermanagh 12.53
Fermat 1.13
ferment 30.53
fermenter 12.76
fermentor 12.76
fermium 24.16
fern 25.53
fernery 4.43
ferny 4.34
ferocious 28.33
ferocity 4.53
Ferranti 4.51
Ferrara 12.64
Ferrari 4.38
Ferrer 12.64
ferret 30.24
ferreter 12.78
ferrety 4.53
ferriage 20.6
ferric 21.15
Ferrier 12.10
ferrous 28.31
ferruginous 28.29
ferrule 23.20
ferry 4.38
ferryman 25.45
ferrymen 25.45
fertile 23.12
fertility 4.53
ferule 23.20
fervency 4.49
fervent 30.56
fervid 16.13
fervor 12.87
fervour 12.87
Fès 35.3
fess 28.3
festal 23.39
fester 12.76
festival 23.40
festive 34.8
festoon 25.33
Festschrift 30.47
Festschriften 25.50
Festus 28.34
feta 12.76
fetal 23.39
fetch 15.3
fetcher 12.23
fête 30.7
fetid 16.12
fetish 29.10

fetishist 31.13
fetishize 35.14
fetlock 21.21
fetor 12.77
fetter 12.76
fetterlock 21.21
fettle 23.39
fettler 12.48
fettuccine 4.31
fetus 28.34
feu 11.1
feud 16.25
feudal 23.28
feudalist 31.8
feudalize 35.12
feu de joie 1.1
feuilleton 25.26
fever 12.85
feverish 29.9
feverous 28.31
few 11.1
fey 3.1
Feydeau 9.11
feyly 4.22
feyness 28.9
Feynman 25.45
fez 35.3
fiacre 12.64
fiancé 3.20
fiancée 3.20
Fianna Fáil 23.19
fiasco 9.16
fiat 30.1
fib 14.7
fibber 12.21
fiber 12.21
fiberboard 16.20
fiberfill 23.8
fiberglass 28.2
fibre 12.21
fibreboard 16.20
fibrefill 23.8
fibreglass 28.2
fibril 23.9
fibrillar 12.43
fibrillary 4.43
fibrillate 30.11
fibro 9.21
fibrous 28.31
fibula 12.46
fiche 29.5
Fichte 30.50
fichu 11.19
fickle 23.32
fictile 23.12
fiction 25.49
fictional 23.34
fictionist 31.10
fictitious 28.33
fictive 34.8
fiddle 23.28

fiddle-de-dee 4.1
fiddler 12.43
fiddlestick 21.17
fiddly 4.27
fideist 31.6
Fidel 23.3
Fidelis 28.8
fidelity 4.53
fidget 30.21
fidgety 4.53
Fido 9.11
fiducial 23.38
fiduciary 4.43
fie 6.1
fief 17.5
fiefdom 24.17
field 16.35
fielder 12.26
fieldfare 2.5
Fielding 26.5
fieldmice 28.13
field mouse 28.16
Fields 35.27
fieldsman 25.45
fieldsmen 25.45
fieldwork 21.31
fieldworker 12.41
fiend 16.41
fiendish 29.6
fiendlike 21.19
fierce 28.23
fiery 4.43
fiesta 12.76
fife 17.7
fifer 12.30
Fifi 4.14
fifteen 25.9
fifteenth 32.19
fifth 32.16
fiftieth 32.6
fifty 4.53
fifty-fifty 4.53
fig 18.6
fight 30.26
fightback 21.2
fighter 12.79
fig leaf 17.5
fig leaves 35.35
figment 30.56
figtree 4.40
figura 12.67
figural 23.36
figurant 30.56
figure 12.31
figurehead 16.3
figurine 25.9
Fiji 4.17
Fijian 25.36
filaria 12.10
filariae 4.3
filarial 23.24

filature 12.24
filbert 30.41
filch 15.15
filcher 12.23
file 23.11
filefish 29.7
filename 24.4
filer 12.44
filet 30.22
filet mignon 25.27
filial 23.24
filibeg 18.3
filibuster 12.81
filicide 16.16
filigree 4.40
filigreed 16.7
filing 26.8
filings 35.32
Filipina 12.54
Filipino 9.19
fill 23.8
fille de joie 1.22
filler 12.43
fillet 30.22
filleter 12.78
filling 26.8
fillip 27.6
fillis 28.8
fillister 12.78
filly 4.24
film 24.18
filmic 21.12
filmmaker 12.38
filmmaking 26.7
film noir 1.1
filmography 4.14
filmset 30.5
filmstrip 27.6
filmy 4.29
filo 9.17
Filofax 28.38
filoselle 23.3
fils 28.6
filter 12.78
filth 32.17
filthy 4.56
filtrate 30.15
fimbriated 16.12
fin 25.13
finagle 23.30
finagler 12.48
final 23.34
finale 4.21
finalist 31.8
finality 4.53
finance 28.44
financial 23.38
financier 12.11
Finbar 1.4
finca 12.39
finch 29.20

find 16.42
finder 12.27
fin de siècle 12.42
finding 26.5
fine 25.21
finery 4.43
fines herbes 14.4
fine-spun 25.35
finesse 28.3
Fingal 23.30
finger 12.31
fingering 26.11
fingerling 26.8
fingernail 23.6
fingerplate 30.11
fingerpost 31.20
fingerprint 30.54
fingerstall 23.15
fingertip 27.6
finial 23.24
finical 23.32
finicking 26.7
finicky 4.19
finis 28.9
finish 29.9
finisher 12.72
Finisterre 2.1
finite 30.29
finitist 31.14
finitude 16.25
fink 21.33
Finland 16.45
Finlay 4.24
Finn 25.13
finnan 25.46
Finney 4.32
Finnic 21.13
Finnish 29.9
finny 4.32
fino 9.19
Finola 12.44
Fiona 12.56
fioritura 12.67
fioriture 4.43
fipple 23.35
fir 13.1
fire 12.13
firearm 24.2
fireback 21.2
fireball 23.14
firebomb 24.8
firebox 28.40
firebrand 16.40
firebreak 21.7
firebrick 21.15
firebug 18.12
firecracker 12.37
firecrest 31.3
firedamp 27.17
firedog 18.8
firefight 30.27

flinders 35.24
fling 26.3
flinger 12.60
flint 30.54
flintlock 21.21
Flintshire 12.5
flinty 4.53
flip 27.6
flipflop 27.8
flippancy 4.48
flippant 30.56
flipper 12.62
flirt 30.45
flirtatious 28.33
flirty 4.55
flit 30.20
flitch 15.6
flitter 12.78
Flo 9.1
float 30.35
floater 12.80
floaty 4.54
floc 21.20
flocci 6.16
flocculate 30.11
floccule 23.20
flocculent 30.56
flocculi 6.11
flocculus 28.27
floccus 28.26
flock 21.20
flocky 4.19
floe 9.1
Floella 12.42
flog 18.8
flogger 12.32
flood 16.27
floodgate 30.9
floodlight 30.28
floodlit 30.22
floor 7.1
floorboard 16.20
flooring 26.11
floozie 4.62
flop 27.8
flophouse 28.16
floppy 4.36
flora 12.66
floral 23.36
floreat 30.1
Florence 28.45
Florentine 25.23
Flores 35.10
florescence 28.45
floret 30.24
Florey 4.41
florid 16.11
Florida 12.27
Floridian 25.37
florilegia 12.6
florin 25.18

Florio 9.4
florist 31.12
floristry 4.40
Florrie 4.41
floruit 30.20
flory 4.41
floss 28.14
Flossie 4.46
flossy 4.46
flotilla 12.43
flotsam 24.20
flounce 28.44
flounder 12.28
flounderer 12.67
flour 12.16
flourish 29.9
flourisher 12.72
floury 4.43
flout 30.34
flow 9.1
flow chart 30.3
flower 12.16
flowerer 12.67
floweret 30.24
flower-like 21.19
flowerpot 30.32
Flowers 35.24
flowery 4.43
flowing 26.3
flown 25.30
flowsheet 30.19
Floyd 16.24
flu 11.1
flub 14.13
fluctuate 30.8
flue 11.1
fluence 28.45
fluency 4.48
fluent 30.56
fluff 17.15
fluffy 4.14
Flügelhorn 25.28
fluid 16.8
fluidity 4.53
fluid ounce 28.44
fluke 21.27
fluky 4.20
flume 24.12
flummery 4.43
flummox 28.41
flump 27.17
flung 26.18
flunk 21.34
flunkey 4.20
fluoresce 28.3
fluorescence 28.45
fluorescent 30.56
fluoridate 30.9
fluoride 16.15
fluorine 25.11
fluorite 30.29

fluorspar 1.15
flurry 4.42
flush 29.16
flusher 12.73
Flushing 26.12
fluster 12.81
flute 30.37
flutist 31.14
flutter 12.81
flutterer 12.67
fluttery 4.43
fluty 4.54
fluvial 23.24
fluviatile 23.12
flux 28.41
fluxional 23.34
fly 6.1
flyable 23.26
flyaway 3.25
flyblown 25.30
flycatcher 12.23
flyer 12.13
flyleaf 17.5
flyleaves 35.35
flyness 28.9
Flynn 25.13
flyover 12.86
flypaper 12.61
fly-past 31.2
flysheet 30.19
flyweight 30.17
flywheel 23.7
foal 23.17
foam 24.11
foamy 4.29
fob 14.9
fobwatch 15.7
focaccia 12.23
focal 23.32
focalize 35.12
Foch 29.11
foci 6.10
fo'c's'le 23.37
focus 28.26
fodder 12.28
foe 9.1
fog 18.8
fog bank 21.33
fogbound 16.43
fogey 4.15
fogeydom 24.17
fogeyish 29.6
foggy 4.19
foghorn 25.28
fohn 25.53
foible 23.26
foie gras 1.1
foil 23.19
foist 31.21
Fokker 12.40
fold 16.37

foldaway 3.25
folder 12.28
folderol 23.13
Foley 4.25
foliaceous 28.33
foliage 20.6
foliate 30.8, 30.41
Folies-Bergère 2.1
folio 9.4
folk 21.24
Folkestone 25.50
folkie 4.20
folkish 29.8
folklore 7.11
folkloric 21.15
folklorist 31.12
folksy 4.47
folktale 23.6
folky 4.20
follicle 23.32
follow 9.17
follower 12.17
following 26.3
follow-my-leader
    12.26
folly 4.25
Folsom 24.20
foment 30.53
fomenter 12.76
fond 16.42
Fonda 12.28
fondant 30.56
fondle 23.28
fondler 12.48
fondue 11.6
font 30.54
fontal 23.39
fontanelle 23.3
Fonteyn 25.8
Foochow 8.1
food 16.25
foodie 4.13
foodstuff 17.15
fool 23.20
foolery 4.43
foolhardy 4.12
foolish 29.8
foolproof 17.13
foolscap 27.1
foot 30.39
footage 20.9
football 23.14
footballer 12.44
footbed 16.3
footbrake 21.7
footbridge 20.8
footer 12.81
footfall 23.15
foothill 23.9
foothold 16.37
footing 26.13

footle 23.39
footlights 28.47
footlocker 12.40
footloose 28.19
footman 25.45
footmark 21.5
footmen 25.45
footnote 30.35
footpad 16.1
footpath 32.2
footplate 30.11
footprint 30.54
footrest 31.3
footsie 4.47
footslog 18.8
footslogger 12.32
footsore 7.16
footstep 27.3
footstool 23.20
footway 3.25
footwear 2.15
footwork 21.31
footy 4.55
foozle 23.41
fop 27.8
foppery 4.43
foppish 29.9
for 7.1
fora 12.66
forage 20.8
forager 12.35
foray 3.19
forbade 16.1
forbear 2.1, 2.3
forbearance 28.45
Forbes 35.26
forbid 16.8
forbidden 25.40
forbidding 26.5
forbore 7.1
forborne 25.28
forbye 6.1
force 28.15
force majeure 13.1
forcemeat 30.18
forceps 28.46
forcer 12.70
forcible 23.26
ford 16.19
fore 7.1
forearm 24.2
forebear 2.3
forebode 16.23
foreboding 26.5
forecast 31.2
forecaster 12.75
forecastle 23.37
foreclose 35.19
foreclosure 12.33
forecourt 30.33
foredeck 21.6

foredoom 24.12
forefather 12.84
forefeet 30.18
forefinger 12.31
forefoot 30.39
forefront 30.55
foregather 12.84
foregoer 12.17
foregoing 26.3
foregone 25.24
foreground 16.43
forehand 16.40
forehead 16.11
forehock 21.20
foreign 25.18
foreigner 12.55
foreknew 11.1
foreknow 9.1
foreknowledge 20.6
foreknown 25.30
foreland 16.45
foreleg 18.3
forelimb 24.6
forelock 21.21
foreman 25.45
foremast 31.2
foremen 25.45
foremost 31.20
forename 24.4
forenoon 25.33
forensic 21.18
forepart 30.3
forepaw 7.14
forepeak 21.8
foreplay 3.15
foreran 25.1
forerun 25.35
forerunner 12.57
foresail 23.6
foresaw 7.1
foresee 4.1
foreseen 25.9
foreseer 12.3
foreshadow 9.11
foresheets 28.47
foreshore 7.17
foreshorten 25.50
foreshow 9.1
foreshown 25.30
foresight 30.30
foresighted 16.12
foreskin 25.15
forest 31.12
forestall 23.14
forestaller 12.44
forestay 3.22
forester 12.78
forestry 4.40
foretaste 31.4
foretell 23.3
foreteller 12.42

forethought 30.33
foretoken 25.43
foretold 16.37
foretop 27.8
forever 12.85
forevermore 7.1
forewarn 25.28
forewarner 12.56
forewent 30.53
forewing 26.14
forewoman 25.45
forewomen 25.17
foreword 16.31
foreyard 16.2
Forfar 12.30
Forfarshire 12.11
forfeit 30.21
forfeiter 12.78
forfeiture 12.23
forfend 16.41
forgave 34.4
forge 20.12
forger 12.35
forgery 4.43
forget 30.4
forget-me-not 30.32
forgetter 12.76
forgive 34.6
forgiven 25.51
forgiver 12.86
forgo 9.1
forgot 30.31
forgotten 25.50
fork 21.22
forlorn 25.28
form 24.9
formal 23.33
formaldehyde 16.14
formalin 25.16
formalist 31.8
format 30.1
Formby 4.10
forme 24.9
former 12.52
Formica 12.40
Formosa 12.71
formula 12.46
formulae 4.26
formulaic 21.9
formularize 35.13
formulary 4.43
formulate 30.11
formwork 21.31
fornicate 30.10
Forrest 31.12
forsake 21.7
forsaken 25.43
forsaker 12.38
forsook 21.28
forsooth 32.12
Forster 12.80

forswear 2.1
forswore 7.1
Forsyth 32.7
forsythia 12.12
fort 30.33
forte 3.22
Fortean 25.37
forth 32.9
forthcoming 26.9
forthright 30.29
forthwith 33.4
fortieth 32.6
fortifier 12.14
fortify 6.7
fortissimo 9.18
fortitude 16.25
fortnight 30.29
fortnightly 4.25
fortress 28.10
fortuitous 28.34
fortuity 4.53
fortunate 30.43
fortune 25.33
forty 4.54
forty-niner 12.55
forum 24.19
forward 16.30
forwarder 12.29
forwards 35.27
forwent 30.53
Fosbury 4.43
fossa 12.70
fosse 28.14
fossick 21.16
fossicker 12.39
fossil 23.37
foster 12.79
fosterage 20.8
fosterer 12.67
Foucault 9.1
fouetté 4.41
fought 30.33
foul 23.16
foulard 1.12
foumart 30.43
found 16.43
founder 12.28
foundling 26.8
foundry 4.41
fount 30.54, 30.55
fountain 25.19
fountainhead 16.3
fountain pen 25.5
four 7.1
fourfold 16.37
Fourier 12.10
fourscore 7.1
foursquare 2.1
fourteen 25.9
fourteenth 32.19
fourth 32.9

fowl 23.16
fowler 12.44
Fowles 35.29
fowling 26.8
fox 28.40
Foxe 28.40
foxglove 34.13
foxhole 23.17
foxhound 16.43
foxlike 21.19
foxtail 23.6
foxtrot 30.32
foxy 4.46
foyer 3.4
Fra 1.1
frabjous 28.25
fracas 1.11
fracases 35.10
fractal 23.39
fraction 25.49
fractional 23.34
fractionalize 35.12
fractionate 30.13
fractious 28.33
fracture 12.23
fragile 23.11
fragility 4.53
fragmentary 4.43
Fragonard 1.14
fragrance 28.45
fragranced 31.30
fragrancy 4.48
fragrant 30.56
frail 23.5
frailty 4.52
fraise 35.3
Fraktur 12.20
frame 24.4
framer 12.50
framework 21.31
Fran 25.1
franc 21.33
France 28.44
Frances 28.11
Francesca 12.37
franchise 35.14
franchisee 4.1
franchiser 12.91
Francine 25.9
Francis 28.11
Franciscan 25.43
francium 24.16
Franck 21.33
Franco 9.16
François 1.22
Françoise 1.22
francolin 25.16
Francophile 23.11
francophone 25.30
frangible 23.26
frangipane 25.8

frangipani 4.31
franglais 3.15
frank 21.33
Frankenstein 25.23
franker 12.37
Frankfort 30.41
Frankfurt 30.45
frankfurter 12.82
Frankie 4.18
frankincense 28.44
Frankish 29.8
franklin 25.16
Franks 28.41
frantic 21.17
frap 27.1
frappé 3.18
Frascati 4.51
Fraser 12.90
frat 30.1
fraternal 23.34
fraternity 4.53
fratricidal 23.28
fratricide 16.16
Frau 8.1
fraud 16.19
fraudster 12.80
fraudulence 28.45
fraudulent 30.56
fraught 30.33
Fräulein 25.22
Fraunhofer 12.30
fray 3.1
Frazier 12.12
frazil 23.10
frazzle 23.41
freak 21.8
freakish 29.8
freaky 4.18
freckle 23.32
freckly 4.22
Fred 16.3
Freddie 4.12
Frederica 12.38
Frederick 21.15
Fredericton 25.50
free 4.1
freebase 28.5
freebie 4.10
freeboard 16.20
freeboot 30.37
freebooter 12.81
freeborn 25.28
freedman 25.2
freedmen 25.5
freedom 24.17
Freefone 25.30
freehand 16.40
freehold 16.37
freeholder 12.28
freelance 28.44
freeload 16.23

freeloader 12.28
Freeman 25.45
Freemason 25.48
freemasonry 4.39
freemen 25.45
Freeport 30.33
Freepost 31.20
freer 12.3
Freer 12.4
freesia 12.12
freestanding 26.5
freestone 25.31
freestyle 23.12
freestyler 12.44
freethinker 12.39
freethinking 26.7
Freetown 25.29
freeware 2.15
freeway 3.25
freewheel 23.7
freewill 23.8
freeze 35.6
freezer 12.90
Freiburg 18.13
freight 30.7
freightage 20.9
freighter 12.77
Fremantle 23.39
Frémont 30.54
French 29.20
Frenchman 25.45
Frenchmen 25.45
Frenchwoman 25.45
Frenchwomen 25.17
Frenchy 4.50
frenetic 21.17
frenzied 16.13
frenzy 4.61
frequency 4.48
frequent 30.53, 30.56
frequenter 12.76
fresco 9.16
fresh 29.3
freshen 25.49
fresher 12.72
freshman 25.45
freshmen 25.45
freshwater 12.80
Fresnel 23.3
Fresno 9.19
fret 30.4
fretboard 16.20
fretsaw 7.16
fretwork 21.31
Freud 16.24
Freudian 25.37
Frey 3.1
Freya 12.2
friable 23.26
friar 12.13
friary 4.43

fribble 23.26
fricandeau 9.11
fricandeaux 35.19
fricassee 4.48
friction 25.49
Friday 3.9
fridge 20.6
Friedan 25.1
Friedman 25.45
Friedrich 21.15
friend 16.41
friendly 4.22
Fries 35.6
Friesian 25.42
Friesland 16.45
frieze 35.6
frig 18.6, 20.6
frigate 30.21
Frigga 12.31
fright 30.26
frighten 25.50
frightener 12.58
frigid 16.10
frigidaria 12.10
frigidarium 24.16
frigidity 4.53
frill 23.8
frilly 4.24
fringe 20.19
fringy 4.17
Frink 21.33
frippery 4.43
frisbee 4.10
Frisch 29.6
frisée 3.27
Frisian 25.37
frisk 21.35
frisker 12.39
frisket 30.21
frisky 4.19
frisson 25.26
frit 30.20
fritillary 4.43
fritter 12.78
fritto misto 9.24
Fritz 28.47
Friuli 4.26
Friulian 25.37
frivolity 4.53
frivolous 28.27
frizz 35.10
frizzle 23.41
frizzly 4.27
frizzy 4.61
Frobisher 12.72
frock 21.20
froe 9.1
Froebel 23.26
frog 18.8
frogging 26.6
froggy 4.15

frogman 25.45
frogmarch 15.2
frogmen 25.45
frogspawn 25.28
frolic 21.11
frolicker 12.39
from 24.8
fromage blanc 25.24
fromage frais 3.1
frond 16.42
front 30.55
frontage 20.9
frontager 12.35
frontal 23.39
frontbench 29.20
front-bencher 12.72
frontier 12.12
frontiersman 25.45
frontiersmen 25.45
frontierswoman
  25.45
frontierswomen
  25.17
frontispiece 28.6
frontlet 30.22
frontline 25.21
frontman 25.2
frontmen 25.5
fronton 25.50
front-runner 12.57
frontward 16.30
frost 31.17
frostbite 30.26
frosting 26.13
frosty 4.54
froth 32.8
frothy 4.56
frottage 19.1
froufrou 11.17
froward 16.28
frown 25.29
frowst 31.19
frowsty 4.54
frowzy 4.61
froze 35.19
frozen 25.52
fructify 6.7
fructose 35.19
fructuous 28.24
frugal 23.30
fruit 30.37
fruitarian 25.37
fruitbat 30.1
fruitcake 21.7
fruiterer 12.67
fruition 25.49
fruitlet 30.22
fruitwood 16.26
fruity 4.54
frump 27.17
frumpish 29.9

frumpy 4.37
frustrate 30.7
frustrater 12.77
fry 6.1
Frye 6.1
fryer 12.13
frypan 25.3
fry-up 27.13
fubsy 4.47
Fuchs 28.40
fuchsia 12.73
fuci 6.16
fuck 21.29
fucker 12.41
fucus 28.26
fuddle 23.28
fuddy-duddy 4.13
fudge 20.16
fuel 23.25
Fuentes 28.5
fug 18.12
fugacious 28.33
fugacity 4.53
fugal 23.30
fuggy 4.15
fugu 11.8
fugue 18.11
Führer 12.67
Fujairah 12.65
Fuji 4.17
Fujian 25.37
Fulani 4.31
Fulbright 30.29
fulcra 12.66
fulcrum 24.19
fulfil 23.8
fulfill 23.8
fulfiller 12.43
fulgent 30.56
fuliginous 28.29
full 23.21
fullback 21.2
fuller 12.46
fully 4.26
fulmar 12.52
fulminate 30.13
fulness 28.29
fulsome 24.20
Fulton 25.50
fulvous 28.35
fumarole 23.18
fumble 23.26
fumbler 12.48
fume 24.12
fumigant 30.56
fumigate 30.9
fumitory 4.43
fumy 4.30
fun 25.35
funambulist 31.8
Funchal 23.2

function 25.49
functional 23.34
functionalist 31.8
functionary 4.43
fund 16.44
fundamentalist 31.8
fundi 6.6
funeral 23.36
funerary 4.43
funereal 23.24
funfair 2.5
fungal 23.30
fungi 6.8
fungicide 16.16
fungiform 24.9
fungo 9.13
fungoid 16.24
fungous 28.25
fungus 28.25
funicular 12.46
funk 21.34
funkster 12.81
funky 4.20
funnel 23.34
funny 4.33
funster 12.81
fur 13.1
furbelow 9.17
furbish 29.6
furbisher 12.72
furcate 30.10
Furies 35.10
furious 28.23
furl 23.42
furless 28.27
furlong 26.15
furlough 9.17
furnace 28.9
furnish 29.9
furnisher 12.72
furnishing 26.12
furnishings 35.32
furniture 12.23
furore 4.41
furores 35.10
furphy 4.14
furrier 12.10
furriery 4.43
furrow 9.21
furrowy 4.7
furry 4.44
further 12.84
furtherance 28.45
furtherer 12.67
furthermore 7.1
furthermost 31.20
furthest 31.14
furtive 34.8
furuncle 23.32
furunculous 28.27
fury 4.43

furze 35.25
furzy 4.62
fuscous 28.26
fuse 35.21
fusee 4.1
fuselage 19.1
fusible 23.26
fusil 23.10
fusilier 12.4
fusillade 16.6
fusilli 4.23
fusion 25.42
fusional 23.34
fusionist 31.10
fuss 28.21
fusser 12.71
fusspot 30.32
fussy 4.47
fustian 25.37
fustic 21.17
fusty 4.55
futile 23.12
futility 4.53
futon 25.26
futtock 21.30
future 12.24
futurist 31.12
futurity 4.53
futz 28.47
fuze 35.21
fuzee 4.1
fuzz 35.23
fuzzy 4.62
Fyfe 17.7
fylfot 30.31

gab 14.1
gabble 23.26
gabbler 12.42
gabbro 9.21
gabbroid 16.24
gabby 4.10
gaberdine 25.10
gabion 25.37
gable 23.26
Gabo 9.9
Gabon 25.24
Gabonese 35.6
Gábor 7.1
Gaborone 4.33
Gabriel 23.24
Gabrielle 23.3
gad 16.1
gadabout 30.34
Gadarene 25.11
Gaddafi 4.14
gadfly 6.11
gadget 30.21

gadgeteer 12.4
gadgetry 4.40
gadgety 4.53
gadid 16.9
gadoid 16.24
gadwall 23.15
gadzooks 28.40
Gael 23.5
Gaeldom 24.17
Gaelic 21.11
Gaeltacht 30.50
Gaenor 12.54
gaff 17.1
gaffe 17.1
gaffer 12.30
gag 18.1
gaga 1.8
Gagarin 25.18
gage 20.4
gaggle 23.30
gagster 12.74
Gaia 12.13
Gaian 25.38
gaiety 4.53
gaijin 25.13
Gail 23.5
gaillardia 12.5
gaily 4.22
gain 25.7
gainer 12.54
gainsaid 16.3
gainsay 3.1
gainsayer 12.2
Gainsborough 12.67
gait 30.7
gaiter 12.77
Gaitskell 23.9
Gaius 28.24
gal 23.1
gala 12.42
galactic 21.17
galago 9.13
galah 1.1
Galahad 16.1
galantine 25.12
Galatea 12.4
Galatia 12.11
Galatian 25.49
galaxy 4.48
Galba 12.21
Galbraith 32.4
gale 23.5
Galen 25.16
galena 12.54
galette 30.4
Galicia 12.11
Galician 25.37
Galilean 25.36
Galilee 4.24
Galileo 9.2
galingale 23.5

gall 23.14
gallant 30.53, 30.56
gallantry 4.43
Galle 23.14
galleon 25.37
galleria 12.3
gallery 4.43
galley 4.21
galliard 16.2
Gallic 21.11
Gallican 25.43
gallimaufry 4.41
Gallipoli 4.27
gallipot 30.32
gallium 24.16
gallivant 30.53
gallon 25.44
galloon 25.33
gallop 27.14
galloper 12.63
galloway 3.25
gallows 35.19
gallstone 25.31
galluses 35.10
galoot 30.37
galop 27.14
galore 7.1
galosh 29.11
Galsworthy 4.57
Galton 25.50
galumph 17.19
Galvani 4.31
galvanic 21.13
Galveston 25.50
Galway 3.25
gam 24.1
gamay 3.16
gamba 12.21
gambado 9.11
Gambia 12.5
Gambian 25.37
gambit 20.20
gamble 23.26
gambler 12.42
gambol 23.26
gambrel 23.36
game 24.4
gamecock 21.20
gamefowl 23.16
gamekeeper 12.61
gamekeeping 26.10
gamelan 25.2
gamesman 25.45
gamesmen 25.45
gamester 12.77
gamete 30.18
gamin 25.17
gamine 25.11
gamma 12.50
gammon 25.45
gammy 4.29

Gamow 9.18
gamp 27.17
gamut 30.43
gamy 4.29
gander 12.25
Gandhi 4.12
gang 26.1
gangboard 16.20
gangbuster 12.81
ganger 12.60
Ganges 35.7
gangland 16.40
gangling 26.8
ganglion 25.37
gangly 4.21
gangplank 21.33
gangrene 25.11
gangsta 12.74
gangster 12.74
gangway 3.25
ganja 12.35
gannet 30.23
gantlet 30.22
gantry 4.38
Ganymede 16.7
gap 27.1
gape 27.4
gaper 12.61
gappy 4.36
gar 1.1
garage 20.2
garb 14.2
garbage 20.6
garbanzo 9.29
garble 23.26
garbler 12.42
Garbo 9.9
garçon 25.26
Garda 12.25
Gardaí 4.1
garden 25.40
gardener 12.58
gardenia 12.8
Gardner 12.53
Gareth 32.13
Garfield 16.35
garfish 29.7
garganey 4.34
gargantuan 25.38
gargle 23.30
gargoyle 23.19
Garibaldi 4.13
garish 29.9
garland 16.45
garlic 21.11
garlicky 4.19
garment 30.56
garner 12.53
garnet 30.23
garnish 29.9
garnishee 4.1

garnishing 26.12
garniture 12.23
Garonne 25.24
garpike 21.19
garret 30.43
Garrick 21.15
garrison 25.48
garrote 30.31
garrotte 30.31
garrulity 4.53
garrulous 28.27
garter 12.75
garth 32.2
Garvey 4.58
Gary 4.38
gas 28.1
gasbag 18.1
Gascogne 25.32
Gascon 25.43
Gascony 4.34
gaseous 28.23
gash 29.1
Gaskell 23.32
gasket 30.21
gaskin 25.15
gaslight 30.28
gasman 25.2
gasmen 25.5
gasoline 25.10
gasometer 12.78
gasp 27.18
gasper 12.61
Gassendi 4.12
gasser 12.69
gassy 4.45
Gasthaus 28.16
gastric 21.15
gastroenteritis
  28.12
gastronome 24.11
gastronomic 21.12
gastronomical 25.52
gastronomy 4.30
gastropod 16.18
gasworks 28.41
gat 30.1
gate 30.7
gateau 9.24
gateaux 35.19
gatecrash 29.1
gatecrasher 12.72
gatefold 16.37
gatehouse 28.16
gatekeeper 12.61
gatelegged 16.33
gatepost 31.20
Gates 28.47
Gateshead 16.3
gateway 3.25
gather 12.84
gatherer 12.67

g

gathering 26.11
Gatling 26.8
Gatwick 21.18
gauche 29.13
gaucherie 4.43
gaucho 9.10
gaud 16.19
Gaudí 4.13
gaudy 4.13
gauge 20.4
gauger 12.35
Gauguin 25.1
Gaul 23.14
Gaulish 29.8
Gaullist 31.8
gaunt 30.54
gauntlet 30.22
gaur 12.16
Gauss 28.16
Gaussian 25.37
gauze 35.17
gauzy 4.61
gave 34.4
gavel 23.40
Gavin 25.19
gavotte 30.31
Gawain 25.8
Gawd 16.19
gawk 21.22
gawky 4.19
gawp 27.9
gawper 12.62
gay 3.1
gayal 23.2
Gaye 3.1
gayety 4.53
gayness 28.9
Gaynor 12.54
gaze 35.5
gazebo 9.9
gazelle 23.3
gazer 12.90
gazette 30.4
gazetteer 12.4
gazpacho 9.10
gazump 27.17
gazumper 12.63
Gdansk 21.35
Gdynia 12.8
gean 25.9
gear 12.4
gearbox 28.40
gearing 26.11
gearstick 21.17
gearwheel 23.7
Geber 12.21
gecko 9.16
gee 4.1
gee-gee 4.17
geek 21.8
Geelong 26.15

geese 28.6
gee-string 26.11
gee-whiz 35.10
geezer 12.90
Gehrig 18.6
Geikie 4.18
geisha 12.72
gel 23.3
gelada 12.25
gelatin 25.19
gelatinize 35.13
gelatinous 28.29
gelato 9.24
geld 16.35
gelding 26.5
gelid 16.10
gelignite 30.29
Gell-Mann 25.1
gelsemium 24.16
gelt 30.51
gem 24.3
Gemara 12.64
gematria 12.10
Gemini 4.32, 6.13
Geminian 25.38
Geminids 35.27
gem-like 21.19
gemsbok 21.20
gemstone 25.31
gemütlich 21.11
gen 25.5
gendarme 24.2
gendarmerie 4.43
gender 12.26
gene 25.9
genealogist 31.7
genealogy 4.17
genera 12.67
general 23.36
generalissimo 9.18
generalist 31.8
generalizer 12.91
generate 30.15
generic 21.15
generosity 4.53
generous 28.31
genesis 28.11
genet 30.23
Genet 3.1
genetic 21.17
geneticist 31.13
Geneva 12.85
genial 23.23, 23.24
genie 4.31
genii 6.3
genital 23.39
genitalia 12.6
genitival 23.40
genius 28.23
genoa 12.17
genocidal 23.28

genocide 16.16
Genoese 35.6
genome 24.11
genotype 27.7
Genova 12.87
genre 12.65
gens 35.31
gent 30.53
genteel 23.7
gentes 35.9
gentian 25.49
gentile 23.12
gentility 4.53
gentle 23.39
gentlefolk 21.24
gentleman 25.45
gentlemanly 4.27
gentlemen 25.45
gentlewoman 25.45
gentlewomen 25.17
gentoo 11.20
gentrifier 12.14
gentrify 6.7
gentry 4.38
genuflect 30.48
genuflection 25.49
genuflector 12.76
genuine 25.13
genus 28.29
geocentric 21.15
geode 16.23
geodesic 21.16
geodic 21.10
Geoff 17.3
Geoffrey 4.38
geographer 12.30
geographic 21.10
geography 4.14
geoid 16.24
geologist 31.7
geology 4.17
geomancy 4.45
geomantic 21.17
geometer 12.78
geometric 21.15
geometrical 23.32
geometry 4.40
geopolitical 23.32
geopolitics 28.39
Geordie 4.13
George 20.12
Georgetown 25.29
Georgette 30.4
Georgia 12.35
Georgian 25.42
Georgiana 12.53
georgic 21.11
Georgie 4.17
Georgina 12.54
geotechnical 23.32
geothermal 23.33

Geraint 30.54
Gerald 16.38
Geraldine 25.10
Geraldton 25.50
geranium 24.16
Gerard 16.2
gerbera 12.67
gerbil 23.8
Gerda 12.29
geriatric 21.15
germ 24.22
Germaine 25.7
German 25.45
germander 12.25
germane 25.7
Germanic 21.13
Germanist 31.10
germanium 24.16
Germany 4.34
germicidal 23.28
germicide 16.16
germinal 23.34
germinate 30.13
Germiston 25.50
Geronimo 9.18
gerontocracy 4.48
Gerry 4.38
gerrymander 12.25
gerrymanderer
  12.67
Gershwin 25.20
Gertrude 16.25
gerund 16.45
gerundive 34.6
Gervaise 35.5
gesso 9.22
gestalt 30.51
Gestapo 9.20
gestate 30.7
gesticulate 30.11
gesticulatory 4.43
gesture 12.23
gesundheit 30.27
get 30.4
getaway 3.25
Gethin 25.19
getter 12.76
Getty 4.51
Gettysburg 18.13
gewgaw 7.7
geyser 12.90
Ghana 12.53
Ghanaian 25.36
ghastly 4.21
ghat 30.3
Ghazi 4.61
ghee 4.1
Ghent 30.53
gherkin 25.15
ghetto 9.24
ghettoize 35.11

Ghibelline 25.10
Ghiberti 4.51
ghillie 4.24
ghost 31.20
ghostlike 21.19
ghostly 4.25
ghostwriter 12.79
ghoul 23.20
ghoulish 29.8
Giacometti 4.51
giant 30.56
giantess 28.12
gibber 12.21
gibberish 29.9
gibbet 30.20
gibbon 25.38
Gibbons 35.31
gibbous 28.24
Gibbs 35.26
giblets 28.47
Gibraltar 12.80
Gibraltarian 25.37
Gibson 25.48
giddy 4.12
Gide 16.7
Gideon 25.37
Gielgud 16.26
gift 30.47
giftware 2.15
giftwrap 27.1
gig 18.6
gigabyte 30.26
gigaflop 27.8
gigantic 21.17
giggle 23.30
giggler 12.48
giggly 4.24
Gigli 4.23
gigolo 9.17
gigot 30.42
Gilbert 30.41
Gilbertian 25.37
gild 16.35
Giles 35.29
gilet 3.1
gilgai 6.8
Gilgamesh 29.3
Gill 23.8
Gillespie 4.36
Gillian 25.37
gillie 4.24
Gillies 35.10
Gillingham 24.19
Gilly 4.24
Gilroy 10.11
gilt 30.51
gilt-edged 16.34
giltwood 16.26
gimbal 23.26
gimcrack 21.3
gimcrackery 4.43

gimlet 30.22
gimme 4.29
gimmick 21.12
gimmickry 4.40
gimmicky 4.19
gimp 27.17
gimpy 4.36
gin 25.13
Gina 12.54
ginger 12.35
gingerbread 16.4
gingerly 4.27
gingery 4.43
gingham 24.19
gingivitis 28.12
gink 21.33
ginkgo 9.16
Ginny 4.32
Gino 9.19
ginormous 28.28
Ginsberg 18.13
ginseng 26.2
Giorgione 4.33
Giotto 9.25
Giovanni 4.31
giraffe 17.2
girandole 23.17
girasol 23.13
gird 16.31
girder 12.29
girdle 23.28
girl 23.42
girlfriend 16.41
girlhood 16.26
girlie 4.28
girlish 29.8
giro 9.21
Gironde 16.42
Girondin 25.14
Girondist 31.6
girt 30.45
girth 32.14
Gisborne 25.53
Giselle 23.3
Gish 29.6
Gissing 26.12
gist 31.6
git 30.20
gîte 30.18
gittern 25.53
Giuseppe 4.36
give 34.6
giveaway 3.25
given 25.51
giver 12.86
gizmo 9.18
gizzard 16.30
glacé 3.20
glacial 23.38
glaciated 16.12
glacier 12.11

glacis 28.11
glad 16.1
gladden 25.40
gladdon 25.40
glade 16.6
gladiatorial 23.24
gladioli 6.11
gladiolus 28.27
Gladstone 25.50
Gladwin 25.20
Gladys 28.7
glair 2.1
glairy 4.39
glam 24.1
glamor 12.50
Glamorgan 25.41
glamorize 35.13
glamorous 28.31
glamour 12.50
glance 28.44
gland 16.40
glanders 35.24
glandular 12.46
glans 35.31
glare 2.1
glary 4.39
Glasgow 9.13
glasnost 31.17
glass 28.2
glasses 35.10
glasshouse 28.16
glassine 25.11
glass-like 21.19
glassware 2.15
glassy 4.45
Glastonbury 4.43
Glaswegian 25.42
glaucoma 12.52
glaucous 28.26
glaze 35.5
glazer 12.90
glazier 12.12
glazy 4.61
gleam 24.5
gleamy 4.29
glean 25.9
gleaner 12.54
gleanings 35.32
glebe 16.6
glee 4.1
glen 25.5
Glenda 12.26
Glendower 12.16
Gleneagles 35.29
glengarry 4.38
Glenn 25.5
Glenrothes 28.12
Glenys 28.9
glib 14.7
glide 16.14
glider 12.27

glim 24.6
glimmer 12.51
glimmering 26.11
glimpse 28.43
Glinka 12.39
glint 30.54
glissade 16.2
glissandi 4.12
glissando 9.11
glissé 3.1
glisten 25.48
glister 12.78
glitch 15.6
glitter 12.78
glitterati 4.51
glittery 4.43
glitz 28.47
glitzy 4.46
gloaming 26.9
gloat 30.35
gloater 12.80
glob 14.9
global 23.26
globe 14.11
globe-like 21.19
globetrotter 12.79
globoid 16.24
globose 28.17
globular 12.46
globule 23.20
globulin 25.16
Glockenspiel 23.7
glom 24.8
gloom 24.12
gloomy 4.30
glop 27.8
Gloria 12.10
Gloriana 12.53
glorifier 12.14
glorify 6.7
gloriole 23.17
glorious 28.23
glory 4.41
gloss 28.14
glossal 23.37
glossary 4.43
glosser 12.70
glossy 4.46
glottal 23.39
glottis 28.12
Gloucester 12.79
glove 34.13
Glover 12.87
glow 9.1
glower 12.16
gloxinia 12.8
Gluck 21.28
glucose 35.19
glue 11.1
gluey 4.8
glug 18.12

g

Glühwein 25.23
glum 24.14
gluon 25.24
glut 30.40
glutamate 30.12
gluteal 23.24
gluten 25.19
glutinous 28.29
glutton 25.50
gluttonize 35.13
gluttonous 28.29
gluttony 4.34
glycerin 25.11
glycerine 25.11
glycine 25.11
glycogen 25.42
glycol 23.13
Glyn 25.13
Glynis 28.9
glyph 17.6
glyptic 21.17
gnamma 12.50
gnarl 23.2
gnarly 4.21
gnash 29.1
gnat 30.1
gnaw 7.1
gneiss 28.13
gnocchi 4.19
gnome 24.11
gnomic 21.12
gnomish 29.8
gnomon 25.25
gnostic 21.17
gnu 11.1
go 9.1
goad 16.23
go-ahead 16.3
goal 23.17
goalball 23.14
goalie 4.25
goalkeeper 12.61
goalkeeping 26.10
goalmouth 32.10
goalpost 31.20
goalscorer 12.66
goalscoring 26.11
goaltending 26.5
Goan 25.38
Goanese 35.6
goat 30.35
goatee 4.1
goatherd 16.31
goatish 29.10
goatskin 25.15
goaty 4.54
gob 14.9
gobbet 30.20
Gobbi 4.10
gobble 23.26
gobbledegook 21.27

gobbler 12.44
Gobelins 35.31
go-between 25.12
Gobineau 9.19
goblet 30.22
goblin 25.16
go-by 6.5
god 16.18
Godard 1.6
godchild 16.36
godchildren 25.47
goddam 24.1
Goddard 16.2
goddess 28.7
Gödel 23.28
godet 30.4
godetia 12.11
godets 28.47
godfather 12.84
God-fearing 26.11
godforsaken 25.43
Godfrey 4.41
Godgiven 25.51
godhead 16.3
Godiva 12.86
godless 28.27
godlike 21.19
godly 4.25
Godman 25.45
godmother 12.84
godown 25.29
godparent 30.56
godsend 16.41
godship 27.6
godson 25.35
Godspeed 16.7
Godunov 17.8
Godwin 25.20
Godwottery 4.43
Godzilla 12.43
Goebbels 35.29
goer 12.17
Goering 26.11
Goethe 12.82
Goethean 25.37
gofer 12.30
goffer 12.30
go-getter 12.76
goggle 23.30
go-go 9.13
Gogol 23.13
going 26.3
goiter 12.81
goitre 12.81
go-kart 30.3
Golan Heights 28.47
Golconda 12.28
gold 16.37
golden 25.40
golden-ager 12.35
goldeneye 6.13

goldenrod 16.18
goldfield 16.35
goldfinch 29.20
goldfish 29.7
Goldie 4.13
Goldilocks 28.40
Golding 26.5
Goldman 25.45
Goldmark 21.5
goldmine 25.22
Goldschmidt 30.23
goldsmith 32.6
Goldwyn 25.20
golem 24.18
golf 17.18
golfer 12.30
Golgotha 12.83
Goliath 32.13
Gollancz 28.41
golliwog 18.8
gollop 27.14
golly 4.25
gombeen 25.9
Gomorrah 12.65
gonad 16.1
gondola 12.48
gondolier 12.4
Gondwanaland 16.40
gone 25.24
goner 12.56
gonfalon 25.44
gong 26.15
gonna 12.56
gonorrhea 12.4
gonorrhoea 12.4
gonzo 9.29
goo 11.1
good 16.26
Goodall 23.14
goodby 6.1
goodbye 6.1
good-hearted 16.12
goodish 29.6
goodly 4.26
good-natured 16.28
goodnight 30.26
good-oh 9.1
goods 35.27
goodwife 17.7
goodwill 23.8
Goodwin 25.20
goodwives 35.35
Goodwood 16.26
goody 4.13
Goodyear 12.12
gooey 4.8
goof 17.13
goofball 23.14
goofy 4.14
google 23.30

googly 4.26
googol 23.13
gook 21.27
goolie 4.26
goon 25.33
goop 27.11
goopy 4.37
goosander 12.25
goose 28.19
gooseberry 4.43
goosebumps 28.46
gooseflesh 29.3
goosefoot 30.39
goosegrass 28.2
goosestep 27.3
goosey 4.47
Goossens 35.31
gopher 12.30
goral 23.36
Gorbachev 17.8
Gorbals 35.29
gorblimey 4.29
gorcock 21.20
Gordimer 12.51
Gordium 24.16
Gordon 25.40
gore 7.1
Gore-tex 28.38
gorge 20.12
gorgeous 28.25
gorger 12.35
Gorgio 9.15
gorgon 25.41
gorgonian 25.37
Gorgonzola 12.44
gorilla 12.43
Goring 26.11
Gorky 4.19
Goronwy 4.59
gorse 28.15
Gorsedd 33.1
gorsy 4.47
gory 4.41
gosh 29.11
goshawk 21.22
gosling 26.8
go-slow 9.1
gospel 23.35
gospeler 12.48
gospeller 12.48
Goss 28.14
gossamer 12.52
gossamery 4.43
gossip 27.6
gossiper 12.62
gossipy 4.36
got 30.31
gotcha 12.24
Goth 32.8
Gotha 12.83
Gotham 24.20

Gothenburg 18.13
Gothic 21.18
gotta 12.79
gouache 29.2
Gouda 12.28
gouge 20.13
gouger 12.35
goujons 35.31
goulash 29.1
Gould 16.37
Gounod 9.19
gourami 4.29
gourd 16.28
gourmand 16.45
gourmandize 35.11
gourmet 3.16
gout 30.34
govern 25.51
governance 28.45
governessy 4.46
governor 12.58
gowan 25.38
gowk 21.23
gown 25.29
Goya 12.18
goyim 24.6
Gozo 9.29
grab 14.1
grabber 12.21
grabble 23.26
grabby 4.10
graben 25.38
Gracchus 28.26
grace 28.5
Gracie 4.45
gracile 23.9
gracious 28.33
grackle 23.32
grad 16.1
gradate 30.7
grade 16.6
grader 12.26
gradient 30.56
gradine 25.10
grading 26.5
gradual 23.25
graduand 16.40
graduate 30.8, 30.41
Graeme 24.15
Graf 17.2
graffiti 4.52
graffitist 31.14
graffito 9.24
graft 30.47
grafter 12.75
Grafton 25.50
graham 24.15
Grail 23.5
grain 25.7
grainer 12.54
Grainger 12.35

grainy 4.31
gram 24.1
grammar 12.50
grammarian 25.37
grammatical 23.32
Grammy 4.29
gramophone 25.30
Grampian 25.37
grampus 28.30
Gramsci 4.50
gran 25.1
Granada 12.25
granary 4.43
Gran Canaria 12.10
Gran Chaco 9.16
grand 16.40
grandad 16.1
grandam 24.1
grandchild 16.36
grandchildren 25.47
granddaughter
    12.80
grandee 4.1
grandeur 12.35
grandfather 12.84
grandfatherly 4.27
grandiloquence
    28.45
grandiloquent 30.56
grandiose 28.17
grandiosity 4.53
grandma 1.13
grand mal 23.1
grandmama 1.13
grandmaster 12.75
grandmother 12.84
grandmotherly 4.27
grandpa 1.15
grandpapa 1.15
grandparent 30.56
Grand Prix 4.1
grandson 25.35
grandstand 16.40
grange 20.19
granita 12.77
granite 30.23
granny 4.31
granola 12.44
grant 30.53
grantee 4.1
granter 12.75
Granth 30.55
Grantha 12.81
grantor 7.1
gran turismo 9.18
granular 12.46
granularity 4.53
granulate 30.11
granule 23.20
Granville 23.10
grape 27.4

grapefruit 30.37
grapeshot 30.32
grapevine 25.23
graph 17.2
graphic 21.10
graphical 23.32
graphite 30.27
grapnel 23.34
grappa 12.61
Grappelli 4.22
grapple 23.35
grappler 12.48
Grasmere 12.7
grasp 27.18
grasper 12.61
grass 28.2
grasscloth 32.8
Grasse 28.2
grasshopper 12.62
grassland 16.40
grass-like 21.19
grassy 4.45
grate 30.7
grater 12.77
graticule 23.20
gratifier 12.14
gratify 6.7
gratin 25.3
gratiné 3.17
grating 26.13
gratis 28.12
gratitude 16.25
gratuitous 28.34
gratuity 4.53
graunch 29.20
gravadlax 28.38
grave 34.2, 34.4
gravedigger 12.31
gravel 23.40
gravelly 4.27
graven 25.51
graver 12.85
Graves 34.2, 35.35
graveside 16.16
gravestone 25.31
graveyard 16.2
gravitas 28.1
gravitate 30.16
gravity 4.53
gravlax 28.38
gravure 12.20
gravy 4.58
gray 3.1
graybeard 16.28
grayish 29.6
grayling 26.8
grayness 28.9
Graz 28.47
graze 35.5
grazer 12.90
grazier 12.12

grease 28.6
greasepaint 30.54
greaseproof 17.13
greaser 12.69
greasy 4.45
great 30.7
greatcoat 30.35
greave 34.5
Greaves 35.35
grebe 14.6
grebo 9.9
Grecian 25.49
Greece 28.6
greed 16.7
greedy 4.12
Greek 21.8
green 25.9
Greenaway 3.25
greenback 21.2
greenbottle 23.39
Greene 25.9
greenery 4.43
greenfeed 16.7
Greenfield 16.35
greenfinch 29.20
greenfly 6.11
greengage 20.4
greengrocer 12.71
greengrocery 4.43
greenhead 16.3
greenheart 30.3
greenhorn 25.28
greenhouse 28.16
greening 26.9
greenish 29.9
greenkeeper 12.61
greenkeeping 26.10
Greenland 16.45
Greenlander 12.29
Greenock 21.30
Greenpeace 28.6
green room 24.12
greensand 16.40
greenshank 21.33
greenskeeper 12.61
greenstone 25.31
greenstuff 17.15
greensward 16.21
Greenwich 15.6
greenwood 16.26
greeny 4.31
Greer 12.4
greet 30.18
greeter 12.77
greeting 26.13
Greg 18.3
gregarious 28.23
Gregor 12.31
Gregory 4.43
greisen 25.52
gremlin 25.16

Grenada 12.26
grenade 16.6
Grenadian 25.37
grenadier 12.4
grenadine 25.10
Grendel 23.28
Grenfell 23.3
Grenoble 23.26
Grenville 23.10
Gresham 24.20
Greta 12.76
Greville 23.10
grew 11.1
grey 3.1
greybeard 16.28
Greyfriars 35.24
greyhound 16.43
greyish 29.6
greylag 18.1
greyness 28.9
Gribble 23.26
gricer 12.70
grid 16.8
griddle 23.28
gridiron 25.38
gridlock 21.21
grief 17.5
Grieg 18.5
Grierson 25.48
grievance 28.45
grieve 34.5
griever 12.85
grievous 28.35
griffin 25.14
Griffith 32.6
griffon 25.41
grift 30.47
grifter 12.78
grig 18.6
grill 23.8
grillade 16.6
grillage 20.6
grille 23.8
griller 12.43
grilling 26.8
grilse 28.42
grim 24.6
grimace 28.28
grimacer 12.71
Grimaldi 4.13
grimalkin 25.15
grime 24.7
Grimes 35.30
Grimm 24.6
Grimond 16.45
Grimsby 4.10
grimy 4.29
grin 25.13
grind 16.42
grinder 12.27
grindstone 25.31

gringo 9.13
grinner 12.55
grip 27.6
gripe 27.7
griper 12.62
gripper 12.62
grippy 4.36
Griqua 12.38
grisaille 23.5
Griselda 12.26
grisette 30.4
griskin 25.15
grisly 4.24
grison 25.52
grissini 4.31
grist 31.6
gristle 23.37
gristly 4.24
gristmill 23.9
grit 30.20
gritter 12.78
gritty 4.53
grizzle 23.41
grizzler 12.43
grizzly 4.24
groan 25.30
groaner 12.56
groat 30.35
grocer 12.71
grocery 4.43
grockle 23.32
Grodno 9.19
grog 18.8
groggy 4.15
grogram 24.19
groin 25.32
grommet 30.23
Gromyko 9.16
Groningen 25.46
groom 24.12
groove 34.12
groovy 4.58
grope 27.10
groper 12.63
Gropius 28.23
grosbeak 21.8
groschen 25.49
grosgrain 25.8
gross 28.17
Grosz 28.17
grot 30.31
grotesque 21.35
grotesquerie 4.43
Grotius 28.23
grotto 9.25
grotty 4.54
grouch 15.9
grouchy 4.11
ground 16.43
grounder 12.28
groundhog 18.8

grounding 26.5
groundling 26.8
groundnut 30.40
grounds 35.31
groundsel 23.37
groundsheet 30.19
groundsman 25.45
groundsmen 25.45
groundswell 23.4
groundwork 21.31
group 27.11
groupage 20.7
grouper 12.63
groupie 4.37
grouping 26.10
grouse 28.16
grouser 12.70
grout 30.34
grouter 12.80
grove 34.11
grovel 23.40
groveler 12.48
groveller 12.48
Grover 12.86
Groves 35.35
grovy 4.58
grow 9.1
growbag 18.1
grower 12.17
growl 23.16
growler 12.44
Growmore 7.12
grown 25.30
grown-up 27.13
growth 32.11
groyne 25.32
Grozny 4.32
grub 14.13
grubber 12.22
grubby 4.10
grubstake 21.7
grudge 20.16
grudger 12.36
gruel 23.25
grueling 26.8
gruelling 26.8
gruff 17.15
grumble 23.26
grumbler 12.47
grumbling 26.8
grumbly 4.26
grump 27.17
grumpish 29.9
grumpy 4.37
grunge 20.19
grungy 4.17
grunion 25.52
grunt 30.55
grunter 12.81

Gruyère 2.16
grysbok 21.20
guacamole 4.25
guacharo 9.21
Guadalajara 12.64
Guadalcanál 23.1
Guadeloupe 27.11
Guadeloupian 25.37
Guam 24.2
guan 25.4
guanaco 9.16
Guangdong 26.15
guano 9.19
guar 1.1
Guarani 4.1
guarantee 4.1
guarantor 7.1
guaranty 4.55
guard 16.2
guardant 30.56
guardhouse 28.16
Guardi 4.12
guardian 25.37
guard rail 23.6
guardroom 24.12
guardsman 25.45
guardsmen 25.45
Guarneri 4.39
Guatemala 12.42
Guatemalan 25.44
guava 12.85
Guayaquil 23.7
gubbins 35.31
gubernatorial 23.24
gudgeon 25.42
Gudrun 25.34
Guelphic 21.10
guenon 25.24
guerdon 25.40
Guernica 12.39
Guernsey 4.62
guerrilla 12.43
guess 28.3
guesser 12.69
guesstimate 30.12, 30.43
guesswork 21.31
guest 31.3
guestbook 21.26
guesthouse 28.16
Guevara 12.64
guff 17.15
guffaw 7.1
Guggenheim 24.7
Guiana 12.53
guidance 28.45
guide 16.14
guidebook 21.28
guideline 25.22
guidepost 31.20
Guider 12.27

guideway 3.25
Guido 9.11
guidon 25.40
Guignol 23.13
guild 16.35
guilder 12.27
Guildford 16.28
guildhall 23.15
guildsman 25.45
guildsmen 25.45
guile 23.11
Guillaume 24.11
guillemot 30.31
guilloche 29.13
guillotine 25.12
guilt 30.51
guilty 4.53
guinea 4.32
Guinean 25.37
Guinevere 12.12
guise 35.11
guitar 1.1
guitarist 31.12
Gujarat 30.3
Gujarati 4.51
Gujranwala 12.42
Gujrat 30.3
gulag 18.1
gulch 15.15
gulden 25.40
gules 35.29
gulf 17.18
gull 23.22
gullet 30.22
gulley 4.26
gullible 23.26
gully 4.26
gulp 27.16
gulper 12.63
gulpy 4.37
gum 24.14
gumbo 9.9
gumboot 30.37
gumdrop 27.8
gummy 4.30
gumption 25.49
gumshield 16.35
gumshoe 11.19
gun 25.35
gunboat 30.35
gundog 18.8
gunfight 30.27
gunfighter 12.79
gunfire 12.14
gunge 20.19
gung-ho 9.1
gungy 4.17
gunk 21.34
gunless 28.27
gunlock 21.21
gunman 25.45

gunmen 25.45
gunmetal 23.39
Gunn 25.35
gunnel 23.34
gunner 12.57
gunnera 12.67
gunnery 4.43
gunny 4.33
gunplay 3.15
gunpoint 30.55
gunpowder 12.28
gunroom 24.12
gunrunner 12.57
gunrunning 26.9
gunsel 23.37
gunship 27.6
gunshot 30.32
gun-shy 6.17
gunsight 30.30
gunslinger 12.60
gunslinging 26.10
gunsmith 32.6
gunstock 21.21
Gunter 12.81
Gunther 12.83
gunwale 23.34
gunyah 12.89
guppy 4.37
Gupta 12.81
gurdwara 12.64
gurgle 23.30
Gurkha 12.41
Gurkhali 4.21
gurnard 16.29
gurney 4.34
guru 11.17
Gus 28.21
gush 29.16
gusher 12.73
gushing 26.12
gushy 4.50
gusset 30.24
gust 31.24
gustatory 4.43
Gustave 34.2
gusto 9.25
gusty 4.55
gut 30.40
Gutenberg 18.13
Guthrie 4.42
Gutiérrez 35.3
gutless 28.27
gutsy 4.47
gutter 12.81
guttersnipe 27.7
gutty 4.55
guv 34.13
guv'nor 12.57
guy 6.1
Guyana 12.53
Guyanese 35.6

Guyenne 25.5
guzzle 23.41
guzzler 12.48
Gwalior 7.3
Gwen 25.5
Gwenda 12.26
Gwendolen 25.16
Gwent 30.53
Gwyn 25.13
Gwynedd 33.9
Gwyneth 32.6
Gwynfor 7.20
gybe 14.8
gym 24.6
gymkhana 12.53
gymnasia 12.12
gymnasial 23.24
gymnasium 24.16
gymnast 31.1
gymnastic 21.17
gymnosophy 4.14
gymnosperm 24.22
gymslip 27.6
gynaecea 12.3
gynaecocracy 4.48
gynaecology 4.17
gynandrous 28.31
gynecocracy 4.48
gynecology 4.17
gyp 27.6
gypsum 24.20
Gypsy 4.46
Gypsyish 29.6
gyrate 30.7
gyration 25.49
gyrator 12.77
gyratory 4.43
gyre 12.13
gyrfalcon 25.43
gyro 9.21
gyropilot 30.42
gyroplane 25.8
gyroscope 27.10
gyroscopic 21.14
gyve 34.9

ha 1.1
Haarlem 24.18
Habakkuk 21.29
habanera 12.65
haberdasher 12.72
haberdashery 4.43
habilitate 30.16
habit 30.20
habitant 30.56
habitat 30.2
habitual 23.25
habituate 30.8

habitude 16.25
habitué 3.6
Habsburg 18.13
hacek 21.6
hacienda 12.26
hack 21.1
hackberry 4.43
hacker 12.37
hackery 4.43
hackle 23.32
hackney 4.31
hacksaw 7.16
had 16.1
haddock 21.30
Hadean 25.37
Hades 35.7
Hadith 32.5
Hadlee 4.21
hadn't 30.56
Hadrian 25.37
haematology 4.17
haemoglobin 25.13
haemophilia 12.6
haemophiliac 21.1
haemorrhage 20.8
haemorrhoid 16.24
haemostat 30.2
hafiz 35.10
haft 30.47
hag 18.1
Hagar 1.8
Haggadah 12.25
Haggadic 21.10
Haggadoth 30.35
Haggai 6.8
haggard 16.28
haggis 28.7
haggish 29.7
haggle 23.30
haggler 12.48
Hagiographa 12.30
hagiographer 12.30
hagiographic 21.10
hagiography 4.14
hagiolatry 4.43
hagiology 4.17
hagridden 25.40
Hague 18.4
hah 1.1
ha-ha 1.1, 1.9
Hahn 25.4
Haida 12.27
Haifa 12.30
Haig 18.4
haik 21.19
haiku 11.12
hail 23.5
hailer 12.43
Haile Selassie 4.45
hailstone 25.31
Hailwood 16.26

h

Haiphong 26.15
hair 2.1
hairbrush 29.16
haircare 2.7
haircloth 32.8
haircut 30.40
hairdo 11.6
hairdresser 12.69
hairdressing 26.12
hairdryer 12.14
hairgrip 27.6
hairline 25.22
hairnet 30.5
hairpiece 28.6
hairpin 25.18
hairspray 3.19
hairstreak 21.8
hairstyle 23.12
hairstyling 26.8
hairstylist 31.8
hairy 4.39
Haiti 4.52
Haitian 25.49
haji 4.17
hajj 20.1
haka 12.37
hake 21.7
Hakenkreuz 28.47
hakim 24.5
Hakka 12.37
Hakluyt 30.37
Hal 23.1
Halacha 1.1
Halafian 25.37
halal 23.2
halation 25.49
halberd 16.28
halcyon 25.37
Haldane 25.7
hale 23.5
Hales 35.29
Haley 4.22
half 17.2
halfback 21.2
halfpence 28.45
halfpenny 4.31
halfpennyworth 32.14
half-time 24.7
half-tone 25.30
half-track 21.3
halfway 3.1
halfwit 30.25
half-witted 16.12
halibut 30.41
Halicarnassus 28.32
Halifax 28.38
halite 30.28
halitosis 28.11
hall 23.14

Hallé 3.15
hallelujah 12.89
Haller 12.42
Halley 4.21
Halliday 3.9
hallmark 21.5
halloo 11.1
hallow 9.17
Halloween 25.9
Hallowes 35.19
hallstand 16.40
Hallstatt 30.3
hallucinate 30.13
hallucinatory 4.43
hallucinogen 25.42
hallucinogenic 21.13
hallway 3.25
halma 12.50
Halmahera 12.65
halo 9.17
halogen 25.42
Hals 28.42
halt 30.51
halter 12.80
halterneck 21.6
halva 12.85
halve 34.2
halyard 16.30
ham 24.1
Hamada 12.25
hamadryad 16.28
hamadryas 28.24
hamartia 12.12
Hamas 28.1
hambone 25.30
Hamburg 18.13
hamburger 12.32
Hamelin 25.16
hames 35.30
Hamilcar 1.11
Hamilton 25.50
Hamish 29.8
Hamite 30.29
hamlet 30.22
hammer 12.50
Hammerfest 31.3
hammerhead 16.3
hammering 26.11
hammerlock 21.21
Hammerstein 25.23
Hammett 30.23
hammock 21.30
Hammond 16.45
hammy 4.29
Hamnett 30.23
hamper 12.61
Hampshire 12.11
Hampstead 16.12
Hampton 25.50

hamster 12.74
hamstring 26.11
hamstrung 26.18
Han 25.1
Hancock 21.20
hand 16.40
handbag 18.1
handball 23.14
handbasin 25.48
handbell 23.3
handbill 23.8
handbook 21.28
handbrake 21.7
handcart 30.3
handclap 27.1
handcraft 30.47
handcuff 17.15
Handel 23.28
handgrip 27.6
handgun 25.35
handhold 16.37
handicap 27.1
handicapper 12.61
handicraft 30.47
handiwork 21.31
handkerchief 17.6
handkerchiefs 28.37
handle 23.28
handlebar 1.4
handler 12.42
handlist 31.8
handmade 16.6
handmaid 16.6
handmaiden 25.40
handout 30.34
handover 12.86
hand-pick 21.9
hand-picked 30.49
handpump 27.17
handrail 23.6
handset 30.5
handshake 21.7
handspike 21.19
handspring 26.11
handstand 16.40
handwork 21.31
handworked 30.49
handwriting 26.13
handwritten 25.50
handy 4.12
handyman 25.2
handymen 25.5
hang 26.1
hangar 12.60
hangdog 18.8
hanger 12.60
hangi 4.35
hanging 26.10
hangman 25.45
hangmen 25.45
hangnail 23.6

hangout 30.34
hangover 12.86
hang-up 27.13
Hangzhou 8.1
hank 21.33
hanker 12.37
hankerer 12.67
hankering 26.11
Hanks 28.41
hanky 4.18
hanky-panky 4.18
Hannah 12.53
Hannibal 23.26
Hanoi 10.1
Hanover 12.86
Hanoverian 25.37
Hans 28.44
Hansard 16.2
Hanse 28.44
hansel 23.37
Hänsel 23.37
hansom 24.20
Hants 28.47
Hanukkah 12.41
Hanuman 25.4
hap 27.1
haphazard 16.30
hapless 28.27
ha'p'orth 32.13
happen 25.46
happening 26.9
happenstance 28.44
happi 4.36
happy 4.36
happy-go-lucky 4.20
hara-kiri 4.40
harangue 26.1
haranguer 12.60
Harare 4.38
harass 28.31
harasser 12.71
harbinger 12.35
harbor 12.21
harborage 20.8
harbour 12.21
harbourage 20.8
harbourmaster (US harbor-master) 12.75
hard 16.2
hardback 21.2
hardball 23.14
hardbitten 25.50
hardboard 16.20
hard-core 7.1
hardcore 7.10
hardcover 12.87
harden 25.40
hardener 12.58

hard hat 30.1
hard-headed 16.9
hard-hearted 16.12
Hardie 4.12
Harding 26.5
hardish 29.6
hardline 25.21
hardliner 12.55
hardstanding 26.5
hard tack 21.4
hardtop 27.8
Hardwar 1.22
hardware 2.15
hardwearing 26.11
hardwood 16.26
hardworking 26.7
hardy 4.12
hare 2.1
harebell 23.3
harebrained 16.41
harelip 27.6
harelipped 30.58
harem 24.19
Harewood 16.26
Hargreaves 35.35
haricot 9.16
Harijan 25.42
hark 21.5
Harlech 22.6
Harlem 24.18
harlequin 25.20
harlequinade 16.6
harlot 30.42
harlotry 4.43
Harlow 9.17
harm 24.2
harmattan 25.50
harmonic 21.13
harmonica 12.39
harmonious 28.23
harmonist 31.10
harmonium 24.16
harmony 4.34
harness 28.9
harnesser 12.70
Harold 16.38
harp 27.2
harper 12.61
harpist 31.11
Harpocrates 35.9
harpoon 25.33
harpooner 12.56
harpsichord 16.21
harpsichordist 31.6
harpy 4.36
harridan 25.40
harrier 12.10
Harries 28.10
Harriet 30.41
Harrington 25.50

Harris 28.10
Harrison 25.48
Harrod 16.29
Harrovian 25.37
harrow 9.21
harrower 12.17
harrumph 17.19
harry 4.38
harsh 29.2
harshen 25.49
hart 30.3
hartal 23.2
Harte 30.3
hartebeest 31.5
Hartford 16.28
Hartlepool 23.20
Hartley 4.21
hartshorn 25.28
harum-scarum 24.19
haruspex 28.38
haruspices 35.8
Harvard 16.29
harvest 31.15
harvester 12.78
harvestman 25.45
harvestmen 25.45
Harvey 4.58
Harwich 20.8
Haryana 12.53
has 35.1, 35.24
Hasdrubal 23.26
Hasek 21.6
hash 29.1
hash-browns 35.31
Hashemite 30.29
hashish 29.5
Hasid 16.11
hasidic 21.10
Hasidim 24.6
haslet 30.22
Hasmonean 25.36
hasn't 30.56
hasp 27.18
Hasselt 30.51
hassle 23.37
hassock 21.30
haste 31.4
hasten 25.48
Hastings 35.32
hasty 4.52
hat 30.1
hatable 23.26
hatband 16.40
hatbox 28.40
hatch 15.1
hatchback 21.2
hatchery 4.43
hatchet 30.20
hatching 26.4
hatchling 26.8
hatchway 3.25

hate 30.7
hater 12.77
hatful 30.47
Hathaway 3.25
Hathor 7.19
hatless 28.27
hatpin 25.18
hatred 16.11
Hatshepsut 30.38
hatstand 16.40
hatter 12.74
Hattie 4.51
Haugh 7.1
haughty 4.54
haul 23.14
haulage 20.6
hauler 12.44
haulier 12.6
haulm 24.9
haunch 29.20
haunt 30.54
haunter 12.80
Hauptmann 25.45
Hausa 12.70
Hausfrau 8.10
hautboy 10.3
haute école 23.13
hauteur 13.1
haut monde 16.42
Havana 12.53
Havant 30.56
have 34.1
Havel 23.40
haven 25.51
haven't 30.56
haver 12.85
Havers 35.24
haversack 21.4
haves 35.35
havildar 1.6
havoc 21.30
haw 7.1
Hawaii 4.4
Hawaiian 25.38
hawfinch 29.20
hawk 21.22
Hawke 21.22
hawker 12.40
Hawking 26.7
Hawkins 35.31
hawkish 29.8
hawkmoth 32.8
Hawksmoor 12.20
Haworth 32.13
hawse 35.17
hawser 12.91
hawthorn 25.28
hay 3.1
haybox 28.40
haycock 21.20
Haydn 25.40

Hayek 21.6
Hayes 35.5
Hayley 4.22
hayloft 30.47
haymaker 12.38
haymaking 26.7
hayrick 21.15
hayride 16.15
Hays 35.5
hayseed 16.7
haystack 21.4
haywire 12.14
Hayworth 32.13
hazard 16.30
hazardous 28.25
haze 35.5
hazel 23.41
hazelnut 30.40
Hazlitt 30.22
hazy 4.61
he 4.1
head 16.3
headache 21.7
headachy 4.18
headage 20.6
headband 16.40
headbanger 12.60
headbanging 26.10
headboard 16.20
headcheese 35.6
headcount 30.55
headdress 28.3
header 12.26
headfirst 31.26
headgear 12.5
headhunt 30.55
headhunter 12.81
heading 26.5
headlamp 27.17
headland 16.45
headlight 30.28
headline 25.22
headliner 12.55
headlock 21.21
headlong 26.15
headman 25.45
headmaster 12.75
headmasterly 4.27
headmen 25.45
headmistress 28.10
headmost 31.20
headnote 30.35
headphone 25.30
headpiece 28.6
headquarter 12.80
headquarters 35.24
headrest 31.3
headroom 24.12
headsail 23.6
headscarf 17.2
headscarves 35.35

h

headset 30.5
headshrinker 12.39
headsman 25.45
headsmen 25.45
headspring 26.11
headsquare 2.15
headstall 23.15
headstock 21.21
headstone 25.31
headstrong 26.15
headteacher 12.23
headward 16.30
headway 3.25
headwind 16.42
headword 16.31
headwork 21.31
heady 4.12
heal 23.7
healer 12.43
health 32.17
healthy 4.56
Heaney 4.31
heap 27.5
hear 12.4
Heard 16.31
hearer 12.67
hearken 25.43
hearsay 3.20
hearse 28.36
heart 30.3
heartache 21.7
heartbeat 30.18
heartbreak 21.7
heartbreaker 12.38
heartbreaking 26.7
heartbroken 25.43
heartburn 25.53
hearten 25.50
heartfelt 30.51
hearth 32.2
hearthrug 18.12
hearthstone 25.31
heartland 16.45
heartrending 26.5
heartsearching 26.4
heartsease 35.8
heartsick 21.16
heartsore 7.16
heartthrob 14.9
heart-to-heart 30.3
heartwarming 26.9
heartwood 16.26
hearty 4.51
heat 30.18
heater 12.77
heath 32.5
heathen 25.51
heathendom 24.17
heathenish 29.9
heather 12.84
heathery 4.43

heathland 16.45
Heathrow 9.1
heathy 4.56
heatproof 17.13
heatstroke 21.24
heatwave 34.4
heave 34.5
heave-ho 9.1
heaven 25.51
heavenly 4.22
heavenward 16.30
heaver 12.85
heavy 4.58
heavy-handed 16.9
heavy-hearted 16.12
heavyish 29.6
heavyset 30.4
heavyweight 30.17
Hebe 4.10
hebetude 16.25
Hebraic 21.9
Hebraist 31.6
Hebrew 11.17
Hebridean 25.36
Hebrides 35.7
Hebron 25.26
Hecate 4.55
hecatomb 24.12
heck 21.6
heckelphone 25.30
heckle 23.32
heckler 12.48
hectarage 20.8
hectare 2.14
hectic 21.17
hector 12.76
Hecuba 12.21
he'd 16.7
heddle 23.28
hedge 20.3
hedgehog 18.8
hedgehop 27.8
hedger 12.35
hedgerow 9.21
Hedges 35.10
Hedley 4.22
hedonist 31.10
heebie-jeebies 35.10
heed 16.7
hee-haw 7.8
heel 23.7
heelball 23.14
heelbar 1.4
heeltap 27.1
heft 30.47
hefty 4.51
Hegel 23.30
Hegelian 25.37
hegemonic 21.13
hegemony 4.34
Hegira 12.65

Heidegger 12.31
Heidelberg 18.13
Heidi 4.12
heifer 12.30
heigh 3.1
heigh-ho 9.1
height 30.26
heighten 25.50
Heilbronn 25.26
Heilong 26.15
Heine 4.32
heinous 28.29
Heinz 35.31
heir 2.1
heirdom 24.17
heiress 28.10
heirloom 24.12
Heisenberg 18.13
heist 31.16
Hekla 12.42
held 16.35
Helen 25.16
Helena 12.55
helenium 24.16
Helga 12.31
Helgoland 16.40
helianthemum 24.19
helianthus 28.35
helical 23.32
helices 35.8
Helicon 25.43
helicopter 12.79
Heligoland 16.40
Heliogabalus 28.27
heliogram 24.1
heliograph 17.2
Heliopolis 28.8
Helios 28.14
heliotrope 27.10
heliotropic 21.14
helipad 16.1
heliport 30.33
helium 24.16
helix 28.39
he'll 23.7
hell 23.3
hellacious 28.33
Helladic 21.10
Hellas 28.1
hellcat 30.1
hellebore 7.4
helleborine 25.11
Hellene 25.10
Hellenic 21.13
Hellenist 31.10
Heller 12.42
Hellespont 30.54
hellfire 12.13
hellhole 23.17
hellhound 16.43

hellion 25.52
hellish 29.8
Hellman 25.45
hello 9.1
hellraiser 12.90
hellraising 26.14
helluva 12.87
hellward 16.30
helm 24.18
helmet 30.23
Helmholtz 28.47
Helms 35.30
helmsman 25.45
helmsmen 25.45
Héloïse 35.6
Helot 30.42
helotry 4.43
help 27.16
helper 12.61
helping 26.10
helpline 25.22
Helpmann 25.45
helpmate 30.12
Helsingborg 18.9
Helsingor 12.60
Helsinki 4.19
helter-skelter 12.76
helve 34.15
Helvetia 12.11
Helvetian 25.49
Helvetic 21.17
hem 24.3
he-man 25.2
hematology 4.17
Hemel Hempstead 16.4
he-men 25.5
Hemingway 3.25
hemipteran 25.47
hemisphere 12.5
hemispheric 21.15
hemispherical 23.32
hemistich 21.17
hemline 25.22
hemlock 21.21
hemoglobin 25.13
hemophilia 12.6
hemophiliac 21.1
hemorrhage 20.8
hemorrhoid 16.24
hemp 27.17
hempen 25.46
hemstitch 15.6
hen 25.5
Henan 25.46
hence 28.44
henceforth 32.9
henceforward 16.30
henchman 25.45
henchmen 25.45
hendiadys 28.7

Hendrix 28.39
Hendry 4.38
henge 20.19
henna 12.53
henpeck 21.6
Henri 4.38
Henrietta 12.76
henry 4.38
Henze 12.69
hep 27.3
hepatic 21.17
hepatica 12.39
hepatitis 28.12
Hepburn 25.53
Hephaestus 28.34
Hepplewhite 30.30
heptad 16.1
heptagon 25.41
heptagonal 23.34
heptameter 12.78
heptarchic 21.11
heptathlete 30.18
heptathlon 25.44
Hepworth 32.14
her 13.1
Hera 12.67
Heracles 35.7
Heraclitus 28.34
Heraklion 25.37
herald 16.38
heraldic 21.10
heraldist 31.6
heraldry 4.43
herb 14.15
herbaceous 28.33
herbage 20.6
herbal 23.26
herbalist 31.8
herbaria 12.10
herbarium 24.16
Herbert 30.41
herbicide 16.16
herbivore 7.20
herbivorous 28.31
herby 4.10
Herculaneum 24.16
Herculean 25.36
Hercules 35.7
herd 16.31
herder 12.29
herdsman 25.45
herdsmen 25.45
Herdwick 21.18
here 12.4
hereabout 30.34
hereafter 12.75
hereat 30.1
hereby 6.1
hereditary 4.43
heredity 4.53
Hereford 16.28

Herefordshire 12.11
herein 25.13
hereof 34.10
heresy 4.46
heretic 21.17
heretical 23.32
hereto 11.1
hereunder 12.29
hereunto 11.20
hereupon 25.24
herewith 33.4
heriot 30.41
heritage 20.9
herky-jerky 4.20
herl 23.42
herm 24.22
Herman 25.45
hermaphrodite 30.26
Hermes 35.7
hermetic 21.17
Hermia 12.7
Hermione 4.34
hermit 30.23
hermitage 20.9
Hermitian 25.49
hermitic 21.17
hernia 12.8
Herning 26.9
hero 9.21
Herod 16.29
Herodotus 28.34
heroic 21.9
heroin 25.13
heroine 25.13
heroize 35.11
heron 25.47
herpes 35.7
Herr 2.1
Herrick 21.15
herring 26.11
herringbone 25.30
Herriot 30.41
hers 35.25
Herschel 23.38
herself 17.18
Hertford 16.28
Hertfordshire 12.11
Hertz 28.47
Herzegovina 12.55
Herzl 23.37
Herzog 18.8
he's 35.6
hesitance 28.45
hesitancy 4.48
hesitant 30.56
hesitate 30.16
hesitater 12.77
Hesketh 32.6
Hesperian 25.37
Hesperides 35.7

Hesperus 28.31
Hesse 28.3
Hessian 25.37
hest 31.3
Hester 12.76
Hesvan 25.51
hetaera 12.67
heteroclite 30.28
heterodox 28.40
heterodoxy 4.46
heterogamy 4.30
heterogeneity 4.53
heterogeneous 28.23
heteronomous 28.28
heteronomy 4.30
heterosexist 31.13
heterosexual 23.25
Hettie 4.51
heuchera 12.67
hew 11.1
hewer 12.19
hex 28.38
hexad 16.1
hexagon 25.41
hexagonal 23.34
hexameter 12.78
hexastyle 23.12
hey 3.1
heyday 3.9
Heyerdahl 23.2
Hezbollah 12.44
hi 6.1
hiatal 23.39
hiatus 28.34
Hiawatha 12.83
hibachi 4.11
hibernate 30.13
Hibernian 25.37
hibiscus 28.26
Hibs 35.26
hic 21.9
hiccup 27.13
hiccupy 4.37
hic jacet 30.5
hick 21.9
hickey 4.19
Hickok 21.20
hickory 4.43
Hicks 28.39
hid 16.8
Hidalgo 9.13
hidden 25.40
hide 16.14
hide-and-seek 21.8
hideaway 3.25
hidebound 16.43
hideous 28.23
hideout 30.34
hider 12.27

hidey-hole 23.17
hiding 26.5
hie 6.1
hierarch 21.5
hierarchic 21.11
hierarchical 23.32
hierarchize 35.11
hierarchy 4.18
hieratic 21.17
hierocracy 4.48
hieroglyph 17.6
hieroglyphic 21.10
Hieronymus 28.28
hierophant 30.53
hi-fi 6.7
higgle 23.30
higgledy-piggledy 4.12
Higgs 35.28
high 6.1
highball 23.14
highbinder 12.27
highborn 25.28
highbrow 8.10
highfalutin 25.19
high-handed 16.9
high-hat 30.1
highland 16.45
Highlander 12.29
Highlandman 25.45
Highlandmen 25.45
highlight 30.28
highlighter 12.79
high-rise 35.13
highroad 16.23
hightail 23.6
highway 3.25
highwayman 25.45
highwaymen 25.45
hijab 14.2
hijack 21.3
hijacker 12.37
hike 21.19
hiker 12.40
hilarious 28.23
hilarity 4.53
Hilary 4.43
Hilda 12.27
hill 23.8
hillbilly 4.24
Hillel 23.3
Hillier 12.6
Hillman 25.45
hillock 21.30
hillocky 4.20
Hills 35.29
hillside 16.16
hilltop 27.8
hillwalker 12.40
hillwalking 26.7
hilly 4.24

h

homicidal 23.28
homicide 16.16
homiletic 21.17
homilist 31.8
homily 4.24
homing 26.9
hominid 16.10
hominoid 16.24
hominy 4.32
Homo 9.18
homoerotic 21.17
homogamy 4.30
homogeneity 4.53
homogeneous 28.23
homogenizer 12.91
homogenous 28.29
homogeny 4.32
homologous 28.25
homonym 24.6
homophobe 14.11
homophobia 12.5
homophobic 21.9
homophone 25.30
homophonic 21.13
homophonous 28.29
homophony 4.34
Homo sapiens 35.31
homosexual 23.25
homunculus 28.27
hon 25.35
honcho 9.10
Honda 12.28
Honduran 25.47
Honduras 28.31
hone 25.30
Honecker 12.39
Honegger 12.31
honest 31.10
honesty 4.53
honey 4.33
honeybee 4.10
honeybun 25.35
honeybunch 29.20
honeycomb 24.11
honeydew 11.22
honeymoon 25.33
honeymooner 12.56
honeysuckle 23.32
Hong Kong 26.15
Honiara 12.64
honied 16.10
honk 21.34
honky 4.19
honky-tonk 21.34
Honolulu 11.13
honor 12.56
honorand 16.40
honoraria 12.10
honorarium 24.16
honorary 4.43
honorific 21.10

honour 12.56
Honshu 11.19
hooch 15.11
hood 16.26
hoodie 4.13
hood-like 21.19
hoodlum 24.18
hoodoo 11.6
hoodwink 21.33
hooey 4.8
hoof 17.13
hoofer 12.30
Hooghly 4.26
hoo-ha 1.9
hook 21.28
hookah 12.41
hooker 12.41
hookey 4.20
hooklet 30.22
hook-like 21.19
hook-up 27.13
hookworm 24.22
hooky 4.20
Hooley 4.26
hooligan 25.41
hoon 25.33
hoop 27.11
Hooper 12.63
hoopla 1.12
hoopoe 11.16
hooray 3.1
hoosegow 8.4
Hoosier 12.33
hoot 30.37
hootenanny 4.31
hooter 12.81
hoover 12.87
hooves 35.35
hop 27.8
hope 27.10
hoper 12.63
hophead 16.3
Hopi 4.36
Hopkin 25.15
Hopkins 35.31
hopper 12.62
hopple 23.35
hopscotch 15.7
Horace 28.10
horary 4.43
Horatian 25.49
Horatio 9.4
horde 16.19
Hordern 25.40
horizon 25.52
horizontal 23.39
Horlicks 28.39
hormonal 23.34
hormone 25.30
Hormuz 35.22
horn 25.28

hornbeam 24.5
hornbill 23.8
hornbook 21.28
hornet 30.23
hornist 31.10
hornpipe 27.7
hornswoggle 23.30
Hornung 26.17
horny 4.32
horologe 20.11
horology 4.17
horoscope 27.10
horoscopic 21.14
horoscopy 4.37
Horowitz 28.47
horrendous 28.25
horrible 23.26
horrid 16.11
horrific 21.10
horrify 6.7
horror 12.65
hors d'oeuvre 34.14
horse 28.15
horseback 21.2
horsebox 28.40
horseflesh 29.3
horsefly 6.11
horsehair 2.6
horseleech 15.5
horselike 21.19
horseman 25.45
horsemen 25.45
horseplay 3.15
horsepower 12.16
horseradish 29.6
horseshoe 11.19
horsetail 23.6
horsewhip 27.6
horsewoman 25.45
horsewomen 25.17
horsey 4.47
Horta 12.80
hortatory 4.43
Hortense 28.44
horticulturalist 31.8
horticulture 12.24
horticulturist 31.12
Horus 28.31
hosanna 12.53
hose 35.19
Hosea 12.4
hosepipe 27.7
hosier 12.12
hosiery 4.43
hospice 28.9
hospital 23.39
hospitaler 12.48
hospitaller 12.48
host 31.20
hostage 20.9
hostel 23.39

hosteler 12.48
hosteller 12.48
hostelry 4.41
hostess 28.34
hostile 23.12
hostility 4.53
hot 30.31
hotbed 16.3
hot-blooded 16.9
hotchpotch 15.7
hotdog 18.8
hotel 23.3
hotelier 12.6
hotfoot 30.39
hothead 16.3
hot-headed 16.9
hothouse 28.16
hotline 25.22
hotly 4.25
hotness 28.29
hotplate 30.11
hotpot 30.32
hotrod 16.18
hot-rodder 12.28
hot-rodding 26.5
hotshot 30.31
hotspot 30.32
hotspur 13.4
Hottentot 30.32
hotter 12.79
hottie 4.54
hottish 29.10
Houdini 4.31
Hough 8.1
hough 21.20
hound 16.43
houndstooth 32.12
hour 12.16
hourglass 28.2
houri 4.43
hourly 4.27
house 28.16, 35.18
houseboat 30.35
housebound 16.43
houseboy 10.3
housebreaker 12.38
housebreaking 26.7
housecarl 23.2
housecoat 30.35
housefly 6.11
household 16.37
householder 12.28
house husband
  16.45
housekeep 27.5
housekeeper 12.61
housekeeping 26.10
housekept 30.58
houseleek 21.8
house lights 28.47
housemaid 16.6

housemaster 12.75
housemate 30.12
housemistress 28.10
housemother 12.84
house plant 30.53
houseroom 24.12
house-sitter 12.78
house-warming 26.9
housewife 17.7
housewifely 4.25
housewifery 4.43
housewives 35.35
housework 21.31
housey-housey 4.61
housing 26.14
Housman 25.45
Houston 25.50
hovel 23.40
hover 12.86
hovercraft 30.47
hoverer 12.67
hoverfly 6.11
hoverport 30.33
how 8.1
Howard 16.28
howbeit 30.20
howdah 12.28
how-do-you-do 11.1
howdy 4.13
Howe 8.1
Howell 23.25
Howes 35.18
however 12.85
howitzer 12.70
howl 23.16
howler 12.44
howsoever 12.85
howzat 30.1
hoy 10.1
hoya 12.18
hoyden 25.40
hoydenish 29.9
Hoyle 23.19
Huascarán 25.4
hub 14.13
Hubble 23.26
hubbub 14.13
hubby 4.10
hubcap 27.1
Hubei 3.1
Hubert 30.41
hubris 28.10
huckaback 21.2
huckleberry 4.43
huckster 12.81
Huddersfield 16.35
huddle 23.28
Hudson 25.48
hue 11.1
Hué 3.1

huff 17.15
huffish 29.7
huffy 4.14
hug 18.12
huge 20.15
hugger 12.32
hugger-mugger 12.32
Huggins 35.31
Hugh 11.1
Hughes 35.21
Hughie 4.8
Hugo 9.13
Huguenot 9.19
huh 12.1
hula 12.45
hula-hoop 27.11
hulk 21.32
hull 23.22
hullabaloo 11.1
hum 24.14
human 25.45
humane 25.7
humanist 31.10
humanitarian 25.37
humanity 4.53
humankind 16.42
humanoid 16.24
Humber 12.22
Humberside 16.16
Humbert 30.41
humble 23.26
Humboldt 30.51
humbug 18.12
humbuggery 4.43
humdinger 12.60
humdrum 24.14
Hume 24.12
humeral 23.36
humerus 28.31
humic 21.12
humid 16.10
humidifier 12.14
humidify 6.7
humidity 4.53
humidor 7.5
humify 6.7
humiliate 30.8
humility 4.53
hummer 12.52
hummingbird 16.31
hummock 21.30
hummocky 4.20
hummus 28.28
humongous 28.25
humor 12.52
humoresque 21.35
humorist 31.12
humorous 28.31
humour 12.52
humous 28.28

hump 27.17
humpback 21.2
humpbacked 30.48
Humperdinck 21.33
humph 17.19
Humphrey 4.42
humpty-dumpty 4.55
humpy 4.37
humus 28.28
Hun 25.35
Hunan 25.1
hunch 29.20
hunchback 21.2
hunchbacked 30.48
hundred 16.29
hundredfold 16.37
hundredth 32.15
hundredweight 30.17
hung 26.18
Hungarian 25.37
Hungary 4.43
hunger 12.32
hungry 4.42
hunk 21.34
hunker 12.41
hunky 4.20
hunky-dory 4.41
Hunnish 29.9
hunt 30.55
hunter 12.81
Huntingdon 25.40
Huntington 25.50
huntress 28.10
huntsman 25.45
huntsmen 25.45
Huntsville 23.10
hurdle 23.28
hurdler 12.48
hurdy-gurdy 4.13
hurl 23.42
hurley 4.28
hurly-burly 4.28
Huron 25.26
hurrah 1.1
hurray 3.1
Hurri 4.41
hurricane 25.43
hurried 16.11
hurry 4.42
Hurst 31.26
Hurston 25.50
hurt 30.45
hurtle 23.39
Husák 21.4
husband 16.45
husbander 12.29
husbandhood 16.26
husbandly 4.27
husbandry 4.43

hush 29.16
hushaby 6.5
hush-hush 29.16
husk 21.35
husky 4.20
huss 28.21
hussar 1.1
Hussein 25.7
Husserl 23.42
Hussite 30.30
hussy 4.47
hustings 35.32
hustle 23.37
hustler 12.47
hut 30.40
hutch 15.13
Hutterite 30.29
Hutton 25.50
Hutu 11.20
Huxley 4.26
Huygens 35.31
huzza 1.1
Hwange 4.15
hwyl 23.8
hyacinth 32.19
hyacinthine 25.23
Hyacinthus 28.35
Hyades 35.7
hybrid 16.11
hybridity 4.53
Hyderabad 16.1
Hydra 12.65
hydrangea 12.35
hydrant 30.56
hydrate 30.7, 30.15
hydraulic 21.11
hydric 21.15
hydrocarbon 25.38
hydrodynamic 21.12
hydrodynamical 23.32
hydroelectric 21.15
hydrofoil 23.19
hydrogen 25.42
hydrogenous 28.29
hydrographic 21.10
hydrography 4.14
hydroid 16.24
hydrologic 21.11
hydrology 4.17
hydromechanics 28.39
hydrophobia 12.5
hydrophobic 21.9
hydroplane 25.8
hydrostatic 21.17
hydrous 28.31
hydroxide 16.16
hydrozoan 25.38
hyena 12.54
hygiene 25.10

hygienic 21.13
hygienist 31.10
Hyksos 28.14
Hyman 25.45
hymen 25.5
hymeneal 23.23
hymn 24.6
hymnal 23.34
hymnary 4.43
hymnic 21.13
hymnodist 31.6
hymnody 4.13
hypaethral 23.36
hypallage 4.17
Hypatia 12.11
hype 27.7
hyperbola 12.48
hyperbole 4.27
hyperbolic 21.11
hyperbolical 23.32
Hyperborean 25.37
hypercritical 23.32
hypergamy 4.30
hypericum 24.18
Hyperion 25.37
hypermarket 30.21
hypersonic 21.13
hyperspace 28.5
hypersthene 25.12
hypertension 25.49
hypertext 31.28
hyperthermia 12.7
hyperventilate 30.11
hypethral 23.36
hyphen 25.41
hyphenate 30.13
Hypnos 28.14
hypnosis 28.11
hypnotherapy 4.37
hypnotic 21.17
hypnotist 31.14
hypo 9.20
hypo-allergenic 21.13
hypocaust 31.18
hypochondria 12.10
hypochondriac 21.1
hypocrisy 4.48
hypocrite 30.24
hypocritical 23.32
hypodermic 21.12
hypoglycaemia 12.7
hypoid 16.24
hypolimnion 25.37
hypostasis 28.11
hypostasize 35.14
hypostatic 21.17
hypostyle 23.12
hypotension 25.49
hypotenuse 28.19

hypothalamus 28.28
hypothecate 30.10
hypothermia 12.7
hypotheses 35.8
hypothesis 28.11
hypothetical 23.32
hyrax 28.38
hysterectomy 4.30
hysteria 12.10
hysteric 21.15
hysterical 23.32
Hywel 23.40

I

I 6.1
iamb 24.1
iambic 21.9
iambus 28.24
Ian 25.36
Iapetus 28.34
Ibadan 25.40
Iban 25.4
Iberia 12.10
Iberian 25.37
ibex 28.38
ibid 16.8
ibis 28.7
Ibiza 12.83
Ibsen 25.48
ibuprofen 25.41
Icarus 28.31
ice 28.13
iceberg 18.13
iceblink 21.33
iceboat 30.35
icebox 28.40
icebreaker 12.38
icefall 23.15
ice house 28.16
Iceland 16.45
Icelander 12.29
Icelandic 21.10
iceman 25.2
icemen 25.5
Iceni 6.13
I Ching 26.3
ichneumon 25.45
ichor 7.10
icicle 23.32
icily 4.24
iciness 28.9
icing 26.12
icky 4.19
icon 25.25
iconic 21.13
iconoclasm 24.21
iconoclast 31.1
iconoclastic 21.17
iconographer 12.30

iconographic 21.10
iconography 4.14
iconolatry 4.43
iconology 4.17
iconostases 35.8
iconostasis 28.11
ictus 28.34
icy 4.46
id 16.8
I'd 16.14
Ida 12.27
Idaho 9.14
Idahoan 25.38
idea 12.4
ideal 23.24
ideality 4.53
idealist 31.8
ideality 4.53
idealizer 12.91
ideate 30.8
ideation 25.49
idée fixe 28.38
idcm 24.3
identical 23.32
identifier 12.14
identify 6.7
identikit 30.21
identity 4.53
ideogram 24.1
ideologist 31.7
ideologue 18.8
ideology 4.17
idcs 35.27
idiocy 4.48
idiolect 30.48
idiom 24.16
idiomatic 21.17
idiosyncrasy 4.48
idiosyncratic 21.17
idiot 30.41
idiotic 21.17
idle 23.28
idler 12.44
idly 4.25
Ido 9.11
idol 23.28
idolater 12.82
idolatrous 28.31
idolatry 4.43
idolizer 12.91
Idomeneus 28.19
idyll 23.8
idyllic 21.11
if 17.6
iffy 4.14
Ifor 7.20
Igbo 9.9
igloo 11.13
Ignatius 28.33
igneous 28.23
ignite 30.26
igniter 12.79

ignition 25.49
ignoble 23.26
ignominious 28.23
ignominy 4.32
ignoramus 28.28
ignorance 28.45
ignorant 30.56
ignore 7.1
ignorer 12.66
Igor 7.7
iguana 12.53
iguanodon 25.25
ilex 28.38
Iliad 16.28
ilk 21.32
I'll 23.11
ill 23.8
illation 25.49
illegal 23.30
illegible 23.26
illegitimacy 4.48
illegitimate 30.43
ill-gotten 25.50
ill-humored 16.29
ill-humoured 16.29
illiberal 23.36
illicit 30.24
Illinois 10.1
Illinoisan 25.38
illiquid 16.13
illiteracy 4.48
illiterate 30.43
ill-natured 16.28
illness 28.9
illogical 23.32
ill-omened 16.41
ill-starred 16.2
illude 16.25
illume 24.12
illuminant 30.56
illuminate 30.13
illuminati 4.51
illumine 25.17
illuminist 31.10
illusion 25.42
illusional 23.34
illusionist 31.10
illusive 34.7
illusory 4.43
illustrate 30.15
illustrious 28.23
Illyria 12.10
Illyrian 25.37
I'm 24.7
image 20.7
imagery 4.43
imaginal 23.34
imaginary 4.43
imagine 25.14
imaginer 12.55
imagines 35.31

h
i

incommunicado 9.11
inconspicuous 28.24
incorporate 30.15
incriminate 30.13
incriminatory 4.43
incubate 30.9
incubatory 4.43
incubi 6.5
incubus 28.24
inculcate 30.10
inculpate 30.14
inculpatory 4.43
incumbency 4.48
incumbent 30.56
incunabula 12.46
incunabulum 24.18
incursion 25.49
incuse 35.21
indaba 12.21
indebted 16.12
indefectible 23.26
indelible 23.26
indemnifier 12.14
indemnity 4.53
index 28.38
indexer 12.69
indexible 23.26
indexical 23.32
India 12.5
Indian 25.37
Indiana 12.53
Indianapolis 28.8
Indic 21.10
indicate 30.10
indicatory 4.43
indices 35.8
indicia 12.11
indict 30.26
indictee 4.1
indicter 12.79
indie 4.12
Indies 35.10
indifferentist 31.14
indigence 28.45
indigene 25.10
indigenize 35.13
indigenous 28.29
indigent 30.56
indigested 16.12
indignant 30.56
indigo 9.13
indite 30.26
indium 24.16
individual 23.25
individualist 31.8
individuate 30.8
Indo-China 12.55
indoctrinate 30.13
indolence 28.45
indolent 30.56

Indonesia 12.12
Indonesian 25.37
indoors 35.17
Indo-Pacific 21.10
Indore 7.1
indorse 28.15
indorser 12.70
Indra 12.65
induce 28.19
inducer 12.71
inducible 23.26
inductance 28.45
inductee 4.1
induction 25.49
indulge 20.18
indulgence 28.45
indulgent 30.56
indulger 12.36
indult 30.51
indurate 30.15, 30.43
Indus 28.25
industrial 23.24
industrialist 31.8
industrious 28.23
industry 4.43
Indy 4.12
Indycar 1.11
inebriate 30.8, 30.41
inebriety 4.53
inept 30.58
ineptitude 16.25
inerrancy 4.48
inert 30.45
inertia 12.73
inertial 23.38
inexpressible 23.26
in extremis 28.8
infamy 4.30
infancy 4.48
infant 30.56
infanta 12.74
infante 4.51
infanticidal 23.28
infanticide 16.16
infantile 23.12
infantility 4.53
infantine 25.23
infantry 4.43
infantryman 25.45
infantrymen 25.45
infatuate 30.8
infect 30.48
infection 25.49
infectious 28.33
infer 13.1
inference 28.45
inferior 12.10
inferiority 4.53
infernal 23.34
inferno 9.19
infest 31.3

infibulate 30.11
infidel 23.3
infighting 26.13
infinite 30.43
infinitesimal 23.33
infinitival 23.40
infinity 4.53
infirmary 4.43
infirmity 4.53
in flagrante delicto 9.24
inflammatory 4.43
inflate 30.7
inflationary 4.43
inflect 30.48
inflection 25.49
inflict 30.49
inflicter 12.78
infliction 25.49
inflow 9.17
influencer 12.71
influential 23.38
influenza 12.90
info 9.12
infomercial 23.38
informant 30.56
informatics 28.39
informatory 4.43
infotech 21.6
infractor 12.74
infrared 16.3
infrastructure 12.24
infringer 12.35
infuriate 30.8
infuser 12.92
ingeminate 30.13
ingenious 28.23
ingénue 11.15
ingenuity 4.53
ingenuous 28.24
ingest 31.3
ingestion 25.39
inglenook 21.28
ingot 30.42
ingrain 25.8
ingrained 16.41
Ingram 24.19
ingrate 30.15
ingratiate 30.8
ingredient 30.56
Ingres 12.64
ingress 28.3
Ingrid 16.11
ingurgitate 30.16
inhalant 30.56
inhaler 12.43
inherence 28.45
inherent 30.56
inherit 30.24
inheritance 28.45
inhibit 30.20

inhibitor 12.78
inhibitory 4.43
inhume 24.12
inimical 23.32
iniquitous 28.34
iniquity 4.53
initial 23.38
initialize 35.12
initiate 30.8, 30.41
initiatory 4.43
inject 30.48
injection 25.49
injector 12.76
Injun 25.42
injunct 30.49
injure 12.35
injurer 12.67
injurious 28.23
ink 21.33
Inkatha 12.75
inker 12.39
inkhorn 25.28
inkling 26.8
inkstand 16.40
inkwell 23.4
inky 4.19
inlander 12.25
in law 7.11
inlay 3.15
inlet 30.22
in loco parentis 28.12
inly 4.24
inmate 30.12
in memoriam 24.1
inn 25.13
innards 35.27
innate 30.7
inner 12.55
innermost 31.20
Innes 28.9
inning 26.9
innit 30.23
innkeeper 12.61
innocence 28.45
innocency 4.48
innocent 30.56
innominate 30.43
innovate 30.16
innovatory 4.43
Innsbruck 21.28
innuendo 9.11
inoculate 30.11
inordinate 30.43
inquirer 12.67
inquiry 4.43
inquisitor 12.78
inrushing 26.12
inscription 25.49
inscriptional 23.34
insecticidal 23.28

insecticide 16.16
insectile 23.12
insectivore 7.20
insectivorous 28.31
inseminate 30.13
insert 30.45
inserter 12.82
insertion 25.49
inset 30.5
inshallah 12.42
insider 12.27
insidious 28.23
insight 30.30
insignia 12.8
insignificancy 4.48
insinuate 30.8
insipid 16.10
insipidity 4.53
insist 31.6
insistence 28.45
insistency 4.48
insistent 30.56
in situ 11.22
insofar 1.1
insole 23.18
insolence 28.45
insolent 30.56
insomnia 12.8
insomniac 21.1
insomuch 15.13
insouciance 28.45
insouciant 30.56
inspan 25.3
inspect 30.48
inspection 25.49
inspector 12.76
inspectorate 30.43
installer 12.44
instance 28.45
instancy 4.48
instant 30.56
instantaneous 28.23
instantiate 30.8
instigate 30.9
instil 23.8
instinct 30.49
instinctual 23.25
institute 30.38
institution 25.49
institutional 23.34
instruct 30.49
instruction 25.49
instructional 23.34
instructor 12.81
instructress 28.10
instrumentalist 31.8
insufflate 30.11
insular 12.46
insularity 4.53
insulate 30.11

insulin 25.16
insult 30.51
insulter 12.81
insurance 28.45
insurer 12.67
insurgence 28.45
insurgency 4.48
insurgent 30.56
insurrection 25.49
insurrectionary 4.43
insurrectionist 31.10
intaglio 9.4
intarsia 12.11
integer 12.35
integral 23.36
integrant 30.56
integrate 30.15
integrity 4.53
intellect 30.48
intellectual 23.25
intellectualist 31.8
intelligence 28.45
intelligent 30.56
intelligential 23.38
intelligentsia 12.11
intelligible 23.26
intendancy 4.48
intendant 30.56
intended 16.9
intensifier 12.14
intensify 6.7
intensive 34.7
intention 25.49
intentional 23.34
inter 13.1
interact 30.48
interactant 30.56
interaction 25.49
inter alia 12.6
interbreed 16.7
intercede 16.7
interceder 12.26
intercensal 23.37
intercept 30.58
interception 25.49
interceptor 12.76
intercessor 12.69
intercessory 4.43
interchange 20.19
intercity 4.53
intercollegiate 30.41
intercom 24.8
intercommunicate 30.10
interconnect 30.48
interconnection 25.49
intercool 23.20

intercooling 26.8
intercorrelate 30.11
intercostal 23.39
intercourse 28.15
intercrop 27.8
intercut 30.40
interdepend 16.41
interdependence 28.45
interdependency 4.48
interdependent 30.56
interdict 30.49
interdiction 25.49
interdigitate 30.16
interdisciplinary 4.43
interest 31.12
interface 28.5
interfacing 26.12
inter-faith 32.4
interfere 12.4
interference 28.45
interferer 12.67
interferon 25.26
interfile 23.11
interfuse 35.21
interfusion 25.42
interim 24.6
interior 12.10
interiorize 35.13
interject 30.48
interjection 25.49
interjectional 23.34
interjectory 4.43
interlace 28.5
Interlaken 25.43
interlard 16.2
interleaf 17.5
interleave 34.5
interline 25.21
interlinear 12.8
Interlingua 12.88
interlink 21.33
interlock 21.20, 21.21
interlocker 12.40
interlocution 25.49
interlocutor 12.81
interlocutory 4.43
interlope 27.10
interloper 12.63
interlude 16.25
intermarriage 20.8
intermarry 4.38
intermediacy 4.48
intermediary 4.43
intermediate 30.41
intermesh 29.3
intermezzo 9.22

intermingle 23.30
intermit 30.20
intermittence 28.45
intermittency 4.48
intermittent 30.56
intermix 28.39
intermixture 12.23
internal 23.34
internationalist 31.8
internecine 25.23
internee 4.1
internode 16.23
interoceanic 21.13
interpellate 30.11
interpersonal 23.34
interplanetary 4.43
interplay 3.15
interpleader 12.26
Interpol 23.13
interpolate 30.11
interpose 35.19
interpret 30.24
interpreter 12.78
interracial 23.38
interregna 12.53
interregnum 24.19
interrelate 30.7
interrogate 30.9
interrogatory 4.43
interrupt 30.58
interrupter 12.81
interruptible 23.26
interruption 25.49
intersect 30.48
intersection 25.49
intersectional 23.34
interspace 28.5
intersperse 28.36
interspersion 25.49
interstate 30.7
interstellar 12.42
interstice 28.12
interstitial 23.38
intertidal 23.28
intertribal 23.26
intertwine 25.21
interval 23.40
intervallic 21.11
intervene 25.9
intervener 12.54
intervenient 30.56
intervention 25.49
interventionist 31.10
interview 11.22
interviewee 4.1
interviewer 12.19
interwar 7.1
interweave 34.5
interwind 16.42

interwound 16.43
interwove 34.11
interwoven 25.51
intestacy 4.48
intestinal 23.34
intestine 25.19
intifada 12.25
intimacy 4.48
intimate 30.12, 30.43
intimidate 30.9
intimidatory 4.43
intinction 25.49
into 11.20
intonate 30.13
in toto 9.25
intoxicant 30.56
intoxicate 30.10
intrados 28.14
Intranet 30.5
intransigence 28.45
intransigency 4.48
intransigent 30.56
intrauterine 25.23
intravenous 28.29
in-tray 3.19
intrepid 16.10
intrepidity 4.53
intricacy 4.48
intricate 30.42
intrigue 18.5
intriguer 12.31
intrinsic 21.16
intro 9.21
introduce 28.19
introducer 12.71
introduction 25.49
introductory 4.43
introit 30.36
introspection 25.49
introversion 25.49
introvert 30.45
introverted 16.12
intrude 16.25
intruder 12.29
intrusion 25.42
intrusive 34.7
intuit 30.20
intuitionist 31.10
intumesce 28.3
Inuit 30.20
Inuk 21.28
Inuktitut 30.39
inundate 30.9
Inupik 21.14
inure 12.20
in utero 9.21
in vacuo 9.8
invade 16.6
invader 12.26

invalid 16.7
Invar 1.1
invasion 25.42
invasive 34.7
invected 16.12
inveigh 3.1
inveigle 23.30
invention 25.49
inventor 12.76
inventory 4.43
invertible 23.26
investigate 30.9
investigatory 4.43
investor 12.76
inveteracy 4.48
inveterate 30.43
invidious 28.23
invigilate 30.11
invigorate 30.15
inviolacy 4.48
inviolate 30.42
invite 30.26
invitee 4.1
inviter 12.79
in vitro 9.21
in vivo 9.27
invocatory 4.43
invoke 21.24
invoker 12.40
involve 34.15
inward 16.30
inwards 35.27
in-your-face 28.5
Io 9.5
iodine 25.10
iodize 35.11
Iolanthe 4.56
ion 25.38
Iona 12.56
Ionesco 9.16
Ionia 12.8
Ionian 25.37
ionic 21.13
ionosphere 12.5
Iorwerth 32.14
iota 12.80
Iowa 12.88
Iowan 25.51
Ipatieff 17.3
Iphigenia 12.3
Ipoh 9.20
ipso facto 9.24
Ipswich 15.6
Iqbal 23.1
Iran 25.4
Irangate 30.9
Iranian 25.37
Iraq 21.5
Iraqi 4.18
irascible 23.26
irate 30.7

ire 12.13
Ireland 16.45
Irene 25.11
Irgun 25.33
iridescence 28.45
iridescent 30.56
iridium 24.16
iridology 4.17
iris 28.10
Irish 29.9
Irishman 25.45
Irishmen 25.45
Irishwoman 25.45
Irishwomen 25.17
irk 21.31
irksome 24.20
Irkutsk 21.35
Irma 12.52
iron 25.38
ironbark 21.5
ironclad 16.1
ironer 12.58
ironic 21.13
ironical 23.32
ironist 31.10
ironize 35.13
ironmonger 12.32
ironmongery 4.43
ironstone 25.31
ironware 2.15
ironwood 16.26
ironwork 21.31
irony 4.34
Iroquoian 25.38
Iroquois 10.14
irradiance 28.45
irradiant 30.56
irradiate 30.8
irrational 23.34
Irrawaddy 4.13
irreducible 23.26
irregular 12.46
irregularity 4.53
irrelevance 28.45
irrelevancy 4.48
irrelevant 30.56
irreligion 25.42
irreligious 28.25
irremissible 23.26
irrepressible 23.26
irresistible 23.26
irresolute 30.37
irresolution 25.49
irresponsible 23.26
irresponsive 34.7
irreverence 28.45
irreverent 30.56
irreverential 23.38
irreversible 23.26

irrigate 30.9
irritant 30.56
irritate 30.16
irrupt 30.58
Irving 26.14
Irvingite 30.29
Irwin 25.20
is 35.10
Isaac 21.30
Isabel 23.3
Isadora 12.66
isagogic 21.11
Isaiah 12.13
Ischia 12.6
Iseult 30.51
Isfahan 25.4
Isherwood 16.26
Ishiguro 9.21
Ishmael 23.5
Ishmaelite 30.28
Ishtar 1.19
Isidore 7.5
Isis 28.11
Isla 12.44
Islam 24.2
Islamabad 16.1
Islamic 21.12
Islamist 31.9
island 16.45
islander 12.29
isle 23.11
islet 30.22
Islwyn 25.13
ism 24.21
Ismaili 4.23
isn't 30.56
isobar 1.4
Isobel 23.3
isochromatic 21.17
Isocrates 35.9
isogeotherm 24.22
isolate 30.11, 30.42
isolationist 31.10
Isolde 12.28
isomer 12.52
isometric 21.15
isopod 16.18
isopropyl 23.11
isosceles 35.7
isothermal 23.33
isotonic 21.13
isotope 27.10
isotopic 21.14
isotropic 21.14
I-spy 6.1
Israel 23.6
Israeli 4.22

i

Israelite 30.28
Issachar 1.11
Issigonis 28.9
issuance 28.45
issuant 30.56
issue 11.19
issuer 12.19
Istanbul 23.21
isthmian 25.37
isthmus 28.28
it 30.20
Italian 25.52
Italianate 30.13
italic 21.11
Italy 4.27
itch 15.6
itchy 4.11
it'd 16.29
item 24.6
itemizer 12.91
iterate 30.15
Ithaca 12.41
itinerancy 4.48
itinerant 30.56
itinerary 4.43
itinerate 30.15
it'll 23.39
Ito 9.24
it's 28.47
its 28.47
itself 17.18
itsy-bitsy 4.46
Ivan 25.1, 25.51
I've 34.9
Ives 35.35
ivied 16.13
Ivor 12.86
ivory 4.43
ivy 4.58
Iwo Jima 12.51
ixia 12.11
Ixion 25.38
Iyyar 1.23
izard 16.30
Izmir 12.4
Iznik 21.13
Izvestia 12.12
Izzy 4.61

J

jab 14.1
Jabalpur 12.20
jabber 12.21
jabberwocky 4.19
Jabez 35.3
jabot 9.9
jacana 12.58
jacaranda 12.25
Jacinta 12.78

jacinth 32.19
jack 21.1
jackal 23.32
jackanapes 28.46
jackaroo 11.1
jackass 28.1
jackboot 30.37
jackdaw 7.5
jacket 30.21
jackfruit 30.37
jackhammer 12.50
Jackie 4.18
jackknife 17.7
jackknives 35.35
Jacklin 25.16
jackpot 30.32
jackrabbit 30.20
Jackson 25.48
Jacksonville 23.10
jackstaff 17.2
jackstone 25.31
jackstraw 7.15
Jacob 14.14
Jacobean 25.36
Jacobi 4.10
Jacobin 25.13
Jacobinic 21.13
Jacobinical 23.32
Jacobite 30.26
Jacobs 35.26
jaconet 30.5
Jacquard 16.2
Jacqueline 25.10
jacquerie 4.43
Jacques 28.38
jacuzzi 4.62
jade 16.6
jadeite 30.26
j'adoube 14.12
Jaeger 12.31
Jaffa 12.30
Jaffna 12.53
jag 18.1
jagged 16.9, 16.33
Jagger 12.31
jaggy 4.15
Jago 9.13
jaguar 12.20
jail 23.5
jailbait 30.9
jailbird 16.31
jailbreak 21.7
jailer 12.43
jailhouse 28.16
Jain 25.7
Jainist 31.10
Jaipur 12.20
Jakarta 12.75
Jake 21.7
Jalalabad 16.1
jalapeño 9.28

jalopy 4.36
jalousie 4.62
jam 24.1
Jamaica 12.38
Jamaican 25.43
jamb 24.1
jambalaya 12.13
jamboree 4.1
James 35.30
Jamestown 25.29
Jamie 4.29
jammer 12.50
Jammu 11.14
jammy 4.29
Jamshid 16.7
Jan 25.1
Jancis 28.11
Jane 25.7
Janet 30.23
Janey 4.31
jangle 23.30
Janice 28.9
Janine 25.9
janissary 4.43
janitor 12.78
janitorial 23.24
Jansen 25.48
Jansenist 31.10
January 4.43
Janus 28.29
Jap 27.1
Japan 25.1
Japanese 35.6
jape 27.4
japery 4.43
Japheth 32.3
japonica 12.39
jar 1.1
jardinière 2.1
jargon 25.41
jargonize 35.13
jarrah 12.64
Jarrow 9.21
Jarvis 28.12
jasmine 25.17
Jason 25.48
jaspé 3.18
jasper 12.61
Jat 30.3
Jataka 12.41
jaundice 28.7
jaunt 30.54
jaunty 4.54
Java 12.85
Javan 25.51
Javanese 35.6
javelin 25.16
jaw 7.1
jawbone 25.30
jawbreaker 12.38
jawline 25.22

jay 3.1
Jaycee 4.1
jaywalk 21.22
jaywalker 12.40
jazz 35.1
jazzer 12.90
jazzman 25.2
jazzmen 25.5
jazzy 4.61
J-cloth 32.8
jealous 28.27
jealousy 4.48
Jean 25.9, 25.24
Jeanette 30.4
Jeanie 4.31
Jeannine 25.9
Jeans 35.31
Jeep 27.5
jeepers 35.24
jeer 12.4
Jeeves 35.35
jeez 35.6
Jeff 17.3
Jefferies 35.10
Jefferson 25.48
Jeffreys 35.10
Jehoshaphat 30.1
Jehovah 12.86
Jehovist 31.10
Jehu 11.22
jejune 25.33
Jekyll 23.32
Jellicoe 9.16
jellify 6.7
jello 9.17
jelly 4.22
jellyfish 29.7
Jem 24.3
Jemima 12.51
Jemma 12.50
jemmy 4.29
Jena 12.54
je ne sais quoi 1.1
Jenkin 25.15
Jenkins 35.31
Jenna 12.53
Jenner 12.53
jennet 30.23
Jennifer 12.30
jenny 4.31
jeopardy 4.13
jerboa 12.17
jeremiad 16.28
Jeremiah 12.13
Jeremy 4.29
Jerez 32.3
Jericho 9.16
jerk 21.31
jerker 12.41
jerkin 25.15
jerky 4.20

Jermaine 25.7
jeroboam 24.17
Jerome 24.11
jerry 4.38
jerrycan 25.2
jersey 4.62
Jerusalem 24.18
Jervis 28.12
Jespersen 25.48
jess 28.3
Jessica 12.39
Jessie 4.45
jest 31.3
jester 12.76
Jesu 11.22
Jesuit 30.20
Jesus 28.35
jet 30.4
jeté 3.22
jetfoil 23.19
Jethro 9.21
jetlag 18.1
jetliner 12.55
jetsam 24.20
jet stream 24.5
jettison 25.48
jetton 25.50
jetty 4.51
jeu d'esprit 4.1
jeunesse dorée 3.1
Jew 11.1
jewel 23.25
jeweler 12.48
jeweller 12.48
jewellery 4.43
jewelry 4.43
Jewess 28.3
Jewish 29.6
Jewry 4.43
Jezebel 23.3
jib 14.7
jibba 12.21
jibber 12.21
jibe 14.8
Jiddah 12.27
jiffy 4.14
jig 18.6
jigger 12.31
jiggery-pokery 4.43
jiggle 23.30
jiggly 4.27
jigsaw 7.16
jihad 16.1
jihadi 4.12
jillion 25.52
jilt 30.51
Jim 24.6
jim-dandy 4.12
jimjams 35.30
Jin 25.13
Jinan 25.1

jingle 23.30
jingly 4.24
jingo 9.13
jingoist 31.6
jink 21.33
jinker 12.39
jinks 28.41
jinn 25.13
Jinnah 12.55
jinx 28.41
jitney 4.32
jitter 12.78
jitterbug 18.12
jittery 4.43
Jivaro 9.21
jive 34.9
jiver 12.86
jizz 35.10
jo 9.1
Joachim 24.6
Joan 25.30
Joanna 12.53
Joanne 25.1
job 14.9
Job 14.11
jobber 12.21
jobbery 4.43
jobcentre 12.76
jobless 28.27
jobsworth 32.14
Jo'burg 18.13
Jocasta 12.74
Jocelyn 25.16
jock 21.20
jockey 4.19
jockstrap 27.1
jocose 28.17
jocosity 4.53
jocular 12.46
jocularity 4.53
jocund 16.45
jocundity 4.53
Jodhpur 12.20
jodhpurs 35.24
Jodie 4.13
Joe 9.1
Joe Bloggs 35.28
Joel 23.17
joey 4.7
jog 18.8
jogger 12.32
joggle 23.30
jogtrot 30.32
Johannesburg 18.13
john 25.24
johnny 4.32
johnnycake 21.7
John o'Groats 28.47
Johns 35.31
Johnson 25.48
Johnsonian 25.37

Johor 7.1
joie de vivre 12.65
join 25.32
joinder 12.28
joiner 12.56
joinery 4.43
joint 30.55
jointer 12.81
jointress 28.10
jointure 12.24
joist 31.21
jojoba 12.21
joke 21.24
joker 12.40
jokey 4.20
Jolene 25.9
jollity 4.53
jolly 4.25
Jolson 25.48
jolt 30.51
jolty 4.54
Jolyon 25.37
Jomon 25.25
Jon 25.24
Jonah 12.56
Jonas 28.29
Jonathan 25.51
Jones 35.31
Joneses 35.10
Jong 26.15
jongleur 13.1
jonquil 23.10
Jonson 25.48
Joplin 25.16
Joppa 12.62
Jordan 25.40
Jordanian 25.37
jorum 24.19
José 3.1
Joseph 17.6
Josephine 25.10
Josephus 28.26
josh 29.11
josher 12.73
Joshua 12.20
Josiah 12.13
Josie 4.61
joss 28.14
josser 12.70
jostle 23.37
jot 30.31
jotter 12.79
Joule 23.20
jounce 28.44
journal 23.34
journalese 35.6
journalist 31.8
journalize 35.12
journey 4.34
journeyer 12.8
journeyman 25.45

journeymen 25.45
journo 9.19
joust 31.19
jouster 12.80
Jove 34.11
jovial 23.24
Jovian 25.37
jowl 23.16
jowly 4.25
joy 10.1
Joyce 28.18
Joycean 25.37
joyful 23.21
joyless 28.8
joyous 28.24
joyride 16.15
joyrider 12.27
joystick 21.17
Juan 25.4
Juanita 12.77
Juárez 35.3
jube 4.10, 14.12
jubilance 28.45
jubilant 30.56
Jubilate 3.22
jubilate 30.11
jubilee 4.24
Judaea 12.4
Judaean 25.37
Judah 12.29
Judaic 21.9
Judaize 35.11
Judas 28.25
Judas Iscariot 30.41
Judas Maccabaeus
  28.22
Judd 16.27
judder 12.29
Jude 16.25
judge 20.16
Judges 35.10
judicatory 4.43
judicature 12.24
judicial 23.38
judiciary 4.43
judicious 28.33
Judith 32.6
judo 9.11
judoka 12.40
Judy 4.13
jug 18.12
Jugendstil 23.7
jugful 23.21
juggernaut 30.33
juggins 35.31
juggle 23.30
juggler 12.47
jugglery 4.43
Jugoslav 34.2
jugular 12.46
Jugurtha 12.83

j

kelvin 25.19
Kemble 23.26
kemp 27.17
kempt 30.52
kempy 4.36
ken 25.5
Kendall 23.28
kendo 9.11
Kendrick 21.15
Keneally 4.23
Kenelm 24.18
Kennedy 4.12
kennel 23.34
Kenneth 32.6
kenning 26.9
Kenny 4.31
keno 9.19
kenosis 28.11
Kensington 25.50
Kentish 29.10
Kenton 25.50
Kentuckian 25.37
Kentucky 4.20
Kenya 12.89
Kenyan 25.52
Kenyatta 12.74
kepi 4.36
Kepler 12.42
kept 30.58
Kerala 12.48
keratin 25.19
kerb 14.15
kerbside 16.16
kerbstone 25.31
kerchief 17.6
kerfuffle 23.29
kermis 28.8
Kermit 30.23
kern 25.53
kernel 23.34
kerosene 25.11
Kerouac 21.1
Kerr 13.1
Kerry 4.38
kersey 4.62
Kes 35.3
Kesey 4.61
kesh 29.4
Kesh 29.3
kestrel 23.36
Keswick 21.18
ketch 15.3
ketchup 27.14
Kettering 26.11
kettle 23.39
kettledrum 24.14
kevel 23.40
Kevin 25.19
key 4.1
keyboard 16.20
keyboarder 12.28

keyboardist 31.6
keyer 12.3
keyholder 12.28
keyhole 23.17
keyless 28.8
Keynes 35.31
Keynesian 25.37
keynote 30.35
keypad 16.1
keypunch 29.20
keyring 26.11
Keys 35.6
keystone 25.31
keystroke 21.24
keyway 3.25
keyword 16.31
Khabarovsk 21.35
Khachaturian 25.37
khaddar 12.25
khaki 4.18
khan 25.4
khanate 30.13
Khartoum 24.12
khazi 4.61
Khedival 23.40
khedive 34.5
Khíos 28.14
Khmer 2.1
Khoikhoi 10.6
Khoisan 25.4
Khomeini 4.31
Khorramshahr 1.1
khoum 24.12
Khrushchev 17.8
Khufu 11.7
kiang 26.1
Kiangsu 11.1
Kia-Ora 12.66
kibble 23.26
kibbutz 28.47
kibbutzim 24.6
kibbutznik 21.13
kibitka 12.39
kibitzer 12.70
kiblah 12.43
kibosh 29.11
kick 21.9
kick-ass 28.2
kickback 21.2
kick-boxing 26.12
kick-down 25.29
kicker 12.39
kick-off 17.8
kick-pleat 30.18
kickshaw 7.17
kickstand 16.40
kick-start 30.3
kid 16.8
Kidd 16.8
kidder 12.27

Kidderminster 12.78
kiddie 4.12
kiddiewink 21.33
kiddle 23.28
kiddush 29.15
kidnap 27.1
kidnaping 26.10
kidnapper 12.61
kidnapping 26.10
kidney 4.32
kidology 4.17
Kiel 23.7
Kielce 12.69
Kieran 25.47
Kierkegaard 16.2
Kiev 17.3
kif 17.6
Kigali 4.21
kike 21.19
Kikuyu 11.22
Kildare 2.1
kilim 24.5
Kilimanjaro 9.21
Kilkenny 4.31
kill 23.8
Killarney 4.31
killer 12.43
killifish 29.7
killing 26.8
killjoy 10.5
Kilmarnock 21.30
kiln 25.44
kilo 9.17
kilobyte 30.26
kilocalorie 4.43
kilogram 24.1
kilohertz 28.47
kilojoule 23.20
kiloliter 12.77
kilolitre 12.77
kilometer 12.77
kilometre 12.77
kilometric 21.15
kiloton 25.35
kilowatt 30.32
Kilroy 10.11
kilt 30.51
kilter 12.78
kiltie 4.53
Kim 24.6
Kimberley 4.27
kimono 9.19
kin 25.13
kina 12.54
kind 16.42
kinda 12.27
Kinder 12.27
kindergarten 25.50
kind-hearted 16.12
kindle 23.28

kindler 12.43
kindling 26.8
kindly 4.25
kindred 16.11
kine 25.21
kinesics 28.39
kinetic 21.17
king 26.3
kingcraft 30.47
kingdom 24.17
kingfish 29.7
kingfisher 12.72
kinghood 16.26
King Kong 26.15
kinglet 30.22
kingly 4.24
kingmaker 12.38
kingpin 25.18
Kingsley 4.24
Kingston 25.50
Kingstown 25.29
kink 21.33
kinkajou 11.11
Kinki 4.19
kinky 4.19
kinless 28.8
Kinsey 4.61
kinsfolk 21.24
Kinshasa 12.69
kinship 27.6
kinsman 25.45
kinsmen 25.45
kinswoman 25.45
kinswomen 25.17
Kintyre 12.13
kiosk 21.35
kip 27.6
Kipling 26.8
kipper 12.62
kir 12.4
kirby grip 27.6
Kirchhoff 17.8
Kirghizia 12.12
Kiribati 4.51
Kirin 25.18
kirk 21.31
Kirkcaldy 4.13
Kirkcudbright 4.41
kirkman 25.45
kirkmen 25.45
Kirkwall 23.15
Kirov 34.10
kirsch 29.17
Kirsten 25.19
Kirstie 4.55
kirtle 23.39
Kirundi 4.13
Kislev 17.3
kismet 30.23
kiss 28.7
kisser 12.70

k

Kissinger 12.35
kissogram 24.1
kissy 4.46
kit 30.20
kitbag 18.1
kitchen 25.13
Kitchener 12.55
kitchenette 30.4
kitchenware 2.15
kite 30.26
Kitemark 21.5
kitsch 15.6
kitschy 4.11
kitten 25.50
kittenish 29.9
kittiwake 21.7
kittle 23.39
kitty 4.53
Kitwe 3.25
Kiwanis 28.9
kiwi 4.59
Klan 25.1
Klansman 25.45
Klansmen 25.45
Klaus 28.16
klaxon 25.48
Klee 3.1
Kleenex 28.38
Klein 25.21
Klemperer 12.67
klepht 30.47
kleptomania 12.8
kleptomaniac 21.1
Klerksdorp 27.9
Klimt 30.52
klipspringer 12.60
Klondike 21.19
Klosters 35.24
kludge 20.15
klutz 28.47
klutzy 4.62
K-meson 25.27
knack 21.1
knacker 12.37
knackwurst 31.26
knap 27.1
knapper 12.61
knapsack 21.4
knapweed 16.7
knar 1.1
knave 34.4
knavery 4.43
knavish 29.10
knawel 23.25
knead 16.7
kneader 12.26
knee 4.1
kneecap 27.1
kneecapping 26.10
kneehole 23.17
kneel 23.7

kneeler 12.43
knee-trembler 12.42
knell 23.3
knelt 30.51
Knesset 30.24
knew 11.1
Knickerbocker 12.40
knick-knack 21.3
knick-knackery 4.43
knife 17.7
knifepoint 30.55
knifer 12.30
knight 30.26
knight-errant 30.56
knight-errantry 4.43
knighthood 16.26
knightly 4.25
Knightsbridge 20.8
knish 29.6
knit 30.20
knitter 12.78
knitwear 2.15
knives 35.35
knob 14.9
knobble 23.26
knobbly 4.25
knobby 4.10
knobkerrie 4.38
knob-like 21.19
knobstick 21.17
knock 21.20
knockabout 30.34
knocker 12.40
knockout 30.34
knoll 23.17
knop 27.8
Knossos 28.14
knot 30.31
knotgrass 28.2
knothole 23.17
knotter 12.79
knotting 26.13
knotty 4.54
knotwork 21.31
knout 30.34
know 9.1
knower 12.17
know-how 8.5
knowing 26.3
knowledge 20.6
known 25.30
Knox 28.40
Knoxville 23.10
knuckle 23.32
knuckle bone 25.30
knucklehead 16.3

knuckly 4.27
knurl 23.42
koala 12.42
koan 25.1
Koch 21.24
koel 23.25
Koestler 12.49
Koh-i-noor 12.20
kohl 23.17
kohlrabi 4.10
koi 10.1
kola 12.44
Kolhapur 12.20
kolinsky 4.19
Köln 25.44
Komodo 9.11
Komsomolsk 21.35
Kongo 9.13
Königsberg 18.13
Kon-Tiki 4.18
kook 21.27
kookaburra 12.66
kooky 4.20
kop 27.8
kopek 21.6
Koran 25.4
Koranic 21.13
Korda 12.28
Kordofan 25.1
Korea 12.4
Korean 25.37
korfball 23.14
Kórinthos 28.14
korma 12.52
koruna 12.56
Kos 28.14
kosher 12.73
Kosovo 9.27
Kostroma 1.13
Kosygin 25.14
Kota 12.80
Kotka 12.40
koto 9.25
Kowloon 25.33
kowtow 8.1
kraal 23.2
kraft 30.47
Krakatoa 12.17
kraken 25.43
Kraków 8.6
Krasnodar 1.1
Krasnoyarsk 21.35
Kraut 30.34
Kray 3.1
Kreisler 12.44
Kremlin 25.16
kriegspiel 23.7
krill 23.8
Krio 9.3
kris 28.6

Krishna 12.55
Krishnamurti 4.55
Kristallnacht 30.50
kroner 12.56
Kronstadt 30.2
Kropotkin 25.15
Kru 11.1
Kruger 12.32
Krugerrand 16.40
Krupp 27.12
krypton 25.26
Kshatriya 12.10
K2 11.1
Kuala Lumpur 12.20
Kubrick 21.15
kuccha 12.24
kudos 28.14
kudu 11.6
kudzu 11.23
Kufic 21.10
kukri 4.41
kulak 21.3
kulan 25.44
Kultur 12.20
Kulturkampf 17.19
Kumamoto 9.25
kumara 12.67
Kümmel 23.33
kumquat 30.32
Kundera 12.67
Kung 26.17
kung fu 11.1
Kunming 26.3
Kuomintang 26.1
kurbash 29.1
Kurd 16.31
Kurdish 29.6
Kurdistan 25.4
Kurgan 25.4
Kurosawa 12.88
Kursaal 23.2
Kurt 30.45
kurta 12.82
kurus 29.15
Kuwait 30.7
Kuwaiti 4.52
kvass 28.2
kvetch 15.3
Kwa 1.1
kwacha 12.23
KwaNdebele 4.23
kwanza 12.90
kwashiorkor 7.10
KwaZulu 11.13
Kweilin 25.13
Kweiyang 26.1
kyat 30.3

kyle 23.11
kylie 4.25
kylin 25.16
kylix 28.39
kyloe 9.17
Kyoto 9.25
Kyrgyz 35.10
Kyrgyzstan 25.4
Kyrie 3.3
Kyushu 11.19

laager 12.31
lab 14.1
Laban 25.38
labarum 24.19
label 23.26
labeler 12.48
labeller 12.48
labia 12.5
labial 23.24
labiate 30.8
labile 23.11
labor 12.21
laboratory 4.43
laborer 12.67
laborious 28.23
Laborite 30.29
labour 12.21
labourer 12.67
Labourite 30.29
Labrador 7.5
La Bruyère 2.1
Labuan 25.38
laburnum 24.19
labyrinth 32.19
labyrinthine 25.23
Lacan 25.1
lace 28.5
lacemaker 12.38
lacemaking 26.7
lacerate 30.15
lacewing 26.14
lacewood 16.26
lacework 21.31
laches 35.10
Lachesis 28.11
Lachlan 25.44
lachrymal 23.33
lachrymatory 4.43
lachrymose 28.17
lacing 26.12
lack 21.1
lackadaisical 23.32
lackey 4.18
lackluster 12.81
lacklustre 12.81
Laconia 12.8
Laconian 25.37

laconic 21.13
La Coruña 12.89
lacquer 12.37
lacquerer 12.67
lacrosse 28.14
lactase 35.5
lactate 30.7, 30.16
lacteal 23.24
lactescent 30.56
lactic 21.17
lactose 28.17
lacuna 12.56
lacunae 4.33
lacunar 12.56
lacustrine 25.23
lacy 4.45
lad 16.1
Ladakh 21.5
ladanum 24.19
ladder 12.25
laddie 4.12
laddish 29.6
lade 16.6
laden 25.40
la-di-da 1.1
Ladin 25.9
lading 26.5
Ladino 9.19
ladle 23.28
ladler 12.48
lady 4.12
ladybird 16.31
ladybug 18.12
lady-fern 25.53
ladyfinger 12.31
ladyfy 6.7
ladykiller 12.43
ladylike 21.19
Ladysmith 32.6
Lae 3.1
Laetitia 12.72
La Fayette 30.4
La Fontaine 25.7
lag 18.1
lagan 25.41
lager 12.31
Lagerlöf 17.11
laggard 16.28
laggardly 4.27
lagger 12.31
lagging 26.6
lagoon 25.33
lagoonal 23.34
Lagos 28.14
Lagrange 20.19
lah 1.1
Lahnda 12.25
Lahore 7.1
Lahu 11.1
laical 23.32
laicize 35.14

laid 16.6
lain 25.7
Laing 26.1
lair 2.1
laird 16.5
lairy 4.39
laissez-faire 2.1
laissez-passer 3.20
laity 4.53
Laius 28.22
lake 21.7
Lakeland 16.45
lakelet 30.22
Laker 12.38
lakeside 16.16
lakh 21.1
Lakshmi 4.29
Lalage 4.15
Lalique 21.8
lam 24.1
lama 12.50
Lamaist 31.6
Lamarck 21.5
Lamaze 35.2
lamb 24.1
lambada 12.25
lambaste 31.4
lambda 12.25
lambent 30.56
lamber 12.50
lambert 30.41
lambkin 25.15
lamblike 21.19
Lambrusco 9.16
lambskin 25.15
lambswool 23.21
lame 24.4
lamé 3.16
lamebrain 25.8
lamellae 4.22
lament 30.53
Lamentations 35.31
lamenter 12.76
laminate 30.13, 30.43
lamington 25.50
Lammas 28.28
lammergeier 12.14
lamp 27.17
lampern 25.46
lamplight 30.28
lamplighter 12.79
lamplit 30.22
lampoon 25.33
lampooner 12.56
lampoonist 31.10
lamp post 31.20
lamprey 4.38
lampshade 16.6
Lana 12.53
Lancashire 12.11
Lancaster 12.82

Lancastrian 25.37
lance 28.44
lancelet 30.22
Lancelot 30.31
lanceolate 30.11
lancer 12.69
lancet 30.24
lancewood 16.26
Lancing 26.12
land 16.40
landau 7.5
landaulet 30.4
Länder 12.26
Landers 35.24
landfall 23.15
landfill 23.8
landform 24.9
landholding 26.5
landing 26.5
landlady 4.12
ländler 12.42
landline 25.22
landlocked 30.49
landlord 16.21
landlubber 12.22
landmark 21.5
landmass 28.1
landmine 25.22
Landor 7.5
landowner 12.56
landowning 26.9
landrail 23.6
landscape 27.4
landscapist 31.11
Landseer 12.11
landslide 16.14
landslip 21.6
landsman 25.45
landsmen 25.45
Landsteiner 12.55
landward 16.30
lane 25.7
Langland 16.45
langlauf 17.10
Langley 4.21
Langmuir 12.20
langouste 31.22
langoustine 25.9
Langton 25.50
Langtry 4.38
language 20.9
langue d'oc 21.20
Languedoc 21.20
languid 16.13
languish 29.10
languisher 12.72
languor 12.31
languorous 28.31
langur 13.3
lank 21.33
lanky 4.18

k

l

lanner 12.53
lanneret 30.24
lanolin 25.16
Lansing 26.12
lantana 12.53
lantern 25.50
lanthanum 24.14
lanyard 16.30
Lanzarote 4.54
Lanzhou 11.1
Lao 8.1
Laocoon 25.24
Laodicean 25.36
Laois 29.5
Laos 28.14
Laotian 25.49
Lao-tzu 11.1
lap 27.1
lapdog 18.8
lapel 23.3
lapful 23.21
lapidary 4.43
lapis lazuli 6.11
Lapith 32.6
Laplace 28.2
Lapland 16.40
Laplander 12.25
Lapp 27.1
Lappish 29.9
lapse 28.46
lapsus linguae 6.21
laptop 27.8
lapwing 26.14
Lara 12.64
Laramie 4.30
larcener 12.55
larcenist 31.10
larcenous 28.29
larceny 4.32
larch 15.2
lard 16.2
lardass 28.2
larder 12.25
lardon 25.40
lardy 4.12
lares 35.7
large 20.2
largesse 28.3
larghetto 9.24
largish 29.7
largo 9.13
lariat 30.41
Larissa 12.70
lark 21.5
Larkin 25.15
larkspur 13.4
larky 4.18
Larousse 28.19
larrikin 25.15
larrup 27.14
Larry 4.38

Lars 35.2
larva 12.85
larvae 4.58
larval 23.40
Larwood 16.26
laryngitis 28.12
larynx 28.41
lasagne 12.89
La Salle 23.1
La Scala 12.42
lascar 12.37
lascivious 28.23
laser 12.90
laserdisc 21.35
LaserVision 25.42
lash 29.1
lasher 12.72
lashing 26.12
Las Palmas 28.28
lass 28.1
lassie 4.45
lassitude 16.25
lasso 11.1
lassoer 12.19
Lassus 28.32
last 31.2
lasting 26.13
Las Vegas 28.25
lat 30.1
Latakia 12.3
latch 15.1
latchet 30.20
latchkey 4.18
late 30.7
latecomer 12.52
latency 4.48
latent 30.56
later 12.77
lateral 23.36
Lateran 25.47
laterite 30.29
latex 28.38
lath 32.2
lathe 33.2
lather 12.84
lathery 4.43
lathi 4.51
Latimer 12.51
Latin 25.19
Latinate 30.13
Latinist 31.10
Latino 9.19
latish 29.10
latitude 16.25
latitudinal 23.34
latitudinarian 25.37
Latium 24.16
latke 12.41
latria 12.13
latrine 25.9
latte 3.22

latter 12.74
lattice 28.12
Latvia 12.12
Latvian 25.37
laud 16.19
Lauda 12.28
laudanum 24.19
laudatory 4.43
laugh 17.2
laugher 12.30
laughing stock 21.21
laughter 12.75
Laughton 25.50
Launceston 25.50
launch 29.20
launcher 12.73
launch pad 16.1
launder 12.28
launderer 12.67
launderette 30.4
laundress 28.10
laundromat 30.1
laundry 4.41
Laura 12.66
laureate 30.41
laurel 23.36
Lauren 25.47
Laurie 4.41
Laurier 12.10
Lausanne 25.1
lav 34.1
lava 12.85
lavabo 9.9
lavation 25.49
lavatorial 23.24
lavatory 4.43
lave 34.4
lavender 12.27
laver 12.85
Lavinia 12.8
lavish 29.10
Lavoisier 3.3
law 7.1
lawful 23.21
lawgiver 12.86
lawless 28.27
lawmaker 12.38
lawman 25.2
lawmen 25.5
lawn 25.28
lawnmower 12.17
lawny 4.32
Lawrence 28.45
lawrencium 24.16
Laws 35.17
lawsuit 30.38
lawyer 12.18
lawyerly 4.27
lax 28.38
laxity 4.53

lay 3.1
layabout 30.34
Layamon 25.45
lay-by 6.5
layer 12.2
layette 30.4
layman 25.45
laymen 25.45
lay-off 17.8
layout 30.34
layover 12.86
layperson 25.48
layshaft 30.47
laywoman 25.45
laywomen 25.17
lazaret 30.4
Lazarus 28.31
laze 35.5
Lazio 9.4
lazy 4.61
lazybones 35.31
L-dopa 12.63
Lea 4.1
leach 15.5
Leacock 21.20
lead 16.3, 16.7
leaden 25.40
leader 12.26
lead-in 25.14
leading 26.5
leaf 17.5
leaflet 30.22
leaf-like 21.19
leafy 4.14
league 18.5
leaguer 12.31
Leah 12.3
leak 21.8
leakage 20.6
leaker 12.38
Leakey 4.18
leaky 4.18
leal 23.7
lean 25.9
Leander 12.25
leaning 26.9
Leanne 25.1
leant 30.53
lean-to 11.20
leap 27.5
leaper 12.61
leapfrog 18.8
leapt 30.58
Lear 12.4
learn 25.53
learned 16.10, 16.46
learner 12.59
learnt 30.57
lease 28.6
leaseback 21.2
leasehold 16.37

leaseholder 12.28
leash 29.5
least 31.5
leastways 35.5
leat 30.18
leather 12.84
leatherette 30.4
leatherjacket 30.21
leathern 25.51
leatherneck 21.6
leathery 4.43
leave 34.5
leaven 25.51
leaver 12.85
leaves 35.35
leavings 35.32
Leavis 28.12
Lebanese 35.6
Lebanon 25.46
Lebensraum 24.10
Leblanc 21.34
Lebowa 12.17
Le Carré 3.19
lech 15.3
lecher 12.23
lecherous 28.31
lechery 4.43
lecithin 25.19
Le Corbusier 3.3
lectern 25.50
lection 25.49
lectionary 4.43
lector 7.18
lecture 12.23
lecturer 12.67
lecythi 6.19
led 16.3
Leda 12.26
Lederhosen 25.52
ledge 20.3
ledger 12.35
lee 4.1
leech 15.5
Leeds 35.27
Lee-Enfield 16.35
leek 21.8
leer 12.4
leery 4.43
lees 35.6
leet 30.18
leeward 16.28, 16.30
leeway 3.25
left 30.47
leftish 29.10
leftist 31.14
leftmost 31.20
left-over 12.86
leftover 12.86
leftward 16.30
lefty 4.51
leg 18.3

legacy 4.48
legal 23.30
legalese 35.6
legalist 31.8
legality 4.53
legate 30.42
legatee 4.1
legatine 25.19
legation 25.49
legato 9.24
legator 12.77
legend 16.45
legendary 4.43
legerdemain 25.7
legged 16.9
legging 26.6
leggy 4.15
leghorn 25.28
legible 23.26
legion 25.42
legionary 4.43
legionnaire 2.1
legislate 30.11
legislature 12.24
legit 30.20
legitimacy 4.48
legitimate 30.43
legitimatize 35.14
legitimist 31.9
legless 28.27
legman 25.2
legmen 25.5
Lego 9.13
legroom 24.12
legume 24.12
leguminous 28.29
legwork 21.31
Lehár 1.1
Le Havre 12.64
lei 3.1
Leibniz 28.47
Leibnizian 25.37
Leicester 12.76
Leicestershire 12.11
Leichhardt 30.3
Leiden 25.40
Leif 17.5
Leigh 4.1
Leighton 25.50
Leila 12.43
Leinster 12.76
Leipzig 18.6
leister 12.77
leisure 12.33
leisurely 4.27
leisurewear 2.15
leitmotif 17.5
Leitrim 24.6
lek 21.6
Leland 16.45
Lely 4.23

leman 25.45
Le Mans 25.24
lemma 12.50
lemmatize 35.14
lemme 4.29
lemming 26.9
Lemmon 25.45
Lemnos 28.14
lemon 25.45
lemonade 16.6
lemony 4.34
lempira 12.67
Lemuel 23.25
lemur 12.51
Len 25.5
Lena 12.54
lend 16.41
lender 12.26
Lendl 23.28
length 32.20
lengthen 25.51
lengthener 12.58
lengthways 35.5
lengthwise 35.15
lengthy 4.56
lenience 28.45
leniency 4.48
lenient 30.56
Lenin 25.18
Leninakan 25.2
Leningrad 16.1
Leninist 31.10
Leninite 30.29
lenity 4.53
Lennon 25.46
Lennox 28.41
Lenny 4.31
Leno 9.19
Le Nôtre 12.65
lens 35.31
lensman 25.45
lensmen 25.45
lent 30.53
Lenten 25.50
lenticular 12.46
lentil 23.9
lento 9.24
Leo 9.3
Leon 25.24
León 25.24
Leona 12.56
Leonard 16.29
Leonardo 9.11
leone 25.30
Leonid 16.10
leonine 25.23
Leonora 12.66
leopard 16.29
Leopold 16.37
Léopoldville 23.10

leotard 16.2
leper 12.61
lepidopteran 25.47
lepidopterist 31.12
Lepidus 28.25
leprechaun 25.28
leprosy 4.48
leprous 28.31
lepton 25.26
Lepus 28.30
Leroy 10.11
Lerwick 21.18
Les 35.3
Lesage 19.1
lesbian 25.37
Lesbos 28.14
lesion 25.42
Lesley 4.22
Leslie 4.22
Lesotho 11.20
less 28.3
lessee 4.1
lessen 25.48
Lesseps 28.46
lesser 12.69
Lessing 26.12
lesson 25.48
lessor 7.1
lest 31.3
Lester 12.76
let 30.4
letdown 25.29
lethal 23.40
lethargic 21.11
lethargy 4.17
Lethe 4.56
Lethean 25.37
Leticia 12.11
Lett 30.4
letter 12.76
letter box 28.40
letterhead 16.3
letterpress 28.3
Lettice 28.12
letting 26.13
lettuce 28.12
let-up 27.13
leu 11.2
leucocyte 30.30
leukaemia 12.7
leukemia 12.7
Leuven 25.5
levant 30.53
levanter 12.74
Levantine 25.23
levee 4.58
level 23.40
leveler 12.48
leveller 12.48
lever 12.85
leverage 20.8

I

leveret 30.24
Leverhulme 24.12
Le Verrier 3.3
Levi 4.58, 6.20
leviathan 25.51
levin 25.19
levirate 30.43
levitate 30.16
Levite 30.30
Leviticus 28.26
levity 4.53
levy 4.58
lewd 16.25
Lewes 28.7
lewis 28.7
lexical 23.32
lexicographer 12.30
lexicography 4.14
lexicon 25.43
Lexington 25.50
Ley 4.1
leylandii 6.3
Leyte 4.52
Lhasa 12.69
liability 4.53
liable 23.26
liaise 35.5
liaison 25.52
Liam 24.15
liana 12.53
Liao 8.1
liar 12.13
Lias 28.24
lib 14.7
libation 25.49
libber 12.21
Libby 4.10
LibDem 24.3
libel 23.26
libeler 12.48
libeller 12.48
libellous 28.27
libelous 28.27
Liberace 4.11
liberal 23.36
liberalist 31.8
liberalizer 12.91
liberate 30.15
liberationist 31.10
Liberia 12.10
Liberian 25.37
libertarian 25.37
libertinage 20.7
libertine 25.12
liberty 4.55
libidinal 23.34
libidinous 28.29
libido 9.11
Libra 12.65
Libran 25.47
librarian 25.37

library 4.43
librettist 31.14
libretto 9.24
Librium 24.16
Libya 12.5
Libyan 25.37
lice 28.13
licence 28.45
license 28.45
licensee 4.1
licenser 12.71
licensor 12.71
licentiate 30.41
licentious 28.33
lichen 25.13
Lichfield 16.35
Lichtenstein 25.23
licit 30.24
lick 21.9
lickerish 29.9
lickety-split 30.20
licking 26.7
lickspittle 23.39
licorice 29.9
lid 16.8
Liddell 23.28
lidless 28.8
lido 9.11
lie 6.1
Liebfraumilch 21.32
Liebig 18.6
Liechtenstein 25.23
Liechtensteiner
   12.55
lied 16.14
Lieder 12.26
lief 17.5
liege 20.5
Liège 19.4
liegeman 25.45
liegemen 25.45
lie-in 25.13
lien 25.36
lieu 11.1
lieutenancy 4.48
lieutenant 30.56
life 17.7
lifebelt 30.51
lifeblood 16.27
lifeboat 30.35
lifeboatman 25.45
lifeboatmen 25.45
lifebuoy 10.3
lifeguard 16.2
lifejacket 30.21
lifelike 21.19
lifeline 25.22
lifelong 26.15
lifer 12.30
lifesaver 12.85
lifespan 25.3

lifestyle 23.12
lifetime 24.7
Liffey 4.14
lift 30.47
lifter 12.78
lig 18.6
ligand 16.45
ligature 12.24
liger 12.31
ligger 12.31
light 30.26
lighten 25.50
lightening 26.9
lighter 12.79
lightfast 31.2
light-footed 16.12
light-headed 16.9
light-hearted 16.12
lighthouse 28.16
lighting 26.13
lightish 29.10
lightning 26.9
lightweight 30.17
ligneous 28.23
lignite 30.29
lignitic 21.17
Liguria 12.10
Ligurian 25.37
likable 23.26
like 21.19
likelihood 16.26
likely 4.25
like-minded 16.9
liken 25.43
likewise 35.15
liking 26.7
Likud 16.26
lilac 21.30
Lilian 25.37
Lilienthal 23.2
Lilith 32.6
Lille 23.7
Lillee 4.24
Lilliputian 25.49
lilo 9.17
lilt 30.51
lily 4.24
lily-livered 16.29
Lima 12.51
Limassol 23.13
limb 24.6
limber 12.21, 12.51
limbo 9.9
Limburger 12.32
lime 24.7
limeade 16.6
limekiln 25.44
limelight 30.28
limepit 30.23
limerick 21.15
limestone 25.31

limewash 29.11
limey 4.29
liminal 23.34
limit 30.23
limitary 4.43
limited 16.12
limiter 12.78
limn 24.6
limner 12.51
limo 9.18
Limoges 19.5
Limousin 25.1
limousine 25.9
limp 27.17
limpet 30.23
limpid 16.10
limpidity 4.53
limpkin 25.15
Limpopo 9.20
limp-wristed 16.12
Linacre 12.41
linage 20.7
linchpin 25.18
Lincoln 25.43
Lincolnshire 12.11
linctus 28.34
Lind 16.42
Linda 12.27
Lindbergh 18.13
linden 25.40
Lindisfarne 25.4
Lindon 25.40
Lindsay 4.61
Lindy 4.12
line 25.21
lineage 20.6
lineal 23.24
linear 12.8
linearity 4.53
linearize 35.13
linebacker 12.37
Lineker 12.39
lineman 25.45
linemen 25.45
linen 25.18
liner 12.55
linesman 25.45
linesmen 25.45
line-up 27.13
Linford 16.28
ling 26.3
Lingala 12.42
lingam 24.18
linger 12.31
lingerer 12.67
lingerie 4.43
lingo 9.13
lingua franca 12.37
lingual 23.40
linguine 4.31
linguist 31.15

linguistician 25.49
lining 26.9
link 21.33
linkage 20.6
linkman 25.2
linkmen 25.5
link-up 27.13
linn 25.13
Linnaean 25.36
Linnaeus 28.22
Linnean 25.36
linnet 30.23
lino 9.19
linocut 30.40
linocutting 26.13
linoleum 24.16
linotype 27.7
linsang 26.1
linseed 16.7
lint 30.54
lintel 23.39
Linton 25.50
linty 4.53
Linus 28.29
liny 4.32
Linz 28.44
lion 25.38
Lionel 23.34
lion-hearted 16.12
lionizer 12.91
lion-like 21.19
Lions 35.31
lip 27.6
lipase 35.5
lipid 16.10
Lipizzaner 12.53
lipless 28.8
lip-like 21.19
liposuction 25.49
Lippi 4.36
Lippmann 25.45
lippy 4.36
lipsalve 34.15
lipstick 21.17
lip-sync 21.33
lip-syncer 12.39
liquefaction 25.49
liquefier 12.14
liquefy 6.7
liquescent 30.56
liqueur 12.20
liquid 16.13
liquidate 30.9
liquidity 4.53
liquor 12.39
liquorice 29.9
lira 12.67
lire 12.67
Lisa 12.69
Lisbon 25.38
Lisburn 25.53

lisente 4.51
lisle 23.11
lisp 27.18
lissom 24.20
list 31.6
listen 25.48
listener 12.58
lister 12.78
listeria 12.10
listing 26.13
Liston 25.50
Liszt 31.6
lit 30.20
litany 4.34
lite 30.26
liter 12.77
literacy 4.48
literage 20.8
literal 23.36
literalist 31.8
literalize 35.12
literary 4.43
literate 30.43
literati 4.51
literatim 24.6
literature 12.23
lithe 33.5
lithium 24.16
litho 9.26
lithograph 17.2
lithographer 12.30
lithographic 21.10
lithography 4.14
Lithuania 12.8
Lithuanian 25.37
litigant 30.56
litigate 30.9
litigious 28.25
litmus 28.28
litotes 35.9
litre 12.77
litreage 20.8
litter 12.78
littérateur 13.1
litterbug 18.12
litter lout 30.34
little 23.39
Little Englander 12.29
Littler 12.43
Littlewood 16.26
littoral 23.36
Littré 3.1
liturgical 23.32
liturgist 31.7
liturgy 4.17
livable 23.26
live 34.6, 34.9
livelihood 16.26
livelong 26.15
lively 4.25

liven 25.51
Liver 12.86
liveried 16.11
liverish 29.9
Liverpool 23.20
Liverpudlian 25.37
liverwort 30.45
livery 4.43
liveryman 25.45
liverymen 25.45
lives 35.35
livestock 21.21
Livia 12.12
livid 16.13
lividity 4.53
living 26.14
Livings 35.32
Livingstone 25.50
Livonia 12.8
Livorno 9.19
Livy 4.58
Liz 35.10
Liza 12.91
lizard 16.30
Lizzie 4.61
Ljubljana 12.53
llama 12.50
Llandudno 9.19
llano 9.19
Llewelyn 25.16
Lloyd 16.24
Lloyd's 35.27
lo 9.1
loach 15.10
load 16.23
loader 12.28
loading 26.5
loaf 17.11
loafer 12.30
loam 24.11
loamy 4.29
loan 25.30
loanee 4.1
loaner 12.56
loan shark 21.5
loanword 16.31
loath 32.11
loathe 33.7
loather 12.84
loaves 35.35
lob 14.9
lobby 4.10
lobbyist 31.6
lobe 14.11
lobo 9.9
lobotomize 35.13
lobotomy 4.30
lobscouse 28.16
lobster 12.79
lobster pot 30.32

lobster thermidor 7.5
lobworm 24.22
local 23.32
locale 23.2
locality 4.53
Locarno 9.19
locate 30.7
location 25.49
locational 23.34
loch 22.4
lochan 25.43
loci 6.16
lock 21.20
lockage 20.6
Locke 21.20
locker 12.40
Lockerbie 4.10
locket 30.21
lockjaw 7.9
locknut 30.40
lockout 30.34
locksmith 32.6
lock-up 27.13
Lockyer 12.89
loco 9.16
locomotion 25.49
locum 24.18
locus 28.26
locust 31.25
locution 25.49
lode 16.23
loden 25.40
lodestar 1.19
lodestone 25.31
lodge 20.11
lodger 12.35
lodging 26.6
loess 28.7
loft 30.47
lofty 4.54
log 18.8
Logan 25.41
loganberry 4.43
logarithm 24.20
logarithmic 21.12
logbook 21.28
loge 19.5
logger 12.32
loggerhead 16.3
loggia 12.6
logia 12.5
logic 21.11
logical 23.32
logician 25.49
logion 25.37
logistic 21.17
logistical 23.32
logjam 24.1
logo 9.13
logomachy 4.20

logon 25.25
logorrheic 21.9
logorrhoeic 21.9
logos 28.14
logotype 27.7
logroller 12.44
logwood 16.26
Lohengrin 25.18
loin 25.32
loincloth 32.8
Loire 1.1
Lois 28.7
loiter 12.81
loiterer 12.67
Loki 4.20
Lola 12.44
Lolita 12.77
loll 23.13
lollapalooza 12.92
Lollard 16.29
Lollardy 4.13
lollipop 27.8
lollop 27.14
lolly 4.25
Lombard 16.2
Lombardic 21.10
Lombardy 4.13
Lombok 21.20
Lomé 3.16
London 25.40
Londonderry 4.38
Londoner 12.58
lone 25.30
lonely 4.25
loner 12.56
long 26.15
longboat 30.35
longbow 9.9
longevity 4.53
Longfellow 9.17
Longford 16.28
longhair 2.6
longhand 16.40
longhorn 25.28
longing 26.10
Longinus 28.29
longish 29.9
longitude 16.25
longitudinal 23.34
longshore 7.17
longshoreman
   25.45
longshoremen 25.45
longstop 27.8
Longton 25.50
longueur 13.1
longways 35.5
Lonnie 4.32
loo 11.1
loofah 12.30
look 21.28

lookalike 21.19
looker 12.41
lookout 30.34
look-see 4.47
lookup 27.13
loom 24.12
loon 25.33
loony 4.33
loop 27.11
looper 12.63
loophole 23.17
loopy 4.37
loose 28.19
loosen 25.48
loosener 12.58
loot 30.37
looter 12.81
lop 27.8
lope 27.10
lopsided 16.9
loquacious 28.33
loquacity 4.53
loquat 30.32
loquitur 12.78
lor 7.1
loran 25.47
Lorca 12.40
Lorcan 25.43
lord 16.19
lord-like 21.19
lordling 26.8
lordly 4.25
Lordy 4.13
lore 7.1
Lorelei 6.11
Loren 25.5
Lorentz 28.45
Lorenz 35.31
Lorenzo 9.29
Loreto 9.24
Loretta 12.76
lorgnette 30.4
lorikeet 30.18
loris 28.10
lorn 25.28
Lorna 12.56
Lorraine 25.7
lorry 4.41
lory 4.41
Los Alamos 28.14
Los Angeles 35.7
lose 35.21
loser 12.92
loss 28.14
lost 31.17
lot 30.31
Lothario 9.4
Lothian 25.37
lotion 25.49
lottery 4.43
Lottie 4.54

lotto 9.25
lotus 28.34
Lou 11.1
louche 29.11
loud 16.22
louden 25.40
loudhailer 12.43
loudmouth 32.10
loudmouthed 16.48
loudspeaker 12.38
Louella 12.42
lough 22.4
Loughborough
   12.67
Loughlin 25.16
Lough Neagh 3.1
Louie 4.8
Louis 4.8
louis 35.10
Louisa 12.90
Louise 35.6
Louisiana 12.53
Louisianan 25.46
Louisville 23.10
lounge 20.19
lounger 12.35
lour 12.16
Lourdes 16.28
Lourenço Marques
   28.38
loury 4.43
louse 28.16
lousy 4.61
lout 30.34
Louth 32.10
loutish 29.10
Louvain 25.1
louver 12.87
louvre 12.87
Louvre 12.66
lovable 23.26
lovage 20.9
lovat 30.44
love 34.13
lovebird 16.31
love bite 30.26
lovechild 16.36
Lovelace 28.5
Lovell 23.40
lovelock 21.21
lovelorn 25.28
lovely 4.26
lover 12.87
lovesick 21.16
lovey 4.58
lovey-dovey 4.58
low 9.1
lowball 23.14
lowboy 10.3
lowbrow 8.10
low-down 25.29

Lowell 23.25
lower 12.16, 12.17
lowermost 31.20
Lowestoft 30.47
lowish 29.6
lowland 16.45
lowlander 12.29
lowlife 17.7
lowlight 30.28
lowly 4.25
lowness 28.29
low-rise 35.11, 35.13
Lowry 4.41
lox 28.40
loyal 23.25
loyalist 31.8
loyalty 4.55
lozenge 20.19
Lualaba 12.21
Luanda 12.25
Luang Prabang 26.1
luau 8.2
lubber 12.22
lubberly 4.27
Lubbock 21.30
lube 14.12
Lübeck 21.6
Lublin 25.16
lubricant 30.56
lubricate 30.10
lubricious 28.33
Lubumbashi 4.50
Lubyanka 12.37
Lucan 25.43
Lucas 28.26
luce 28.19
lucency 4.47
lucent 30.56
Lucerne 25.53
Lucia 12.3, 12.11
Lucian 25.37
lucid 16.11
lucidity 4.53
Lucifer 12.30
Lucille 23.7
Lucinda 12.27
Lucius 28.23
luck 21.29
Lucknow 8.9
lucky 4.20
lucre 12.41
Lucrece 28.6
Lucretia 12.72
Lucretius 28.33
Lucy 4.47
Luda 12.29
Luddite 30.26
Ludendorff 17.9
ludic 21.10
ludicrous 28.31
ludo 9.11

Ludovic 21.18
Ludwig 18.6
luff 17.15
Luftwaffe 12.30
lug 18.12
Lugano 9.19
luge 20.15
Luger 12.32
luggage 20.6
lugger 12.32
lughole 23.17
lugsail 23.6
lugubrious 28.23
lugworm 24.22
Lukács 15.1
Luke 21.27
lukewarm 24.9
lull 23.22
lullaby 6.5
Lully 4.26
lulu 11.13
lum 24.14
lumbago 9.13
lumbar 12.22
lumber 12.22
lumberer 12.67
lumberjack 21.3
lumbermen 25.45
lumen 25.17
luminaire 2.1
luminary 4.43
luminescence 28.45
luminescent 30.56
luminosity 4.53
luminous 28.29
lumme 4.30
lummox 28.41
lump 27.17
lumpen 25.46
lumpenproletariat 30.41
lumper 12.63
lumpfish 29.7
lumpish 29.9
lumpy 4.37
Luna 12.56
lunacy 4.48
lunar 12.56
lunate 30.13
lunatic 21.17
lunation 25.49
lunch 29.20
luncheon 25.49
luncheonette 30.4
luncher 12.73
lunchtime 24.7
Lund 16.43, 16.44
Lundy 4.13
lunette 30.4
lung 26.18
lunge 20.19

lungfish 29.7
lungi 4.15
lungworm 24.22
lungwort 30.45
lunisolar 12.44
lunker 12.41
Luo 9.7
Lupercalia 12.6
lupin 25.18
lupine 25.18, 25.23
lupus 28.30
lurch 15.14
lurcher 12.24
lure 12.20
Lurex 28.38
lurgy 4.15
lurid 16.11
lurk 21.31
lurker 12.41
Lusaka 12.37
luscious 28.33
lush 29.16
Lusitania 12.8
lust 31.24
luster 12.81
lustral 23.36
lustrate 30.7
lustre 12.81
lustrous 28.31
lustrum 24.19
lusty 4.55
lute 30.37
lutein 25.13
lutetium 24.16
Luther 12.83
Lutheran 25.47
Luton 25.50
Lutyens 35.31
Lutz 28.47
luvvy 4.58
lux 28.41
luxe 28.41
Luxembourg 18.13
Luxembourger 12.32
Luxor 7.16
luxuriance 28.45
luxuriant 30.56
luxuriate 30.8
luxurious 28.23
luxury 4.43
Luzon 25.24
lwei 3.1
Lyall 23.25
lycanthrope 27.10
lycanthropy 4.37
lycée 3.20
lyceum 24.15
lychee 4.1
lychgate 30.9
lychnis 28.9

Lycia 12.11
Lycian 25.37
lycopene 25.11
Lycra 12.65
Lycurgus 28.25
lyddite 30.26
Lydgate 30.9
Lydia 12.5
Lydian 25.37
lye 6.1
lying 26.3
Lyle 23.11
Lyly 4.24
lymph 17.19
lymphangitis 28.12
lymphatic 21.15
lymphoma 12.52
lynch 29.20
lyncher 12.72
lynching 26.12
Lynette 30.4
Lynn 25.13
Lynsey 4.61
lynx 28.41
Lyon 25.38
lyonnaise 35.5
Lyons 25.24, 35.31
Lyra 12.65
lyre 12.13
lyrebird 16.31
lyric 21.15
lyrical 23.32
lyricist 31.13
lyrist 31.12
Lysander 12.25
Lysenko 9.16
Lysippus 28.30
Lysol 23.13
Lytton 25.50

ma 1.1
ma'am 24.2
Maas 28.2
Maastricht 30.50
Maat 30.3
Mabel 23.26
Mabinogion 25.24
mac 21.1
macabre 12.64
macadam 24.17
macadamia 12.7
Macanese 35.6
Macao 8.1
macaque 21.5
macaroni 4.33
macaronic 21.13
macaroon 25.33
MacArthur 12.83

macassar 12.69
Macau 8.1
Macaulay 4.25
macaw 7.1
Macbeth 32.3
Maccabean 25.36
Maccabees 35.6
MacDiarmid 16.10
Macdonald 16.38
mace 28.5
macédoine 25.4
Macedon 25.40
Macedonia 12.8
Macedonian 25.37
macer 12.69
macerate 30.15
mach 21.1
machete 4.51
Machiavelli 4.22
Machiavellian 25.37
machinate 30.13
machine 25.9
machinery 4.43
machinist 31.10
machismo 9.18
Machmeter 12.77
macho 9.10
Machu Picchu 11.5
Mackay 6.1
Mackenzie 4.61
mackerel 23.36
mackinaw 7.13
mackintosh 29.11
mackle 23.32
Maclean 25.9
Macleod 16.22
Macmillan 25.44
MacNeice 28.6
Macquarie 4.41
macramé 4.29
macro 9.21
macrobiotic 21.17
macrocosm 24.21
macrocosmic 21.12
macron 25.26
macropod 16.18
macroscopic 21.14
mad 16.1
Madagascan 25.43
Madagascar 12.37
madam 24.17
Madame 24.17
madcap 27.1
madden 25.40
madder 12.25
made 16.6
Madeira 12.67
Madeiran 25.47
madeleine 25.16
mademoiselle 23.3

l
m

made-to-measure 12.33
Madge 20.1
madhouse 28.16
Madhya Pradesh 29.3
Madison 25.48
madly 4.21
madman 25.45
madmen 25.45
madness 28.29
Madras 28.2
madrasa 12.69
Madrid 16.8
madrigal 23.30
madrigalian 25.37
Madura 12.67
Madurese 35.6
madwomen 25.17
Mae 3.1
Maecenas 28.29
maelstrom 24.19
maenad 16.1
maenadic 21.10
maestro 9.21
Maeterlinck 21.33
Maeve 34.4
Mafeking 26.7
Mafia 12.5
mafiosi 4.61
mafioso 9.29
mag 18.1
magazine 25.9
Magdalen 25.16
Magdalena 12.54
Magdalenian 25.37
Magdeburg 18.13
mage 20.4
Magellan 25.44
magenta 12.76
Maggie 4.15
maggot 30.42
maggoty 4.55
Maghrib 14.6
magi 6.9
magian 25.37
magic 21.11
magical 23.32
magician 25.49
magisterial 23.24
magisterium 24.16
magistracy 4.48
magistrate 30.15
magistrature 12.23
maglev 34.3
magma 12.50
Magna Carta 12.75
magna cum laude 3.9
magnanimity 4.53
magnanimous 28.28

magnate 30.13
magnesia 12.72
magnesite 30.30
magnesium 24.16
magnet 30.23
magnetic 21.17
magnetite 30.30
magneto 9.24
magneton 25.26
Magnificat 30.1
magnificence 28.45
magnificent 30.56
magnifico 9.16
magnifier 12.14
magnify 6.7
magniloquence 28.45
magniloquent 30.56
magnitude 16.25
magnolia 12.6
Magnox 28.40
magnum 24.19
Magnus 28.29
magpie 6.14
Magritte 30.18
maguey 3.1
magus 28.25
Magyar 1.23
Mahabharata 12.82
Mahalia 12.6
mahant 30.55
maharaja 12.35
maharani 4.31
Maharashtra 12.64
Maharashtrian 25.37
maharishi 4.50
mahatma 12.50
Mahaweli 4.22
Mahayana 12.53
Mahdi 4.12
Mahfouz 35.21
mah-jong 26.15
Mahler 12.42
mahogany 4.34
Mahon 25.4
mahonia 12.8
mahout 30.34
mahseer 12.11
Maia 12.13
maid 16.6
maidan 25.4
maiden 25.40
maidenhair 2.6
maidenhead 16.3
maidenhood 16.26
maidenish 29.9
maidenly 4.22
maidservant 30.56
Maidstone 25.50
maigre 12.31

mail 23.5
mailbag 18.1
mailboat 30.35
mailbox 28.40
mailer 12.43
mailing 26.8
maillot 9.1
mailman 25.2
mailmen 25.5
mailshot 30.32
maim 24.4
Maimonides 35.7
main 25.7
Main 25.21
Maine 25.7
mainframe 24.4
mainland 16.45
mainlander 12.29
mainline 25.22
mainliner 12.55
mainmast 31.2
mainplane 25.8
mainsail 23.37
mainsheet 30.19
mainspring 26.11
mainstay 3.22
mainstream 24.5
maintain 25.7
maintainer 12.54
maintenance 28.45
Maintenon 25.26
maintop 27.8
Mainz 28.47
maiolica 12.39
Maisie 4.61
maisonette 30.4
Maithili 4.24
maître d'hôtel 23.3
maize 35.5
majestic 21.17
majesty 4.53
Majlis 28.7
majolica 12.39
major 12.35
Majorca 12.40
Majorcan 25.43
majordomo 9.18
majorette 30.4
majoritarian 25.37
majority 4.53
majuscular 12.46
majuscule 23.20
Makassar 12.69
make 21.7
make-believe 34.5
makeover 12.86
maker 12.38
makeshift 30.47
make-up 27.13
making 26.7
mako 9.16

Malabo 9.9
Malachi 6.10
malachite 30.27
Malachy 4.20
maladjusted 16.12
maladminister 12.78
maladroit 30.36
malady 4.13
mala fide 4.12
Málaga 12.32
Malagasy 4.45
malaise 35.5
Malamud 16.26
malamute 30.38
malapert 30.45
malaprop 27.8
malapropos 9.1
malaria 12.10
malarial 23.24
malarkey 4.18
Malawi 4.59
Malawian 25.37
Malay 3.1
Malaya 12.2
Malayalam 24.18
Malayan 25.36
Malaysia 12.12
Malaysian 25.37
Malcolm 24.18
malcontent 30.53
malcontented 16.12
mal de mer 2.1
Maldivian 25.37
male 23.5
malediction 25.49
maledictory 4.43
malefaction 25.49
malefactor 12.74
malefic 21.10
maleficence 28.45
maleficent 30.56
malevolence 28.45
malevolent 30.56
malfeasance 28.45
malfeasant 30.56
malformed 16.39
malfunction 25.49
Malherbe 14.4
Mali 4.21
Malian 25.37
Malibu 11.4
malice 28.8
malice aforethought 30.33
malicious 28.33
malign 25.21
malignancy 4.48
malignant 30.56
maligner 12.55

malignity 4.53
Malin 25.16
Malines 25.9
malinger 12.31
malingerer 12.67
Malinowski 4.19
malison 25.52
mall 23.1
mallam 24.18
mallard 16.2
Mallarmé 3.1
mallee 4.21
mallet 30.22
mallow 9.17
malm 24.2
Malmö 9.18
malnourished 30.59
malodorous 28.31
Malory 4.43
Malpighi 4.15
Malplaquet 3.14
malpractice 28.12
malt 30.51
Malta 12.80
Maltese 35.6
malthouse 28.16
Malthus 28.35
Malthusian 25.37
malting 26.13
maltreat 30.18
maltreater 12.77
Malvinas 28.29
mam 24.1
mama 1.1
mamaguy 6.8
mamba 12.21
mambo 9.9
Mamet 30.23
Mamie 4.29
mamillary 4.43
mamma 1.1, 12.50
mammae 4.29
mammal 23.33
mammalian 25.37
mammary 4.43
mammee 4.29
mammogram 24.1
Mammon 25.45
Mammonist 31.10
mammoth 32.13
mammy 4.29
man 25.1
mana 12.53
manacle 23.32
manage 20.7
manager 12.35
manageress 28.3
managerial 23.24
managing 26.6
Managua 12.20
manakin 25.15

mañana 12.53
Manasseh 4.45
man-at-arms 35.30
manatee 4.1
Manaus 28.16
Manawatu 11.20
Manchester 12.78
manchineel 23.7
Manchu 11.1
Manchuria 12.10
manciple 23.35
Mancunian 25.37
Mandaean 25.36
mandala 12.48
Mandalay 3.1
mandarin 25.18
mandatary 4.43
mandate 30.7, 30.9
mandatory 4.43
Mandean 25.36
Mandela 12.42
Mandeville 23.10
mandible 23.26
mandola 12.44
mandolin 25.13
mandoline 25.13
mandolinist 31.10
mandrake 21.7
mandrel 23.9
mandrill 23.9
manducate 30.10
Mandy 4.12
mane 25.7
manège 19.4
manes 35.5
Manet 3.17
maneuver 12.87
maneuverer 12.67
maneuvering 26.11
Manfred 16.11
manful 23.21
manga 12.31
manganese 35.7
manganic 21.13
manganite 30.29
mange 20.19
mangel 23.30
mangel-wurzel
   23.41
manger 12.35
mangetout 11.1
mangle 23.30
mangler 12.48
mango 9.13
mangold 16.37
mangosteen 25.12
mangrove 34.11
mangy 4.17
manhandle 23.28
Manhattan 25.50
manhole 23.17

manhood 16.26
man-hour 12.16
manhunt 30.55
mania 12.8
maniac 21.1
maniacal 23.32
manic 21.13
Manichee 4.1
manicure 12.20
manicurist 31.12
manifest 31.3
manifesto 9.24
manifold 16.37
manikin 25.15
Manila 12.43
manilla 12.43
manioc 21.20
maniple 23.35
manipulate 30.11
manipulatory 4.43
Manipur 12.20
Manipuri 4.43
Manitoba 12.21
Manitoban 25.38
manitou 11.20
mankind 16.42
manky 4.18
manless 28.27
Manley 4.21
manlike 21.19
manly 4.21
man-made 16.6
Mann 25.1
manna 12.53
manned 16.40
mannequin 25.15
manner 12.53
mannerist 31.12
mannerly 4.27
Mannheim 24.7
Manning 26.9
mannish 29.9
Mano 9.19
manoeuvre 12.87
manoeuvrer 12.67
manoeuvring 26.11
manometer 12.78
manor 12.53
manorial 23.24
man-o'-war 7.1
manpower 12.16
manqué 3.14
mansard 16.2
Mansart 30.3
manse 28.44
Mansell 23.37
manservant 30.56
Mansfield 16.35
mansion 25.49
manslaughter 12.80
Manson 25.48

manta 12.74
manteau 9.24
Mantegna 12.89
mantel 23.39
mantelletta 12.76
mantellette 3.22
mantelpiece 28.6
mantelshelf 17.18
mantelshelves 35.35
mantic 21.17
manticore 7.10
mantilla 12.43
mantis 28.12
mantle 23.39
mantlet 30.22
mantling 26.8
mantra 12.64
mantrap 27.1
mantua 12.20
Manu 11.15
manual 23.25
Manuel 23.3
manufactory 4.43
manufacture 12.23
manufacturer 12.67
manuka 12.41
manumit 30.20
manure 12.20
manuscript 30.58
Manx 28.41
many 4.31
manyfold 16.37
Manzoni 4.33
Maoism 24.21
Maoist 31.6
Maori 4.41
Mao Zedong 26.15
map 27.1
maple 23.35
mapless 28.27
Mappa Mundi 4.13
mapper 12.61
Maputo 9.25
maquette 30.4
maquillage 19.1
maquis 4.1
mar 1.1
marabou 11.4
marabout 11.4, 30.37
maraca 12.37
Maracaibo 9.9
Maradona 12.56
Maramba 12.21
maraschino 9.19
Marat 1.16
Maratha 12.75
Marathi 4.51
marathon 25.51
marathoner 12.58
maraud 16.19
marauder 12.28

m

Marbella 12.2
marble 23.26
marbling 26.8
marbly 4.27
marc 21.5
Marcan 25.43
marcasite 30.30
Marceau 9.1
marcel 23.3
march 15.2
marcher 12.23
Marches 35.10
Marcia 12.11
Marciano 9.19
Marconi 4.33
Marcos 28.14
Marcus 28.26
Marcuse 12.92
Mardi Gras 1.1
Marduk 21.30
mardy 4.12
mare 2.1, 3.19
maremma 12.50
Marengo 9.13
Margaret 30.24
margarine 25.9
margarita 12.77
Margate 30.9
margate 30.21
marge 20.2
margin 25.14
marginal 23.34
marginalia 12.6
Margot 9.13
marguerite 30.18
Mari 4.38
Maria 12.4
Marian 25.37
Marianas 35.24
Marianne 25.1
Marie 4.1
Marie-Antoinette 30.4
marigold 16.37
marijuana 12.53
Marilyn 25.16
marimba 12.21
marina 12.54
marinade 16.6
marinara 12.64
marinate 30.13
marine 25.9
mariner 12.55
Marinetti 4.51
Mario 9.4
marionette 30.4
Marisa 12.70
Marist 31.12
marital 23.39
maritime 24.7
Maritimes 35.30

Maritsa 12.70
Marius 28.23
marjoram 24.19
Marjorie 4.43
mark 21.5
markdown 25.29
marked 30.48
marker 12.37
market 30.21
marketeer 12.4
marketer 12.78
marketing 26.13
marketplace 28.5
marking 26.7
markka 1.11
Markova 12.86
Marks 28.38
marksman 25.45
marksmen 25.45
markup 27.13
marl 23.2
Marlborough 12.67
Marlene 12.54, 25.10
Marley 4.21
marlin 25.16
marline 25.16
marlinspike 21.19
Marlon 25.44
Marlowe 9.17
marly 4.21
Marmaduke 21.27
marmalade 16.6
marmite 30.29
marmoreal 23.24
marmoset 30.5
marmot 30.43
Marne 25.4
marocain 25.7
Maronite 30.29
maroon 25.33
marque 21.5
marquee 4.1
Marquesas 35.24
marquess 28.12
marquetry 4.40
Marquette 30.4
marquis 28.12
marquisate 30.43
marquise 35.6
marquisette 30.4
Marrakesh 29.3
Marrano 9.19
marriage 20.8
married 16.11
marrow 9.21
marrowbone 25.30
marry 4.38
Marryat 30.41
Mars 35.2
Marsala 12.42
Marseillaise 35.5

Marseilles 3.1
marsh 29.2
Marsha 12.72
marshal 23.38
marshland 16.40
marshmallow 9.17
marshy 4.50
marsupial 23.24
mart 30.3
martello 9.17
marten 25.19
Martens 35.31
Martha 12.83
martial 23.38
Martian 25.49
martin 25.19
Martina 12.54
Martineau 9.19
martinet 30.4
martingale 23.5
martini 4.31
Martinique 21.8
Martinmas 28.1
martlet 30.22
martyr 12.75
martyrdom 24.17
martyrize 35.13
martyry 4.43
marvel 23.40
marveler 12.48
Marvell 23.40
marveller 12.48
marvellous 28.27
marvelous 28.27
Marvin 25.19
Marx 28.38
Marxist 31.13
Mary 4.39
Maryland 16.45
Mary Magdalene 25.16
marzipan 25.3
Masada 12.25
Masai 6.16
masala 12.42
Masaryk 21.15
Mascagni 4.60
mascara 12.64
Mascarene 25.9
mascarpone 4.33
mascle 23.32
mascot 30.31
masculine 25.16
masculinity 4.53
masculinize 35.13
Masefield 16.35
Maseru 11.17
mash 29.1
masher 12.72
mashie 4.50
Mashona 12.56

Mashonaland 16.40
mask 21.35
masker 12.37
masochist 31.7
mason 25.48
Masonic 21.13
masonry 4.39
masque 21.35
masquerade 16.6
masquerader 12.26
mass 28.1
Massachusetts 28.47
massacre 12.41
massage 20.2
massager 12.36
Massawa 12.88
massé 4.45
masseur 13.1
massif 17.5
Massine 25.9
Massinger 12.35
massive 34.7
Masson 25.48
massy 4.45
mast 31.2
mastaba 12.22
mastectomy 4.30
master 12.75
masterclass 28.2
masterly 4.27
mastermind 16.42
masterpiece 28.6
Masters 35.24
masterstroke 21.24
masterwork 21.31
mastery 4.43
masthead 16.3
mastic 21.17
masticate 30.10
masticatory 4.43
mastiff 17.6
mastodon 25.25
mastoid 16.24
masturbate 30.9
masturbatory 4.39
mat 30.1
Matabele 4.23
Matabeleland 16.40
matador 7.5
Mata Hari 4.38
matamata 12.74
match 15.1
matchbox 28.40
matchlock 21.21
matchmaker 12.38
matchmaking 26.7
matchplay 3.15
matchstick 21.17
matchwood 16.26
mate 30.7

maté 3.22
matelot 9.17
matelote 30.35
mater 12.77
materfamilias 28.1
material 23.24
materialist 31.8
matériel 23.3
maternal 23.34
maternity 4.53
matey 4.52
math 32.1
mathematical 23.32
mathematician 25.49
mathematics 28.39
Mathias 28.24
maths 28.48
Matilda 12.27
matinée 3.17
matins 35.31
Matisse 28.6
Mato Grosso 9.22
matriarch 21.5
matriarchal 23.32
matriarchy 4.18
matrices 35.8
matricidal 23.28
matricide 16.16
matriculate 30.11
matrilineal 23.24
matrimonial 23.24
matrimony 4.34
matrix 28.39
matron 25.47
matronly 4.27
matsuri 4.41
Matsuyama 12.50
matt 30.1
matte 30.1
matted 16.12
matter 12.74
Matterhorn 25.28
matter-of-fact 30.48
Matthew 11.22
Matthews 35.21
matting 26.13
mattock 21.30
mattress 28.10
mature 12.20
maturity 4.53
matzo 12.70
maudlin 25.16
Maugham 24.9
maul 23.14
mauler 12.44
Mau Mau 8.8
maunder 12.28
maundering 26.11
Maundy 4.13
Maupassant 25.26

Maura 12.66
Maureen 25.11
Mauriac 21.1
Maurice 28.10
Mauritania 12.8
Mauritanian 25.37
Mauritian 25.49
Mauritius 28.33
Maury 4.41
Maurya 12.10
Mauser 12.92
mausoleum 24.15
mauve 34.11
maven 25.51
maverick 21.15
mavis 28.12
maw 7.1
mawkish 29.8
max 28.38
maxi 4.45
maxillary 4.43
maxim 24.6
maxima 12.51
maximal 23.33
maximalist 31.8
Maximilian 25.37
maximizer 12.91
maximum 24.19
Maxine 25.9
maxixe 28.38
Maxwell 23.4
may 3.1
Maya 12.2, 12.13
Mayan 25.38
maybe 4.10
mayday 3.9
Mayer 12.2, 12.13
Mayfair 2.5
mayflower 12.16
mayfly 6.11
mayhap 27.1
mayhem 24.3
Maynard 16.2
Maynooth 32.12
mayn't 30.56
Mayo 9.2
mayonnaise 35.5
mayor 2.1
mayoral 23.36
mayoralty 4.55
mayoress 28.31
Mayotte 30.31
maypole 23.18
Mays 35.5
Mazar-e-Sharif 17.5
Mazarin 25.18
maze 35.5
mazer 12.90
mazurka 12.41
mazy 4.61
mazzard 16.30

Mazzini 4.31
Mbabane 4.31
McAleese 28.6
McCarthy 4.56
McCarthyite 30.26
McCartney 4.31
McEnroe 9.21
McEwan 25.38
McGonagall 23.30
McIntosh 29.11
McKinlay 4.24
McLuhan 25.38
me 4.1
mea culpa 12.63
mead 16.7
meadow 9.11
meadowlark 21.5
meadowsweet 30.19
meadowy 4.7
meager 12.31
meagre 12.31
meal 23.7
mealie 4.23
mealtime 24.1
mealworm 24.22
mealy 4.23
mealy-mouthed 16.48
mean 25.9
meander 12.25
meandering 26.11
meanie 4.31
meaning 26.9
means 35.31
meant 30.53
meantime 24.7
meanwhile 23.12
measles 35.29
measly 4.23
measure 12.33
meat 30.18
meatball 23.14
Meath 33.3
meathead 16.3
meaty 4.52
mecca 12.37
meccano 9.19
mechanic 21.13
mechanical 23.32
mechanician 25.49
mechanist 31.10
mechanizer 12.91
mechatronics 28.39
Mechlin 25.16
Mecklenburg 18.13
Med 16.3
medal 23.28
medalist 31.8
medallic 21.11
medallion 25.37
medallist 31.8

Medawar 12.88
meddle 23.28
meddler 12.48
Mede 16.7
Medea 12.4
Medellín 25.9
Medevac 21.4
media 12.5
medial 23.24
median 25.37
mediant 30.56
mediate 30.8
mediatory 4.43
medic 21.10
Medicaid 16.6
medical 23.32
Medicare 2.7
medicate 30.10
Medicean 25.36
Medici 4.11
medicinal 23.34
medicine 25.19
medick 21.10
medieval 23.40
medievalist 31.8
medievalize 35.12
Medina 12.54, 12.55
mediocre 12.40
mediocrity 4.53
meditate 30.16
Mediterranean 25.37
medium 24.16
medlar 12.42
medley 4.22
Médoc 21.20
medulla 12.47
medusa 12.92
medusae 4.62
meed 16.7
meek 21.8
meerkat 30.1
meerschaum 24.20
Meerut 30.43
meet 30.18
meeting 26.13
meeting house 28.16
Meg 18.3
mega 12.31
megabuck 21.29
megabyte 30.26
megadeath 32.3
Megaera 12.67
megaflop 27.8
megahertz 28.47
megalith 25.8
megalithic 21.18
megalomania 12.8
megalomaniac 21.1

megalomaniacal 23.32
megalopolis 28.8
megalopolitan 25.50
megalosaurus 28.31
Megan 25.41
megaphone 25.30
megastar 1.19
megastore 7.18
megaton 25.35
megavolt 30.51
megawatt 30.32
Megger 12.31
megohm 24.11
megrim 24.6
meiosis 28.11
meiotic 21.17
Meir 12.4
Meissen 25.48
Mekong 26.15
melamine 25.22
melancholia 12.6
melancholic 21.11
melancholy 4.27
Melanchthon 25.51
Melanesia 12.89
Melanesian 25.52
mélange 19.7
Melanie 4.34
melanin 25.18
melanoma 12.52
Melbourne 25.38
Melchior 7.3
meld 16.35
Meleager 12.31
melee 3.15
melic 21.11
melick 21.11
Melilla 12.4
melilot 30.31
Melinda 12.27
meliorate 30.15
meliorist 31.12
Melissa 12.70
melliferous 28.31
mellifluence 28.45
mellifluent 30.56
mellifluous 28.24
Mellon 25.44
mellotron 25.26
mellow 9.17
melodeon 25.37
melodic 21.10
melodica 12.39
melodious 28.23
melodize 35.11
melodrama 12.50
melodramatic 21.17
melodramatist 31.14

melodramatize 35.14
melody 4.13
melon 25.44
Melos 28.14
Melpomene 4.32
melt 30.51
meltdown 25.29
melter 12.76
melton 25.50
Melville 23.10
Melvin 25.19
member 12.21
membrane 25.8
membranous 28.29
meme 24.5
memento 9.24
memento mori 6.15
Memnon 25.26
memo 9.18
memoir 1.22
memoirist 31.12
memorabilia 12.6
memoranda 12.25
memorandum 24.17
memorial 23.24
memorialist 31.8
memorialize 35.12
memorizer 12.91
memory 4.43
Memphis 28.7
memsahib 14.7
men 25.5
menace 28.9
menacer 12.70
ménage 19.1
ménage à trois 1.1
menagerie 4.43
Menander 12.25
menarche 4.18
Mencken 25.43
mend 16.41
mendacious 28.33
mendacity 4.53
Mendel 23.28
Mendeleev 34.3
Mendelian 25.37
Mendelssohn 25.48
mender 12.26
mendicancy 4.48
mendicant 30.56
Mendoza 12.92
Menelaus 28.22
Menes 35.7
menfolk 21.24
menhir 12.5
menial 23.24
meningitis 28.12
meniscus 28.26
Mennonite 30.29
menopausal 23.41

menopause 35.17
menorah 12.66
Mensa 12.69
menses 35.8
Menshevik 21.18
menstrual 23.25
menstruate 30.8
menswear 2.15
mental 23.39
mentalist 31.8
menthol 23.13
mentholated 16.12
mention 25.49
mentor 7.18
menu 11.22
Menuhin 25.13
Menzies 35.10
Mephistophelian 25.37
mephitic 21.17
mercantile 23.12
Mercedes 35.7
mercenary 4.43
mercer 12.71
mercerize 35.13
mercery 4.43
merchandise 28.13, 35.11
merchandiser 12.91
merchant 30.56
Mercia 12.11
Mercian 25.37
Merckx 28.41
mercurial 23.24
mercury 4.41
mercy 4.49
mere 12.4
Meredith 32.6
meretricious 28.33
merge 20.17
merger 12.36
Mérida 12.27
meridian 25.37
meridional 23.34
Meriel 23.24
meringue 26.1
merino 9.19
merit 30.24
meritocracy 4.48
meritocratic 21.17
meritorious 28.23
merkin 25.15
merle 23.42
merlin 25.16
merlon 25.44
Merlot 30.42
mermaid 16.6
merman 25.2
mermen 25.5
Merovingian 25.37
Merrill 23.9

merry 4.38
merry-go-round 16.43
merrymaker 12.38
merrymaking 26.7
Mersey 4.62
Merseyside 16.16
Merthyr Tydfil 23.10
Mervyn 25.19
mesa 12.69
mésalliance 28.45
mescal 23.1
mescaline 25.16
mesdames 24.1
mesdemoiselles 23.3
mesh 29.3
mesic 21.18
Mesmer 12.50
mesmeric 21.15
mesmerist 31.12
mesmerizer 12.91
mesne 25.9
mesocephalic 21.11
Mesolithic 21.18
Mesopotamia 12.7
Mesopotamian 25.37
Mesozoic 21.9
mesquite 30.18
mess 28.3
message 20.9
Messalina 12.54
messenger 12.35
Messiaen 25.27
messiah 12.13
messianic 21.13
messieurs 35.25
Messina 12.54
messmate 30.12
Messrs 35.24
messy 4.45
met 30.4
metabolic 21.11
metacarpus 28.30
metal 23.39
metalize 35.12
metallic 21.11
metallize 35.12
metallurgical 23.32
metallurgist 31.7
metallurgy 4.17
metalwork 21.31
metalworker 12.41
metalworking 26.7
metamorphic 21.10
metamorphose 35.19
metamorphosis 28.11
metaphor 12.30

metaphoric 21.15
metaphorical 23.32
metaphysic 21.18
metaphysical 23.32
metaphysician 25.49
metastasize 35.14
metatarsal 23.37
metathesis 28.11
metathetical 23.32
mete 30.18
metempsychosis 28.11
meteor 12.12
meteoric 21.15
meteorite 30.29
meteoroid 16.24
meteorology 4.17
meter 12.77
meterage 20.8
methadone 25.30
methane 25.8
methanol 23.13
Methedrine 25.11
methinks 28.41
method 16.29
methodic 21.10
methodical 23.32
Methodist 31.6
methodize 35.11
methodizer 12.91
methodology 4.17
methought 30.33
meths 28.48
methuselah 12.48
metic 21.17
metical 23.32
meticulous 28.27
métier 3.3
metol 23.13
metonym 24.6
metonymy 4.30
metre 12.77
metreage 20.8
metric 21.15
metrical 23.32
metricate 30.10
metro 9.21
metronome 24.11
metronomic 21.12
metronymic 21.12
Metropole 23.18
metropolis 28.8
metropolitan 25.50
Metternich 21.13
mettle 23.39
Metz 28.47
meunière 2.1
Meurig 18.6
Meuse 35.25
mew 11.1
mewl 23.20

mews 35.21
Mexicali 4.21
Mexican 25.43
Mexico 9.16
Meyerhof 17.8
mezuzah 12.92
mezuzoth 30.35
mezzanine 25.11
mezza voce 3.8
mezzo 9.22
Mezzogiorno 9.19
mezzotint 30.54
mho 9.1
Mia 12.4
Miami 4.29
miaow 8.1
miasma 12.50
miasmal 23.33
miasmatic 21.17
miasmic 21.12
miaul 23.14
mic 21.19
mica 12.40
Micawber 12.21
Micawberish 29.9
mice 28.13
Michael 23.32
Michaelmas 28.28
Michel 23.3
Michelangelo 9.17
Michelin 25.16
Michelle 23.3
Michelson 25.48
Michigan 25.41
Michoacán 25.4
mick 21.9
mickey 4.19
mickle 23.32
micro 9.21
microbe 14.11
microbial 23.24
microchip 27.6
microcline 25.22
microcosm 24.21
microcosmic 21.12
microdot 30.31
microfiche 29.5
microfilm 24.18
microform 24.9
microgram 24.1
micrograph 17.2
microlight 30.28
micromesh 29.3
micrometer 12.77, 12.78
micrometre 12.77
micrometry 4.40
micron 25.26
Micronesia 12.89
Micronesian 25.52
microphone 25.30

microprocessor 12.69
microscope 27.10
microscopic 21.14
microscopy 4.37
microsecond 16.45
microsurgery 4.43
microtone 25.31
microwave 34.4
mid 16.8
mid-air 2.1
Midas 28.25
midday 3.1
midden 25.40
middle 23.28
middlebrow 8.10
middleman 25.2
middlemen 25.5
middle-of-the-road 16.23
Middlesbrough 12.65
Middlesex 28.38
Middleton 25.50
middleweight 30.17
middling 26.8
middy 4.12
Mideast 31.5
midfield 16.35
midfielder 12.26
Midgard 16.2
midge 20.6
midget 30.21
midgut 30.40
Midi 4.1
midi 4.12
midiron 25.38
midland 16.45
midlander 12.29
midlife 17.7
Midlothian 25.37
midmost 31.20
midnight 30.29
midpoint 30.55
Midrash 29.1
Midrashim 24.6
midriff 17.6
midship 27.6
midshipman 25.45
midshipmen 25.45
midships 28.46
midst 31.27
midstream 24.5
midsummer 12.52
midterm 24.22
midtown 25.29
Midway 3.25
midway 3.1
midweek 21.8
Midwest 31.3
Midwestern 25.50

midwicket 30.21
midwife 17.7
midwifery 4.43
midwinter 12.78
midwives 35.35
mien 25.9
miff 17.6
MI5 34.9
might 30.26
mightn't 30.56
mighty 4.54
migraine 25.8
migrant 30.56
migrate 30.7
migratory 4.43
Miguel 23.3
mihrab 14.2
Mikado 9.11
mike 21.19
Mikhail 23.11
mil 23.8
milady 4.12
Milan 25.1
Milanese 35.6
milch 29.19
mild 16.36
mildew 11.22
mildewy 4.8
mildish 29.6
Mildred 16.11
mile 23.11
mileage 20.6
milepost 31.20
miler 12.44
Miles 35.29
Milesian 25.37
milestone 25.31
Miletus 28.34
milfoil 23.19
Milhaud 9.3
milieu 13.5
militancy 4.48
militant 30.56
militarist 31.12
military 4.43
militate 30.16
militia 12.72
militiaman 25.45
militiamen 25.45
milk 21.32
milker 12.39
milkmaid 16.6
milkman 25.45
milkmen 25.5
milkshake 21.7
milksop 27.8
milkwort 30.45
milky 4.19
mill 23.8
Millais 3.15
millefeuille 5.2

m

millenarian 25.37
millenary 4.43
millennial 23.24
millennialist 31.8
millennium 24.16
millepore 7.14
miller 12.43
millet 30.22
millhand 16.40
milliampere 2.10
millibar 1.4
Millicent 30.56
Milligan 25.41
milligram 24.1
Millikan 25.43
milliliter 12.77
millilitre 12.77
millimeter 12.77
millimetre 12.77
milliner 12.55
millinery 4.43
million 25.52
millionaire 2.1
millionfold 16.37
millionth 32.19
millipede 16.7
millisecond 16.45
millpond 16.42
millrace 28.5
Mills 35.29
millstone 25.31
millstream 24.5
millwheel 23.7
millwright 30.29
Milne 25.44
milo 9.17
milometer 12.78
milord 16.19
Milton 25.50
Miltonian 25.37
Miltonic 21.13
Milwaukee 4.19
Mimas 28.28
mime 24.7
mimer 12.51
mimesis 28.11
mimetic 21.17
Mimi 4.29
mimic 21.12
mimicker 12.39
mimicry 4.40
mimosa 12.92
mimulus 28.27
Min 25.13
minaret 30.4
minareted 16.12
mince 28.44
mincemeat 30.18
mincer 12.70
Minch 29.20
mind 16.42

Mindanao 8.1
minder 12.27
mind-numbing 26.9
Mindoro 9.21
mind-reader 12.26
mindset 30.5
mine 25.21
minefield 16.35
minelayer 12.2
minelaying 26.3
miner 12.55
mineral 23.36
mineralize 35.12
mineralogist 31.7
mineralogy 4.17
Minerva 12.87
minestrone 4.33
minesweeper 12.61
minesweeping 26.10
Ming 26.3
mingle 23.30
Mingus 28.25
mingy 4.17
mini 4.32
miniature 12.23
miniaturist 31.12
minibar 1.4
minibus 28.21
minicab 14.1
minicam 24.1
minidress 28.3
minikin 25.15
minim 24.6
minima 12.51
minimal 23.33
minimalist 31.8
minimax 28.38
minimizer 12.91
minimum 24.19
minion 25.52
mini-pill 23.9
miniseries 35.10
miniskirt 30.45
minister 12.78
ministerial 23.24
ministrant 30.56
ministry 4.40
minivan 25.3
miniver 12.86
mink 21.33
minke 4.19
Minkowski 4.19
Minneapolis 28.8
Minnesinger 12.31
Minnesota 12.80
Minnesotan 25.50
Minnie 4.32
minnow 9.19
Minoan 25.38
minor 12.55
Minorca 12.40

Minorcan 25.43
Minorite 30.29
minority 4.53
Minos 28.14
Minotaur 7.18
Minsk 21.35
minster 12.78
minstrel 23.36
minstrelsy 4.48
mint 30.54
mintage 20.9
Minter 12.78
Minton 25.50
minty 4.53
minuet 30.4
minus 28.29
minuscular 12.46
minuscule 23.20
minute 30.23, 30.37
minutiae 6.3
minx 28.41
minxish 29.9
Miocene 25.11
Mir 12.4
Mirabeau 9.9
mirabelle 23.3
miracle 23.32
miraculous 28.27
mirador 7.1
mirage 19.1
Miranda 12.25
mire 12.13
mirepoix 1.1
Miriam 24.16
mirid 16.11
mirk 21.31
mirky 4.20
Miró 9.1
mirror 12.65
mirth 32.14
miry 4.43
misadventure 12.23
misalliance 28.45
misanthrope 27.10
misanthropic 21.14
misanthropical
    23.32
misanthropist 31.11
misanthropy 4.37
misapply 6.1
misapprehend 16.41
misapprehension
    25.49
misappropriate 30.8
misbegotten 25.50
misbehave 34.4
misbehavior 12.89
misbehaviour 12.89
misbelief 17.5
miscalculate 30.11
miscall 23.14

miscarriage 20.8
miscarry 4.38
miscast 31.2
miscellanea 12.8
miscellaneous 28.23
miscellany 4.34
mischance 28.44
mischief 17.6
mischievous 28.35
miscible 23.26
misconceive 34.5
misconception
    25.49
misconduct 30.49
misconstruction
    25.49
misconstrue 11.1
miscount 30.55
miscreant 30.56
miscue 11.1, 11.22
misdate 30.7
misdeal 23.7
misdealt 30.51
misdeed 16.7
misdemeanor 12.54
misdemeanour
    12.54
misdescription
    25.49
misdiagnose 35.19
misdiagnoses 35.8
misdiagnosis 28.11
misdirect 30.48
misdirection 25.49
misdoing 26.3
misdoubt 30.34
mise en scène 25.7
miser 12.91
misère 2.1
miserere 4.39
misericord 16.21
miserly 4.27
misery 4.43
misfield 16.35
misfire 12.13, 12.14
misfit 30.21
misfortune 25.33
misgave 34.4
misgive 34.6
misgiven 25.51
misgiving 26.14
misgovern 25.51
misguidance 28.45
misguide 16.14
misguided 16.9
mishandle 23.28
mishap 27.1
mishear 12.4
misheard 16.31
mishit 30.20
mishmash 29.1

Mishnah 12.55
Mishnaic 21.9
misidentify 6.7
misinform 24.9
misinterpret 30.24
misinterpreter 12.78
MI6 28.39
misjudge 20.16
miskick 21.9
Miskito 9.24
mislay 3.1
mislead 16.7
misleader 12.26
misleading 26.5
misled 16.3
mislike 21.19
mismanage 20.7
mismatch 15.1
mismated 16.12
misname 24.4
misnomer 12.52
misogamist 31.9
misogamy 4.30
misogynist 31.10
misogynous 28.29
misogyny 4.32
misplace 28.5
misplay 3.1, 3.15
misprint 30.54
misprision 25.42
misprize 35.11
mispronounce 28.44
misquote 30.35
misread 16.3, 16.7
misreport 30.33
misrepresent 30.53
misrule 23.20
miss 28.7
missal 23.37
misshape 27.4
misshapen 26.46
missile 23.11
mission 25.49
missionary 4.43
missioner 12.58
Mississippi 4.36
Mississippian 25.37
missive 34.7
Missolonghi 4.35
Missouri 4.43
Missourian 25.37
misspell 23.3
misspelling 26.8
misspend 16.41
misspent 30.53
misstate 30.7
misstep 27.3
missus 35.10
missy 4.46
mist 31.6

mistake 21.7
mistaken 25.43
mister 12.78
mistime 24.7
mistitle 23.39
mistletoe 9.24
mistook 21.28
mistranslate 30.7
mistreat 30.18
mistress 28.10
mistrial 23.25
mistrust 31.24
misty 4.53
mistype 27.7
misunderstand 16.40
misunderstanding 26.5
misunderstood 16.26
misusage 20.9
misuse 28.19, 35.21
misuser 12.92
Mitch 15.6
Mitchell 23.27
Mitchum 24.17
mite 30.26
miter 12.79
Mitford 16.28
Mithraic 21.9
Mithraist 31.6
Mithras 28.1
mitigate 30.9
mitigatory 4.43
Mitla 12.43
mitochondria 12.10
mitre 12.79
mitt 30.20
mitten 25.50
Mitterrand 25.26
Mitzi 4.46
mitzvah 12.88
mitzvoth 30.35
mix 28.39
mixable 23.26
mixer 12.70
Mixtec 21.6
mixture 12.23
Mizoram 24.19
mizuna 12.56
mizzen 25.52
mizzenmast 31.2
mizzle 23.41
mnemonic 21.13
mo 9.1
moa 12.17
Moab 14.1
Moabite 30.26
moan 25.30
moaner 12.56
moat 30.35

mob 14.9
mobber 12.21
mobile 23.11
mobility 4.53
mobilizer 12.91
mobocracy 4.48
mobster 12.79
Mobutu 11.20
moccasin 25.19
mocha 12.40
mock 21.20
mocker 12.40
mockery 4.43
mockingbird 16.31
mod 16.18
modal 23.28
modality 4.53
mod cons 35.31
mode 16.23
model 23.28
modeler 12.48
modeller 12.48
modem 24.3
Modena 12.55
moderate 30.15, 30.43
moderato 9.24
modern 25.40
modernist 31.10
modernity 4.53
modernizer 12.91
modest 31.6
modesty 4.53
modicum 24.18
modificatory 4.43
modifier 12.14
modify 6.7
Modigliani 4.31
modillion 25.52
modish 29.6
modiste 31.5
Mods 35.27
modular 12.46
modulate 30.11
module 23.20
modulo 9.17
modus operandi 4.12
modus vivendi 4.12
Mogadishu 11.19
Mogadon 25.25
moggie 4.15
mogul 23.30
mohair 2.6
Mohammedan 25.40
mohawk 21.22
Mohican 25.43
Moho 9.14
Mohs 9.1
moiety 4.53
moil 23.19

Moira 12.66
moire 1.1
moist 31.21
moisten 25.48
moisture 12.24
Mojave 4.58
mojo 9.15
moke 21.24
moko 9.16
moksha 12.73
mol 23.17
molar 12.44
molasses 35.10
mold 16.37
Moldau 8.3
Moldavia 12.12
Moldavian 25.37
moldboard 16.20
molder 12.28
molding 26.5
Moldova 12.86
moldy 4.13
mole 23.17
molecular 12.46
molecule 23.20
molehill 23.9
moleskin 25.15
molest 31.3
molester 12.76
Molière 2.2
moline 25.21
Moline 25.9
moll 23.13
Mollie 4.25
mollifier 12.14
mollify 6.7
mollusc 21.35
molluscan 25.43
mollusk 21.35
molluskan 25.43
molly 4.25
mollycoddle 23.28
Molotov 17.8
molt 30.51
molten 25.50
molto 9.25
Moluccas 35.24
moly 4.25
molybdenum 24.19
mom 24.8
Mombasa 12.69
moment 30.56
momentary 4.43
momentous 28.34
momentum 24.20
momma 12.51
Mommsen 25.48
mommy 4.29
Mon 25.30
Mona 12.56
Monaco 9.16

m

monad 16.1
Monaghan 25.42
monarch 21.30
monarchal 23.32
monarchial 23.24
monarchic 21.11
monarchical 23.32
monarchist 31.7
monarchy 4.20
monastery 4.43
monastic 21.17
Monck 21.34
mondaine 25.7
Monday 3.9
mondial 23.24
Monégasque 21.35
Monel 23.34
Monet 3.17
monetarist 31.12
monetary 4.43
money 4.33
moneybags 35.28
moneychanger 12.35
moneymaker 12.38
moneymaking 26.7
Mongol 23.30
Mongolia 12.6
Mongolian 25.37
mongoloid 16.24
mongoose 28.19
mongrel 23.36
mongrelize 35.12
monial 23.24
Monica 12.39
moniker 12.39
monism 24.21
monist 31.10
monistic 21.17
monition 25.49
monitor 12.78
monitorial 23.24
monitory 4.43
monk 21.34
monkey 4.20
monkeyish 29.6
monkfish 29.7
Mon-Khmer 2.1
monkish 29.8
Monks 28.41
Monmouth 32.13
Monmouthshire 12.11
Mono 9.19
monocausal 23.41
Monoceros 28.31
monochord 16.21
monochromatic 21.17
monochrome 24.11
monochromic 21.12

monocle 23.32
monocoque 21.20
monocotyledon 25.40
monocracy 4.48
monocratic 21.17
monocycle 23.32
monodic 21.10
monodist 31.6
monofil 23.8
monogamous 28.28
monogamy 4.30
monogenean 25.36
monoglot 30.31
monogram 24.1
monogrammatic 21.17
monograph 17.2
monographic 21.10
monographist 31.7
monohull 23.22
monokini 4.31
monolingual 23.40
monolith 32.6
monolithic 21.18
monologic 21.11
monologue 18.8
monomania 12.8
monomaniac 21.1
monomer 12.52
mononucleosis 28.11
Monophysite 30.30
monoplane 25.8
monopod 16.18
Monopole 23.18
monopolist 31.8
monopolizer 12.91
monopoly 4.27
monopteros 28.14
monorail 23.6
monosyllabic 21.9
monotheist 31.6
Monothelite 30.28
monotint 30.54
monotone 25.31
monotonic 21.13
monotonous 28.29
monotony 4.34
monotreme 24.5
Monotype 27.7
monoxide 16.16
Monroe 9.1
Monrovia 12.12
Mons 35.31
Monseigneur 13.1
monsieur 13.1
Monsignor 12.89
monsignori 4.41
monsoon 25.33
monsoonal 23.34

monster 12.79
monstera 12.67
monstrance 28.45
monstrosity 4.53
monstrous 28.31
montage 19.1
Montagna 12.89
Montagnard 16.2
Montague 11.22
Montaigne 25.7
Montana 12.53
Montanan 25.46
montane 25.8
Mont Blanc 25.24
Montcalm 24.2
Monte 4.54
Monte Cassino 9.19
Montenegrin 25.18
Montenegro 9.21
Monterrey 3.1
Montesquieu 13.1
Montessori 4.41
Monteverdi 4.12
Montevideo 9.2
Montez 35.3
Montgolfier 12.5
Montgomery 4.43
month 32.19
monthly 4.26
Montmartre 12.64
Montmorency 4.45
Montpelier 12.6
Montpellier 12.6
Montreal 23.14
Montreux 13.1
Montrose 35.19
Montserrat 30.1
Montserratian 25.37
Monty 4.54
monumentalize 35.12
moo 11.1
mooch 15.11
moocher 12.24
mood 16.25
moody 4.13
moolah 12.45
mooli 4.26
moon 25.33
moonbeam 24.5
mooncalf 17.2
mooncalves 35.35
Moonie 4.33
moonlight 30.28
moonlighter 12.79
moonlit 30.22
moonquake 21.7
moonrise 35.13
moonscape 27.4
moonset 30.5
moonshine 25.23

moonshiner 12.55
moonstone 25.31
moonstruck 21.29
moony 4.33
moor 12.20
moorage 20.8
moorcock 21.20
Moore 12.20
moorfowl 23.16
moorhen 25.5
mooring 26.11
Moorish 29.9
moorland 16.45
moory 4.43
moose 28.19
moot 30.37
mop 27.8
mope 27.10
moped 16.3
moper 12.63
mophead 16.3
moppet 30.23
moppy 4.36
moquette 30.4
mor 7.1
Morag 18.1
moraine 25.7
moral 23.36
morale 23.2
moralist 31.8
morality 4.53
moralizer 12.91
Moran 25.1
morass 28.1
moratoria 12.10
moratorium 24.16
Moravia 12.12
Moravian 25.37
moray 3.19
morbid 16.8
morbidity 4.53
mordacious 28.33
mordancy 4.47
mordant 30.56
Mordecai 6.10
mordent 30.56
Mordred 16.11
more 7.1
moreen 25.9
moreish 29.9
morel 23.3
morello 9.17
moreover 12.86
mores 35.5
Moresque 21.35
Morgan 25.41
morgen 25.41
morgue 18.9
moribund 16.44
moribundity 4.53
morion 25.37

Morisco 9.16
Morley 4.25
Mormon 25.45
morn 25.28
Morna 12.56
Mornay 3.17
morning 26.9
Moro 9.21
Moroccan 25.43
Morocco 9.16
moron 25.26
Moroni 4.33
moronic 21.13
morose 28.17
Morpeth 32.13
morph 17.9
morpheme 24.5
Morpheus 28.23
morphine 25.10
morphing 26.6
Morrison 25.48
morrow 9.21
morse 28.15
morsel 23.37
mort 30.33
mortadella 12.42
mortal 23.39
mortar 12.80
mortar board 16.20
mortgage 20.6
mortgagee 4.1
mortgagor 7.1
mortician 25.49
mortify 6.7
Mortimer 12.51
mortise 28.12
Morton 25.50
mortuary 4.43
Morwenna 12.53
mosaic 21.9
moschatel 23.3
Moscow 9.16
Moseley 4.25
Moselle 23.3
Moses 35.10
mosey 4.61
mosh 29.11
moshav 34.2
Moskva 12.86
mosque 21.35
mosquito 9.24
moss 28.14
Mossad 16.1
mossie 4.61
mossy 4.46
most 31.20
Mostyn 25.19
Mosul 23.37
mot 9.1
mote 30.35
motel 23.3

motet 30.4
moth 32.8
mothball 23.14
mother 12.84
motherboard 16.20
motherfucker 12.41
motherfucking 26.7
motherhood 16.26
motherland 16.40
motherly 4.27
mothproof 17.13
mothy 4.56
motif 17.5
motion 25.49
motional 23.34
motivate 30.16
motive 34.8
mot juste 31.22
motley 4.25
motmot 30.31
moto perpetuo 9.8
motor 12.80
motorbike 21.19
motorboat 30.35
motorcade 16.6
motorcar 1.11
motorcycle 23.32
motorcycling 26.8
motorcyclist 31.8
motorhome 24.11
motorist 31.12
motorize 35.13
motorman 25.2
motormen 25.5
motormouth 32.10
motorway 3.25
Motown 25.29
motte 30.31
mottle 23.39
motto 9.25
Motu 11.20
moue 11.1
mouflon 25.25
mould 16.37
mouldboard 16.20
moulder 12.28
moulding 26.5
mouldy 4.13
moulin 25.16
Moulmein 25.8
moult 30.51
mound 16.43
mount 30.55
mountain 25.19
mountaineer 12.4
mountainous 28.29
mountainside 16.16
mountainy 4.32
Mountbatten 25.50
mountebank 21.33

mountebankery
  4.43
mounter 12.80
Mountie 4.54
mounting 26.13
Mount Isa 12.91
mourn 25.28
mourner 12.56
mourning 26.9
mouse 28.16
mouser 12.70
mousetrap 27.1
moussaka 12.37
mousse 28.19
mousseline 25.10
moustache 29.2
mousy 4.47
mouth 32.10, 33.6
mouthbrooder
  12.29
mouther 12.84
mouthpiece 28.6
mouth-to-mouth
  32.10
mouthwash 29.11
mouthy 4.57
movable 23.26
move 34.12
mover 12.87
movie 4.58
mow 8.1, 9.1
mower 12.17
mowing 26.3
mown 25.30
moxie 4.46
Mozambican 25.43
Mozambique 21.8
Mozarabic 21.9
Mozart 30.3
Mozartian 25.37
mozzarella 12.42
mph 15.4
Ms 35.10
MSc 4.1
MS-DOS 28.14
mu 11.1
Mubarak 21.3
much 15.13
mucilage 20.6
muck 21.29
mucker 12.41
muckle 23.32
muckrake 21.7
muckraker 12.38
mucky 4.20
mucous 28.26
mucus 28.26
mud 16.27
mudbank 21.33
mudbath 32.2
muddle 23.28

muddler 12.48
muddy 4.13
Mudéjar 1.9
Mudéjares 28.3
mudfish 29.7
mudflap 27.1
mudflat 30.1
mudflow 9.17
mudguard 16.2
mudlark 21.5
mudpack 21.3
mudskipper 12.62
mud-slinger 12.60
mud-slinging 26.10
mudstone 25.31
muesli 4.26
muezzin 25.20
muff 17.15
muffin 25.14
muffle 23.29
muffler 12.47
mufti 4.55
mug 18.12
Mugabe 4.10
mugful 23.21
mugger 12.32
mugging 26.6
muggins 35.31
muggy 4.15
Mughal 23.30
mugshot 30.32
mugwump 27.17
Muhammad 16.29
Muir 12.20
mujahedin 25.9
Mukden 25.40
mulatto 9.24
mulberry 4.43
mulch 29.19
mulct 30.49
Muldoon 25.33
mule 23.20
muleteer 12.4
mulga 12.32
mulish 29.8
mull 23.22
mullah 12.47
mullein 25.16
Müller 12.46
Muller 12.47
mullet 30.22
mulligan 25.41
mulligatawny 4.32
mullion 25.37
mulloway 3.25
Mulroney 4.33
multichannel 23.34
multicolor 12.47
multicolored 16.29
multicolour 12.47
multicoloured 16.29

m

multiculturalist 31.8
multi-ethnic 21.13
multifaceted 16.12
multifarious 28.23
multifoil 23.19
multiform 24.9
multiformity 4.53
multifunction 25.49
multifunctional 23.34
multigrade 16.6
multihull 23.22
multilateral 23.36
multilateralist 31.8
multi-layered 16.28
multilingual 23.40
multimedia 12.5
multimillion 25.52
multimillionaire 2.1
multipartite 30.30
multiphase 35.5
multiple 23.35
multiplex 28.38
multiplier 12.14
multiply 6.11
multipolar 12.44
multipurpose 28.30
multiracial 23.38
multistage 20.4
multistorey 4.41
multitude 16.25
multitudinous 28.29
multivalve 34.15
multum in parvo 9.27
mum 24.14
mumble 23.26
mumbler 12.48
Mumbles 35.29
mumbling 26.8
mumbo-jumbo 9.9
mummer 12.52
mummery 4.43
mummify 6.7
mumming 26.9
mummy 4.30
mumps 28.46
munch 29.20
Munch 21.34
München 25.49
munchies 35.10
Munda 12.29
mundane 25.7
mundanity 4.53
mungo 9.13
Munich 21.13
municipal 23.35
municipalize 35.12
munificence 28.45

munificent 30.56
munition 25.49
munitioner 12.58
Munro 9.1
munshi 4.50
Munster 12.81
Münster 12.81
mural 23.36
muralist 31.8
murder 12.29
murderer 12.67
murderess 28.3
murderous 28.31
Murdo 9.11
Murdoch 21.20
mure 12.20
murex 28.38
Murgatroyd 16.24
Muriel 23.24
Murillo 9.17
murk 21.31
murky 4.20
Murmansk 21.35
murmur 12.52
murmurer 12.67
murmurous 28.31
murphy 4.14
murrain 25.18
Murray 4.42
murre 13.1
Murrumbidgee 4.17
Mururoa 12.17
Muscadet 3.9
muscadine 25.21
muscat 30.1
muscatel 23.3
muscle 23.37
muscly 4.27
muscovado 9.11
Muscovite 30.30
Muscovy 4.58
muscular 12.46
musculature 12.24
muse 35.21
musette 30.4
museum 24.15
mush 29.15, 29.16
mushroom 24.12
mushroomy 4.30
mushy 4.50
music 21.18
musical 23.32
musicale 23.2
musicalize 35.12
musician 25.49
musicianly 4.24
musicology 4.17
musing 26.14
musk 21.35
musket 30.21
musketeer 12.4

Muskogean 25.37
muskrat 30.2
musky 4.20
Muslim 24.6
muslin 25.16
muso 9.29
musquash 29.11
muss 28.21
mussel 23.37
Mussolini 4.31
Mussorgsky 4.19
mussy 4.47
must 31.24
mustache 29.2
mustang 26.1
mustard 16.29
muster 12.81
musterer 12.67
Mustique 21.8
mustn't 30.56
musty 4.55
Mut 30.40
mutable 23.26
mutant 30.56
mutate 30.7
mutation 25.49
mutch 15.13
mute 30.37
mutilate 30.11
mutineer 12.4
mutinous 28.29
mutiny 4.32
mutt 30.40
mutter 12.81
mutterer 12.67
muttering 26.11
mutton 25.50
muttonhead 16.3
muttony 4.34
mutual 23.25
mutualist 31.8
mutule 23.20
muumuu 11.14
Muzak 21.4
muzhik 21.11
muzzle 23.41
muzzy 4.62
my 6.1
myalgia 12.6
myall 23.25
Mycenae 4.31
Mycenaean 25.37
Mycenean 25.37
Myfanwy 4.59
Mykonos 28.14
Mylar 1.12
mynah 12.55
myope 27.10
myopia 12.9
myopic 21.14
myosotis 28.12

Myra 12.65
myriad 16.28
myriapod 16.18
Myrmidon 25.40
Myrna 12.59
myrobalan 25.44
Myron 25.47
myrrh 13.1
myrtle 23.39
myself 17.18
Mysia 12.11
Mysian 25.37
Mysore 7.1
mysterious 28.23
mystery 4.43
mystic 21.17
mystical 23.32
mystify 6.7
mystique 21.8
myth 32.6
mythi 6.19
mythic 21.18
mythical 23.32
mythicist 31.13
mythicize 35.14
mythologer 12.36
mythologic 21.11
mythologize 35.11
mythologizer 12.91
mythology 4.17
mythopoeic 21.9
Mytilene 25.10
myxomatosis 28.11

nab 14.1
Nabataean 25.36
Nabatean 25.36
Nablus 28.27
nabob 14.9
Nabokov 34.10
nacelle 23.3
nacho 9.10
nacre 12.38
Na-Dene 3.1
Nader 12.26
Nadia 12.5
Nadine 25.9
nadir 12.5
naff 17.1
nag 18.1
naga 12.31
Nagaland 16.40
Nagasaki 4.18
nagger 12.31
Nagorno-Karabakh 21.1
Nagoya 12.18
Nagpur 12.20

Nahuatl 23.39
Nahum 24.18
naiad 16.1
naif 17.5
nail 23.5
nailer 12.43
nailery 4.43
nainsook 21.28
Naipaul 23.14
naira 12.65
Nairobi 4.10
naive 34.5
naivety 4.53
Najaf 17.1
naked 16.10
Nakuru 11.17
Namaqualand 16.40
namby-pamby 4.10
name 24.4
namedrop 27.8
name-dropper 12.62
nameplate 30.11
namesake 21.7
Namibia 12.5
Namibian 25.37
Namur 12.20
nan 25.1
nana 12.53
Nanak 21.3
nance 28.44
Nanchang 26.1
Nancy 4.45
Nandi 4.12
Nanette 30.4
Nanga Parbat 30.1
Nanjing 26.3
nankeen 25.9
nanny 4.31
nanny goat 30.35
nanometer 12.77
nanometre 12.77
nanosecond 16.46
Nansen 25.48
Nantes 30.53
Nantucket 30.21
naoi 10.2
Naomi 4.29
nap 27.1
napalm 24.2
nape 27.4
napery 4.43
Naphtali 6.11
naphtha 12.83
naphthalene 25.10
Napier 12.9
napkin 25.15
Naples 35.29
napoleon 25.37
Napoleonic 21.13
nappa 12.61
nappe 27.1

napper 12.61
nappy 4.36
Nara 12.64
Narayan 25.38
Narbonne 25.24
narc 21.5
narcissi 6.16
narcissist 31.13
narcissus 28.32
narcolepsy 4.45
narcotic 21.17
narcotize 35.14
nard 16.2
nardoo 11.1
nark 21.5
narky 4.18
Narragansett 30.24
narrate 30.7
narrow 9.21
narrowcasting 26.13
narrowish 29.6
Narvik 21.18
narwhal 23.40
nary 4.39
nasal 23.41
nascent 30.56
Naseby 4.10
Nash 29.1
Nashville 23.10
Nasmyth 32.6
Nassau 7.16, 8.11
Nasser 12.69
nasturtium 24.20
nasty 4.51
Nat 30.1
natal 23.39
Natal 23.1
Natalie 4.27
natality 4.53
Natasha 12.72
natation 25.49
natatorial 23.24
natatorium 24.14
natatory 4.43
natch 15.1
Nathan 25.51
Nathaniel 23.24
nation 25.49
national 23.34
nationalist 31.8
nationalizer 12.91
nationhood 16.26
nationwide 16.14
native 34.8
nativist 31.15
nativity 4.53
natron 25.26
natter 12.74
natterer 12.67
natty 4.51
natural 23.36

naturalist 31.8
nature 12.23
naturist 31.12
naught 30.33
Naughton 25.50
naughty 4.54
Nauru 11.17
nausea 12.11
nauseate 30.8
nauseous 28.23
nautch 15.8
nautical 23.32
nautilus 28.27
Navajo 9.14
naval 23.40
navarin 25.18
Navarino 9.19
Navarre 1.1
nave 34.4
navel 23.40
navicular 12.46
navigate 30.9
Navrátilová 12.86
navvy 4.58
navy 4.58
nawab 14.2
Náxos 28.14
nay 3.1
naysay 3.20
naysayer 12.2
Nazarene 25.9
Nazareth 32.13
Nazi 4.45
Nazify 6.7
Nazirite 30.29
Nazism 24.21
Ndebele 4.23
N'Djamena 12.54
Ndola 12.44
né 3.1
neanderthal 23.2
neap 27.5
Neapolitan 25.50
near 12.4
nearby 6.1
nearish 29.9
nearside 16.16
neat 30.18
neaten 25.50
neath 32.5
nebbish 29.6
Nebraska 12.37
Nebraskan 25.43
Nebuchadnezzar 12.90
nebula 12.46
nebulosity 4.53
nebulous 28.27
nebuly 4.26
necessarian 25.37
necessary 4.43

necessitarian 25.37
necessitate 30.16
necessitous 28.34
necessity 4.53
neck 21.6
Neckar 12.37
neckband 16.40
Necker 12.37
neckerchief 17.6
necklace 28.8
necklet 30.22
neckline 25.22
necktie 6.18
neckwear 2.15
necrology 4.17
necromancer 12.69
necromancy 4.45
necromantic 21.17
necrophile 23.11
necrophilia 12.6
necrophiliac 21.1
necrophilic 21.11
necrophilist 31.8
necropolis 28.8
necrosis 28.11
nectar 12.76
nectarine 25.11
nectarous 28.31
Ned 16.3
neddy 4.12
née 3.1
need 16.7
Needham 24.17
needle 23.28
needlecord 16.21
needlecraft 30.47
needlepoint 30.55
Needles 35.29
needlework 21.31
needn't 30.56
needy 4.12
neep 27.5
ne'er 2.1
ne'er-do-well 23.4
nefarious 28.23
Nefertiti 4.52
negate 30.7
negation 25.49
negativist 31.15
negator 12.77
negatory 4.43
Negev 34.3
neglect 30.48
negligee 3.12
negligence 28.45
negligent 30.56
negligible 23.26
Negombo 9.9
negotiant 30.56
negotiate 30.8
Negrillo 9.17

n

Negro 9.21
negus 28.25
Nehemiah 12.13
Nehru 11.17
neigh 3.1
neighbor 12.21
neighborhood 16.26
neighborly 4.27
neighbour 12.21
neighbourhood
  16.26
neighbourly 4.27
Neil 23.7
neither 12.84
Nell 23.3
nelly 4.22
Nelson 25.48
nematode 16.23
Nembutal 23.1
nemertean 25.37
nemertine 25.23
nemeses 35.8
nemesia 12.5
nemesis 28.11
Nene 25.5, 25.9
Nennius 28.23
neoclassic 21.16
neoclassical 23.32
neoclassicist 31.13
neocolonial 23.24
neocolonialist 31.8
neocon 25.25
neolithic 21.18
neon 25.24
neonatal 23.39
neonate 30.13
neophyte 30.27
neoplastic 21.17
Neoplatonist 31.10
Nepal 23.14
Nepalese 35.6
Nepali 4.25
nepheline 25.10
nephew 11.22
nephrite 30.29
nephritis 28.12
nepotist 31.14
Neptune 25.33
Neptunian 25.37
neptunium 24.16
nerd 16.31
nerdy 4.13
nereid 16.8
Nereus 28.23
Nerissa 12.69
Nernst 31.30
Nero 9.21
Neruda 12.29
Nerva 12.87
nerve 34.14
nerve-racking 26.7

Nervi 4.58
nervous 28.35
nervy 4.58
Nerys 28.10
Nesbit 30.20
nescience 28.45
nescient 30.56
nesh 29.3
ness 28.3
Nessie 4.45
nest 31.3
Nestlé 3.15
nestle 23.37
nestling 26.8
Nestor 12.76
Nestorian 25.37
net 30.4
netball 23.14
nether 12.84
Netherlander 12.25
Netherlandish 29.6
Netherlands 35.31
nethermost 31.20
netherworld 16.38
netsuke 4.20
Nettie 4.51
nettle 23.39
network 21.31
networker 12.41
neume 24.12
neural 23.36
neuralgia 12.35
neuralgic 21.11
neurasthenia 12.8
neuritis 28.12
neurology 4.17
neuron 25.26
neuroscience 28.45
neuroses 35.8
neurosis 28.11
neurotic 21.17
neuter 12.81
neutral 23.36
neutralist 31.8
neutralizer 12.91
neutrino 9.19
neutron 25.26
Neva 12.85
Nevada 12.25
Nevadan 25.40
Neve 34.5
névé 3.24
never 12.85
nevermore 7.1
never-never 12.85
Neville 23.10
Nevis 28.12
new 11.1
Newark 21.5, 21.30
newbie 4.10
newborn 25.28

Newby 4.10
Newcastle 23.37
Newcomen 25.45
newcomer 12.52
newel 23.25
newel post 31.20
newfangled 16.38
Newfoundland
  16.45
Newfoundlander
  12.29
Newgate 30.9
newish 29.6
newlaid 16.6
Newlands 35.31
newly 4.26
newly-wed 16.4
Newman 25.45
Newmarket 30.21
newness 28.29
New Orleans 35.31
Newport 30.33
Newry 4.43
news 35.21
newsagent 30.56
newsboy 10.3
newscast 31.2
newscaster 12.75
newsflash 29.1
newshound 16.43
newsletter 12.76
newsman 25.2
newsmen 25.5
newspaper 12.61
newspaperman 25.2
newspapermen 25.5
newspeak 21.8
newsprint 30.54
newsreader 12.26
newsreel 23.7
newsroom 24.12
news sheet 30.19
news stand 16.40
newsvendor 12.26
newsworthy 4.57
newsy 4.62
newt 30.37
newton 25.50
Newtonian 25.37
Newtown 25.29
next 31.28
nexus 28.32
Ney 3.1
ngaio 9.5
Ngamiland 16.40
Nguni 4.33
niacin 25.19
Niagara 12.64
Niall 23.25
Niamey 3.16
nib 14.7

nibble 23.26
nibbler 12.48
Nibelung 26.17
Nibelungenlied
  16.7
niblick 21.11
nicad 16.1
Nicaea 12.3
Nicam 24.1
Nicaragua 12.20
Nicaraguan 25.38
nice 28.13
Nice 28.6
niceish 29.9
nicety 4.53
niche 29.5
Nicholas 28.27
Nicholson 25.48
Nichrome 24.11
nick 21.9
nickel 23.32
nickelodeon 25.37
nicker 12.39
Nicklaus 28.27
nickname 24.4
Nicky 4.19
Nicobar 1.4
Nicola 12.48
Nicole 23.17
Nicosia 12.3
nicotine 25.12
nide 16.14
nidi 6.6
nidus 28.25
niece 28.6
niello 9.17
Nielsen 25.48
Niemeyer 12.14
Niersteiner 12.55
Nietzsche 12.23
Nietzschean 25.37
niff 17.6
niffy 4.14
nifty 4.53
Nigel 23.31
Nigella 12.42
Niger 2.1, 12.35
Nigeria 12.10
Nigerian 25.37
niggard 16.28
niggardly 4.27
niggle 23.30
niggly 4.24
nigh 6.1
night 30.26
nightbird 16.31
nightcap 27.1
nightclothes 35.19
nightclub 14.13
nightdress 28.3
nightfall 23.15

nightgown 25.29
nighthawk 21.22
nightie 4.54
nightingale 23.5
nightjar 1.10
nightlife 17.7
night light 30.28
nightly 4.25
nightmare 2.9
nightmarish 29.9
nightshade 16.6
nightshirt 30.45
nightspot 30.32
nightstick 21.17
nighttime 24.7
nightwear 2.15
nigrescent 30.56
nihilist 31.8
nihility 4.53
Nijinsky 4.19
Nijmegen 25.41
Nike 4.19
nil 23.8
nil desperandum 24.17
Nile 23.11
Nilsson 25.48
nim 24.6
nimbi 6.5
nimble 23.26
nimbostratus 28.34
nimbus 28.24
nimby 4.10
Nîmes 24.5
niminy-piminy 4.32
Nimrod 16.18
Nina 12.54
nincompoop 27.11
nine 25.21
ninefold 16.37
nineteen 25.9
nineteenth 32.19
ninetieth 32.6
ninety 4.54
Nineveh 12.86
Ninian 25.37
ninja 12.35
ninny 4.32
ninon 25.26
ninth 32.19
Niobe 4.10
nip 27.6
nipper 12.62
nipple 23.35
nipplewort 30.45
Nippon 25.26
Nipponese 35.6
nippy 4.36
nirvana 12.53
Nisan 25.4
nisi 6.16

nit 30.20
nite 30.26
niterie 4.43
nitpick 21.14
nitrate 30.15
nitric 21.15
nitrite 30.29
nitrogen 25.42
nitroglycerin 25.11
nitroglycerine 25.11
nitty-gritty 4.53
nitwit 30.25
nitwitted 16.12
Niue 3.5
Niven 25.51
niveous 28.23
nix 28.39
Nixon 25.48
Nkomo 9.18
Nkrumah 12.52
no 9.1
no-account 30.55
Noah 12.17
Noam 24.17
nob 14.9
no-ball 23.14
nobble 23.26
nobbler 12.48
Nobel 23.3
nobelium 24.16
nobility 4.53
noble 23.26
nobleman 25.45
noblemen 25.45
noblesse 28.3
noblewomen 25.17
nobly 4.25
nobody 4.13
nock 21.20
noctambulist 31.8
noctuid 16.8
noctule 23.20
nocturn 25.53
nocturnal 23.34
nocturne 25.53
nocuous 28.24
nod 16.18
noddle 23.28
noddy 4.13
node 16.23
nodular 12.46
nodule 23.20
Noel 23.3, 23.25
noes 35.19
nog 18.8
noggin 25.14
nogging 26.6
Noh 9.1
no-hoper 12.63
nohow 8.5
noil 23.19

noir 1.1
noise 35.20
noisette 30.4
noisome 24.20
noisy 4.61
Nolan 25.44
nolens volens 35.31
nomad 16.1
nomadic 21.10
no-man's-land 16.40
nombril 23.9
nom de guerre 2.1
Nome 24.11
nomen 25.5
nomenclature 12.24
nomenklatura 12.67
nominal 23.34
nominalist 31.8
nominate 30.13
nominee 4.1
nonage 20.7
nonagenarian 25.37
nonaligned 16.42
nonce 28.44
nonchalance 28.45
nonchalant 30.56
non-com 24.8
nonda 12.28
nondescript 30.58
none 25.35
nones 35.31
nonesuch 15.13
nonet 30.4
nong 26.15
no-no 9.19
nonpareil 23.5
nonsense 28.45
nonsensical 23.32
non sequitur 12.78
non-U 11.1
noodle 23.28
nook 21.28
nooky 4.20
noon 25.33
noonday 3.9
noontide 16.17
noontime 24.7
noose 28.19
nopal 23.35
nope 27.10
nor 7.1
Nora 12.66
noradrenalin 25.16
Norbert 30.41
Nordic 21.10
Noreen 25.11
Norfolk 21.30
Noriega 12.31
nork 21.22
norm 24.9
Norma 12.52

normal 23.33
normalcy 4.47
Norman 25.45
Normandy 4.13
Norn 25.28
Norris 28.10
Norroy 10.11
Norse 28.15
Norseman 25.45
Norsemen 25.45
north 32.9
Northampton 23.50
Northamptonshire 12.11
Northants 28.47
northbound 16.43
Northcliffe 17.6
northeast 31.5
northeastern 25.50
northeastward 16.30
northerly 4.27
northern 25.51
northerner 12.58
northernmost 31.20
northing 26.14
Northland 16.45
Northumberland 16.45
Northumbria 12.10
Northumbrian 25.37
northward 16.30
northwest 31.3
northwestern 25.50
northwestward 16.30
Norway 3.25
Norwegian 25.42
Norwich 20.8
nose 35.19
nosebag 18.1
noseband 16.40
nosebleed 16.7
nosedive 34.9
nosegay 3.11
nosh 29.11
noshery 4.43
no-show 9.1
nosh-up 27.13
nostalgia 12.6
nostalgic 21.11
nostoc 21.21
Nostradamus 28.28
nostril 23.9
nostrum 24.19
nosy 4.61
nosy parker 12.37
not 30.31
nota bene 3.17
notable 23.26
notarial 23.24

notarize 35.13
notary 4.43
notate 30.7
notation 25.49
notch 15.7
notchy 4.11
note 30.35
notebook 21.28
notecase 28.5
notelet 30.22
notepad 16.1
notepaper 12.61
noteworthy 4.57
nothing 26.14
notice 28.12
noticeboard 16.20
notify 6.7
notion 25.49
notional 23.34
notoriety 4.53
notorious 28.23
Notre-Dame 24.2
Nottingham 24.19
Nottinghamshire 12.11
notwithstanding 26.5
nougat 1.8
nougatine 25.9
nought 30.33
Nouméa 12.2
noumena 12.55
noumenal 23.34
noumenon 25.26
noun 25.29
nounal 23.34
nourish 29.9
nourisher 12.72
nous 28.16
nouveau riche 29.5
nova 12.86
Nova Scotian 25.49
novel 23.40
novelette 30.4
novelist 31.8
novelize 35.12
novella 12.42
Novello 9.17
novelty 4.54
November 12.21
novena 12.54
Novgorod 16.18
novice 28.12
novitiate 30.41
novocaine 25.7
Novokuznetsk 21.35
Novosibirsk 21.35
Novotný 4.32
now 8.1
nowadays 35.5
noway 3.1

nowhere 2.15
no-win 25.13
nowise 35.15
nowt 30.34
noxious 28.33
nozzle 23.41
nth 32.19
nu 11.1
nuance 28.44
nub 14.13
Nuba 12.21
nubble 23.26
nubbly 4.26
nubby 4.10
Nubia 12.5
Nubian 25.37
nubile 23.11
nubility 4.53
nuclear 12.6
nucleate 30.8
nuclei 6.3
nucleon 25.24
nucleotide 16.17
nucleus 28.23
nuddy 4.13
nude 16.25
nudge 20.16
nudger 12.36
nudism 24.21
nudist 31.6
nudity 4.53
nudnik 21.13
Nuer 12.19
Nuffield 16.35
nugatory 4.43
nugget 30.21
nuisance 28.45
nuke 21.27
Nuku'alofa 12.30
null 23.22
nullah 12.47
nullifier 12.14
nullify 6.7
nullity 4.53
numb 24.14
numbat 30.1
number 12.22
number plate 30.11
numbskull 23.22
numdah 12.29
numen 25.45
numeracy 4.48
numeral 23.36
numerate 30.43
numeric 21.15
numerical 23.32
numerology 4.17
numerous 28.31
Numidia 12.5
Numidian 25.37
numina 12.55

numinous 28.29
numismatic 21.17
numismatist 31.14
nun 25.35
nunciature 12.20
nuncio 9.4
Nuneaton 25.50
nunlike 21.19
nunnery 4.43
nunnish 29.9
Nupe 3.18
nuptial 23.38
Nuremberg 18.13
Nureyev 17.3
Nurofen 25.5
nurse 28.36
nurseling 26.8
nursemaid 16.6
nursery 4.43
nurseryman 25.45
nurserymen 25.45
nursling 26.8
nurture 12.24
nurturer 12.67
nut 30.40
nutation 25.49
nutcase 28.5
nutcracker 12.37
nuthouse 28.16
nutmeg 18.3
nutrient 30.56
nutritionist 31.10
nutritious 28.33
nutshell 23.3
nutter 12.81
Nutting 26.13
nutty 4.55
nuzzle 23.41
nyala 12.42
Nyasaland 16.40
Nye 6.1
Nyerere 4.39
nylon 25.25
nymph 17.19
nymphal 23.29
nymphean 25.37
nymphet 30.4
nympho 9.12
nympholepsy 4.45
nympholeptic 21.17
nymphomania 12.8
nymphomaniac 21.1
Nynorsk 21.35
Nyree 4.40
Nyx 28.39

oaf 17.11
oafish 29.7

Oahu 11.10
oak 21.24
oaken 25.43
Oakland 16.45
Oakley 4.25
Oaks 28.40
oakum 24.18
oar 7.1
oarless 28.27
oarlock 21.21
oarsman 25.45
oarsmen 25.45
oarswoman 25.45
oarswomen 25.17
oases 35.8
oasis 28.11
oast 31.20
oast house 28.16
oat 30.35
oatcake 21.7
oaten 25.50
Oates 28.47
oath 32.11
oatmeal 23.7
oaty 4.54
Oaxaca 12.37
Obadiah 12.13
obbligati 9.4
obbligato 9.24
obduracy 4.48
obdurate 30.43
obedience 28.45
obedient 30.56
obeisance 28.45
obeisant 30.56
obelisk 21.35
obelus 28.27
Oberammergau 8.4
Oberon 25.26
obese 28.6
obesity 4.53
obey 3.1
obeyer 12.2
obfuscate 30.10
obfuscatory 4.43
obi 4.10
obit 30.20
obituarist 31.12
obituary 4.43
object 30.48, 30.49
objection 25.49
objectivist 31.15
objectivize 35.14
objector 12.76
objet d'art 1.1
objurgate 30.9
objurgatory 4.43
oblast 31.1
oblate 30.11
oblation 25.49

oblational 23.34
obligate 30.9
obligati 4.51
obligato 9.24
obligatory 4.43
oblige 20.10
obligee 4.1
obliger 12.35
obliging 26.6
obligor 7.1
oblique 21.8
obliquity 4.53
obliterate 30.15
oblivion 25.37
oblivious 28.23
oblong 26.15
obloquy 4.59
obnoxious 28.33
oboe 9.9
oboist 31.6
obol 23.13
O'Brien 25.38
obscene 25.9
obscenity 4.53
obscurant 30.56
obscurantist 31.14
obscure 12.20
obscurity 4.53
obsequies 35.10
obsequious 28.23
observance 28.45
observant 30.56
observatory 4.43
observe 34.14
observer 12.87
obsess 28.3
obsessional 23.34
obsessive 34.7
obsidian 25.37
obsolescence 28.45
obsolescent 30.56
obsolete 30.18
obstacle 23.32
obstetric 21.15
obstetrician 25.49
obstinacy 4.48
obstinate 30.43
obstreperous 28.31
obstruct 30.49
obstruction 25.49
obstructionist 31.10
obstructor 12.81
obtain 25.7
obtainer 12.54
obtention 25.49
obtrude 16.25
obtruder 12.29
obtrusion 25.42
obtrusive 34.7
obtuse 28.19
obverse 28.36

obviate 30.8
obvious 28.23
ocarina 12.54
O'Casey 4.45
Occam 24.18
occasion 25.42
occasional 23.34
occidentalize 35.12
Occitan 25.50
occlude 16.25
occlusion 25.42
occult 30.51
occultist 31.14
occupancy 4.48
occupant 30.56
occupier 12.14
occupy 6.14
occur 13.1
occurrence 28.45
occurrent 30.56
ocean 25.49
Oceania 12.8
Oceanian 25.37
oceanic 21.13
Oceanid 16.10
oceanographer 12.30
oceanography 4.14
Oceanus 28.29
oceanward 16.30
ocelot 30.31
och 22.4
oche 4.19
ocher 12.40
ocherish 29.9
ocherous 28.31
ochery 4.41
ochone 25.30
ochre 12.40
ochreish 29.9
ochrous 28.31
ochry 4.41
ocker 12.40
o'clock 21.20
O'Connell 23.34
O'Connor 12.56
octad 16.1
octagon 25.41
octagonal 23.34
octahedron 25.47
octane 25.8
Octans 35.31
octant 30.56
octave 34.8
Octavia 12.12
Octavian 25.37
Octavius 28.23
octavo 9.27
octet 30.4
October 12.21
octodecimo 9.18

octogenarian 25.37
octopus 28.30
octuple 23.35
ocular 12.46
oculist 31.8
od 16.18
odalisque 21.35
odd 16.18
oddball 23.14
Oddfellow 9.17
oddish 29.6
oddity 4.53
oddly 4.25
oddment 30.56
oddness 28.29
odds and ends 35.27
odds-on 25.24
ode 16.23
O'Dea 3.1
odea 12.5
Odense 12.71
Odeon 25.37
Oder 12.28
Odessa 12.69
Odets 28.47
Odette 30.4
odeum 24.16
Odin 25.14
odious 28.23
odium 24.16
Odonata 12.75
odonate 30.13
odor 12.28
odoriferous 28.31
odorous 28.31
odour 12.28
Odyssean 25.37
Odysseus 28.19
odyssey 4.46
oedema 12.51
Oedipal 23.35
Oedipus 28.30
Oenone 25.30
oenophilist 31.8
o'er 12.17
oesophagus 28.25
oestrogen 25.42
oeuvre 12.68
of 34.10
off 17.8
Offa 12.30
offal 23.29
Offaly 4.27
offbeat 30.18
offcut 30.40
Offenbach 21.5
offence 28.44
offend 16.41
offender 12.26
offense 28.44
offensive 34.7

offer 12.30
offerer 12.67
offering 26.11
offertory 4.43
offhand 16.40
offhanded 16.9
office 28.7
officer 12.70
official 23.38
officialdom 24.17
officialese 35.6
officiant 30.56
officiate 30.8
officinal 23.34
officious 28.33
offing 26.6
offish 29.7
offload 16.23
offprint 30.54
off-putting 26.13
offset 30.5
offshoot 30.38
offshore 7.1
offside 16.14
offspring 26.11
offstage 20.4
Ofgas 28.1
oft 30.47
Oftel 23.4
often 25.41
oftentimes 35.30
Ofwat 30.32
Ogaden 25.5
ogee 4.17
ogham 24.18
ogle 23.30
ogler 12.44
ogre 12.32
ogreish 29.9
oh 9.1
O'Higgins 35.31
Ohio 9.5
Ohioan 25.38
ohm 24.11
ohmic 21.12
oho 9.1
oi 10.1
oik 21.25
oil 23.19
oilcake 21.7
oilcan 25.2
oilcloth 32.8
oiler 12.44
oilfield 16.35
oilman 25.2
oilmen 25.5
oilrig 18.6
oilseed 16.7
oilskin 25.15
oily 4.25
oink 21.34

o

o

oratorio 9.4
oratory 4.43
orb 14.10
orbit 30.20
orbital 23.39
orc 21.22
orca 12.40
Orcadian 25.37
orchard 16.28
orchestra 12.65
orchestral 23.36
orchestrate 30.15
orchid 16.10
orchil 23.9
Orczy 4.47
ordain 25.7
ordainer 12.54
ordeal 23.7
order 12.28
ordering 26.11
orderly 4.27
ordinal 23.34
ordinance 28.45
ordinand 16.40
ordinary 4.43
ordnance 28.45
ordonnance 28.45
Ordovician 25.37
ordure 12.20
ore 7.1
oread 16.1
oregano 9.19
Oregon 25.41
Oregonian 25.37
Orenburg 18.13
Oreo 9.4
Orestes 35.9
orfe 17.9
Orff 17.9
organ 25.41
organdie 4.13
organdy 4.13
organelle 23.3
organic 21.13
organist 31.10
organizer 12.91
organon 25.26
organum 24.19
organza 12.90
organzine 25.12
orgasm 24.21
orgasmic 21.12
orgastic 21.17
orgeat 30.41
orgiastic 21.17
orgy 4.17
Oriana 12.53
oribi 4.10
oriel 23.24
Orient 30.56
orient 30.53

Oriental 23.39
orientalist 31.8
orientalize 35.12
orientate 30.16
orienteer 12.4
orienteering 26.11
orifice 28.7
oriflamme 24.1
origami 4.29
origanum 24.19
Origen 25.5
origin 25.14
original 23.34
originate 30.13
Orinoco 9.16
oriole 23.17
Orion 25.38
orison 25.52
Orissa 12.70
Oriya 12.3
Orkney 4.32
Orlando 9.11
orle 23.14
Orléans 35.31
Orlon 25.25
ormolu 11.13
ornamentalist 31.8
ornate 30.7
ornery 4.43
ornithology 4.17
Orontes 35.9
orotund 16.44
orphan 25.41
orphanage 20.7
Orphean 25.36
Orpheus 28.23
Orphic 21.10
orphrey 4.41
orpine 25.23
Orpington 25.50
orris 28.10
Orson 25.48
ortanique 21.8
Ortega 12.31
orthodontist 31.14
orthodox 28.40
orthodoxy 4.46
orthogonal 23.34
orthographic 21.10
orthography 4.14
orthopaedic 21.10
orthopedic 21.10
ortolan 25.44
Orton 25.50
orts 28.47
Oruro 9.21
Orvieto 9.24
Orville 23.10
Orwell 23.4
Orwellian 25.37
oryx 28.39

Osage 20.4
Osaka 12.37
Osbert 30.41
Osborne 25.28
Oscar 12.40
oscillate 30.11
oscillatory 4.43
oscular 12.46
osculate 30.11
osier 12.12
Osiris 28.10
Oslo 9.17
Osmanli 4.21
Osmond 16.45
osmosis 28.11
osmotic 21.17
Osnabrück 21.28
osprey 3.19
Ossa 12.70
osseous 28.23
Ossian 25.37
ossify 6.7
osso buco 9.16
ossuary 4.43
Ostade 16.2
Ostend 16.41
ostensible 23.26
ostensive 34.7
ostensory 4.43
ostentatious 28.33
osteoarthritis 28.12
osteopath 32.1
osteopathy 4.56
osteoporosis 28.11
Ostia 12.12
ostinato 9.24
ostler 12.44
Ostmark 21.5
Ostpolitik 21.8
Ostrava 12.87
ostrich 15.6
Ostwald 16.38
Oswald 16.38
Otago 9.13
other 12.84
otherwhere 2.15
otherwise 35.15
Otho 9.26
otiose 28.17
Otis 28.12
Otomi 4.1
O'Toole 23.20
Ott 30.31
ottava rima 12.51
Ottawa 12.88
otter 12.79
Otto 9.25
Ottoline 25.16
ottoman 25.45
Otway 3.25
Ouagadougou 11.8

oubliette 30.4
ouch 15.9
Oudenarde 16.2
Oudh 16.25
ought 30.33
oughtn't 30.56
Oulu 11.13
ounce 28.44
our 12.16
ours 35.24
ourself 17.18
ourselves 35.35
Ouse 35.21
oust 31.19
ouster 12.80
out 30.34
outage 20.9
out-and-out 30.34
outback 21.2
outbacker 12.37
outbalance 28.45
outbid 16.8
outboard 16.20
outbound 16.43
outbrave 34.4
outbreak 21.7
outbuilding 26.5
outburst 31.26
outcast 31.2
outcaste 31.2
outclass 28.2
outcome 24.14
outcompete 30.18
outcrop 27.8
outcry 6.15
outdance 28.44
outdated 16.12
outdid 16.8
outdistance 28.45
outdo 11.1
outdoes 35.23
outdone 25.35
outdoor 7.1
outdoors 35.17
outdoorsman 25.45
outdoorsmen 25.45
outer 12.80
outermost 31.20
outerwear 2.15
outface 28.5
outfall 23.15
outfield 16.35
outfielder 12.26
outfight 30.26
outfit 30.21
outfitter 12.78
outflank 21.33
outflew 11.1
outflow 9.17
outflown 25.30
outflung 26.18

outfly 6.1
outfought 30.33
outfox 28.40
outgo 9.1
outgoing 26.3
outgone 25.24
outgrew 11.1
outgrow 9.1
outgrown 25.30
outgrowth 32.11
outguess 28.3
outgun 25.35
outhouse 28.16
outie 4.54
outing 26.13
outjump 27.17
outlander 12.25
outlandish 29.6
outlast 31.2
outlaw 7.11
outlawry 4.41
outlay 3.1, 3.15
outlet 30.4
outlier 12.14
outline 25.22
outlive 34.6
outlook 21.28
outlying 26.3
outmanoeuvre 12.87
outmatch 15.1
outmoded 16.9
outmost 31.20
outnumber 12.22
outpace 28.5
outpatient 30.56
outperform 24.9
outperformance 28.45
outplay 3.1
outpoint 30.55
outport 30.33
outpost 31.20
outpouring 26.11
output 30.39
outrage 20.4
outrageous 28.25
outran 25.1
outrank 21.33
outré 3.19
outreach 15.5
outridden 25.40
outride 16.14
outrider 12.27
outrigged 16.33
outrigger 12.31
outright 30.26
outrival 23.40
outrode 16.23
outrun 25.35
outrush 29.16

outsail 23.5
outsat 30.1
outsell 23.3
outset 30.5
outshine 25.21
outshone 25.24
outshoot 30.37
outshot 30.31
outside 16.14
outsider 12.27
outsit 30.20
outsize 35.11
outskirts 28.47
outsmart 30.3
outsold 16.37
outsource 28.15
outspan 25.1, 25.3
outspoken 25.43
outspread 16.3
outstanding 26.5
outstare 2.1
outstay 3.1
outstep 27.3
outstretch 15.3
outstretched 30.46
outstrip 27.6
outswing 26.14
out-take 21.7
outvote 30.35
outwalk 21.22
outward 16.30
outwards 35.27
outwatch 15.7
outwear 2.1
outweigh 3.1
outwent 30.53
outwit 30.20
outwith 32.6
outwore 7.1
outwork 21.31
outworker 12.41
outworking 26.7
outworn 25.28
ouzel 23.41
ouzo 9.29
ova 12.86
oval 23.40
ovarian 25.37
ovary 4.43
ovate 30.16
ovation 25.49
oven 25.51
ovenproof 17.13
oven-ready 4.12
Ovens 35.31
ovenware 2.15
over 12.86
overage 20.8
overall 23.15
overcall 23.15
overdramatize 35.14

overeaten 25.50
overfall 23.15
overflight 30.28
overflow 9.17
overgeneralize 35.12
overhaul 23.15
overheard 16.31
overinflated 16.12
overjoyed 16.24
overkill 23.9
overlander 12.25
overlay 3.15
overleaped 30.58
overlord 16.21
overnighter 12.79
overparted 16.12
overqualified 16.14
overseas 35.6
overseer 12.11
oversexed 31.28
overshoe 11.19
overside 16.16
oversight 30.30
oversoul 23.18
overspecialize 35.12
overspill 23.9
overt 30.45
overthrow 9.21
overtone 25.31
overtrick 21.15
overture 12.20
overview 11.22
overweening 26.9
overwhelm 24.18
Ovid 16.13
Oviedo 9.11
oviform 24.9
ovoid 16.24
ovulate 30.11
ovum 24.20
ow 8.1
owe 9.1
Owen 25.13
Owens 35.31
owl 23.16
owlet 30.22
owlish 29.8
own 25.30
owner 12.56
owt 30.34
ox 28.40
oxbow 9.9
Oxbridge 20.8
oxen 25.48
Oxfam 24.1
Oxford 16.28
Oxfordshire 12.11
oxhide 16.14
oxidant 30.56
oxide 16.16

oxlip 27.6
Oxon 25.26
Oxonian 25.37
oxtail 23.6
oxter 12.79
ox tongue 26.18
oxygen 25.42
oxygenate 30.13
oxygenous 28.29
oxymoron 25.26
oxytocin 25.19
oyez 3.1
oyster 12.81
oystercatcher 12.23
Oz 35.16
Ozalid 16.10
ozone 25.31

pa 1.1
Pablo 9.17
Pablum 24.18
pabulum 24.18
paca 12.37
pacarana 12.53
pace 4.45, 28.5
pacemaker 12.38
pacemaking 26.7
pacer 12.69
pace-setting 26.13
Pachelbel 23.3
pachyderm 24.22
pachydermal 23.33
pacific 21.10
pacificatory 4.43
pacifier 12.14
pacifist 31.7
pacify 6.7
Pacino 9.19
pack 21.1
package 20.6
packager 12.35
packer 12.37
packet 30.21
packhorse 28.15
packice 28.13
packing 26.7
packing case 28.5
packman 25.2
packmen 25.5
packsaddle 23.28
Pac-man 25.2
pact 30.48
pacy 4.45
pad 16.1
paddle 23.28
paddler 12.48
paddock 21.30
paddy 4.12

Paderewski 4.18
padlock 21.21
Padma 12.50
padre 3.19
padrone 4.33
Padua 12.20
Paduan 25.38
paean 25.36
paediatric 21.15
paediatrician 25.49
paedophile 23.11
paedophilia 12.6
paella 12.42
paeon 25.36
Pagalu 11.13
pagan 25.41
Paganini 4.31
paganish 29.9
paganize 35.13
page 20.4
pageant 30.56
pageantry 4.43
pageboy 10.3
pager 12.35
paginal 23.34
paginate 30.13
pagoda 12.28
pah 1.1
Pahang 26.1
Pahlavi 4.58
paid 16.6
Paige 20.4
Paignton 25.50
pail 23.5
pain 25.7
Paine 25.7
painkiller 12.43
painkilling 26.8
painstaking 26.7
paint 30.54
paintball 23.14
paintbox 28.40
paintbrush 29.16
painter 12.77
painterly 4.27
painting 26.13
paintwork 21.31
painty 4.52
pair 2.1
pairing 26.11
paisa 1.17
paise 12.70
paisley 4.22
Paiute 30.37
pakeha 1.9
Pakistan 25.4
Pakistani 4.31
pakora 12.66
pal 23.1
palace 28.8
paladin 25.14

Palaeocene 25.11
palaeographer 12.30
palaeographic 21.10
palaeography 4.14
Palaeolithic 21.18
Palaeozoic 21.9
palaestra 12.65
palais 3.15
palanquin 25.9
palatalize 35.12
palate 30.42
palatial 23.38
Palatinate 30.43
Palatine 25.23
Palau 8.1
palaver 12.85
Palawan 25.38
pale 23.5
paleface 28.5
Palekh 21.6
Palembang 26.1
Palenque 4.18
Paleocene 25.11
paleographer 12.30
paleographic 21.10
paleography 4.14
Paleolithic 21.18
Paleozoic 21.9
Palermo 9.18
Palestine 25.23
Palestinian 25.37
palestra 12.65
Palestrina 12.54
palette 30.22
palfrey 4.41
Palgrave 34.4
Pali 4.21
palimony 4.34
palimpsest 31.3
palindrome 24.11
palindromic 21.12
palindromist 31.0
paling 26.8
palisade 16.6
Palisades 35.27
palish 29.8
pall 23.14
Palladian 25.37
Palladio 9.4
palladium 24.16
Pallas 28.27
pallbearer 12.65
pallet 30.22
palletize 35.14
pallia 12.6
pallial 23.24
palliasse 28.1
palliate 30.8
pallid 16.10
pallium 24.16
pall-mall 23.1

pallor 12.42
pally 4.21
palm 24.2
Palma 12.50
Palmerston 25.50
palmist 31.9
palmistry 4.40
palmtop 27.8
palmy 4.29
palmyra 12.65
palomino 9.19
palooka 12.41
Palouse 28.19
palpate 30.14
palpitant 30.56
palpitate 30.16
palsgrave 34.4
palsied 16.13
palsy 4.61
palsy-walsy 4.61
palter 12.80
palterer 12.67
paltry 4.41
Paludrine 25.18
Pam 24.1
Pamela 12.43
Pamirs 35.24
pampas 28.30
pamper 12.61
Pampers 35.24
pamphlet 30.22
pamphleteer 12.4
Pamphylian 25.37
Pamplona 12.56
pan 25.4
Pan 25.1
panacea 12.4
panache 29.1
panada 12.25
Panadol 23.13
Panaji 4.17
Panama 1.1
Panamanian 25.37
panatella 12.42
pancake 21.7
panchromatic 21.17
Pancras 28.31
pancreas 28.23
pancreatic 21.17
panda 12.25
pandanus 28.29
Pandarus 28.31
pandemic 21.12
pandemonium 24.16
pander 12.25
pandit 30.21
Pandora 12.66
pane 25.7
paneer 12.4
panegyric 21.15
panegyrical 23.32

panegyrist 31.12
panegyrize 35.13
panel 23.34
panelist 31.8
panellist 31.8
panettone 3.17
panettoni 4.33
panforte 3.22
pan-fried 16.14
panfry 6.15
panful 23.21
pang 26.1
panga 12.31
Pangaea 12.3
pangolin 25.16
panhandle 23.28
panhandler 12.48
panic 21.13
panicky 4.19
Panini 4.31, 4.32
panjandrum 24.19
Pankhurst 31.26
panlike 21.19
pannage 20.7
panne 25.1
pannier 12.8
pannikin 25.15
panoply 4.27
panoptic 21.17
panorama 12.50
panoramic 21.12
panstick 21.17
pansy 4.61
pant 30.53
pantalets 28.47
pantalettes 28.47
pantechnicon 25.43
Pantelleria 12.3
pantheist 31.6
pantheon 25.37
panther 12.83
pantile 23.12
panto 9.24
pantomime 24.7
pantomimic 21.12
pantry 4.38
pants 28.47
pantsuit 30.38
pantyhose 35.19
Panzer 12.90
pap 27.1
papa 1.1
papacy 4.48
papal 23.35
papalist 31.8
paparazzi 4.45
paparazzo 9.22
papaya 12.13
paper 12.61
paperback 21.2
paperboy 10.3

p

paperchase 28.5
paperclip 27.6
paperer 12.67
paperhanger 12.60
paperknife 17.7
paperknives 35.35
paperweight 30.17
paperwork 21.31
papery 4.43
papier-mâché 3.21
papillae 4.24
papillon 25.25
papism 24.21
papist 31.11
papistical 23.32
papistry 4.40
papoose 28.19
pappardelle 3.15
pappy 4.36
paprika 12.39
Papua 12.20
Papuan 25.38
papyri 6.15
papyrus 28.31
par 1.1
Pará 1.1
para 12.64
parabases 35.8
parable 23.26
parabola 12.48
parabolic 21.11
Paracelsus 28.32
paracetamol 23.13
parachute 30.38
parachutist 31.14
paraclete 30.18
parade 16.6
parader 12.26
paradiddle 23.28
paradigm 24.7
paradigmatic 21.17
paradisal 23.37
paradise 28.13
paradisiacal 23.32
parador 7.5
paradox 28.40
paradoxical 23.32
paraffin 25.14
paraglide 16.14
paraglider 12.27
paragliding 26.5
paragon 25.41
paragraph 17.2
Paraguay 6.21
Paraguayan 25.38
parakeet 30.18
paralegal 23.30
paralipsis 28.11
parallax 28.38
parallel 23.3
parallelogram 24.1

Paralympics 28.39
paralyse 35.12
paralyses 35.8
paralysis 28.11
paralytic 21.17
paramedic 21.10
paramedical 23.32
parameter 12.78
paramilitary 4.43
paramo 9.18
paramount 30.55
paramountcy 4.47
paramour 12.20
Paraná 1.1
parang 26.1
paranoia 12.18
paranoid 16.24
paranormal 23.33
parapet 30.23
paraph 17.1
paraphernalia 12.6
paraphrase 35.5
paraplegia 12.35
paraplegic 21.11
paraquat 30.32
parasailing 26.8
parascend 16.41
parascender 12.26
parasite 30.30
parasitic 21.17
parasiticide 16.16
parasitology 4.17
parasol 23.13
parathion 25.24
paratrooper 12.63
paravane 25.8
par avion 25.27
parboil 23.19
parbuckle 23.32
parcel 23.37
parch 15.2
Parcheesi 4.61
parclose 35.19
pard 16.2
pardon 25.40
pardoner 12.58
pare 2.1
paren 25.5
parent 30.56
parentage 20.9
parental 23.39
parentheses 35.8
parenthesis 28.11
parenthesize 35.14
parenthetic 21.17
parenthetical 23.32
parenthood 16.26
parer 12.65
parfait 3.10
parfleche 29.3
parfumerie 4.43

pariah 12.13
Parian 25.37
paring 26.11
Paris 28.10
parish 29.9
parishioner 12.58
Parisian 25.37
parity 4.53
park 21.5
parka 12.37
parkin 25.15
parkland 16.45
Parks 28.38
parkway 3.25
parky 4.18
parlance 28.45
parlay 3.15
parley 4.21
parliamentarian 25.37
parliamentary 4.43
parlor 12.42
parlormaid 16.6
parlour 12.42
parlourmaid 16.6
parlous 28.27
Parma 12.50
Parmenides 35.7
Parmentier 12.12
parmesan 25.1
Parnassian 25.37
Parnell 23.3
parochial 23.24
parodic 21.10
parodist 31.6
parody 4.13
parol 23.17
parole 23.17
parolee 4.1
paroxysm 24.21
paroxysmal 23.33
parpen 25.46
parquet 3.14
parquetry 4.40
parricidal 23.28
parricide 16.16
parrot 30.43
parrotfish 29.7
parry 4.38
parse 35.2
Parsee 4.1
parser 12.90
Parsifal 23.1
parsimonious 28.23
parsimony 4.34
parsnip 27.6
parson 25.48
parsonage 20.7
Parsons 35.31
part 30.3
partake 21.7

partaken 25.43
partaker 12.38
parterre 2.1
part-exchange 20.19
parthenogenesis 28.11
Parthenon 25.46
Parthia 12.12
Parthian 25.37
partial 23.38
partible 23.26
participant 30.56
participate 30.14
participatory 4.43
participial 23.24
participle 23.35
particle 23.32
particolored 16.29
particoloured 16.29
particular 12.46
particularist 31.12
particularity 4.53
parting 26.13
parti pris 4.1
partisan 25.1
partite 30.30
partitioner 12.58
partitionist 31.10
partner 12.53
Parton 25.50
partook 21.28
partridge 20.8
part song 26.15
part-time 24.7
part-timer 12.51
parturient 30.56
part-way 3.1
part-work 21.31
party 4.51
party-pooper 12.63
parvenu 11.15
parvis 28.12
pas 1.1
Pasadena 12.54
Pascal 23.2
paschal 23.32
pas de deux 13.1
pash 29.1
pasha 12.72
Pashto 9.25
paso doble 3.15
paspalum 24.18
pasquinade 16.6
pass 28.2
passage 20.9
passageway 3.25
Passamaquoddy 4.13
passant 30.54, 30.56
passata 12.75
passbook 21.28

Passchendaele 23.5
passé 3.20
passel 23.37
passementerie 4.43
passenger 12.35
passe-partout 11.20
passer 12.69
passer-by 6.1
passerine 25.23
pas seul 23.42
passible 23.26
passim 24.6
passing 26.12
passion 25.49
passional 23.34
passionate 30.43
passion flower 12.16
passion fruit 30.37
passive 34.7
passkey 4.18
Passover 12.86
passport 30.33
password 16.31
past 31.2
pasta 12.74
paste 31.4
pasteboard 16.20
pastel 23.39
pastern 25.50
Pasternak 21.3
Pasteur 13.1
pasticcio 9.10
pastiche 29.5
pastie 4.52
pastille 23.9
pastime 24.7
pasting 26.13
pastis 28.12
pastmaster 12.75
pastor 12.75
pastoral 23.36
pastorale 23.2
pastorate 30.43
pastrami 4.29
pastry 4.39
pasturage 20.8
pasture 12.23
pasty 4.51, 4.52
pat 30.1
pat a cake 21.7
Patagonia 12.8
Patagonian 25.37
patball 23.14
patch 15.1
patcher 12.23
patchouli 4.26
patchwork 21.31
patchy 4.11
pâté 3.22
Pate 30.7

pâté de foie gras 1.1
patella 12.42
paten 25.50
patency 4.45
patent 30.56
patentee 4.1
pater 12.77
paterfamilias 28.1
paternal 23.34
paternalist 31.8
paternity 4.53
paternoster 12.79
path 32.2
Pathan 25.4
Pathé 3.23
pathetic 21.17
pathfinder 12.27
pathogenesis 28.11
pathologic 21.11
pathology 4.17
pathos 28.14
pathway 3.25
patience 28.45
patient 30.56
patina 12.55
patio 9.4
pâtisserie 4.43
patly 4.21
Pátmos 28.14
Patna 12.53
patness 28.29
patois 1.22
Paton 25.50
patrial 23.24
patriarch 21.5
patriarchal 23.32
patriarchate 30.42
patriarchy 4.18
Patricia 12.72
patrician 25.49
patriciate 30.41
patricidal 23.28
patricide 16.16
Patrick 21.15
patrilineal 23.24
patrimonial 23.24
patrimony 4.34
patriot 30.41
patriotic 21.17
Patroclus 28.27
patrol 23.17
patroller 12.44
patrolman 25.2
patrolmen 25.5
patron 25.47
patronage 20.7
patronal 23.34
patronizer 12.91
patronymic 21.12
patsy 4.45

pattée 3.22
patten 25.50
patter 12.74
pattern 25.50
patty 4.51
patulous 28.27
paucity 4.53
Paul 23.14
Paula 12.44
Paulette 30.4
Pauli 4.25
Pauline 25.10, 25.22
Pauling 26.8
paunch 29.20
paunchy 4.50
pauper 12.62
pauperdom 24.17
pauperize 35.13
Pausanias 28.23
pause 35.17
pavage 20.9
pavane 25.1
Pavarotti 4.54
pavé 3.24
pave 34.4
paver 12.85
pavilion 25.37
paving 26.14
pavior 12.12
paviour 12.12
Pavlov 34.10
Pavlova 12.86
Pavlovian 25.37
pavonine 25.23
paw 7.1
pawky 4.19
pawl 23.14
pawn 25.28
pawnbroker 12.40
pawnbroking 26.7
Pawnee 4.1
pawnshop 27.8
pawpaw 7.14
pax 28.38
Paxton 25.50
pay 3.1
payable 23.26
payback 21.2
payday 3.9
pay dirt 30.45
payee 4.1
payer 12.2
payload 16.23
paymaster 12.75
payment 30.56
paynim 24.6
payoff 17.8
payola 12.44
payout 30.34
payphone 25.30
payroll 23.18

paysage 19.1
payslip 27.6
Paz 35.2
pea 4.1
peace 28.6
peacekeeper 12.61
peacekeeping 26.10
peacemaker 12.38
peacemaking 26.7
peacenik 21.13
peacetime 24.7
peach 15.5
peachick 21.9
peachy 4.11
peacock 21.20
peafowl 23.16
peahen 25.5
peak 21.8
Peake 21.8
peakload 16.23
peaky 4.18
peal 23.7
pecan 25.36
peanut 30.40
pear 2.1
Pearce 28.23
pearl 23.42
pearler 12.49
pearlescent 30.56
Pearl Harbor 12.21
pearlite 30.28
pearlized 16.50
pearly 4.28
Pears 35.4, 35.24
pearshaped 30.58
Pearson 25.48
peart 30.41
peasant 30.56
peasantry 4.38
peasanty 4.51
pease 35.6
peasepudding 26.5
peashooter 12.81
pea-souper 12.63
peat 30.18
peatland 16.40
peatmoss 28.14
peaty 4.52
peau-de-soie 1.1
pebble 23.26
pebbledash 29.1
pebbly 4.27
pecan 25.1
peccadillo 9.17
peccant 30.56
peccary 4.43
peck 21.6
pecker 12.37
peckish 29.8
pecorino 9.19
pecten 25.19

p

pectin 25.19
pectinate 30.43
pectoral 23.36
peculiar 12.6
peculiarity 4.53
pecuniary 4.43
pedagogic 21.11
pedagogue 18.8
pedagogy 4.17
pedal 23.28
pedalo 9.17
pedant 30.56
pedantic 21.17
pedantry 4.38
peddle 23.28
pederast 31.1
pederastic 21.17
pederasty 4.51
pedestal 23.39
pedestrian 25.37
pediatric 21.15
pediatrician 25.49
pedicab 14.1
pedicure 12.20
pedicurist 31.12
pedigree 4.40
pedlar 12.42
pedlary 4.43
pedologist 31.7
pedometer 12.78
pedophile 23.11
pedophilia 12.6
Pedro 9.21
peduncle 23.32
pee 4.1
peek 21.8
peekaboo 11.1
peel 23.7
peeler 12.43
peeling 26.8
Peelite 30.28
peen 25.9
peep 27.5
peep-bo 9.20
peeper 12.61
peephole 23.17
peep show 9.23
peepul 23.35
peer 12.4
peerage 20.8
peeress 28.10
peer group 27.11
peeve 34.5
peevish 29.10
peewee 4.59
peewit 30.25
peg 18.3
Pegasus 28.32
Peg-board 16.20
pegboard 16.20
Peggy 4.15

peg-leg 18.3
Pegu 11.22
Pei 3.1
peignoir 1.22
Peirce 28.23
pekan 25.43
Pekinese 35.6
Peking 26.3
pekoe 9.16
Pelagian 25.37
Pelagius 28.23
pelargonium 24.16
Pelé 3.15
Peleus 28.35
pelham 24.18
pelican 25.43
Pelion 25.37
pelisse 28.6
pelite 30.28
pellagra 12.64
pellet 30.22
pelletize 35.14
pell-mell 23.3
pellucid 16.11
pelmet 30.23
Peloponnese 35.6
Pelops 28.46
pelorus 28.31
pelota 12.79
peloton 25.26
pelt 30.51
pelta 12.76
peltate 30.16
peltry 4.38
pelvic 21.18
pelvis 28.12
Pemba 12.21
Pembroke 21.28
pen 25.5
penal 23.34
penalty 4.51
penance 28.45
Penang 26.1
penates 35.9
pence 28.44
penchant 25.26
pencil 23.37
penciler 12.48
penciller 12.48
pendant 30.56
pendency 4.48
pendent 30.56
pendragon 25.41
pendulous 28.27
pendulum 24.18
Penelope 4.37
penetrate 30.15
penfriend 16.41
penguin 25.20
penicillin 25.16
penile 23.11

peninsula 12.46
penis 28.9
Penistone 25.50
penitence 28.45
penitent 30.56
penitential 23.38
penitentiary 4.43
penknife 17.7
penknives 35.35
penlight 30.28
penman 25.45
penmen 25.45
Penn 25.5
pennant 30.56
penne 4.31
penniä 1.2
pennies 35.10
pennon 25.46
Pennsylvania 12.8
Pennsylvanian
   25.37
penny 4.31
pennyfarthing 26.14
pennyweight 30.17
pennyworth 32.13
penpusher 12.73
pensée 3.20
pension 25.27, 25.49
pensioner 12.58
pensive 34.7
penstock 21.21
pent 30.53
pentachord 16.21
pentacle 23.32
pentad 16.1
pentagon 25.41
pentagram 24.1
pentameter 12.78
pentangle 23.30
Pentateuch 21.27
pentateuchal 23.32
pentathlete 30.18
pentathlon 25.44
Pentecost 31.17
Pentecostal 23.39
Pentecostalist 31.8
penthouse 28.16
Pentothal 23.1
penult 30.51
penultimate 30.43
penumbra 12.66
penumbrae 4.42
penurious 28.23
penury 4.41
Penza 12.90
Penzance 28.44
peon 25.36
peony 4.34
people 23.35
pep 27.3
Pepe 3.18

peplum 24.18
pepper 12.61
pepperbox 28.40
peppercorn 25.28
peppermint 30.54
pepperminty 4.53
pepperoni 4.33
pepperpot 30.32
peppery 4.43
peppy 4.36
peptalk 21.22
peptic 21.17
peptide 16.17
Pepys 28.46
per 13.1
peradventure 12.23
Perak 12.65
perambulate 30.11
perambulatory 4.43
per annum 24.19
per capita 12.78
per caput 30.39
perceive 34.5
perceiver 12.85
percent 30.53
percentage 20.9
percentile 23.12
percept 30.58
perceptible 23.26
perception 25.49
perceptional 23.34
perceptual 23.25
perch 15.14
perchance 28.44
percher 12.24
Percheron 25.26
percipience 28.45
percipient 30.56
Percival 23.40
percolate 30.11
percussionist 31.10
percussive 34.7
Percy 4.49
per diem 24.3
Perdita 12.78
père 2.1
peregrinate 30.13
peregrine 25.18
Perelman 25.45
peremptory 4.43
perennial 23.24
Peres 35.3
perestroika 12.39
perfect 30.48, 30.49
perfecter 12.76
perfectible 23.26
perfection 25.49
perfectionist 31.10
perfecto 9.24
perfervid 16.13
perfidious 28.23

perfidy 4.12
perfin 25.14
perforate 30.15, 30.43
perforce 28.15
perform 24.9
performance 28.45
performer 12.52
perfume 24.12
perfumer 12.52
perfumery 4.43
perfumy 4.30
perfunctory 4.43
perfuse 35.21
Pergamum 24.19
pergola 12.48
perhaps 28.46
peri 4.43
periapt 30.58
pericarditis 28.12
periclase 35.5
Periclean 25.36
Pericles 35.7
pericope 4.37
peridot 30.31
peril 23.9
perilous 28.27
perimeter 12.78
period 16.28
periodic 21.10
periodical 23.32
periodize 35.11
peripatetic 21.17
peripeteia 12.13
peripheral 23.36
periphery 4.43
periphrases 35.8
periphrasis 28.11
periphrastic 21.17
peripteral 23.36
periscope 27.10
perish 29.9
perisher 12.72
peristyle 23.12
peritoneal 23.23
peritoneum 24.15
peritonitis 28.12
periwig 18.6
periwinkle 23.32
perjure 12.36
perjurer 12.67
perjurious 28.23
perjury 4.43
perk 21.31
Perkin 25.15
Perks 28.41
perky 4.20
perlite 30.28
perlocution 25.49
perm 24.22
permafrost 31.17

permanence 28.45
permanency 4.48
permanent 30.56
permeate 30.8
Permian 25.37
permissible 23.26
permissive 34.7
permit 30.20, 30.23
permittee 4.1
permitter 12.78
permutate 30.16
permute 30.37
pernicious 28.33
pernickety 4.53
pernoctate 30.16
Pernod 9.19
Perón 25.24
perorate 30.15
peroxide 16.16
perpend 16.41
perpendicular 12.46
perpetrate 30.15
perpetual 23.25
perpetuance 28.45
perpetuate 30.8
perpetuity 4.53
perplex 28.38
perplexity 4.53
perquisite 30.25
Perrault 9.1
Perrin 25.3, 25.18
perron 25.47
perry 4.38
per se 3.1
perse 28.36
persecute 30.38
persecution 25.49
persecutor 12.81
persecutory 4.43
Perseids 35.27
Persephone 4.34
Persepolis 28.8
Perseus 28.23
perseverance 28.45
persevere 12.4
Persia 12.73
Persian 25.49
persiflage 19.1
persimmon 25.45
persist 31.6
persistence 28.45
persistency 4.48
persistent 30.56
person 25.48
persona 12.56
personae 6.13
personage 20.7
personal 23.34
personalty 4.55
persona non grata 12.75

personate 30.13
personifier 12.14
personify 6.7
personnel 23.3
perspectival 23.40
perspex 28.38
perspicacious 28.33
perspicacity 4.53
perspicuity 4.53
perspicuous 28.24
perspiratory 4.43
perspire 12.13
persuade 16.6
persuader 12.26
persuasible 23.26
persuasion 25.42
persuasive 34.7
pert 30.45
pertain 25.7
Perth 32.14
pertinacious 28.33
pertinacity 4.53
pertinence 28.45
pertinency 4.48
pertinent 30.56
perturb 14.15
Peru 11.1
Perugia 12.6
peruke 21.27
perusal 23.41
peruse 35.21
peruser 12.92
Perutz 28.47
Peruvian 25.37
perv 34.14
pervade 16.6
pervasion 25.42
pervasive 34.7
perverse 28.36
perversion 25.49
perversity 4.53
pervert 30.45
perverter 12.82
pervious 28.23
Pesach 21.5
peseta 12.77
pesky 4.18
peso 9.22
pessary 4.43
pessimist 31.9
pest 31.3
pester 12.76
pesterer 12.67
pesticidal 23.28
pesticide 16.16
pestiferous 28.31
pestilence 28.45
pestilent 30.56
pestilential 23.38
pestle 23.37
pesto 9.24

pet 30.4
Peta 12.77
Pétain 25.1
petal 23.39
pétanque 21.34
petard 16.2
petasus 28.32
petcock 21.20
Pete 30.18
peter 12.77
Peterborough 12.67
Peters 35.24
petersham 24.20
Peterson 25.48
petit 4.51
petite 30.18
petition 25.49
petitionary 4.43
petitioner 12.58
petit mal 23.1
Petra 12.64
Petrarch 21.5
Petrarchan 25.43
petrel 23.36
Petrie 4.39
petrifaction 25.49
petrify 6.7
petrochemical 23.32
Petrograd 16.1
petrol 23.36
petrolatum 24.20
petroleum 24.16
Petronius 28.23
petter 12.76
petticoat 30.35
pettifog 18.8
pettifogger 12.32
pettifoggery 4.43
pettish 29.10
petty 4.51
Petula 12.45
petulance 28.45
petulant 30.56
petunia 12.8
Pevsner 12.53
pew 11.1
pewter 12.81
peyote 4.54
Pfennig 18.6
pH 15.4
Phaedra 12.65
Phaethon 25.51
phaeton 25.50
phagocyte 30.30
phalanger 12.35
phalangist 31.7
phalanx 28.41
phalli 6.11
phallic 21.11
phallocentric 21.15
phallus 28.27

p

phantasm 24.21
phantasmagoria 12.10
phantasmagoric 21.15
phantasmagorical 23.32
phantasmal 23.33
phantasmic 21.12
phantasy 4.48
phantom 24.20
pharaoh 9.21
Pharisaic 21.9
Pharisaical 23.32
Pharisee 4.46
pharmaceutical 23.32
pharmacist 31.13
pharmacology 4.17
pharmacopoeia 12.3
pharmacy 4.48
pharos 28.14
pharyngitis 28.12
pharynx 28.41
phase 35.5
phasic 21.18
Phasmida 12.27
pheasant 30.56
pheasantry 4.38
phenobarbital 23.39
phenomena 12.55
phenomenal 23.34
phenomenalist 31.8
phenomenalize 35.12
phenomenon 25.46
phenotype 27.7
pheromone 25.30
phi 6.1
phial 23.25
Phidias 28.1
Phil 23.8
Philadelphia 12.5
Philadelphian 25.37
philander 12.25
philanderer 12.67
philanthrope 27.10
philanthropic 21.14
philanthropist 31.11
philanthropize 35.13
philanthropy 4.37
philatelic 21.11
philatelist 31.8
philately 4.27
Philby 4.10
Philemon 25.45
philhellene 25.10
Philip 27.6
Philippa 12.62

Philippi 6.14
philippic 21.14
Philippine 25.11
Philistine 25.23
Phillida 12.27
Phillips 28.46
Philly 4.24
philogynist 31.10
philologian 25.37
Philomela 12.43
Philomena 12.54
philosopher 12.30
philosophic 21.10
philosophizer 12.91
philosophy 4.14
philter 12.78
philtre 12.78
Phineas 28.23
phiz 35.10
phizog 18.8
phlegm 24.3
phlegmatic 21.17
phlox 28.40
Phnom Penh 25.5
phobia 12.5
phobic 21.9
Phobos 28.14
phoebe 4.10
Phoebus 28.24
Phoenicia 12.72
Phoenician 25.49
phoenix 28.39
phon 25.24
phone 25.30
phonecard 16.2
phone-in 25.18
phoneme 24.5
phonetic 21.17
phoney 4.33
phonic 21.13
phono 9.19
phonograph 17.2
phonolite 30.28
phooey 4.8
phosgene 25.10
phosphate 30.9
phosphor 12.30
phosphoresce 28.3
phosphorescence 28.45
phosphorescent 30.56
phosphoric 21.15
phosphorite 30.29
phosphorous 28.31
phosphorus 28.31
photic 21.17
Photius 28.23
photo 9.25
photocall 23.15

photochemical 23.32
photochemistry 4.40
photochromic 21.12
photocopier 12.9
photocopy 4.36
photoelectric 21.15
photofit 30.21
photogenic 21.13
photogram 24.1
photograph 17.2
photographer 12.30
photographic 21.10
photography 4.14
photogravure 12.20
photojournalist 31.8
photometer 12.78
photomontage 19.1
photon 25.26
photoset 30.5
photosetter 12.76
photosetting 26.13
photostat 30.2
photostatic 21.17
photosynthesis 28.11
photosynthesize 35.14
photosynthetic 21.17
phototropic 21.14
phrasal 23.41
phrase 35.5
phrase book 21.28
phraseology 4.17
phrasing 26.14
phrenology 4.17
Phrygia 12.6
Phrygian 25.37
Phuket 30.4
phut 30.40
phylactery 4.43
Phyllis 28.8
phyllite 30.28
phylum 24.18
physical 23.32
physicalist 31.8
physician 25.49
physicist 31.13
physio 9.4
physiognomic 21.12
physiognomical 23.32
physiognomist 31.9
physiognomy 4.30
physiology 4.17
physiotherapist 31.11
physiotherapy 4.37
physique 21.8

phytoplankton 25.50
pi 6.1
Piaf 17.1
piaffe 17.1
Piaget 3.12
pianissimo 9.18
pianist 31.10
piano 9.19
pianoforte 4.54
pianola 12.44
piaster 12.74
piastre 12.74
piazza 12.69
pibroch 21.21
pic 21.9
pica 12.40
picador 7.5
Picard 16.2
Picardy 4.13
picaresque 21.35
Picasso 9.22
picayune 25.33
Piccadilly 4.24
piccalilli 4.24
piccolo 9.17
pick 21.9
pickaback 21.2
pickax 28.38
pickaxe 28.38
picker 12.39
pickerel 23.36
Pickering 26.11
picket 30.21
picketer 12.78
Pickford 16.28
pickings 35.32
pickle 23.32
pickler 12.48
Pickles 35.29
pick-me-up 27.13
pickpocket 30.21
pickpocketing 26.13
pickup 27.13
Pickwickian 25.37
picky 4.19
picnic 21.13
picnicker 12.39
picot 9.16
picquet 30.4, 30.21
Pict 30.49
Pictish 29.10
pictograph 17.2
pictographic 21.10
pictorial 23.24
picture 12.23
picture book 21.28
picturesque 21.35
piddle 23.28
piddler 12.48
piddock 21.30

pidgin 25.14
pie 6.1
piebald 16.36
piece 28.6
pièce de résistance 28.44
piecemeal 23.7
piecer 12.69
piecework 21.31
pied 16.14
pied-à-terre 2.1
piedmont 30.54
Piedmontese 35.6
pie-eyed 16.14
pier 12.4
pierce 28.23
piercer 12.71
Pierre 2.1, 12.4
Pierrot 9.21
Piers 35.24
pietà 1.1
pietist 31.14
piety 4.53
piffle 23.29
piffling 26.8
pig 18.6
pigeon 25.14
pigeonhole 23.17
piggery 4.43
piggish 29.7
Piggott 30.42
piggy 4.15
piggyback 21.2
piggy bank 21.33
pig-headed 16.9
piglet 30.22
piglike 21.19
pigment 30.53, 30.56
pigpen 25.5
pigskin 25.15
pigsty 6.18
pigswill 23.10
pigtail 23.6
pika 12.40
pike 21.19
pikelet 30.22
pikeperch 15.14
piker 12.40
pikestaff 17.2
pilaf 17.1
pilaster 12.74
Pilate 30.42
pilchard 16.28
pile 23.11
piledriver 12.86
piledriving 26.14
pile-up 27.13
pilfer 12.30
pilferage 20.8
pilferer 12.67
pilgrim 24.6

pilgrimage 20.7
piling 26.8
pill 23.8
pillage 20.6
pillager 12.35
pillar 12.43
pillar box 28.40
pillaret 30.4
pillbox 28.40
Pilling 26.8
pillion 25.52
pillock 21.30
pillory 4.43
pillow 9.17
pillowcase 28.5
pillowslip 27.6
pillowy 4.7
pillwort 30.45
pilot 30.42
pilotage 20.9
Pilsen 25.52
Pilsner 12.55
Pima 12.51
pimiento 9.24
pimp 27.17
pimpernel 23.3
pimple 23.35
pimply 4.24
pin 25.13
piña colada 12.25
pinafore 7.6
pinball 23.14
pince-nez 3.1
pincer 12.70
pincette 30.4
pinch 29.20
pinchbeck 21.6
pinchpenny 4.31
pincushion 25.49
Pindar 1.6
Pindaric 21.15
pine 25.21
pineapple 23.35
pine cone 25.30
Pinero 9.21
pinery 4.43
pinetree 4.40
pinewood 16.26
pinfold 16.37
ping 26.3
pinger 12.60
pingpong 26.15
pinhead 16.3
pinheaded 16.9
pinhole 23.17
pinion 25.52
pink 21.33
Pinkerton 25.50
pink-eye 6.10
pinkie 4.19
pinkish 29.8

pinko 9.16
pinky 4.19
pinnace 28.9
pinnacle 23.32
pinny 4.32
Pinochet 3.21
pinochle 23.32
pinole 4.25, 23.17
piñon 25.24
Pinot Blanc 25.24
Pinot Noir 1.1
pinpoint 30.55
pinprick 21.15
pinstripe 27.7
pint 30.54
Pinta 12.78
pintail 23.6
Pinter 12.78
pintle 23.39
pinto 9.24
pin-up 27.13
pinwheel 23.7
piny 4.32
Pinyin 25.13
pioneer 12.4
pious 28.24
pip 27.6
pipe 27.7
pipeclay 3.15
pipecleaner 12.54
pipefish 29.7
pipeline 25.22
piper 12.62
pipette 30.4
pipistrelle 23.3
pipit 30.23
pipkin 25.15
Pippa 12.62
pippin 25.18
pipsqueak 21.8
pipy 4.36
piquancy 4.40
piquant 30.56
piqué 3.14
pique 21.8
piquet 30.4, 30.21
piracy 4.48
Piraeus 28.22
Pirandello 9.17
Piranesi 4.61
piranha 12.53
pirate 30.43
piratic 21.17
piratical 23.32
piripiri 4.40
pirog 18.10
pirogue 18.10
pirouette 30.4
Pisa 12.90
pis aller 3.15
Pisano 9.19

piscatorial 23.24
piscatory 4.43
Piscean 25.37
piscean 25.36
Pisces 35.8
pisciculture 12.24
pisciculturist 31.12
piscina 12.54
piscine 25.11, 25.23
pisco 9.16
pish 29.6
Pisidian 25.37
piss 28.7
Pissarro 9.21
pissoir 1.22
piss-taker 12.38
piss-taking 26.7
piss-up 27.13
pistachio 9.4
piste 31.5
pisteur 13.1
pistil 23.9
pistol 23.39
pistole 23.18
pistoleer 12.4
piston 25.50
pistou 11.20
pit 30.20
pit-a-pat 30.1
pitch 15.6
pitchblack 21.1
pitcher 12.23
pitchfork 21.22
pitchman 25.45
pitchmen 25.45
pitchpine 25.23
pitchpipe 27.7
pitchstone 25.31
pitchy 4.11
piteous 28.23
pitfall 23.15
pith 32.6
pithead 16.3
pithy 4.56
pitman 25.45
pitmen 25.45
piton 25.26
Pitt 30.20
pitta 12.78
pittance 28.45
pitter-patter 12.74
Pitti 4.53
pittosporum 24.19
Pittsburgh 18.13
pity 4.53
pivot 30.44
pivotal 23.39
pix 28.39
pixel 23.37
pixie 4.46
pixilated 16.12

p

Pizarro 9.21
pizza 12.69
pizzazz 35.1
pizzeria 12.3
pizzicato 9.24
pizzle 23.41
placard 16.2
placate 30.7
placatory 4.43
place 28.5
placebo 9.9
placenta 12.76
placer 12.69
placet 30.5
placid 16.11
placidity 4.53
placing 26.12
placket 30.21
plafond 25.24
plage 19.1
plagiarist 31.12
plagiarizer 12.91
plague 18.4
plaguy 4.15
plaice 28.5
plaid 16.1
plaided 16.9
plain 25.7
plainchant 30.53
plainclothes 35.19
plainsman 25.45
plainsmen 25.45
plainsong 26.15
plain-spoken 25.43
plaint 30.54
plaintiff 17.6
plait 30.1
plan 25.1
planar 12.54
planarian 25.37
planchet 30.24
planchette 30.4
Planck 21.33
plane 25.7
planer 12.54
planet 30.23
planetarium 24.16
planetary 4.43
planetoid 16.24
plangency 4.48
plangent 30.56
planisphere 12.5
plank 21.33
plankton 25.50
planner 12.53
plant 30.53
Plantagenet 30.23
plantain 25.19
planter 12.75
planting 26.13
plantlet 30.22

plant-like 21.19
plaque 21.1
plash 29.1
plashy 4.50
plasma 12.50
plasmodia 12.5
plasmodial 23.24
plasmodium 24.16
plaster 12.75
plasterboard 16.20
plasterer 12.67
plasterwork 21.31
plastery 4.43
plastic 21.17
Plasticine 25.11
plasticky 4.19
plastral 23.36
plastron 25.47
plat 30.1
plat du jour 12.20
plate 30.7
plateau 9.24
plateaux 35.19
platelet 30.22
platen 25.50
plater 12.77
plateresque 21.35
platform 24.9
Plath 32.1
plating 26.13
platinum 24.19
platitude 16.25
platitudinize 35.13
platitudinous 28.29
Plato 9.24
Platonic 21.13
Platonist 31.10
platoon 25.33
platteland 16.40
platter 12.74
platypus 28.30
plaudit 30.21
plausible 23.26
Plautus 28.34
play 3.1
playa 12.13
play-act 30.48
playback 21.2
playbill 23.8
playbook 21.28
playboy 10.3
player 12.2
Playfair 2.5
playfellow 9.17
playground 16.43
playgroup 27.11
playhouse 28.16
playlet 30.22
playlist 31.8
playmaker 12.38
playmate 30.12

playoff 17.8
playpen 25.5
playroom 24.12
playschool 23.20
playsuit 30.38
plaything 26.14
playtime 24.7
playwright 30.29
plaza 12.90
plc 4.1
plea 4.1
pleach 15.5
plead 16.7
pleader 12.26
pleading 26.5
pleasance 28.45
pleasant 30.56
pleasantry 4.38
please 35.6
pleasure 12.33
pleat 30.18
pleb 14.3
plebby 4.10
plebe 14.6
plebeian 25.36
plebiscitary 4.43
plebiscite 30.24
plectra 12.64
plectrum 24.19
pledge 20.3
pledgee 4.1
pledger 12.35
Pleiades 35.7
plein-air 2.1
Pleistocene 25.11
plenary 4.43
plenipotentiary
  4.43
plenitude 16.25
plenteous 28.23
plenty 4.51
plenum 24.19
pleonasm 24.21
pleonastic 21.17
plesiosaur 7.16
plethora 12.67
pleurisy 4.48
Pleven 25.51
plew 11.1
plexus 28.28
pliable 23.26
pliancy 4.48
pliant 30.56
plié 3.2
pliers 35.24
plight 30.26
plimsoll 23.37
plink 21.33
plinth 32.19
Pliny 4.32
Pliocene 25.11

plissé 3.20
plod 16.18
plodder 12.28
plonk 21.34
plonker 12.40
plop 27.8
plosive 34.7
plot 30.31
Plotinus 28.29
plotter 12.79
plough 8.1
plougher 12.16
ploughman 25.45
ploughmen 25.45
ploughshare 2.13
plover 12.87
plow 8.1
plower 12.16
plowman 25.45
plowmen 25.45
plowshare 2.13
ploy 10.1
pluck 21.29
plucker 12.41
plucky 4.20
plug 18.12
plugger 12.32
plughole 23.17
plug-ugly 4.26
plum 24.14
plumage 20.7
plumb 24.14
plumber 12.52
plumb line 25.22
plume 24.12
plummet 30.23
plummy 4.30
plump 27.17
plumpish 29.9
plumpy 4.37
plumy 4.30
plunder 12.29
plunderer 12.67
plundering 26.11
plunge 20.19
plunger 12.36
plunk 21.34
pluperfect 30.49
plural 23.36
pluralist 31.8
plus 28.21
plus-fours 35.17
plush 29.16
plushy 4.50
Plutarch 21.5
Pluto 9.25
plutocracy 4.48
plutocrat 30.2
plutocratic 21.17
Plutonian 25.37
Plutonic 21.13

p

plutonium 24.16
pluvial 23.24
ply 6.1
Plymouth 32.13
plywood 16.26
pneumatic 21.17
pneumonia 12.8
Pnyx 28.39
po 9.1
poach 15.10
poacher 12.24
poblano 9.19
Pocahontas 28.34
pochard 16.28
pochette 30.4
pock 21.20
pocket 30.21
pocketbook 21.28
pockmark 21.5
pocky 4.19
poco 9.16
pod 16.18
podgy 4.17
podia 12.5
podiatry 4.43
podium 24.16
Poe 9.1
poem 24.6
poesy 4.61
poet 30.20
poetess 28.12
poetic 21.17
poetical 23.32
poeticize 35.14
poetize 35.14
poetry 4.40
po-faced 31.4
pogo 9.13
pogrom 24.19
poi 10.1
poignance 28.45
poignancy 4.48
poignant 30.56
poind 16.43
Poindexter 12.76
poinsettia 12.12
point 30.55
point-blank 21.33
pointe 30.53
pointer 12.81
pointes 30.53
pointillist 31.15
point-to-point 30.55
pointy 4.54
poise 35.20
poison 25.52
poisoner 12.58
poisoning 26.9
poisonous 28.29
Poitier 3.3

Poitiers 3.3
Poitou 11.1
poke 21.24
poker 12.40
pokey 4.20
poky 4.20
pol 23.13
Poland 16.45
Polanski 4.18
polar 12.44
Polaris 28.10
polarity 4.53
Polaroid 16.24
polder 12.28
pole 23.17
poleaxe 28.38
polecat 30.1
polemic 21.12
polemical 23.32
polemicist 31.13
polemicize 35.14
polenta 12.76
polevault 30.51
pole-vaulter 12.80
poleward 16.30
police 28.6
policeman 25.45
policemen 25.45
policewoman 25.45
policewomen 25.17
policy 4.46
policyholder 12.28
polio 9.4
polis 28.8
Polisario 9.4
Polish 29.8
polisher 12.72
Politburo 9.21
polite 30.26
politesse 28.3
politic 21.17
political 23.32
politician 25.49
politicking 26.7
politico 9.16
polity 4.53
polka 12.40
polka dot 30.31
poll 23.13, 23.17
pollack 21.30
pollan 25.44
pollard 16.29
pollee 4.1
pollen 25.44
pollinate 30.13
polliwog 18.8
pollock 21.30
pollster 12.80
pollutant 30.56
pollute 30.37
polluter 12.81

pollution 25.49
Pollux 28.41
polly 4.25
Pollyanna 12.53
Pollyannaish 29.6
polo 9.17
polonaise 35.5
polonium 24.16
polony 4.33
poltergeist 31.16
poltroon 25.33
poltroonery 4.43
poly 4.25
polyamide 16.14
polyandrous 28.31
polyandry 4.38
polyanthus 28.35
Polybius 28.23
polychaete 30.18
polychromatic 21.17
polychrome 24.11
polychromy 4.29
Polyclitus 28.34
polycyclic 21.11
polyester 12.76
Polyfilla 12.43
polygamist 31.9
polygamous 28.28
polygamy 4.30
polygeny 4.32
polyglot 30.31
polygon 25.41
polygonum 24.19
polygraph 17.2
polygynous 28.29
polygyny 4.32
polyhedron 25.47
polymath 32.1
polymathic 21.18
polymathy 4.56
polymer 12.51
polymerase 35.5
polymorphic 21.10
polymorphous 28.25
Polynesia 12.89
Polynesian 25.52
polyp 27.6
polyphase 35.5
Polyphemus 28.28
polyphonic 21.13
polyphonous 28.29
polyphony 4.34
polyptych 21.17
polystyrene 25.11
polysyllabic 21.9
polytechnic 21.13
polytheist 31.6
polythene 25.12
polytonal 23.34
polyunsaturate
 30.15

polyunsaturates
 28.47
polyurethane 25.8
pom 24.8
pomace 28.8
pomade 16.2
pomander 12.25
pomatum 24.20
pomegranate 30.23
pomelo 9.17
Pomerania 12.8
Pomeranian 25.37
pomfret 30.24
pommel 23.33
pommie 4.29
pommy 4.29
pomp 27.17
Pompadour 12.20
pompano 9.19
Pompeii 4.2
Pompey 4.36
Pompidou 11.6
pompom 24.8
pomposity 4.53
pompous 28.30
ponce 28.44
poncey 4.46
poncho 9.23
pond 16.42
ponder 12.28
pondering 26.11
ponderosa 12.92
ponderosity 4.53
ponderous 28.31
Pondicherry 4.38
pondweed 16.7
pone 25.30
pong 26.15
ponga 12.60
pongal 23.30
pongo 9.13
pongy 4.35
poniard 16.30
pons asinorum
 24.19
pont 30.54
Pontianak 21.3
pontifex 28.38
pontiff 17.6
pontifical 23.32
pontificate 30.10,
 30.42
pontifices 35.8
Pontine Marshes
 35.10
pontoon 25.33
Pontormo 9.18
Pontus 28.34
pony 4.33
ponytail 23.6
pooch 15.11
poodle 23.28

pooh 11.1
pooh-bah 1.1
pooh-pooh 11.1
pooka 12.41
pool 23.20
Poole 23.20
poolroom 24.12
poolside 16.16
poon 25.33
Poona 12.56
poop 27.11
pooper-scooper 12.63
poor 7.1
poorhouse 28.16
poorly 4.25
Pooterish 29.9
pootle 23.39
pop 27.8
popcorn 25.28
pope 27.10
popedom 24.17
Popemobile 23.7
popery 4.43
popeyed 16.14
popgun 25.35
popinjay 3.13
poplar 12.44
poplin 25.16
Popocatépetl 23.39
popover 12.86
poppa 12.62
poppadom 24.17
popper 12.62
poppet 30.23
poppied 16.10
popple 23.35
poppy 4.36
poppycock 21.20
Popsicle 23.32
popsy 4.46
populace 28.27
popular 12.46
popularity 4.53
popularizer 12.91
populate 30.11
populist 31.8
populous 28.27
porbeagle 23.30
porcelain 25.16
porcellaneous 28.23
porcellanous 28.29
porch 15.8
porcine 25.23
porcini 4.31
porcupine 25.23
pore 7.1
porgy 4.15
Pori 4.41
pork 21.22
porker 12.40

porkling 26.8
porky 4.19
porn 25.28
porno 9.19
pornographer 12.30
pornographic 21.10
pornography 4.14
porosity 4.53
porous 28.31
porphyry 4.40
porpoise 28.30
porridge 20.8
porridgy 4.17
porringer 12.35
Porsche 29.12
Porsena 12.55
port 30.33
portage 20.9
Portakabin 25.13
portal 23.39
portamenti 4.51
portamento 9.24
Port-au-Prince 28.44
portcullis 28.8
Porte 30.33
portend 16.41
portent 30.53
portentous 28.34
porter 12.80
porterage 20.8
porterhouse 28.16
portfolio 9.4
Port Harcourt 30.33
porthole 23.17
Portia 12.73
portico 9.16
portion 25.49
Portland 16.45
portly 4.25
portmanteau 9.24
portmanteaux 35.19
Port Moresby 4.10
Porto 9.25
Porto Alegre 12.64
Portobello 9.17
Port-of-Spain 25.7
portolan 25.44
Porto Novo 9.27
portrait 30.15
portraitist 31.14
portraiture 12.23
portray 3.1
portrayal 23.23
portrayer 12.2
Portsmouth 32.13
Portugal 23.30
Portuguese 35.6
pose 35.19
Poseidon 25.40
poser 12.92

poseur 13.1
posey 4.61
posh 29.11
posit 30.25
position 25.49
positional 23.34
positioner 12.58
positivist 31.15
positron 25.26
posse 4.46
possess 28.3
possessive 34.7
possessor 12.69
possessory 4.43
posset 30.24
possible 23.26
possum 24.20
post 31.20
postage 20.9
postal 23.39
poster 12.80
poste restante 30.54
posterior 12.10
posterity 4.53
postern 25.50
post hoc 21.20
postie 4.54
postil 23.9
postilion 25.37
posting 26.13
postlude 16.25
postman 25.45
postmen 25.45
postmortem 24.20
post-partum 24.20
postponer 12.56
postulant 30.56
postulate 30.11, 30.42
posture 12.24
posturer 12.67
posturing 26.11
posy 4.61
pot 30.31
potable 23.26
potage 19.1
potager 12.36
potash 29.1
potassic 21.16
potassium 24.16
potation 25.49
potato 9.24
pot-au-feu 13.1
potboiler 12.44
poteen 25.9
Potemkin 25.15
potence 28.45
potency 4.47
potent 30.56
potentate 30.16
potential 23.38

potentiate 30.8
potful 23.21
pother 12.84
potherb 14.15
pothole 23.17
potholer 12.44
pothouse 28.16
potion 25.49
Potiphar 12.30
Potomac 21.3
potoroo 11.1
potpourri 4.41
Potsdam 24.1
potsherd 16.31
potshot 30.32
pottage 20.9
potter 12.79
potterer 12.67
Potteries 35.10
pottery 4.43
pottle 23.39
potty 4.54
pouch 15.9
pouchy 4.11
pouffe 17.13, 17.14
Poulenc 21.33
poult 30.51
poult-de-soie 1.1
poulterer 12.67
poultice 28.12
poultry 4.41
pounce 28.44
pouncer 12.70
pound 16.43
poundage 20.6
poundal 23.28
pounder 12.28
pour 7.1
pourboire 1.22
pourer 12.66
pousada 12.25
Poussin 25.3
pout 30.34
pouter 12.80
pouty 4.54
poverty 4.55
pow 8.1
powder 12.28
powder puff 17.15
powdery 4.43
Powell 23.25
power 12.16
powerboat 30.35
powerhouse 28.16
power pack 21.3
Powers 35.24
powwow 8.12
Powys 28.7
pox 28.40
poxy 4.46
Poznan 25.2

practical 23.32
practice 28.12
practicer 12.70
practicum 24.18
practise 28.12
practiser 12.70
practitioner 12.58
Prado 9.11
praecipe 4.36
praemunire 4.43
praenomen 25.5
praetor 12.77
practorian 25.37
pragmatic 21.17
pragmatist 31.14
Prague 18.2
Praha 1.9
Praia 12.13
prairie 4.39
praise 35.5
praiser 12.90
praiseworthy 4.57
Prakrit 30.24
praline 25.10
pram 24.1
prana 12.53
pranayama 12.50
prance 28.44
prancer 12.69
prandial 23.24
Prandtl 23.39
prang 26.1
prank 21.33
prankish 29.8
prankster 12.74
prase 35.5
prat 30.1
prate 30.7
pratfall 23.15
pratie 4.52
pratique 21.8
prattle 23.39
prattler 12.48
Pravda 12.25
prawn 25.28
praxis 28.11
Praxiteles 35.7
pray 3.1
prayer 2.1, 12.2
preach 15.5
preacher 12.23
preachify 6.7
preaching 26.4
preachy 4.11
preambular 12.46
prebend 16.45
prebendal 23.28
prebendary 4.43
precarious 28.23
precatory 4.43
precedence 28.45

precedent 30.56
precentor 12.76
precept 30.58
preceptor 12.76
precinct 30.49
preciosity 4.53
precious 28.33
precipice 28.9
precipitancy 4.48
precipitant 30.56
precipitate 30.16, 30.43
precipitous 28.34
precis 4.45
precise 28.13
precisian 25.42
precision 25.42
preclude 16.25
preclusion 25.42
preclusive 34.7
precocial 23.38
precocious 28.33
precocity 4.53
predatory 4.43
predecessor 12.69
predella 12.42
predestinarian 25.37
predestinate 30.13
predicant 30.56
predicate 30.10, 30.42
predict 30.49
predictor 12.78
predigested 16.12
predilection 25.49
preemie 4.29
pre-empt 30.52
pre-emption 25.49
pre-emptor 12.76
preen 25.9
preface 28.7
prefatory 4.43
prefect 30.48
prefectoral 23.36
prefectorial 23.24
prefecture 12.20
prefer 13.1
preference 28.45
preferential 23.38
pregnancy 4.48
pregnant 30.56
prehensile 23.11
prehension 25.49
prejudice 28.7
prelacy 4.48
prelapsarian 25.37
prelate 30.42
prelatic 21.17
prelatical 23.32
prelature 12.24

prelim 24.6
preliminary 4.43
prelude 16.25
preludial 23.24
premature 12.24
premed 16.3
premier 12.7
première 2.2
premise 28.8
premium 24.16
prentice 28.12
pre-owned 16.43
prep 27.3
preparatory 4.43
prepense 28.44
preponderance 28.45
preponderant 30.56
preponderate 30.15
preposterous 28.31
preppy 4.36
prequel 23.40
Pre-Raphaelite 30.28
presage 20.9
presager 12.35
presbyter 12.78
presbyteral 23.36
presbyterate 30.43
presbyterial 23.24
Presbyterian 25.37
presbytery 4.43
pre-schooler 12.45
prescient 30.56
prescind 16.42
prescription 25.49
prescriptivist 31.15
presence 28.45
present 30.56
presentee 4.1
presenter 12.76
preservationist 31.10
preset 30.5
presidency 4.48
president 30.56
presidential 23.38
Presley 4.22
press 28.3
Pressburg 18.13
pressgang 26.1
pressing 26.12
pressman 25.45
pressmen 25.45
press-up 27.13
pressure 12.72
prestige 20.5
prestigious 28.25
presto 9.24
Preston 25.50
Prestonpans 35.31

prestressed 31.3
Prestwick 21.18
presume 24.12
presumption 25.49
prêt-à-porter 3.22
pretence 28.44
pretense 28.44
pretentious 28.33
preterit 30.24
preterite 30.24
pretermit 30.20
pretor 12.77
Pretoria 12.10
pretorian 25.37
prettifier 12.14
prettify 6.7
pretty 4.53
prettyish 29.6
pretzel 23.37
prevalent 30.56
prevaricate 30.10
prevenient 30.56
preventer 12.76
prevention 25.49
preview 11.22
Previn 25.19
previous 28.23
previse 35.11
prexy 4.45
prey 3.1
preyer 12.2
prezzie 4.61
Priam 24.1
priapic 21.14
Priapus 28.30
price 28.13
pricer 12.70
pricey 4.46
prick 21.9
pricker 12.39
pricket 30.21
prickle 23.32
prickly 4.24
pride 16.14
prie-dieu 13.1
priest 31.5
priestcraft 30.47
priestess 28.3
priesthood 16.26
Priestley 4.23
priestly 4.23
prig 18.6
priggery 4.43
priggish 29.7
prim 24.6
primacy 4.48
prima donna-ish 29.6
prima facie 4.3
primal 23.33
primary 4.43

primate 30.12, 30.43
primatial 23.38
primavera 12.65
prime 24.7
primer 12.51
primeval 23.40
primitivist 31.15
primo 9.18
primogenital 23.39
primogenitary 4.43
primogenitor 12.78
primogeniture 12.23
primordial 23.24
primp 27.17
primrose 35.19
primula 12.46
primus 28.28
primus inter pares 35.7
prince 28.44
princedom 24.17
princelike 21.19
princeling 26.8
princely 4.24
princess 28.3
principal 23.35
principate 30.43
Príncipe 3.18
principle 23.35
prink 21.33
print 30.54
printer 12.78
printery 4.43
printing 26.13
printmaker 12.38
printmaking 26.7
printout 30.34
printworks 28.41
prion 25.24, 25.38
prior 12.13
priorate 30.43
priority 4.53
priory 4.43
Priscian 25.37
Priscilla 12.43
prise 35.11
prism 24.21
prismatic 21.17
prismoid 16.24
prison 25.52
prisoner 12.55
prissy 4.46
Pristina 12.55
pristine 25.12
Pritchett 30.20
prithee 4.57
privacy 4.48
private 30.25
privateer 12.4
privateering 26.11

privateersman 25.45
privateersmen 25.45
privatizer 12.91
privet 30.25
privilege 20.6
privileged 16.34
privy 4.58
prix fixe 28.39
prize 35.11
prizefight 30.27
prizefighter 12.79
prizefighting 26.13
prizewinner 12.55
prizewinning 26.9
pro 9.1
proa 12.17
proaction 25.49
pro-am 24.1
probate 30.9
probationary 4.43
probationer 12.58
probe 14.11
probing 26.4
probit 30.20
probity 4.53
problem 24.18
problematic 21.17
problematical 23.32
problematize 35.14
proboscis 28.11
procedure 12.35
proceed 16.7
proceedings 35.32
proceeds 35.27
process 28.3
processional 23.34
processor 12.69
procès-verbal 23.2
pro-choice 28.18
proclaim 24.4
proclaimer 12.50
proclamatory 4.43
Procne 4.32
proconsul 23.37
proconsulate 30.42
Procopius 28.23
procrastinate 30.13
procrastinatory 4.43
procreate 30.8
Procrustean 25.37
Procrustes 35.9
proctor 12.79
procure 12.20
procurer 12.67
procuress 28.3
prod 16.18
prodder 12.28
prodigal 23.30
prodigious 28.25
prodigy 4.17
produce 28.19

producer 12.71
producible 23.26
product 30.49
production 25.49
proem 24.3
proemial 23.24
profane 25.7
profaner 12.54
profanity 4.53
profess 28.3
professional 23.34
professionalize 35.12
professor 12.69
professorate 30.43
professorial 23.24
professoriate 30.41
proffer 12.30
proficiency 4.46
proficient 30.56
profile 23.11
profiler 12.44
profit 30.21
profiteer 12.4
profiterole 23.18
profligacy 4.48
profligate 30.42
pro-forma 12.52
profound 16.43
profundity 4.53
profuse 28.19
profusion 25.42
prog 18.8
progenitor 12.78
progeniture 12.23
progeny 4.32
progesterone 25.30
prognoses 35.8
prognosis 28.11
prognostic 21.17
prognosticate 30.10
prognosticatory 4.43
program 24.1
programmatic 21.17
programme 24.1
programmer 12.50
progress 28.3
progressional 23.34
progressionist 31.10
progressive 34.7
progressivist 31.15
prohibit 30.20
prohibiter 12.78
prohibitionary 4.43
prohibitionist 31.10
prohibitory 4.43
project 30.48
projectile 23.12
projection 25.49

projectionist 31.10
projector 12.76
Prokofiev 17.3
prolapse 28.46
prole 23.17
prolegomena 12.55
prolegomenon 25.46
prolepsis 28.11
proleptic 21.17
proletarian 25.37
proletarianize 35.13
proletariat 30.41
pro-life 17.7
proliferate 30.15
prolific 21.10
prolificacy 4.48
prolix 28.39
prolixity 4.53
prolog 18.8
prologue 18.8
prolong 26.15
prolonger 12.60
prolusion 25.42
prom 24.8
promenade 16.2
promenader 12.25
Promethean 25.37
Prometheus 28.23
promethium 24.16
prominence 28.45
prominency 4.48
prominent 30.56
promiscuity 4.53
promiscuous 28.24
promise 28.8
promisee 4.1
promiser 12.70
promissory 4.43
prommer 12.51
promo 9.18
promontory 4.43
promote 30.35
promoter 12.80
promotion 25.49
promotional 23.34
prompt 30.52
prompter 12.79
prompting 26.13
promptitude 16.25
promulgate 30.9
promulge 20.18
pronaoi 10.2
prone 25.30
prong 26.15
pronominal 23.34
pronominalize 35.12
pronoun 25.29
pronounce 28.44
pronouncer 12.70
pronto 9.25

proof 17.13
proofread 16.4, 16.7
proofreader 12.26
prop 27.8
propaganda 12.25
propagandist 31.6
propagandize 35.11
propagate 30.9
propane 25.8
propel 23.3
propellant 30.56
propellent 30.56
propeller 12.42
propensity 4.53
proper 12.62
propertied 16.12
Propertius 28.23
property 4.55
prophecy 4.46
prophesier 12.14
prophesy 6.16
prophet 30.21
prophetess 28.3
prophetic 21.17
prophetical 23.32
prophylactic 21.17
propinquity 4.53
propitiate 30.8
propitiatory 4.43
propitious 28.33
propjet 30.4
proponent 30.56
proportion 25.49
proportional 23.34
proportionate 30.43
proposal 23.41
propose 35.19
proposer 12.92
propound 16.43
propounder 12.28
proprietary 4.43
proprietor 12.82
proprietorial 23.24
propriety 4.55
propulsion 25.49
propulsive 34.7
propulsor 12.71
propyla 12.43
propylaeum 24.15
propylon 25.25
prorate 30.7
prorogue 18.10
prosaic 21.9
prosaist 31.6
proscenia 12.8
proscenium 24.16
prosciutto 9.25
proscribe 14.8
proscription 25.49
prose 35.19
prosecute 30.38

prosecution 25.49
prosecutor 12.81
proselyte 30.28
proselytizer 12.91
proser 12.92
prosimian 25.37
prosodic 21.10
prosodist 31.6
prosody 4.13
prospect 30.48
prospector 12.76
prospectus 28.34
prosper 12.62
prosperity 4.53
Prospero 9.21
prosperous 28.31
Prost 31.17
prostate 30.16
prosthesis 28.11
prostitute 30.38
prostitution 25.49
prostitutor 12.81
prostrate 30.7, 30.15
prosy 4.61
protagonist 31.10
protases 35.8
protasis 28.11
protea 12.12
protean 25.37
protect 30.48
protectant 30.56
protection 25.49
protectionist 31.10
protector 12.76
protectoral 23.36
protectorate 30.43
protectress 28.3
protégé 3.12
protein 25.12
proteinous 28.29
pro tem 24.3
protest 31.3
Protestant 30.56
protester 12.76
Proteus 28.23
prothalamium 24.16
protheses 35.8
prothesis 28.11
prothetic 21.17
protist 31.14
protium 24.16
protocol 23.13
proton 25.26
protonotary 4.43
prototypal 23.35
prototype 27.7
prototypic 21.14
prototypical 23.32
protozoa 12.17
protozoan 25.38
protozoon 25.38

protract 30.48
protracted 16.12
protraction 25.49
protractor 12.74
protrude 16.25
protrusion 25.42
protuberance 28.45
protuberant 30.56
proud 16.22
Proudhon 25.25
Proust 31.22
Prout 30.34
prove 34.12
proven 25.51
provenance 28.45
Provençal 23.2
Provence 28.44
provender 12.27
provenience 28.45
proverb 14.15
proverbial 23.24
Proverbs 35.26
provide 16.14
providence 28.45
provident 30.56
providential 23.38
provider 12.27
province 28.44
provincial 23.38
provincialist 31.8
provision 25.42
provisional 23.34
provisioner 12.58
proviso 9.29
provisor 12.91
provisory 4.43
Provo 9.27
provoke 21.24
provoker 12.40
provost 31.25
prow 8.1
prowess 28.7
prowl 23.16
prowler 12.44
proximate 30.43
proximity 4.53
proximo 9.18
proxy 4.46
Prozac 21.4
prude 16.25
prudence 28.45
prudent 30.56
prudential 23.38
prudery 4.43
prudish 29.6
prune 25.33
pruner 12.56
prurience 28.45
pruriency 4.48
prurient 30.56
Prussia 12.73

Prussian 25.49
pry 6.1
psalm 24.2
psalmic 21.12
psalmist 31.9
psalmodic 21.10
psalmodist 31.6
psalmody 4.13
psalter 12.80
psaltery 4.43
pseud 16.25
pseudo 9.11
pseudomorph 17.9
pseudonym 24.6
pseudonymity 4.53
pseudonymous
28.28
psi 6.1
psittacosis 28.11
psoriasis 28.11
psych 21.19
psyche 4.19, 21.19
psychedelia 12.6
psychedelic 21.11
psychiatric 21.15
psychiatrist 31.12
psychiatry 4.43
psychic 21.11
psychical 23.32
psycho 9.16
psychoanalyse 35.12
psychoanalysis
28.11
psychoanalyst 31.8
psychoanalytic
21.17
psychoanalyze 35.12
psychobabble 23.26
psychodynamic
21.12
psychokinesis 28.11
psychokinetic 21.17
psychologize 35.11
psychology 4.17
psychometric 21.15
psychometrist 31.12
psychometry 4.40
psychopath 32.1
psychopathic 21.18
psychoses 35.8
psychosexual 23.25
psychosis 28.11
psychosocial 23.38
psychosomatic
21.17
psychotherapeutic
21.17
psychotherapist
31.11
psychotherapy 4.37
psychotic 21.17
psyllium 24.16

p

ptarmigan 25.41
pteranodon 25.25
pterodactyl 23.9
Ptolemaic 21.9
Ptolemy 4.30
pub 14.13
pub crawl 23.15
puberty 4.55
pubes 35.6
pubescence 28.45
pubescent 30.56
pubic 21.9
pubis 28.7
public 21.11
publican 25.43
publicist 31.13
publish 29.8
publisher 12.72
Puccini 4.31
puccoon 25.33
puce 28.19
puck 21.29
pucker 12.41
puckery 4.43
puckish 29.8
pud 16.26
pudding 26.5
puddingy 4.35
puddle 23.28
puddler 12.48
puddly 4.27
pudenda 12.26
pudeur 13.1
pudge 20.16
pudgy 4.17
pudic 21.10
Puebla 12.42
pueblo 9.17
puerile 23.11
puerility 4.53
Puerto Rican 25.43
Puerto Rico 9.16
puff 17.15
puffball 23.14
puffer 12.30
puffery 4.43
puffin 25.14
puffy 4.14
pug 18.12
puggish 29.7
puggy 4.15
pugilist 31.8
Pugin 25.14
pugnacious 28.33
pugnacity 4.53
puissance 28.45
puissant 30.56
puja 12.35
puke 21.27
pukey 4.20
pukka 12.41

pul 23.20
pula 12.46
Pulaski 4.18
pulchritude 16.25
pulchritudinous 28.29
pule 23.20
puli 4.26
Pulitzer 12.70
pull 23.21
puller 12.46
pullet 30.22
pulley 4.26
Pullman 25.45
pull-out 30.34
pullover 12.86
pull-up 27.13
pulmonaria 12.10
pulmonary 4.43
pulmonate 30.43
pulp 27.16
pulper 12.63
pulpit 30.23
pulpy 4.37
pulsar 1.17
pulsate 30.7
pulsatory 4.43
pulse 28.42
pultrude 16.25
pulverizer 12.91
puma 12.52
pumice 28.8
pummel 23.33
pump 27.17
pumpernickel 23.32
pumpkin 25.15
pumpkinseed 16.7
pun 25.35
puna 12.56
punch 29.20
punchbag 18.1
punchball 23.14
punchbowl 23.17
punch-drunk 21.34
puncher 12.73
Punchinello 9.17
punchline 25.22
punch-up 27.13
punchy 4.50
punctilio 9.4
punctilious 28.23
punctual 23.25
punctuate 30.8
puncture 12.24
pundit 30.21
punditry 4.40
pungency 4.48
pungent 30.56
Punic 21.13
punish 29.9
punisher 12.72

Punjab 14.2
Punjabi 4.10
punk 21.34
punkah 12.41
punkish 29.8
punky 4.20
punner 12.57
punnet 30.23
punster 12.81
punt 30.55
Punta Arenas 28.29
punter 12.81
puny 4.33
pup 27.13
pupa 12.63
pupae 4.37
pupal 23.35
pupate 30.7
pupil 23.35
pupilage 20.6
pupillage 20.6
puppet 30.23
puppeteer 12.4
puppeteering 26.11
puppetry 4.40
puppy 4.37
puppyhood 16.26
puppyish 29.6
Purana 12.53
Puranic 21.13
purblind 16.42
Purcell 23.37
purchase 28.7
purchaser 12.70
purdah 1.6
pure 12.20
pure-bred 16.3, 16.4
purée 3.19
purgatory 4.43
purge 20.17
purger 12.36
purificatory 4.43
purifier 12.14
purify 6.7
Purim 24.6
purism 24.21
purist 31.12
puristic 21.17
puritan 25.50
puritanical 23.32
purity 4.53
purl 23.42
purler 12.49
purlieu 11.22
purlieux 35.21
purlin 25.16
purloin 25.32
purloiner 12.56
purple 23.35
purplish 29.8
purply 4.27

purport 30.33
purpose 28.30
purposive 34.7
purpure 12.20
purr 13.1
purse 28.36
purser 12.71
purslane 25.16
pursuance 28.45
pursuant 30.56
pursue 11.1
pursuer 12.19
pursuit 30.37
pursuivant 30.56
pursy 4.49
purulent 30.56
purvey 3.1
purveyance 28.45
purveyor 12.2
purview 11.22
pus 28.21
Pusan 25.1
Pusey 4.62
push 29.15
pushbike 21.19
pushcart 30.3
pushchair 2.4
pusher 12.73
Pushkin 25.15
pushover 12.86
pushpin 25.18
push-pull 23.21
pushrod 16.18
push-start 30.3
pushy 4.50
pusillanimity 4.53
pusillanimous 28.28
puss 28.20
pussy 4.47
pussycat 30.1
pussyfoot 30.39
pussyfooter 12.81
pustular 12.46
pustulate 30.11
pustule 23.20
put 30.39
put-down 25.29
putrefaction 25.49
putrefy 6.7
putrescence 28.45
putrescent 30.56
putrid 16.11
putridity 4.53
putsch 15.12
putt 30.40
puttee 4.55
putter 12.81
putti 4.55
putting green 25.11
Puttnam 24.19
putto 9.25

putty 4.55
putz 28.47
puzzle 23.41
puzzler 12.47
puzzling 26.8
pya 1.1
Pygmalion 25.37
pygmy 4.29
pyknic 21.13
pylon 25.44
Pyongyang 26.1
pyramid 16.10
pyramidal 23.28
Pyramus 28.28
pyre 12.13
Pyrenean 25.36
Pyrenees 35.6
pyrethrin 25.18
pyrethrum 24.19
Pyrex 28.38
pyrite 30.29
pyrites 35.9
pyritic 21.17
pyrogenic 21.13
pyromania 12.8
pyromaniac 21.1
pyrometer 12.78
pyrometric 21.15
pyrometry 4.40
pyrophoric 21.15
pyrotechnic 21.13
pyrotechnical 23.32
pyrotechnist 31.10
pyrotechny 4.31
pyroxene 25.11
Pyrrhic 21.15
Pyrrho 9.21
Pyrrhus 28.31
Pythagoras 28.31
Pythagorean 25.36
Pythia 12.12
Pythian 25.37
python 25.51
Pythonesque 21.35
pyx 28.39

Q

Qatar 1.19
Qatari 4.38
Qinghai 6.1
qua 3.1
Quaalude 16.25
quack 21.1
quackery 4.43
quackish 29.8
quad 16.18
quadragenarian 25.37
quadrangle 23.30

quadrangular 12.46
quadrant 30.56
quadraphonic 21.13
quadrat 30.43
quadrate 30.7, 30.15
quadratic 21.17
quadrennia 12.8
quadriceps 28.46
quadrilateral 23.36
quadrille 23.8
quadripartite 30.30
quadriplegia 12.6
quadriplegic 21.11
quadruped 16.3
quadruple 23.35
quadruplet 30.22
quadruplicate 30.10, 30.42
quadrupole 23.18
quaestor 12.77
quaff 17.8
quaffer 12.30
quag 18.1
quagga 12.31
quaggy 4.15
quagmire 12.14
quaich 22.2
Quai d'Orsay 3.1
quail 23.5
quaint 30.54
quake 21.7
Quaker 12.38
Quakerish 29.9
quaky 4.18
qualificatory 4.43
qualifier 12.14
qualify 6.7
quality 4.53
qualm 24.2
quandary 4.43
quango 9.13
quant 30.54
quantifier 12.14
quantify 6.7
quantity 4.53
quantum 24.20
quarantine 25.12
quark 21.5
quarrel 23.36
quarreler 12.48
quarreller 12.48
quarry 4.41
quarryman 25.45
quarrymen 25.45
quart 30.33
quartan 25.50
quarte 30.3
quarter 12.80
quarterage 20.8
quarterback 21.2
quarterdeck 21.6

quarterfinal 23.34
quartering 26.11
quarterly 4.27
quartermaster 12.75
quartern 25.50
quartet 30.4
quarto 9.25
quartz 28.47
quartzite 30.30
quasar 1.24
quash 29.11
Quasimodo 9.11
quassia 12.11
quaternary 4.43
quatorze 35.17
quatrain 25.8
quaver 12.85
quavery 4.43
quay 4.1
quayage 20.6
quayside 16.16
quean 25.9
queasy 4.61
Québec 21.6
Quebecker 12.37
Quechua 12.88
Quechuan 25.51
queen 25.9
queendom 24.17
queenie 4.31
queen-like 21.19
queenly 4.23
Queens 35.31
queen-size 35.14
Queensland 16.45
Queenslander 12.29
queer 12.4
queerish 29.9
quell 23.3
queller 12.42
quench 29.20
quenelle 23.3
Quentin 25.19
querist 31.12
quern 25.53
querulous 28.27
query 4.43
quest 31.3
Quested 16.12
quester 12.76
question 25.39
questioner 12.58
questionnaire 2.1
Quetta 12.76
queue 11.1
quibble 23.26
quibbler 12.48
quiche 29.5
quick 21.9
quicken 25.43
quickie 4.19

quicklime 24.7
quicksand 16.40
quickset 30.4
quicksilver 12.86
quickstep 27.3
quick-witted 16.12
quid 16.8
quiddity 4.53
quidnunc 21.34
quid pro quo 9.1
quiescence 28.45
quiescent 30.56
quiet 30.41
quieten 25.50
quietist 31.14
quietude 16.25
quietus 28.34
quiff 17.6
quill 23.8
quilling 26.8
quilt 30.51
quilter 12.78
quim 24.6
quin 25.13
quinary 4.43
quince 28.44
quincunx 28.41
quinella 12.42
quinine 25.11
quinquagenarian 25.37
quinquennia 12.8
quint 30.54
quintain 25.19
quintal 23.39
quintessence 28.45
quintessential 23.38
quintet 30.4
quintile 23.9
Quintilian 25.37
Quinton 25.50
quintuple 23.35
quintuplet 30.22
quintuplicate 30.10
Quintus 28.34
quip 27.6
quipster 12.78
quipu 11.16
quire 12.13
quirk 21.31
quirkish 29.8
quirky 4.20
quirt 30.45
quisling 26.8
quit 30.20
quitch 15.6
quite 30.26
Quito 9.24
quittance 28.45
quitter 12.78
quiver 12.86

p
q

quivering 26.11
quivery 4.43
quixotic 21.17
quixotry 4.41
quiz 35.10
quizmaster 12.75
quizzer 12.90
quizzical 23.32
Qum 24.13
Qumran 25.4
quod 16.18
quodlibet 30.4
quodlibetarian 25.37
quoin 25.32
quoit 30.36
quokka 12.40
quondam 24.1
Quonset 30.24
quorate 30.15
Quorn 25.28
quorum 24.19
quota 12.80
quote 30.35
quoth 32.11
quotidian 25.37
quotient 30.56
Qwaqwa 12.88

R

Rabat 30.1
Rabaul 23.16
rabbet 30.20
rabbi 6.5
Rabbie 4.10
rabbinate 30.43
rabbinic 21.13
rabbinical 23.32
rabbit 30.20
rabbity 4.53
rabble 23.26
rabble-rouser 12.92
Rabelais 3.15
Rabelaisian 25.37
rabid 16.8
rabidity 4.53
rabies 35.6
Rabin 25.9
raccoon 25.33
race 28.5
racecard 16.2
racecourse 28.15
racegoer 12.17
racehorse 28.15
raceme 24.5
racer 12.69
racetrack 21.3
Rachel 23.27
Rachmaninov 17.8

racial 23.38
racialist 31.8
Racine 25.9
racism 24.21
racist 31.13
rack 21.1
racket 30.21
racketeer 12.4
rackety 4.53
Rackham 24.18
racon 25.25
raconteur 13.1
racquetball 23.14
racy 4.45
rad 16.1
radar 1.6
Radcliffe 17.6
radial 23.24
radian 25.37
radiance 28.45
radiancy 4.48
radiant 30.56
radiate 30.8
radical 23.32
radicalize 35.12
radicchio 9.4
radices 35.8
radii 6.3
radio 9.4
radiocarbon 25.38
radiogenic 21.13
radiogram 24.1
radiograph 17.2
radiographer 12.30
radiography 4.14
radioisotope 27.10
radiology 4.17
radio-telephone 25.30
radiotherapy 4.37
radish 29.6
radium 24.16
radius 28.23
radix 28.39
radome 24.11
radon 25.25
Rae 3.1
Raeburn 25.53
Raelene 25.10
Rafe 17.4
raffia 12.5
raffish 29.7
raffle 23.29
Raffles 35.29
Rafsanjani 4.31
raft 30.47
rafter 12.75
raftsman 25.45
raftsmen 25.45
rag 18.1
raga 12.31

ragamuffin 25.14
ragbag 18.1
rage 20.4
ragged 16.9
raggedy 4.12
raggle-taggle 23.30
raglan 25.44
ragman 25.2
ragmen 25.5
Ragnarök 21.21
ragout 11.8
ragstone 25.31
ragtag 18.1
ragtime 24.7
ragtop 27.8
ragweed 16.7
ragworm 24.22
ragwort 30.45
rah 1.1
rah-rah 1.16
rai 6.1
raid 16.6
raider 12.26
rail 23.5
railage 20.6
railcar 1.11
railcard 16.2
railer 12.43
railhead 16.3
railing 26.8
raillery 4.43
railman 25.45
railmen 25.45
railroad 16.23
railway 3.25
railwayman 25.45
railwaymen 25.45
raiment 30.56
rain 25.7
rainbow 9.9
raincoat 30.35
raindrop 27.8
Raine 25.7
rainfall 23.15
rainforest 31.12
Rainier 3.3, 12.8
rainmaker 12.38
rainproof 17.13
rainstorm 24.9
rainswept 30.58
rainwater 12.80
rainwear 2.15
rainy 4.31
Raisa 12.69
raise 35.5
raisin 25.52
raisiny 4.34
raison d'être 12.64
raj 20.2
raja 12.35
Rajasthan 25.4

Rajasthani 4.31
Rajneesh 29.5
Rajput 30.39
Rajshahi 4.16
rake 21.7
raker 12.38
raki 4.18
rakish 29.8
raku 11.12
Raleigh 4.21
rallier 12.6
rally 4.21
rallycross 28.14
Ralph 17.18
ram 24.1
Rama 12.50
Ramadan 25.1
Ramakrishna 12.55
Ramayana 12.58
Rambert 2.3
ramble 23.26
rambler 12.42
rambling 26.8
Rambo 9.9
rambunctious 28.33
rambutan 25.50
Rameau 9.18
ramekin 25.15
ramen 25.5
rami 6.12
ramie 4.29
ramify 6.7
Ramillies 35.7
ramin 25.9
ramjet 30.4
rammer 12.50
rammy 4.29
Ramón 25.24
Ramona 12.56
ramp 27.17
rampage 20.4
rampageous 28.25
rampager 12.35
rampancy 4.48
rampant 30.56
rampart 30.3
rampion 25.37
ram raid 16.6
ramrod 16.18
Ramsay 4.61
ramshackle 23.32
ran 25.1
ranch 29.20
rancher 12.72
ranchero 9.21
Ranchi 4.50
rancid 16.11
rancidity 4.53
rancor 12.37
rancorous 28.31
rancour 12.37

religious 28.25
relinquish 29.10
reliquary 4.43
reliquiae 4.3
relish 29.8
reluctance 28.45
reluctant 30.56
rely 6.1
rem 24.3
remainder 12.26
remand 16.41
Rembrandt 30.53
remedy 4.12
rememberer 12.67
remembrance 28.45
remembrancer 12.71
reminisce 28.7
reminiscence 28.45
reminiscent 30.56
reminiscer 12.70
remise 35.11
remissible 23.26
remit 30.20, 30.23
remittal 23.39
remittance 28.45
remitter 12.78
remnant 30.56
remonetize 35.14
remonstrate 30.15
remontant 30.56
remora 12.67
removal 23.40
remunerate 30.15
Remus 28.28
Renaissance 28.45
renal 23.34
renascence 28.45
Renata 12.75
renationalize 35.12
Renault 9.19
rend 16.41
Rendell 23.28
render 12.26
renderer 12.67
rendering 26.11
rendezvous 11.21
René 3.17
renegade 16.6
renegado 9.11
renege 18.5
reneger 12.31
renewal 23.25
renewer 12.19
renminbi 4.10
Rennes 25.5
rennet 30.23
Rennie 4.31
Reno 9.19
Renoir 1.22
renounce 28.44

renouncer 12.70
renovate 30.16
renown 25.29
rent 30.53
rental 23.39
rentboy 10.3
renter 12.76
renunciant 30.56
renunciatory 4.43
renvoi 1.22
rep 27.3
repairer 12.65
repairman 25.2
repairmen 25.5
repartee 4.1
repatriate 30.8
repeater 12.77
repêchage 19.1
repel 23.3
repellence 28.45
repellency 4.48
repellent 30.56
repeller 12.42
repentance 28.45
repentant 30.56
repenter 12.76
repertoire 1.22
repertory 4.43
repetend 16.41
répétiteur 13.1
repetitious 28.33
replay 3.15
replenish 29.9
replenisher 12.72
replete 30.18
repletion 25.49
replevin 25.19
replica 12.39
replicate 30.10
replier 12.13
repo 9.20
reportage 20.2
reportorial 23.24
repository 4.43
repoussé 3.20
reprehend 16.41
reprehensible 23.26
representa-
tionalist 31.8
representationist 31.10
represser 12.69
repressible 23.26
repressive 34.7
reprieve 34.5
reprimand 16.41
reprisal 23.41
reprise 35.6
repro 9.21
reproach 15.10
reproacher 12.24

reprographic 21.10
reprography 4.14
reprover 12.87
reproving 26.14
reptile 23.12
reptilian 25.37
Repton 25.50
repudiate 30.8
repugnance 28.45
repugnant 30.56
repulsion 25.49
repulsive 34.7
repute 30.37
requiem 24.16
requiescat 30.1
requirer 12.67
requisite 30.25
requisitioner 12.58
requisitionist 31.10
requital 23.39
reredos 28.14
resale 23.6
rescind 16.42
rescue 11.22
rescuer 12.19
resemblant 30.56
resemble 23.26
reservist 31.15
reservoir 1.22
residence 28.45
residency 4.48
resident 30.56
residential 23.38
residentiary 4.43
residua 12.20
residual 23.21
residuary 4.41
residue 11.22
residuum 24.17
resigned 16.42
resile 23.11
resilience 28.45
resiliency 4.48
resilient 30.56
resin 25.20
resinate 30.13
resinous 28.29
resist 31.6
resistance 28.45
resistant 30.56
resistible 23.26
resistor 12.78
resit 30.24
resolute 30.37
resonance 28.45
resonant 30.56
resonate 30.13
respect 30.48
respecter 12.76
respiratory 4.43
respite 30.29

resplendence 28.45
resplendency 4.48
respond 16.42
respondent 30.56
responder 12.28
response 28.44
responsible 23.26
responsive 34.7
responsory 4.43
respray 3.19
res publica 12.39
rest 31.3
restaurant 30.53
restaurateur 13.1
restitution 25.49
restive 34.8
restorationist 31.10
restraint 30.54
restriction 25.49
restrictionist 31.10
restroom 24.12
restructuring 26.11
result 30.51
resultant 30.56
résumé 3.16
resume 3.16, 24.12
resumption 25.49
resurgence 28.45
resurgent 30.56
resurrect 30.48
resurrection 25.49
resuscitate 30.16
ret 30.4
retail 23.6
retailer 12.43
retain 25.7
retainer 12.54
retaliate 30.8
retaliatory 4.43
retard 16.2
retarded 16.9
retarder 12.25
retch 15.3
retention 25.49
retiarius 28.23
reticence 28.45
reticent 30.56
reticle 23.32
reticule 23.20
retiform 24.9
retina 12.55
retinue 11.22
retiral 23.36
retiree 4.1
retiring 26.11
retortion 25.49
retread 16.4
retribution 25.49
retributory 4.43
retrieval 23.40
retrieve 34.5

r

r

ringlet 30.22
ringletted 16.12
ringlety 4.53
ringmaster 12.75
ring pull 23.21
ringside 16.16
ringsider 12.27
ringtail 23.6
ringtone 25.31
ringworm 24.22
rink 21.33
rinkhals 28.42
rinky dink 21.33
rinse 28.44
rinser 12.70
Rio 9.3
Rio de Janeiro 9.21
Río de la Plata 12.75
Río Grande 4.12
Rioja 12.40
Riordan 25.40
riot 30.41
rioter 12.82
riotous 28.34
rip 27.6
riparian 25.37
ripcord 16.21
ripe 27.7
ripen 25.46
ripieno 9.19
rip-off 17.8
riposte 31.17
ripper 12.62
ripple 23.35
ripplet 30.22
ripply 4.27
riproaring 26.11
ripsaw 7.16
ripsnorter 12.80
ripsnorting 26.13
ripstop 27.8
riptide 16.17
rise 35.11
risen 25.52
riser 12.91
risible 23.26
rising 26.14
risk 21.35
risky 4.19
Risorgimento 9.24
risotto 9.25
risqué 3.14
rissole 23.18
Rita 12.77
Ritalin 25.16
rite 30.26
ritenuto 9.25
ritual 23.25
ritualize 35.12
Ritz 28.47

ritzy 4.46
rival 23.40
rivalry 4.40
rive 34.9
riven 25.51
river 12.86
Rivera 12.65
riverbank 21.33
riverboat 30.35
riverine 25.23
Rivers 35.24
riverside 16.16
rivet 30.25
riveter 12.78
Riviera 12.65
rivière 2.1
rivulet 30.22
Riyadh 16.1
riyal 23.2
roach 15.10
road 16.23
roadbed 16.3
roadblock 21.21
roadhog 18.8
roadholding 26.5
roadhouse 28.16
roadie 4.13
roadkill 23.9
roadroller 12.44
roadrunner 12.57
roadshow 9.23
roadside 16.16
roadstead 16.4
roadster 12.80
road test 31.3
roadway 3.25
roadwork 21.31
roadworthy 4.57
Roald 16.38
roam 24.11
roamer 12.52
roan 25.30
roar 7.1
roarer 12.66
roaring 26.11
roast 31.20
roaster 12.80
roasting 26.13
rob 14.9
robber 12.21
robbery 4.43
Robbins 35.31
robe 14.11
Robert 30.41
Roberts 28.47
Robeson 25.48
Robespierre 2.2
Robey 4.10
robin 25.13
Robin Goodfellow 9.17

Robinson 25.48
Robinson Crusoe 9.22
robot 30.31
robotic 21.17
robotize 35.14
Robsart 30.3
Robson 25.48
robust 31.24
roc 21.20
rocaille 6.1
rocambole 23.17
Rocco 9.16
Rochelle 23.3
Rochester 12.78
rochet 30.20
rock 21.20
rockabilly 4.24
Rockall 23.15
rock-bottom 24.20
rock cake 21.7
Rockefeller 12.42
rocker 12.40
rockery 4.43
rocket 30.21
rocketeer 12.4
rocketry 4.40
rockfall 23.15
rockfish 29.7
Rockhampton 25.50
Rockies 35.10
rock-like 21.19
rockling 26.8
Rockwell 23.4
rocky 4.19
rococo 9.16
rod 16.18
Roddenberry 4.43
Roddick 21.10
rode 16.23
rodent 30.56
rodeo 9.4
Roderick 21.15
Rodgers 35.24
rodham 24.17
Rodin 25.1
rodless 28.27
rodlet 30.22
rod-like 21.19
Rodney 4.32
rodomontade 16.2
roe 9.1
roebuck 21.29
Roedean 25.10
roe-deer 12.5
roentgen 25.52
rogation 25.49
roger 12.35
Roget 3.12
rogue 18.10
roguery 4.43

roguish 29.7
roil 23.19
roister 12.81
roisterer 12.67
roistering 26.11
roisterous 28.31
Roland 16.45
rôle 23.17
Rolf 17.18
roll 23.17
rollaway 3.25
rollback 21.2
rollbar 1.4
rollcall 23.15
roller 12.44
rollerball 23.14
rollerblade 16.6
rollerblader 12.26
rollick 21.11
rollmop 27.8
Rollo 9.17
roll-on 25.25
roll-on roll-off 17.8
Rolls 35.29
roly-poly 4.25
Rom 24.8
Roma 12.52
Romaic 21.9
romaine 25.7
Roman 25.45
roman-à-clef 3.1
Romance 28.44
romancer 12.69
Romanesque 21.35
roman-fleuve 34.14
Romania 12.8
Romanian 25.37
Romanic 21.13
Romano 9.19
Romanov 17.8
Romansh 29.20
romantic 21.17
romanticist 31.13
Romany 4.34
Romberg 18.13
Rome 24.11
Romeo 9.4
romer 12.52
Rommel 23.33
Romney 4.32
romp 27.17
Romulus 28.27
Ronald 16.38
Ronan 25.46
Roncesvalles 23.2
rondavel 23.40
ronde 16.42
rondeau 9.11
rondel 23.28
rondo 9.11
Rondônia 12.8

r

rone 25.30
ronin 25.18
Ronnie 4.32
roo 11.1
rood 16.25
rood screen 25.11
roof 17.13
roofer 12.30
roofing 26.6
roofscape 27.4
rooftop 27.8
rooibos 28.14
rook 21.28
rookery 4.43
rookie 4.20
room 24.12
roomer 12.52
roomette 30.4
roomie 4.30
room-mate 30.12
roomy 4.30
Rooney 4.33
Roosevelt 30.51
roost 31.22
rooster 12.81
root 30.37
rootbeer 12.5
rooter 12.81
rootle 23.39
root-like 21.19
rootstock 21.21
rootsy 4.47
rooty 4.54
rope 27.10
rope-walk 21.22
roping 26.10
ropy 4.36
roque 21.24
Roquefort 7.6
rorqual 23.40
rort 30.33
rorty 4.54
Rory 4.41
Ros 35.16
Rosa 12.92
rosace 28.5
Rosaleen 25.10
Rosalie 4.27
Rosalind 16.42
rosaline 25.10
Rosalyn 25.16
Rosamund 16.44
Rosanna 12.53
Rosanne 25.1
rosaria 12.10
rosarian 25.37
Rosario 9.4
rosarium 24.16
rosary 4.43
Roscius 28.23
roscoe 9.16

Roscommon 25.45
rose 35.19
rosé 3.27
roseate 30.41
rosebay 3.7
Rosebery 4.43
rosehip 27.6
rose-like 21.19
rosella 12.42
rosemary 4.43
rosette 30.4
rosetted 16.12
rosewater 12.80
rosewood 16.26
Rosh Hashana 12.53
Rosicrucian 25.49
Rosie 4.61
rosin 25.20
Roskilde 16.35
Ross 28.14
Rossellini 4.31
Rossetti 4.51
Rossini 4.31
Rosslare 2.1
roster 12.79
Rostock 21.21
rostra 12.65
rostral 23.36
rostrum 24.19
Roswell 23.4
rosy 4.61
rot 30.31
rota 12.80
Rotarian 25.37
rotary 4.43
rotate 30.7
rotation 25.49
rotational 23.34
rotator 12.77
rotatory 4.43
rotavate 30.16
rote 30.35
rotgut 30.40
Roth 32.8
Rotherham 24.19
Rothko 9.16
Rothschild 16.36
roti 4.54
rotisserie 4.43
rotogravure 12.20
rotor 12.80
rotten 25.50
rotter 12.79
Rotterdam 24.1
Rottweiler 12.44
rotund 16.44
rotunda 12.29
rotundity 4.53
Rouault 9.1
rouble 23.26
roué 3.5

Rouen 25.24
rouge 19.6
rough 17.15
roughage 20.6
rough-and-tumble
  23.26
roughcast 31.2
roughen 25.41
roughie 4.14
roughish 29.7
roughneck 21.6
roughrider 12.27
roughshod 16.18
roughy 4.14
rouille 4.8
roulade 16.2
rouleau 9.17
rouleaux 35.19
roulette 30.4
round 16.43
roundabout 30.34
roundel 23.28
roundelay 3.15
rounder 12.28
Roundhead 16.3
roundish 29.6
roundsman 25.45
roundsmen 25.45
round-up 27.13
roundworm 24.22
roup 27.11
roupy 4.37
rouse 35.18
Rouse 28.16
rouser 12.92
Rousse 28.19
Rousseau 9.22
Roussillon 25.27
roust 31.19
roustabout 30.34
rout 30.34
route 30.37
routine 25.9
routinize 35.13
roux 11.1
rove 34.11
rover 12.86
row 8.1, 9.1
rowan 25.38
rowboat 30.35
rowdy 4.13
Rowe 9.1
rowel 23.25
rowen 25.38
Rowena 12.54
rower 12.17
Rowlandson 25.48
Rowley 4.25
rowlock 21.30
Rowntree 4.41
Roy 10.1

royal 23.25
royalist 31.8
royalty 4.55
Royce 28.18
Royle 23.19
Royston 25.50
Roz 35.16
rozzer 12.91
rub 14.13
rubato 9.24
rubber 12.22
rubberize 35.13
rubberneck 21.6
rubbery 4.43
rubbing 26.4
rubbish 29.6
rubbishy 4.50
rubble 23.26
rubbly 4.27
Rubbra 12.66
rube 14.12
rubella 12.42
rubellite 30.28
Rubens 35.31
rubeola 12.48
Rubicon 25.43
rubicund 16.45
rubicundity 4.53
rubidium 24.16
rubiginous 28.29
Rubinstein 25.23
rubric 21.15
rubrical 23.32
rubricate 30.10
ruby 4.10
ruche 29.14
ruck 21.29
ruckle 23.32
rucksack 21.4
ruckus 28.26
ruction 25.49
rudbeckia 12.6
rudd 16.27
rudder 12.29
ruddle 23.28
ruddy 4.13
rude 16.25
rudery 4.43
Rudi 4.13
rudimentary 4.43
Rudolph 17.18
rue 11.1
rueful 23.21
ruff 17.15
ruffian 25.37
ruffle 23.29
rufous 28.25
Rufus 28.25
rug 18.12
rugby 4.10
Rügen 25.42

rugged 16.9
rugger 12.32
Ruhr 12.20
ruin 25.13
ruinous 28.29
rule 23.20
ruler 12.45
ruling 26.8
rum 24.14
rumba 12.22
rumble 23.26
rumbler 12.48
rumbling 26.8
rumbustious 28.24
ruminant 30.56
ruminate 30.13
rumly 4.26
rummage 20.7
rummager 12.35
rummer 12.52
rummy 4.30
rumness 28.29
rumor 12.52
rumour 12.52
rump 27.17
rumple 23.35
rumply 4.27
rumpus 28.30
rumpy-pumpy 4.37
run 25.35
runabout 30.34
runaround 16.43
runaway 3.25
Runcorn 25.28
rundown 25.29
run-down 25.29
rune 25.33
rung 26.18
runic 21.13
run-in 25.18
runlet 30.22
runnel 23.34
runner 12.57
running board 16.20
runny 4.33
Runnymede 16.7
runt 30.55
run-through 11.17
runty 4.55
run-up 27.13
runway 3.25
Runyon 25.52
rupee 4.1
Rupert 30.43
rupiah 12.3
rupture 12.24
rural 23.36
ruralist 31.8
rurality 4.53
ruralize 35.12

Rurik 21.15
Ruritania 12.8
Ruritanian 25.37
rusa 12.71
ruse 35.21
rush 29.16
Rushdie 4.13
rusher 12.73
rush hour 12.16
rushlight 30.28
rushy 4.50
rusk 21.35
Ruskin 25.15
Russ 28.21
Russell 23.37
russet 30.24
russety 4.53
Russia 12.73
Russian 25.49
Russophile 23.11
rust 31.24
rust belt 30.51
rust bucket 30.21
rustic 21.17
rusticate 30.10
rustle 23.37
rustler 12.47
rustling 26.8
rustproof 17.13
rusty 4.55
rut 30.40
rutabaga 12.31
ruth 32.12
ruthenium 24.16
Rutherford 16.28
rutherfordium 24.16
rutile 23.12
Rutland 16.45
rutty 4.55
Rwanda 12.25
Rwandan 25.40
Rwandese 35.6
Ryan 25.38
Ryder 12.27
rye 6.1
ryegrass 28.2
Ryle 23.11
ryokan 25.43
ryot 30.41

Saadi 4.12
Saar 1.1
Saarbrücken 25.43
Saarland 16.40
Saba 12.21
Sabaean 25.36
Sabah 12.21

Sabaoth 32.8
sabayon 25.27
sabbatarian 25.37
sabbath 32.13
sabbatical 23.32
Sabellian 25.37
saber 12.21
Sabian 25.37
Sabine 25.9, 25.21
sable 23.26
sabot 9.9
sabotage 20.2
saboteur 13.1
sabra 12.64
sabre 12.21
sabretooth 32.12
sabreur 13.1
Sabrina 12.54
sac 21.1
saccade 16.2
saccharide 16.15
saccharin 25.18
saccharine 25.18
sacerdotal 23.39
sachem 24.17
sachet 3.21
Sacheverell 23.36
Sachs 28.38
Sachsen 25.48
sack 21.1
sackbut 30.40
sackcloth 32.8
sacking 26.7
sacra 12.65
sacral 23.36
Sacramento 9.24
sacraria 12.10
sacred 16.11
sacrifice 28.13
sacrificial 23.38
sacrilege 20.6
sacrilegious 28.25
sacrist 31.12
sacristan 25.50
sacristy 4.53
sacroiliac 21.1
sacrosanct 30.49
sacrosanctity 4.53
sacrum 24.19
sad 16.1
Sadat 30.1
sadden 25.40
saddish 29.6
saddle 23.28
saddleback 21.2
saddlebag 18.1
saddlecloth 32.8
saddler 12.42
saddlery 4.43
Sadducean 25.36

Sadducee 4.47
Sade 16.2
sadhu 11.6
Sadie 4.12
sadism 24.21
sadist 31.6
sadistic 21.17
sadly 4.21
sadness 28.29
sadomasochist 31.7
safari 4.38
safe 17.4
safebreaker 12.38
safe-conduct 30.49
safecracker 12.37
safeguard 16.2
safekeeping 26.10
safety 4.52
safflower 12.16
saffron 25.47
saffrony 4.34
sag 18.1
saga 12.31
sagacious 28.33
sagacity 4.53
sagamore 7.12
Sagan 25.1
Sagar 12.31
sage 20.4
sagebrush 29.16
saggar 12.31
saggy 4.15
sagittal 23.39
Sagittarian 25.37
Sagittarius 28.23
sago 9.13
Sahara 12.64
Saharan 25.47
Sahel 23.3
Sahelian 25.37
sahib 14.2
said 16.3
Said 16.14
Saida 12.27
saiga 12.31
Saigon 25.24
sail 23.5
sailboard 16.20
sailboarder 12.28
sailboarding 26.5
sailboat 30.35
sailcloth 32.8
sailer 12.43
sail-fluke 21.27
sailing 26.8
sailmaker 12.38
sailor 12.43
sailorly 4.27
sailplane 25.8
Sainsbury 4.43

r

s

saint 30.54
saintdom 24.17
sainted 16.12
sainthood 16.26
saintly 4.22
Saint-Saëns 25.24
Saipan 25.1
sake 21.7
saké 4.18
saker 12.38
Sakhalin 25.10
Sakharov 17.8
saki 4.18
sal 23.1
salaam 24.2
salable 23.26
salacious 28.33
salad 16.29
salade 16.2
Saladin 25.14
Salamanca 12.37
salamander 12.25
salamandrine 25.23
salami 4.29
Salamis 28.8
salariat 30.41
salary 4.43
salat 30.3
Salazar 1.1
sale 23.5
Salem 24.18
Salerno 9.19
saleroom 24.12
salesclerk 21.5
salesgirl 23.42
Salesian 25.37
saleslady 4.12
salesman 25.45
salesmen 25.45
salesperson 25.48
salesroom 24.12
saleswoman 25.45
saleswomen 25.17
Salford 16.28
Salian 25.37
Salic 21.11
salience 28.45
saliency 4.48
salient 30.56
Salieri 4.39
Salina 12.55
Salinas 28.29
saline 25.22
Salinger 12.35
salinity 4.53
Salisbury 4.43
Salish 29.8
saliva 12.86
salivary 4.43
salivate 30.16

sallow 9.17
sallowish 29.6
sallowy 4.7
Sallust 31.25
sally 4.21
salmanazar 12.90
salmon 25.45
salmonella 12.42
salmonid 16.10
salmony 4.34
Salome 4.29
salon 25.25
Salonica 12.39
saloon 25.33
Salop 27.14
Salopian 25.37
salsa 12.69
salsify 4.14
salt 30.51
salt-and-pepper
    12.61
saltbox 28.40
saltbush 29.15
saltcellar 12.42
salter 12.80
saltern 25.50
saltimbocca 12.40
saltine 25.9
salting 26.13
saltire 12.14
saltish 29.10
saltlick 21.11
Saltmarsh 29.2
saltpan 25.3
saltpeter 12.77
saltpetre 12.77
saltus 28.34
saltwater 12.80
salty 4.54
salubrious 28.23
salubrity 4.53
saluki 4.20
salutary 4.43
salutatorian 25.37
salutatory 4.43
salute 30.37
saluter 12.81
Salvador 7.5
Salvadorean 25.37
salvage 20.9
salvager 12.35
salvationist 31.10
salve 34.15
salver 12.85
salvia 12.12
salvo 9.27
salvor 12.85
Salyut 30.37
Salzburg 18.13
Sam 24.1

samadhi 4.12
Samantha 12.83
Samar 12.50
Samara 12.64
Samaria 12.10
Samaritan 25.50
Samarkand 16.40
samba 12.21
sambar 12.21
sambhar 12.21
same 24.4
samey 4.29
samfu 11.7
Samhain 25.13
Samian 25.37
samisen 25.5
samite 30.29
samizdat 30.1
Sammy 4.29
Samnite 30.29
Samoa 12.17
Samoan 25.38
Sámos 28.14
samosa 12.71
samovar 1.21
samoyed 16.3
Samoyedic 21.10
samp 27.17
sampan 25.3
sample 23.35
sampler 12.42
sampling 26.8
samsara 12.64
samsaric 21.15
samskara 12.64
Samson 25.48
Samuel 23.25
samurai 6.15
Sana'a 1.1
sanatoria 12.10
sanatorium 24.16
Sancho 9.23
sanctifier 12.14
sanctify 6.7
sanctimonious
    28.23
sanctimony 4.34
sanction 25.49
sanctitude 16.25
sanctity 4.53
sanctuary 4.43
sanctum 24.20
Sanctus 28.34
sand 16.40
Sand 25.24
sandal 23.28
sandalwood 16.26
sandarac 21.3
sandbag 18.1
sandbagger 12.31

sandbank 21.33
sandbar 1.4
sand bath 32.2
sandblast 31.2
sandblaster 12.75
sandbox 28.40
sandboy 10.3
sandcastle 23.37
sander 12.25
sanderling 26.8
sanders 35.24
sandfly 6.11
Sandford 16.28
sandglass 28.2
sandhi 4.12
sandhog 18.8
Sandhurst 31.26
Sandinista 12.78
sandlot 30.31
sandman 25.2
sandpaper 12.61
sandpiper 12.62
sandpit 30.23
Sandra 12.64
Sands 35.27
sandshoe 11.19
sandstone 25.31
sandstorm 24.9
sandwich 20.9
Sandwich 15.6
sandwich board
    16.20
sandy 4.12
sandyish 29.6
sane 25.7
Sanford 16.28
San Francisco 9.16
sang 26.1
sangar 12.31
Sanger 12.60
sang-froid 1.1
sangha 12.32
Sango 9.13
sangrail 23.5
sangría 12.3
sanguinary 4.43
sanguine 25.20
sanguineous 28.23
Sanhedrin 25.18
sanicle 23.32
sanidine 25.10
sanitarian 25.37
sanitarium 24.16
sanitary 4.43
sanitizer 12.91
sanity 4.53
sank 21.33
San Marino 9.19
sans 35.31
sans-culotte 30.31

Sanskrit 30.24
Sanskritic 21.17
Sanskritist 31.14
Sansovino 9.19
Santa 12.74
Santa Claus 35.17
Santa Fé 3.1
Santander 2.1
Santayana 12.53
Santiago 9.13
Santiago de
  Compostela 12.42
santonica 12.39
santonin 25.18
Santoríni 4.31
Santos 28.14
São Paulo 9.17
sap 27.1
sapele 4.23
sapid 16.10
sapient 30.56
sapiential 23.38
Sapir 12.4
sapling 26.8
sapodilla 12.43
saponaceous 28.33
sapper 12.61
Sapphic 21.10
sapphire 12.14
sapphirine 25.23
Sappho 9.12
Sapporo 9.21
sappy 4.36
saprophyte 30.27
saprophytic 21.17
sapwood 16.26
saraband 16.40
Saracen 25.48
Saragossa 12.70
Sarah 12.65
Sarajevo 9.27
saran 25.1
sarangi 4.15
Saransk 21.35
Saranwrap 27.1
Saratoga 12.32
Sarawak 21.4
sarcasm 24.21
sarcastic 21.17
sarcoma 12.52
sarcophagi 6.8
sarcophagus 28.25
sard 16.2
Sardanapalus 28.27
Sardegna 12.89
sardelle 23.3
sardine 25.9, 25.21
Sardinia 12.8
Sardinian 25.37
Sardis 28.7

sardonic 21.13
sardonyx 28.39
Sargasso 9.22
sarge 20.2
Sargent 30.56
Sargodha 12.28
Sargon 25.25
sari 4.38
sarin 25.9
sark 21.5
sarking 26.7
sarky 4.18
Sarmatian 25.49
sarnie 4.31
sarod 16.23
sarong 26.15
Saros 28.14
sarrusophone 25.30
sarsaparilla 12.43
sarsen 25.48
sartorial 23.24
Sartre 12.64
Sarum 24.19
sash 29.1
Sasha 12.72
sashay 3.21
sashimi 4.29
sasine 25.19
Saskatchewan 25.38
Saskatoon 25.33
Saskia 12.6
sasquatch 15.1
sass 28.1
sassafras 28.1
Sassanian 25.37
Sassanid 16.10
Sassenach 22.1
Sassoon 25.33
sassy 4.45
sastrugi 4.15
sat 30.1
Satan 25.50
satang 26.1
satanic 21.13
satanist 31.10
satanize 35.13
satay 3.22
satchel 23.27
sate 30.7
sateen 25.9
satellite 30.28
satiate 30.8, 30.41
Satie 4.51
satiety 4.53
satin 25.19
satinette 30.4
satinized 16.50
satinwood 16.26
satiny 4.32
satire 12.14

satiric 21.15
satirical 23.32
satirist 31.12
satisfaction 25.49
satisfactory 4.43
satisfy 6.7
satnav 34.1
satori 4.41
satrap 27.14
satrapy 4.37
satsuma 12.52
saturate 30.15
Saturday 3.9
Saturn 25.50
Saturnalia 12.6
saturnalian 25.37
Saturnian 25.37
saturnine 25.23
satyr 12.74
satyric 21.15
sauce 28.15
sauceboat 30.35
saucepan 25.46
saucer 12.70
saucy 4.47
Saudi 4.13
sauerkraut 30.34
Saul 23.14
Saumur 12.20
sauna 12.56
Saunders 35.24
saunter 12.80
saunterer 12.67
sauropod 16.18
saury 4.41
sausage 20.9
Saussure 12.20
sauté 3.22
Sauternes 25.53
Sauveterrian 25.37
Sauvignon 25.27
savable 23.26
savage 20.9
savagery 4.43
savannah 12.53
savant 30.56
savante 30.56
savarin 25.18
savate 30.3
save 34.4
saveloy 10.7
saver 12.85
Savery 4.43
savin 25.19
saving 26.14
savior 12.89
saviour 12.89
savoir faire 2.1
Savonarola 12.44
savor 12.85
savory 4.43

savour 12.85
savoury 4.43
savoy 10.1
Savoyard 16.2
savvy 4.58
saw 7.1
sawbill 23.8
sawbones 35.31
sawbuck 21.29
sawdust 31.24
sawgrass 28.2
sawhorse 28.15
sawmill 23.9
sawn 25.28
sawtooth 32.12
sawtoothed 30.60
sawyer 12.89
sax 28.38
saxe 28.38
saxifrage 20.4
saxist 31.13
Saxon 25.48
Saxonist 31.10
saxony 4.34
saxophone 25.30
saxophonic 21.13
saxophonist 31.10
say 3.1
sayable 23.26
Sayers 35.24
saying 26.3
says 35.3
say-so 9.22
scab 14.1
scabbard 16.28
scabby 4.10
scabies 35.10
scabious 28.23
scabrous 28.31
scad 16.1
scaffold 16.37
scaffolder 12.25
scaffolding 26.5
scagliola 12.44
scald 16.36
scale 23.5
scalene 25.10
scaler 12.43
Scaliger 12.35
scallawag 18.1
scallion 25.37
scallop 27.14
scalloper 12.63
scallywag 18.1
scalp 27.16
scalpel 23.35
scalper 12.61
scaly 4.22
scam 24.1
scammony 4.34

scamp 27.17
scamper 12.61
scampi 4.36
scampish 29.9
scan 25.1
scandal 23.28
scandalmonger 12.32
scandalous 28.27
Scandinavia 12.12
Scandinavian 25.37
scandium 24.16
scanner 12.53
scansion 25.49
scant 30.53
scantling 26.8
scanty 4.51
scapegoat 30.35
scapula 12.46
scapulary 4.43
scar 1.1
scarab 14.14
scarabaeid 16.8
scaramouch 29.14
Scarborough 12.67
scarce 28.4
scarcity 4.53
scare 2.1
scarecrow 9.21
scaredy-cat 30.1
scaremonger 12.32
scaremongering 26.11
scarer 12.65
scarf 17.2
scarifier 12.14
scarify 6.7
scarlatina 12.54
Scarlatti 4.51
scarlet 30.22
Scarlett 30.22
scarp 27.2
scarper 12.61
Scart 30.3
scarves 35.35
scary 4.39
scat 30.1
scathe 33.2
scathing 26.14
scatology 4.17
scatter 12.74
scatterbrain 25.8
scatterer 12.67
scattergun 25.35
scatty 4.51
scaup 27.9
scaur 7.1
scavenge 20.19
scavenger 12.35
scena 12.54
scenario 9.4

scenarist 31.12
scene 25.9
scenery 4.43
scenester 12.77
scenic 21.13
scent 30.53
scepter 12.76
sceptic 21.17
sceptical 23.32
sceptre 12.76
Schadenfreude 12.28
schappe 27.1
schedule 23.21
scheduler 12.46
Scheele 12.43
Scheherazade 12.25
Scheldt 30.51
schema 12.51
schemata 12.82
schematic 21.17
scheme 24.5
schemer 12.51
scheming 26.9
scherzo 9.22
Schiaparelli 4.22
Schiele 12.43
Schiller 12.43
Schilling 26.8
schism 24.21
schismatic 21.17
schist 31.6
schizo 9.22
schizoid 16.24
schizophrenia 12.8
schizophrenic 21.13
Schlegel 23.30
schlemiel 23.7
schlepp 27.3
Schleswig 18.6
Schliemann 25.45
schlieren 25.47
schlock 21.20
schlocky 4.19
schmaltz 28.47
schmaltzy 4.47
schmooze 35.21
schmuck 21.29
schnapps 28.46
schnauzer 12.70
schnitzel 23.37
schnook 21.28
schnozz 35.16
Schoenberg 18.13
scholar 12.44
scholarly 4.27
scholastic 21.17
scholiastic 21.17
school 23.20
schoolboy 10.3

schoolchild 16.36
schoolchildren 25.47
schoolfellow 9.17
schoolgirl 23.42
schoolhouse 28.16
schoolie 4.26
schooling 26.8
schoolman 25.2
schoolmarm 24.2
schoolmarmish 29.8
schoolmaster 12.75
schoolmastering 26.11
schoolmasterly 4.27
schoolmate 30.12
schoolmistress 28.10
schoolroom 24.12
schoolteacher 12.23
schoolteaching 26.4
schooner 12.56
Schopenhauer 12.16
schorl 23.14
schottische 29.5
Schroder 12.28
Schrödinger 12.60
schtuck 21.28
Schubert 30.41
Schulz 28.47
Schumacher 12.37
Schumann 25.45
schuss 28.20
Schütz 28.47
schwa 1.1
Schwann 25.24
Schwarzkopf 17.8
Schwarzwald 16.35
Schweitzer 12.70
sciatic 21.17
sciatica 12.39
science 28.45
sciential 23.38
scientific 21.10
scientist 31.14
Scientology 4.17
sci-fi 6.7
scilicet 30.5
scilla 12.43
Scillies 35.10
scimitar 12.78
scintilla 12.43
scintillate 30.11
scion 25.38
Scipio 9.4
scissel 23.37
scission 25.42
scissor 12.90
scleroses 35.8
sclerosis 28.11

sclerotic 21.17
scoff 17.8
scoffer 12.30
scold 16.37
scolder 12.28
scolding 26.5
scollop 27.14
sconce 28.44
Scone 25.33
scone 25.24
scoop 27.11
scooper 12.63
scoot 30.37
scooter 12.81
scooterist 31.12
scope 27.10
scorch 15.8
scorcher 12.24
score 7.1
scoreboard 16.20
scorebook 21.28
scorecard 16.2
scorer 12.66
scoring 26.11
scorn 25.28
scorner 12.56
scorp 27.9
Scorpian 25.37
Scorpio 9.4
scorpion 25.37
Scorpius 28.23
scorzonera 12.67
Scot 30.31
scotch 15.7
scoter 12.80
scot-free 4.1
Scotia 12.73
Scotland 16.45
Scots 28.47
Scotsman 25.45
Scotsmen 25.45
Scotswoman 25.45
Scotswomen 25.17
Scott 30.31
Scottie 4.54
Scottish 29.10
scoundrel 23.36
scoundrelly 4.27
scour 12.16
scourer 12.67
scourge 20.17
scourger 12.36
Scouser 12.70
scout 30.34
scouter 12.80
Scoutmaster 12.75
scow 8.1
scowl 23.16
scowler 12.44
scrabble 23.26
scrag 18.1

S

scrag-end 16.41
scraggly 4.21
scraggy 4.15
scram 24.1
scramble 23.26
scrambler 12.42
scramjet 30.4
scran 25.1
Scranton 25.50
scrap 27.1
scrapbook 21.28
scrape 27.4
scraper 12.61
scraperboard 16.20
scrapheap 27.5
scrapie 4.36
scraping 26.10
scrapper 12.61
scrapple 23.35
scrappy 4.36
scrapyard 16.2
scratch 15.1
scratchboard 16.20
scratcher 12.23
scratch pad 16.1
scratchy 4.11
scrawl 23.14
scrawly 4.25
scrawny 4.32
scream 24.5
screamer 12.51
scree 4.1
screech 15.5
screecher 12.23
screechy 4.11
screed 16.7
screen 25.9
screener 12.54
screening 26.9
screenplay 3.15
screen print 30.54
screenwriter 12.79
screenwriting 26.13
screw 11.1
screwball 23.14
screwdriver 12.86
screwer 12.19
screwtop 27.8
screw-top 27.8
screw worm 24.22
screwy 4.8
Scriabin 25.13
scribal 23.26
scribble 23.26
scribbler 12.48
scribbling 26.8
scribbly 4.27
scribe 14.8
scriber 12.21
scrim 24.6

scrimmage 20.7
scrimmager 12.35
scrimp 27.17
scrimshank 21.33
scrimshanker 12.37
scrimshaw 7.17
scrip 27.6
script 30.58
scriptoria 12.10
scriptorial 23.24
scriptorium 24.16
scripture 12.23
Scriptures 35.24
scriptwriter 12.79
scriptwriting 26.13
scrivener 12.58
scrod 16.18
scrofulous 28.27
scroll 23.17
scroller 12.44
scrooge 20.15
scrotum 24.20
scrounge 20.19
scrounger 12.35
scrub 14.13
scrubber 12.22
scrubby 4.10
scrubland 16.40
scruff 17.15
scruffy 4.14
scrum 24.14
scrum half 17.2
scrummage 20.7
scrummager 12.35
scrummy 4.30
scrump 27.17
scrumple 23.35
scrumptious 28.33
scrumpy 4.37
scrunch 29.20
scruple 23.35
scrupulosity 4.53
scrupulous 28.27
scrutineer 12.4
scrutinizer 12.91
scrutiny 4.32
scry 6.1
scryer 12.13
scuba 12.21
scuba-dive 34.9
scud 16.27
scuff 17.15
scuffle 23.29
scull 23.22
sculler 12.47
scullery 4.43
scullion 25.37
sculpt 30.58
sculptor 12.81
sculpture 12.24

sculpturesque 21.35
scum 24.14
scumbag 18.1
scumble 23.26
scummy 4.30
scuncheon 25.49
scunge 20.19
scungy 4.17
scunner 12.57
Scunthorpe 27.9
scup 27.13
scupper 12.63
scurf 17.17
scurfy 4.14
scurrilous 28.27
scurry 4.42
scurvy 4.58
scut 30.40
Scutari 4.38
scutch 15.13
scutcheon 25.39
scutcher 12.24
scutter 12.81
scuttle 23.39
scuttlebutt 30.40
scuzzy 4.62
scythe 33.5
Scythia 12.12
Scythian 25.37
sea 4.1
seabed 16.3
seabird 16.31
seaboard 16.20
seaborne 25.28
seacock 21.20
seadog 18.8
seafarer 12.65
seafaring 26.11
seafood 16.25
seafront 30.55
seagoing 26.3
seagull 23.22
sea horse 28.15
seal 23.7
sealant 30.56
sealer 12.43
sealskin 25.15
Sealyham 24.16
seam 24.5
seaman 25.45
seamanlike 21.19
seamanly 4.27
seamark 21.5
seamen 25.45
seamer 12.51
seamstress 28.10
Seamus 28.28
seamy 4.29
Sean 25.28
Seanad 16.29

séance 28.44
seaplane 25.8
seaport 30.33
seaquake 21.7
sear 12.4
search 15.14
searcher 12.24
searchlight 30.28
Searle 23.42
Sears 35.24
seascape 27.4
seashell 23.4
seashore 7.17
seasick 21.16
seaside 16.16
season 25.52
seasonal 23.34
seasoning 26.9
seat 30.18
seat belt 30.51
Seattle 23.39
seawall 23.14
seaward 16.30
seawater 12.80
seaway 3.25
seaweed 16.7
seaworthy 4.57
sebaceous 28.33
Sebastian 25.37
Sebastopol 23.13
Sebat 30.1
sec 21.6
secateurs 35.25
secco 9.16
secede 16.7
seceder 12.26
secessional 23.34
secessionist 31.10
seclude 16.25
seclusion 25.42
seclusive 34.7
second 16.42, 16.45
secondary 4.43
secondee 4.1
seconder 12.29
secondi 4.13
secondo 9.11
secrecy 4.46
secret 30.24
secretaire 2.1
secretarial 23.24
secretariat 30.41
secretary 4.43
secrete 30.18
secretion 25.49
secretor 12.77
sect 30.48
sectarian 25.37
sectarianize 35.13
section 25.49

S

sectional 23.34
sectionalist 31.8
sectionalize 35.12
sector 12.76
sectorial 23.24
secular 12.46
secularist 31.12
secularity 4.53
secularize 35.13
secure 12.20
securitize 35.14
security 4.53
sedan 25.1
sedate 30.7
sedation 25.49
sedentary 4.43
Seder 12.26
sederunt 30.56
sedge 20.3
Sedgemoor 7.12
Sedgwick 21.18
sedgy 4.17
sedilia 12.6
sedimentary 4.43
sedition 25.49
seditious 28.33
seduce 28.19
seducer 12.71
seducible 23.26
seduction 25.49
seductress 28.10
sedulity 4.53
sedulous 28.27
see 4.1
seeable 23.26
seed 16.7
seedbed 16.3
seedcake 21.7
seedcorn 25.28
seeder 12.26
seedling 26.8
seedsman 25.45
seedsmen 25.45
seedy 4.12
Seeger 12.31
seek 21.8
seeker 12.38
seel 23.7
seem 24.5
seemly 4.23
seen 25.9
seep 27.5
seepage 20.7
seer 12.3, 12.4
seersucker 12.41
seesaw 7.16
seethe 33.3
see-through 11.17
segment 30.53, 30.56
segmentalize 35.12

segmentary 4.43
Segovia 12.12
segregate 30.9
segue 3.25
seguidilla 12.89
sei 3.1
seif 17.5
seigneur 13.1
seigneurial 23.24
Seine 25.7
seiner 12.54
seise 35.6
seisin 25.20
seismic 21.12
seismical 23.32
seismograph 17.2
seismology 4.17
seize 35.6
seizer 12.90
seizure 12.33
seldom 24.17
select 30.48
selection 25.49
selector 12.76
Selene 4.31
selenide 16.14
selenite 30.29
selenium 24.16
Seleucid 16.11
self 17.18
self-absorbed 16.32
self-addressed 31.3
self-adjusting 26.13
self-aggrandizing 26.14
self-appointed 16.12
self-assured 16.28
self-catering 26.11
self-centered 16.29
self-centred 16.29
self-cocking 26.7
self-colored 16.29
self-coloured 16.29
self-confessed 31.3
self-contained 16.41
self-controlled 16.37
self-deceiving 26.14
self-defeating 26.13
self-denying 26.3
self-deprecating 26.13
self-educated 16.12
self-effacing 26.12
self-employed 16.24
self-faced 31.4
self-feeding 26.5
self-fulfilling 26.8
self-governed 16.45
self-governing 26.9

self-imposed 16.50
self-induced 31.22
self-inflicted 16.12
self-interested 16.12
selfish 29.7
self-mocking 26.7
self-motivated 16.12
self-perpetuating 26.13
self-pitying 26.3
self-possessed 31.3
self-proclaimed 16.39
self-propelled 16.35
self-propelling 26.8
self-regarding 26.5
self-regulating 26.13
self-respecting 26.13
self-restrained 16.41
Selfridge 20.8
self-righting 26.13
self-sacrificing 26.12
self-satisfied 16.14
self-sealing 26.8
self-seeking 26.7
self-selecting 26.13
self-styled 16.36
self-supporting 26.13
self-sustained 16.41
self-sustaining 26.9
self-willed 16.35
Selima 12.51
Selina 12.54
Seljuk 21.27
Selkirk 21.31
sell 23.3
Sellafield 16.35
seller 12.42
Sellers 35.24
sellotape 27.4
sell-out 30.34
Selma 12.50
Selous 11.1
seltzer 12.69
Selvas 28.35
selvedge 20.9
selves 35.35
Selwyn 25.20
Selznick 21.13
semantic 21.17
semaphore 7.6
semaphoric 21.15
Semarang 26.1
semblance 28.45
Semele 4.24

semen 25.45
semester 12.76
semi 4.29
semi-automatic 21.17
semibreve 34.5
semicircle 23.32
semicircular 12.46
semicolon 25.44
semiconductor 12.81
semi-detached 30.46
semi-final 23.34
semi-finalist 31.8
Semillon 25.27
seminal 23.34
seminar 1.14
seminarian 25.37
seminarist 31.12
seminary 4.43
Seminole 23.17
semiology 4.17
semiotic 21.17
semi-precious 28.33
semiquaver 12.85
semi-retired 16.28
Semite 30.29
Semitic 21.17
Semitist 31.14
semitone 25.31
semi-tropical 23.32
semi-tropics 28.39
semivowel 23.25
semmit 30.23
semolina 12.54
sempervivum 24.20
semplice 4.11
sempre 3.19
sempstress 28.10
Semtex 28.38
senarius 28.23
senary 4.43
senate 30.23
senator 12.78
senatorial 23.24
send 16.41
Sendai 6.6
sendal 23.28
sender 12.26
Seneca 12.39
Senegal 23.14
Senegalese 35.6
seneschal 23.38
senhor 7.1
senhora 23.14
Senhorita 12.77
senile 23.11
senility 4.53
senior 12.8
seniority 4.53

senna 12.53
Sennacherib 14.7
sennet 30.23
sennight 30.29
sennit 30.23
señor 7.1
señora 12.66
señores 35.5
señorita 12.77
sensate 30.15
sensationalist 31.8
sense 28.44
sensible 23.26
sensitizer 12.91
sensor 12.69
sensory 4.43
sensual 23.25
sensualist 31.8
sensualize 35.12
sensum 24.20
sensuous 28.24
sent 30.53
sente 4.51
sentence 28.45
sentential 23.38
sententious 28.33
sentience 28.45
sentient 30.56
sentimentalist 31.8
sentinel 23.34
sentry 4.38
Senussi 4.47
Seoul 23.17
sepal 23.35
separate 30.15, 30.43
separatist 31.14
Sephardic 21.10
sepia 12.9
sepoy 10.10
sepsis 28.11
sept 30.58
September 12.21
septenary 4.43
septennia 12.8
septet 30.4
septic 21.17
septicaemia 12.7
septicemia 12.7
septillion 25.52
septimal 23.33
septime 24.5
Septimus 28.28
septuagenarian 25.37
Septuagint 30.54
septum 24.20
septuple 23.35
septuplet 30.22
sepulcher 12.37
sepulchral 23.36

sepulchre 12.37
sepulture 12.23
sequacious 28.33
sequacity 4.53
sequel 23.40
sequence 28.45
sequencer 12.71
sequent 30.56
sequential 23.38
sequester 12.76
sequestrate 30.15
sequin 25.20
sequoia 12.18
sera 12.67
serac 21.3
seraglio 9.4
serai 6.1
serape 4.36
seraph 17.16
seraphic 21.10
seraphim 24.6
Seraphina 12.54
Serapis 28.9
Serb 14.15
Serbia 12.5
Serbian 25.37
Serbo-Croat 30.1
Serbo-Croatian 25.49
sere 12.4
Seremban 25.1
Serena 12.54
serenade 16.6
serenader 12.26
serenata 12.75
serendipitous 28.34
serendipity 4.53
serene 25.9
Serengeti 4.51
serenity 4.53
serf 17.17
serfdom 24.17
serge 20.17
sergeant 30.56
sergeant major 12.35
Sergei 3.11
Sergio 9.4
serial 23.24
serialist 31.8
seriatim 24.6
sericulture 12.24
sericulturist 31.12
series 35.10
serif 17.6
serigraph 17.2
serigrapher 12.30
serin 25.18
serious 28.23
sermon 25.45
sermonizer 12.91

serotine 25.23
serotonin 25.18
Serpens 35.31
serpent 30.56
serpentine 25.23
serrate 30.7, 30.15
serried 16.11
serum 24.19
serval 23.40
servant 30.56
serve 34.14
server 12.87
servery 4.43
Servian 25.37
service 28.12
serviceman 25.45
servicemen 25.45
servicewoman 25.45
servicewomen 25.17
serviette 30.4
servile 23.12
servility 4.53
serving 26.14
servitude 16.25
servo 9.27
sesame 4.30
sesamum 24.19
Sesotho 9.25
sesquipedalian 25.37
session 25.49
sessional 23.34
sesterce 28.36
sestertii 6.3
sestertius 28.23
sestet 30.4
set 30.4
setaceous 28.33
setback 21.2
Seth 32.3
set piece 28.6
setsquare 2.15
Setswana 12.53
sett 30.4
settee 4.1
setter 12.76
setting 26.13
settle 23.39
settler 12.48
settlor 12.48
set-to 11.1
set-up 27.13
Seurat 1.16
seven 25.51
sevenfold 16.37
seventeen 25.9
seventeenth 32.19
seventh 32.19
seventieth 32.6
seventy 4.51
sever 12.85

several 23.36
severalty 4.55
severance 28.45
severe 12.4
severity 4.53
Severn 25.51
Severus 28.31
severy 4.43
seviche 3.8
Seville 23.8
Sèvres 12.64
sew 9.1
sewage 20.6
sewellel 23.33
sewer 12.17, 12.19
sewerage 20.8
sewn 25.30
sex 28.38
sexagenarian 25.37
sexism 24.21
sexist 31.13
sexless 28.27
sexologist 31.7
sexpartite 30.30
sexpot 30.32
sext 31.28
Sextans 35.31
sextant 30.56
sextet 30.4
sextile 23.12
sextillion 25.52
sextodecimo 9.18
sexton 25.50
sextuple 23.35
sextuplet 30.22
sexual 23.25
sexualize 35.12
sexy 4.45
Seychelles 35.29
Seychellois 1.1
Seymour 7.12
sez 35.3
sforzandi 4.12
Shaba 12.21
shabbat 30.1
shabbos 28.24
shabby 4.10
shack 21.1
shackle 23.32
Shackleton 25.50
shad 16.1
shadbush 29.15
shaddock 21.30
shade 16.6
shading 26.5
shadoof 17.13
shadow 9.11
shadow-box 28.40
shadower 12.17
shadowy 4.7

S

shady 4.12
shaft 30.47
Shaftesbury 4.43
shag 18.1
shagger 12.31
shaggy 4.15
shagreen 25.9
shah 1.1
shahdom 24.17
Shaka 12.37
shake 21.7
shakedown 25.29
shaken 25.43
shaker 12.38
Shakespeare 12.9
Shakespearean 25.37
shake-up 27.13
shako 9.16
shaky 4.18
shale 23.5
shall 23.1
shallop 27.14
shallot 30.31
shallow 9.17
shalom 24.8
shalwar 1.21
shaly 4.22
sham 24.1
shaman 25.45
shamanic 21.13
shamanist 31.10
shamateur 12.82
shamble 23.26
shambolic 21.11
shame 24.4
shamefaced 31.4
Shamir 12.4
shammer 12.50
shammy 4.29
shampoo 11.1
shamrock 21.21
shamus 28.28
Shan 25.4
shandy 4.12
Shane 25.7
Shang 26.1
shanghai 6.1
Shangri-La 1.1
shank 21.33
Shankar 1.11
Shankly 4.21
Shanks 28.41
Shannon 25.46
shan't 30.53
shantung 26.18
shanty 4.51
shanty town 25.29
Shanxi 4.1
shape 27.4

shapely 4.22
shaper 12.61
shaping 26.10
shard 16.2
share 2.1
sharecrop 27.8
sharecropper 12.62
shareholder 12.28
shareholding 26.5
sharer 12.65
shareware 2.15
sharia 12.3
Sharif 17.5
Sharjah 1.10
shark 21.5
sharkskin 25.15
Sharman 25.45
Sharon 25.47
sharp 27.2
Shar Pei 3.1
sharpen 25.46
sharpener 12.58
sharpening 26.9
sharper 12.61
sharpie 4.36
sharpish 29.9
sharpshooter 12.81
sharpshooting 26.13
Shastra 12.64
shat 30.1
Shatt al-Arab 14.14
shatter 12.74
shatterer 12.67
shatterproof 17.13
shave 34.4
shaven 25.51
shaver 12.85
Shavian 25.37
shaving 26.14
Shavuoth 28.24
shaw 7.1
shawl 23.14
shawm 24.9
Shawnee 4.1
shay 3.1
shchi 4.1
she 4.1
shea 4.1
sheading 26.5
sheaf 17.5
shear 12.4
shearer 12.67
shearing 26.11
shearling 26.8
shearwater 12.80
sheath 32.5
sheathe 33.3
sheathing 26.14
sheave 34.5
Sheba 12.21

shebang 26.1
shebeen 25.9
shed 16.3
she'd 16.7
shedder 12.26
she-devil 23.40
sheen 25.9
Sheena 12.54
sheeny 4.31
sheep 27.5
sheepdip 27.6
sheepdog 18.8
sheepfold 16.37
sheepish 29.9
sheeplike 21.19
sheep run 25.35
sheepshank 21.33
sheepskin 25.15
sheep walk 21.22
sheer 12.4
sheer legs 35.28
sheet 30.18
Sheetrock 21.21
Sheffield 16.35
sheikh 21.7
sheikhdom 24.17
sheila 12.43
shekel 23.32
Shekinah 12.55
Shelagh 12.43
Sheldon 25.40
shelduck 21.29
shelf 17.18
shelf-life 17.7
she'll 23.7
shell 23.3
shellac 21.1
shellback 21.2
Shelley 4.22
shellfire 12.14
shellfish 29.7
shell shock 21.21
shelly 4.22
Shelta 12.76
shelter 12.76
shelterer 12.67
sheltie 4.51
shelve 34.15
shelves 35.35
Shem 24.3
Shema 12.50
shemozzle 23.41
Shenandoah 12.17
shenanigans 35.31
Shenyang 26.1
Shenzhen 25.5
shepherd 16.29
shepherdess 28.3
Sher 13.1
Sheraton 25.50

sherbet 30.41
shereef 17.5
Sheridan 25.40
sheriff 17.6
Sherman 25.45
sherpa 12.63
Sherrington 25.50
sherry 4.38
Sheryl 23.9
she's 35.6
Shetland 16.45
Shetlander 12.29
Shevardnadze 12.90
shew 9.1
Shia 12.3
shiatsu 11.18
shibboleth 32.3
shicker 12.39
shied 16.14
shield 16.35
Shields 35.27
shieling 26.8
shift 30.47
shifter 12.78
shifty 4.53
shih-tzu 11.1
Shiism 24.21
Shiite 30.26
shikar 1.1
shikara 12.64
shikari 4.38
Shikoku 11.12
shill 23.8
shillelagh 12.43
shilling 26.8
Shillong 26.15
Shilluk 21.28
shilly-shally 4.21
shilly-shallyer 12.6
Shilton 25.50
shim 24.6
shimmer 12.51
shimmery 4.43
shimmy 4.29
shin 25.13
shin bone 25.30
shindig 18.6
shindy 4.12
shine 25.21
shiner 12.55
shingle 23.30
shingly 4.24
shinny 4.32
shin splints 28.47
Shinto 9.24
Shintoist 31.6
shinty 4.53
shiny 4.32
ship 27.6
shipboard 16.20

shipbroker 12.40
shipbuilder 12.27
shipbuilding 26.5
Shipley 4.24
shipload 16.23
shipmate 30.12
shipowner 12.56
shipper 12.62
ship-rigged 16.33
shipshape 27.4
ship-to-shore 7.1
shipway 3.25
shipwreck 21.6
shipwright 30.29
shipyard 16.2
Shiraz 35.1
shire 12.13
shire horse 28.15
shirk 21.31
shirker 12.41
Shirley 4.28
shirr 13.1
shirt 30.45
shirtdress 28.3
shirting 26.13
shirtsleeve 34.5
shirt tail 23.6
shirtwaist 31.4
shirtwaister 12.77
shirty 4.55
shit 30.20
shite 30.26
shit-scared 16.5
shitty 4.53
shiv 34.6
Shiva 12.85
shiver 12.86
shiverer 12.67
shivery 4.43
shoal 23.17
shoaly 4.25
shoat 30.35
shock 21.20
shocker 12.40
shocking 26.7
shockproof 17.13
shod 16.18
shoddy 4.13
shoe 11.1
shoebill 23.8
shoeblack 21.3
shoebox 28.40
shoehorn 25.28
shoelace 28.5
shoemaking 26.7
shoeshine 25.23
shoestring 26.11
shoetree 4.41
shofar 12.30
shofroth 30.35

shogun 25.35
Sholto 9.25
Shona 12.56
shone 25.24
shonky 4.19
shoo 11.1
shoo-in 25.13
shook 21.28
shoot 30.37
shooter 12.81
shooting 26.13
shoot-out 30.34
shop 27.8
shopaholic 21.11
shopfitter 12.78
shopfitting 26.13
shop-floor 7.1
shopfront 30.55
shopkeeper 12.61
shopkeeping 26.10
shoplift 30.47
shoplifter 12.78
shopper 12.62
shopsoiled 16.37
shopwalker 12.40
shopworker 12.41
shopworn 25.28
shore 7.1
shorebird 16.31
shoreline 25.22
shoreward 16.30
shoring 26.11
shorn 25.28
short 30.33
shortage 20.9
short-arm 24.2
shortbread 16.4
shortcake 21.7
short-change 20.19
short-circuit 30.21
shortcoming 26.9
shortcut 30.40
shorten 25.50
shortfall 23.15
shorthair 2.6
shorthand 16.40
short-handed 16.9
shorthaul 23.15
shorthold 16.37
shorthorn 25.28
shortish 29.10
shortlist 31.8
shortsighted 16.12
shortstop 27.8
shortwave 34.4
short weight 30.7
shorty 4.54
Shoshone 4.33
Shostakovich 15.6
shot 30.31

shotgun 25.35
should 16.26
shoulder 12.28
shouldn't 30.56
shout 30.34
shouter 12.80
shove 34.13
shove-halfpenny
  4.31
shovel 23.40
shovelboard 16.20
shoveler 12.48
shoveller 12.48
show 9.1
show-and-tell 23.3
showband 16.40
showbiz 35.10
showboat 30.35
showcard 16.2
showcase 28.5
showdown 25.29
shower 12.16, 12.17
showerproof 17.13
showery 4.43
showgirl 23.42
showground 16.43
showing 26.3
showjump 27.17
showjumper 12.63
showjumping 26.10
showman 25.45
showmen 25.45
shown 25.30
show-off 17.8
showpiece 28.6
showplace 28.5
showroom 24.12
show-stopper 12.62
show-stopping
  26.10
showy 4.7
shoyu 11.22
shrank 21.33
shrapnel 23.34
shred 16.3
shredder 12.26
Shreveport 30.33
shrew 11.1
shrewd 16.25
shrewish 29.6
Shrewsbury 4.43
shriek 21.8
shrieker 12.38
shrieval 23.40
shrift 30.47
shrike 21.19
shrill 23.8
shrimp 27.17
shrimper 12.62
shrine 25.21

shrink 21.33
shrinkage 20.6
shrinker 12.39
shrinking 26.7
shrive 34.9
shrivel 23.40
shriven 25.51
Shropshire 12.11
shroud 16.22
shrove 34.11
Shrovetide 16.17
shrub 14.13
shrubbery 4.43
shrubby 4.10
shrug 18.12
shrunk 21.34
shrunken 25.43
shtick 21.9
shuck 21.29
shucker 12.41
shudder 12.29
shuddery 4.43
shuffle 23.29
shuffleboard 16.20
shuffler 12.48
shuffling 26.8
shufti 4.55
shul 23.20
Shula 12.45
Shumen 25.5
shun 25.35
shunt 30.55
shunter 12.81
shush 29.16
shut 30.40
shutdown 25.29
Shute 30.37
shut-eye 6.18
shut-out 30.34
shutter 12.81
shutterbug 18.12
shuttle 23.39
shuttlecock 21.20
shy 6.1
shyer 12.13
Shylock 21.21
shyly 4.25
shyness 28.9
shyster 12.79
si 4.1
Siam 24.1
Siamese 35.6
Siân 25.4
sib 14.7
Sibelius 28.23
Siberia 12.10
Siberian 25.37
sibilance 28.45
sibilant 30.56
sibilate 30.11

S

sibling 26.8
sibyl 23.8
sibylline 25.22
sic 21.9
sice 28.13
Sichuan 25.4
Sicilian 25.37
siciliano 9.19
Sicily 4.24
sick 21.9
sickbay 3.7
sickbed 16.3
sicken 25.43
sickener 12.58
Sickert 30.42
sickie 4.19
sickish 29.8
sickle 23.32
sickly 4.24
sicko 9.16
sickroom 24.12
Siddons 35.31
side 16.14
sidearm 24.2
sidebar 1.4
sideboard 16.20
sideburn 25.53
sidecar 1.11
sidehill 23.9
sidekick 21.11
sidelamp 27.17
sidelight 30.28
sideline 25.22
sidelong 26.15
side-on 25.24
sidereal 23.24
side-saddle 23.28
sideshow 9.23
side-slip 27.6
side-splitting 26.13
sidestep 27.3
sidestepper 12.61
sidestroke 21.24
sideswipe 27.7
sidetrack 21.3
sidewalk 21.22
sideward 16.30
sideways 35.5
sidewinder 12.27
sidewise 35.15
siding 26.5
sidle 23.28
Sidmouth 32.13
Sidney 4.32
Sidon 25.40
siege 20.5
Siegfried 16.7
Sieg Heil 23.11
Siemens 35.31
Siena 12.53

Sienese 35.6
sienna 12.53
sierra 12.64
Sierra Madre 3.19
siesta 12.76
sieve 34.6
sievert 30.44
sifaka 12.37
sift 30.47
sifter 12.78
sigh 6.1
sight 30.26
sighter 12.79
sighting 26.13
sight line 25.22
sightly 4.25
sight-reader 12.26
sight screen 25.11
sightsee 4.46
sightseeing 26.3
sightseer 12.3
sigil 23.9
Sigismund 16.45
sigla 12.43
sigma 12.51
Sigmund 16.45
sign 25.21
signal 23.34
signaler 12.48
signalize 35.12
signaller 12.48
signalman 25.45
signalmen 25.45
signatory 4.43
signature 12.24
signboard 16.20
signer 12.55
signet 30.23
significance 28.45
significant 30.56
signified 16.14
signifier 12.14
signify 6.7
signing 26.9
signor 7.1
signora 12.66
signorina 12.54
signpost 31.20
signwriter 12.79
signwriting 26.13
Sigurd 16.31
Sihanouk 21.28
sika 12.38
Sikh 21.8
Sikkim 24.6
Sikkimese 35.6
Sikorsky 4.19
silage 20.6
Silas 28.27
Silchester 12.78

sild 16.35
silence 28.45
silencer 12.71
silent 30.56
Silesia 12.12
Silesian 25.37
silex 28.38
silhouette 30.4
silica 12.39
silicate 30.42
siliceous 28.33
silicon 25.43
silicone 25.30
siliqua 12.88
siliquose 28.17
silk 21.32
silken 25.43
silkscreen 25.11
silkworm 24.22
silky 4.19
sill 23.8
Sillitoe 9.24
Sills 35.29
silly 4.24
silo 9.17
Siloam 24.17
silt 30.51
siltstone 25.31
silty 4.53
Silurian 25.37
Silvanus 28.29
silver 12.86
silverfish 29.7
silvern 25.51
silverside 16.16
silversmith 32.6
silversmithing 26.14
Silverstone 25.31
silverware 2.15
silverweed 16.7
silvery 4.43
silviculture 12.24
silviculturist 31.12
Sim 24.6
simcha 12.23
Simenon 25.26
Simeon 25.37
simian 25.37
similar 12.43
similarity 4.53
simile 4.24
similitude 16.25
Simla 12.43
simmer 12.51
simoleon 25.37
Simon 25.45
Simone 25.30
Simonides 35.7
simon-pure 12.20
simony 4.34

simp 27.17
simpatico 9.16
simper 12.62
simple 23.35
simple-minded 16.9
simpleton 25.50
simplex 28.38
simplify 6.7
Simplon 25.25
Simpson 25.48
Sims 35.30
simulacra 12.65
simulacrum 24.19
simulate 30.11
simulcast 31.2
simultaneity 4.53
simultaneous 28.23
sin 25.13
Sinai 6.3
Sinatra 12.64
Sinbad 16.1
sin bin 25.13
since 28.44
sincere 12.4
sincerity 4.53
Sinclair 2.8
Sind 16.42
Sindebele 4.23
Sindhi 4.12
Sindy 4.12
sine 25.21
Sinéad 16.6
sinecure 12.20
sinecurist 31.12
sine qua non 25.24
sinew 11.22
sinewy 4.8
sinfonia 12.8
sinfonietta 12.76
sinful 23.21
sing 26.3
singalong 26.15
Singapore 7.1
Singaporean 25.37
singe 20.19
singer 12.60
Singh 26.3
single 23.30
single-minded 16.9
singlet 30.22
singleton 25.50
singsong 26.15
singular 12.46
singularity 4.53
singularize 35.13
Sinhala 12.43
Sinhalese 35.6
sinister 12.78
sinistral 23.36
sink 21.33

sinkage 20.6
sinker 12.39
sinkhole 23.17
sinking 26.7
sinless 28.8
sinner 12.55
sinnet 30.23
Sinn Fein 25.7
Sinn Feiner 12.54
Sintra 12.65
sinuosity 4.53
sinuous 28.24
sinus 28.29
sinusitis 28.12
Siouan 25.38
Sioux 11.1
sip 27.6
sipe 27.7
siphon 25.41
siphonic 21.13
sipper 12.62
sippet 30.23
sir 13.1
sirdar 1.6
sire 12.13
siren 25.47
Sirius 28.23
sirloin 25.32
sirocco 9.16
sirrah 12.65
sirree 4.1
sirup 27.14
sirupy 4.37
sis 28.7
sisal 23.37
siskin 25.15
Sisley 4.24
sissified 16.14
sissy 4.46
sissyish 29.6
sister 12.78
sisterhood 16.26
sister-in-law 7.11
sisterly 4.27
Sistine 25.12
sistra 12.65
sistrum 24.19
Sisyphean 25.36
Sisyphus 28.25
sit 30.20
Sita 12.77
sitar 1.19
sitarist 31.12
sitcom 24.8
sit-down 25.29
site 30.26
sit-in 25.19
Sitka 12.39
Sittang 26.1
sitter 12.78

sitting 26.13
situate 30.8, 30.41
situationist 31.10
sit-up 27.13
Sitwell 23.4
Sitzkrieg 18.5
Sivaite 30.26
Sivan 25.51
Siwash 29.11
six 28.39
sixain 25.8
sixer 12.70
sixfold 16.37
sixgun 25.35
sixpence 28.45
sixpenny 4.34
six-shooter 12.81
sixteen 25.9
sixteenth 32.19
sixth 32.22
sixth-former 12.52
sixtieth 32.6
sixty 4.53
sizable 23.26
size 35.11
sizer 12.91
Sizewell 23.4
sizzle 23.41
sizzler 12.48
sjambok 21.20
ska 1.1
Skagerrak 21.3
Skanda 12.25
skarn 25.4
skat 30.1
skate 30.7
skateboard 16.20
skateboarder 12.28
skatepark 21.5
skater 12.77
skean 25.36
skean dhu 11.1
sked 16.3
skedaddle 23.28
skeet 30.18
skeeter 12.77
skeg 18.3
skein 25.7
skeletal 23.39
skeleton 25.50
Skelton 25.50
skep 27.3
skeptic 21.17
skeptical 23.32
skerrick 21.15
sketch 15.3
sketchbook 21.28
sketcher 12.23
sketch pad 16.1
sketchy 4.11

skew 11.1
skewbald 16.36
skewer 12.19
skew-whiff 17.6
ski 4.1
skiable 23.26
skibob 14.9
skid 16.8
skidlid 16.10
skidoo 11.1
skidpan 25.3
skier 12.3
skiff 17.6
skiffle 23.29
ski-jump 27.17
skilift 30.47
skill 23.8
skillet 30.22
skilly 4.24
skim 24.6
skimmer 12.51
skimp 27.17
skimpy 4.36
skin 25.13
skincare 2.7
skin-deep 27.5
skinflick 21.11
skinflint 30.54
skinhead 16.3
skink 21.33
skinner 12.55
skinny 4.32
skinny-dip 27.6
skint 30.54
skintight 30.26
skip 27.6
skipjack 21.3
ski-plane 25.8
skipper 12.62
skippet 30.23
skipping-rope 27.10
skirl 23.42
skirmish 29.8
skirmisher 12.72
skirr 13.1
skirret 30.24
skirt 30.45
skirting 26.13
skit 30.20
skite 30.26
skitter 12.78
skittery 4.43
skittish 29.10
skittle 23.39
skive 34.9
skiver 12.86
Skivvies 35.10
skivvy 4.58
skoal 23.17
skol 23.13

skua 12.19
skulduggery 4.43
skulk 21.32
skulker 12.41
skull 23.22
skullcap 27.1
skunk 21.34
sky 6.1
skydive 34.9
skydiver 12.86
skydiving 26.14
Skye 6.1
skyer 12.13
skyey 4.4
sky-high 6.1
skyhook 21.28
skyjack 21.3
skyjacker 12.37
Skylab 14.1
skylark 21.5
skyless 28.8
skylight 30.28
skyline 25.22
skyrocket 30.21
skysail 23.6
skyscape 27.4
skyscraper 12.61
skywalk 21.22
skyward 16.30
skywatch 15.7
skyway 3.25
skywriting 26.13
slab 14.1
slack 21.1
slacken 25.43
slacker 12.37
slag 18.1
slaggy 4.15
slagheap 27.5
slain 25.7
slàinte 12.35
slake 21.7
slalom 24.18
slam 24.1
slambang 26.1
slammer 12.50
slander 12.25
slanderer 12.67
slanderous 28.31
slang 26.1
slangy 4.35
slant 30.53
slantwise 35.15
slap 27.1
slapdash 29.1
slap-happy 4.36
slapshot 30.32
slapstick 21.17
slap-up 27.13
slash 29.1

S

slasher 12.72
slat 30.1
slate 30.7
slater 12.77
slather 12.84
slating 26.13
slattern 25.50
slatternly 4.21
slaty 4.52
slaughter 12.80
slaughterer 12.67
slaughterhouse 28.16
slaughterous 28.31
Slav 34.2
slave 34.4
slave-driver 12.86
slaver 12.85
slavery 4.43
slavey 4.58
Slavic 21.18
slavish 29.10
Slavonic 21.13
slay 3.1
slayer 12.2
slaying 26.3
sleaze 35.6
sleazy 4.61
sled 16.3
sledge 20.3
sledgehammer 12.50
sleek 21.8
sleeky 4.18
sleep 27.5
sleeper 12.61
sleepover 12.86
sleepwalk 21.22
sleepwalker 12.40
sleepwalking 26.7
sleepy 4.36
sleepyhead 16.3
sleet 30.18
sleety 4.52
sleeve 34.5
sleigh 3.1
sleight 30.26
slender 12.26
slenderize 35.13
slept 30.58
sleuth 32.12
slew 11.1
sley 3.1
slice 28.13
slicer 12.70
slick 21.9
slicker 12.39
slid 16.8
slide 16.14
slider 12.27

slight 30.26
slightish 29.10
Sligo 9.13
slim 24.6
slime 24.7
slimline 25.22
slimmer 12.51
slimy 4.29
sling 26.3
slingback 21.2
slinger 12.60
slingshot 30.32
slink 21.33
slinky 4.19
slip 27.6
slipcase 28.5
slipcover 12.87
slip knot 30.32
slipover 12.86
slippage 20.7
slipper 12.62
slippery 4.43
slippy 4.36
slipshod 16.18
slipstream 24.5
slipway 3.25
slit 30.20
slither 12.84
slithery 4.43
slitter 12.78
slitty 4.53
sliver 12.86
slivovitz 28.47
Sloane 25.30
Sloaney 4.33
slob 14.9
slobber 12.21
slobbery 4.43
slobbish 29.6
sloe 9.1
sloe-eyed 16.14
slog 18.8
slogan 25.41
slogger 12.32
slo-mo 9.18
sloop 27.11
sloosh 29.14
sloot 30.37
slop 27.8
slope 27.10
sloppy 4.36
slosh 29.11
sloshy 4.50
slot 30.31
sloth 32.11
slouch 15.9
slouchy 4.11
slough 17.15
Slough 8.1
Slovak 21.4

Slovakia 12.6
sloven 25.51
Slovene 25.12
Slovenia 12.8
Slovenian 25.37
slovenly 4.26
slow 9.1
slowcoach 15.10
slowdown 25.29
slowish 29.6
slowpoke 21.24
slow-worm 24.22
slub 14.13
sludge 20.16
sludgy 4.17
slug 18.12
sluggard 16.28
sluggardly 4.27
slugger 12.32
sluggish 29.7
sluice 28.19
sluicegate 30.9
sluiceway 3.25
slum 24.14
slumber 12.22
slumberer 12.67
slumberous 28.31
slumgullion 25.52
slumlord 16.21
slummock 21.30
slummy 4.30
slump 27.17
slung 26.18
slunk 21.34
slur 13.1
slurp 27.15
slurry 4.42
slush 29.16
slushy 4.50
slut 30.40
sluttish 29.10
sly 6.1
slyboots 28.47
slyly 4.25
slyness 28.9
slype 27.7
smack 21.1
smacker 12.37
small 23.14
smallholder 12.28
smallholding 26.5
smallish 29.8
small-minded 16.9
smallpox 28.40
small talk 21.22
smalt 30.51
smarm 24.2
smarmy 4.29
smart 30.3
smart-alecky 4.19

smart-arse 28.2
smarten 25.50
smartish 29.10
smarty-pants 28.47
smash 29.1
smash-and-grab 14.1
smasher 12.72
smatter 12.74
smattering 26.11
smear 12.4
smearer 12.67
smeary 4.43
smell 23.3
smeller 12.42
smelly 4.22
smelt 30.51
Smersh 29.18
Smetana 12.58
smew 11.1
smidgen 25.14
smile 23.11
smiler 12.44
Smiles 35.29
smiley 4.25
Smily 4.25
smirch 15.14
smirk 21.31
smirker 12.41
smirky 4.20
smite 30.26
smiter 12.79
smith 32.6
smithereens 35.31
Smithers 35.24
Smithfield 16.35
smithy 4.57
smitten 25.50
smock 21.20
smog 18.8
smoggy 4.15
smoke 21.24
smokehouse 28.16
smoker 12.40
smokescreen 25.11
smokestack 21.4
smoky 4.20
smolder 12.28
Smolensk 21.35
Smollett 30.22
smolt 30.51
smooch 15.11
smoocher 12.24
smoochy 4.11
smoodge 20.15
smooth 33.8
smoother 12.84
smooth-faced 31.4
smoothie 4.57
smoothish 29.10

S

smooth-talk 21.22
smooth-tongued 16.47
smorgasbord 16.20
smote 30.35
smother 12.84
smoulder 12.28
smriti 4.53
smudge 20.16
smudgy 4.17
smug 18.12
smuggle 23.30
smuggler 12.48
smut 30.40
Smuts 28.47
smutty 4.55
Smyrna 12.59
snack 21.1
snaffle 23.29
snafu 11.1
snag 18.1
snaggle-toothed 30.60
snaggy 4.15
snail 23.5
snake 21.7
snakebite 30.26
snake-charmer 12.50
snakeroot 30.37
snakeskin 25.15
snaky 4.18
snap 27.1
snapdragon 25.41
snapper 12.61
snappish 29.9
snappy 4.36
snapshot 30.32
snare 2.1
snarer 12.65
snark 21.5
snarl 23.2
snarler 12.42
snarl-up 27.13
snarly 4.21
snatch 15.1
snatcher 12.23
snatchy 4.11
snazzy 4.61
sneak 21.8
sneaker 12.38
sneaky 4.18
sneck 21.6
sneer 12.4
sneerer 12.67
sneeze 35.6
Snell 23.3
snib 14.7
snick 21.9
snicker 12.39
Snickers 35.24

snicket 30.21
snide 16.14
sniff 17.6
sniffer 12.30
sniffle 23.29
sniffler 12.43
sniffly 4.24
sniffy 4.14
snifter 12.78
snig 18.6
snigger 12.31
sniggerer 12.67
sniggle 23.30
snip 27.6
snipe 27.7
sniper 12.62
snippet 30.23
snippety 4.53
snipping 26.10
snippy 4.36
snit 30.20
snitch 15.6
snivel 23.40
sniveler 12.48
sniveller 12.48
snob 14.9
snobbery 4.43
snobbish 29.6
snobby 4.10
Sno-Cat 30.1
snog 18.8
snood 16.25
snook 21.27
snooker 12.41
snoop 27.11
snooper 12.63
snoopy 4.37
snoot 30.37
snooty 4.54
snooze 35.21
snoozer 12.92
snoozy 4.62
snore 7.1
snorer 12.66
snorkel 23.32
snorkeler 12.48
snorkeller 12.48
snort 30.33
snorter 12.80
snot 30.31
snotty 4.54
snout 30.34
snouty 4.54
snow 9.1
snowball 23.14
snowberry 4.43
snowblind 16.42
snowblower 12.17
snowboard 16.20
snowboarder 12.28

snowboarding 26.5
snow boot 30.37
snowbound 16.43
snowcap 27.1
snow-capped 30.58
snow cone 25.30
Snowdon 25.40
Snowdonia 12.8
snowdrift 30.47
snowdrop 27.8
snowfall 23.15
snowfield 16.35
snowflake 21.7
snowline 25.22
snowman 25.2
snowmen 25.5
snowmobile 23.7
snowplough 8.7
snowplow 8.7
snowscape 27.4
snowshoe 11.19
snowshoer 12.19
snowstorm 24.9
Snow-white 30.26
snowy 4.7
snub 14.13
snubber 12.22
snuff 17.15
snuffbox 28.40
snuffer 12.30
snuffle 23.29
snuffler 12.48
snuffly 4.27
snuffy 4.14
snug 18.12
snuggery 4.43
snuggle 23.30
so 9.1
soak 21.24
soakage 20.6
soaker 12.40
soaking 26.7
so-and-so 9.22
Soane 25.30
soap 27.10
soapbox 28.40
soapstone 25.31
soapsuds 35.27
soapy 4.36
soar 7.1
soarer 12.66
sob 14.9
sober 12.21
Sobers 35.24
sobriety 4.53
sobriquet 3.14
soca 12.40
so-called 16.36
soccer 12.40
social 23.38

socialist 31.8
socialite 30.28
societal 23.39
society 4.55
sociology 4.17
sociometric 21.15
sociometrist 31.12
sociometry 4.40
sociopath 32.1
socio-political 23.32
sock 21.20
socket 30.21
sockeye 6.10
socko 9.16
Socotra 12.66
Socrates 35.9
Socratic 21.17
sod 16.18
soda 12.28
sodden 25.40
Soddy 4.13
sodium 24.16
Sodom 24.17
sodomite 30.29
sodomize 35.13
sodomy 4.30
Sodor 7.5
sofa 12.30
sofa bed 16.3
Sofar 1.7
soffit 30.21
Sofia 12.5
soft 30.47
softback 21.2
softball 23.14
softcore 7.1
soften 25.41
softener 12.56
softie 4.54
softish 29.10
softly softly 4.25
software 2.15
softwood 16.26
soggy 4.15
soh 9.1
Soho 9.14
soi-disant 25.27
soigné 3.26
soignée 3.26
soil 23.19
soilpipe 27.7
soirée 3.19
soixante-neuf 17.17
sojourn 25.42
sojourner 12.58
soke 21.24
sol 23.13
sola 12.44
solace 28.8
solar 12.44

S

solaria 12.10
solarium 24.16
solarize 35.13
solatia 12.11
solatium 24.16
sold 16.37
solder 12.28
soldier 12.35
soldierly 4.27
soldiery 4.43
sole 23.17
Soledad 16.1
solemn 24.18
solemnity 4.53
solenoid 16.24
Solent 30.56
sol-fa 1.1
solfeggi 4.17
soli 4.25
solicit 30.24
solicitor 12.78
solicitous 28.34
solicitude 16.25
solid 16.10
solidarity 4.53
solidi 6.6
solidifier 12.14
solidify 6.7
solidity 4.53
solidus 28.25
Solihull 23.22
soliloquist 31.15
soliloquize 35.15
soliloquy 4.59
solipsist 31.13
solitaire 2.1
solitary 4.43
solitude 16.25
solmizate 30.17
solo 9.17
soloist 31.6
Solomon 25.45
Solon 25.25
solstice 28.12
solstitial 23.38
Solti 4.54
soluble 23.26
solus 28.27
solution 25.49
solve 34.15
solvency 4.48
solvent 30.56
solver 12.86
Solzhenitsyn 25.19
soma 12.52
Somali 4.21
Somalia 12.6
Somalian 25.37
somatic 21.17
somber 12.21

sombre 12.21
sombrero 9.21
some 24.14
somebody 4.13
someday 3.9
somehow 8.5
someone 25.35
someplace 28.5
somersault 30.51
Somerset 30.5
something 26.14
sometime 24.7
sometimes 35.30
someway 3.25
somewhat 30.32
somewhen 25.5
somewhere 2.15
Somme 24.8
sommelier 12.6
somnambulant 30.56
somnambulist 31.8
somniferous 28.31
somnolence 28.45
somnolent 30.56
Somoza 12.92
son 25.35
sonar 1.14
sonata 12.75
sonatina 12.54
Sondheim 24.7
sone 25.30
son et lumière 2.2
song 26.15
songbird 16.31
songbook 21.28
songsmith 32.6
songster 12.79
song thrush 29.16
songwriter 12.79
songwriting 26.13
Sonia 12.8
sonic 21.13
son-in-law 7.11
sonnet 30.23
sonneteer 12.4
sonny 4.33
sonogram 24.1
Sonora 12.66
sonority 4.53
sonorous 28.31
sonsy 4.46
Sontag 18.1
sool 23.20
soon 25.33
soonish 29.9
soot 30.39
sooth 32.12
soothe 33.8
soother 12.84
soothsayer 12.2

sooty 4.55
sop 27.8
Sophia 12.13
Sophie 4.14
sophist 31.7
sophisticate 30.10
sophistry 4.40
Sophocles 35.7
sophomore 7.12
sophomoric 21.15
soporific 21.10
sopping 26.10
soppy 4.36
soprano 9.19
Sopwith 32.6
sora 12.66
sorb 14.10
sorbet 3.7
Sorbian 25.37
sorbitol 23.13
Sorbonne 25.24
sorcerer 12.67
sorcerous 28.31
sorcery 4.43
sordid 16.9
sordor 12.28
sore 7.1
sorehead 16.3
sorel 23.36
sorghum 24.18
sori 6.15
sorority 4.53
sorption 25.49
sorrel 23.36
Sorrento 9.24
sorrow 9.21
sorry 4.41
sort 30.33
sorter 12.80
sortie 4.54
sortilege 20.6
sorus 28.31
so-so 9.22
sostenuto 9.25
sot 30.31
Sothic 21.18
Sotho 11.20
sottish 29.10
sotto voce 4.11
sou 11.1
soubrette 30.4
souchong 26.15
soufflé 3.15
Soufrière 2.1
sough 8.1
sought 30.33
sought-after 12.75
souk 21.27
soukous 28.26
soul 23.17

soulmate 30.12
soulster 12.80
sound 16.43
soundalike 21.19
soundbite 30.26
soundboard 16.20
soundbox 28.40
soundcheck 21.6
sounder 12.28
soundhole 23.17
sounding 26.5
soundproof 17.13
soundtrack 21.3
soup 27.11
soupçon 25.26
soupspoon 25.33
soupy 4.37
sour 12.16
source 28.15
sourcebook 21.28
sourdough 9.11
sourish 29.9
sourpuss 28.20
Sousa 12.92
sousaphone 25.30
sousaphonist 31.10
souse 28.16
souslik 21.11
Sousse 28.19
soutache 29.1
soutane 25.4
souteneur 13.1
souter 12.81
south 32.10
Southampton 25.50
southbound 16.43
South Carolina 12.55
Southdown 25.29
southeast 31.5
southeastern 25.50
southeastward 16.30
southerly 4.27
southern 25.51
southerner 12.58
southernmost 31.20
Southey 4.57
southing 26.14
southpaw 7.14
southward 16.30
southwest 31.3
southwestern 25.50
southwestward 16.30
souvenir 12.4
souvlaki 4.18
souvlakia 12.6
sou'wester 12.76
sovereign 25.18
sovereignty 4.53

soviet 30.41
sow 8.1, 9.1
sowbread 16.4
sower 12.17
Sowetan 25.50
Soweto 9.24
sowing 26.3
sown 25.30
soy 10.1
soya 12.18
soybean 25.9
Soyinka 12.39
Soyuz 35.22
sozzled 16.38
spa 1.1
space 28.5
space-age 20.4
spacecraft 30.47
spaceman 25.2
spacer 12.69
spacesuit 30.38
space walk 21.22
spacey 4.45
spacing 26.12
spacious 28.33
spade 16.6
spadework 21.31
spadille 23.8
spae 3.1
spaewife 17.7
spaewives 35.35
spaghetti 4.51
spaghettini 4.31
spahi 4.16
Spain 25.7
spalpeen 25.11
Spam 24.1
span 25.1
spanakopita 12.78
spandrel 23.36
spang 26.1
spangle 23.30
Spanglish 29.8
spangly 4.27
Spaniard 16.30
spaniel 23.40
Spanish 29.9
spank 21.33
spanker 12.37
spanking 26.7
spanner 12.53
spar 1.1
spare 2.1
sparer 12.65
sparerib 14.7
sparge 20.2
sparing 26.11
spark 21.5
sparkish 29.8
sparkle 23.32

sparkler 12.42
sparkly 4.21
Sparks 28.38
sparky 4.18
sparling 26.8
sparrow 9.21
sparrowhawk 21.22
sparry 4.38
sparse 28.2
sparsity 4.53
Sparta 12.75
Spartacus 28.26
spartan 25.50
spasm 24.21
spasmodic 21.10
spastic 21.17
spat 30.1
spatchcock 21.20
spate 30.7
spathe 33.2
spatial 23.38
spatialize 35.12
spatio-temporal
    23.36
Spätlesen 25.52
spatter 12.74
spatterdash 29.1
spatula 12.46
spatulate 30.42
spavin 25.19
spawn 25.28
spawning 26.9
spay 3.1
speak 21.8
speakeasy 4.61
speaker 12.38
speakerphone 25.30
spear 12.4
spearfish 29.7
speargun 25.35
spearhead 16.3
spearmint 30.54
Spears 35.24
spec 21.6
special 23.38
specialist 31.8
specialty 4.51
species 35.10
specific 21.10
specifier 12.14
specify 6.7
specimen 25.17
specious 28.33
speck 21.6
speckle 23.32
specs 28.38
spectacle 23.32
spectacular 12.46
spectate 30.7
specter 12.76

Spector 12.76
spectra 12.64
spectral 23.36
spectre 12.76
spectrograph 17.2
spectrum 24.19
specular 12.46
speculate 30.11
speculum 24.18
sped 16.3
speech 15.5
speechifier 12.14
speechify 6.7
speed 16.7
speedball 23.14
speedboat 30.35
speeder 12.26
speedo 9.11
speedometer 12.78
speedster 12.77
speedway 3.25
speedwell 23.4
speedy 4.12
speiss 28.13
Speke 21.8
spell 23.3
spellbind 16.42
spellbinder 12.27
spellbound 16.43
speller 12.42
spelling 26.8
spelt 30.51
spelunker 12.41
spelunking 26.7
spence 28.44
spend 16.41
spender 12.26
spendthrift 30.47
Spenser 12.69
Spenserian 25.37
spent 30.53
sperm 24.22
spermatozoa 12.17
spermatozoid 16.8
spermatozoon 25.38
spermicide 16.16
spew 11.1
spewer 12.19
Spey 3.1
sphenoid 16.24
spheral 23.36
sphere 12.4
spheric 21.15
spherical 23.32
spheroid 16.24
sphincter 12.78
sphinx 28.41
spic 21.9
spice 28.13
spicebush 29.15

spick-and-span 25.1
spicy 4.46
spider 12.27
spiderish 29.9
spidery 4.43
spiel 23.7
Spielberg 18.13
spieler 12.43
spiffing 26.6
spifflicate 30.10
spiffy 4.14
spignel 23.34
spigot 30.42
spike 21.19
spiky 4.19
spile 23.11
spill 23.8
spillage 20.6
Spillane 25.7
spiller 12.43
spillikin 25.15
spillover 12.86
spilt 30.51
spin 25.13
spina bifida 12.27
spinach 20.7
spinal 23.34
spindle 23.28
spindleshanks 28.41
spindly 4.24
spindrift 30.47
spin-dry 6.1
spine 25.21
spinel 23.3
spinet 30.4
spinifex 28.38
spinnaker 12.41
spinner 12.55
spinneret 30.4
spinney 4.32
spin-off 17.8
spin-out 30.34
Spinoza 12.92
spinster 12.78
spinsterhood 16.26
spinsterish 29.9
spiny 4.32
spiraea 12.3
spiral 23.36
spire 12.13
spirea 12.3
spirit 30.24
spiritist 31.14
spiritous 28.34
spiritual 23.25
spiritualist 31.8
spiritualize 35.12
spirituous 28.24
spirogyra 12.65
spirt 30.45

spiry 4.43
spit 30.20
spit-and-polish 29.8
spitball 23.14
spite 30.26
spitfire 12.14
Spithead 16.3
Spitsbergen 25.41
spitter 12.78
spittle 23.39
spittoon 25.33
spitty 4.53
spitz 28.47
spiv 34.6
spivvish 29.10
spivvy 4.58
splake 21.7
splash 29.1
splashback 21.2
splashy 4.50
splat 30.1
splatter 12.74
splay 3.1
splay-feet 30.18
splay-foot 30.39
splay-footed 16.12
spleen 25.9
splendent 30.56
splendid 16.9
splendiferous 28.31
splendor 12.26
splendour 12.26
splenetic 21.17
splice 28.13
splicer 12.70
spliff 17.6
spline 25.21
splint 30.54
splint bone 25.30
splinter 12.78
splintery 4.43
split 30.20
split-level 23.40
split-second 16.45
splitter 12.78
splodge 20.11
splodgy 4.17
splosh 29.11
splotch 15.7
splotchy 4.11
splurge 20.17
splutter 12.81
splutterer 12.67
Spock 21.20
Spode 16.23
spoil 23.19
spoilage 20.6
spoiler 12.44
spoilsport 30.33
spoilt 30.51

Spokane 25.1
spoke 21.24
spoken 25.43
spokesman 25.45
spokesmen 25.45
spokesperson 25.48
spokeswoman 25.45
spokeswomen 25.17
spondaic 21.9
spondee 4.13
spondulicks 28.39
sponge 20.19
sponge-like 21.19
sponger 12.36
spongiform 24.9
spongy 4.17
sponson 25.48
sponsor 12.70
spontaneity 4.53
spontaneous 28.23
spoof 17.13
spoofer 12.30
spoofery 4.43
spook 21.27
spooky 4.20
spool 23.20
spoon 25.33
spoonbill 23.8
spooner 12.56
spoonfed 16.3
spoonfeed 16.7
spoony 4.33
spoor 12.20
Sporades 35.7
sporadic 21.10
sporangia 12.6
spore 7.1
sporran 25.47
sport 30.33
sporter 12.80
sportif 17.5
sportscast 31.2
sportscaster 12.75
sportsman 25.45
sportsmanlike 21.19
sportsmen 25.45
sportspeople 23.35
sportsperson 25.48
sportswear 2.15
sportswoman 25.45
sportswomen 25.17
sporty 4.54
spot 30.31
spot-check 21.6
spotlamp 27.17
spotlight 30.28
spot-on 25.24
spotter 12.79
spotty 4.54
spot-weld 16.35

spot-welder 12.26
spousal 23.41
spouse 28.16
spout 30.34
spouter 12.80
sprag 18.1
sprain 25.7
sprang 26.1
sprat 30.1
sprawl 23.14
spray 3.1
spray-dry 6.15
sprayer 12.2
spray-paint 30.54
spread 16.3
spread eagle 23.30
spreader 12.26
spreadsheet 30.19
spree 4.1
sprig 18.6
spriggy 4.15
sprightly 4.25
spring 26.3
springboard 16.20
springbok 21.20
spring-clean 25.9,
  25.10
spring-cleaning 26.9
springe 20.19
springer 12.60
Springfield 16.35
springlet 30.22
springlike 21.19
spring-loaded 16.9
Springs 35.32
Springsteen 25.12
springtail 23.6
springtide 16.17
springtime 24.7
springy 4.35
sprinkle 23.32
sprinkler 12.43
sprinkling 26.8
sprint 30.54
sprinter 12.78
sprit 30.20
sprite 30.26
spritsail 23.37
spritz 28.47
spritzer 12.70
sprocket 30.21
sprog 18.8
sprout 30.34
spruce 28.19
sprucer 12.71
sprue 11.1
spruik 21.27
spruit 30.7
sprung 26.18
spry 6.1

spud 16.27
spumante 4.51
spume 24.12
spumous 28.28
spumy 4.30
spun 25.35
spunk 21.34
spunky 4.20
spur 13.1
spurge 20.17
spurious 28.23
spurn 25.53
spurner 12.59
spurrier 12.10
spurt 30.45
sputnik 21.13
sputter 12.81
sputum 24.20
spy 6.1
spyglass 28.2
spyhole 23.17
spymaster 12.75
squab 14.9
squabble 23.26
squabbler 12.48
squad 16.18
squaddie 4.13
squadron 25.47
squalid 16.10
squall 23.14
squally 4.25
squalor 12.44
squander 12.28
squanderer 12.67
square 2.1
square-bashing
  26.12
square dance 28.44
square-eyed 16.14
squarer 12.65
square-rigged 16.33
squarish 29.9
squash 29.11
squashy 4.50
squat 30.31
squatter 12.79
squaw 7.1
squawk 21.22
squawker 12.40
squeak 21.8
squeaker 12.38
squeaky 4.18
squeal 23.7
squealer 12.43
squeamish 29.8
squeegee 4.17
squeeze 35.6
squeezebox 28.40
squeezer 12.90
squelch 15.15
squelchy 4.11

squib 14.7
squid 16.8
squidgy 4.17
squiffed 30.47
squiffy 4.14
squiggle 23.30
squiggly 4.27
squill 23.8
squillion 25.52
squinch 29.20
squint 30.54
squire 12.13
squirearch 21.5
squireen 25.9
squirl 23.42
squirm 24.22
squirmer 12.52
squirmy 4.30
squirrel 23.36
squirrelly 4.27
squirt 30.45
squish 29.6
squishy 4.50
squit 30.20
squitters 35.24
squiz 35.10
Sri Lanka 12.37
Sri Lankan 25.43
Srinagar 12.32
stab 14.1
stabber 12.21
stabbing 26.4
stabile 23.11
stability 4.53
stable 23.26
stablemate 30.12
stablish 29.8
staccato 9.24
Stacey 4.45
stack 21.1
stacker 12.37
staddle 23.28
stadia 12.5
stadium 24.16
staff 17.2
Staffa 12.30
staffage 20.6
staffer 12.30
Stafford 16.28
Staffordshire 12.11
staffroom 24.12
stag 18.1
stage 20.4
stagecoach 15.10
stagecraft 30.47
stagehand 16.40
stage-manage 20.7
stager 12.35
stagestruck 21.29
stagger 12.31

staggerer 12.67
staging 26.6
stagnancy 4.48
stagnant 30.56
stagnate 30.7
stagy 4.17
staid 16.6
stain 25.7
stained-glass 28.2
stair 2.1
staircase 28.5
stairhead 16.3
stairlift 30.47
stairway 3.25
stairwell 23.4
stake 21.7
stakeholder 12.28
stakeout 30.34
staker 12.38
stalactite 30.30
Stalag 18.1
stalagmite 30.29
St Albans 35.31
stale 23.5
stalemate 30.12
Stalin 25.16
Stalingrad 16.1
Stalinist 31.10
stalk 21.22
stalker 12.40
stall 23.14
stallage 20.6
stallholder 12.28
stallion 25.52
stalwart 30.44
Stamboul 23.20
stamen 25.45
stamina 12.55
stammer 12.50
stammerer 12.67
stamp 27.17
stampede 16.7
stampeder 12.26
stamper 12.61
stance 28.44
stanchion 25.49
stand 16.40
standard 16.28
standardizer 12.91
standby 6.5
standee 4.1
stander 12.25
stand-in 25.14
standing 26.5
Standish 29.6
stand-off 17.8
standoffish 29.7
standout 30.34
standpipe 27.7
standpoint 30.55

standstill 23.9
stand-to 11.20
Stanford 16.28
Stanhope 27.14
Stanislas 28.1
Stanislavsky 4.18
stank 21.33
Stanley 4.21
Stanleyville 23.10
Stansted 16.4
stanza 12.90
stanzaic 21.9
staple 23.35
stapler 12.48
star 1.1
starboard 16.28
starburst 31.26
starch 15.2
starcher 12.23
starchy 4.11
star-crossed 31.17
stardom 24.17
stardust 31.24
stare 2.1
starer 12.65
starfish 29.7
stargaze 35.5
stargazer 12.90
stargazing 26.14
stark 21.5
starkers 35.24
starlet 30.22
starlight 30.28
starlike 21.19
starling 26.8
starlit 30.22
Starr 1.1
starry 4.38
starry-eyed 16.14
Stars and Bars 35.2
Stars and Stripes
   28.46
start 30.3
starter 12.75
startle 23.39
startler 12.48
start-up 27.13
starve 34.2
starveling 26.8
stash 29.1
Stasi 4.61
stasis 28.11
stat 30.1
state 30.7
statecraft 30.47
statehood 16.26
statehouse 28.16
statelet 30.22
stately 4.22
stater 12.77

stateroom 24.12
stateside 16.16
statesman 25.45
statesmanlike 21.19
statesmen 25.45
stateswoman 25.45
stateswomen 25.17
statewide 16.14
static 21.17
statice 4.46
station 25.49
stationary 4.43
stationer 12.58
stationery 4.43
station-keeping
   26.10
statist 31.14
statistician 25.49
Statius 28.23
stative 34.8
stats 28.47
statuary 4.43
statue 11.5
statuesque 21.35
statuette 30.4
stature 12.23
status 28.34
status quo 9.1
statute 30.37
statutory 4.43
staunch 29.20
Stavanger 12.60
stave 34.4
stavesacre 12.38
stay 3.1
stayer 12.2
staysail 23.37
stead 16.3
steadfast 31.2
steadier 12.5
steading 26.5
steady 4.12
steak 21.7
steakhouse 28.16
steal 23.7
stealer 12.43
stealth 32.17
stealthy 4.56
steam 24.5
steamboat 30.35
steamer 12.51
steaming 26.9
steamroller 12.44
steamy 4.29
stearin 25.18
Stedman 25.45
steed 16.7
steel 23.7
Steele 23.7
steelworks 28.41
steely 4.23

S

steelyard 16.30
Steen 25.9
steenbok 21.20
steep 27.5
steepen 25.46
steepish 29.9
steeple 23.35
steeplechase 28.5
steeplechaser 12.69
steeplechasing 26.12
steeplejack 21.3
steer 12.4
steerage 20.8
steerageway 3.25
steerer 12.67
steersman 25.45
steersmen 25.45
steeve 34.5
stegosaur 7.16
stegosaurus 28.31
stein 25.21
Steinbeck 21.6
Steiner 12.55
Steinway 3.25
Stella 12.42
stellar 12.42
stem 24.3
stemma 12.50
stemple 23.35
stench 29.20
stencil 23.37
Stendhal 23.2
steno 9.19
stenographer 12.30
stenographic 21.10
stenography 4.14
stenotype 27.7
stent 30.53
stentor 7.18
stentorian 25.37
step 27.3
stepbrother 12.84
stepchild 16.36
stepchildren 25.47
stepdaughter 12.80
stepfamily 4.24
stepfather 12.84
Stephanie 4.34
stepladder 12.25
stepmother 12.84
step-parent 30.56
steppe 27.3
stepping stone 25.31
stepsister 12.78
stepson 25.35
stepwise 35.15
steradian 25.37
stere 12.4
stereo 9.4

stereobate 30.9
stereophonic 21.13
stereopticon 25.25
stereoscope 27.10
stereoscopy 4.37
stereotype 27.7
stereotypic 21.14
stereotypical 23.32
sterile 23.11
sterility 4.53
sterling 26.8
stern 25.53
Sterne 25.53
Sterno 9.19
sternpost 31.20
sternum 24.19
sternway 3.25
steroid 16.24
stertorous 28.31
stet 30.4
stethoscope 27.10
Stetson 25.48
Steve 34.5
stevedore 7.5
Steven 25.51
Stevenage 20.7
Stevens 35.31
Stevenson 25.48
stew 11.1
steward 16.28
stewardess 28.7
Stewart 30.41
stewpot 30.32
St Helens 35.31
St Helier 12.6
stichomythia 12.12
stick 21.9
stickball 23.14
sticker 12.39
stick-in-the-mud 16.27
stickleback 21.2
stickler 12.43
stickpin 25.18
stickum 24.18
stick-up 27.13
sticky 4.19
stickybeak 21.8
Stieglitz 35.33
stifado 9.11
stiff 17.6
stiffen 25.41
stiffener 12.58
stiffening 26.9
stiffish 29.7
stiffy 4.14
stifle 23.29
stifler 12.44
stigma 12.51
stigmata 12.82

stigmatic 21.17
stigmatist 31.14
stilb 14.16
stile 23.11
Stiles 35.29
stiletto 9.24
still 23.8
stillage 20.6
stillbirth 32.14
stillborn 25.28
still-life 17.7
Stillson 25.48
stilly 4.24
stilt 30.51
stilted 16.12
Stilton 25.50
stimulant 30.56
stimulate 30.11
stimuli 6.11
stimulus 28.27
sting 26.3
stinger 12.60
stingray 3.19
stingy 4.17, 4.35
stink 21.33
stink bomb 24.8
stinker 12.39
stinko 9.16
stinkpot 30.32
stinkweed 16.7
stinkwood 16.26
stinky 4.19
stint 30.54
stipend 16.41
stipendiary 4.43
stipple 23.35
stippler 12.48
stipulate 30.11
stir 13.1
stir-crazy 4.61
stir-fry 6.15
stirk 21.31
Stirling 26.8
stirrer 12.68
stirring 26.11
stirrup 27.14
stitch 15.6
stitcher 12.23
stitchery 4.43
St John's 35.31
St Kilda 12.27
St Kitts 28.47
St Leger 12.35
stoat 30.35
stob 14.9
stock 21.20
stockade 16.6
stockbreeder 12.26
stockbreeding 26.5
stockbroker 12.40

stockcar 1.11
stocker 12.40
Stockhausen 25.52
stockholder 12.28
Stockholm 24.11
stockinet 30.4
stocking 26.7
stock-in-trade 16.6
stockist 31.7
stockman 25.45
stockmen 25.45
stockpile 23.11
stockpiler 12.44
Stockport 30.33
stockpot 30.32
stockroom 24.12
Stocks 28.40
stock-still 23.8
stocktake 21.7
stocktaking 26.7
Stockton-on-Tees 35.6
stocky 4.19
stockyard 16.2
stodge 20.11
stodgy 4.17
stoep 27.11
stogy 4.15
Stoic 21.9
stoical 23.32
stoke 21.24
stokehole 23.17
Stoke-on-Trent 30.53
Stoker 12.40
stokes 28.40
Stokowski 4.19
stole 23.17
stolen 25.44
stolid 16.10
stolidity 4.53
Stollen 25.44
stomach 21.30
stomacher 12.41
stomp 27.17
stomper 12.62
stone 25.30
stone-broke 21.24
stonecrop 27.8
stonefish 29.7
stoneground 16.43
Stonehenge 20.19
stonemason 25.48
stonemasonry 4.39
stoner 12.56
stonewall 23.14
stonewaller 12.44
stoneware 2.15
stonewashed 30.59
stonework 21.31

stoneworker 12.41
stonker 12.40
stonking 26.7
stony 4.33
stony-broke 21.24
stood 16.26
stooge 20.15
stook 21.27
stool 23.20
stoolball 23.14
stoolie 4.26
stool pigeon 25.14
stoop 27.11
stop 27.8
stopcock 21.20
Stopes 28.46
stopgap 27.1
stopover 12.86
stoppage 20.7
Stoppard 16.2
stopper 12.62
stopping 26.10
stopple 23.35
stopwatch 15.7
storage 20.8
storax 28.38
store 7.1
storefront 30.55
storehouse 28.16
storekeeper 12.61
storeman 25.45
storemen 25.45
storer 12.66
storeroom 24.12
storey 4.41
storiated 16.12
storied 16.11
stork 21.22
storksbill 23.8
storm 24.9
stormbound 16.43
stormdoor 7.5
stormer 12.52
stormproof 17.13
stormy 4.29
Stornoway 3.25
story 4.41
storyboard 16.20
storybook 21.28
storyline 25.22
storyteller 12.42
storytelling 26.8
stot 30.31
stotinka 12.39
stotinki 4.19
stoup 27.11
Stour 12.16, 12.17, 12.20
stout 30.34
stoutish 29.10
stove 34.11

stovepipe 27.7
stow 9.1
stowage 20.6
stowaway 3.25
Stowe 9.1
St Petersburg 18.13
Strabo 9.9
Strachey 4.11
Strad 16.1
straddle 23.28
straddler 12.48
Stradivari 4.38
Stradivarius 28.23
strafe 17.2
strafing 26.6
straggle 23.30
straggler 12.48
straggly 4.27
straight 30.7
straightaway 3.1, 3.25
straight edge 20.3
straighten 25.50
straightener 12.54
straightforward 16.30
straightish 29.10
straight-up 27.13
straightway 3.1
strain 25.7
strainer 12.54
strait 30.7
straiten 25.50
straitjacket 30.21
strait-laced 31.4
strake 21.7
strand 16.40
stranding 26.5
strange 20.19
stranger 12.35
strangle 23.30
stranglehold 16.37
strangler 12.42
strangling 26.8
strangulate 30.11
Stranraer 1.1
strap 27.1
strap-hang 26.1
straphanger 12.60
straphanging 26.10
strapline 25.22
strapper 12.61
strappy 4.36
Strasberg 18.13
Strasbourg 18.13
strata 12.75
stratagem 24.18
stratal 23.39
strategic 21.11
strategical 23.32

strategist 31.7
strategy 4.17
Stratford-upon-Avon 25.51
strath 32.1
Strathclyde 16.14
strathspey 3.1
stratify 6.7
stratocumulus 28.27
stratosphere 12.5
stratospheric 21.15
stratum 24.20
stratus 28.34
Strauss 28.16
Stravinsky 4.19
straw 7.1
strawberry 4.43
strawboard 16.20
straw boss 28.14
strawman 25.2
strawmen 25.5
strawy 4.5
stray 3.1
strayer 12.2
streak 21.8
streaker 12.38
streaky 4.18
stream 24.5
streamer 12.51
streamlet 30.22
streamline 25.22
Streep 27.5
street 30.18
streetcar 1.11
street light 30.28
streetwalker 12.40
streetwalking 26.7
streetwise 35.15
Streisand 16.40
strength 32.20
strengthen 25.51
strengthener 12.58
strenuous 28.24
strep 27.3
streptocarpus 28.30
stress 28.3
stretch 15.3
stretcher 12.23
stretchy 4.11
strew 11.1
strewer 12.19
strewth 32.12
striated 16.12
stricken 25.43
strickle 23.32
strict 30.49
stricture 12.23
stridden 25.40
stride 16.14
stridency 4.46

strident 30.56
strider 12.27
stridor 12.27
strife 17.7
strigil 23.9
strike 21.19
strikebreaker 12.38
strikebreaking 26.7
strikeout 30.34
striker 12.40
strimmer 12.51
Strindberg 18.13
Strine 25.21
string 26.3
stringboard 16.20
stringency 4.48
stringent 30.56
stringer 12.60
stringhalt 30.51
string like 21.19
stringy 4.35
stringy-bark 21.5
strip 27.6
stripe 27.7
stripling 26.8
stripper 12.62
striptease 35.9
stripteaser 12.90
stripy 4.36
strive 34.9
striver 12.86
strobe 14.11
strobilus 28.27
stroboscope 27.10
strode 16.23
Stroganoff 17.8
stroke 21.24
stroke play 3.15
stroll 23.17
stroller 12.44
Stromboli 4.27
strong 26.15
strongbox 28.40
stronghold 16.37
strongish 29.9
strongman 25.2
strongmen 25.5
strongpoint 30.55
strongroom 24.12
strongyle 23.9
strontium 24.16
strop 27.8
strophe 4.14
strophic 21.10
stroppy 4.36
Stroud 16.22
strove 34.11
strow 9.1
strown 25.30
struck 21.29

S

structuralist 31.8
structure 12.24
strudel 23.28
struggle 23.30
struggler 12.48
strum 24.14
strummer 12.52
strumous 28.28
strumpet 30.23
strung 26.18
strut 30.40
strutter 12.81
strychnine 25.11
stub 14.13
stubble 23.26
stubbly 4.27
stubborn 25.38
Stubbs 35.26
stubby 4.10
stucco 9.16
stuck 21.29
stuck-up 27.13
stud 16.27
student 30.56
studio 9.4
studious 28.23
study 4.13
stuff 17.15
stuffing 26.6
stuffy 4.14
Stuka 12.41
stultifier 12.14
stultify 6.7
stum 24.13, 24.14
stumble 23.26
stumblebum 24.14
stumbler 12.47
stumer 12.52
stump 27.17
stumper 12.63
stumpy 4.37
stun 25.35
stung 26.18
stunk 21.34
stunner 12.57
stunt 30.55
stuntman 25.2
stuntmen 25.5
stupa 12.63
stupe 27.11
stupefaction 25.49
stupefier 12.14
stupefy 6.7
stupendous 28.25
stupid 16.10
stupidity 4.53
stupor 12.63
stuporous 28.31
sturdy 4.13
sturgeon 25.42

Sturm und Drang
26.1
Sturt 30.45
stutter 12.81
stutterer 12.67
Stuttgart 30.3
sty 6.1
Stygian 25.37
style 23.11
styler 12.44
stylet 30.22
styli 6.11
stylish 29.8
stylist 31.8
stylite 30.28
Stylites 35.9
stylobate 30.9
stylograph 17.2
stylus 28.27
stymie 4.29
styptic 21.17
Styria 12.10
Styrofoam 24.11
Styx 28.39
suable 23.26
suasion 25.42
suave 34.2
suavity 4.53
sub 14.13
subacute 30.37
subaltern 25.50
subantarctic 21.17
sub-aqua 12.88
sub-aquatic 21.17
subaqueous 28.23
subarctic 21.17
subatomic 21.12
Subbuteo 9.4
subcategorize 35.13
subcategory 4.43
subclass 28.2
subcommittee 4.53
subconscious 28.33
subcontinent 30.56
subcontract 30.48
subcontractor 12.74
subcritical 23.32
subculture 12.24
subcutaneous 28.23
subdivide 16.14
subdivision 25.42
subdue 11.1
subedit 30.21
subeditor 12.78
subfamily 4.24
subfloor 7.11
subframe 24.4
subfusc 21.35
subgroup 27.11
sub-head 16.3

sub-heading 26.5
subhuman 25.45
subject 30.48, 30.49
subjection 25.49
subjectivist 31.15
subjoin 25.32
sub judice 4.46
subjugate 30.9
sublease 28.6
sublet 30.4
sublimate 30.12
sublime 24.7
subliminal 23.34
sublunary 4.43
submarginal 23.34
submarine 25.9
submariner 12.55
submerge 20.17
submergence 28.45
submergible 23.26
submerse 28.36
submersible 23.26
submersion 25.49
submissive 34.7
submit 30.20
submitter 12.78
subnormal 23.33
sub-nuclear 12.6
subordinary 4.43
subordinate 30.13,
30.43
suborn 25.28
suborner 12.56
sub-plot 30.31
subpoena 12.54
subrogate 30.9
subscribe 14.8
subscriber 12.21
subscript 30.58
subscription 25.49
subsection 25.49
subsequence 28.45
subsequent 30.56
subserve 34.14
subservience 28.45
subserviency 4.48
subservient 30.56
subset 30.5
subside 16.14
subsidence 28.45
subsidiarity 4.53
subsidiary 4.43
subsidizer 12.91
subsidy 4.12
subsist 31.6
subsistence 28.45
subsistent 30.56
subsoil 23.19
subsonic 21.13
subspecies 35.10

substance 28.45
sub-standard 16.28
substantial 23.38
substantialist 31.8
substantialize 35.12
substantiate 30.8
substantival 23.40
substitute 30.38
substitution 25.49
substitutional 23.34
substitutionary 4.43
substrata 12.75
substrate 30.15
substratum 24.20
substructure 12.24
subsume 24.12
subsystem 24.6
subtenancy 4.48
subtenant 30.56
subtend 16.41
subterfuge 20.15
subterranean 25.37
subtext 31.28
subtitle 23.39
subtle 23.39
subtlety 4.55
subtonic 21.13
subtopia 12.9
subtopian 25.37
subtotal 23.39
subtract 30.48
subtraction 25.49
subtropical 23.32
subtropics 28.39
subtype 27.7
suburb 14.15
suburban 25.38
suburbanite 30.29
suburbanize 35.13
suburbia 12.5
subvention 25.49
subversion 25.49
subversive 34.7
subvert 30.45
subverter 12.82
subway 3.25
sub-zero 9.21
succeed 16.7
succeeder 12.26
success 28.3
successional 23.34
successive 34.7
successor 12.69
succinct 30.49
succor 12.41
succory 4.43
succotash 29.1
Succoth 30.35
succour 12.41
succubi 6.5

succubus 28.24
succulence 28.45
succulent 30.56
succumb 24.14
succursal 23.37
such 15.13
suchlike 21.19
suck 21.29
sucker 12.41
suckle 23.32
suckler 12.47
Suckling 26.8
sucre 3.19
sucrose 35.19
suction 25.49
Sudan 25.4
Sudanese 35.6
sudarium 24.16
sudatoria 12.10
sudatorium 24.16
Sudbury 4.43
sudd 16.27
sudden 25.40
Sudetenland 16.40
Sudra 12.66
suds 35.27
sudsy 4.62
sue 11.1
suede 16.6
suer 12.19
suet 30.20
Suetonius 28.23
suety 4.53
Suez 35.10
suffer 12.30
sufferance 28.45
sufferer 12.67
suffering 26.11
suffice 28.13
sufficiency 4.46
sufficient 30.56
suffix 28.39, 31 28, 35.10
suffocate 30.10
suffocating 26.13
Suffolk 21.30
suffrage 20.8
suffragette 30.4
suffragist 31.7
suffuse 35.21
suffusion 25.42
Sufi 4.14
Sufic 21.10
Sufism 24.21
sugar 12.32
sugar beet 30.18
sugar cane 25.7
sugarcoated 16.12
sugarloaf 17.11
sugarplum 24.14

sugary 4.43
suggest 31.3
suggester 12.76
suggestible 23.26
suggestion 25.39
Sui 3.1
suicidal 23.28
suicide 16.16
suit 30.37
suitcase 28.5
suite 30.18
suiting 26.13
suitor 12.81
Sukarno 9.19
Sukhotai 6.1
Sukie 4.20
sukiyaki 4.18
Sukkur 12.41
Sulawesi 4.45
sulfur 12.30
sulfureous 28.23
sulfuric 21.15
sulfurous 28.31
sulfury 4.43
sulk 21.32
sulker 12.41
sulky 4.20
Sulla 12.47
sullen 25.44
Sullivan 25.51
sully 4.26
sulphur 12.30
sulphureous 28.23
sulphuric 21.15
sulphurous 28.31
sulphury 4.43
sultan 25.50
sultana 12.53
sultanate 30.43
sultry 4.42
sum 24.14
sumac 21.3
Sumatra 12.64
Sumatran 25.47
Sumer 12.52
Sumerian 25.37
summa 12.52
summa cum laude 3.9
summarizer 12.91
summary 4.43
summer 12.52
summerhouse 28.16
Summers 35.24
summertime 24.7
summery 4.43
summing-up 27.13
summit 30.23
summiteer 12.4
summon 25.45

summoner 12.58
summons 35.31
summum bonum 24.19
sumo 9.18
sump 27.17
sumptuary 4.43
sumptuosity 4.53
sumptuous 28.24
sun 25.35
sun-baked 30.48
sunbathe 33.2
sunbather 12.84
sunbeam 24.5
sunbed 16.3
sunbelt 30.51
sunblind 16.42
sunblock 21.21
sunburn 25.53
sunburnt 30.57
sunburst 31.26
sundae 3.9
Sundanese 35.6
Sunday 3.9
sundeck 21.6
sunder 12.29
Sunderland 16.45
sundial 23.25
sundown 25.29
sundowner 12.56
sundress 28.3
sun-dried 16.15
sundry 4.42
sunfast 31.2
sunflower 12.16
sung 26.18
sunglasses 35.10
sun hat 30.1
sunk 21.34
sunken 25.43
sunlamp 27.17
sunless 28.27
sunlight 30.28
sunlike 21.19
sunlit 30.22
sunlounger 12.35
Sunna 12.56
Sunni 4.33
Sunnite 30.29
sunny 4.33
sunray 3.19
sunrise 35.13
sunroof 17.13
sunroom 24.12
sunscreen 25.11
sunset 30.5
sunshade 16.6
sunshine 25.23
sunshiny 4.32
sunspot 30.32

sunstar 1.19
sunstone 25.31
sunstroke 21.24
suntan 25.3
suntrap 27.1
sunup 27.13
sunward 16.30
Sun Yat-sen 25.5
sup 27.13
super 12.63
superannuate 30.8
superb 14.15
supercilious 28.23
supererogatory 4.43
superficial 23.38
superficies 35.6
superfluity 4.53
superfluous 28.24
superglue 11.13
superintendence 28.45
superintendency 4.48
superintendent 30.56
superior 12.10
superiority 4.53
superlunary 4.43
Superman 25.2
supernal 23.34
supernumerary 4.43
superordinate 30.43
superscription 25.49
supersede 16.7
superstar 1.19
superstate 30.16
superstitious 28.33
superstore 7.18
supervene 25.9
supervention 25.49
supervise 35.14
supervisory 4.43
supine 25.23
supper 12.63
supplant 30.53
supplanter 12.75
supple 23.35
supplementary 4.43
suppletion 25.49
suppliant 30.56
supplicant 30.56
supplicate 30.10
supplicatory 4.43
supplier 12.13
supply 6.1
support 30.33
supporter 12.80
suppose 35.19
suppositious 28.33
suppository 4.43
suppress 28.3

S

S

Switzerland 16.45
swive 34.9
swivel 23.40
swizz 35.10
swizzle 23.41
swollen 25.44
swoon 25.33
swoop 27.11
swoosh 29.14
sword 16.19
swordbearer 12.65
swordfish 29.7
swordplay 3.15
swordsman 25.45
swordstick 21.17
swore 7.1
sworn 25.28
swot 30.31
swum 24.14
swung 26.18
sybarite 30.29
sybaritic 21.17
sycamore 7.12
syce 28.13
sycophancy 4.48
sycophant 30.56
sycophantic 21.17
Sydney 4.32
syenitic 21.17
syllabi 6.5
syllabic 21.9
syllabub 14.13
syllabus 28.24
syllepses 35.8
syllepsis 28.11
syllogize 35.11
sylph 17.18
sylphlike 21.19
sylvan 25.51
sylvatic 21.17
Sylvester 12.76
Sylvia 12.12
Sylvie 4.58
symbioses 35.8
symbiosis 28.11
symbiotic 21.17
symbol 23.26
symbolic 21.11
symbolical 23.32
symbolist 31.8
symbology 4.17
symmetrical 23.32
symmetry 4.40
Symons 35.31
sympathetic 21.17
sympathizer 12.91
sympathy 4.56
symphonic 21.13
symphonist 31.10
symphony 4.34

symposia 12.12
symposiast 31.1
symposium 24.16
symptom 24.20
symptomatic 21.17
synaesthesia 12.12
synagogal 23.30
synagogue 18.8
synapse 28.46
synapsis 28.11
synaptic 21.17
synarchy 4.18
sync 21.33
synchro 9.21
synchromesh 29.3
synchronizer 12.91
synchronous 28.29
synchrony 4.34
syncopal 23.35
syncopate 30.14
syncope 4.37
syncretic 21.17
syncretist 31.14
syncretize 35.14
syndetic 21.17
syndic 21.10
syndical 23.32
syndicalist 31.8
syndicate 30.10,
   30.42
syndrome 24.11
syne 25.21
synecdoche 4.20
synecdochic 21.11
synergy 4.17
Synge 26.3
synod 16.29
synodal 23.28
synodical 23.32
synonym 24.6
synonymous 28.28
synonymy 4.29
synopses 35.8
synopsis 28.11
synopsize 35.14
synoptic 21.17
synoptical 23.32
synoptist 31.14
synovial 23.24
syntactic 21.17
syntactical 23.32
syntax 28.38
synth 32.19
syntheses 35.8
synthesis 28.11
synthesist 31.13
synthesize 35.14
synthetic 21.17
synthetical 23.32
synthetize 35.14

syphilis 28.8
syphilitic 21.17
Syracuse 28.19, 35.21
Syria 12.10
Syriac 21.1
Syrian 25.37
syringe 20.19
syrup 27.14
syrupy 4.37
system 24.6
systematic 21.17
systematist 31.14
systematizer 12.91
systemic 21.12
systemize 35.13
systemizer 12.91
systole 4.27
Szeged 16.3

ta 1.1
Taal 23.2
tab 14.1
tabard 16.28
Tabasco 9.16
tabby 4.10
tabernacle 23.32
Tabitha 12.83
tabla 12.42
tablature 12.24
table 23.26
tableau 9.17
tableau vivant 25.26
tableaux 35.19
tablecloth 32.8
table d'hôte 30.35
tablespoon 25.33
tablet 30.22
tabletop 27.8
tableware 2.15
tablier 3.3
tabloid 16.24
taboo 11.1
tabor 12.21
Tabriz 35.6
tabular 12.46
tabula rasa 12.90
tabulate 30.11
tacet 30.24
tach 21.1
tacho 9.16
tachograph 17.2
tachometer 12.78
tachycardia 12.5
tachygraphy 4.14
tacit 30.24
taciturn 25.53
taciturnity 4.53

Tacitus 28.34
tack 21.1
tacker 12.37
tackle 23.32
tackler 12.42
tacky 4.18
taco 9.16
tact 30.48
tactic 21.17
tactical 23.32
tactician 25.49
tactile 23.12
tactility 4.53
tactual 23.25
tad 16.1
tadpole 23.18
Taff 17.1
taffeta 12.78
taffy 4.14
tafia 12.5
Taft 30.47
tag 18.1
Taganrog 18.8
tagliatelle 4.22
Tagore 7.1
Tagus 28.25
Tahiti 4.52
Tahitian 25.49
tahr 1.1
Tai 6.1
Tai'an 25.4
t'ai chi ch'uan 25.4
Taichung 26.17
taig 18.4
taiga 12.31
tail 23.5
tailback 21.2
tailboard 16.20
tail bone 25.30
tailcoat 30.35
tail end 16.41
tailgate 30.9
tailgater 12.77
tailing 26.8
Tailleferre 2.1
tail light 30.28
tailor 12.43
tailor-made 16.6
tailpiece 28.6
tailpipe 27.7
tailplane 25.8
tailspin 25.18
tailstock 21.21
tailwind 16.42
Tainan 25.1
taint 30.54
taipan 25.3
Taipei 3.1
Taiwan 25.4
Taiwanese 35.6

s

t

taj 20.2
Tajik 21.11
Tajikistan 25.4
Taj Mahal 23.2
Tajo 9.14
taka 1.11
takable 23.26
takahe 4.16
take 21.7
takeaway 3.25
takedown 25.29
taken 25.43
take-off 17.8
takeout 30.34
takeover 12.86
taker 12.38
take-up 27.13
taking 26.7
Taklimakan 25.4
tala 12.42
talapoin 25.32
talc 21.32
talcy 4.18
tale 23.5
talebearing 26.11
talent 30.56
tales 35.7
talipot 30.32
talisman 25.45
talismanic 21.13
talk 21.22
talkathon 25.26
talkback 21.2
talker 12.40
talkfest 31.3
talkie 4.19
tall 23.14
tallage 20.6
Tallahassee 4.45
tallboy 10.3
Talleyrand 16.40
Tallinn 25.16
Tallis 28.8
tallish 29.8
tallith 32.6
tallow 9.17
tallowy 4.7
Tallulah 12.45
tally 4.21
tally-ho 9.1
tallyman 25.45
tallymen 25.45
Talmud 16.26
Talmudic 21.10
Talmudical 23.32
Talmudist 31.6
talon 25.44
talus 28.27
tam 24.1
tamale 4.21

tamandua 12.20
Tamar 1.13
Tamara 12.64
tamarack 21.3
tamari 4.38
tamarillo 9.17
tamarin 25.18
tamarind 16.42
tamarisk 21.35
tambala 12.42
Tambo 9.9
tambour 12.20
tamboura 12.67
tambourin 25.18
tambourine 25.9
tambourinist 31.10
tame 24.4
tamer 12.50
Tamerlane 25.8
Tamil 23.9
Tamilian 25.37
Tamil Nadu 11.6
Tammany 4.34
tam-o'-shanter
    12.74
tamp 27.17
Tampa 12.61
tamper 12.61
Tampere 12.67
tamperer 12.67
tampering 26.11
Tampico 9.16
tampion 25.37
tampon 25.26
tam-tam 24.1
Tamworth 32.13
tan 25.1
tanager 12.36
Tanagra 12.67
Tananarive 34.5
tanbark 21.5
tandem 24.17
tandoor 12.20
tandoori 4.43
tang 26.1
tanga 12.31
Tanganyika 12.38
tangelo 9.17
tangent 30.56
tangential 23.38
tangerine 25.9
tangible 23.26
Tangier 12.4
tangle 23.30
tangly 4.21
tango 9.13
tangram 24.1
tangy 4.35
tank 21.33
tanka 12.37

tankage 20.6
tankard 16.28
tanker 12.37
tanktop 27.8
tanner 12.53
tannery 4.43
Tannhäuser 12.92
tannin 25.18
tannish 29.9
tannoy 10.9
tansy 4.61
tantalic 21.11
tantalite 30.28
tantalizer 12.91
tantalum 24.18
tantalus 28.27
tantamount 30.55
tant mieux 13.1
tant pis 4.1
tantra 12.64
tantric 21.15
tantrist 31.12
tantrum 24.19
Tanya 12.8
Tanzania 12.3
Tanzanian 25.36
Tao 8.1
Taoiseach 21.30
Taoism 24.21
Taoist 31.6
Taoistic 21.17
Taormina 12.54
tap 27.1
tapas 28.30
tap-dance 28.44
tape 27.4
taper 12.61
tape-record 16.21
tapestry 4.40
tapeworm 24.22
tapioca 12.40
tapir 12.9
tapis 4.36
tapper 12.61
tapping 26.10
taproom 24.12
tapu 11.16
taqueria 12.3
tar 1.1
Tara 12.64
taradiddle 23.28
tarakihi 4.16
taramasalata 12.75
tarantass 28.1
tarantella 12.42
tarantula 12.46
tarboosh 29.14
Tardis 28.7
tardy 4.12
tare 2.1

target 30.21
Targum 24.18
tariff 17.6
Tarmac 21.3
tarmacadam 24.17
tarn 25.4
tarnish 29.9
taro 9.21
tarot 9.21
tarp 27.2
tarpan 25.3
tarpaulin 25.16
Tarpeia 12.3
tarpon 25.46
Tarquin 25.20
tarragon 25.41
Tarrasa 12.69
tarrier 12.10
tarry 4.38
tarsal 23.37
tarsier 12.11
tarsus 28.32
tart 30.3
tartan 25.50
tartar 12.75
tartare 1.1
Tartarus 28.31
Tartary 4.43
tartlet 30.22
Tartuffe 17.13
tarty 4.51
Tarzan 25.52
Tashkent 30.53
task 21.35
taskmaster 12.75
Tasman 25.45
Tasmania 12.8
Tasmanian 25.37
tass 28.1
tassel 23.37
Tasso 9.22
taste 31.4
taster 12.77
tasting 26.13
tasty 4.52
tat 30.1
tata 1.1
Tatar 12.75
Tatarstan 25.4
Tate 30.7
tater 12.77
Tati 4.51
Tatiana 12.53
Tatras 28.31
tatterdemalion
    25.37
tattersall 23.15
tattery 4.43
tattie 4.51
tattle 23.39
tattler 12.48

tattletale 23.6
tattoo 11.1
tattooer 12.19
tattooist 31.6
tatty 4.51
Tatum 24.20
tau 7.1
taught 30.33
taunt 30.54
taunter 12.80
Taunton 25.50
taupe 27.10
Tauranga 12.31
Taurean 25.37
taurine 25.11, 25.23
Taurus 28.31
taut 30.33
tauten 25.50
tautog 18.8
tautologize 35.11
tautologous 28.25
tautology 4.17
tavern 25.51
taverna 12.59
Taverner 12.58
taw 7.1
tawdry 4.41
tawer 12.15
tawny 4.32
taws 35.17
tawse 35.17
tax 28.38
taxable 23.26
taxation 25.49
tax-deductible 23.26
taxi 4.45
taxicab 14.1
taxidermal 23.33
taxidermic 21.12
taxidermist 31.9
taxidermy 4.30
taxis 28.11
taxiway 3.25
taxman 25.2
taxmen 25.5
taxonomic 21.12
taxonomy 4.30
taxpayer 12.2
Tay 3.1
Taylor 12.43
Tayside 16.16
tazza 12.69
Tbilisi 4.45
Tchaikovsky 4.19
tea 4.1
tea bag 18.1
teabread 16.4
teacake 21.7
teach 15.5
teacher 12.23
teacherly 4.27

teaching 26.4
teacup 27.13
tea garden 25.40
teak 21.8
teal 23.7
tea leaf 17.5
tea leaves 35.35
team 24.5
teammate 30.12
teamster 12.77
teamwork 21.31
teapot 30.32
teapoy 10.10
tear 2.1, 12.4
tearaway 3.25
teardrop 27.8
tearer 12.65
teargas 28.1
tearjerker 12.41
tear-jerking 26.7
tearoom 24.12
tearstained 16.41
teary 4.43
tease 35.6
teasel 23.41
teaser 12.90
teaset 30.5
Teasmade 16.6
teaspoon 25.33
teat 30.18
teatime 24.7
tec 21.6
tech 21.6
techie 4.18
technetium 24.16
technic 21.13
technical 23.32
technician 25.49
technicist 31.13
technicolor 12.47
technique 21.8
techno 9.19
technobabble 23.26
technocracy 4.48
technocrat 30.2
technocratic 21.17
technology 4.17
technophile 23.11
technophobe 14.11
technophobia 12.5
technophobic 21.9
technospeak 21.8
tectonic 21.13
ted 16.3
tedder 12.26
teddy 4.12
Te Deum 24.15
tedious 28.23
tedium 24.16
tee 4.1

tee-hee 4.1
teem 24.5
teen 25.9
teenage 20.4
teenager 12.35
teensy 4.61
teeny 4.31
teenybopper 12.62
teeny-weeny 4.31
Tees 35.6
Teesside 16.16
teeter 12.77
teeth 32.5
teethe 33.3
teetotal 23.39
teetotaler 12.44
teetotaller 12.44
teetotum 24.20
teff 17.3
Teflon 25.25
teg 18.3
Tehran 25.4
Teilhard de
  Chardin 25.1
Te Kanawa 12.88
telamon 25.45
Tel Aviv 34.5
telecast 31.2
telecaster 12.75
telecine 4.32
Telecom 24.8
telecommute 30.37
telecommuter 12.81
telecoms 35.30
Telefax 28.38
telefilm 24.18
telegenic 21.13
telegram 24.1
telegraph 17.2
telegrapher 12.30
telegraphese 35.6
telegraphic 21.10
telekinesis 28.11
telekinetic 21.17
Telemachus 28.26
Telemann 25.2
telemark 21.5
telemarketing 26.13
teleologic 21.11
teleost 31.17
telepath 32.1
telepathic 21.18
telepathist 31.14
telepathize 35.14
telepathy 4.56
telephone 25.30
telephonist 31.10
telephony 4.34
teleplay 3.15
teleport 30.33

teleprinter 12.78
teleprompter 12.79
telerecord 16.21
telerecording 26.5
telesales 35.29
telescope 27.10
telescopic 21.14
teletext 31.28
telethon 25.26
televangelist 31.8
televise 35.14
television 25.42
televisual 23.25
telework 21.31
teleworker 12.41
Telex 28.38
Telford 16.28
tell 23.3
teller 12.42
telling 26.8
telling-off 17.8
telltale 23.6
tellurian 25.37
telluric 21.15
telluride 16.15
tellurium 24.16
telly 4.22
telnet 30.5
telos 28.14
Telstar 1.19
Telugu 11.8
temerarious 28.23
temerity 4.53
temp 27.17
temper 12.61
tempera 12.67
temperance 28.45
temperate 30.43
temperature 12.23
temperer 12.67
tempest 31.11
tempestuous 28.24
tempi 4.36
Templar 12.42
template 30.11
temple 23.35
tempo 9.20
temporal 23.36
temporary 4.43
temporizer 12.91
tempt 30.52
tempter 12.76
tempting 26.13
temptress 28.10
tempura 12.67
ten 25.5
tenable 23.26
tenace 28.5
tenacious 28.33
tenacity 4.53

Theobald 16.36
theocentric 21.15
theocracy 4.48
theocrat 30.2
theocratic 21.17
Theocritus 28.34
theodicean 25.36
theodicy 4.46
Theodora 12.66
Theodorákis 28.7
Theodore 7.5
theogony 4.34
theologian 25.42
theologist 31.7
theologize 35.11
theology 4.17
theomachy 4.20
theophany 4.34
Theophilus 28.27
theophoric 21.15
Theophrastus 28.34
theorem 24.19
theoretic 21.17
theoretical 23.32
theoretician 25.49
theorist 31.12
theorizer 12.91
theory 4.43
theosopher 12.30
theosophic 21.10
theosophist 31.7
theosophy 4.14
Thera 12.67
therapeutic 21.17
therapeutical 23.32
therapeutist 31.14
therapist 31.11
therapy 4.37
Theravada 12.25
there 2.1
thereabout 30.34
thereabouts 28.47
thereafter 12.75
thereat 30.1
thereby 6.1
therefore 7.6
therefrom 24.8
therein 25.13
thereinto 11.20
theremin 25.17
thereof 34.10
thereon 25.24
thereout 30.34
Theresa 12.90
thereto 11.1
thereunder 12.29
thereunto 11.20
thereupon 25.24
therewith 33.4
therewithal 23.15

theriac 21.1
therm 24.22
thermae 4.30
thermal 23.33
thermic 21.12
thermionic 21.13
thermite 30.29
thermodynamic 21.12
thermometer 12.78
thermonuclear 12.6
Thermos 28.28
thermosphere 12.5
thermostat 30.2
thermostatic 21.17
thesauri 6.15
thesaurus 28.31
these 35.6
theses 35.8
Theseus 28.23
thesis 28.11
thespian 25.37
Thespis 28.9
Thessalian 25.37
Thessaloníki 4.18
Thessaly 4.27
theta 12.77
Thetis 28.12
theurgist 31.7
thew 11.1
they 3.1
they'd 16.6
they'll 23.5
they're 2.1
they've 34.4
thiamine 25.11
thick 21.9
thicken 25.43
thickener 12.58
thickening 26.9
thicket 30.21
thickhead 16.3
thickheaded 16.9
thickish 29.8
thicko 9.16
thickset 30.4
thick-skulled 16.37
thief 17.5
thieve 34.5
thievery 4.43
thieves 35.35
thievish 29.10
thigh 6.1
thigh bone 25.30
thill 23.8
thimble 23.26
thimblerig 18.6
thin 25.13
thine 25.21
thing 26.3

thingamabob 14.9
thingamajig 18.6
thingummy 4.30
thingy 4.35
think 21.33
thinker 12.39
think tank 21.33
thinner 12.55
thinning 26.9
thinnish 29.9
third 16.31
thirdhand 16.40
thirst 31.26
thirsty 4.55
thirteen 25.9
thirteenth 32.19
thirtieth 32.6
thirty 4.55
this 28.7
Thisbe 4.10
thistle 23.37
thistledown 25.29
thistly 4.27
thither 12.84
thole 23.17
tholos 28.14
Thom 24.8
Thomas 28.28
Thompson 25.48
thong 26.15
Thor 7.1
thoraces 35.8
thoracic 21.16
thorax 28.38
Thoreau 9.21
thorn 25.28
Thorndike 21.19
thorny 4.32
thorough 12.66
thoroughbred 16.4
thoroughfare 2.5
thoroughgoing 26.3
Thorpe 27.9
those 35.19
Thoth 32.11
thou 8.1
though 9.1
thought 30.33
thought-provoking 26.7
thousand 16.45
thousandfold 16.37
thousandth 32.19
Thrace 28.5
Thracian 25.49
thraldom 24.17
thrall 23.14
thrash 29.1
thrasher 12.72
thrashing 26.12

thrawn 25.28
thread 16.3
threadbare 2.3
threader 12.26
thread-like 21.19
threadworm 24.22
thready 4.12
threat 30.4
threaten 25.50
threatener 12.58
three 4.1
three-dimensional 23.34
threefold 16.37
threepence 28.45
threepenny 4.34
three-quarter 12.80
threescore 7.1
threnodic 21.10
threnodist 31.6
threnody 4.13
thresh 29.3
thresher 12.72
threshold 16.37
threw 11.1
thrice 28.13
thrift 30.47
thrifty 4.53
thrill 23.8
thriller 12.43
thrips 28.46
thrive 34.9
thriven 25.51
thro 11.1
throat 30.35
throaty 4.54
throb 14.9
thrombose 35.19
thrombosis 28.11
throne 25.30
throng 26.15
throstle 23.37
throttle 23.39
throttler 12.48
through 11.1
throughout 30.34
throughput 30.39
throughway 3.25
throw 9.1
throwaway 3.25
throwback 21.2
thrower 12.17
throw-in 25.13
thrown 25.30
thru 11.1
thrum 24.14
thrush 29.16
thrust 31.24
thruster 12.81
thrutch 15.13

t

Thucydides 35.7
thud 16.27
thug 18.12
thuggee 4.1
thuggery 4.43
thuggish 29.7
Thule 4.26, 23.20
thulium 24.16
thumb 24.14
thumbnail 23.6
thumbprint 30.54
thumbscrew 11.17
thumbtack 21.4
thump 27.17
thumper 12.63
thunder 12.29
thunderbird 16.31
thunderbolt 30.51
thunderbox 28.40
thunderbug 18.12
thunderclap 27.1
thundercloud 16.22
thunderer 12.67
thunderflash 29.1
thundering 26.11
thunderous 28.31
thunderstorm 24.9
thunderstruck 21.29
thundery 4.43
thunk 21.34
Thurber 12.22
thurible 23.26
thurifer 12.30
Thuringia 12.6
Thursday 3.9
Thurso 9.22
thus 28.21
thwack 21.1
Thwaite 30.7
thwart 30.33
thy 6.1
Thyestean 25.37
Thyestes 35.9
thylacine 25.23
thyme 24.7
thymus 28.28
thymy 4.29
thyroid 16.24
thyrsi 6.16
thyrsus 28.32
thyself 17.18
tiara 12.64
Tiber 12.21
Tiberius 28.23
Tibet 30.4
Tibetan 25.50
tibia 12.5
Tibullus 28.27
tic 21.9
tick 21.9

ticker 12.39
ticker tape 27.4
ticket 30.21
tickety-boo 11.1
ticking 26.7
tickle 23.32
tickler 12.48
ticklish 29.8
tickly 4.27
tick-tock 21.21
ticky-tacky 4.18
tic-tac 21.4
tic-tac-toe 9.1
tidal 23.28
tidbit 30.20
tiddledywink 21.33
tiddler 12.48
tiddly 4.24
tiddlywink 21.33
tide 16.14
tideline 25.22
tidemark 21.5
tidewater 12.80
tideway 3.25
tidings 35.32
tidy 4.12
tie 6.1
tieback 21.2
tiebreak 21.7
tie-breaker 12.38
tie-dye 6.6
tieless 28.8
Tientsin 25.13
tiepin 25.18
tier 12.4, 12.13
tierce 28.23
Tierney 4.34
Tierra del Fuego
    9.13
tiff 17.6
tiffany 4.34
tiffin 25.14
tig 18.6
tiger 12.31
tigerish 29.9
Tigers 35.24
tiger's-eye 6.22
tight 30.26
tighten 25.50
tight-fisted 16.12
tightrope 27.10
tightwad 16.18
tigon 25.41
Tigray 3.19
Tigrayan 25.36
tigress 28.10
Tigrinya 12.89
Tigris 28.10
Tijuana 12.53
tiki 4.18

tikka 12.38
Tilburg 18.13
tilbury 4.43
Tilda 12.27
tilde 12.27
tile 23.11
tiler 12.44
tiling 26.8
till 23.8
tillage 20.6
tiller 12.43
Tilly 4.24
Tilsit 30.24
tilt 30.51
tilter 12.78
tilth 32.17
Tim 24.6
Timaru 11.17
timbal 23.26
timbale 23.2
timber 12.21
timberland 16.40
timberline 25.22
timbre 12.21
timbrel 23.36
Timbuktu 11.1
time 24.7
timekeeper 12.61
timekeeping 26.10
timely 4.25
timeous 28.28
timeout 30.34
timepiece 28.6
timer 12.51
Times 35.30
timescale 23.5
time-server 12.87
time-serving 26.14
timeshare 2.13
time-sharing 26.11
time sheet 30.19
time-worn 25.28
timid 16.10
timidity 4.53
timing 26.9
Timmy 4.29
Timor 7.12
Timorese 35.6
timorous 28.31
timothy 4.56
timpani 4.34
timpanist 31.10
tin 25.13
tinamou 11.14
tincture 12.23
tinder 12.27
tinderbox 28.40
tindery 4.43
tine 25.21
tinfoil 23.19

ting 26.3
tinge 20.19
tingle 23.30
tingly 4.24
tinhorn 25.28
tinker 12.39
tinkerer 12.67
tinkering 26.11
tinkle 23.32
tinkling 26.8
tinkly 4.24
tinnitus 28.34
tinny 4.32
tinpot 30.32
tinsel 23.37
tinselly 4.27
Tinseltown 25.31
tinsmith 32.6
tint 30.54
Tintagel 23.31
tinter 12.78
Tintoretto 9.24
tinware 2.15
tiny 4.32
tip 27.6
tipper 12.62
Tipperary 4.39
tippet 30.23
Tippett 30.23
Tipp-Ex 28.38
tipple 23.35
tippler 12.48
tippy 4.36
tipstaff 17.2
tipster 12.78
tipsy 4.46
tipsy cake 21.7
tiptoe 9.24
tiptop 27.8
tirade 16.6
tiramisu 11.1
Tirana 12.53
tire 12.13
Tiree 4.1
Tiresias 28.23
Tirol 23.17
tisane 25.1
Tishri 4.40
tissue 11.19
tit 30.20
titan 25.50
Titania 12.8
titanic 21.13
titanium 24.16
titbit 30.20
titch 15.6
titchy 4.11
titfer 12.30
tit-for-tat 30.1
tithe 33.5

t

tithing 26.14
Tithonus 28.29
titi 4.52
Titian 25.49
titillate 30.11
titivate 30.16
titlark 21.5
title 23.39
titling 26.8
titmice 28.13
titmouse 28.16
Tito 9.24
Titograd 16.1
Titoist 31.6
titter 12.78
titterer 12.67
tittle 23.39
tittle-tattle 23.39
tittup 27.14
titty 4.53
titular 12.46
Titus 28.34
tizz 35.10
tizzy 4.61
T-junction 25.49
Tlemcen 25.5
Tlingit 30.21
to 11.1
toad 16.23
toadflax 28.38
toad-in-the-hole 23.17
toadish 29.6
toadlet 30.22
toadstool 23.20
toady 4.13
toadyish 29.6
to-and-fro 9.1
toast 31.20
toaster 12.80
toastie 4.54
toastmaster 12.75
toastmistress 28.10
toasty 4.54
tobacco 9.16
tobacconist 31.10
Tobago 9.13
Tobagonian 25.37
Tobias 28.24
Tobit 30.20
toboggan 25.41
tobogganer 12.58
tobogganist 31.10
Tobruk 21.28
tocsin 25.19
tod 16.18
today 3.1
Todd 16.18
toddle 23.28
toddler 12.48

toddlerhood 16.26
toddy 4.13
todger 12.35
to-do 11.1
tody 4.13
toe 9.1
toecap 27.1
toehold 16.37
toeless 28.27
toenail 23.6
toey 4.7
toff 17.8
toffee 4.14
toffee-nosed 16.50
toft 30.47
tofu 11.7
tog 18.8
toga 12.32
together 12.84
toggery 4.43
toggle 23.30
Togo 9.13
Togolese 35.6
toil 23.19
toile 23.2
toiler 12.44
toilet 30.22
toilette 30.4
toilworn 25.28
toing and froing 26.3
Tojo 9.15
tokay 3.1
toke 21.24
Tokelau 8.7
token 25.43
Tokugawa 12.88
Tokyo 9.4
tolbooth 33.8
told 16.37
Toledo 9.11
tolerance 28.45
tolerant 30.56
tolerate 30.15
Tolkien 25.10
toll 23.17
tollbooth 33.8
tollbridge 20.8
toll gate 30.9
Tolstoy 10.12
Toltec 21.6
tom 24.8
tomahawk 21.22
tomato 9.24
tomatoey 4.7
tomb 24.12
Tombaugh 7.4
tombola 12.44
tombolo 9.17
tomboy 10.3

tomboyish 29.6
Tombs 35.30
tombstone 25.31
tomcat 30.1
tome 24.11
tomfool 23.20
tomfoolery 4.43
tommy 4.29
tommyrot 30.32
tomorrow 9.21
Toms 35.30
Tomsk 21.35
tomtit 30.24
tomtom 24.8
ton 25.24, 25.35
tonal 23.34
tonality 4.53
tondi 4.13
tondo 9.11
tone 25.30
tonearm 24.2
tone-deaf 17.3
toner 12.56
tong 26.15
tonga 12.60
Tongan 25.46
tongue 26.18
tongue-in-cheek 21.8
tongue-lashing 26.12
tongue tie 6.18
tonguing 26.10
Toni 4.33
tonic 21.13
tonight 30.26
Tonkin 25.13, 25.15
Tonks 28.41
tonnage 20.7
tonne 25.35
tonneau 9.19
tonsil 23.37
tonsillectomy 4.30
tonsillitis 28.12
tonsorial 23.24
tonsure 12.73
tontine 25.12
Tonton Macoute 30.37
ton-up 27.13
tony 4.33
too 11.1
toodle-oo 11.1
toodle-pip 27.6
took 21.28
tool 23.20
toolbox 28.40
toolkit 30.21
toolmaking 26.7
toot 30.37
tooter 12.81

tooth 32.12
toothache 21.7
toothbrush 29.16
toothcomb 24.11
toothglass 28.2
tooth-like 21.19
toothpaste 31.4
toothpick 21.14
toothy 4.56
Tooting 26.13
tootle 23.39
tootsie 4.47
Toowoomba 12.21
top 27.8
topaz 35.1
top boot 30.37
topcoat 30.35
top-dress 28.3
tope 27.10
Topeka 12.38
toper 12.63
top-heavy 4.58
Tophet 30.21
topi 4.36
topiarian 25.37
topiarist 31.12
topiary 4.43
topic 21.14
topical 23.32
topknot 30.32
topless 28.27
topmast 31.2
topmost 31.20
topnotch 15.7
top-notcher 12.24
topo 9.20
topographer 12.30
topography 4.14
topoi 10.10
topology 4.17
topos 28.14
topper 12.62
topping 26.10
topple 23.35
topsail 23.6
topside 16.16
topsoil 23.19
topspin 25.18
topstitch 15.6
topsy-turvy 4.58
top-up 27.13
toque 21.24
tor 7.1
Torah 12.66
Torbay 3.1
torc 21.22
torch 15.8
torch-bearer 12.65
torchlight 30.28
torchlit 30.22

t

torchon 25.26
tore 7.1
toreador 7.5
torero 9.21
torgoch 22.4
tori 6.15
torii 4.3
Torino 9.19
torment 30.53
tormentil 23.9
tormentor 12.76
torn 25.28
tornado 9.11
Tornio 9.4
Toronto 9.25
torpedo 9.11
torpid 16.10
torpidity 4.53
torpor 12.62
Torquay 4.1
torque 21.22
Torquemada 12.25
torr 7.1
torrent 30.56
torrential 23.38
Torricelli 4.22
torrid 16.11
torridity 4.53
torse 28.15
Tórshavn 25.51
torsion 25.49
torso 9.22
tort 30.33
torte 12.80
Tortelier 3.3
tortellini 4.31
torten 25.50
tortilla 12.89
tortious 28.33
tortoise 28.34
tortoiseshell 23.4
Tortola 12.44
tortrices 35.8
tortrix 28.39
tortuous 28.24
torture 12.24
torturer 12.67
torturous 28.31
torulae 4.26
torus 28.31
Tory 4.41
Toscanini 4.31
tosh 29.11
Tosk 21.35
toss 28.14
tosser 12.70
tosspot 30.32
toss-up 27.13
tostada 12.25
tostone 6.13

tot 30.31
total 23.39
totalitarian 25.37
totality 4.53
totalize 35.12
totalizer 12.91
tote 30.35
totem 24.20
totemic 21.12
totemist 31.9
t'other 12.84
totter 12.79
totterer 12.67
tottery 4.43
totting-up 27.13
totty 4.54
toucan 25.43
touch 15.13
touch-and-go 9.1
touchback 21.2
touchdown 25.29
touché 3.21
toucher 12.24
touchline 25.22
touch-me-not 30.32
touch pad 16.1
touchstone 25.31
touchy 4.11
Tough 17.15, 22.5
toughen 25.41
toughener 12.58
toughie 4.14
toughish 29.7
tough-minded 16.9
Toulon 25.24
Toulouse 35.21
Toulouse-Lautrec 21.6
toupée 3.18
tour 12.20
tourer 12.67
tourist 31.12
touristy 4.53
tourmaline 25.10
Tournai 3.1
tournedos 9.11
tourney 4.34
tourniquet 3.14
Tours 12.20
tousle 23.41
tout 30.34
touter 12.80
tow 9.1
towable 23.26
towage 20.6
toward 16.19
towards 35.27
towbar 1.4
towel 23.25
toweling 26.8

towelling 26.8
tower 12.16, 12.17
Towers 35.24
towery 4.43
towhee 4.16
towline 25.22
town 25.29
Townes 35.31
town house 28.16
townie 4.32
townish 29.9
townlet 30.22
townscape 27.4
townsfolk 21.24
townsman 25.45
townsmen 25.45
townspeople 23.35
Townsville 23.10
townswoman 25.45
townswomen 25.17
townward 16.30
towpath 32.2
towplane 25.8
towrope 27.10
towy 4.7
Towy 4.6
toxic 21.16
toxicity 4.53
toxicology 4.17
toxin 25.19
toxophily 4.24
toxoplasmosis 28.11
toy 10.1
toyboy 10.3
toylike 21.19
Toynbee 4.10
toyshop 27.8
toytown 25.29
trace 28.5
tracer 12.69
tracery 4.43
trachea 12.3
tracheotomy 4.30
tracing 26.12
track 21.1
trackage 20.6
trackbed 16.3
tracker 12.37
tracking 26.7
tracklayer 12.2
trackman 25.45
trackmen 25.45
trackside 16.16
tracksuit 30.38
trackway 3.25
tract 30.48
tractate 30.16
traction 25.49
tractor 12.74
Tracy 4.45

trad 16.1
trade 16.6
trademark 21.5
trader 12.26
tradesman 25.45
tradesmen 25.45
tradespeople 23.35
tradewind 16.42
traditionalist 31.8
traditionary 4.43
traditionist 31.10
traduce 28.19
traducer 12.71
Trafalgar 12.31
traffic 21.10
trafficker 12.39
tragedian 25.37
tragedy 4.12
tragic 21.11
tragical 23.32
tragicomedy 4.12
tragicomic 21.12
tragopan 25.3
Traherne 25.53
trail 23.5
trailblazer 12.90
trailblazing 26.14
trailer 12.43
train 25.7
trainee 4.1
trainer 12.54
trainload 16.23
traipse 28.46
trait 3.1
traitor 12.77
traitorous 28.31
Trajan 25.42
trajectory 4.43
tra-la 1.1
Tralee 4.1
tram 24.1
tramcar 1.11
tramline 25.22
trammel 23.33
tramontana 12.53
tramp 27.17
tramper 12.61
trampish 29.9
trample 23.35
trampler 12.42
trampoline 25.10
trampolinist 31.10
tramway 3.25
trance 28.44
tranche 29.20
tranny 4.31
tranquil 23.10
tranquility 4.53
tranquilize 35.12
tranquillity 4.53

tranquillize 35.12
transact 30.48
transaction 25.49
transactional 23.34
transactor 12.74
transatlantic 21.17
transaxle 23.37
transcend 16.41
transcendence 28.45
transcendency 4.48
transcendent 30.56
transcendentalist 31.0
transcendentalize 35.12
transcribe 14.8
transcriber 12.21
transcript 30.58
transcription 25.49
transect 30.48
transection 25.49
transept 30.58
transeptal 23.39
transfer 13.1, 13.2
transferee 4.1
transference 28.45
transferor 12.68
transferral 23.36
transferrer 12.68
transfigure 12.31
transfinite 30.29
transfix 28.39
transfixion 25.49
transform 24.9
transformer 12.52
transfuse 35.21
transfusion 25.42
transgress 28.3
transgressive 34.7
transgressor 12.69
transience 28.45
transiency 4.48
transient 30.56
transistor 12.78
transit 30.24
transitionary 4.43
transitory 4.43
Transkei 6.1
translate 30.7
transliterate 30.15
translocate 30.7
translucence 28.45
translucency 4.47
translucent 30.56
transmarine 25.9
transmigrant 30.6
transmigrate 30.7
transmigratory 4.43
transmissible 23.26
transmit 30.20

transmitter 12.78
transmogrify 6.7
transmute 30.37
transmuter 12.81
transoceanic 21.13
transom 24.20
transonic 21.13
transpacific 21.10
transparence 28.45
transparency 4.48
transparent 30.56
transpersonal 23.34
transpire 12.13
transplant 30.53
transplanter 12.75
transpontine 25.23
transport 30.33
transporter 12.80
transpose 35.19
transsexual 23.25
transubstantiate 30.8
transude 16.25
Transvaal 23.2
transversal 23.37
transverse 28.36
transvestist 31.14
transvestite 30.30
Transylvania 12.8
Transylvanian 25.37
trap 27.1
trapdoor 7.1
trapes 28.46
trapeze 35.6
trapezium 24.16
trapezoid 16.24
trap-like 21.19
trapper 12.61
trappings 35.32
Trappist 31.11
trash 29.1
trash can 25.2
trashy 4.50
trattoria 12.3
trauma 12.52
traumata 12.82
traumatic 21.17
travail 23.6
travel 23.40
traveler 12.48
traveller 12.48
travelogue 18.8
Travers 35.24
traversal 23.37
traverse 28.35
traverser 12.71
travertine 25.12
travesty 4.53
Travis 28.12
trawl 23.14

trawler 12.44
trawlerman 25.45
tray 3.1
treacherous 28.31
treachery 4.43
treacle 23.32
treacly 4.27
tread 16.3
treader 12.26
treadle 23.28
treadmill 23.9
treadwheel 23.7
treason 25.52
treasonous 28.29
treasure 12.33
treasurer 12.67
treasury 4.43
treat 30.18
treater 12.77
treatise 35.10
treaty 4.52
Trebizond 16.42
treble 23.26
Treblinka 12.39
trebly 4.22
trebuchet 30.5
tree 4.1
treecreeper 12.61
treehouse 28.16
treeline 25.22
treen 25.9
treenail 23.6
treetop 27.8
trefa 12.30
trefoil 23.19
trek 21.6
trekker 12.37
trellis 28.8
trematode 16.23
tremble 23.26
trembler 12.42
trembling 26.8
trembly 4.22
tremendous 28.25
tremolo 9.17
tremor 12.50
tremulous 28.27
trench 29.20
trenchancy 4.48
trenchant 30.56
Trenchard 16.2
trencher 12.72
trencherman 25.45
trenchermen 25.45
trend 16.41
trendsetter 12.76
trendsetting 26.13
trendy 4.12
Trent 30.53
Trento 9.24

Trenton 25.50
trepan 25.1
trepang 26.1
trespass 28.30
trespasser 12.71
tress 28.3
tressy 4.45
trestle 23.37
tret 30.4
Trevelyan 25.37
Trevino 9.19
Trevor 12.85
trews 35.21
trey 3.1
triable 23.26
triacetate 30.16
triad 16.1
triadic 21.10
triage 19.1
trial 23.25
trialist 31.8
triangle 23.30
triangular 12.46
triangulate 30.11, 30.42
Trianon 25.26
Trias 28.1
Triassic 21.16
triathlete 30.18
triathlon 25.44
triaxial 23.24
tribade 16.28
tribal 23.26
tribalist 31.8
tribe 14.8
tribesman 25.45
tribesmen 25.45
tribeswoman 25.45
tribeswomen 25.17
triblet 30.22
tribrach 21.3
tribunal 23.34
tribunate 30.43
tribune 25.33
tributary 4.43
tribute 30.38
tricar 1.11
trice 28.13
Tricel 23.3
triceps 28.46
triceratops 28.46
trichinosis 28.11
trichomonad 16.1
trichotomous 28.28
trichotomy 4.30
Tricia 12.72
trick 21.9
tricker 12.39
trickery 4.43
trickle 23.32

t

trickster 12.78
tricksy 4.46
tricky 4.19
triclinia 12.8
tricolor 12.48
tricolour 12.48
tricorne 25.28
tricot 9.16
tricycle 23.32
tricyclist 31.8
trident 30.56
Tridentine 25.23
triduum 24.17
tried 16.14
triennia 12.8
triennial 23.24
Trier 12.4
trier 12.13
Trieste 31.3
triffid 16.9
trifle 23.29
trifler 12.44
trifoliate 30.41
triform 24.9
trig 18.6
trigamous 28.28
trigamy 4.30
trigger 12.31
triglyphic 21.10
trigon 25.41
trigonal 23.34
trigonometry 4.40
trike 21.19
trilateral 23.36
trilby 4.10
trill 23.8
Trilling 26.8
trillion 25.52
trillionth 32.19
trillium 24.16
trilogy 4.17
trim 24.6
trimaran 25.3
trimester 12.76
trimetrical 23.32
trimmer 12.51
trimming 26.9
Trimurti 4.55
Trincomalee 4.1
trine 25.21
Trini 4.31
Trinidad 16.1
Trinidadian 25.37
Trinitarian 25.37
trinity 4.53
trinket 30.21
trinketry 4.40
trio 9.3
triode 16.23
triolet 30.4

trip 27.6
tripartite 30.30
tripe 27.7
Tripitaka 12.41
triplane 25.8
triple 23.35
triplet 30.22
triplex 28.38
triplicate 30.10, 30.42
tripod 16.18
tripodal 23.28
tripoli 4.27
Tripolitanian 25.37
tripos 28.14
tripper 12.62
trippy 4.36
triptych 21.17
Tripura 12.66
tripwire 12.14
trishaw 7.17
triskelion 25.37
Tristan da Cunha 12.56
tristesse 28.3
Tristram 24.19
trite 30.26
triton 25.50
tritone 25.31
triturate 30.15
triumph 17.19
triumphal 23.29
triumphalist 31.8
triumphant 30.56
triumvir 12.87
triumviral 23.36
triumvirate 30.43
triune 25.33
trivet 30.25
trivia 12.12
trivial 23.24
Trixie 4.46
trochaic 21.9
trochee 4.20
trod 16.18
trodden 25.40
trog 18.8
troglodyte 30.26
troglodytes 35.9
troglodytic 21.17
troika 12.40
Troilus 28.27
Trojan 25.42
troll 23.13, 23.17
troller 12.44
trolley 4.25
trolleybus 28.21
trollop 27.14
Trollope 27.14
trombone 25.30

trombonist 31.10
tromp 27.17
trompe l'œil 10.1
tronc 21.34
Trondheim 24.7
Troon 25.33
troop 27.11
trooper 12.63
trope 27.10
trophic 21.10
trophy 4.14
tropic 21.14
tropical 23.32
troppo 9.20
Trossachs 28.41
trot 30.31
troth 32.11
Trotsky 4.19
Trotskyist 31.6
Trotskyite 30.26
trotter 12.79
troubadour 7.5
trouble 23.26
troublemaker 12.38
troublemaking 26.7
troubler 12.47
troubleshoot 30.38
troubleshooter 12.81
troubleshot 30.32
troublous 28.27
trough 17.8
trounce 28.44
trouncer 12.70
troupe 27.11
trouper 12.63
trouser 12.92
trousseau 9.22
trout 30.34
trove 34.11
trover 12.86
trow 9.1
Trowbridge 20.8
trowel 23.25
troy 10.1
truancy 4.48
truant 30.56
truce 28.19
Trucial States 28.47
truck 21.29
truckage 20.6
trucker 12.41
truckle 23.32
truckload 16.23
truculence 28.45
truculent 30.56
Trudeau 9.11
trudge 20.16
trudgen 25.42
trudger 12.36
Trudy 4.13

true 11.1
true-blue 11.1
Trueman 25.45
Truffaut 9.12
truffle 23.29
trug 18.12
truism 24.21
truistic 21.17
Trujillo 9.28
trull 23.22
truly 4.26
trump 27.17
trumpery 4.43
trumpet 30.23
trumpeter 12.78
trumpeting 26.13
truncate 30.7
truncheon 25.49
trundle 23.28
trunk 21.34
trunking 26.7
Truro 9.21
truss 28.21
trusser 12.71
trust 31.24
trustee 4.1
truster 12.81
trusting 26.13
trustworthy 4.57
trusty 4.55
truth 32.12
try 6.1
trysail 23.37
tryst 31.6
tryster 12.78
tsar 1.1
tsardom 24.17
tsarevich 15.6
tsarina 12.54
tsarist 31.12
tsessebi 4.10
tsetse 4.45
T-shirt 30.45
T-square 2.15
tsunami 4.29
Tsushima 12.51
Tswana 12.53
tub 14.13
tuba 12.21
tubby 4.10
tube 14.12
tuber 12.21
tubercular 12.46
tuberculosis 28.11
tuberose 35.19
tuberous 28.31
tubful 23.21
tubifex 28.38
tubing 26.4
tubular 12.46

tuck 21.29
tucker 12.41
tucket 30.21
Tucson 25.26
Tudor 12.29
Tuesday 3.9
tufa 12.30
tuff 17.15
tuffet 30.21
tuft 30.47
tufty 4.55
tug 18.12
tugboat 30.35
tugger 12.32
tug-of-love 34.13
tug-of-war 7.1
tugrik 21.8
Tuileries 4.43
tuition 25.49
tuitional 23.34
Tula 12.45
tulip 27.6
Tull 23.22
Tullamore 7.12
tulle 23.20
Tulsa 12.71
tum 24.14
tumble 23.26
tumbledown 25.29
tumble-dry 6.1
tumble-dryer 12.13
tumbler 12.47
tumbleweed 16.7
tumbril 23.9
tumefaction 25.49
tumefy 6.7
tumescence 28.45
tumescent 30.56
tumid 16.10
tummy 4.30
tumor 12.52
tumour 12.52
tump 27.17
tumult 30.51
tumultuous 28.24
tumulus 28.27
tun 25.35
tuna 12.56
tunable 23.26
tundra 12.66
tune 25.33
tuner 12.56
tungsten 25.50
tunic 21.13
tunicate 30.10
tunicle 23.32
tuning 26.9
Tunis 28.9
Tunisia 12.12
Tunisian 25.37

tunnel 23.34
tunneler 12.48
tunneller 12.48
tunny 4.33
tup 27.13
Tupamaro 9.21
tupelo 9.17
Tupi 4.37
tuppence 28.45
tuppenny 4.34
Tupperware 2.15
tuque 21.27
turaco 9.16
Turanian 25.37
turban 25.38
turbary 4.43
turbid 16.8
turbine 25.21
turbo 9.9
turbocharge 20.2
turbocharger 12.35
turbocharging 26.6
turbofan 25.1
turbojet 30.4
turboprop 27.8
turboshaft 30.47
turbot 30.41
turbulence 28.45
turbulent 30.56
Turco 9.16
turd 16.31
tureen 25.9
turf 17.17
turfman 25.45
turfmen 25.45
turfy 4.14
Turgenev 17.3
turgescent 30.56
turgid 16.10
turgidity 4.53
Turin 25.13
Turing 26.11
Turk 21.31
Turkestan 25.4
turkey 4.20
Turkic 21.11
Turkish 29.8
Turkmenistan 25.4
Turkoman 25.45
turmeric 21.15
turmoil 23.19
turn 25.53
turnabout 30.34
turnaround 16.43
turnbuckle 23.32
turncoat 30.35
turner 12.59
turning 26.9
turnip 27.6
turnipy 4.36

turnkey 4.20
turnout 30.34
turnover 12.86
turnpike 21.19
turnsole 23.18
turnspit 30.23
turnstile 23.12
turnstone 25.31
turnup 27.13
turpentine 25.23
Turpin 25.18
turpitude 16.25
turps 28.46
turquoise 35.20
turret 30.24
turtle 23.39
turtle dove 34.13
turtleneck 21.6
turves 35.35
Tuscan 25.43
Tuscany 4.34
Tuscarora 12.66
tush 29.16
tusk 21.35
tusker 12.41
tussle 23.37
tussock 21.30
tussocky 4.20
tut 30.40
Tutankhamen 25.45
tutee 4.1
tutelage 20.6
tutelary 4.43
tutor 12.81
tutorage 20.8
tutorial 23.24
tutsan 25.48
Tutsi 4.47
tutti 4.55
tutti-frutti 4.54
tutu 11.20
Tuva 12.87
tu-whit tu-whoo 11.1
tux 28.41
tuxedo 9.11
Twa 1.1
twaddle 23.28
twaddler 12.48
twain 25.7
twang 26.1
twangy 4.35
twat 30.31
tweak 21.8
twee 4.1
tweed 16.7
tweedy 4.12
tweeny 4.31
tweet 30.18

tweeter 12.77
twelfth 32.16
twelve 34.15
twelvefold 16.37
twelvemonth 32.19
twentieth 32.6
twenty 4.51
twentyfold 16.37
twenty-twenty 4.51
twerp 27.15
Twi 4.1
twice 28.13
twiddle 23.28
twiddler 12.48
twiddly 4.27
twig 18.6
twilight 30.28
twilit 30.22
twill 23.8
twin 25.13
twine 25.21
twiner 12.55
twinge 20.19
Twining 26.9
twinkle 23.32
twinkler 12.43
twinkly 4.24
twinning 26.9
twinset 30.5
twintub 14.13
twirl 23.42
twirler 12.49
twirly 4.28
twist 31.6
twister 12.78
twisting 26.13
twisty 4.53
twit 30.20
twitch 15.6
twitcher 12.23
twitchy 4.11
twite 30.26
twitter 12.78
twitterer 12.67
twittery 4.43
twittish 29.10
twizzle 23.41
two 11.1
two-bit 30.20
two-by-four 7.1
two-dimensional 23.34
twofold 16.37
twoness 28.29
twopence 28.45
twopenny 4.33
twopenny-halfpenny 4.31
two-piece 28.6

t

t
u

uncircumcised 16.50
unclaimed 16.39
unclassified 16.14
uncle 23.32
unclimbed 16.39
unclouded 16.9
uncluttered 16.29
unco 9.16
uncollected 16.12
uncolored 16.29
uncoloured 16.29
uncombed 16.39
uncommitted 16.12
uncompensated 16.12
uncomplaining 26.9
uncompleted 16.12
uncomplicated 16.12
uncomprehending 26.5
uncompromising 26.14
unconcealed 16.35
unconditioned 16.45
unconfined 16.42
unconfirmed 16.39
unconnected 16.12
unconquered 16.28
unconsecrated 16.12
unconsenting 26.13
unconsidered 16.28
unconstrained 16.41
unconstricted 16.12
unconsumed 16.39
unconsummated 16.12
uncontaminated 16.12
uncontested 16.12
uncontrived 16.49
uncontrolled 16.37
uncontroverted 16.12
unconverted 16.12
unconvinced 31.30
unconvincing 26.12
uncooked 30.49
uncoordinated 16.12
uncorrected 16.12
uncorroborated 16.12
uncorrupted 16.12
uncounted 16.12
uncovenanted 16.12
uncreased 31.5
uncredited 16.12

uncrowded 16.9
uncrumpled 16.38
unction 25.49
unctuous 28.24
uncultivated 16.12
uncultured 16.28
uncured 16.28
uncurtained 16.42
undamaged 16.34
undated 16.12
undaunted 16.12
undecided 16.9
undeclared 16.5
undecorated 16.12
undefeated 16.12
undefended 16.9
undefiled 16.36
undefined 16.42
undelivered 16.29
undemanding 26.5
undented 16.12
under 12.29
underachieve 34.5
underachiever 12.85
underact 30.48
under-age 20.4
underarm 24.2
underbelly 4.22
underbid 16.8
underbred 16.3
undercarriage 20.8
undercharge 20.2
underclass 28.2
underclothes 35.19
underclothing 26.14
undercoat 30.35
undercook 21.28
undercover 12.87
undercroft 30.47
undercurrent 30.56
undercut 30.40
underdeveloped 30.58
underdog 18.8
underdone 25.35
underdrawing 26.3
underdress 28.3
undereducated 16.12
underemphasis 28.11
underemployed 16.24
underestimate 30.12, 30.43
underexpose 35.19
underfed 16.3
underfelt 30.51
underfloor 7.1
underflow 9.17
underfoot 30.39

underframe 24.4
underfunded 16.9
underfunding 26.5
undergird 16.31
underglaze 35.5
undergo 9.1
undergone 25.24
undergrad 16.1
undergraduate 30.41
underground 16.43
undergrowth 32.11
underhand 16.40
underhanded 16.9
underlain 25.7
underlay 3.1, 3.15
underlease 28.6
underlet 30.4
underlie 6.1
underline 25.21, 25.22
underlinen 25.18
underling 26.8
undermanned 16.40
undermanning 26.9
undermentioned 16.45
undermine 25.21
undermost 31.20
underneath 32.5
undernourished 30.59
underpaid 16.6
underpainting 26.13
underpants 28.44
underpart 30.3
underpass 28.2
underperform 24.9
underpin 25.13
underpinning 26.9
underplant 30.53
underpopulated 16.12
underpowered 16.28
underprepared 16.5
underprice 28.13
underpriced 31.16
underprivileged 16.34
underproduction 25.49
underproof 17.13
underprop 27.8
underrate 30.7
under-rehearsed 31.26
under-represented 16.12
under-resourced 31.18

underscore 7.1, 7.10
undersea 4.1
underseal 23.7
undersecretary 4.43
undersell 23.3
undersexed 31.28
undershirt 30.45
undershoot 30.37
undershorts 28.47
undershot 30.31
underside 16.16
undersigned 16.42
undersized 16.50
underskirt 30.45
underslung 26.18
undersold 16.37
undersow 9.1
undersown 25.30
underspend 16.41
underspent 30.53
understaffed 30.47
understaffing 26.6
understairs 35.4
understand 16.40
understander 12.25
understanding 26.5
understate 30.7
understater 12.77
understood 16.26
understorey 4.41
understudy 4.13
undersubscribed 16.32
undersurface 28.7
undertake 21.7
undertaker 12.38
undertaking 26.7
underthings 35.32
undertone 25.31
undertook 21.28
undertow 9.25
undertrained 16.41
undertrick 21.15
underused 16.50
underutilize 35.12
undervalue 11.22
undervest 31.3
underwater 12.80
underwear 2.15
underweight 30.7
underwent 30.53
underwhelm 24.18
underwing 26.14
underwire 12.14
underwired 16.28
underwood 16.26
underwork 21.31
underworld 16.38
underwrite 30.26
underwriter 12.79

u

underwritten 25.50
undeserved 16.49
undesigned 16.42
undesired 16.28
undetected 16.12
undetermined 16.42
undeterred 16.31
undeveloped 30.58
undeviating 26.13
undiagnosed 16.50
undies 35.10
undifferentiated 16.12
undigested 16.12
undiluted 16.12
undiminished 30.59
undimmed 16.39
undine 25.10
undirected 16.12
undischarged 16.34
undisclosed 16.50
undiscovered 16.29
undiscriminating 26.13
undiscussed 31.24
undisguised 16.50
undismayed 16.6
undisputed 16.12
undissolved 16.49
undistinguished 30.59
undistorted 16.12
undistributed 16.12
undisturbed 16.32
undivided 16.9
undocumented 16.12
undomesticated 16.12
undoubted 16.12
undrained 16.41
undraped 30.58
undreamed 16.39
undulant 30.56
undulate 30.11
undy 4.13
undyed 16.14
unearned 16.46
uneaten 25.50
unedifying 26.3
unedited 16.12
uneducated 16.12
unelected 16.12
unembarrassed 31.25
unembellished 30.59
unemployed 16.24
unenclosed 16.50
unencumbered 16.28

unendowed 16.22
unengaged 16.34
unenlightened 16.45
unenlightening 26.9
unenvied 16.13
unequalize 35.12
unequipped 30.58
unerring 26.11
unescorted 16.12
unestablished 30.59
unexamined 16.42
unexampled 16.38
unexciting 26.13
unexecuted 16.12
unexpected 16.12
unexpired 16.28
unexplained 16.41
unexploded 16.9
unexploited 16.12
unexplored 16.19
unexposed 16.50
unexpressed 31.3
unexpurgated 16.12
unfading 26.5
unfancied 16.11
unfathomed 16.39
unfazed 16.50
unfeigned 16.41
unfenced 31.30
unfermented 16.12
unfilled 16.35
unfiltered 16.29
unfinished 30.59
unfitted 16.12
unflagging 26.6
unflattering 26.11
unflavored 16.29
unflavoured 16.29
unfledged 16.34
unfleshed 30.59
unflinching 26.12
unfocused 31.25
unforced 31.18
unforgiving 26.14
unformed 16.39
unformulated 16.12
unfortified 16.14
unfounded 16.9
unframed 16.39
unfrequented 16.12
unfulfilled 16.35
unfulfilling 26.8
unfunded 16.9
unfurnished 30.59
ungainly 4.22
ungifted 16.12
unglazed 16.50
ungloved 16.49
unglued 16.25

ungrounded 16.9
ungrudging 26.6
unguent 30.56
unguided 16.9
ungulate 30.42
unhallowed 16.23
unhampered 16.29
unharmed 16.39
unhatched 30.46
unhealed 16.35
unheard 16.31
unheated 16.12
unhedged 16.34
unheeded 16.9
unheeding 26.5
unheralded 16.9
unhesitating 26.13
unhindered 16.28
unhonoured 16.29
unhooded 16.9
unhoped 30.58
unhyphenated 16.12
uni 4.33
Uniate 30.41
unicameral 23.36
unicorn 25.28
unicycle 23.32
unicyclist 31.8
unidentified 16.14
unidirectional 23.34
unifier 12.14
uniflow 9.17
uniform 24.9
uniformity 4.53
unify 6.7
unilateral 23.36
unilateralist 31.8
unilluminated 16.12
unillustrated 16.12
unimpaired 16.5
unimpassioned 16.45
unimpeded 16.9
unimposing 26.14
unimpressed 31.3
unimproved 16.49
unincorporated 16.12
uninflected 16.12
uninfluenced 31.30
uninformed 16.39
uninhabited 16.12
uninhibited 16.12
uninitiated 16.12
uninjured 16.28
uninspired 16.28
uninspiring 26.11
uninstructed 16.12
uninsulated 16.12

uninsured 16.28
uninterested 16.12
uninteresting 26.13
uninterrupted 16.12
uninvestigated 16.12
uninvited 16.12
uninviting 26.13
uninvolved 16.49
union 25.37
unionist 31.10
uniplanar 12.54
unipod 16.18
unique 21.8
unironed 16.45
unisex 28.38
unisexual 23.25
unison 25.48
unit 30.23
Unitarian 25.37
unitarity 4.53
unitary 4.43
unite 30.26
United Nations 35.31
United States 28.47
unitive 34.8
unitize 35.14
unity 4.53
univalve 34.15
universal 23.37
universalist 31.8
universe 28.36
university 4.53
univocal 23.32
unjustified 16.14
unlabeled 16.38
unlabelled 16.38
unlamented 16.12
unleaded 16.9
unleavened 16.45
unlettered 16.29
unliberated 16.12
unlicensed 31.30
unlighted 16.12
unlined 16.42
unlisted 16.12
unlooked 30.49
unloved 16.49
unloving 26.14
unmanaged 16.34
unmannered 16.29
unmapped 30.58
unmarred 16.2
unmatched 30.46
unmeasured 16.28
unmediated 16.12
unmelted 16.12
unmentioned 16.45
unmerited 16.12

unmetalled 16.38
unmitigated 16.12
unmixed 31.28
unmodernized 16.50
unmodified 16.14
unmodulated 16.12
unmolested 16.12
unmotivated 16.12
unmounted 16.12
unmourned 16.42
unmoved 16.49
unmoving 26.14
unmurmuring 26.11
unnamed 16.39
unneeded 16.9
unnoticed 31.14
unnumbered 16.28
Uno 9.19
unobscured 16.28
unobserved 16.49
unobstructed 16.12
unoccupied 16.14
unoffending 26.5
unoiled 16.37
unopened 16.45
unopposed 16.50
unordered 16.28
unornamented 16.12
unowned 16.43
unpadded 16.9
unpainted 16.12
unpaired 16.5
unparalleled 16.35
unpatented 16.12
unpatronizing 26.14
unpaved 16.49
unpeeled 16.35
unpersuaded 16.9
unperturbed 16.32
unpitying 26.3
unplaced 31.4
unplanned 16.40
unplanted 16.12
unplayed 16.6
unpleasing 26.14
unploughed 16.22
unplowed 16.22
unplumbed 16.39
unpointed 16.12
unpolished 30.59
unpolled 16.37
unpolluted 16.12
unpopulated 16.12
unposed 16.50
unpowered 16.28
unpracticed 31.14
unpractised 31.14

unprecedented 16.12
unpredicted 16.12
unprejudiced 31.6
unpremeditated 16.12
unprepared 16.5
unprepossessing 26.12
unpressed 31.3
unpressurized 16.50
unpretending 26.5
unprimed 16.39
unprincipled 16.38
unprinted 16.12
unprocessed 31.3
unpromising 26.12
unprompted 16.12
unprotected 16.12
unprotesting 26.13
unprovided 16.9
unprovoked 30.49
unpublicized 16.50
unpublished 30.59
unpunctuated 16.12
unpunished 30.59
unpurified 16.14
unqualified 16.14
unquantified 16.14
unquenched 30.59
unquestioned 16.45
unquestioning 26.9
unrated 16.12
unreciprocated 16.12
unreclaimed 16.39
unreconciled 16.36
unreconstructed 16.12
unrecorded 16.9
unredeemed 16.39
unrefined 16.42
unreflecting 26.13
unreformed 16.39
unregarded 16.9
unregistered 16.29
unregulated 16.12
unrehearsed 31.26
unrelated 16.12
unrelaxed 31.28
unreleased 31.5
unrelenting 26.13
unrelieved 16.49
unremarked 30.48
unremembered 16.28
unremitting 26.13
unreported 16.12
unrepresented 16.12
unrequested 16.12

unrequited 16.12
unresisted 16.12
unresisting 26.13
unresolved 16.49
unresting 26.13
unrestored 16.19
unrestrained 16.41
unrestricted 16.12
unreturned 16.46
unrevealed 16.35
unrevised 16.50
unrewarded 16.9
unrewarding 26.5
unrhymed 16.39
unrivaled 16.38
unrivalled 16.38
unruffled 16.38
unruly 4.26
unsalaried 16.11
unsalted 16.12
unsanctified 16.14
unsanctioned 16.45
unsatisfied 16.14
unsatisfying 26.3
unsaturated 16.12
unsaved 16.49
unscaled 16.35
unscarred 16.2
unscathed 16.48
unscented 16.12
unscheduled 16.37
unschooled 16.37
unscreened 16.41
unscripted 16.12
unsealed 16.35
unseasoned 16.45
unsecured 16.28
unseeded 16.9
unseeing 26.3
unsegregated 16.12
unselected 16.12
unselfconscious 28.33
unseparated 16.12
unshaded 16.9
unshared 16.5
unshaved 16.49
unsheltered 16.29
unshielded 16.9
unsighted 16.12
unsigned 16.42
unsized 16.50
unskilled 16.35
unskimmed 16.39
unsleeping 26.10
unsliced 31.16
unsmiling 26.8
unsmoked 30.49
unsoiled 16.37
unsolicited 16.12

unsolved 16.49
unsophisticated 16.12
unsorted 16.12
unspeaking 26.7
unspecialized 16.50
unspecified 16.14
unspoiled 16.37
unsponsored 16.29
unsporting 26.13
unspotted 16.12
unsprayed 16.6
unstaffed 30.47
unstained 16.41
unstamped 30.52
unstated 16.12
unstinted 16.12
unstinting 26.13
unstirred 16.31
unstrained 16.41
unstressed 31.3
unstructured 16.28
unstudied 16.9
unstuffed 30.47
unsubdued 16.25
unsubstantiated 16.12
unsugared 16.28
unsuited 16.12
unsullied 16.10
unsummoned 16.45
unsupervised 16.50
unsupported 16.12
unsurfaced 31.7
unsurpassed 31.2
unsurprised 16.50
unsuspected 16.12
unsuspecting 26.13
unsustained 16.41
unswayed 16.6
unsweetened 16.45
unswerving 26.14
untainted 16.12
untalented 16.12
untamed 16.39
untanned 16.40
untapped 30.58
untarnished 30.59
untasted 16.12
untempered 16.29
untended 16.9
untenured 16.30
untested 16.12
unthanked 30.49
unthinking 26.7
unthreatening 26.9
until 23.8
untilled 16.35
untinged 16.34
untiring 26.11

u

untitled 16.38
unto 11.20
untouched 30.46
untraced 31.4
untracked 30.48
untrained 16.41
untrammeled 16.38
untrammelled 16.38
untransformed 16.39
untraveled 16.38
untravelled 16.38
untreated 16.12
untrimmed 16.39
untroubled 16.38
untuned 16.43
unturned 16.46
untutored 16.29
unuttered 16.29
unvalued 16.25
unvarnished 30.59
unvarying 26.3
unventilated 16.12
unverified 16.14
unversed 31.26
unvisited 16.12
unvitiated 16.12
unvoiced 31.21
unwaged 16.34
unwalled 16.36
unwanted 16.12
unwarned 16.42
unwarranted 16.12
unwashed 30.59
unwatched 30.46
unwatered 16.29
unwavering 26.11
unweaned 16.41
unwearied 16.11
unwearying 26.3
unwedded 16.9
unwhipped 30.58
unwinking 26.7
unwitnessed 31.10
unworked 30.49
unworried 16.11
unwounded 16.9
unwrinkled 16.38
up 27.13
up-anchor 12.37
up-and-coming 26.9
up-and-over 12.86
up-and-under 12.29
Upanishad 16.1
upas 28.30
upbeat 30.18
upbraid 16.6
upbraiding 26.5
upbringing 26.10
upbuild 16.35

upbuilt 30.51
upcast 31.2
upchuck 21.29
upcoming 26.9
upcountry 4.42
update 30.7, 30.9
Updike 21.19
upend 16.41
upfield 16.35
up-front 30.55
upgrade 16.6
upgrader 12.26
upgrowth 32.11
upheaval 23.40
upheave 34.5
upheld 16.35
uphill 23.8
uphold 16.37
upholder 12.28
upholster 12.80
upholsterer 12.67
upholstery 4.43
upkeep 27.5
upland 16.45
uplift 30.47
uplifter 12.78
uplighter 12.79
upload 16.23
upmarket 30.21
upmost 31.20
upon 25.24
upper 12.63
upper case 28.5
upper-class 28.2
uppercut 30.40
uppermost 31.20
uppish 29.9
uppity 4.53
Uppsala 12.42
upraise 35.5
uprate 30.7
uprating 26.13
upright 30.29
uprise 35.11
uprisen 25.52
uprising 26.14
upriver 12.86
uproar 7.15
uproarious 28.23
uproot 30.37
uprooter 12.81
uprose 35.19
uprush 29.16
upscale 23.5
upset 30.4, 30.5
upsetter 12.76
upshift 30.47
upshot 30.32
upside 16.16

upside-down 25.29
upsides 35.27
upsilon 25.44
upstage 20.4
upstairs 35.4
upstanding 26.5
upstart 30.3
upstate 30.7
upstater 12.77
upstream 24.5
upstroke 21.24
upsurge 20.17
upswept 30.58
upswing 26.14
upsy-daisy 4.61
uptake 21.7
uptempo 9.20
upthrow 9.21
upthrust 31.24
uptight 30.26
up-to-date 30.7
uptown 25.29
uptowner 12.56
upturn 25.53
upturned 16.46
upward 16.30
upwelling 26.8
upwind 16.42
Ur 13.1
uraei 6.2
uraemia 12.7
uraeus 28.22
Uralic 21.11
Urania 12.8
uranium 24.16
Uranus 28.29
urban 25.38
urbane 25.7
urbanist 31.10
urbanite 30.29
urbanity 4.53
urchin 25.13
Urdu 11.6
urea 12.3
ureter 12.77
urethra 12.65
urethral 23.36
Urey 4.43
urge 20.17
urgency 4.48
urgent 30.56
urger 12.36
urging 26.6
Uriah 12.13
Uriel 23.24
urinal 23.34
urinary 4.43
urinate 30.13
urine 25.18

urn 25.53
urogenital 23.39
urology 4.17
ursine 25.23
Ursula 12.46
Ursuline 25.22
Uruguay 6.21
Uruguayan 25.38
Uruk 21.28
us 28.21
usability 4.53
usable 23.26
usage 20.9
usance 28.45
use 28.19, 35.21
used 16.50, 31.22
useful 23.21
useless 28.27
user 12.92
user-friendly 4.22
usher 12.73
usherette 30.4
usquebaugh 7.4
Ustashe 4.50
Ustinov 17.8
usual 23.25
usurer 12.67
usurious 28.23
usurp 27.15
usurper 12.63
usury 4.43
Utah 7.18
Ute 30.37
utensil 23.9
uterine 25.23
uterus 28.31
utile 23.12
utilitarian 25.37
utility 4.53
utilizer 12.91
utmost 31.20
Utopia 12.9
Utopian 25.37
Utrecht 30.48
Utrillo 9.17
Utsire 12.67
Uttar Pradesh 29.3
utter 12.81
utterance 28.45
utterer 12.67
uttermost 31.20
Uttley 4.26
U-turn 25.53
uvula 12.46
uvulae 4.26
uxorial 23.24
uxoricidal 23.28
uxoricide 16.16

uxorious 28.23
Uzbek 21.6
Uzbekistan 25.4
Uzi 4.62

 V

Vaal 23.2
Vaasa 12.69
vac 21.1
vacancy 4.48
vacant 30.56
vacate 30.7
vacation 25.49
vacationer 12.58
vacationist 31.10
vaccinate 30.13
vaccine 25.11
vacillate 30.11
vacua 12.20
vacuity 4.53
vacuous 28.24
vacuum 24.12
vade mecum 24.18
Vaduz 35.21
vagabond 16.42
vagabondage 20.6
vagary 4.43
vagina 12.55
vaginal 23.34
vagrancy 4.48
vagrant 30.56
vague 18.4
vaguish 29.7
vail 23.5
vain 25.7
vainglorious 28.23
vainglory 4.41
Vaishnava 12.87
Vaisya 12.89
Val 23.1
valance 28.45
valanced 31.30
Valda 12.25
Valdemar 1.13
vale 23.5
valediction 25.49
valedictorian 25.37
valedictory 4.43
valence 28.45
valency 4.48
valentine 25.23
Valentino 9.19
valerian 25.37
Valerie 4.43
valet 30.22
valetudinarian 25.37

valetudinary 4.43
Valhalla 12.42
valiant 30.56
valid 16.10
validate 30.9
validity 4.53
valise 35.6
valium 24.16
Valkyrie 4.40
Valletta 12.76
valley 4.21
vallum 24.18
Valois 1.22
Valona 12.56
valonia 12.8
valor 12.42
valorous 28.31
valour 12.42
Valparaiso 9.29
valse 28.42
valuate 30.8
value 11.22
valuer 12.20
valve 34.15
vamoose 28.19
vamp 27.17
vampire 12.14
vampiric 21.15
vampish 29.9
vampy 4.36
van 25.1
vanadium 24.16
Vanbrugh 12.64
Van Buren 25.47
Vancouver 12.87
Vanda 12.25
vandal 23.28
Vandalic 21.11
Vanderbilt 30.51
Van Dyck 21.19
vandyke 21.19
vane 25.7
Vanessa 12.69
vang 26.1
vanguard 16.2
vanilla 12.43
vanish 29.9
vanity 4.53
vanquish 29.10
vanquisher 12.72
vantage 20.9
vantage point 30.55
Vanuatu 11.20
Vanya 12.89
vapid 16.10
vapidity 4.53
vapor 12.61
vaporetti 4.51
vaporetto 9.24
vaporish 29.9

vaporous 28.31
vapory 4.43
vapour 12.61
vapourish 29.9
vapoury 4.43
Varah 12.64
Varèse 35.3
Vargas 28.1
variance 28.45
variant 30.56
varicolored 16.29
varicoloured 16.29
varicose 28.17
varied 16.11
varietal 23.39
varietist 31.14
variety 4.53
varifocal 23.32
variform 24.9
various 28.23
varlet 30.22
varletry 4.40
varmint 30.54
varna 12.53
varnish 29.9
Varro 9.21
varsity 4.53
vary 4.39
Vasari 4.38
Vasco da Gama 12.50
vascular 12.46
vas deferens 35.31
vase 35.2
vasectomy 4.30
vaseline 25.10
vassal 23.37
vast 31.2
vat 30.1
Vatican 25.43
Vaticanist 31.10
vaticinal 23.34
Vättern 25.53
vaudeville 23.10
vaudevillian 25.37
Vaudois 1.22
Vaughan 25.28
vault 30.51
vaulter 12.80
vaunt 30.54
vaunter 12.80
vavasory 4.43
veal 23.7
Veblen 25.44
vector 12.76
vectorial 23.24
vectorize 35.13
Veda 12.26
Vedanta 12.75
Vedantic 21.17

Vedda 12.26
vedette 30.4
Vedic 21.10
veep 27.5
veer 12.4
veg 20.3
Vega 12.31
vegan 25.41
Vegeburger 12.32
Vegemite 30.29
vegetal 23.39
vegetarian 25.37
vegetate 30.16
veggie 4.17
vehemence 28.45
vehicle 23.32
vehicular 12.46
veil 23.5
veiling 26.8
vein 25.7
vein like 21.19
veiny 4.31
velar 12.43
Velázquez 35.10
velcro 9.21
veld 30.51
veldskoen 25.33
veleta 12.77
vellum 24.18
Velma 12.50
velocimeter 12.78
velocipede 16.7
velocity 4.53
velodrome 24.11
velour 12.20
velouté 3.22
velum 24.18
velvet 30.25
velveteen 25.9
velvety 4.53
vena cava 12.85
venae cavae 4.58
venal 23.34
venality 4.53
vend 16.41
Venda 12.26
vendace 28.7
vendetta 12.76
vendeuse 35.25
vendible 23.26
vendor 7.5
vendue 11.1
veneer 12.4
venerate 30.15
venereal 23.24
venery 4.43
Venetia 12.72
venetian 25.49
Venezuela 12.43
Venezuelan 25.44

u
v

vengeance 35.31
venial 23.24
Venice 28.9
venison 25.48
venom 24.19
venomous 28.28
venous 28.29
vent 30.53
ventiduct 30.49
ventil 23.9
ventilate 30.11
Ventolin 25.16
ventouse 28.19
ventral 23.36
ventricle 23.32
ventriloquial 23.24
ventriloquist 31.15
ventriloquize 35.15
ventriloquy 4.59
venture 12.72
venturer 12.67
venue 11.22
Venus 28.29
Venusian 25.37
Vera 12.67
veracious 28.33
veracity 4.53
Veracruz 35.21
veranda 12.25
verb 14.15
verbal 23.26
verbalist 31.8
verbalizer 12.91
verbatim 24.6
verbena 12.54
verbiage 20.6
verbose 28.17
verbosity 4.53
verboten 25.50
verdancy 4.49
verdant 30.56
Verdelho 11.22
Verdi 4.12
verdict 30.49
verdigris 4.40
Verdun 25.35
verdure 12.36
verdurous 28.31
Vere 12.4
Vereeniging 26.6
verge 20.17
verger 12.36
verglas 1.12
veridical 23.32
veriest 31.6
verifier 12.14
verify 6.7
verisimilar 12.43
verisimilitude 16.25
verism 24.21

verismo 9.18
veristic 21.17
verity 4.53
verjuice 28.19
Verlaine 25.7
Vermeer 12.4
vermeil 23.5
vermian 25.37
vermicelli 4.22
vermicular 12.46
vermilion 25.37
vermin 25.17
verminate 30.13
verminous 28.29
Vermont 30.54
vermouth 32.13
vernacular 12.46
vernacularity 4.53
vernacularize 35.13
vernal 23.34
vernalize 35.12
Verne 25.53
Verner 12.59
vernicle 23.32
vernissage 19.1
Vernon 25.46
Verny 4.34
Verona 12.56
Veronese 4.61
veronica 12.39
veronique 21.8
verruca 12.41
verrucae 4.20
Versailles 6.1
versant 30.56
versatile 23.12
versatility 4.53
verse 28.36
verselet 30.22
verset 30.24
versicle 23.32
versicolored 16.29
versicoloured 16.29
versifier 12.14
versify 6.7
version 25.49
versional 23.34
vers libre 12.65
verso 9.22
verst 31.26
versus 28.32
vert 30.45
vertebra 12.65
vertebrae 3.19
vertebrate 30.43
vertex 28.38
vertical 23.32
verticalize 35.12
vertices 35.8
vertiginous 28.29

vertigo 9.13
vervain 25.8
verve 34.14
Verwoerd 30.41
very 4.38
Vesalius 28.23
vesicle 23.32
Vespa 12.61
Vespasian 25.42
vesper 12.61
vespertine 25.23
Vespucci 4.11
vessel 23.37
vest 31.3
vesta 12.76
vestal 23.39
vestee 4.1
vestiary 4.43
vestibule 23.20
vestige 20.9
vestigial 23.24
vestiture 12.23
vestry 4.38
vestryman 25.45
vestrymen 25.45
vesture 12.23
Vesuvius 28.23
vet 30.4
vetch 15.3
vetchling 26.8
veteran 25.47
veterinarian 25.37
veterinary 4.43
veto 9.24
vetoer 12.17
vex 28.38
vexation 25.49
vexatious 28.33
vexer 12.69
vexilla 12.43
vexillum 24.18
Vi 6.1
via 12.13
viability 4.53
viable 23.26
Via Dolorosa 12.71
viaduct 30.49
Viagra 12.64
vial 23.25
viand 16.45
viatica 12.39
viaticum 24.18
vibe 14.8
vibes 35.26
vibist 31.6
vibrancy 4.48
vibrant 30.56
vibraphone 25.30
vibraphonist 31.10
vibrate 30.7

vibrato 9.24
vibratory 4.43
Vic 21.9
vicar 12.39
vicarage 20.8
vicarial 23.24
vicariate 30.41
vicarious 28.23
vice 4.46, 28.13
vice-like 21.19
viceregal 23.30
vicereine 25.7
viceroy 10.11
viceroyal 23.25
vice versa 12.71
Vichy 4.50
vichyssoise 35.2
vicinal 23.34
vicinity 4.53
vicious 28.33
vicissitude 16.25
vicissitudinous 28.29
Vicksburg 18.13
Vicky 4.19
Vico 9.16
vicomte 30.54
vicomtesse 28.3
victim 24.6
victimizer 12.91
victor 12.78
victoria 12.10
Victorian 25.37
Victoriana 12.53
victorious 28.23
victory 4.43
victual 23.39
victualer 12.48
victualler 12.48
vicuña 12.56
Vidal 23.2
vide 4.12
videlicet 30.5
video 9.4
videoconferencing 26.12
videophone 25.30
video recorder 12.28
videorecording 26.5
videotape 27.4
vie 6.1
vielle 23.3
Vienna 12.53
Viennese 35.6
Vientiane 25.4
Vietcong 26.15
Vietminh 25.13
Vietnam 24.1
Vietnamese 35.6

V

Voltaire 2.1
volte 30.51
volte-face 28.2
voluble 23.26
volume 24.12
voluminous 28.29
voluntarist 31.12
voluntary 4.43
volunteer 12.4
voluptuary 4.43
voluptuous 28.24
volute 30.37
voluted 16.12
volution 25.49
volvox 28.40
vomit 30.23
vomitoria 12.10
vomitorium 24.16
vomitory 4.43
Vonnegut 30.40
voodoo 11.6
voodooist 31.6
voracious 28.33
voracity 4.53
vortex 28.38
vortical 23.32
vortices 35.8
vorticist 31.13
vorticose 28.17
Vosges 19.5
Vostok 21.21
votarist 31.12
votary 4.43
vote 30.35
voter 12.80
votive 34.8
vouch 15.9
voucher 12.24
vouchsafe 17.4
Vouvray 3.19
vow 8.1
vowel 23.25
vox populi 4.26
voyage 20.6
voyager 12.35
voyageur 13.1
voyeur 13.1
vroom 24.12
V-sign 25.23
Vulcan 25.43
Vulcanian 25.37
vulgar 12.32
vulgarian 25.37
vulgarity 4.53
vulgate 30.9
vulpine 25.23
vulture 12.24
vulturine 25.23
vulturish 29.9
vulturous 28.31

vulva 12.87
vying 26.3

Waal 23.2
wack 21.1
wacko 9.16
wacky 4.18
wad 16.18
wadding 26.5
waddle 23.28
waddler 12.48
wade 16.6
wader 12.26
wadi 4.13
Wadi Halfa 12.30
wafer 12.30
wafery 4.43
waffle 23.29
waffler 12.48
waffly 4.27
waft 30.47
wag 18.1
wage 20.4
wager 12.35
Wagga Wagga 12.32
waggish 29.7
waggle 23.30
waggly 4.27
Wagnerian 25.37
wagon 25.41
wagoner 12.58
wagonette 30.4
wagon-lit 4.1
wagonload 16.23
wagtail 23.6
Wahhabi 4.10
wahine 4.31
wahoo 11.1
wah-wah 1.22
waif 17.4
waifish 29.7
waiflike 21.19
Waikato 9.24
Waikiki 4.1
wail 23.5
wailer 12.43
wailing 26.8
wain 25.7
wainscot 30.42
wainwright 30.29
waist 31.4
waistband 16.40
waistcoat 30.35
waistline 25.22
wait 30.7
waiter 12.77

waitress 28.10
waive 34.4
waiver 12.85
wake 21.7
Wakefield 16.35
waken 25.43
waker 12.38
wakey-wakey 4.18
Waldemar 1.13
Waldenses 35.8
Waldensian 25.37
Waldheim 24.7
Waldo 9.11
wale 23.5
Wales 35.29
walk 21.22
walkabout 30.34
walkathon 25.26
walker 12.40
walkies 35.10
walkie-talkie 4.19
walk-in 25.15
Walkman 25.45
walk-on 25.25
walkout 30.34
walkover 12.86
walk-through 11.17
walk-up 27.13
walkway 3.25
wall 23.14
wallaby 4.10
Wallace 28.8
Wallachia 12.6
wallah 12.44
wallaroo 11.1
Wallasey 4.48
wallchart 30.3
wallcovering 26.11
Wallenberg 18.13
Waller 12.44
wallet 30.22
wall eye 6.11
wall-eyed 16.14
wallflower 12.16
Walloon 25.33
wallop 27.14
walloper 12.63
wallow 9.17
wallpaper 12.61
Walls 35.29
wally 4.25
walnut 30.40
Walpole 23.18
walrus 28.31
Walsall 23.15
Walsh 29.19
Walsingham 24.19
Walter 12.80
Walton 25.50
waltz 28.42

waltzer 12.70
wampum 24.19
wan 25.24
wand 16.42
Wanda 12.28
wander 12.28
wanderer 12.67
wandering 26.11
wanderlust 31.24
wane 25.7
waney 4.31
Wanganui 4.8
wangle 23.30
wangler 12.48
wank 21.33
wanker 12.37
wanky 4.18
wanly 4.25
wanna 12.56
wannabe 4.10
wanness 28.29
want 30.54
wanter 12.79
wanton 25.50
wapentake 21.7
war 7.1
waratah 1.1
Warbeck 21.6
warble 23.26
warbler 12.44
Warburg 18.13
warby 4.10
ward 16.19
warden 25.40
warder 12.28
wardrobe 14.11
ware 2.1
warehouse 28.16
warehouseman 25.45
warehousemen 25.45
warfare 2.5
warfarin 25.18
Wargrave 34.4
warhead 16.3
Warhol 23.17
warhorse 28.15
Waring 26.11
warlike 21.19
warlock 21.21
warlord 16.21
warm 24.9
warm-blooded 16.9
warmer 12.52
warm-hearted 16.12
warmish 29.8
warmonger 12.32
warmth 32.18
warm-up 27.13
warn 25.28

warner 12.56
warning 26.9
warp 27.9
warpage 20.7
warpaint 30.54
warpath 32.2
warper 12.62
warplane 25.8
warrant 30.56
warrantee 4.1
warranter 12.82
warrantor 7.1
warranty 4.55
warren 25.47
warrigal 23.30
Warrington 25.50
warrior 12.10
Warsaw 7.16
warship 27.6
wart 30.33
warthog 18.8
wartime 24.7
wartorn 25.28
warty 4.54
Warwick 21.15, 21.18
Warwickshire 12.11
wary 4.39
was 35.16
wash 29.11
washbag 18.1
washbasin 25.48
washboard 16.20
washcloth 32.8
washday 3.9
washer 12.73
washerman 25.45
washermen 25.45
washerwoman 25.45
washerwomen 25.17
Washington 25.50
Washingtonian 25.37
washing-up 27.13
washland 16.40
washout 30.34
washroom 24.12
washstand 16.40
washtub 14.13
wash-up 27.13
washy 4.50
wasn't 30.56
wasp 27.18
waspie 4.36
waspish 29.9
waspy 4.36
wassail 23.6
wassail-bowl 23.17
wassailer 12.43
wastage 20.9
waste 31.4

wasteland 16.40
waster 12.77
wastrel 23.36
Wat 30.31
watch 15.7
watch chain 25.7
watchdog 18.8
watcher 12.24
watchfire 12.14
watchmaker 12.38
watchman 25.45
watchmen 25.45
watchnight 30.29
watch spring 26.11
watchtower 12.16
watchword 16.31
water 12.80
waterbed 16.3
waterbird 16.31
waterborne 25.28
watercolor 12.47
watercolour 12.47
watercourse 28.15
watercraft 30.47
watercress 28.3
waterer 12.67
waterfall 23.15
waterfowl 23.16
waterfront 30.55
watergate 30.9
waterhole 23.17
Waterhouse 28.16
watering 26.11
waterline 25.22
waterlogged 16.33
Waterloo 11.1
waterman 25.45
watermark 21.5
watermelon 25.44
watermen 25.45
watermill 23.9
water power 12.16
waterproof 17.13
waterproofer 12.30
water-repellent 30.56
water-resistant 30.56
Waters 35.24
watershed 16.4
waterside 16.16
waterspout 30.34
watertight 30.30
waterway 3.25
waterweed 16.7
waterwheel 23.7
water wings 35.32
waterworks 28.41
watery 4.43
Watford 16.28

Watkin 25.15
Watson 25.48
Watt 30.31
wattage 20.9
Watteau 9.25
wattle 23.39
Watts 28.47
Watusi 4.47
Waugh 7.1
waul 23.14
wave 34.4
waveband 16.40
wavelength 32.20
wavelet 30.22
waver 12.85
waverer 12.67
wavery 4.43
wavy 4.58
wax 28.38
waxberry 4.43
waxbill 23.8
waxcloth 32.8
waxen 25.48
waxer 12.69
waxing 26.12
waxwing 26.14
waxwork 21.31
waxy 4.45
way 3.1
waybill 23.8
wayfarer 12.65
wayfaring 26.11
waylay 3.1
waylayer 12.2
waymark 21.5
waymarker 12.37
Wayne 25.7
way-out 30.34
wayside 16.16
wayward 16.30
wazzock 21.30
we 4.1
weak 21.8
weaken 25.43
weakener 12.58
weakish 29.8
weak-kneed 16.7
weakling 26.8
weakly 4.23
weal 23.7
wealden 25.40
wealth 32.17
wealthy 4.56
wean 25.9
weaner 12.54
weapon 25.46
weaponry 4.43
wear 2.1
Wear 12.4
wearer 12.65

wearing 26.11
weary 4.43
weasel 23.41
weaselly 4.27
weather 12.84
weatherbeaten 25.50
weatherboard 16.20
weatherbound 16.43
weathercock 21.20
weathergirl 23.42
weather glass 28.2
weatherly 4.27
weatherman 25.2
weathermen 25.5
weatherproof 17.13
weatherstrip 27.6
weathervane 25.8
weave 34.5
weaver 12.85
weaverbird 16.31
weaving 26.14
web 14.3
Webb 14.3
Weber 12.21
weblog 18.8
website 30.30
Webster 12.76
we'd 16.7
wed 16.3
wedding 26.5
Wedekind 16.42
wedge 20.3
wedgie 4.17
Wedgwood 16.26
wedlock 21.21
Wednesday 3.9
wee 4.1
weed 16.7
weeder 12.26
weedkiller 12.43
weedy 4.12
week 21.8
weekday 3.9
weekend 16.41
weekender 12.26
weekly 4.23
Weeks 28.38
ween 25.9
weeny 4.31
weep 27.5
weeper 12.61
weepy 4.36
weever 12.85
weevil 23.10
weevily 4.24
weewee 4.59
weft 30.47
Wehrmacht 30.48

Wei 3.1
weigh 3.1
weigher 12.2
weigh-in 25.13
weight 30.7
weighting 26.13
weightlifter 12.78
weightlifting 26.13
weight-watchers 35.24
weighty 4.52
Weil 23.11
Weimar 1.13
weir 12.4
weird 16.28
weirdo 9.11
Weismann 25.45
Weissmuller 12.46
weka 12.37
welcome 24.18
welcomer 12.52
weld 16.35
welder 12.26
welfare 2.5
welfarist 31.12
welkin 25.15
well 23.3
we'll 23.7
well-being 26.3
wellington 25.50
Wells 35.29
wellspring 26.11
well-to-do 11.1
well-wisher 12.72
welly 4.22
welsh 29.19
welsher 12.72
Welshman 25.45
Welshmen 25.45
Welshwoman 25.45
Welshwomen 25.17
welt 30.51
welter 12.76
welterweight 30.17
Weltschmerz 28.47
Wenceslas 28.27
wench 29.20
wencher 12.72
wend 16.41
Wenda 12.26
Wendell 23.28
Wendic 21.10
Wendish 29.6
Wendy 4.12
Wensleydale 23.5
went 30.53
wept 30.58
were 13.1
we're 12.4
weren't 30.57

werewolf 17.18
werewolves 35.35
Werner 12.59
Weser 12.90
Wesker 12.37
Wesley 4.22
Wesleyan 25.37
Wessex 28.39
west 31.3
westbound 16.43
West Bromwich 20.7
westerly 4.27
western 25.50
westerner 12.58
westernizer 12.91
westernmost 31.20
westing 26.13
Westmeath 32.5
Westminster 12.78
Westmorland 16.45
Weston-super-Mare 2.1
Westphalia 12.6
Westphalian 25.37
westward 16.30
wet 30.4
wetback 21.2
wether 12.84
wetland 16.40
wet look 21.28
wetly 4.22
wetness 28.29
wet nurse 28.36
wetsuit 30.38
wetting 26.13
wettish 29.10
we've 34.5
Wexford 16.28
wey 3.1
Weymouth 32.13
whack 21.1
whacker 12.37
whacking 26.7
whacko 9.1
whale 23.5
whaleback 21.2
whaleboat 30.35
whalebone 25.30
whaler 12.43
wham 24.1
whammy 4.29
whang 26.1
Whangarei 3.1
whare 4.41
wharf 17.9
wharfie 4.14
wharfinger 12.35
Wharton 25.50
wharves 35.35

what 30.31
whatever 12.85
whatnot 30.32
whatsit 30.24
whatsoever 12.85
whaup 27.9
wheat 30.18
wheatear 12.12
wheaten 25.50
wheatgerm 24.22
wheatgrass 28.2
wheatmeal 23.7
Wheatstone 25.31
whee 4.1
wheedle 23.28
wheedler 12.48
wheel 23.7
wheelbarrow 9.21
wheelbase 28.5
wheelchair 2.4
wheel clamp 27.17
wheeler 12.43
wheeler-dealer 12.43
wheeler-dealing 26.8
wheelhouse 28.16
wheelie 4.23
wheeling 26.8
wheelsman 25.45
wheelsmen 25.45
wheelspin 25.18
wheelwright 30.29
Wheen 25.9
wheeze 35.6
wheezer 12.90
wheezy 4.61
whelk 21.32
whelp 27.16
when 25.5
whence 28.44
whenever 12.85
whensoever 12.85
where 2.1
whereabouts 28.47
whereafter 12.75
whereas 35.1
whereat 30.1
whereby 6.1
wherefore 7.6
wherefrom 24.8
wherein 25.13
whereof 34.10
whereon 25.24
wheresoever 12.85
whereto 11.1
whereupon 25.24
wherever 12.85
wherewith 33.4

wherewithal 23.14, 23.15
wherry 4.38
whet 30.4
whether 12.84
whetstone 25.31
whetter 12.76
whew 11.1
whey 3.1
which 15.6
whichever 12.85
whichsoever 12.85
whicker 12.39
whiff 17.6
whiffle 23.29
whiffy 4.61
Whig 18.6
whiggery 4.43
whiggish 29.7
while 23.11
whilom 24.18
whilst 31.29
whim 24.6
whimbrel 23.36
whimper 12.62
whimperer 12.67
whimpering 26.11
whimsical 23.32
whimsy 4.61
whim-wham 24.1
whin 25.13
whinchat 30.1
whine 25.21
whiner 12.55
whinge 20.19
whinger 12.35
whingy 4.17
whinny 4.32
whinstone 25.31
whiny 4.32
whip 27.6
whipcord 16.21
whiplash 29.1
whipper 12.62
whipper-in 25.13
whippersnapper 12.61
whippet 30.23
whipping 26.10
whippoorwill 23.10
whippy 4.36
whip-round 16.43
whipsaw 7.16
whirl 23.42
whirler 12.49
whirligig 18.6
whirlpool 23.20
whirlwind 16.42
whirlybird 16.31
whirr 13.1

whisht 30.59
whisk 21.35
whisker 12.39
whiskery 4.43
whisky 4.19
whisper 12.62
whisperer 12.67
whispering 26.11
whist 31.6
whistle 23.37
whistler 12.48
whistle-stop 27.8
whit 30.20
Whitby 4.10
white 30.26
whitebait 30.9
whiteboard 16.20
whitecap 27.1
white-collar 12.44
white currant 30.56
whiteface 28.5
whitefish 29.7
whitefly 6.11
Whitehall 23.15
whitehead 16.3
Whitehorse 28.15
White House 28.16
whiten 25.50
whitener 12.58
white-out 30.34
whitethroat 30.35
whitewall 23.15
whitewash 29.11
whitewasher 12.73
Whitewater 12.80
whitewood 16.26
whitey 4.54
whither 12.84
whiting 26.13
whitish 29.10
Whitlam 24.18
Whitman 25.45
Whitney 4.32
Whitsun 25.48
Whitsuntide 16.17
Whittier 12.12
Whittington 25.50
whittle 23.39
Whitworth 32.14
whiz-bang 26.1
whizz 35.10
whizz-kid 16.10
whizzo 9.29
who 11.1
whoa 9.1
who'd 16.25
whodunit 30.23
whodunnit 30.23
whoever 12.85
whole 23.17

wholefood 16.25
wholegrain 25.8
wholehearted 16.12
wholemeal 23.7
wholesale 23.6
wholesaler 12.43
wholewheat 30.19
whom 24.12
whomever 12.85
whomp 27.17
whomsoever 12.85
whoop 27.11
whoopee 4.1, 4.37
whooper 12.63
whoops 28.46
whoosh 29.15
whop 27.8
whopper 12.62
who're 12.19
whore 7.1
whoredom 24.17
whorehouse 28.16
whoremonger 12.32
Whorf 17.9
whorish 29.9
whorl 23.42
whortleberry 4.38
who's 35.21
whose 35.21
whosoever 12.85
whump 27.17
why 6.1
Whyalla 12.42
whydah 12.27
Whymper 12.62
Wicca 12.39
Wiccan 25.43
Wichita 7.18
wick 21.9
wicked 16.10
wicker 12.39
wickerwork 21.31
wicket 30.21
wicketkeeper 12.61
wicketkeeping 26.10
Wicklow 9.17
Wicks 28.39
widdershins 35.31
wide 16.14
wide-angle 23.30
wideawake 21.7
widen 25.40
widener 12.58
widening 26.9
widescreen 25.11
widespread 16.4
widget 30.21
widish 29.6
Widnes 28.9

widow 9.11
widower 12.17
widowhood 16.26
width 32.15
widthways 35.5
Wieland 16.45
wield 16.35
wielder 12.26
wieldy 4.12
wiener 12.54
Wiesbaden 25.40
Wiesel 23.37
Wiesenthal 23.2
wife 17.7
wifehood 16.26
wifely 4.25
wife-swapping 26.10
wig 18.6
Wigan 25.41
wigeon 25.14
wigging 26.6
wiggle 23.30
wiggler 12.48
wiggly 4.25
wight 30.26
Wigtownshire 12.11
wigwag 18.1
wigwam 24.1
Wilberforce 28.15
Wilbur 12.21
Wilcox 28.40
wild 16.36
wildcat 30.1
Wilde 16.36
wildebeest 31.5
Wilder 12.27
wildfire 17.14
wildfowl 23.16
wilding 26.5
wildish 29.6
wildlife 17.7
wildwood 16.26
wile 23.11
Wilfred 16.11
wilful 23.21
Wilhelmina 12.54
Wilhelmshaven 25.51
Wilkie 4.19
Wilkins 35.31
will 23.8
Willa 12.43
Willard 16.2
willer 12.43
willet 30.22
willful 23.21
William 24.20
Williams 35.30

Williamsburg 18.13
Williamson 25.48
willing 26.8
will-o'-the-wisp 27.18
Willoughby 4.10
willow 9.17
willowherb 14.15
willowy 4.7
willpower 12.16
Wills 35.29
willy 4.24
willy-nilly 4.24
Wilma 12.51
Wilmer 12.51
Wilmot 30.31
Wilson 25.48
wilt 30.51
Wilton 25.50
Wiltshire 12.5
wily 4.25
Wimbledon 25.40
wimp 27.17
wimpish 29.9
wimple 23.35
wimpy 4.36
win 25.13
wince 28.44
wincer 12.70
wincey 4.46
winceyette 30.4
winch 29.20
wincher 12.72
Winckelmann 25.2
wind 16.42
windage 20.6
Windaus 28.16
windbag 18.1
windbound 16.43
windbreak 21.7
Windbreaker 12.38
windcheater 12.77
wind chill 23.8
winder 12.27
Windermere 12.7
windfall 23.15
wind farm 24.2
Windhoek 21.28
windhover 12.86
windjammer 12.50
windlass 28.27
windmill 23.9
window 9.11
windowpane 25.8
window seat 30.18
window-shop 27.8
window-shopper 12.62
windowsill 23.9
windpipe 27.7

W

windproof 17.13
windrow 9.21
windsail 23.37
Windscale 23.5
windscreen 25.11
windshield 16.35
windsock 21.21
Windsor 12.90
windstorm 24.9
windsurf 17.17
windsurfer 12.30
windswept 30.58
wind-up 27.13
windward 16.30
windy 4.12
wine 25.21
winebibber 12.21
winebibbing 26.4
wine glass 28.2
winegrower 12.17
winemaking 26.7
winery 4.43
wineskin 25.15
wing 26.3
wingback 21.2
wingding 26.5
winged 16.10, 16.47
winger 12.35, 12.60
wing half 17.2
winglet 30.22
wing-like 21.19
wingman 25.2
wingmen 25.5
wing nut 30.40
wingover 12.86
wingspan 25.3
wingspread 16.4
wingtip 27.6
Winifred 16.11
wink 21.33
winker 12.39
winkle 23.32
winkler 12.43
winless 28.8
Winnebago 9.13
winner 12.55
winning 26.9
Winnipeg 18.3
winnow 9.19
winnower 12.17
wino 9.19
Winona 12.56
winsome 24.20
Winston 25.50
winter 12.78
winterbourne 25.28
wintergreen 25.11
winterize 35.13
winterly 4.27
Winters 35.24

wintertime 24.7
Winthrop 27.8
Winton 25.50
wintry 4.40
wipe 27.7
wipeout 30.34
wiper 12.62
wire 12.13
wire-draw 7.15
wire-drawn 25.28
wireman 25.2
wiremen 25.5
wirepuller 12.46
wirepulling 26.8
wirer 12.67
wiring 26.11
Wirral 23.36
wiry 4.43
Wisconsin 25.19
Wisden 25.40
wisdom 24.17
wise 35.11
wiseacre 12.38
wisecrack 21.3
wisecracker 12.37
Wiseman 25.45
wish 29.6
wishbone 25.30
wishing well 23.4
wish-list 31.8
wish-wash 29.11
wishy-washy 4.50
wisp 27.18
wispy 4.36
wist 31.6
wisteria 12.10
wit 30.20
witan 25.50
witch 15.6
witchcraft 30.47
witchdoctor 12.79
witchery 4.43
witchetty 4.53
witch-hunt 30.55
witchlike 21.19
with 33.4
withal 23.14
withdraw 7.1
withdrawal 23.25
withdrawn 25.28
withdrew 11.1
wither 12.84
withers 35.24
withheld 16.35
withhold 16.37
withholder 12.28
within 25.13
without 30.34
withstand 16.40
withstander 12.25

withstood 16.26
withy 4.57
witless 28.8
witling 26.8
witness 28.9
Wittenberg 18.13
witter 12.78
wittering 26.11
Wittgenstein 25.23
witting 26.13
witty 4.53
Witwatersrand 16.40
wives 35.35
wiz 35.10
wizard 16.30
wizardly 4.27
wizardry 4.43
wizened 16.45
wo 9.1
woad 16.23
wobble 23.26
wobbler 12.48
wobbly 4.27
Wodehouse 28.16
wodge 20.11
woe 9.1
woebegone 25.25
woeful 23.21
wog 18.8
woggle 23.30
wok 21.20
woke 21.24
woken 25.43
Woking 26.7
wold 16.37
Wolf 17.18
wolfcub 14.13
Wolfe 17.18
Wolfgang 26.1
wolfhound 16.43
wolfish 29.7
wolf-like 21.19
wolfram 24.19
wolfskin 25.15
Wolfson 25.48
Wollaston 25.50
Wollongong 26.15
Wollstonecraft 30.47
Wolof 17.8
Wolsey 4.62
Wolverhampton 25.50
wolverine 25.11
wolves 35.35
woman 25.45
womanhood 16.26
womanish 29.9
womanizer 12.91

womankind 16.42
womanlike 21.19
womanly 4.27
womb 24.12
wombat 30.1
women 25.17
womenfolk 21.24
womenswear 2.15
won 25.24, 25.35
wonder 12.29
wonderer 12.67
wondering 26.11
wonderland 16.40
wondrous 28.31
wonky 4.19
won't 30.55
wont 30.55
wonted 16.12
wonton 25.24
woo 11.1
wooable 23.26
wood 16.26
woodbine 25.21
woodblock 21.21
woodcarver 12.85
woodcarving 26.14
woodchip 27.6
woodchuck 21.29
woodcock 21.20
woodcraft 30.47
woodcut 30.40
woodcutter 12.81
woodcutting 26.13
wooded 16.9
wooden 25.40
wooden-head 16.3
wooden-headed 16.9
woodland 16.45
woodlander 12.29
woodlark 21.5
woodlice 28.13
woodlouse 28.16
woodman 25.45
woodmen 25.45
woodnote 30.35
woodpecker 12.37
wood pigeon 25.14
woodpile 23.11
Woodrow 9.21
woodruff 17.15
woodrush 29.16
Woods 35.27
woodscrew 11.17
woodshed 16.4
woodsman 25.45
woodsmen 25.45
woodsmoke 21.24
Woodstock 21.21
woodsy 4.62

woodturner 12.59
woodturning 26.9
Woodward 16.30
woodwasp 27.18
woodwind 16.42
woodwork 21.31
woodworker 12.41
woodworm 24.22
woody 4.13
woodyard 16.2
wooer 12.19
woof 17.13, 17.14
woofer 12.30
wool 23.21
woolen 25.44
Woolf 17.18
woolgathering 26.11
woollen 25.44
Woolley 4.26
wool-like 21.19
woolly 4.26
woolpack 21.3
woolsack 21.4
woolshed 16.4
Woolworth 32.13
woomera 12.67
woosh 29.15
woozy 4.62
wop 27.8
Worcester 12.81
Worcestershire 12.11
word 16.31
wordage 20.6
wordbook 21.28
wording 26.5
word-perfect 30.49
wordplay 3.15
wordsearch 15.14
wordsmith 32.6
Wordsworth 32.13
wordy 4.13
wore 7.1
work 21.31
workaday 3.9
workaholic 21.11
workbench 29.20
workboat 30.35
workbook 21.28
workbox 28.40
workday 3.9
worker 12.41
workflow 9.17
workforce 28.15
workhorse 28.15
workhouse 28.16
working 26.7
Workington 25.50
workload 16.23

workman 25.45
workmanlike 21.19
workmate 30.12
workmen 25.45
workout 30.34
workpeople 23.35
workpiece 28.6
workplace 28.5
workroom 24.12
worksheet 30.19
workshop 27.8
work-shy 6.17
worksite 30.30
workspace 28.5
worktop 27.8
workwear 2.15
workweek 21.8
world 16.38
worldly 4.28
worldwide 16.14
worm 24.22
worm cast 31.2
wormer 12.52
wormhole 23.17
worm-like 21.19
Worms 35.30
wormwood 16.26
wormy 4.30
worn 25.28
worrier 12.10
worrit 30.24
worry 4.42
worrywart 30.33
worse 28.36
worsen 25.48
worship 27.6
worshiper 12.62
worshipper 12.62
worst 31.26
worsted 16.12
wort 30.45
worth 32.14
Worthing 26.14
worthwhile 23.11
worthy 4.57
wot 30.31
wotcha 12.24
would 16.26
would-be 4.10
wouldn't 30.56
wouldst 31.27
wound 16.43
wounding 26.5
wove 34.11
woven 25.51
wow 8.1
wowser 12.92
wrack 21.1
wraith 32.4
wraithlike 21.19

wrangle 23.30
wrangler 12.42
wrangling 26.8
wrap 27.1
wrapper 12.61
wrapping 26.10
wrasse 28.1
wrath 32.8
wrathy 4.56
wreak 21.8
wreaker 12.38
wreath 32.5
wreathe 33.3
wreck 21.6
wreckage 20.6
wrecker 12.37
wren 25.5
wrench 29.20
wrest 31.3
wrestle 23.37
wrestler 12.42
wrestling 26.8
wretch 15.3
wretched 16.8
Wrexham 24.20
wriggle 23.30
wriggler 12.48
wriggly 4.27
wright 30.26
wring 26.3
wringer 12.60
wrinkle 23.32
wrinkly 4.24
wrist 31.6
wristband 16.40
wristlet 30.22
wristwatch 15.7
wristy 4.53
writ 30.20
write 30.26
writer 12.79
writerly 4.27
writhe 33.5
writhing 26.14
writing 26.13
written 25.50
Wroclaw 34.2
wrong 26.15
wrongdoer 12.19
wrongdoing 26.3
wronger 12.60
wrong-foot 30.16
wrong-footed 16.12
wrong-headed 16.9
wrong'un 25.46
wrote 30.35
wrought 30.33
wrung 26.18
wry 6.1
wryly 4.25

wryness 28.9
Wu 11.1
Wuhan 25.1
wunderkind 16.42
Wuppertal 23.2
Wurlitzer 12.70
wurst 31.26
Würzburg 18.13
wuss 28.20
Wyandot 30.31
Wyatt 30.41
wychelm 24.18
Wycherley 4.27
wych hazel 23.41
Wyclif 17.6
Wye 6.1
wynd 16.42
Wyndham 24.17
Wynne 25.13
Wyoming 26.9
Wystan 25.50

Xanadu 11.6
Xanthe 4.56
Xanthippe 4.36
Xavier 12.12
xenon 25.26
Xenophanes 35.7
xenophobe 14.11
xenophobia 12.5
xenophobic 21.9
Xenophon 25.25
xeric 21.15
xerographic 21.10
xerox 28.40
Xhosa 12.70
xi 6.1
Xian 25.1
Xingtai 6.1
Xining 26.3
Xinjiang 26.1
Xizang 26.1
xoanon 25.26
X-rated 16.12
X-ray 3.19
Xuzhou 9.1
xylophone 25.30
xylophonist 31.10

yabber 12.21
yabby 4.10
yacht 30.31
yachtie 4.54
yachtsman 25.45

Z

Oxford Paperback Reference

The Concise Oxford Dictionary of English Etymology
T. F. Hoad

A wealth of information about our language and its history, this reference source provides over 17,000 entries on word origins.

'A model of its kind'

Daily Telegraph

A Dictionary of Euphemisms
R. W. Holder

This hugely entertaining collection draws together euphemisms from all aspects of life: work, sexuality, age, money, and politics.

Review of the previous edition
'This ingenious collection is not only very funny but extremely instructive too'

Iris Murdoch

The Oxford Dictionary of Slang
John Ayto

Containing over 10,000 words and phrases, this is the ideal reference for those interested in the more quirky and unofficial words used in the English language.

'hours of happy browsing for language lovers'

Observer

OXFORD

Oxford Paperback Reference

The Concise Oxford Dictionary of Quotations
Edited by Elizabeth Knowles

Based on the highly acclaimed *Oxford Dictionary of Quotations*, this
paperback edition maintains its extensive coverage of literary and
historical quotations, and contains completely up-to-date material. A
fascinating read and an essential reference tool.

The Oxford Dictionary of Humorous Quotations
Edited by Ned Sherrin

From the sharply witty to the downright hilarious, this sparkling
collection will appeal to all senses of humour.

Quotations by Subject
Edited by Susan Ratcliffe

A collection of over 7,000 quotations, arranged thematically for easy
look-up. Covers an enormous range of nearly 600 themes from 'The
Internet' to 'Parliament'.

The Concise Oxford Dictionary of Phrase and Fable
Edited by Elizabeth Knowles

Provides a wealth of fascinating and informative detail for over 10,000
phrases and allusions used in English today. Find out about anything
from the 'Trojan horse' to 'ground zero'.

AskOxford.*com*

Oxford Dictionaries Passionate about language

For more information about the background to Oxford Quotations and Language Reference Dictionaries, and much more about Oxford's commitment to language exploration, why not visit the world's largest language learning site, www.AskOxford.com

Passionate about English?

What were the original 'brass monkeys'?   **Ask**Oxford.*com*

How do new words enter the dictionary?   **Ask**Oxford.*com*

How is 'whom' used?   **Ask**Oxford.*com*

Who said, 'For also knowledge itself is power?'   **Ask**Oxford.*com*

How can I improve my writing?   **Ask**Oxford.*com*

If you have a query about the English language, want to look up a word, need some help with your writing skills, are curious about how dictionaries are made, or simply have some time to learn about the language, bypass the rest and ask the experts at www.AskOxford.com.

Passionate about language?

If you want to find out about writing in French, German, Spanish, or Italian, improve your listening and speaking skills, learn about other cultures, access resources for language students, or gain insider travel tips from those   **Ask**Oxford.*com* in the know, ask the experts at

OXFORD